If you bought a new copy of this text, the card will give you Total Access to all of the resources that you'll need to learn music theory, starting with an intera[...]

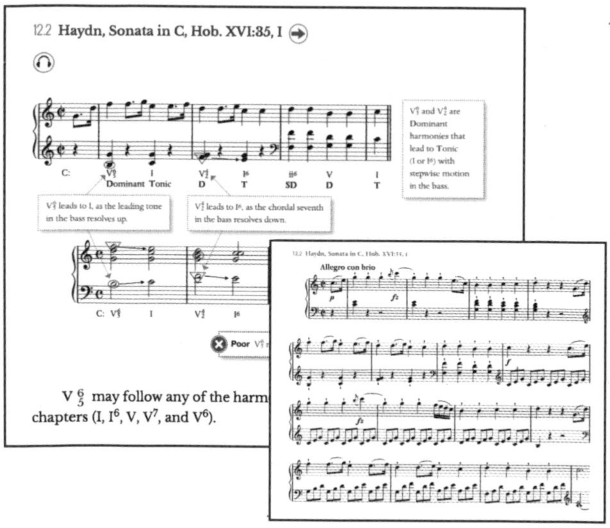

12.2 Haydn, Sonata in C, Hob. XVI:35, I
C: V$^6_5$ I V$^4_3$ I^6 ii^6 V I
Dominant Tonic D T SD D T
V$^6_5$ and V$^4_3$ are Dominant harmonies that lead to Tonic (I or I^6) with stepwise motion in the bass.
V$^6_5$ leads to I, as the leading tone in the bass resolves up.
V$^4_3$ leads to I^6, as the chordal seventh in the bass resolves down.
Poor
V $^6_5$ may follow any of the harm
chapters (I, I^6, V, V^7, and V^6).
Allegro con brio

◀ [...] readable on a variety of devices, the ebook includes a number of exciting enhancements. MUSICAL EXAMPLES accompanied by ➔ are expandable: clicking or tapping on the icon reveals an extended version of the excerpt.

RECORDINGS are available of every example in the book. Clicking or tapping on the player icon launches the recording. ▶

SEVENTH CHORDS

SEVENTH CHORD CONSTRUCTION

A **seventh chord** can be understood as either a triad plus a seventh over its root or a triad with an additional third stacked on top of its fifth. Seventh chords can be written on four consecutive staff lines or four consecutive spaces. When a seventh chord is stacked in thirds, the lowest note is called the root, followed by the **third**, the **fifth**, and the **seventh**.

3.10

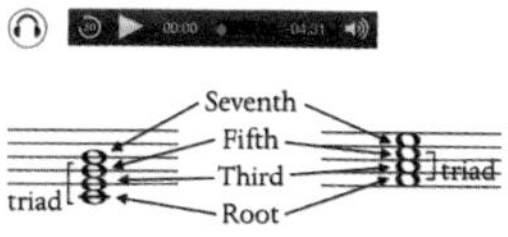

Seventh
Fifth
Third
Root
triad
triad

Know It? Show It!

Focus by working through the tutorials on:

- Triad Qualities
- Triad Inversions
- Seventh Chord Qualities
- Seventh Chord Inversions
- Finding Chords in the Key

Learn with inQuizitive.

Apply what you've learned to complete the assignments:

- Identifying Triad Quality
- Writing Triads
- Triad Inversions
- Triads in Major and Minor Keys
- Identifying Seventh-Chord quality
- Seventh Chords by Root and Quality
- Seventh-Chord Inversions

◀ The ebook is also the launching pad for the KNOW IT? SHOW IT! online pedagogy that accompanies the text. You'll find links to Know It? Show It! pedagogy at the end of every chapter.

ONE CODE. TOTAL ACCESS.

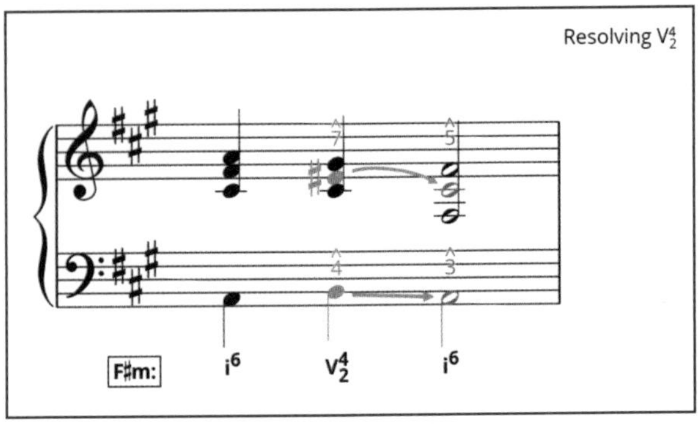

First, as you read the text, VIDEO TUTORIALS illustrate concepts, help you hear the harmonies discussed in the text, and explain voice-leading procedures that you'll use in Assignments.

Then, FORMATIVE QUIZZES—powered by Norton InQuizitive—prepare you for homework assignments. Quizzes feature a variety of question types—many include musical notation—and robust feedback helps you avoid pitfalls. With InQuizitive, you can answer questions until you've mastered the skills you'll need to complete your homework.

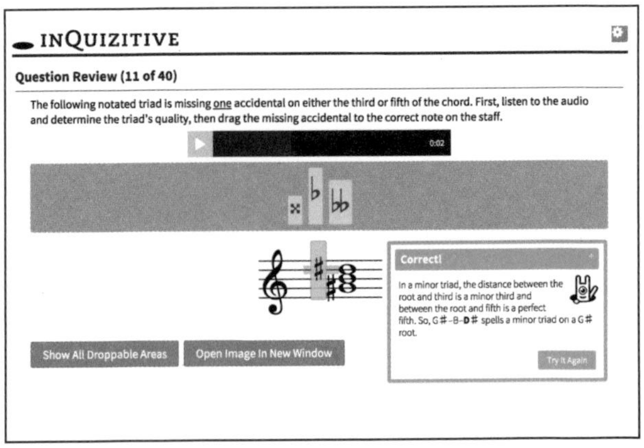

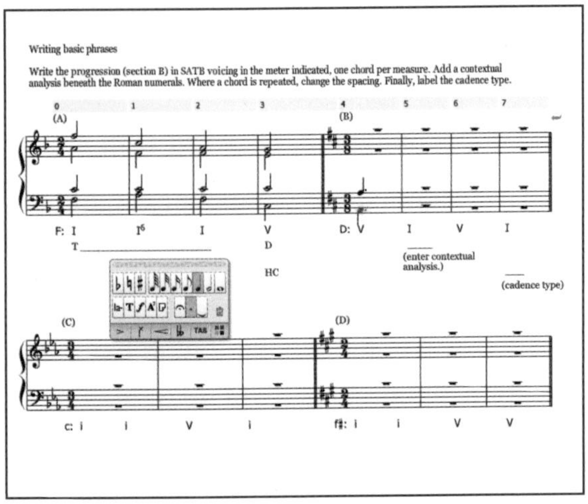

Finally, you can complete workbook exercises in the printed workbook or with NOTEFLIGHT. If you use the online workbook, you can instantly share completed assignments with your professor, who can then grade them electronically.

All of this and more is accessible by going to **digital.wwnorton.com/conciseharmony** and registering your Total Access code.

Concise Introduction to Tonal Harmony

Concise Introduction to Tonal Harmony

L. POUNDIE BURSTEIN
Graduate Center and Hunter College
City University of New York

JOSEPH N. STRAUS
Graduate Center
City University of New York

W. W. NORTON & COMPANY
NEW YORK • LONDON

W. W. Norton & Company has been independent since its founding in 1923, when William Warder Norton and Mary D. Herter Norton first published lectures delivered at the People's Institute, the adult education division of New York City's Cooper Union. The firm soon expanded its program beyond the Institute, publishing books by celebrated academics from America and abroad. By midcentury, the two major pillars of Norton's publishing program—trade books and college texts—were firmly established. In the 1950s, the Norton family transferred control of the company to its employees, and today—with a staff of four hundred and a comparable number of trade, college, and professional titles published each year—W. W. Norton & Company stands as the largest and oldest publishing house owned wholly by its employees.

Editor: Justin Hoffman
Project Editors: Jennifer Barnhardt, Debra Nichols
Assistant Editor: Michael Fauver
Manuscript Editor: Jodi Beder
Managing Editor, College: Marian Johnson
Managing Editor, College Digital Media: Kim Yi
Production Manager: Diana Spiegle
Media Editor: Steve Hoge
Media Project Editor: Meg Wilhoite
Media Editorial Assistant: William Paceley
Marketing Manager, Music: Mary Dudley
Design Director: Rubina Yeh
Art Direction: Jillian Burr
Design: Wendy Lai

Composition and Music Engraving: David Botwinik
Manufacturing: LSC Communications–Kendallville

Library of Congress Cataloging-in-Puclication Data
Burstein, L. Poundie.
Concise introduction to tonal harmony / L. Poundie Burstein, Joseph N. Straus.—First edition.
pages cm
Includes index
ISBN: 978-0-393-26476-0 (hardcover)
1. Harmony. 2. Music theory—Elementary works. I. Straus, Joseph Nathan. II. Title.
MT50.B979C66 2016
781.2'5—dc23 2015022960

W. W. Norton & Company, Inc., 500 Fifth Avenue, New York, NY 10110-0017
wwnorton.com
W. W. Norton & Company Ltd., 15 Carlisle Street, London W1D 3BS

5 6 7 8 9 0

Contents in Brief

Contents

Part Five Form 329

Preface

Concise Introduction to Tonal Harmony represents a new, concise approach to the tonal harmony textbook. Rather than a sprawling, encyclopedic compendium, this is a guidebook to the most important things that students need to know. Our text introduces all of the topics typically covered in the undergraduate theory sequence—fundamentals, diatonic and chromatic harmony, and form—but it approaches each topic with focus and concision. No frills and no nonsense—just the essentials. When it comes to textbooks, less can be more, and this is a text that students will be able to read and comprehend, freeing up class time for enriching activities.

Online resources offer yet another way to make class time more efficient, and with this new text, we've collaborated with two colleagues who have made extensive use of online tools in their own classrooms—Anna Gawboy (Ohio State University) and Inessa Bazayev (Louisiana State University)—to create the best set of online resources for music theory available today. At the end of each chapter, students will find innovative Know It? Show It! activities. **Video tutorials** and adaptive **online quizzes** help students understand the content of the chapter and prepare them for the workbook assignments, which can be completed online or on paper.

FEATURES

- Each carefully crafted chapter is just a few pages long and isolates a particular harmony and the voice-leading issues associated with it. Students quickly grasp the essential concepts, and instructors have the flexibility to teach chapters in a different order from the one that appears in the text.

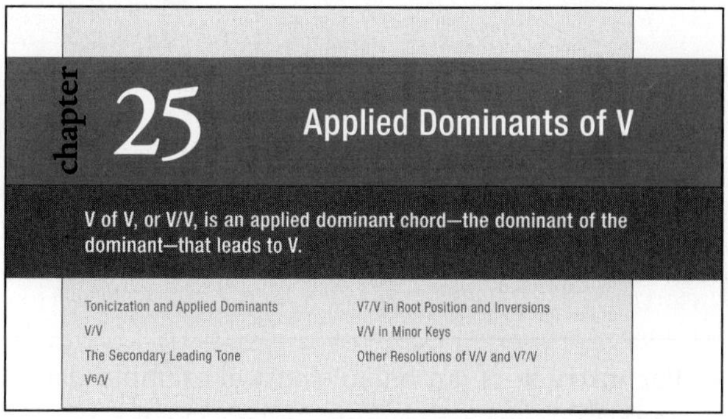
chapter 25 Applied Dominants of V

V of V, or V/V, is an applied dominant chord—the dominant of the dominant—that leads to V.

Tonicization and Applied Dominants
V/V
The Secondary Leading Tone
V^6/V
V^7/V in Root Position and Inversions
V/V in Minor Keys
Other Resolutions of V/V and V^7/V

- Explanations are concise and clearly worded, with key terms in **bold**. In the ebook, students can tap on or mouse over boldface terms to reveal definitions.

BINARY FORM

In **binary form** an entire movement is divided into two parts, each of which is usually repeated. Each part of a binary form consists of one or more phrases and ends with a cadence. The first part may end conclusively with an authentic cadence in the main key. Usually, however, it is harmonically open-ended, closing with either a half cadence in the main key or an authentic cadence in another key (most often, the key of V or—in minor-key pieces—the relative major). The second part of a binary form almost always ends with a perfect authentic cadence in the main key.

37.1
BINARY FORM

𝄆 FIRST PART 𝄇	𝄆 SECOND PART 𝄇
Ends with a PAC in the new key or HC in the main key or PAC (or IAC) in the main key	Ends with a PAC in the main key

- Concepts are illustrated with short musical examples, carefully selected to illustrate the topic at hand and to expose students to diverse composers (nationality, historical period, gender) and works (genre, instrumentation). Annotations draw attention to key features of each example. Extended versions of examples, offering opportunities for additional study, appear in the ebook and are indicated by the ➔ symbol.

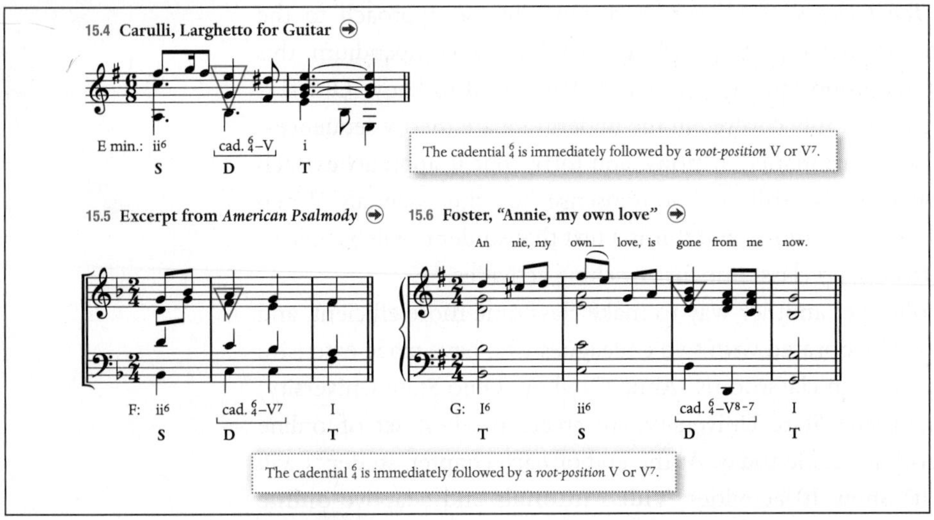

- Musical examples provide models of correct usage, but they also anticipate mistakes, showing students common errors and how to avoid them.

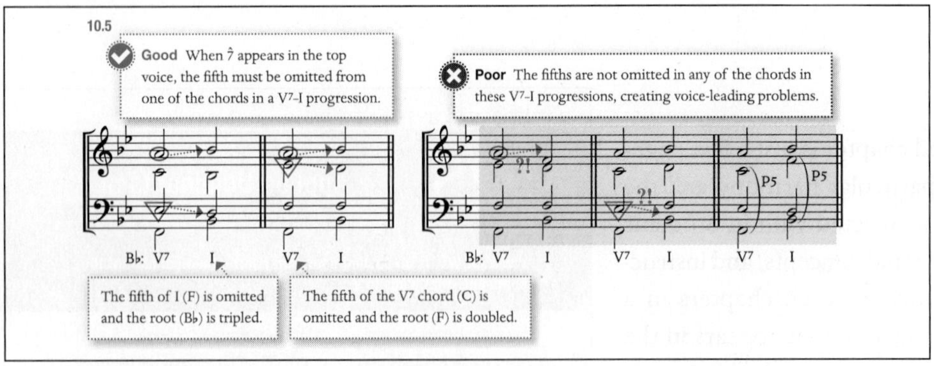

- For instructors, an online musical-example database supplements the text with additional musical examples indexed by the theoretical concepts they exemplify. It can be accessed at wwnorton.com/instructors.

- Each chapter ends with a list of **Points for Review**.

POINTS FOR REVIEW

- **A modulation is a substantial change of key that is confirmed by a cadence.**
- **Modulations are usually signaled by accidentals, rather than by a new key signature.**
- **After a modulation has begun, the harmonies and scale degrees are labeled in the new key.**
- **The key that appears at the start and end of the movement is known as the main key. The keys to which there are modulations are identified by their relationship to the main key.**
- **In a major key piece, the most common modulation is to the dominant key (the key of V).**
- **In modulating between two keys, often the last chord of the first key is the same as the first chord of the new key. This shared chord is known as a pivot chord and must be diatonic to both keys.**
- **Compared to tonicizations, modulations are changes of key that tend to be more substantial, involve a pivot chord, and have a cadence in the new key.**

- Every chapter ends with a **Test Yourself** activity, to ensure that students understand the concepts covered in the chapter. Answers appear in the back of the printed text, or can be revealed in the ebook.

TEST YOURSELF

1. Which of the following statements are true?
   a. In a sequence, doubled leading tones are permissible.
   b. In a sequence, parallel fifths and octaves are permissible.
   c. In a sequence, you might find chord successions that are normally forbidden in standard functional harmonic progressions.
   d. In minor-key sequences, $\hat{7}$ must be raised to become a leading tone.
   e. In a sequence, chordal sevenths need not resolve down by step.
2. Excerpts (a)–(f) show the first five chords of various sequential patterns (two full units of the pattern and half of the third). If the sequences continued in the same fashion, what would the next chord be?

a.

b.

- The accompanying workbook, which is available both online and in print, includes more exercises than could ever be used in a theory class. Error detection, chord spelling, figured bass and Roman numeral realization, composition, harmonization, and analysis exercises appear throughout the workbook, at all levels of difficulty. Review questions invite students to explain key concepts and processes in their own words.

- An Instructor's Edition of the workbook offers sample solutions to workbook exercises.

ONLINE RESOURCES

An ebook, included with every copy of the text, allows students to read on a wide variety of devices. Special ebook enhancements include:

- Links to **RECORDINGS** of every musical example in the text.
- **EXTENDED MUSICAL EXAMPLES**, allowing students to see and hear longer versions of the short excerpts that appear in the text. These examples can even be used instead of an anthology.
- **A CLOSER LOOK** features, which go into more detail about selected topics, such as less common or exceptional uses of the harmonies discussed.

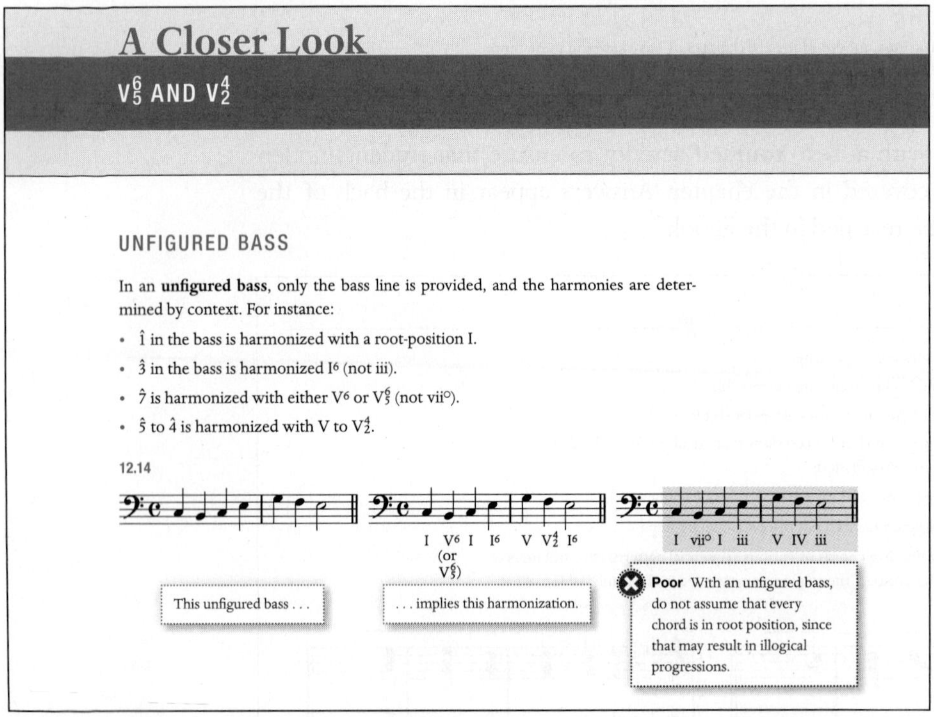

A Closer Look

V^6_5 AND V^4_2

UNFIGURED BASS

In an **unfigured bass**, only the bass line is provided, and the harmonies are determined by context. For instance:

- $\hat{1}$ in the bass is harmonized with a root-position I.
- $\hat{3}$ in the bass is harmonized I^6 (not iii).
- $\hat{7}$ is harmonized with either V^6 or V^6_5 (not vii°).
- $\hat{5}$ to $\hat{4}$ is harmonized with V to V^4_2.

12.14

I V6 I I6 V V4/2 I6
(or V6/5)
I vii° I iii V IV iii
This unfigured bass . . .
. . . implies this harmonization.
Poor With an unfigured bass, do not assume that every chord is in root position, since that may result in illogical progressions.

As part of its media package, *Concise Introduction to Tonal Harmony* also features Know It? Show It! pedagogy, which is designed to enhance student learning.

- As they read the chapter, students watch short **VIDEO TUTORIALS**, created by Anna Gawboy and keyed to each topic discussed in the text. Tutorials show students how to work through the problems they will encounter in their homework assignments.
- Students take carefully graduated **ADAPTIVE ONLINE QUIZZES** to deepen their understanding and demonstrate mastery of the material. InQuizitive, a new formative assessment tool, with questions written by Inessa Bazayev, asks students questions until they've demonstrated that they understand the chapter material. When students have trouble, tailored feedback points them back to the book and tutorials. And once students complete the activity, rich data about their performance can be reported to your campus learning management system.

- In addition to the print workbook, the **online workbook** makes all workbook activities available in Noteflight, an online notation program that allows students to complete their homework and send it to their instructor electronically. Instructors can grade work and return it to students paperlessly.

> **Know It? Show It!**
>
> **Focus by working through the tutorials on:**
> - Triad Qualities
> - Triad Inversions
> - Seventh Chord Qualities
> - Seventh Chord Inversions
> - Finding Chords in the Key
>
> **Learn with inQuizitive.**
>
> **Apply what you've learned to complete the assignments:**
> - Identifying Triad Quality
> - Writing Triads
> - Triad Inversions
> - Triads in Major and Minor Keys
> - Identifying Seventh-Chord qualites
> - Seventh Chords by Root and Quality
> - Seventh-Chord Inversions

With **Total Access**, all students who purchase a new book—regardless of format—will receive access to all of the media, including the ebook and Know It? Show It! pedagogy. Students can access the media in a variety of ways:

- The **ebook** includes links to all of the accompanying media.
- With Norton **Coursepacks**, instructors can bring the media into their campus learning management systems.
- At digital.wwnorton.com/conciseharmony, students and instructors can launch all of the online resources included with the text.

ACKNOWLEDGMENTS

We acknowledge the following reviewers, whose feedback helped to shape this text: Kyle Adams (Indiana University), Allen Anderson (The University of North Carolina at Chapel Hill), John Anderson (Wayne State University), Mark Anson-Cartwright (Queens College), Matthew Arndt (University of Iowa), Daniel Arthurs (University of Tulsa), Ellen Bakulina (University of North Texas), Nicole Biamonte (McGill University), Stephen Burnaman (Huston-Tillotson University), Michael Callahan (Michigan State University), Michael Chikinda (University of Utah), Brian Chin (Seattle Pacific University), Howard Cinnamon (Hofstra University), Robin Cox (California State University, Long Beach), Diego Cubero (University of North Texas), Michael Cuthbert (Massachusetts Institute of Technology), Mark Dal Porto (Eastern New Mexico University), Clare Eng (Belmont University), Cathy Ann Elias (DePaul University), Nathan Fleshner (Stephen F. Austin State University), Neil Flory (Jamestown Community College), Arnold Friedman (Berklee College of Music), Joel Galand (Florida International University),

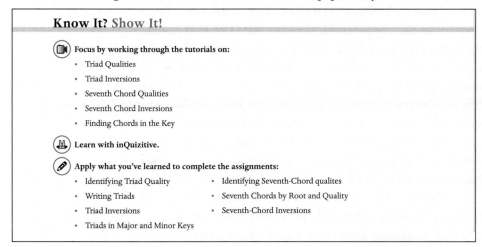

Chris Garmon (Career Center High School, Winston-Salem, NC), Anna Gawboy (Ohio State University), Emily Gertsch (University of Georgia), Jeffrey Gillespie (Butler University), Robert Glarner (Radford University), Cynthia Gonzales (Texas State University), Deborah Grabeel (Virginia Episcopal School), Kristin Grahm (Irondequoit High School), Joshua Groffman (Montclair State University), Bente Hansen (University of Lethbridge), Douglas Harbin (Arizona State University), Ryan Hare (Washington State University), Jared Hartt (Oberlin Conservatory of Music), Richard Hermann (University of New Mexico), Huck Hodge (University of Washington), Bryn Hughes (University of Miami), Brian Hulse (College of William and Mary), Samantha Inman (University of North Texas), Jennifer Iverson (University of Iowa), Rebecca Jemian (University of Louisville), Daniel Jenkins (University of South Carolina), Kyle Jenkins (Georgia State University), Elizabeth Kelly (Texas Woman's University), Stanley Kleppinger (University of Nebraska), George Lam (York College, City University of New York), Justin Lavacek (University of North Texas), Christopher Lee (Newtown High School), Anatole Leikin (University of California, Santa Cruz), Cherise Leiter (Metropolitan State College of Denver), Benjamin Levy (University of California, Santa Barbara), Zachary Lyman (Pacific Lutheran University), Liviu Marinescu (California State University, Northridge), David Martin (Sussex County College), William Marvin (Eastman School of Music), A. J. McCaffrey (California State University, Northridge), Greg McCandless (Full Sail University), Mark McFarland (Georgia State University), Brent Milam (Georgia State University), Neil Minturn (University of Missouri-Columbia), Jan Miyake (Oberlin Conservatory), Michael Murray (Missouri State University), Paul Nauert (University of California, Santa Cruz), Sam Nichols (University of California, Davis), Catherine Nolan (University of Western Ontario), John Odom (Starr's Mill High School), Janet Peachey (Duke Ellington School of the Arts), Stephen Peles (University of Alabama), Richard Pellegrin (University of Missouri-Columbia), Mika Pelo (University of California, Davis), Jeffrey Perry (Louisiana State University), Larry Phifer (Rend Lake College), Ève Poudrier (Yale University), André Redwood (University of Notre Dame), John Reef (Nazareth College), Thomas Robinson (University of Alabama), James Romig (Western Illinois University), Robert Ross (Community College of Philadelphia), Ciro Scotto (University of South Florida), Philip Seward (Columbia College Chicago), Alan Shockley (California State University, Long Beach), Louie Silvestri (Fossil Ridge High School), Andrew Simpson (Catholic University of America), Daphne Tan (Indiana University), David Thurmaier (University of Missouri-Kansas City), Donald Traut (University of Arizona), Ben Wadsworth (Kennesaw State University), Barbara Wallace (Dallas Baptist University), and Kurt Westerberg (DePaul University). We would also like to thank the students and professors at DePaul University, Fort Valley State University, Kennesaw State University, Louisiana State University, McGill University, University of Massachusetts at Amherst, University of Oklahoma, and University of Washington, who have used earlier versions of this text in their classes. Their feedback has resulted in numerous improvements throughout the book.

At W.W. Norton, an editorial dream team turned our vision of a concise introduction to tonal harmony into a tangible (and virtual) reality. We conceived the project in discussions with Maribeth Payne. Our editor, Justin Hoffman (a brilliant music theorist in his own right) worked with an experienced and capable team, including Jennifer Barnhardt, Jodi Beder, David Botwinik, Jillian Burr, Mary Dudley, Michael Fauver, Steve Hoge, Marian Johnson, William Paceley, Diana Spiegle, Debra Nichols, and Meg Wilhoite. We benefitted from their professionalism and expertise in countless ways, large and small, and we are deeply grateful to all of them. We also had assistance from several of our talented doctoral students at the CUNY Graduate Center: Ellen Bakulina, Megan Lavengood, Christina Lee, Andrew Moylan, and Simon Prosser.

part one

Fundamentals

chapter 0 Notation of Pitch and Rhythm

Musical pitches and rhythms are notated in standard ways.

THE STAFF

Music is written on a five-line **staff**. **Pitches**—specific points on the continuum of audible sound—are represented by notes written on the lines and spaces of the staff. As notes go higher on the staff the pitches ascend, and as notes go lower the pitches descend.

0.1

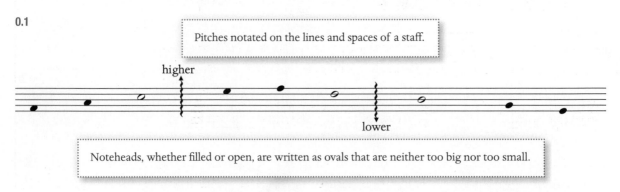

Pitches notated on the lines and spaces of a staff.

Noteheads, whether filled or open, are written as ovals that are neither too big nor too small.

Pitches that are too high or too low for the staff are written on **ledger lines** (temporary extensions of the staff).

0.2

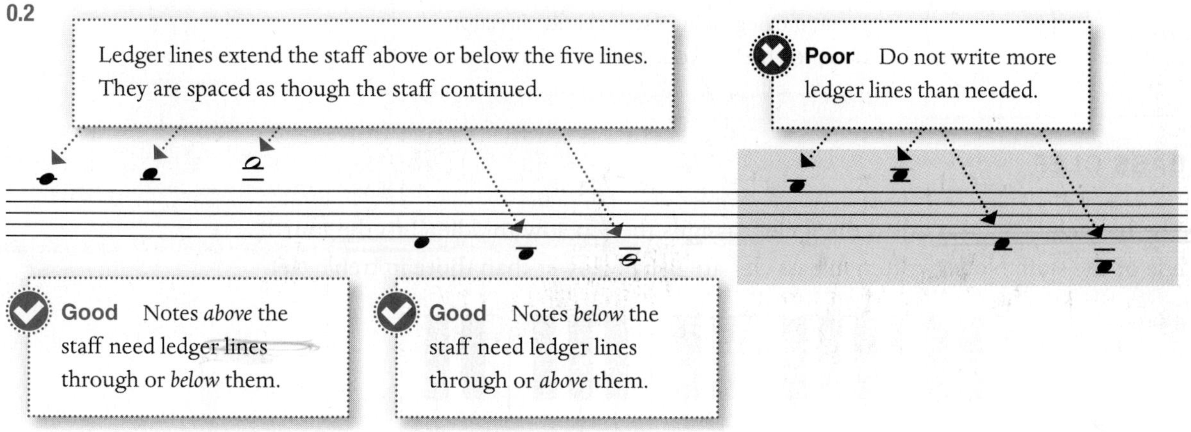

Ledger lines extend the staff above or below the five lines. They are spaced as though the staff continued.
Poor Do not write more ledger lines than needed.
Good Notes *above* the staff need ledger lines through or *below* them.
Good Notes *below* the staff need ledger lines through or *above* them.

NOTATING PITCHES

TREBLE CLEF

Musicians use letters from A to G to identify the notes on the white keys of the piano. As a point of reference, the C in the middle of the piano keyboard is called **middle C**. A **clef** associates lines and spaces on the staff with specific pitches. The **treble clef** (𝄞, also called the G clef), assigns the G above middle C to the second line of the staff.

0.3

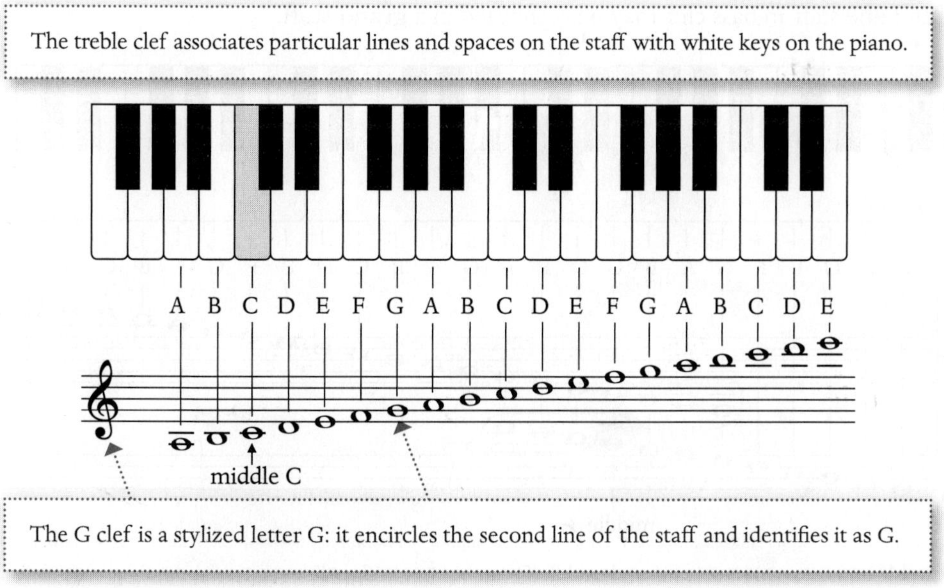

The treble clef associates particular lines and spaces on the staff with white keys on the piano.
A B C D E F G A B C D E F G A B C D E
middle C
The G clef is a stylized letter G: it encircles the second line of the staff and identifies it as G.

As pitches ascend, the letter names repeat once every eight notes, or **octave**.

0.4

Starting on any note, and including the starting point, moving eight notes in either direction takes you back to your starting point.

BASS CLEF

The **bass clef** (𝄢, also called the F clef) assigns the F below middle C to the fourth line of the staff. Notes written in bass clef are usually lower than those in treble clef.

0.5

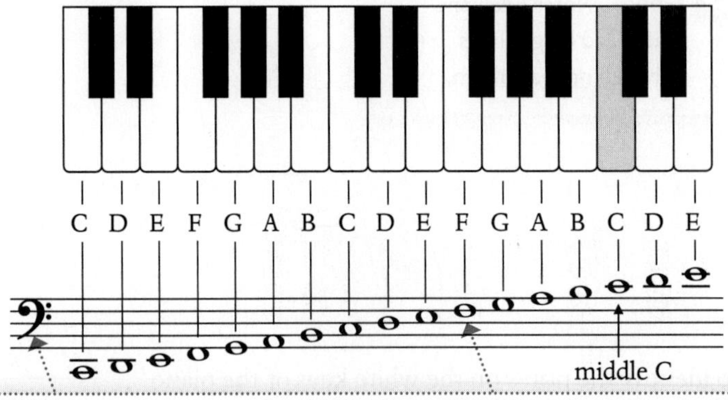

The F clef is a stylized letter F: it is centered on the fourth line of the staff and identifies it as F.

GRAND STAFF

One staff in treble clef and one staff in bass clef may be combined in a **grand staff**.

0.6

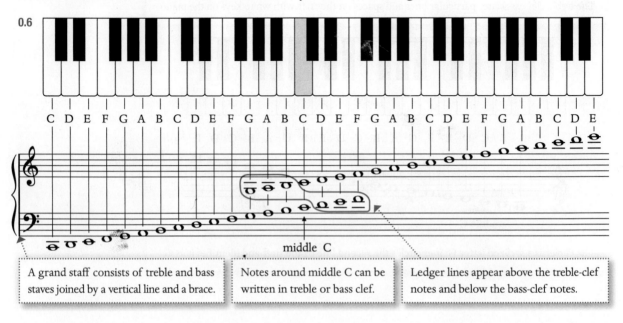

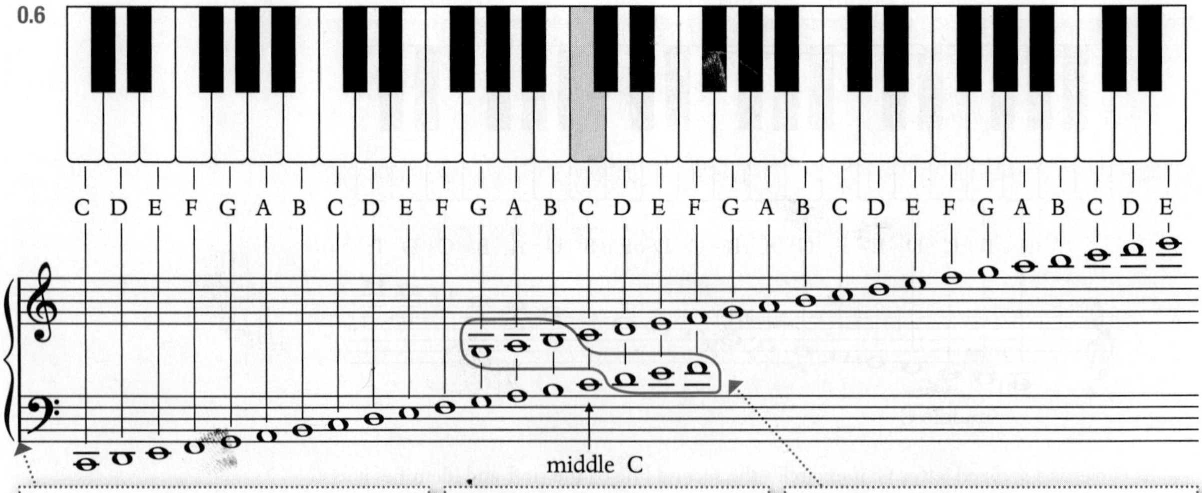

A grand staff consists of treble and bass staves joined by a vertical line and a brace.

Notes around middle C can be written in treble or bass clef.

Ledger lines appear above the treble-clef notes and below the bass-clef notes.

C CLEFS

In addition to the treble and bass clefs, several clefs known as **C clefs** show the placement of middle C on the staff. Of these, the most important are the **alto clef**, with middle C on the third line of the staff, and the **tenor clef**, with middle C on the fourth line. Violists usually play in alto clef, while cellists, bassoonists, and trombonists play in tenor clef when their music is too high to be comfortably notated in bass clef.

0.7

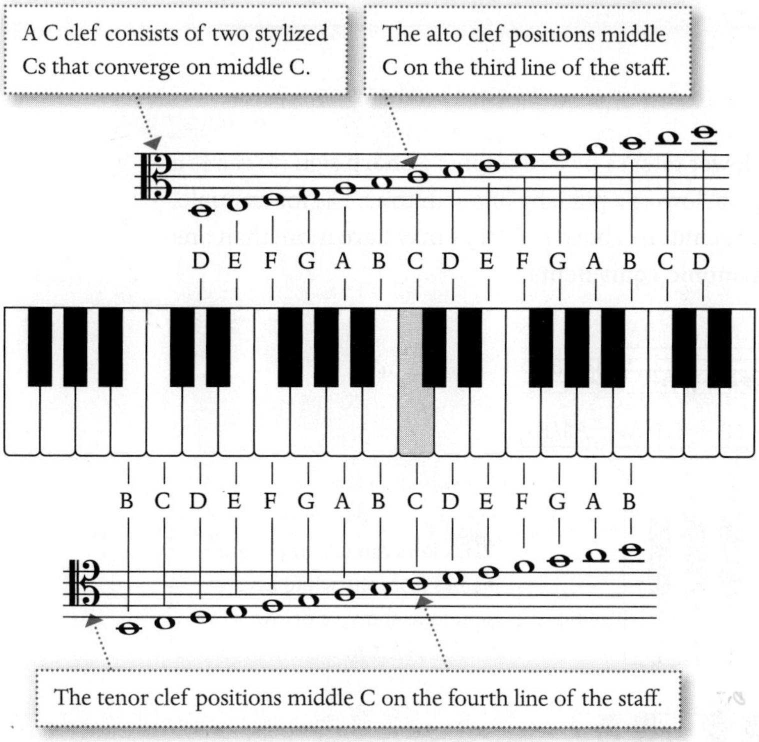

A C clef consists of two stylized Cs that converge on middle C.
The alto clef positions middle C on the third line of the staff.
D E F G A B C D E F G A B C D
B C D E F G A B C D E F G A B
The tenor clef positions middle C on the fourth line of the staff.

SEMITONES (HALF STEPS) AND WHOLE TONES (WHOLE STEPS)

The pitches on the keyboard are separated by either a **semitone** (**half step**) or a **whole tone** (**whole step**). A semitone is the smallest possible space between two notes. Any two adjacent keys on the piano keyboard comprise a semitone, and there are twelve semitones in the octave. Two semitones make up a whole tone. Among the white keys, E-F and B-C are separated by a semitone. All other pairs of white keys are a whole tone apart.

0.8

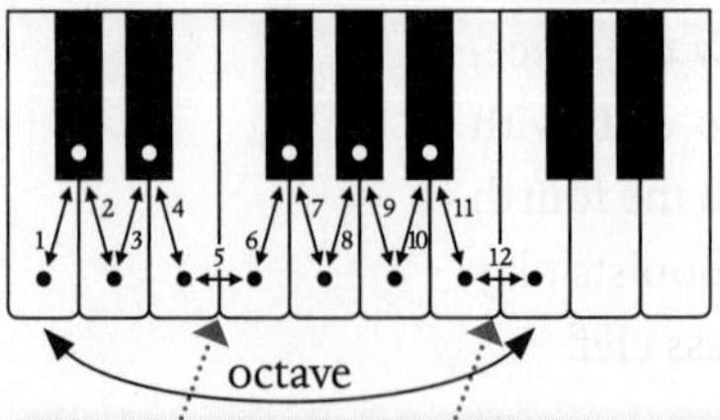

Adjacent keys on the keyboard are a semitone apart. Two semitones comprise a whole tone.

There are twelve semitones in an octave.

E–F and B–C are semitones. All other pairs of adjacent white keys are whole tones.

ACCIDENTALS

Accidentals are used to raise or lower pitches by a semitone: a **sharp** sign (♯) raises a pitch by one semitone; a **flat** sign (♭) lowers a pitch by one semitone. D♭, for example, is a semitone below D, and F♯ is a semitone above F. Pitches may have more than one name (different names are **enharmonic equivalents**).

0.9

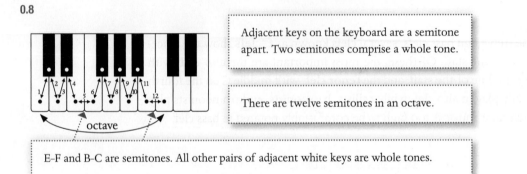

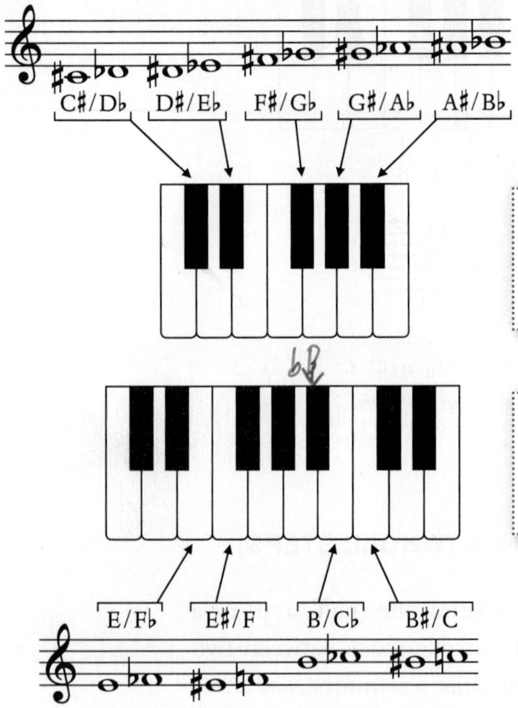

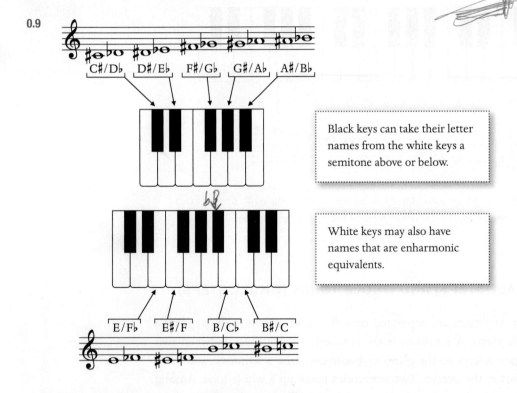

Black keys can take their letter names from the white keys a semitone above or below.

White keys may also have names that are enharmonic equivalents.

On the staff, accidentals are written *before* the note, but when you say (or write) the name of a note, the accidental comes *after* the letter name, as in "F-sharp" or "G-flat." A note that is neither sharp nor flat is **natural**, and is identified by a natural sign (♮). Most often, the natural sign is used to cancel a previous sharp or flat, so C♮ tells you that the C is no longer sharp or flat, but has been restored to its usual unmodified state.

0.10

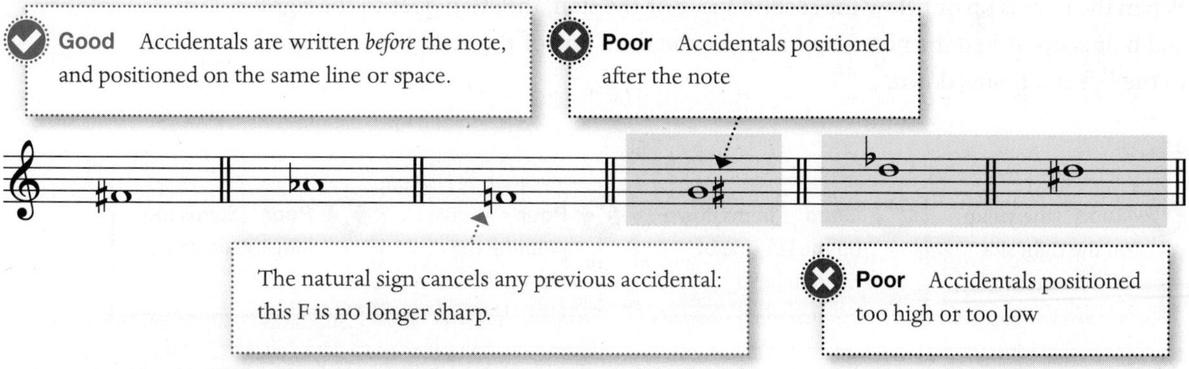
Good Accidentals are written *before* the note, and positioned on the same line or space.
Poor Accidentals positioned after the note
The natural sign cancels any previous accidental: this F is no longer sharp.
Poor Accidentals positioned too high or too low

It is also possible to raise a note by two semitones using a **double sharp** sign (𝄪) or to lower a note by two semitones using a **double flat** sign (𝄫).

0.11

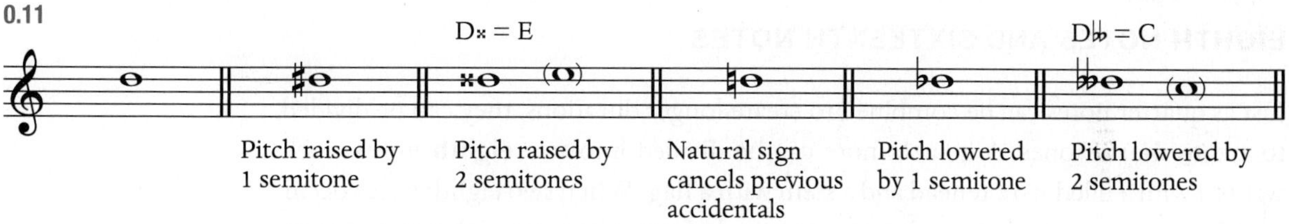
D𝄪 = E
D𝄫 = C
Pitch raised by 1 semitone
Pitch raised by 2 semitones
Natural sign cancels previous accidentals
Pitch lowered by 1 semitone
Pitch lowered by 2 semitones

RHYTHMIC DURATION

QUARTER NOTES, HALF NOTES, AND WHOLE NOTES

The basic unit of musical duration is a **quarter note**, written with a filled-in notehead and a stem. Two quarter notes together make a **half note**, written as an open note-head with a stem. Two half notes combine to make a **whole note**, written as an open notehead with no stem.

0.12

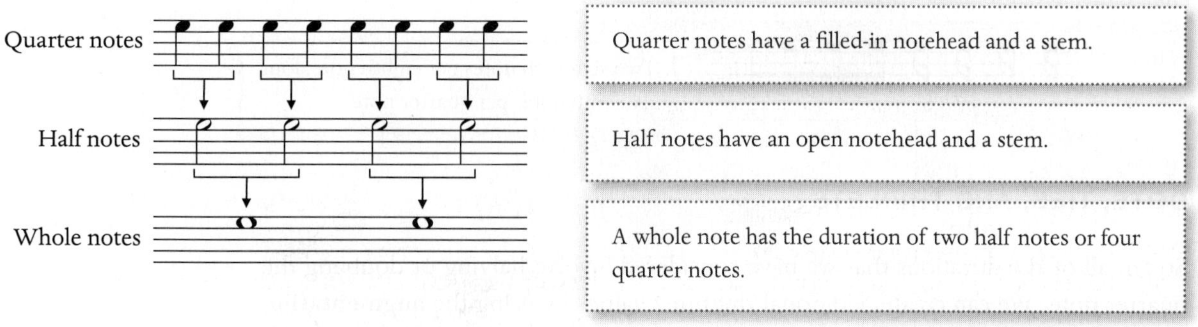
Quarter notes
Half notes
Whole notes
Quarter notes have a filled-in notehead and a stem.
Half notes have an open notehead and a stem.
A whole note has the duration of two half notes or four quarter notes.

When writing quarter notes and half notes, make the stem an octave in length. When the note is on or below the second space of the staff, the stem goes to the right and points up. When the note is on or above the third line of the staff, the stem goes to the left and points down.

0.13

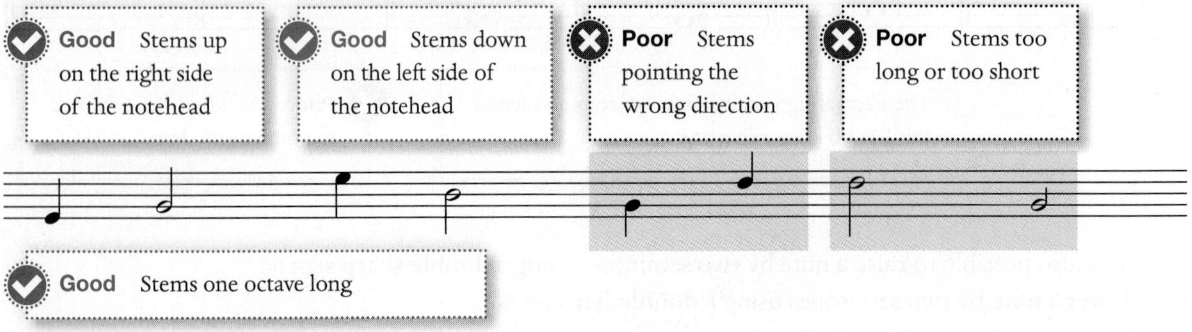

EIGHTH NOTES AND SIXTEENTH NOTES

Just as quarter notes can be combined to create longer durations, they can be divided to create shorter ones. A quarter note can be divided into two **eighth notes**, each written with a filled-in notehead and a stem with a **flag**. When two eighth notes occur together as a pair, join them with a **beam** instead of using flags. An eighth note can be divided into two **sixteenth notes**, each written as a filled-in notehead with a double flag or, in pairs or groups of four, joined together with a double beam. (Further subdivisions—thirty-second notes and sixty-fourth notes—are also possible.)

0.14

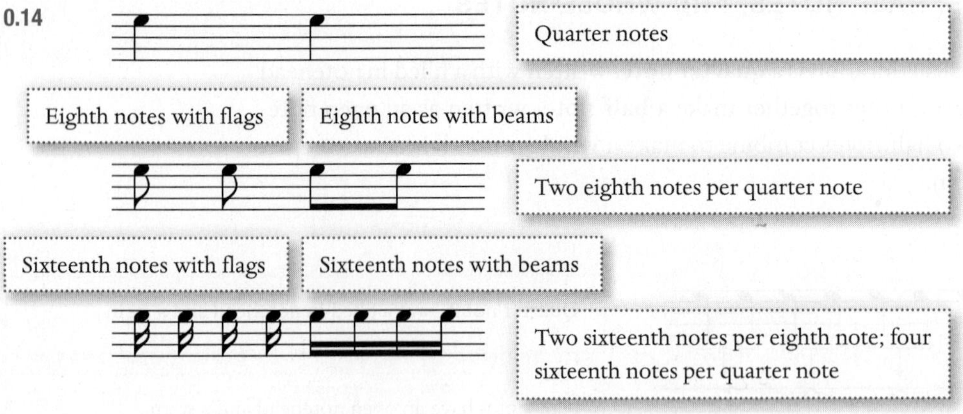

DOTS, TIES, AND TRIPLETS

So far, all of the durations that we have considered involve halving or doubling the quarter note. We can create additional rhythmic values by using the **augmentation dot**. A dot placed directly after a note increases the duration of that note by one half.

0.15

$$\text{𝅗𝅥.} = \text{𝅗𝅥} + \text{♩}$$

$$\text{♩.} = \text{♩} + \text{♪}$$

$$\text{♪.} = \text{♪} + \text{♬}$$

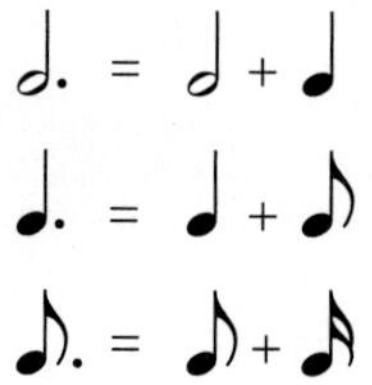

Dotted rhythms often divide a duration into two unequal parts.

0.16

Dotted-half + quarter = whole

Dotted-quarter + eighth = half

Dotted-eighth + sixteenth = quarter
The dotted-eighth and sixteenth are frequently beamed together.

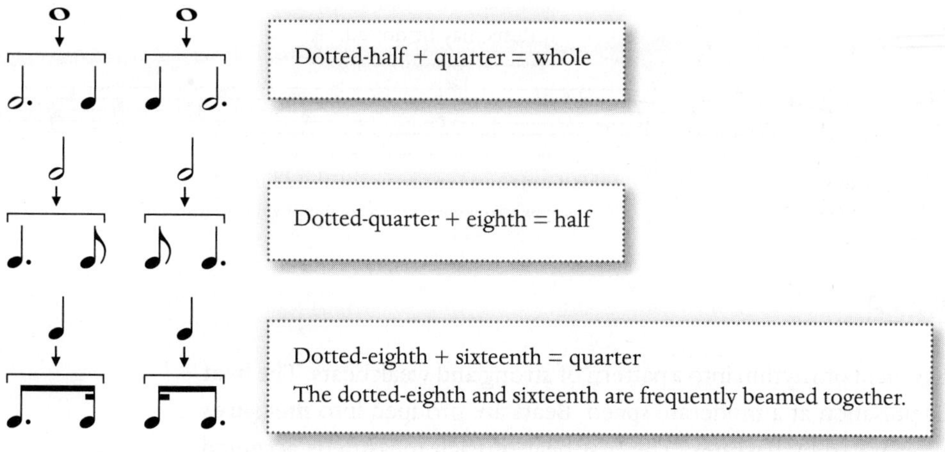

Still more rhythmic values become available with **ties**. A tie connecting two notes combines their durations into a single note.

0.17

$$\text{𝅝} \frown \text{♩} = \text{𝅝} + \text{♩}$$

$$\text{♪} \frown \text{𝅗𝅥} = \text{♪} + \text{𝅗𝅥}$$

$$\text{♩} \frown \text{♬} = \text{♩} + \text{♬}$$

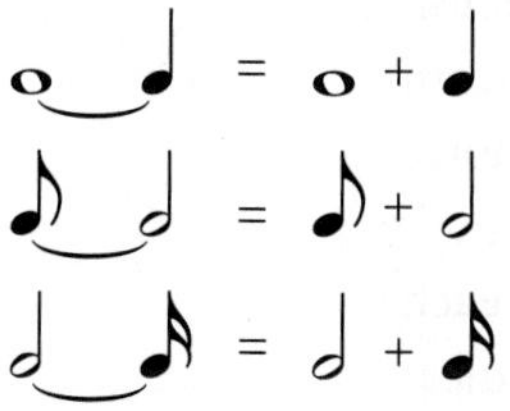

Triplets divide a rhythmic unit—usually a half or quarter note—into three parts instead of two.

0.18

Half note divided into triplet quarter notes

Quarter note divided into triplet eighth notes

The number 3 within the bracket tells you that these notes divide a longer note into three equal parts.

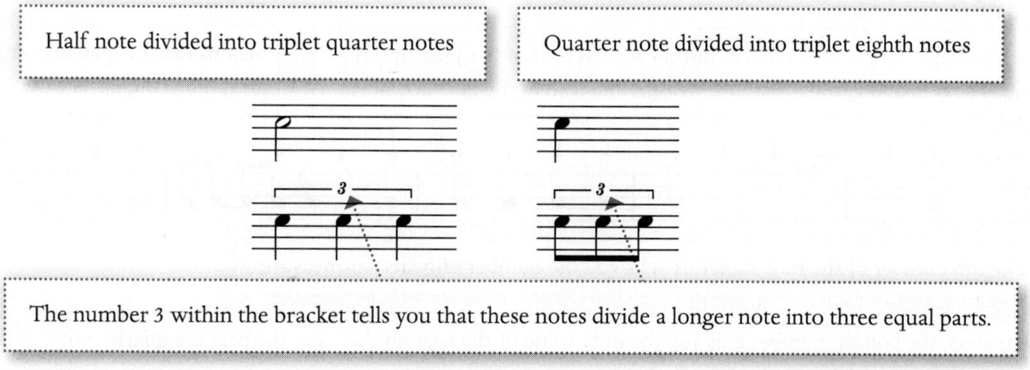

RESTS

A **rest** indicates a duration of silence. Rests can correspond to any rhythmic value. They are written in the middle of the staff.

0.19

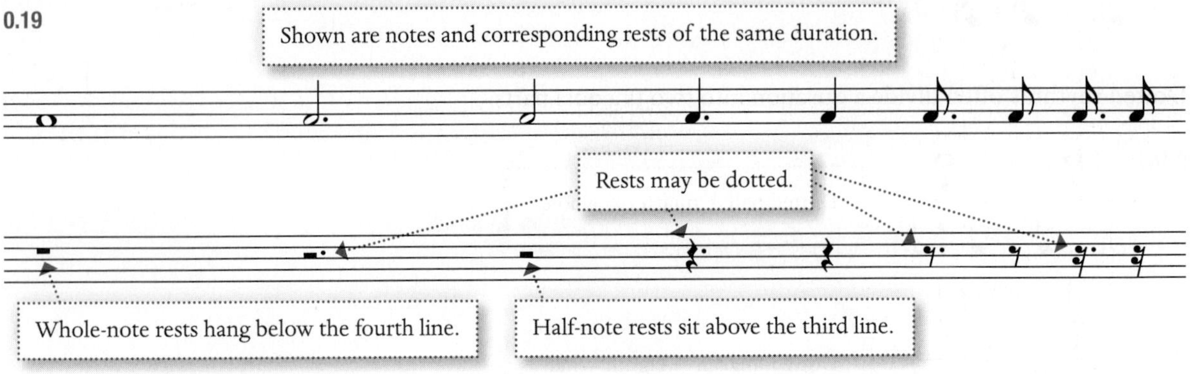
Shown are notes and corresponding rests of the same duration.
Rests may be dotted.
Whole-note rests hang below the fourth line.
Half-note rests sit above the third line.

SIMPLE METER

Meter is the arrangement of rhythm into a pattern of strong and weak beats. The **beat** is a steady, regular pulsation at a moderate speed. Beats are grouped into **measures** (also called bars), separated by **barlines**. The first beat of each measure is accented and called the **downbeat**. The remaining beats of the measure are weaker and lead to the downbeat of the following measure.

A **time signature**, consisting of two stacked numbers, defines the meter. The bottom number determines the note value of each beat. If the beat unit is *not dotted*, the meter is **simple**. In simple meters, the quarter note–indicated by a 4 at the bottom of the time signature–is the most common beat, but eighth notes (8) and half notes (2) can also function as the beat.

The top number of a time signature determines the number of beats in each measure. In simple meters, this number is 2, 3, or 4. If there are four beats per measure, a 4 appears at the top of the time signature, and the meter is **quadruple**. For quadruple simple meters, the most common time signature is $\frac{4}{4}$, which indicates four quarter notes per measure. $\frac{4}{4}$ is sometimes called "common time" and labeled **C**.

0.20

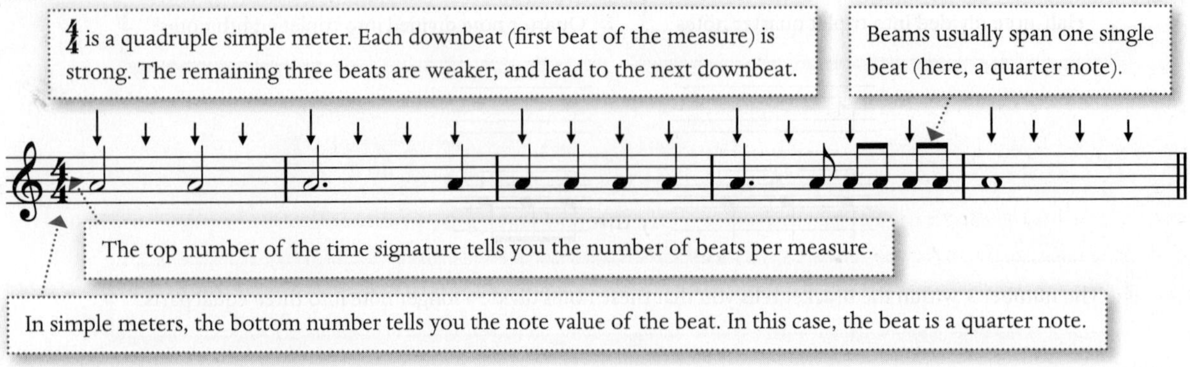
4/4 is a quadruple simple meter. Each downbeat (first beat of the measure) is strong. The remaining three beats are weaker, and lead to the next downbeat.
Beams usually span one single beat (here, a quarter note).
The top number of the time signature tells you the number of beats per measure.
In simple meters, the bottom number tells you the note value of the beat. In this case, the beat is a quarter note.

If there are three beats per measure, a 3 appears at the top of the time signature and the meter is **triple**.

0.21

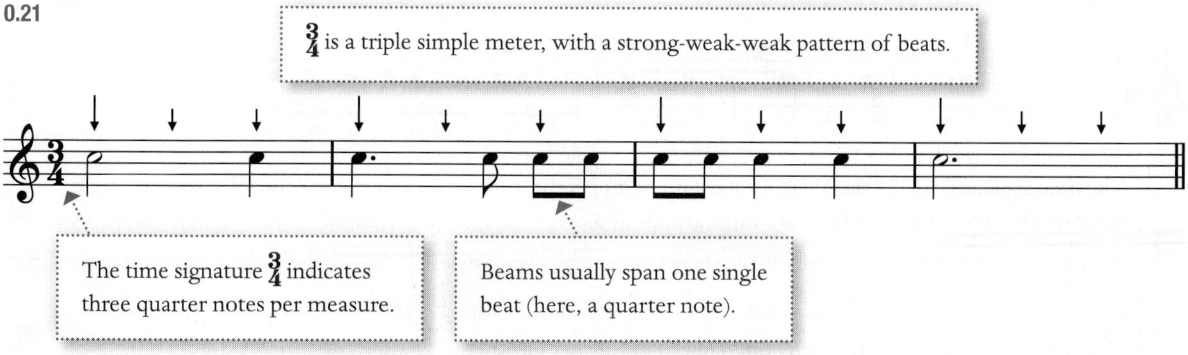
3/4 is a triple simple meter, with a strong-weak-weak pattern of beats.
The time signature 3/4 indicates three quarter notes per measure.
Beams usually span one single beat (here, a quarter note).

Duple meters have two beats per measure.

0.22

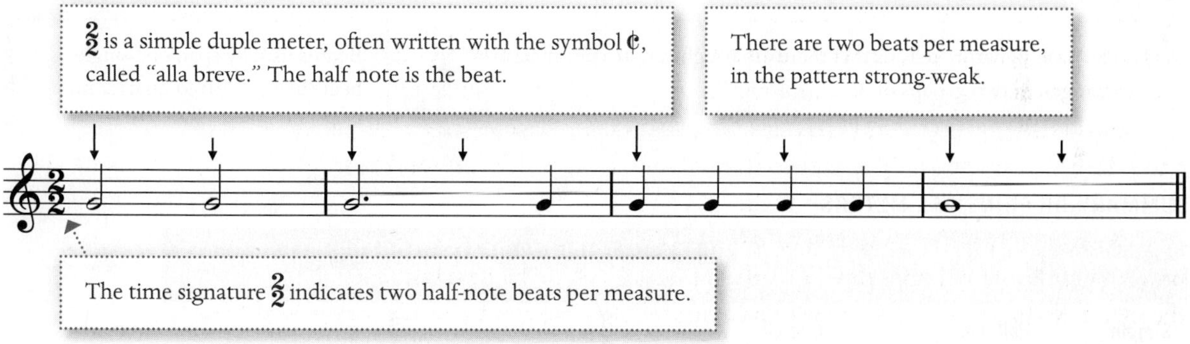
2/2 is a simple duple meter, often written with the symbol ¢, called "alla breve." The half note is the beat.
There are two beats per measure, in the pattern strong-weak.
The time signature 2/2 indicates two half-note beats per measure.

COMPOUND METER

In simple meters, the beat is divided into *two parts*: quarter-note beats contain two eighth notes, and half-note beats contain two quarter notes. In **compound meters**, the beat is divided into *three parts*, and the beat itself is a dotted note. Because the bottom number of a time signature cannot show a dotted beat unit, compound time signatures show instead the divisions of the beat. If the bottom number of a compound time signature is 8, the beat will be a dotted-quarter note, which is three eighth notes grouped together. Other beat units are also possible: a dotted-half note can be divided into three quarter notes (4), or a dotted-eighth note into three sixteenths (16).

The top number of a compound meter signature is 6, 9, or 12 and shows the number of *beat divisions* in each measure. Divide by three to find the number of beats in each measure. Like simple meters, compound meters may be duple (6 in the time signature), triple (9), or quadruple (12).

0.23

9/8 is a triple compound meter: three dotted-quarter beats per measure, in a pattern of strong-weak-weak.

The time signature tells us that there are 9 eighth notes per measure; these divide a dotted-quarter beat into three groups of 3.

Beams usually span one single beat (here, a dotted-quarter note).

6/8 is a duple compound meter: two dotted-quarter beats per measure in a pattern of strong-weak.

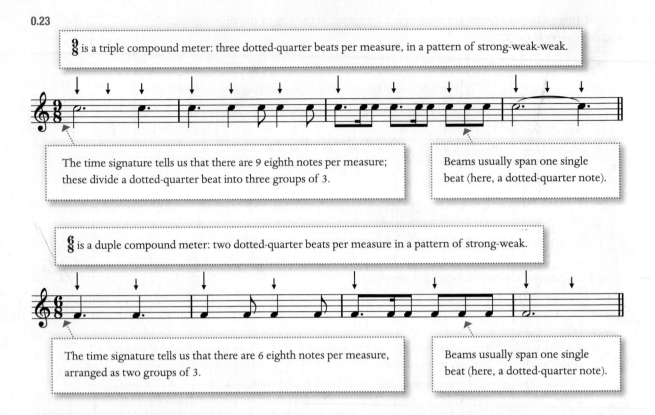

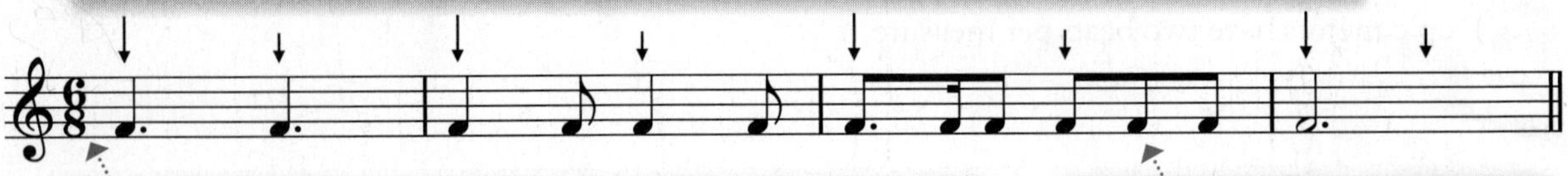

The time signature tells us that there are 6 eighth notes per measure, arranged as two groups of 3.

Beams usually span one single beat (here, a dotted-quarter note).

SUMMARY OF PRINCIPAL METERS

	NOTE VALUE OF THE BEAT	DUPLE (2 BEATS PER MEASURE)	TRIPLE (3 BEATS PER MEASURE)	QUADRUPLE (4 BEATS PER MEASURE)
Simple	Half note	2/2 or ¢	3/2	4/2
Simple	Quarter note	2/4	3/4	4/4 or **C**
Simple	Eighth note	2/8	3/8	4/8
Compound	Dotted-half note	6/4	9/4	12/4
Compound	Dotted-quarter note	6/8	9/8	12/8
Compound	Dotted-eighth note	6/16	9/16	12/16

ANACRUSIS

A piece of music in any meter may begin on the downbeat (first beat) of a measure, or it may begin in the middle of an incomplete measure. This incomplete measure is called an **anacrusis** (or, more familiarly, an upbeat or a pickup). Usually, a piece that begins with an anacrusis ends with an incomplete measure. Taken together, the incomplete first and last measures add up to one complete measure.

0.24

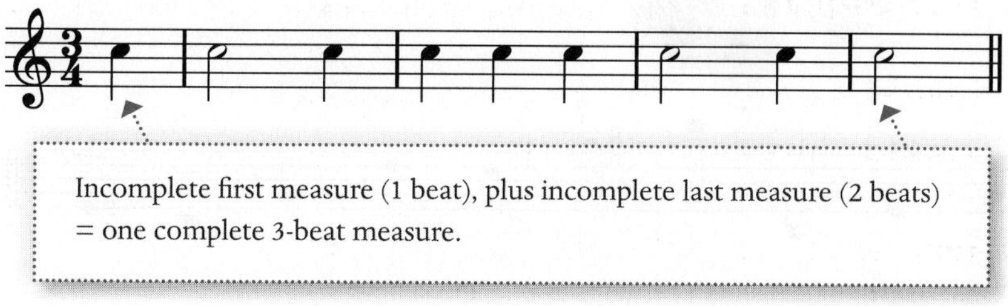
Incomplete first measure (1 beat), plus incomplete last measure (2 beats)
= one complete 3-beat measure.

review and interact

POINTS FOR REVIEW

- **Pitches are written on the lines and spaces of the five-line staff.**
- **Clefs determine the location of pitches on the staff. The most commonly used clefs are the treble clef (second line = G above middle C) and the bass clef (fourth line = F below middle C).**
- **The C clefs locate middle C on the staff: the alto clef assigns it to the third line; the tenor clef assigns it to the fourth line.**
- **Accidentals (sharps and flats) raise or lower pitches by a semitone. Less commonly, double sharps and double flats raise or lower pitches by two semitones. Naturals are neither sharp nor flat.**
- **The most common durational value is the quarter note. The other common values—whole notes, half notes, eighth notes, and sixteenth notes—are made by doubling or halving quarter notes.**
- **Augmentation dots, ties, and triplets create additional durations.**
- **In simple meters, the beat unit is not dotted and divides into two parts. The top number of a simple time signature is 2, 3, or 4 and indicates the number of beats per measure. The bottom number shows the beat unit (8 = eighth note; 4 = quarter note; 2 = half note).**
- **Compound meters have a dotted note as the beat, which divides into three parts. The top number of a compound time signature is 6, 9, or 12 and indicates the number of beat divisions; divide by three to find the number of beats. The bottom number indicates the unit of beat divisions (16 = sixteenth note; 8 = eighth note; 4 = quarter note); group three of them together to find the beat unit.**
- **An anacrusis is an incomplete initial measure.**

TEST YOURSELF

1. Identify each note.

2. Write a note that is enharmonically equivalent to each given note.

3. Insert barlines to create complete measures in the indicated time signatures.

4. There are blank spots in some of these measures (indicated by arrows). Fill them in by inserting a single note of the proper duration.

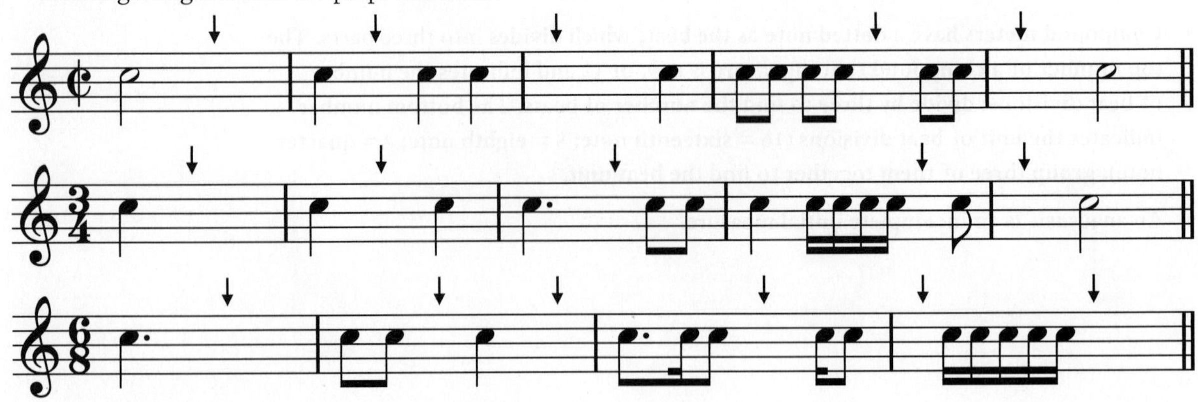

Know It? Show It!

Focus by working through the tutorials on:

- Whole tones and semitones
- Rhythmic notation
- Meter

Learn with inQuizitive.

Apply what you've learned to complete the assignments:

- Identifying Note Names
- Writing Notes
- Pitch and Keyboard
- Enharmonic Notes
- Barlines
- Writing Time Signatures
- Beams
- Writing Rhythms

chapter 1

Scales

Major and minor scales are the basic building blocks of tonal music.

A **scale** is a collection of notes, organized with reference to a central, **tonic** pitch and used as the basis for a musical composition. Scales are typically written in ascending order within an octave. There are two scales commonly used in tonal music: major and minor. In both major and minor scales, each of the seven letter names (A, B, C, D, E, F, and G) occurs only once and none is omitted. Major and minor scales thus contain seven different notes, although the first note is generally written again an octave higher at the end.

MAJOR SCALE

ORDER OF WHOLE TONES AND SEMITONES

Built above a principal pitch (the tonic), a **major scale** consists of a sequence of whole tones and semitones: W-W-S-W-W-W-S. For example, the C-major scale uses that sequence of whole tones and semitones written starting on C. It is the only major scale that can be written without accidentals (sharps or flats).

1.1

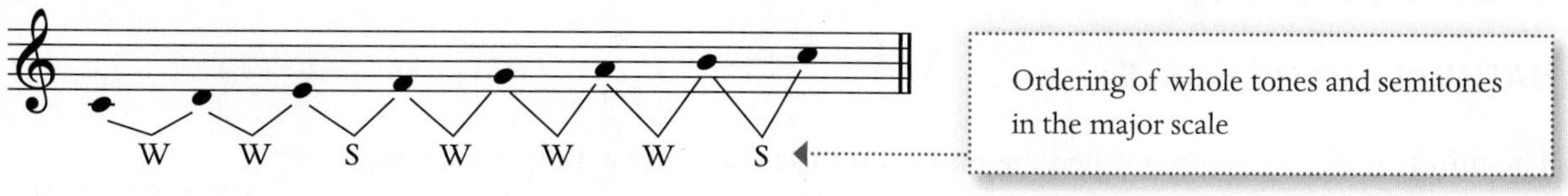

SCALE DEGREES

The notes of the scale, known as **scale degrees**, can be identified either with traditional **scale-degree names** or with **scale-degree numbers**, written beneath a caret sign (ˆ). The first scale degree, for instance, is known either as tonic or as $\hat{1}$. The two semitones of the major scale may be found between $\hat{3}$ and $\hat{4}$ and between $\hat{7}$ and $\hat{8}$.

1.2

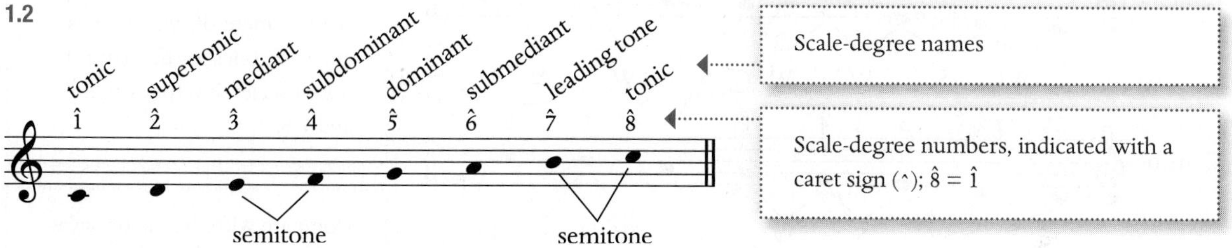

Distances between scale degrees are usually counted in **steps**. Adjacent scale degrees (like $\hat{1}$ and $\hat{2}$ or $\hat{5}$ and $\hat{6}$) span two steps of the scale (this interval is also called a second—see Chapter 2); scale degrees that fall on adjacent lines or spaces (like $\hat{2}$ and $\hat{4}$ or $\hat{5}$ and $\hat{7}$) span three steps of the scale (this interval is also called a third); and so on.

TRANSPOSITION

Any note can serve as the tonic of a major scale. In other words, the C-major scale can be **transposed** to any of the remaining eleven notes. Some of the notes will have to be altered with sharps or flats, however, to preserve C major's pattern of whole tones and semitones.

1.3

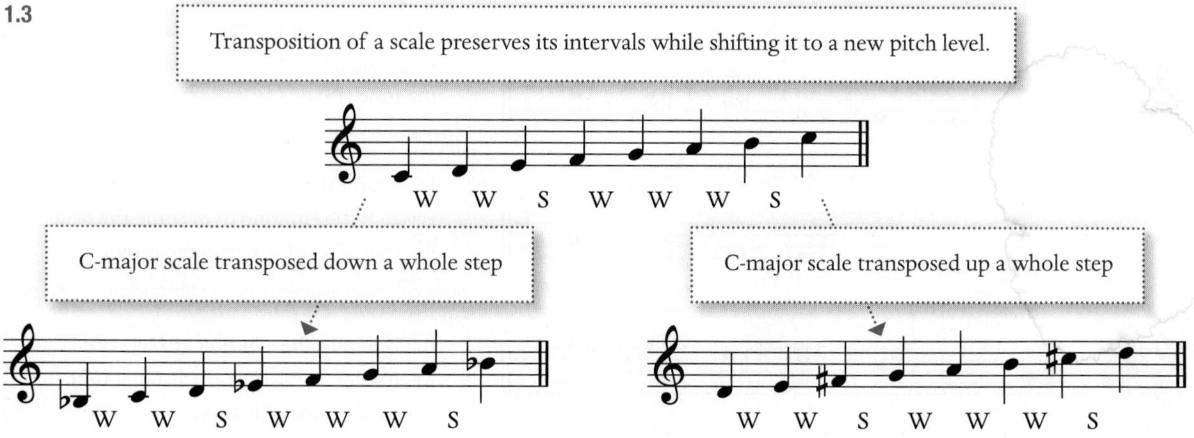

MINOR SCALES

NATURAL MINOR SCALE

The **minor scale** (sometimes called the **natural minor scale**) has a different arrangement of semitones and whole tones than the major scale. The minor scale has semitones between $\hat{2}$ and $\hat{3}$ and between $\hat{5}$ and $\hat{6}$, while the major scale has semitones between $\hat{3}$ and $\hat{4}$ and between $\hat{7}$ and $\hat{8}$.

1.4

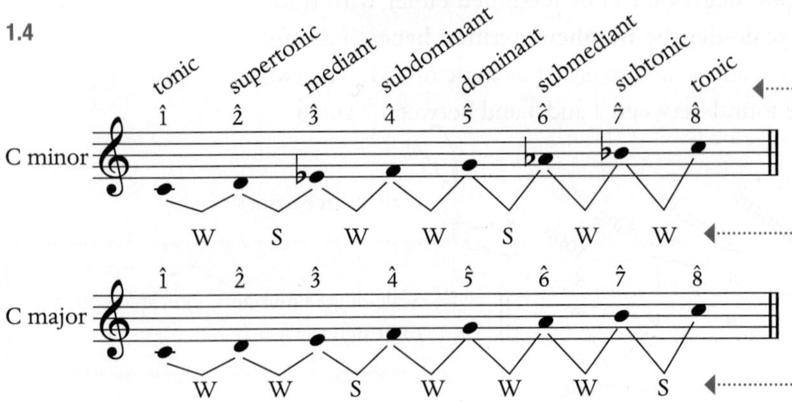

Scale-degree names and numbers. In the natural minor, $\hat{7}$ is called **subtonic**.

Arrangement of whole tones and semitones for the natural minor scale: semitones at $\hat{2}$–$\hat{3}$ and $\hat{5}$–$\hat{6}$.

Compare with the major scale: semitones at $\hat{3}$–$\hat{4}$ and $\hat{7}$–$\hat{8}$.

Note that $\hat{7}$ in natural minor is called the subtonic rather than the leading tone. Because the subtonic is a whole tone rather than a semitone below $\hat{1}$, it lacks a sense of directed movement toward the tonic.

HARMONIC MINOR SCALE

The subtonic often is raised by one semitone, turning it into a leading tone. Depending on the scale, raising the subtonic to a leading tone may require a natural (if the subtonic is flat), a sharp (if the subtonic is natural), or a double sharp (if the subtonic is sharp).

1.5

In C natural minor, the subtonic (B♭) is raised by a semitone to become the leading tone (B♮) of C harmonic minor.

In A natural minor, the subtonic (G) is raised by a semitone to become the leading tone (G♯) of A harmonic minor.

In G♯ minor, the subtonic (F♯) is raised by a semitone to become the leading tone (F𝄪) of G♯ harmonic minor.

The scale that results from raising $\hat{7}$ is called **harmonic minor**. In a harmonic minor scale, there are semitones between $\hat{2}$ and $\hat{3}$ and between $\hat{5}$ and $\hat{6}$ (as in natural minor), as well as between $\hat{7}$ and $\hat{8}$ (as in major, but not natural minor). There is also a gap, spanning three semitones, between $\hat{6}$ and $\hat{7}$. This gap is called an **augmented second** (see Chapter 2).

1.6 The harmonic minor scale has three semitones and an augmented second.

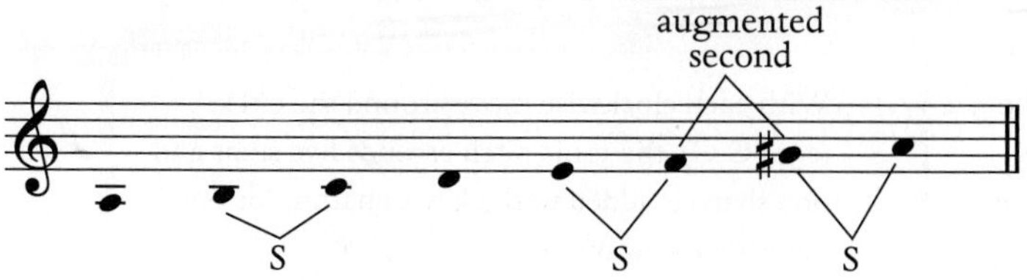

ASCENDING MELODIC MINOR SCALE

Sometimes, the gap between $\hat{6}$ and $\hat{7}$ in the harmonic minor scale is smoothed out by also raising $\hat{6}$. Note that $\hat{6}$ is typically raised only in conjunction with $\hat{7}$. Raising both $\hat{6}$ and $\hat{7}$ creates a second variant of the minor scale called **ascending melodic minor**. Like natural minor, the ascending melodic minor scale contains only two semitones: $\hat{2}$-$\hat{3}$ and $\hat{7}$-$\hat{8}$. Melodic minor is particularly suitable for singing or playing a melody that ascends to the tonic. Like raised $\hat{7}$, raised $\hat{6}$ always requires an accidental: if $\hat{6}$ in natural minor is flat, it must be made natural; if it is natural, it must be made sharp; if it is sharp, it must be made double sharp.

1.7 The ascending melodic minor raises both $\hat{6}$ and $\hat{7}$.

A final variant of the minor scale is called **descending melodic minor**. When descending melodically, the upward tendencies of raised $\hat{6}$ and $\hat{7}$ may no longer be musically desirable. Therefore, when descending, $\hat{6}$ and $\hat{7}$ revert to their natural minor form. As a result, the descending melodic minor is identical to natural minor.

KEY SIGNATURES FOR MAJOR KEYS

CIRCLE OF FIFTHS

A piece or passage that makes consistent reference to a particular major or minor scale is said to be in that **key**. So, for example, music that uses the B♭-major scale is in the key of B♭ major and music that uses the E-minor scale is in the key of E minor. The sharps and flats (accidentals) needed for a major scale (or major key) can be conveniently summarized in a **key signature**, written directly after the clef at the beginning of each line of a musical staff.

1.8

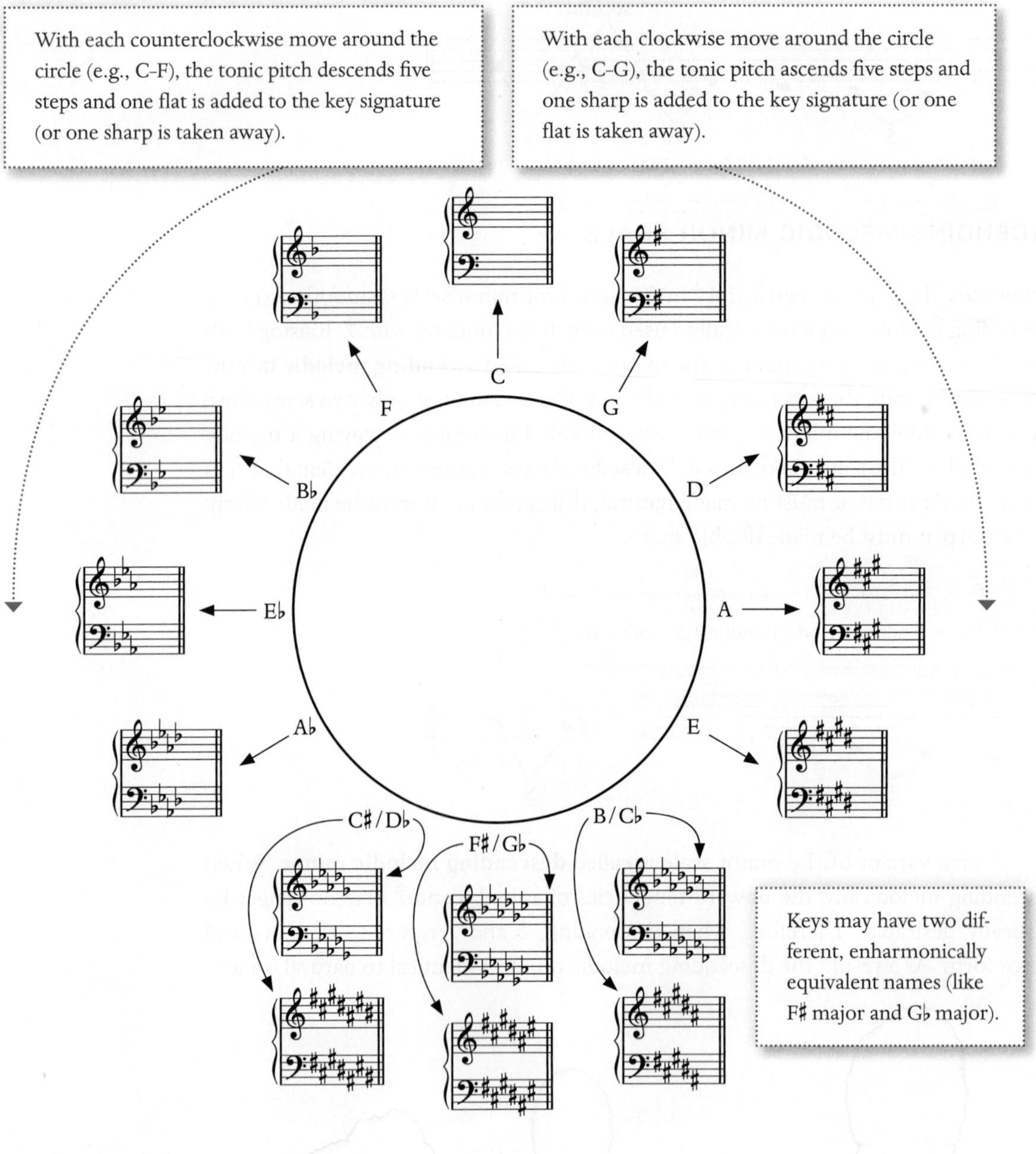

With each counterclockwise move around the circle (e.g., C–F), the tonic pitch descends five steps and one flat is added to the key signature (or one sharp is taken away).
With each clockwise move around the circle (e.g., C–G), the tonic pitch ascends five steps and one sharp is added to the key signature (or one flat is taken away).
C
G
D
A
E
B/C♭
F♯/G♭
C♯/D♭
A♭
E♭
B♭
F
Keys may have two different, enharmonically equivalent names (like F♯ major and G♭ major).

The key signature directs performers to consistently perform notes with sharps or flats, unless they are cancelled by another accidental. Transposing a scale up five steps adds one sharp to the key signature (or removes one flat). Transposing a scale down five steps adds one flat to the key signature (or removes one sharp). As a result, all of the major key signatures can be arranged around a **circle of fifths**.

The accidentals in the key signature must be written in the correct position on the staff and in the proper order. The order in which sharps and flats are written follows the circle of fifths. Sharps move clockwise from F♯: F♯-C♯-G♯-D♯-A♯-E♯-B♯. Flats move counterclockwise from B♭: B♭-E♭-A♭-D♭-G♭-C♭-F♭.

1.9

Good Key signatures for E major and D♭ major written with accidentals in the correct, circle-of-fifths order and in the correct octave

Poor Key signatures for E major and D♭ major written with accidentals in the wrong order and (often) in the wrong octave

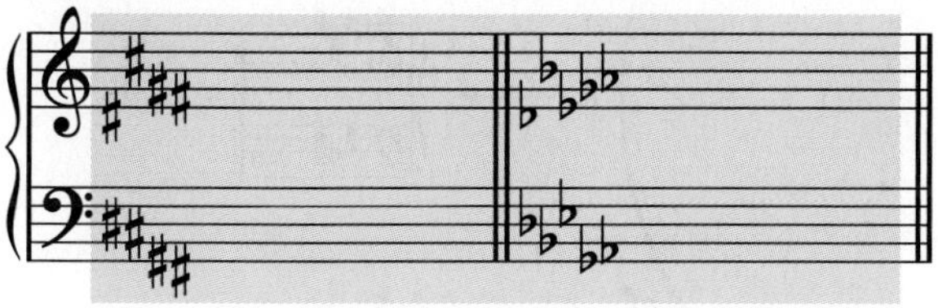

KEY SIGNATURES FOR MINOR KEYS

CIRCLE OF FIFTHS

As with the major scale, the natural minor scale (and its variants) can be transposed to start on any of the twelve notes. As with major, the circle of fifths can show the accidentals needed to write minor scales (or minor keys) gathered into a key signature. (The illustration uses a common shorthand of lowercase letters to represent minor keys.)

1.10

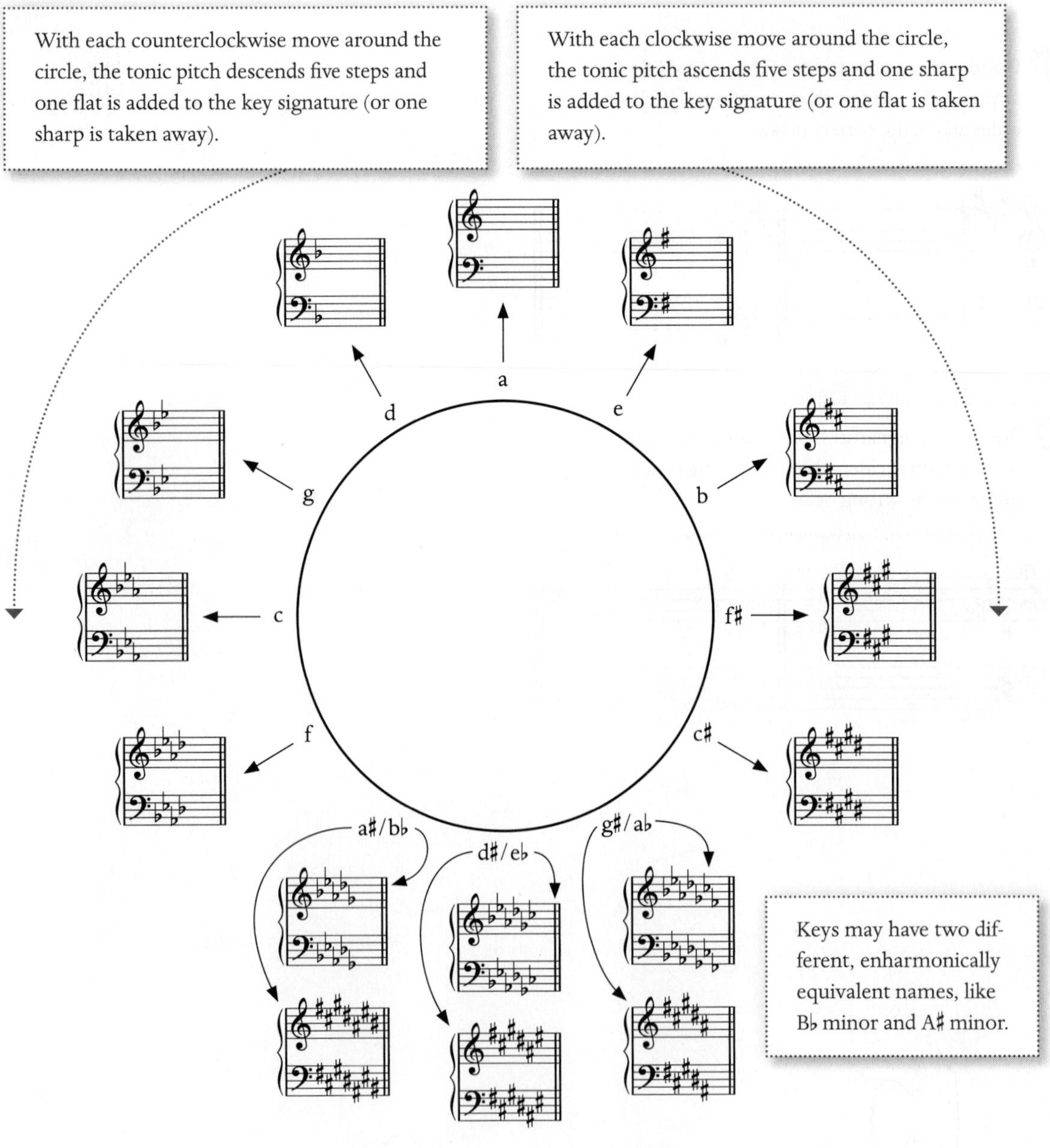
With each counterclockwise move around the circle, the tonic pitch descends five steps and one flat is added to the key signature (or one sharp is taken away).
With each clockwise move around the circle, the tonic pitch ascends five steps and one sharp is added to the key signature (or one flat is taken away).
a
e
b
f♯
c♯
g♯/a♭
d♯/e♭
a♯/b♭
f
c
g
d
Keys may have two different, enharmonically equivalent names, like B♭ minor and A♯ minor.

When writing a minor key signature, use only the accidentals from natural minor. This is the basic form of the minor scale—the others (harmonic minor and ascending melodic minor) are variants that result from altering $\hat{7}$ or both $\hat{6}$ and $\hat{7}$.

RELATIVE AND PARALLEL KEYS

RELATIVE KEYS

Major and minor keys with the same key signature are called **relative keys**. For example, G major and E minor both use the same seven notes (the only accidental is F♯), but each starts on a different note.

1.11

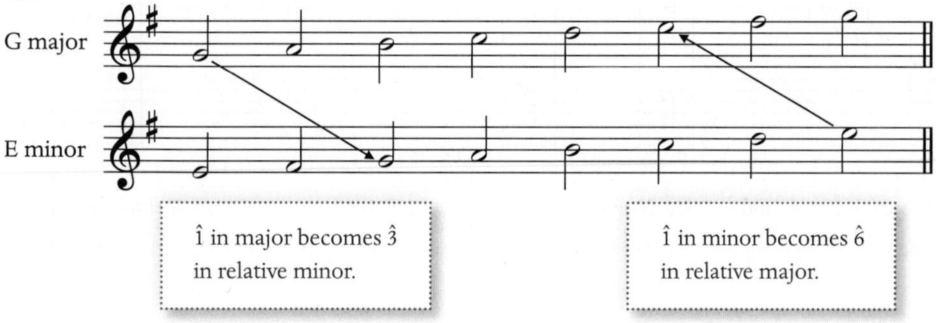

A double circle of fifths can show all of the relative major and minor keys and the key signature they share.

1.12

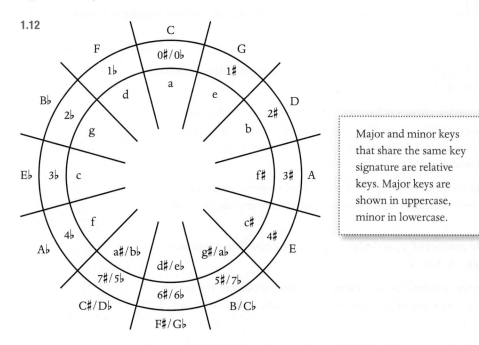

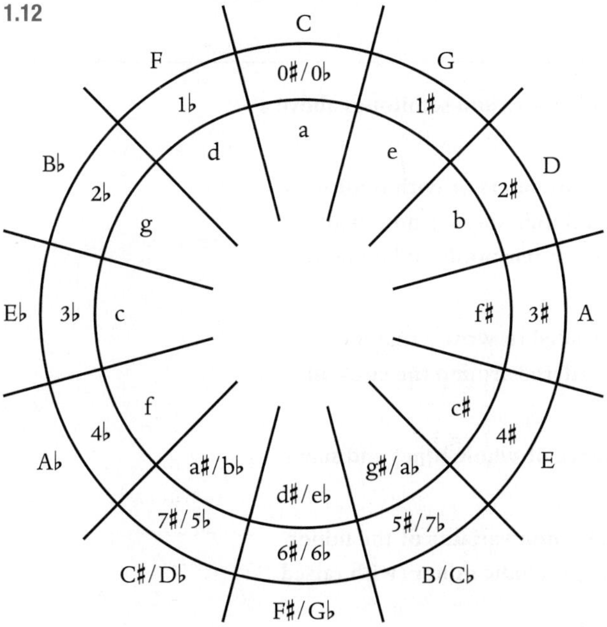

Major and minor keys that share the same key signature are relative keys. Major keys are shown in uppercase, minor in lowercase.

PARALLEL KEYS

Major and minor keys that share the same tonic are called **parallel keys**. Looking back to the double circle of fifths, if you start on a minor key and move three fifths clockwise, you will find its parallel major, and if you start on a major key and move three fifths counterclockwise you will find its parallel minor. Although their key signatures are different (unlike relative keys), parallel keys share not only $\hat{1}$, but also $\hat{2}$, $\hat{4}$, and $\hat{5}$. Indeed, they differ only in $\hat{3}$, $\hat{6}$, and $\hat{7}$.

1.13

G major and G minor are parallel keys (major and minor scales with the same tonic).

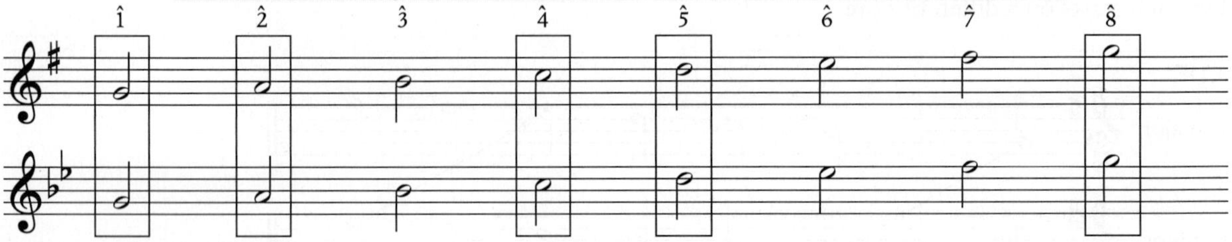

Parallel keys have the same $\hat{1}$, $\hat{2}$, $\hat{4}$, and $\hat{5}$. Scale degrees $\hat{3}$, $\hat{6}$, and $\hat{7}$ are a half step lower in the parallel minor.

review and interact

POINTS FOR REVIEW

- **A major scale consists of a particular sequence of whole tones and semitones above a tonic pitch: W-W-S-W-W-W-S.**
- **Scale degrees can be identified either with scale-degree numbers or with traditional names: $\hat{1}$ = tonic; $\hat{2}$ = supertonic; $\hat{3}$ = mediant; $\hat{4}$ = subdominant; $\hat{5}$ = dominant; $\hat{6}$ = submediant; and $\hat{7}$ = leading tone (in major, as well as harmonic and melodic minor) or subtonic (natural minor).**
- **A key signature lists the accidentals (sharps or flats) needed to write a major or minor scale beginning on a tonic. Key signatures are ordered around the circle of fifths.**
- **The natural minor scale consists of a particular sequence of whole tones and semitones above a tonic pitch: W-S-W-W-S-W-W.**
- **Minor key signatures refer to natural minor scales. Common variants of the minor scale are harmonic minor (with raised $\hat{7}$) and ascending melodic minor (with raised $\hat{6}$ and $\hat{7}$).**
- **Relative keys have the same key signature. Parallel keys have the same tonic ($\hat{1}$).**

TEST YOURSELF

1. Write scales as indicated. Use appropriate accidentals (do not use key signatures).

A major | F minor (natural)

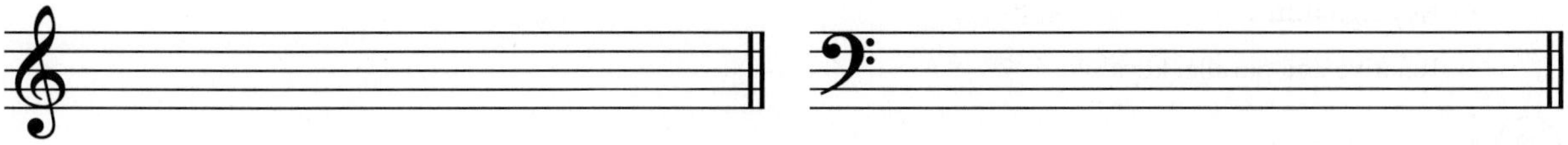

B minor (ascending melodic) | G♯ minor (harmonic)

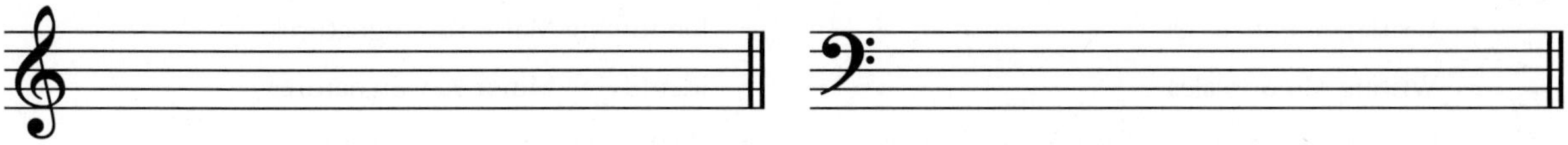

2. Given the name of a major or minor scale and a scale-degree number, write the appropriate note.

F major: $\hat{4}$ | F♯ minor: $\hat{6}$ (natural minor) | G minor: $\hat{7}$ (harmonic minor) | A♭ major: $\hat{3}$ | D minor: $\hat{6}$ (ascending melodic minor) | E major: $\hat{5}$

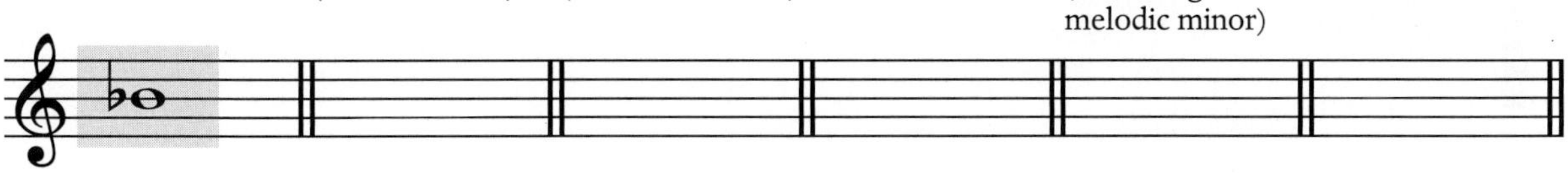

3. Write key signatures for these keys.

B minor | E♭ major | F minor | E minor | F♯ major | D minor

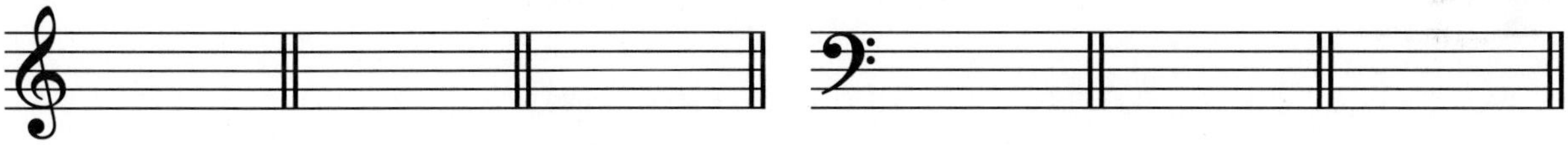

4. Name the two keys, one major and one minor, represented by each of these key signatures. Use uppercase to indicate the major key, lowercase for minor.

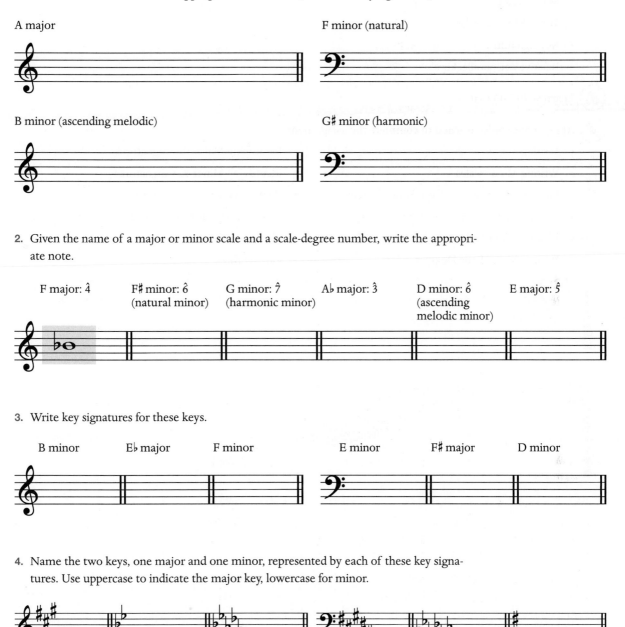

A, f♯ ______ ______ ______ ______ ______

Know It? Show It!

Focus by working through the tutorials on:

- Major scales
- Writing minor scales
- Key signatures
- Relative and parallel keys

Learn with inQuizitive.

Apply what you've learned to complete the assignments:

- Writing Major Scales
- Writing Minor scales
- Identifying Major Keys from Scale Degrees
- Identifying Minor Keys from Scale Degrees
- Writing Major Scale Degrees
- Writing Minor Scale Degrees
- Identifying Major Key Signatures
- Identifying Minor Key Signatures
- Writing Major Key Signatures
- Writing Minor Key Signatures
- Identifying Relative Keys
- Parallel Keys

chapter 2

Intervals

Intervals measure the size and quality of the distance between notes.

Interval Size

Simple and Compound Intervals

Interval Quality

- Major and minor intervals (seconds, thirds, sixths, sevenths)
- Perfect intervals (unisons, fourths, fifths, octaves)
- Interval inversion
- Natural (white-key) intervals
- Enharmonic intervals

Consonant and Dissonant Intervals

Intervals in a Key

INTERVAL SIZE

An **interval** is the distance between two tones. If the tones occur simultaneously, the interval is a **harmonic interval**; if the tones occur one after the other, the interval is a **melodic interval**. The size of an interval is the number of letter names it spans, counting either up or down (including the first note in the count). To determine the size of an interval, ignore any accidentals. Interval sizes are named using ordinal numbers (for example, an interval that spans two steps is a second or 2nd).

2.1

SIZE	NUMBER OF STEPS (LETTER NAMES) SPANNED	EXAMPLES
Unison	1 (C-C)	
Second	2 (C-D)	
Third	3 (C-D-E)	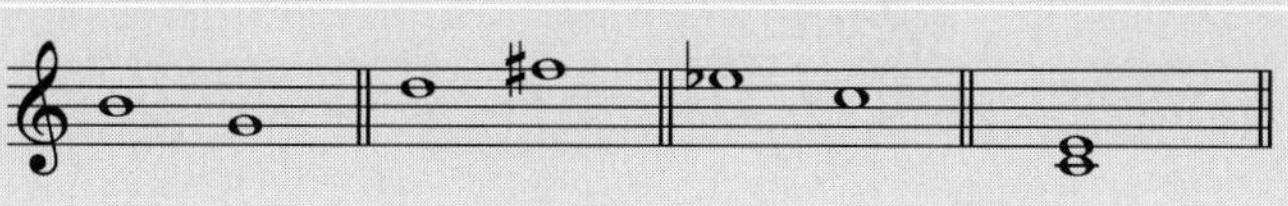

SIZE	NUMBER OF STEPS (LETTER NAMES) SPANNED	EXAMPLES
Fourth	4 (C-D-E-F)	
Fifth	5 (C-D-E-F-G)	
Sixth	6 (C-D-E-F-G-A)	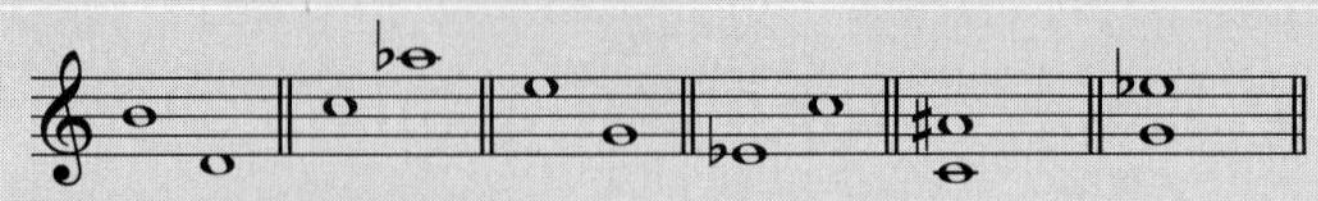
Seventh	7 (C-D-E-F-G-A-B)	
Octave	8 (C-D-E-F-G-A-B-C)	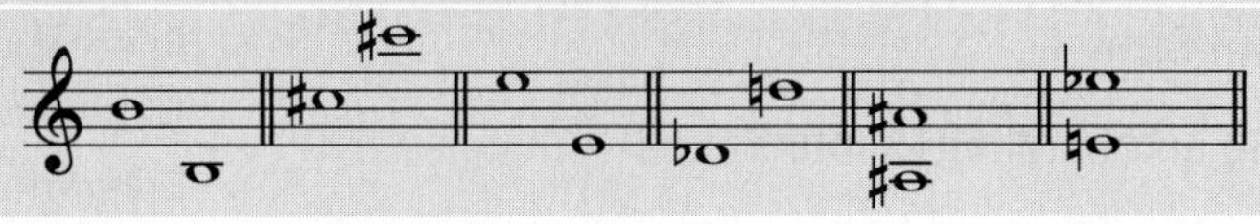

SIMPLE AND COMPOUND INTERVALS

Intervals smaller than an octave are **simple intervals**. Intervals larger than an octave are **compound intervals**; they contain a simple interval plus one or more octaves. You can identify a compound interval as you do a simple interval, by counting the total number of letter names it contains. Alternatively, compound intervals may be identified by the simple interval they contain, ignoring any extra octaves. When adding an octave to a simple interval, the arithmetic will look a little odd. For example, a second plus an octave is a ninth, not a tenth.

2.2

SIMPLE NAME (STEPS)	EXAMPLE	COMPOUND NAME (STEPS)	EXAMPLE
Second (2)		Ninth (9 = 2 + 8)	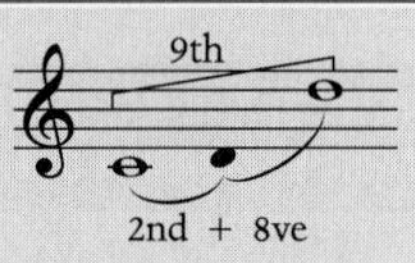
Third (3)		Tenth (10 = 3 + 8)	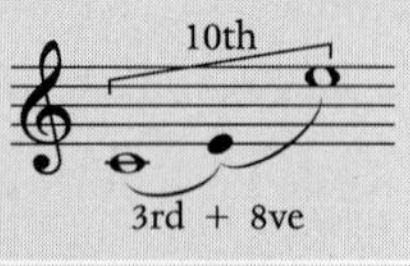
Fourth (4)		Eleventh (11 = 4 + 8)	

SIMPLE NAME (STEPS)	EXAMPLE	COMPOUND NAME (STEPS)	EXAMPLE
Fifth (5)		Twelfth (12 = 5 + 8)	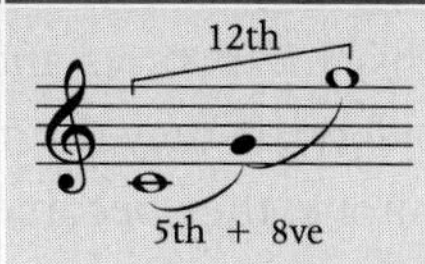
Sixth (6)		Thirteenth (13 = 6 + 8)	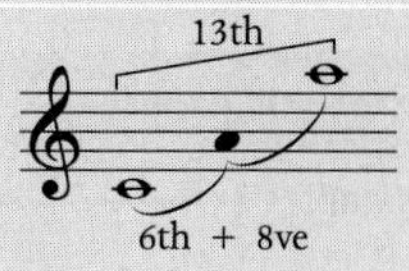
Seventh (7)		Fourteenth (14 = 7 + 8)	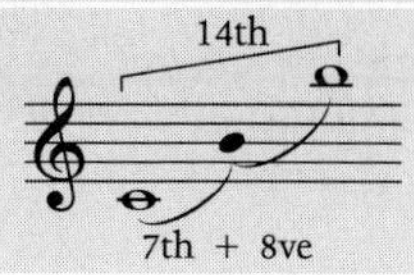

INTERVAL QUALITY

MAJOR AND MINOR INTERVALS (SECONDS, THIRDS, SIXTHS, SEVENTHS)

Intervals of the same numerical size may vary in **quality** depending on how many semitones they contain. Seconds, thirds, sixths, and sevenths are usually **minor** (smaller) or **major** (larger) in quality. If a minor interval shrinks by a semitone, it becomes **diminished**; if a major interval expands by semitone, it becomes **augmented**. Note that the same thing is true of the equivalent compound intervals. For instance, a ninth (compound second) may be diminished, minor, major, or augmented.

2.3

DIMINISHED (d)	MINOR (m)	MAJOR (M)	AUGMENTED (A)
smaller ←			→ **larger**

We focus on seconds and thirds.

2.4

Seconds span two steps (between a line and the adjacent space).

The two notes of a second are written side by side, with any accidentals placed before both notes.

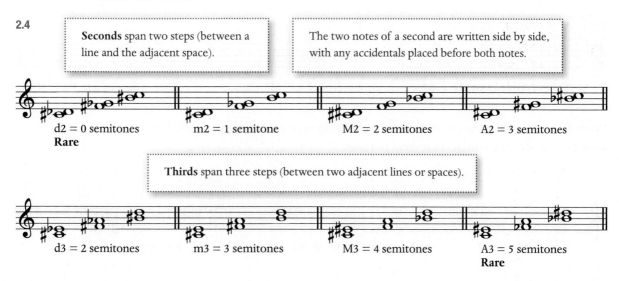

d2 = 0 semitones **Rare** | m2 = 1 semitone | M2 = 2 semitones | A2 = 3 semitones

Thirds span three steps (between two adjacent lines or spaces).

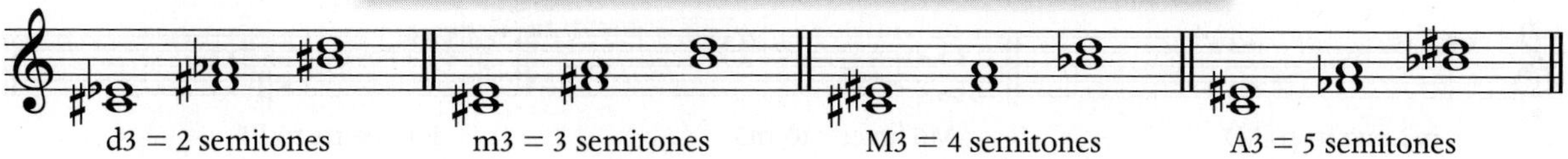

d3 = 2 semitones | m3 = 3 semitones | M3 = 4 semitones | A3 = 5 semitones **Rare**

PERFECT INTERVALS (UNISONS, FOURTHS, FIFTHS, OCTAVES)

Unisons, fourths, fifths, and octaves and their compounds are usually perfect (*they may never be minor or major*). If they shrink by a semitone, they become diminished; if they expand by a semitone, they become augmented.

2.5

DIMINISHED (d)	PERFECT (P)	AUGMENTED (A)
smaller ←	———	→ larger

We focus on fourths and fifths.

2.6

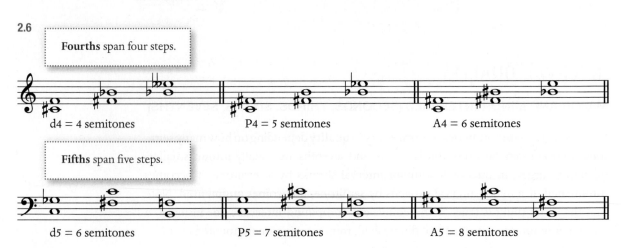

Fourths span four steps.

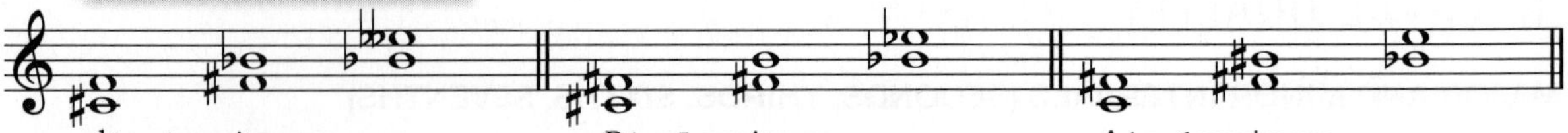

d4 = 4 semitones   P4 = 5 semitones   A4 = 6 semitones

Fifths span five steps.

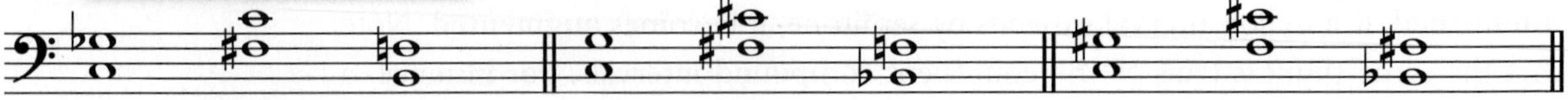

d5 = 6 semitones   P5 = 7 semitones   A5 = 8 semitones

INTERVAL INVERSION

If you divide an octave into two smaller intervals, the two intervals are related by **inversion**.

2.7

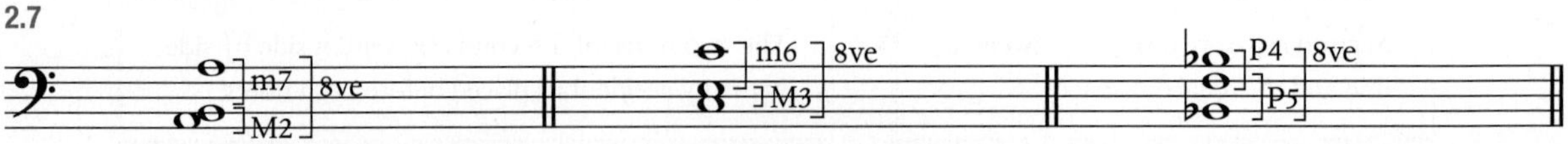

Octave divided into M2 + m7   Octave divided into M3 + m6   Octave divided into P5 + P4

To invert an interval, either shift the lower note up an octave, or the upper note down an octave, so that the two notes reverse position.

2.8

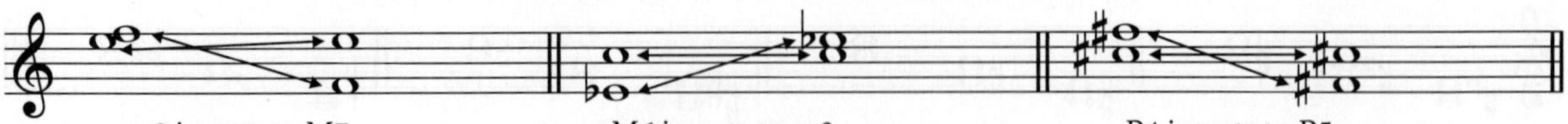

m2 inverts to M7   M6 inverts to m3   P4 inverts to P5

When intervals are inverted, their size and quality change in predictable ways.

2.9

EFFECT OF INVERSION ON INTERVAL SIZE (INTERVAL SIZES SUM TO 9)
Unison ← inverts to → Octave
Second ← inverts to → Seventh
Third ← inverts to → Sixth
Fourth ← inverts to → Fifth

EFFECT OF INVERSION ON INTERVAL QUALITY
Major ← inverts to → Minor
Augmented ← inverts to → Diminished
Perfect ← inverts to → Perfect

NATURAL (WHITE-KEY) INTERVALS

Knowing the **natural** qualities of intervals—written without accidentals, using only the white keys on the piano—can be an efficient way to identify or write intervals of a particular quality.

2.10

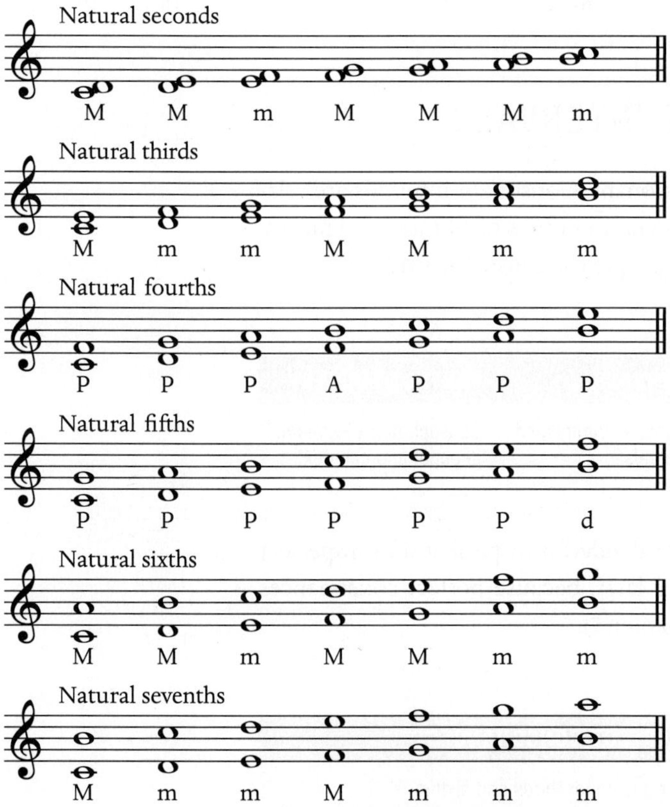

Adding a sharp to the upper note of an interval, or a flat to the lower note, causes the interval to expand. Conversely, adding a flat to the upper note, or a sharp to the lower note, causes the interval to contract.

2.11

D–F expands to D–F♯ or D♭–F C–G contracts to C–G♭ or C♯–G
(m3) (M3) (M3) (P5) (d5) (d5)

ENHARMONIC INTERVALS

Intervals of different sizes (spanning a different number of letter names) but that contain the same number of semitones are **enharmonic**. For example, A6 and m7—one a sixth and the other a seventh—both span 10 semitones.

2.12

Enharmonic intervals include the same number of semitones but span a different number of scale steps.

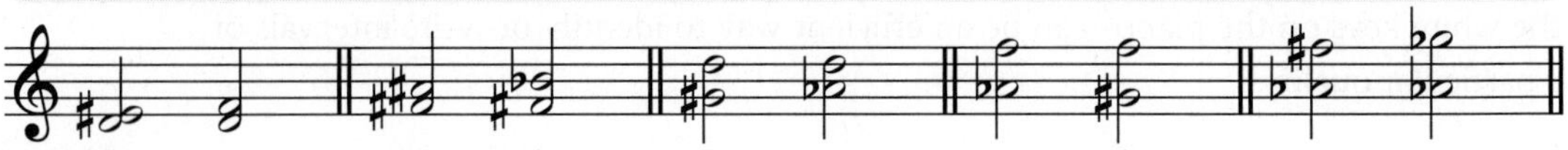

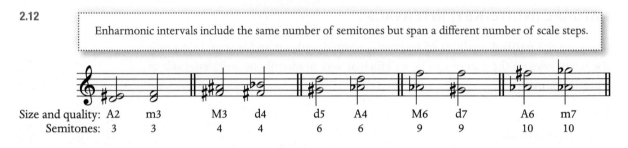

Size and quality:	A2	m3	M3	d4	d5	A4	M6	d7	A6	m7
Semitones:	3	3	4	4	6	6	9	9	10	10

CONSONANT AND DISSONANT INTERVALS

Music treats intervals as either consonant or dissonant. Consonant intervals are relatively stable—they appear at beginnings and especially endings of phrases and pieces. Dissonant intervals are relatively unstable: they propel the music forward.

2.13

CONSONANT INTERVALS	DISSONANT INTERVALS	PERFECT FOURTH
Perfect unisons, fifths, and octaves; major and minor thirds and sixths	Seconds and sevenths; all diminished and augmented intervals	Consonant or dissonant, depending on context

The consonant intervals are often further divided into perfect and imperfect consonances. This distinction will be important later, because perfect consonances can be approached only in certain ways (see Chapter 5).

2.14

PERFECT CONSONANCES	IMPERFECT CONSONANCES
Perfect unisons, perfect fifths, perfect octaves	Major and minor thirds and sixths

When two intervals are enharmonic, at least one is always dissonant.

INTERVALS IN A KEY

In major keys, the intervals above the tonic are all major or perfect.

2.15

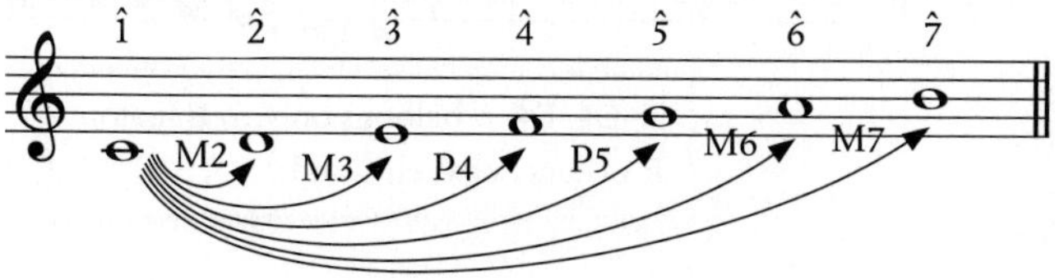

This information can be useful in calculating the quality of intervals. Imagine that the lowest note of an interval is the tonic of a major scale, and compare the upper note to the degrees of the scale.

2.16

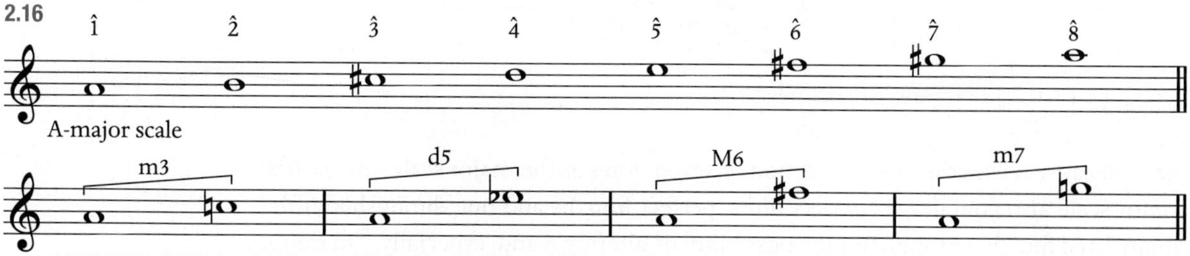

C♮ is a semitone lower than $\hat{3}$ in A major, so A–C is a m3.

E♭ is a semitone lower than $\hat{5}$ in A major, so A–E♭ is a d5.

F♯ is $\hat{6}$ in A major, so A–F♯ is a M6.

G♮ is a semitone lower than $\hat{7}$ in A major, so A–G is a m7.

All of the fifths in a major key are perfect, except for the fifth between $\hat{7}$ and $\hat{4}$, which is diminished. (Similarly, all of the fourths are perfect except for the fourth between $\hat{4}$ and $\hat{7}$, which is augmented.)

2.17

Six perfect fifths above scale degrees $\hat{1}$, $\hat{2}$, $\hat{3}$, $\hat{4}$, $\hat{5}$, and $\hat{6}$. One diminished fifth, between scale degrees $\hat{7}$ and $\hat{4}$.

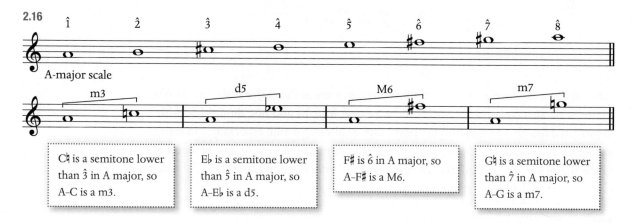

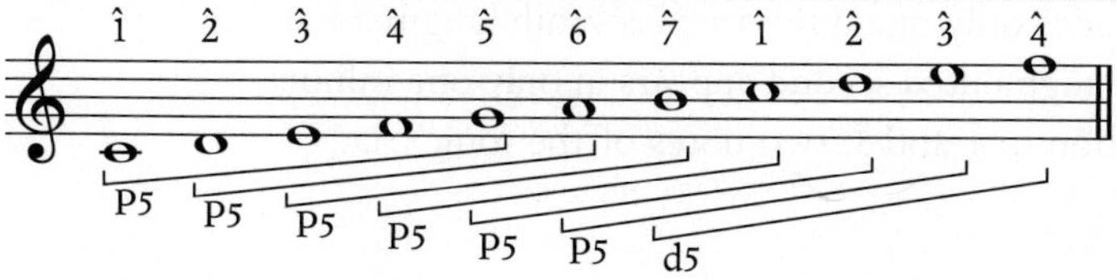

The diminished fifth/augmented fourth between $\hat{7}$ and $\hat{4}$ plays a unique role in defining the key. Each major scale includes only one diminished fifth/augmented fourth, and each diminished fifth/augmented fourth is part of only one major scale. As a dissonance, it seeks resolution to $\hat{1}$ and $\hat{3}$, two notes of the tonic triad (a topic for future chapters). The diminished fifth/augmented fourth is sometimes called a **tritone**, because an augmented fourth contains three whole tones.

2.18

The tritone C–F♯ identifies G major.

The tritone A–D♯ identifies E major.

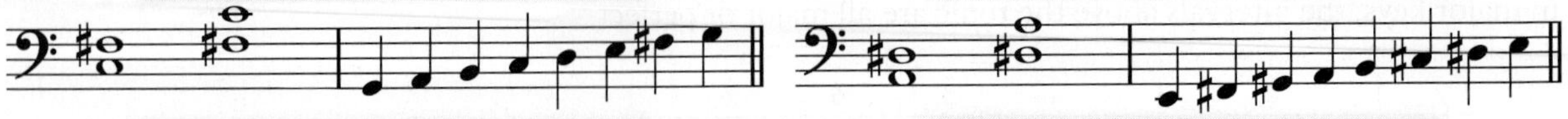

C–F♯/F♯–C belongs only to G major. It occurs between $\hat{7}$ and $\hat{4}$.

A–D♯/D♯–A belongs only to E major. It occurs between $\hat{7}$ and $\hat{4}$.

In the natural minor scale, the intervals formed above the tonic are minor and perfect, except for the major second between $\hat{1}$ and $\hat{2}$.

2.19

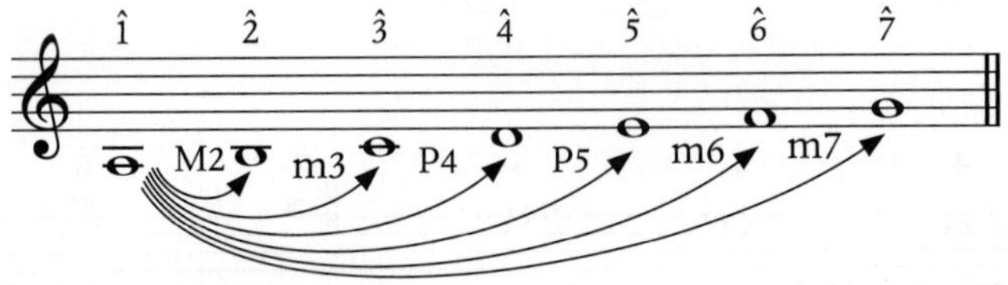

Because it uses the same collection of seven notes as the major scale, the natural minor scale also contains six perfect fifths/perfect fourths and one diminished fifth/augmented fourth (tritone). But the possibility of altering $\hat{6}$ and, especially, $\hat{7}$ in minor allows for the creation of new intervals. Like the diminished fifth/augmented fourth in the major key, the diminished seventh/augmented second between raised $\hat{7}$ and $\hat{6}$ is important in defining a minor key.

2.20

d7/A2 are formed between $\hat{7}$ and $\hat{6}$ in harmonic minor.

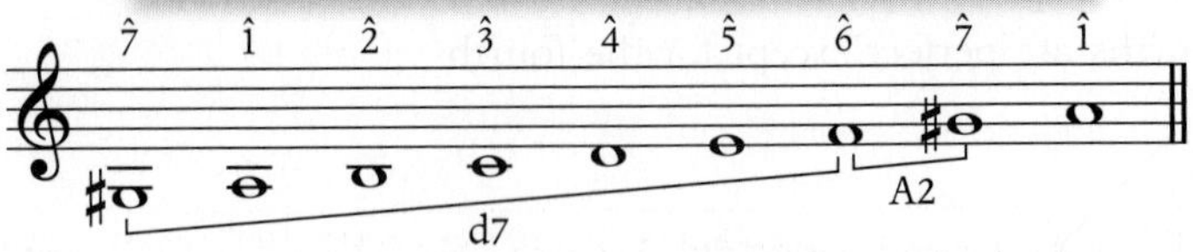

Each harmonic minor scale includes only one diminished seventh/augmented second, and each diminished seventh/augmented second appears in only one minor scale. As a dissonance, it seeks resolution to $\hat{1}$ and $\hat{5}$, two notes of the tonic triad (a topic for future chapters).

2.21

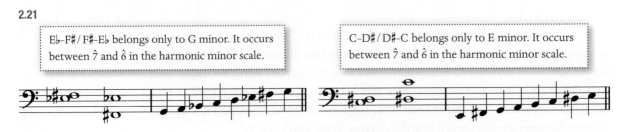

E♭–F♯/F♯–E♭ belongs only to G minor. It occurs between $\hat{7}$ and $\hat{6}$ in the harmonic minor scale.

C–D♯/D♯–C belongs only to E minor. It occurs between $\hat{7}$ and $\hat{6}$ in the harmonic minor scale.

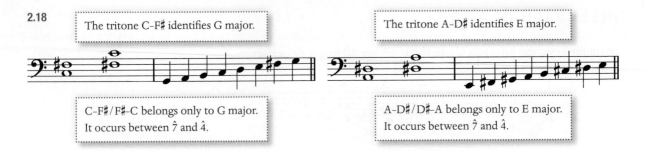

review and interact

POINTS FOR REVIEW

- The size of an interval is the number of letter names it spans, irrespective of accidentals.
- Intervals smaller than an octave are simple intervals. Intervals larger than an octave are compound intervals, because they contain a simple interval plus one or more octaves.
- Seconds, thirds, sixths, sevenths, and their compounds may be diminished, minor, major, or augmented.
- Fourths, fifths, octaves, and their compounds may be diminished, perfect, or augmented.
- Dividing the octave in two smaller parts produces two intervals related by inversion. Intervals related by inversion have sizes that sum to 9 (like seconds and sevenths, thirds and sixths, and fourths and fifths) and qualities that are related in predictable ways (diminished becomes augmented and vice versa; minor becomes major and vice versa; perfect remains perfect).
- Enharmonic intervals contain the same number of semitones but have different names.
- Major and minor thirds and sixths are consonant (imperfect consonances), as are perfect fifths and octaves (perfect consonances). Seconds, sevenths, and all augmented and diminished intervals are dissonant. The perfect fourth may be consonant or dissonant depending on context.
- Intervals may be calculated with reference either to the natural (white-key) intervals or the major scale of which the interval's lowest note is the tonic.
- A major scale has only major and perfect intervals above the tonic. The diminished fifth/augmented fourth uniquely defines a major scale.
- A minor scale has mostly minor and perfect intervals above the tonic. The diminished seventh/augmented second uniquely defines a harmonic minor scale.

TEST YOURSELF

1. Identify these intervals by numerical size and quality (d = diminished; m = minor; M = major; P = perfect; A = augmented). If the interval is larger than an octave (compound), give its simple size and quality.

2. Write the requested interval above the given note.

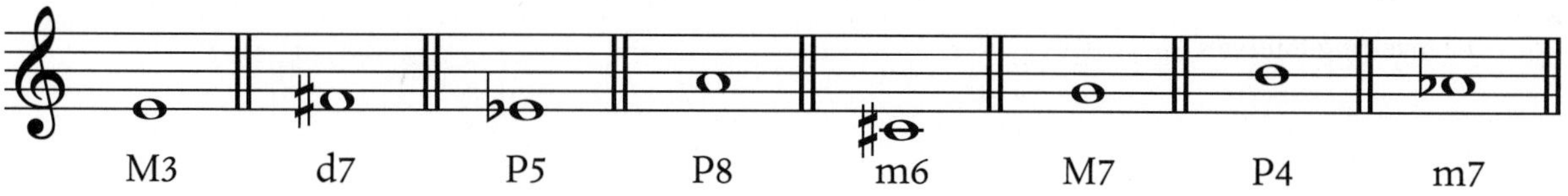

3. Name the notes and the interval between these pairs of scale degrees in a major key (ascending from the first to the second):
   a. F major: $\hat{2}$-$\hat{6}$
   b. B♭ major: $\hat{4}$-$\hat{7}$
   c. E major: $\hat{1}$-$\hat{6}$
   d. D major: $\hat{3}$-$\hat{5}$
4. Name the notes and interval between these pairs of scale degrees in a minor key (ascending from the first to the second):
   a. G♯ minor: $\hat{2}$-$\hat{6}$ (natural minor)
   b. B♭ minor: $\hat{7}$-$\hat{6}$ (harmonic minor)
   c. D minor: $\hat{1}$-$\hat{5}$
   d. C♯ minor: $\hat{4}$-$\hat{7}$ (harmonic minor)
5. Identify the major key that uniquely contains each of these diminished fifths/augmented fourths.
   a. C♯-G
   b. D-A♭
   c. D-G♯
   d. G-D♭
6. Identify the minor key whose harmonic minor scale uniquely contains each of these diminished sevenths/augmented seconds.
   a. E♭-F♯
   b. B♭-C♯
   c. A♯-G
   d. D♯-C

Know It? Show It!

Focus by working through the tutorials on:

- Interval basics
- Recognizing intervals
- Writing simple intervals

Learn with inQuizitive.

Apply what you've learned to complete the assignments:

- Identifying Interval Size
- Writing Intervals
- Inverting Intervals
- Identifying Enharmonic Intervals
- Identifying Intervals in a Key

chapter

3 Triads and Seventh Chords

Triads and seventh chords are the basic harmonies of most Western music.

TRIADS

TRIAD CONSTRUCTION

A **triad** consists of three different pitches: a fifth divided into two thirds, or two thirds stacked to make a fifth. Triads can appear on three consecutive lines or spaces on the staff. When a triad is stacked in thirds, the lowest note is the **root**, the middle note is the **third**, and the highest note is the **fifth**.

3.1

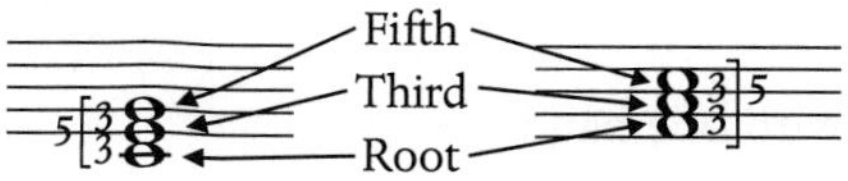

TRIAD QUALITIES

Triads are classified by **quality**: depending on the qualities of the thirds and fifths they contain, triads may be **diminished**, **minor**, **major**, or **augmented**. You can refer to a triad by its name and quality, for example, C♯-major triad or D-minor triad.

3.2

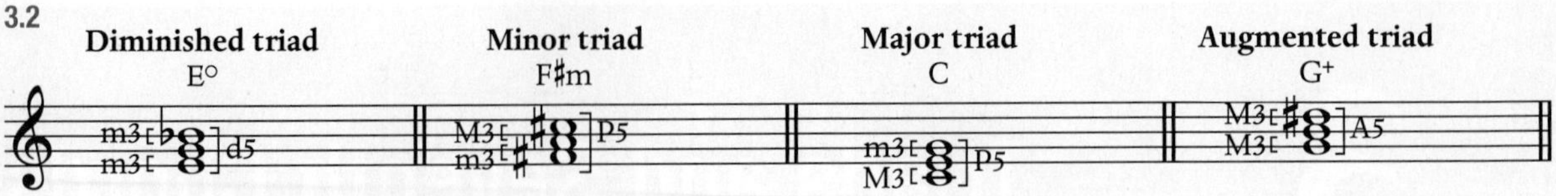

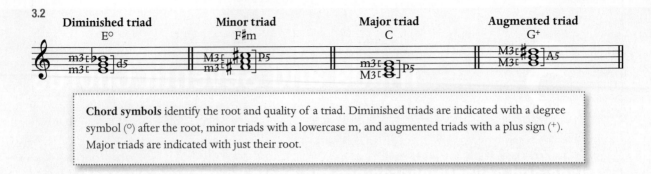

> **Chord symbols** identify the root and quality of a triad. Diminished triads are indicated with a degree symbol (°) after the root, minor triads with a lowercase m, and augmented triads with a plus sign (+). Major triads are indicated with just their root.

NATURAL (WHITE-KEY) TRIADS

Knowing the **natural triads**—without accidentals—can be helpful in identifying triad quality.

3.3

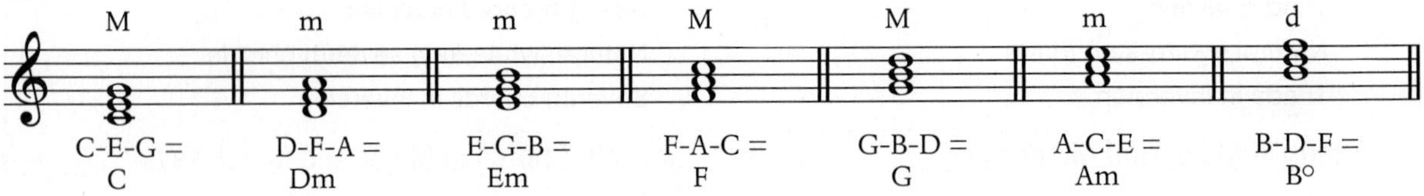

Every triad uses one of those seven groups of letter names: CEG, DFA, EGB, FAC, GBD, ACE, BDF. To spell a triad, start with a white-key triad and, if necessary, add an accidental to match the root requested. Then check the intervals of the triad, adding accidentals as needed for the proper quality of the third and the fifth.

3.4

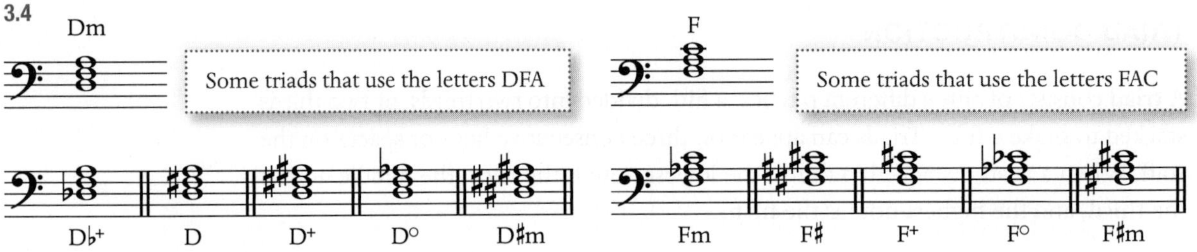

TRIADS IN INVERSION

Triads can be arranged in a variety of ways, from three notes played with one hand at the piano to being spread out over an entire orchestra. However they are arranged, the lowest-sounding note of a triad is called the **bass**; any one of a triad's three notes can sound in the bass. The bass note of a triad determines its **position**. When the root of a triad is in the bass, the triad is in **root position**. When the third of a triad is in the bass, the triad is in **first inversion**. When the fifth of a triad is in the bass, the triad is in **second inversion**. It does not matter which notes are on the top or in the middle of the chord: the position is determined solely by the bass.

3.5

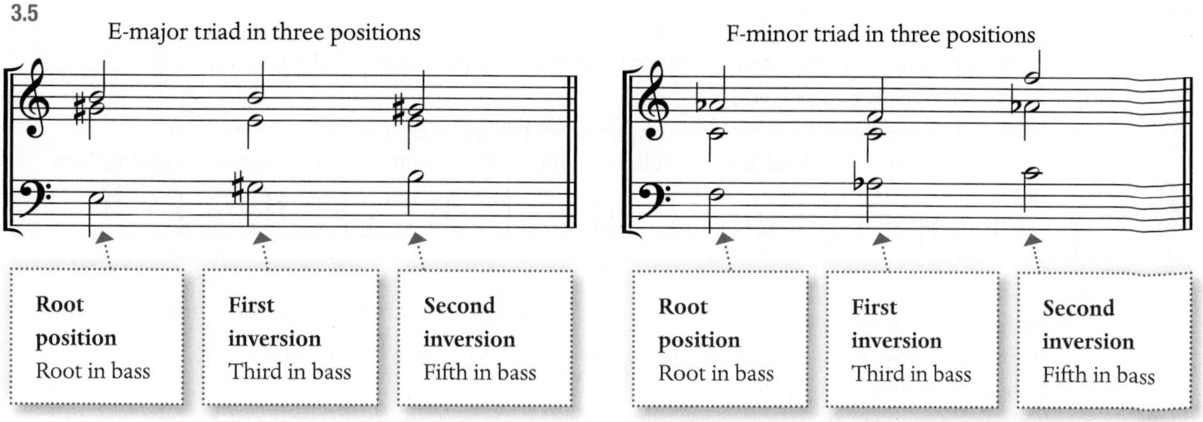

Triad positions are commonly labeled with a stack of two Arabic numbers, or a **figure**: $\substack{5\\3}$ = root position; $\substack{6\\3}$ = first inversion; $\substack{6\\4}$ = second inversion. These numbers correspond to the intervals formed above the lowest-sounding note.

3.6

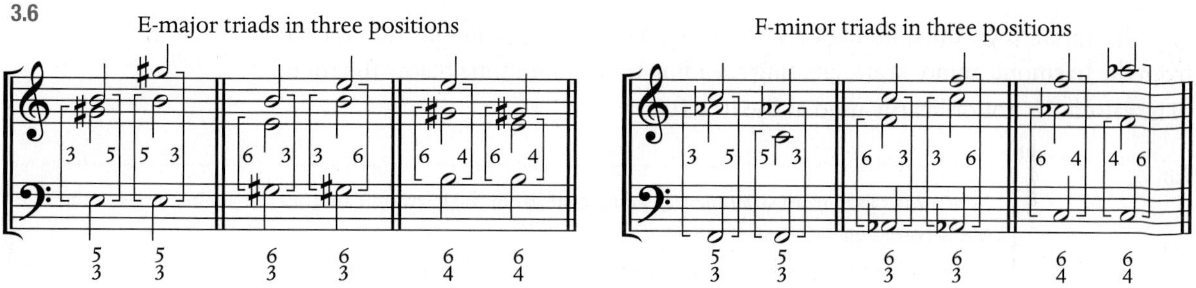

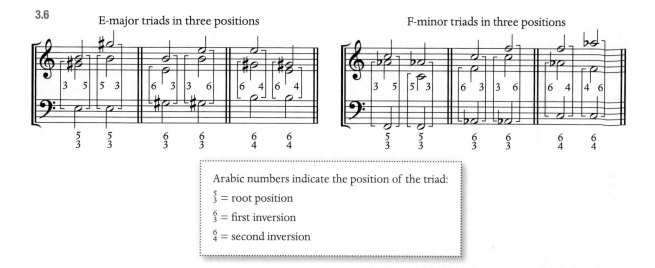

Arabic numbers indicate the position of the triad:

$\substack{5\\3}$ = root position

$\substack{6\\3}$ = first inversion

$\substack{6\\4}$ = second inversion

TRIADS IN MAJOR AND MINOR KEYS

ROMAN NUMERALS

Within a major or minor key, **Roman numerals**—corresponding to the root—identify triads. Major triads are indicated with uppercase Roman numerals; lowercase Roman numerals indicate minor triads; and lowercase Roman numerals followed by a degree symbol (°) indicate diminished triads. (Augmented triads require accidentals and occur only under special, rare conditions.)

3.7

In every major key, there are three major triads (I, IV, V), three minor triads (ii, iii, vi), and one diminished triad (vii°).

Tonic | Supertonic | Mediant | Subdominant | Dominant | Submediant | Leading Tone

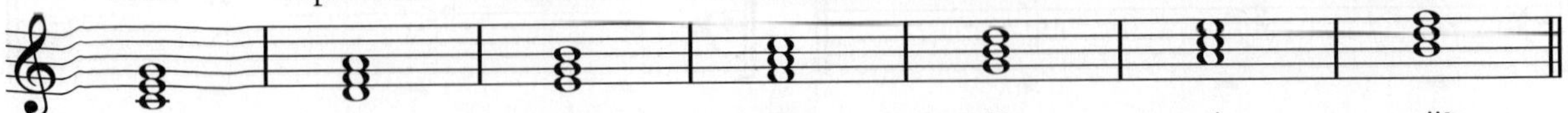

C major: I | ii | iii | IV | V | vi | vii°

In every minor key, there are three major triads (III, VI, VII), three minor triads (i, iv, v), and one diminished triad (ii°).

Tonic | Supertonic | Mediant | Subdominant | Dominant | Submediant | Subtonic

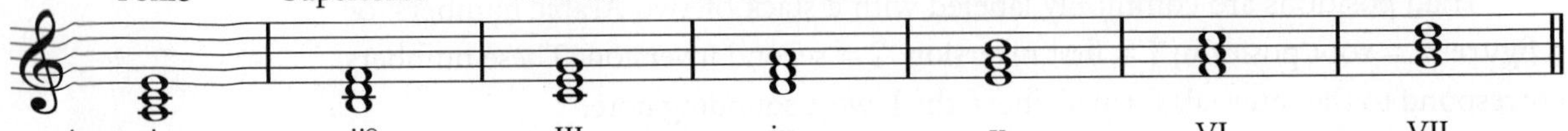

A minor: i | ii° | III | iv | v | VI | VII

In minor keys, the dominant and subtonic harmonies usually include raised $\hat{7}$ from the harmonic minor scale, creating a leading tone (a semitone below the tonic). (The raised $\hat{7}$ is not ordinarily used in the III triad.)

3.8

When $\hat{7}$ is raised from subtonic to leading tone (as in the harmonic minor scale), v becomes V and VII becomes vii°.

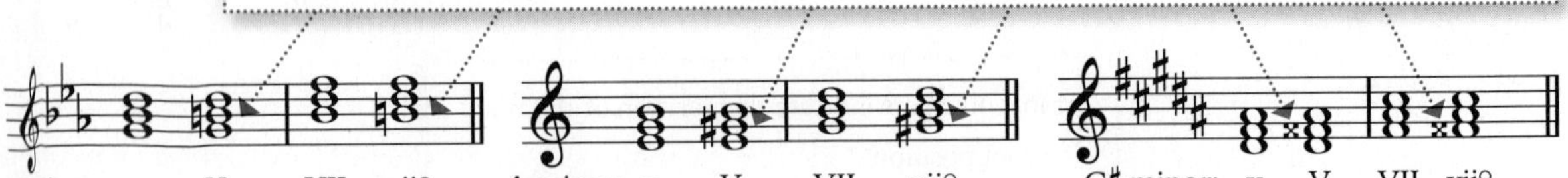

C minor: v V VII vii° | A minor: v V VII vii° | G♯ minor: v V VII vii°

ROMAN NUMERALS AND INVERSIONS

A Roman numeral can be combined with a figure that consists of Arabic numbers to show the root, quality, and position of a triad.

3.9

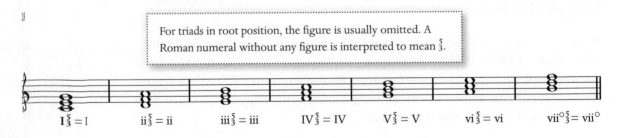

For triads in root position, the figure is usually omitted. A Roman numeral without any figure is interpreted to mean $^5_3$.

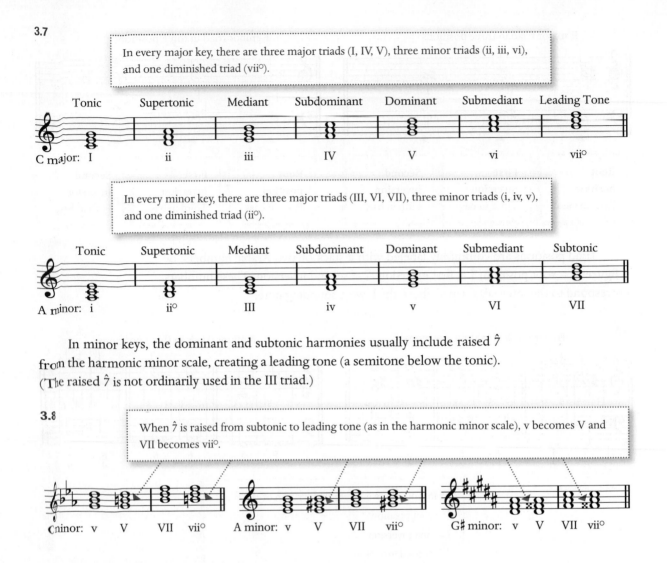

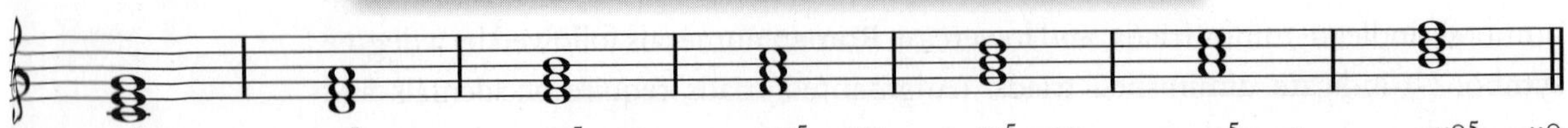

$I^5_3 = I$ | $ii^5_3 = ii$ | $iii^5_3 = iii$ | $IV^5_3 = IV$ | $V^5_3 = V$ | $vi^5_3 = vi$ | $vii^{o5}_{3} = vii^o$

For triads in first inversion, $^6_3$ is usually abbreviated to ^{6}.

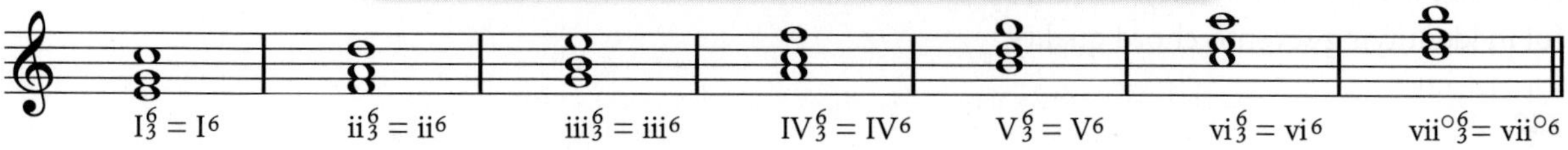

For triads in second inversion, $^6_4$ appears with the Roman numeral and is not abbreviated.

SEVENTH CHORDS

SEVENTH-CHORD CONSTRUCTION

A **seventh chord** can be understood as either a triad plus a seventh over its root or a triad with an additional third stacked on top of its fifth. Seventh chords can be written on four consecutive staff lines or four consecutive spaces. When a seventh chord is stacked in thirds, the lowest note is called the root, followed by the **third**, the **fifth**, and the **seventh**.

3.10

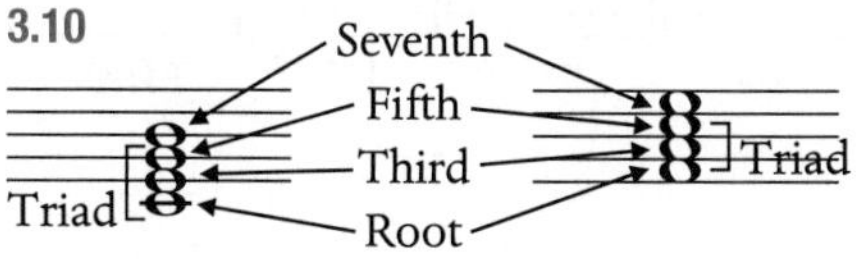

SEVENTH-CHORD QUALITIES

Like triads, seventh chords are classified by quality. Depending on the qualities of the triads and sevenths they contain, seventh chords may be **fully diminished** (diminished triad + diminished seventh), **half-diminished** (diminished triad + minor seventh), minor (minor triad + minor seventh), **dominant** (major triad + minor seventh), or **major** (major triad + major seventh). As with triads, you can refer to a seventh chord by its root and quality.

3.11

Chord symbols: $^{\circ 7}$ = fully diminished; ^{ø7} = half-diminished; m^{7} = minor seventh; ^{7} = dominant; maj^{7} = major seventh

NATURAL (WHITE-KEY) SEVENTH CHORDS

Knowing the qualities of **natural seventh chords**—without accidentals—can be helpful in identifying seventh-chord quality.

3.12

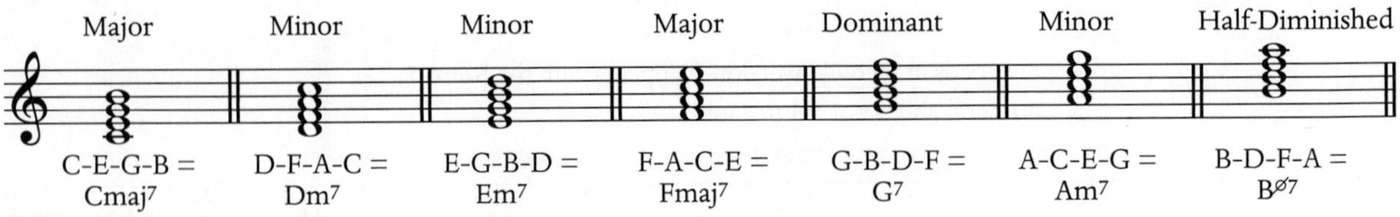

Every seventh chord uses one of those seven groups of letter names: CEGB, DFAC, EGBD, FACE, GBDF, ACEG, BDFA. To spell a seventh chord, start with a white-key seventh chord and, if necessary, add an accidental to match the root requested. Then check the intervals of the seventh chord, adding accidentals as needed for the proper quality of third, fifth, and seventh.

3.13

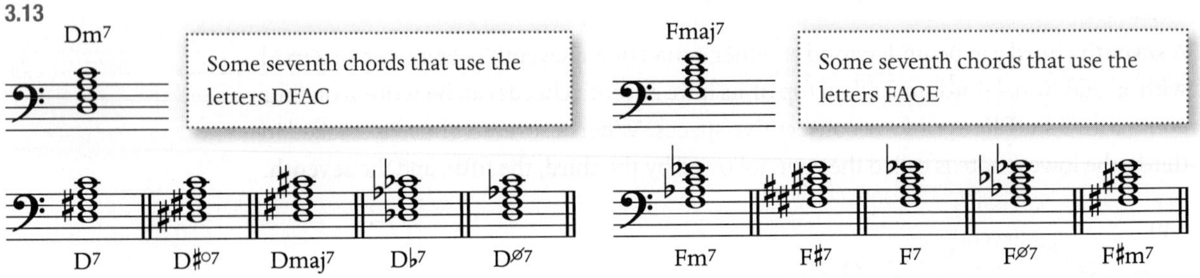

SEVENTH CHORDS IN INVERSION

Like triads, seventh chords can appear in inversion as well as root position; any of the four notes of a seventh chord can sound in the bass. A figure (stack of three Arabic numbers) is used to identify these inversions: $\substack{7\\5\\3}$ = root position; $\substack{6\\5\\3}$ = first inversion; $\substack{6\\4\\3}$ = second inversion; $\substack{6\\4\\2}$ = third inversion.

3.14

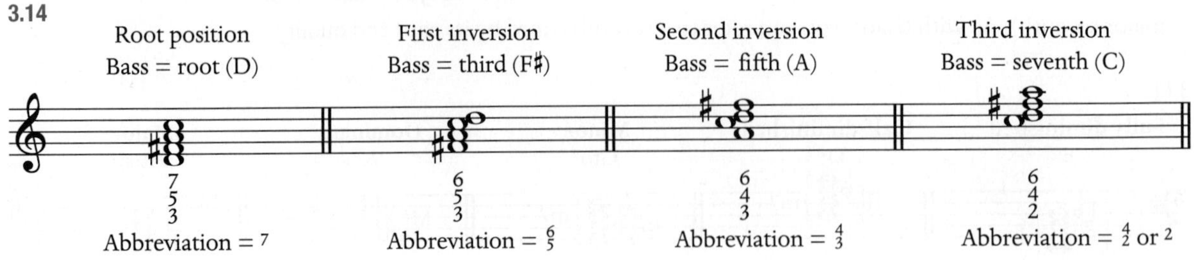

SEVENTH CHORDS IN MAJOR AND MINOR KEYS

ROMAN NUMERALS AND INVERSIONS

For seventh chords as for triads, a combination of a Roman numeral and a figure indicates the root, quality, and position (although there is no longer any typographical distinction between major seventh chords and dominant seventh chords). Seventh chords built on $\hat{2}$, $\hat{4}$, $\hat{5}$, and $\hat{7}$ are more common than those on $\hat{1}$, $\hat{3}$, or $\hat{6}$.

3.15

In every major key, ii^7 is minor, IV^7 is major, V^7 is dominant, and vii^{ø7} is half-diminished.

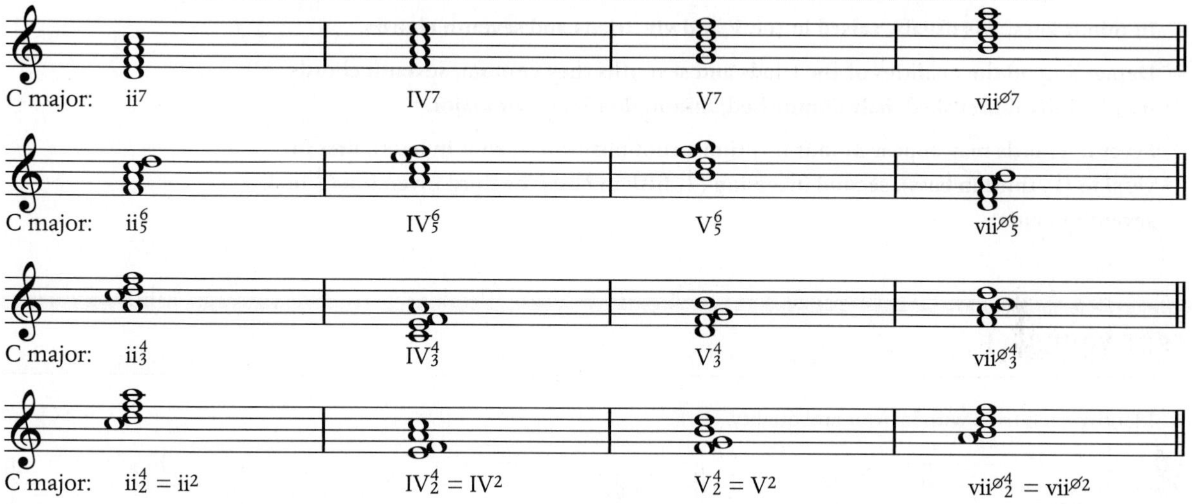

3.16

In every minor key, ii^{ø7} is half-diminished, and iv^7 is minor. The seventh chords on $\hat{5}$ and $\hat{7}$ usually use the raised $\hat{7}$, the leading tone, from the harmonic minor scale; thus V^7 is dominant, and vii^{o7} is fully diminished.

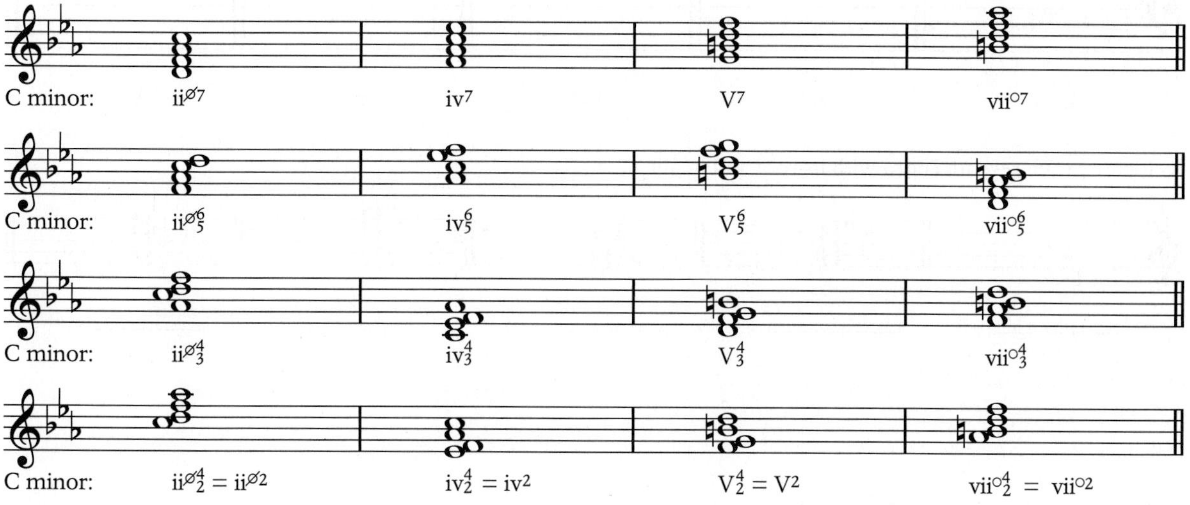

review and interact

POINTS FOR REVIEW

- **Depending on the qualities of the thirds and fifths they contain, triads may be diminished, minor, major, or augmented.**
- **Triads may appear in three positions: root position ($^5_3$, root in bass), first inversion ($^6_3$, third in bass), or second inversion ($^6_4$, fifth in bass).**
- **Roman numerals combined with figures (stacks of Arabic numbers) identify the root (as a scale degree in a major or minor scale), quality, and inversion of a triad or seventh chord.**
- **In minor keys, $\hat{7}$ is usually raised in the V and vii° triads and seventh chords.**
- **Depending on the qualities of the triads and sevenths they contain, seventh chords may be fully diminished, half-diminished, minor, dominant, or major.**
- **Seventh chords may appear in four positions: root position (^{7}, root in bass), first inversion ($^6_5$, third in bass), second inversion ($^4_3$, fifth in bass), or third inversion ($^4_2$ or ^{2}, seventh in bass).**

TEST YOURSELF

1. Identify each triad with its root and quality.

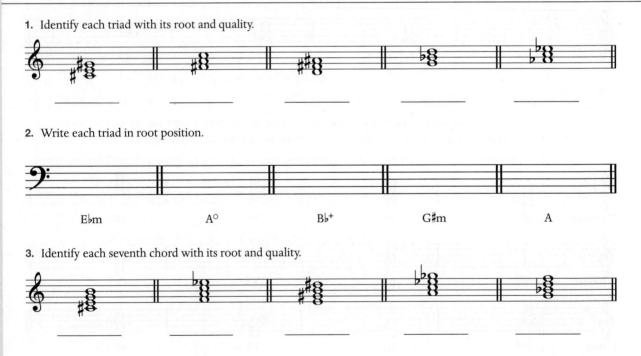

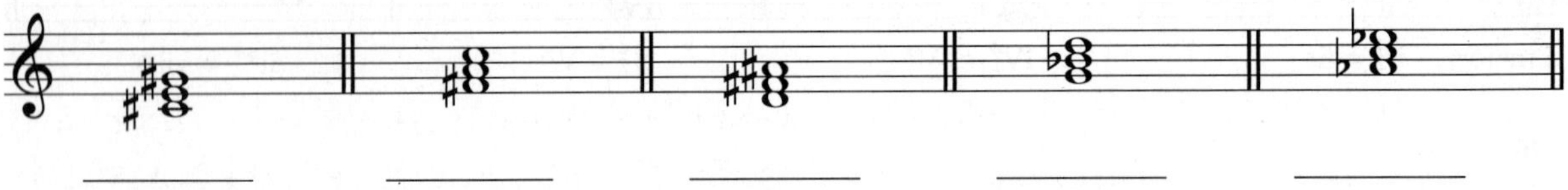

2. Write each triad in root position.

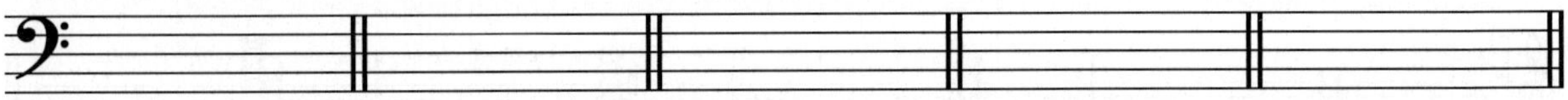

E♭m A° B♭+ G♯m A

3. Identify each seventh chord with its root and quality.

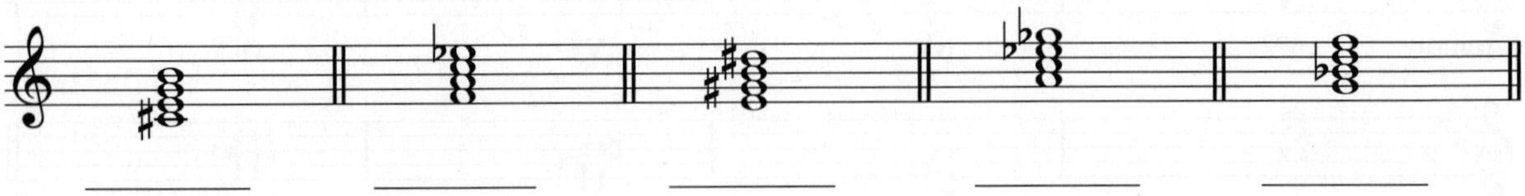

4. Write each seventh chord in root position.

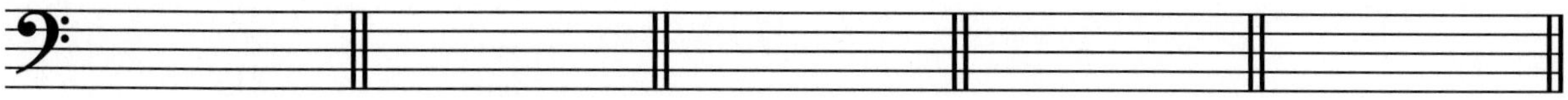

F♯m^7 A♭maj^7 B^{o7} F^{ø7} E♭^{7}

5. Use a Roman numeral with a figure to identify each triad or seventh chord in the key indicated.

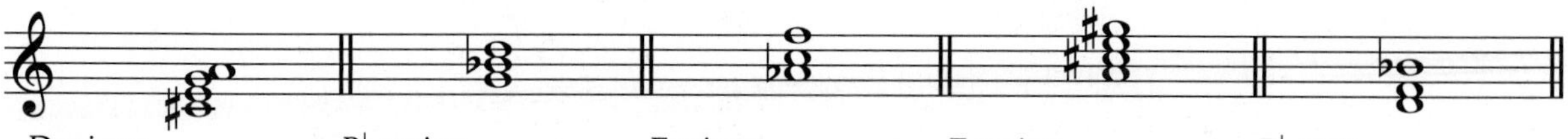

D minor: B♭ major: F minor: E major: E♭ major:

6. Write each triad or seventh chord in the key indicated. Use accidentals rather than key signatures.

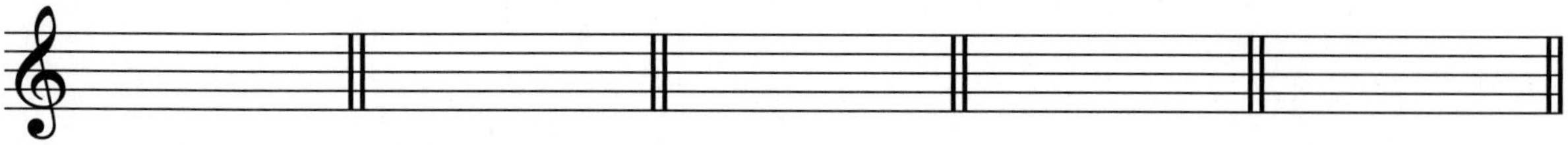

C minor: ii^{o6} D major: V^7 E♭ major: IV G minor: V$^4_2$ A major: I^6

Know It? Show It!

Focus by working through the tutorials on:

- Triad Qualities
- Triad Inversions
- Seventh Chord Qualities
- Seventh Chord Inversions
- Finding Chords in the Key

Learn with inQuizitive.

Apply what you've learned to complete the assignments:

- Identifying Triad Quality
- Writing Triads
- Triad Inversions
- Triads in Major and Minor Keys
- Identifying Seventh-Chord qualites
- Seventh Chords by Root and Quality
- Seventh-Chord Inversions

part two

Overview of Harmony and Voice Leading

chapter

4 Four-Part Harmony

The conventions of four-part harmony are useful for understanding tonal music.

WRITING CHORDS IN FOUR PARTS

Tonal music often is discussed in relation to **four-part harmony**. In four-part harmony, each chord uses four notes, with the same basic rhythm in all four parts, as in a typical hymn.

4.1 From *The Chorale Book for England*

A standard four-part harmony setting includes four notes in each chord. All four voices share the same basic rhythm.

Four-part harmony is useful as a model for harmonic practices found in settings that are more elaborate as well, and forms the basis of most traditional exercises in tonal harmony.

FORMATS FOR WRITING FOUR-PART HARMONY

Four-part writing is traditionally studied in either of two formats: SATB (chorale) format and keyboard format.

SATB FORMAT

Four-part harmony is typically notated in **SATB** (or **chorale**) **format**, for a vocal choir consisting of a soprano, alto, tenor, and bass. In SATB format, the soprano and alto parts are written on the treble staff and the tenor and bass parts on the bass staff. On each staff, the upper part (soprano or tenor) is written with stems up and the lower part (alto or bass) with stems down.

4.2

Good Soprano and tenor are always stemmed upward; alto and bass are always stemmed downward.

Poor No matter how high or low the notes are, soprano and tenor should never be stemmed downward; alto and bass should never be stemmed upward.

Poor No matter how high the notes are, the tenor voice should not be written in treble clef; no matter how low, the alto voice should not be written in bass clef.

Range Each voice in SATB writing remains within a specified **range**, so that the notes are not too high or too low to be sung comfortably by singers in a standard choir.

4.3

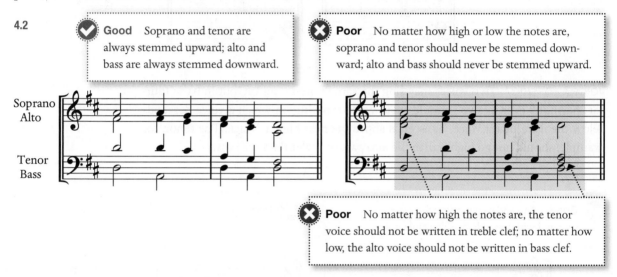

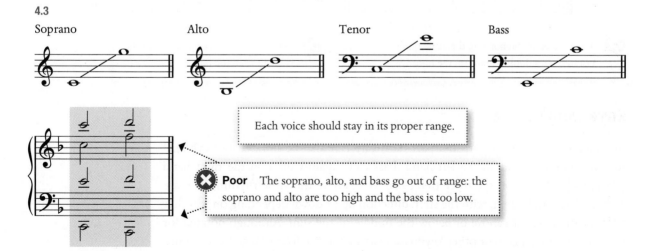

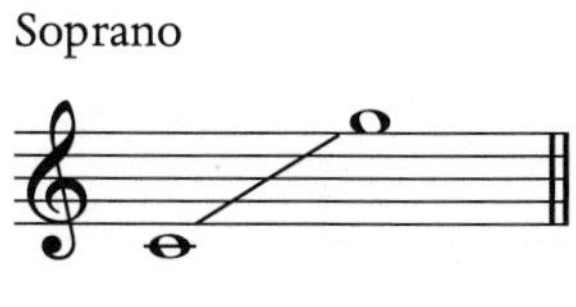

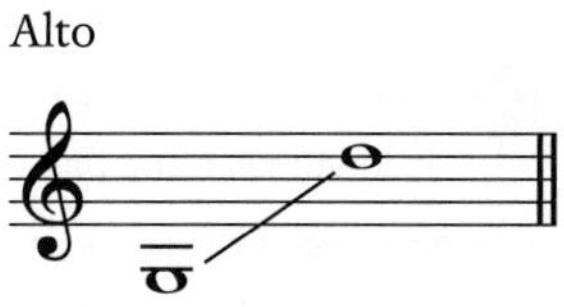

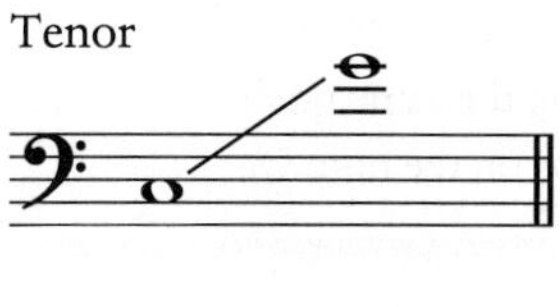

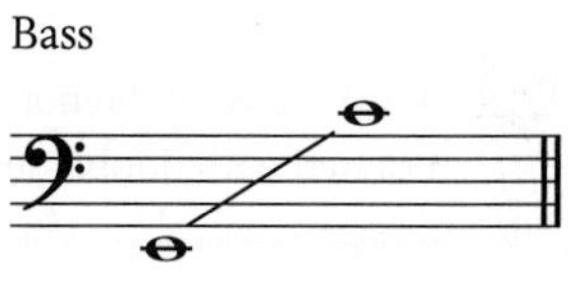

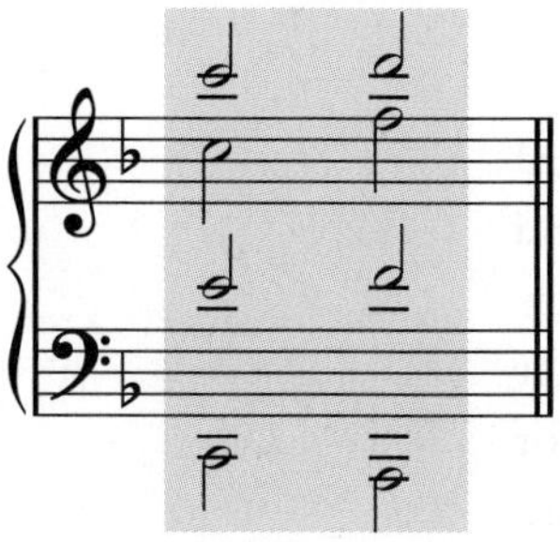

Each voice should stay in its proper range.

Poor The soprano, alto, and bass go out of range: the soprano and alto are too high and the bass is too low.

Spacing Every chord should have a proper **spacing**; the notes of adjacent upper parts (soprano + alto; alto + tenor) should never be more than an octave apart. The tenor and bass can be more than an octave apart.

4.4

Good Pitches are within proper range; and alto and soprano are always within an octave of each other, as are tenor and alto.

Poor Pitches of the alto and tenor are more than an octave apart in the first chord, as are the pitches of the soprano and alto in the second chord.

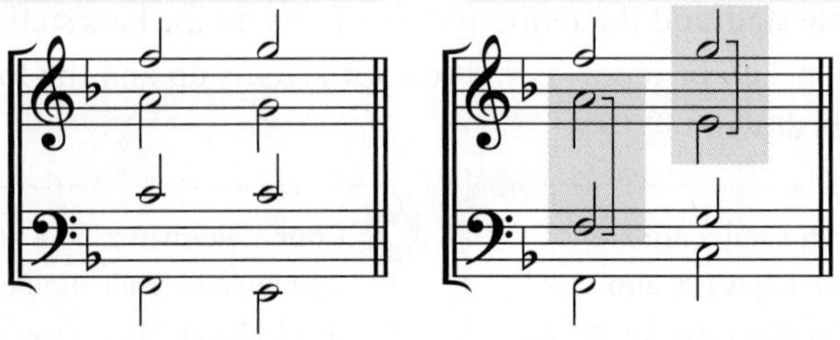

Voice Crossing Two voices may sing the same note in unison, but in basic four-part harmony exercises you should avoid **voice crossing**, in which a voice descends below the next lowest voice, or ascends above the next highest voice. The tenor, for example, should not go higher than the alto part or lower than the bass.

4.5

Good Alto and soprano sing the same pitch (notated with two side-by-side whole notes).

Poor Voice crossing: the last two notes in the alto are lower than the last two notes in the tenor.

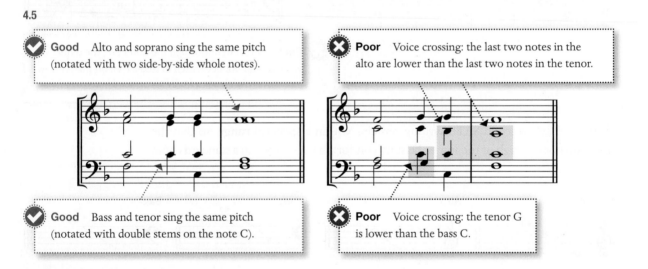

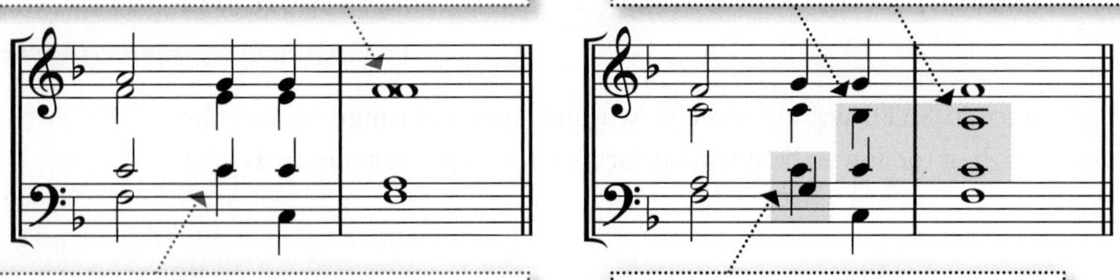

Good Bass and tenor sing the same pitch (notated with double stems on the note C).

Poor Voice crossing: the tenor G is lower than the bass C.

KEYBOARD FORMAT

In addition to SATB format, four-part harmony can also be notated in **keyboard format**, with one note in the left hand (bass clef) against three in the right hand (treble clef). As long as the three treble-clef voices have the same rhythm, they are notated on a single stem, with the stem direction up or down depending on whether most of the notes are above or below the middle of the staff. Although notated for performance on a piano or other keyboard instrument, the four notes of each chord in keyboard format are nonetheless regarded as distinct voices that often are referred to as soprano, alto, tenor, and bass. Thus when two of the upper voices are on the same pitch, the notehead may be written twice.

4.6

In the second chord, both soprano and alto are on E.

Keyboard notation: one voice is in bass clef, three voices are in treble.

When an interval of a second appears within a chord, one of the notes is written on the side of the stem opposite the others; the upper note of the second is always placed on the right side of the stem.

4.7

Good Because of the harmonic second between G and F, G is on the opposite side of the stem from F and B.

Poor G and F are crammed together, making them hard to read.

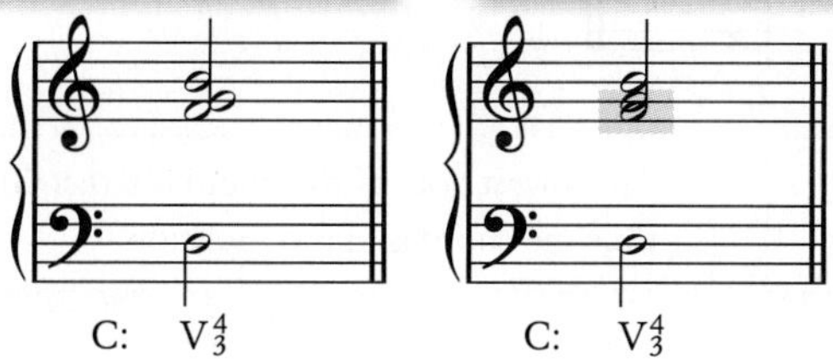

If one of the upper voices has a rhythm different from the others within the same chord, it is stemmed separately and in the opposite direction.

4.8

Good On beats 1 and 2, the alto has two quarter notes while the soprano and tenor each have a half note; these rhythms are stemmed in opposite directions.

Poor Different rhythms are stemmed together, which is visually confusing and even ambiguous. On the third beat it is unclear which are quarter notes and which are eighths.

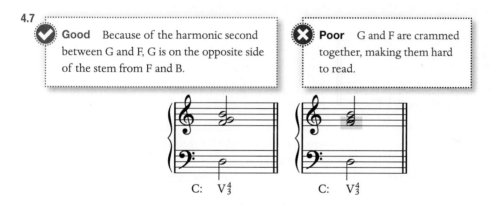

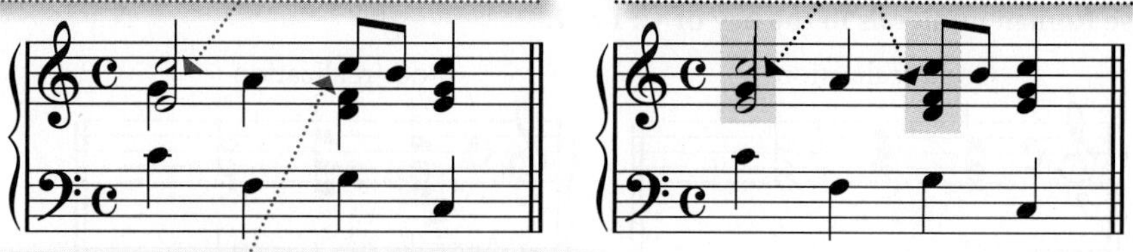

Good On beat 3, the soprano has two eighth notes while the alto and tenor each have a quarter note; these different rhythms are stemmed in opposite directions.

Spacing In standard keyboard format, spacing is the main constraint: the upper three voices (soprano, alto, and tenor) are placed within an octave so that they can be comfortably played by the right hand alone.

4.9

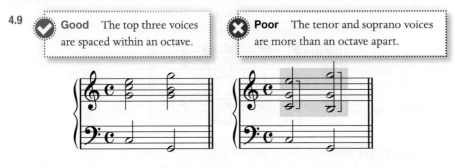

Good The top three voices are spaced within an octave.

Poor The tenor and soprano voices are more than an octave apart.

Inversions A chord's inversion is always determined by its lowest note, *not* by the lowest note in the treble part. Keep this in mind when writing for keyboard, where the lowest note of the right hand is not the same as the lowest note of the chord.

4.10

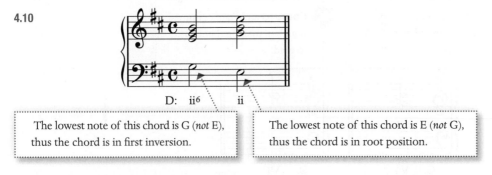

The lowest note of this chord is G (*not* E), thus the chord is in first inversion.

The lowest note of this chord is E (*not* G), thus the chord is in root position.

REALIZING ROMAN NUMERALS IN FOUR-PART HARMONY

DETERMINING THE CORRECT NOTES

In studying four-part harmony, you often are asked to **realize** a series of Roman numerals—that is, to compose a passage based on indicated chords. Each chord should use the notes indicated by the Roman numeral, with the correct bass determined by the inversion of the chord.

4.11

***Task*: Realize these Roman numerals in the key of C: I–V–I.**

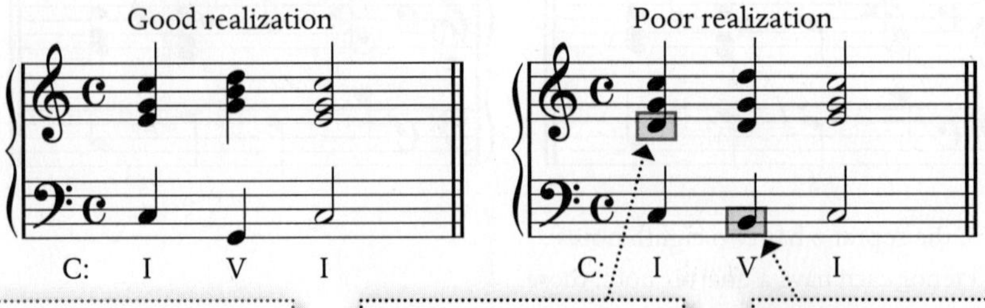

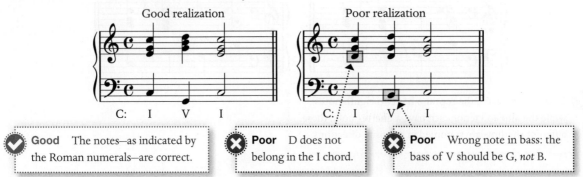

Good The notes—as indicated by the Roman numerals—are correct.

Poor D does not belong in the I chord.

Poor Wrong note in bass: the bass of V should be G, *not* B.

In minor keys, $\hat{7}$ is most often raised to create a leading tone, so that the triad on $\hat{5}$ is V (major rather than minor). Depending on the key signature, this requires a natural, sharp, or double sharp.

4.12

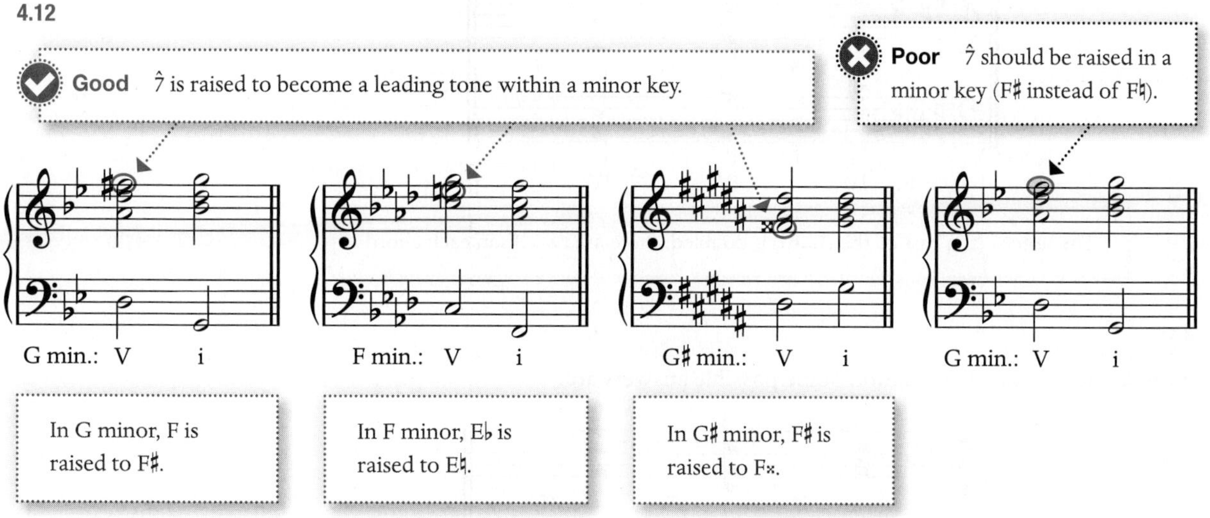
Good $\hat{7}$ is raised to become a leading tone within a minor key.
Poor $\hat{7}$ should be raised in a minor key (F♯ instead of F♮).
G min.: V i
F min.: V i
G♯ min.: V i
G min.: V i
In G minor, F is raised to F♯.
In F minor, E♭ is raised to E♮.
In G♯ minor, F♯ is raised to F𝄪.

DOUBLING

When three notes of a triad are distributed among four voices, one of the notes must be **doubled**—that is, it appears in two different voices (regardless of octave) at the same time. Since seventh chords have four different notes, they do not require any doubling.

4.13

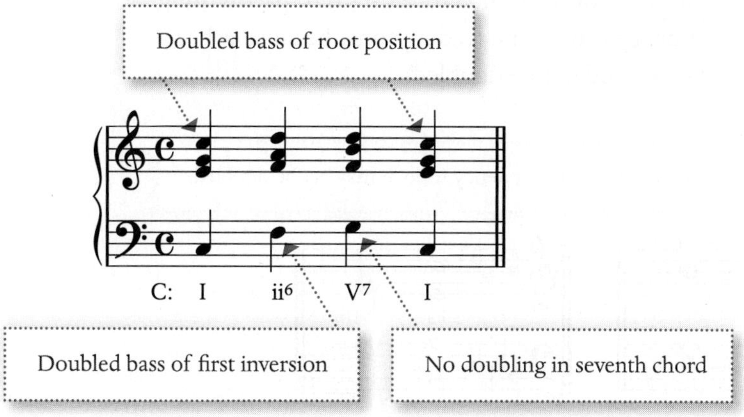
Doubled bass of root position
C: I ii6 V7 I
Doubled bass of first inversion
No doubling in seventh chord

It is preferable to double the *bass* of root-position and second-inversion triads. In first-inversion triads, you can usually double any note.

4.14

***Task*: Write a IV chord in E major. Since IV in E has the notes A-C♯-E (with A in the bass), some possible answers are:**

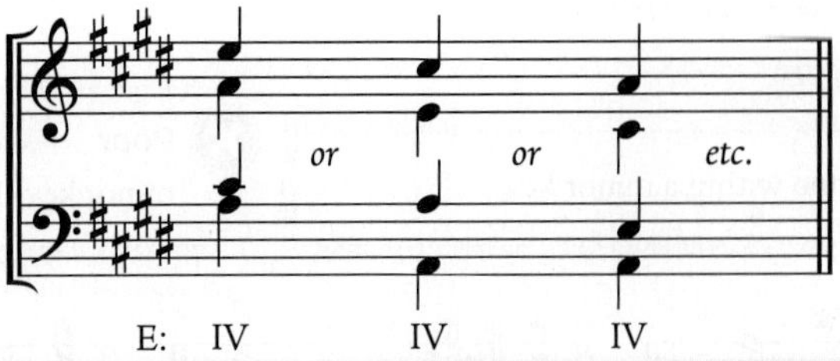

The note A (the bass of the chord) is doubled; there are two A's in each chord.

4.15

***Task*: Write a i^6 chord in F minor. Some possible answers are:**

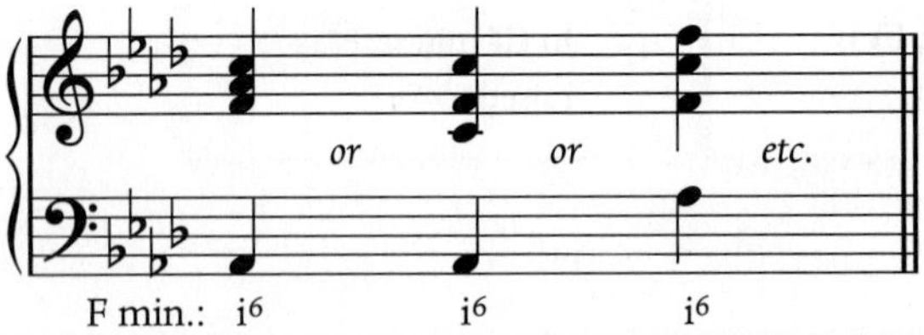

Note: in a first-inversion chord, usually any note (root, third, or fifth) may be doubled.

TENDENCY TONES (LEADING TONES AND CHORDAL DISSONANCE)

In four-part harmony, you should never double **tendency tones**, that is, notes that need to move stepwise either up or down. Doubling such tones leads to part-writing errors (see Chapter 5). One such tendency tone is the leading tone: because it has a strong tendency to move up by step, it should not be doubled.

4.16

In A♭ major, the leading tone ($\hat{7}$) is G. Since it is a tendency tone, it may *not* be doubled.

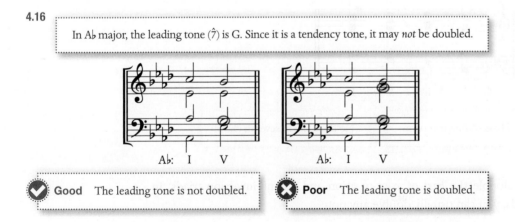

Good The leading tone is not doubled.

Poor The leading tone is doubled.

Another type of tendency tone is a **chordal dissonance**, which is a dissonant member of a chord, such as the seventh of a seventh chord. A chordal dissonance has a strong tendency to resolve down by step, and thus may not be doubled.

4.17

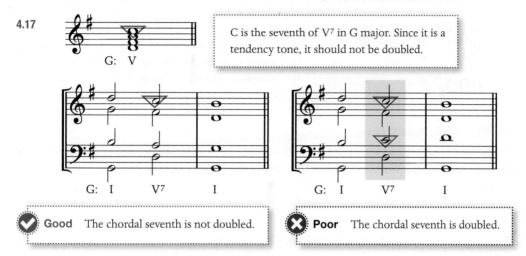

C is the seventh of V^7 in G major. Since it is a tendency tone, it should not be doubled.

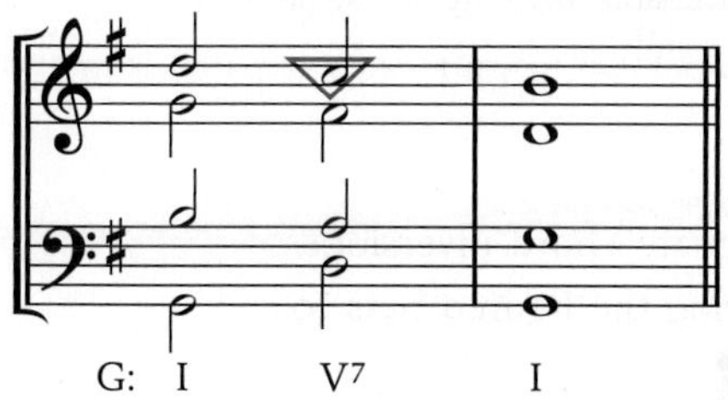

Good The chordal seventh is not doubled.

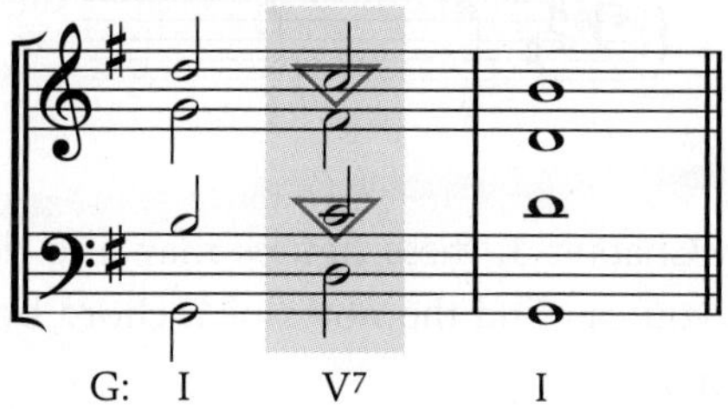

Poor The chordal seventh is doubled.

REALIZING FIGURED BASS

DETERMINING THE CORRECT NOTES

In addition to Roman numerals, you will often be asked to realize chord progressions from a **figured bass**. Figured bass uses numerals to designate the upper notes of chords by indicating the intervals above the bass notes. Thus, for instance, the figure $^5_3$ indicates the upper notes of the chord should be a fifth and a third (or their compound equivalents) above the bass. When you see an accidental preceding a figure, alter the note as indicated. The rules for doubling are the same in realizing a figured bass as they are for realizing Roman numerals.

4.18

***Task*: Realize this figured bass in SATB format.**

Some possible answers are:

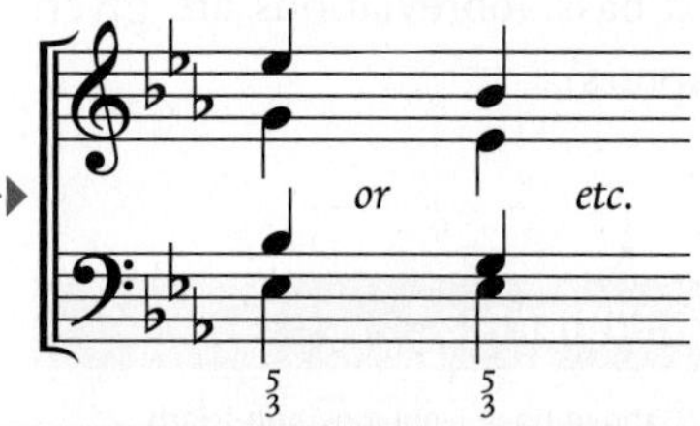

In this key, 5 above E♭ is B♭, and 3 above E♭ is G. Though 5 is the top note of the figure, the 5 above the bass (B♭) does *not* have to be the highest note of the chord.

The bass is doubled in root position.

4.19

***Task*: Realize this figured bass in keyboard format.**

Some possible answers are:

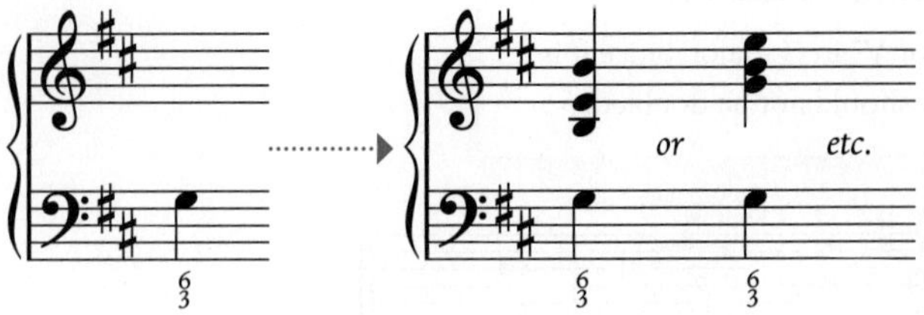

6 above G is E, and 3 above G is B. These notes can appear in any register. Because the chord is in first inversion, any note can be doubled.

As you saw in Chapter 3, these figures may also designate chord inversions. Thus in most cases you can find the notes of a chord by using the figured bass to determine the inversion.

4.20

***Task*: Realize this figured bass in keyboard format, determining the notes by using chord inversion.**

Some possible answers are:

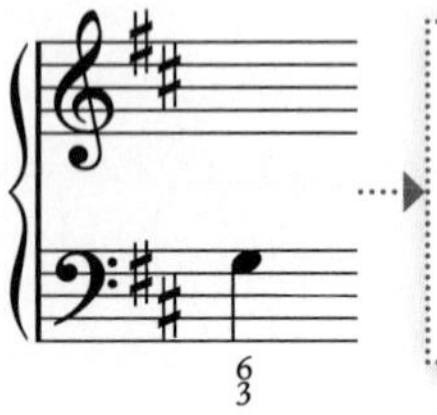

(1) $^6_3$ = first-inversion triad; (2) therefore the bass G is the third of the chord, and E must be the root; (3) thus the notes of chord are E–G–B.

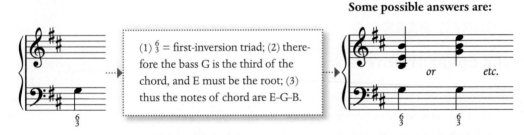

Notice that both of the methods described above for finding the notes of figured bass produce the same results. However, it is not always possible to realize a figured bass by first finding the root of the chord. Especially with more-complex figures, the chord may need to be determined by the intervals above the bass.

ABBREVIATED FIGURES

As you saw in Chapter 3, the most common figures are abbreviated. You should memorize these abbreviations. The most common figured bass abbreviations are given below (others are discussed in Chapter 3 and later chapters).

4.21

FIGURE ABBREVIATION . . .	STANDS FOR . . .	WHICH INDICATES . . .
(no figure)	$^5_3$	5 and 3 above bass (root-position triad)
6	$^6_3$	6 and 3 above bass (triad in first inversion)
7	$^7_{\substack{5\\3}}$	7, 5, and 3 above bass (root-position seventh chord)

4.22

This figured bass:

is an abbreviated form of this:

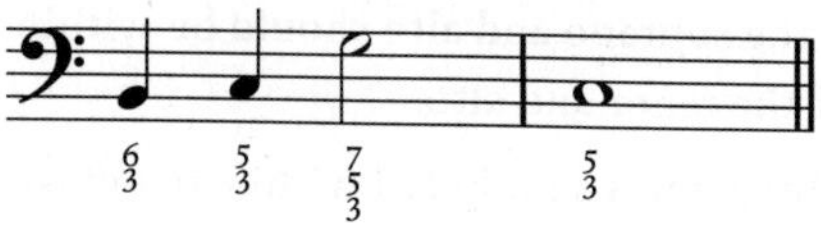

ACCIDENTALS IN FIGURED BASS

An accidental alone, with no number following it, applies to the third above the bass.

4.23

FIGURE ABBREVIATION . . .	STANDS FOR . . .	WHICH INDICATES . . .
♯	$\begin{smallmatrix}5\\ \sharp 3\end{smallmatrix}$	5 and ♯3 above bass
♭	$\begin{smallmatrix}5\\ \flat 3\end{smallmatrix}$	5 and ♭3 above bass
$\begin{smallmatrix}6\\ \sharp\end{smallmatrix}$	$\begin{smallmatrix}6\\ \sharp 3\end{smallmatrix}$	6 and ♯3 above bass
$\begin{smallmatrix}7\\ \natural\end{smallmatrix}$	$\begin{smallmatrix}7\\ 5\\ \natural 3\end{smallmatrix}$	7, 5, and ♮3 above bass

4.24

This figured bass:

is an abbreviated form of this:

4.25

***Task*: Realize the figured bass in keyboard format.**

Some possible answers are:

(1) $\begin{smallmatrix}7\\ \sharp\end{smallmatrix}$ is an abbreviated form of $\begin{smallmatrix}7\\ 5\\ \sharp 3\end{smallmatrix}$; (2) thus notes in the chord above D are C, A, and F♯.

review and interact

POINTS FOR REVIEW

- **Four-part harmony exercises are traditionally notated in either SATB or keyboard format; strict guidelines govern each of these formats.**

- **Parts written in SATB format should be singable, with the notes for each of the voices (soprano, alto, tenor, bass) lying within an appropriate range.**
- **In SATB format, the notes of the soprano and alto should be within an octave of each other, as should notes of the tenor and alto.**
- **In keyboard format, the top three notes should fall within an octave (the tenor and soprano should not be more than an octave apart).**
- **A note is doubled if it appears in two different voices. In root-position and second-inversion chords, double the bass. In first-inversion chords, any note may usually be doubled. In seventh chords, no doubling is needed.**
- **Tendency tones—such as leading tones and chordal dissonances—may *not* be doubled.**
- **In minor keys, the seventh scale degree ($\hat{7}$) is usually raised by a half step (with a sharp, natural, or double sharp) so as to create a leading tone.**
- **Roman numerals indicate the root of the chord, with figures further indicating the chord's inversion; figured bass indicates the intervals that appear above a given bass note.**
- **Often figured bass symbols are abbreviated.**

TEST YOURSELF

1. The following questions refer to the SATB chord below:
   a. Which voice is too high?
   b. Which pair of voices are too far apart?
   c. Which notes are stemmed incorrectly?
   d. Which note is doubled: root, third, or fifth?
   e. Assume that this key is B♭ major. Label the chord with the appropriate Roman numeral and figures to indicate its inversion.

2. Which of these figured bass realizations (a–e) are correct?

3. Which of these chords are written correctly?

Know It? Show It!

Focus by working through the tutorials on:

- Chords on the grand staff: SATB (chorale) format
- Chords on the grand staff: Keyboard format
- Realizing Roman numerals
- Realizing figured bass

Learn with inQuizitive.

Apply what you've learned to complete the assignments:

- Identifying Chords and Doublings
- Leading Tones and Chordal Sevenths
- Notation in SATB and Keyboard Formats
- Realizing Roman Numerals
- Realizing Figured Bass

chapter 5

Voice Leading

Successions of notes, intervals, and chords in tonal music follow conventional guidelines.

MOVING BETWEEN HARMONIES (VOICE LEADING)

HARMONIC PROGRESSION

In tonal music, a chord is understood to move to the one that follows, so that a series of chords form a **harmonic progression** or **chord progression**. When one chord moves to another, each note in the first chord moves to a note in the next. In four-part harmony, this creates four separate melodic lines, called voices.

5.1

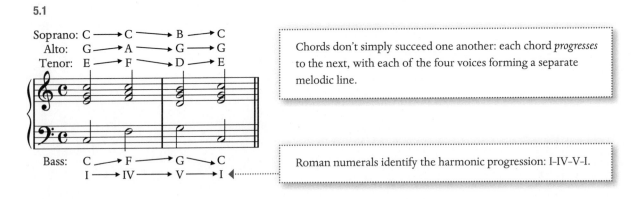

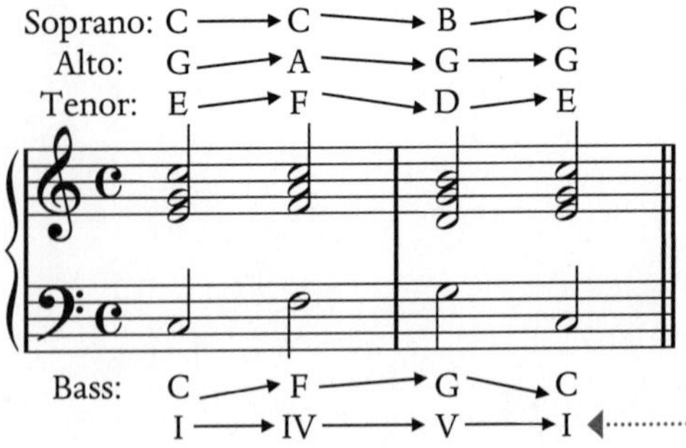

Chords don't simply succeed one another: each chord *progresses* to the next, with each of the four voices forming a separate melodic line.

Roman numerals identify the harmonic progression: I–IV–V–I.

The manner in which one chord, note, or interval moves to the next is called **voice leading**. The guidelines for voice leading in four-part harmony exercises—discussed here and in subsequent chapters—help develop sensitivity to standard harmonic procedures of tonal music. Naturally, these guidelines tend to be somewhat stricter than actual musical practice, where the specific artistic contexts often give rise to exceptions (or seeming exceptions) to these rules.

STEPS AND LEAPS

In four-part harmony, the three upper voices (soprano, alto, and tenor) should move smoothly, mostly with small melodic intervals. Usually, upper voices either stay on the same note or move by step or third, and they never use leaps greater than a sixth. The bass line, on the other hand, frequently uses melodic leaps.

5.2

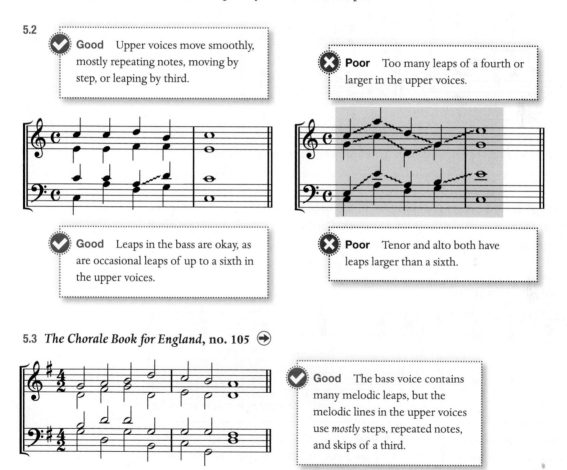

Good Upper voices move smoothly, mostly repeating notes, moving by step, or leaping by third.

Poor Too many leaps of a fourth or larger in the upper voices.

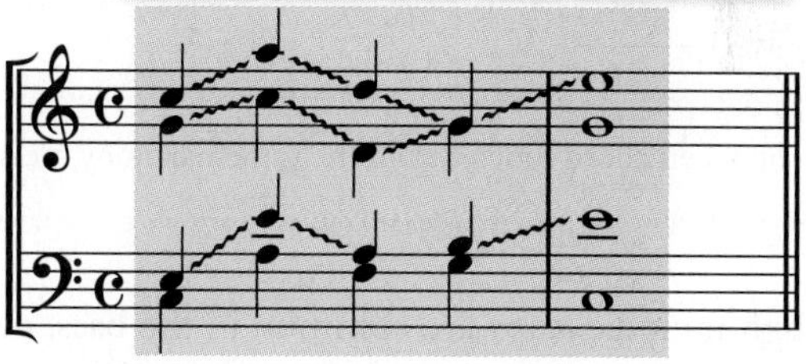

Good Leaps in the bass are okay, as are occasional leaps of up to a sixth in the upper voices.

Poor Tenor and alto both have leaps larger than a sixth.

5.3 ***The Chorale Book for England*, no. 105**

Good The bass voice contains many melodic leaps, but the melodic lines in the upper voices use *mostly* steps, repeated notes, and skips of a third.

When a chord repeats or is sustained, on the other hand, melodic leaps in one or more of the upper voices are not a problem. These leaps are called **chord skips**.

5.4

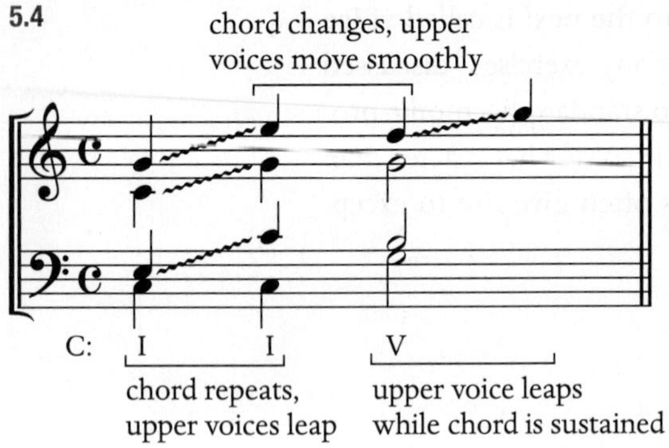

Good Within chords that repeat or are sustained, large melodic leaps in upper voices (chord skips) are okay.

5.5 J. S. Bach, Chorale 270

J. S. Bach, Chorale 222

Leaps between chord tones within the same harmony are known as a chord skips.

Although melodic leaps are common in the bass, even there you should avoid leaps greater than an octave or leaps of a seventh. Furthermore, melodic augmented intervals (including the augmented second) should not appear in any voice.

5.6

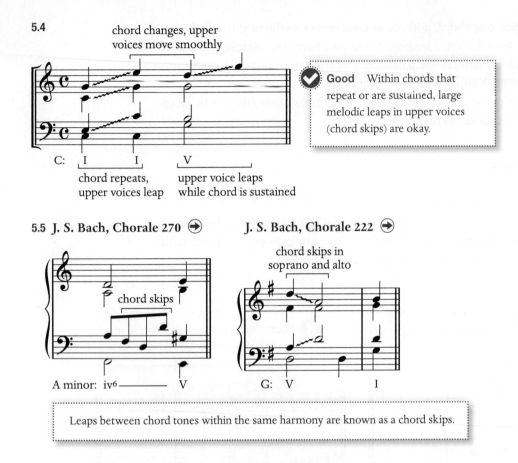

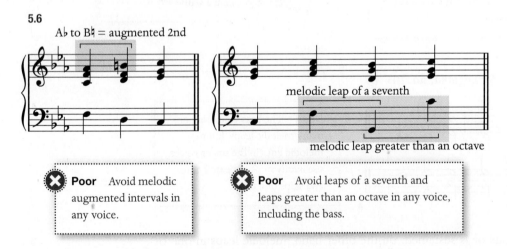

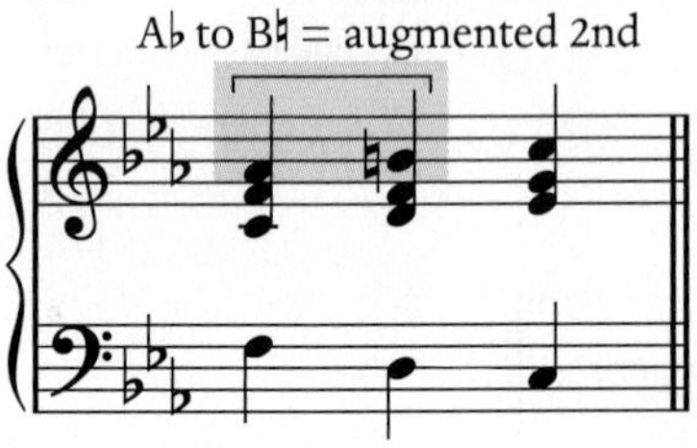

Poor Avoid melodic augmented intervals in any voice.

Poor Avoid leaps of a seventh and leaps greater than an octave in any voice, including the bass.

In all voices, you should also avoid approaching a leading tone with an ascending melodic leap of more than a third.

5.7

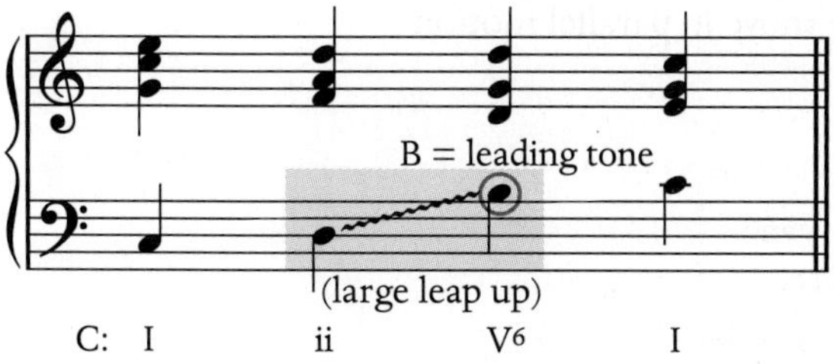

Poor Avoid *upward* leaps larger than a third to the leading tone.

KINDS OF MOTION

MOTION BETWEEN INTERVALS

Instead of thinking about all four voices at once, it can be helpful to think about them in pairs, like soprano + alto, or soprano + bass. For each pair of voices, you should think about the intervals formed and how these intervals are approached. Each interval may be approached in one of five different ways:

1. **Contrary motion**: one voice moves up and the other moves down.
2. **Parallel motion**: the two voices move in same direction and the same distance.
3. **Similar motion**: the voices move in the same direction but different distances.
4. **Oblique motion**: one voice remains on the same note while the other moves up or down.
5. **Stationary motion**: both voices remain on the same note.

5.8

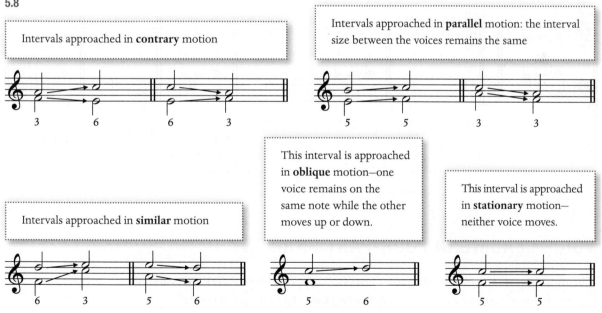

Intervals approached in **contrary** motion

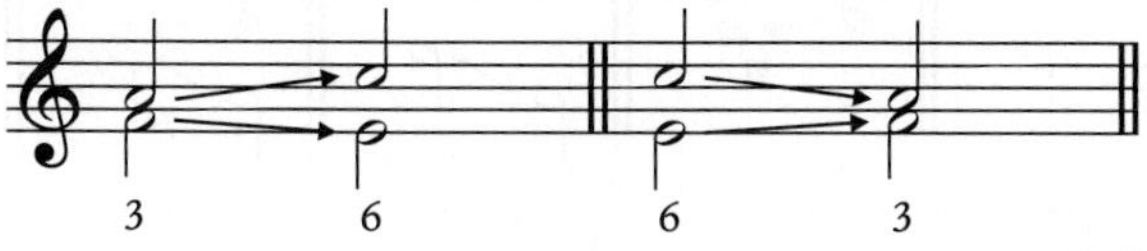

Intervals approached in **parallel** motion: the interval size between the voices remains the same

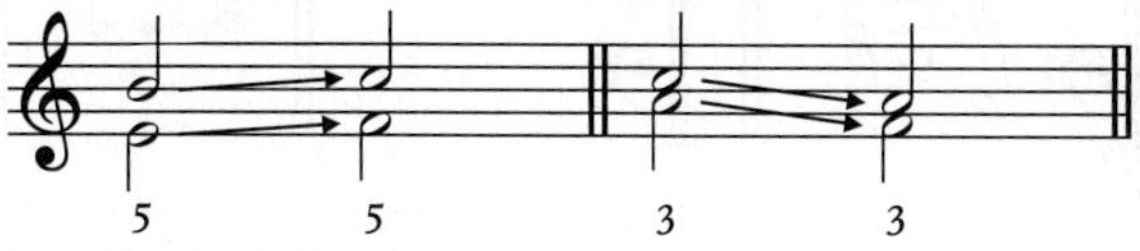

Intervals approached in **similar** motion

This interval is approached in **oblique** motion—one voice remains on the same note while the other moves up or down.

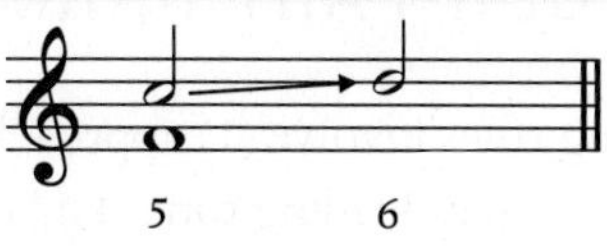

This interval is approached in **stationary** motion—neither voice moves.

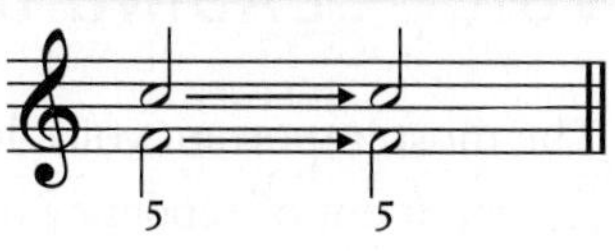

Note that in parallel motion the interval size stays the same, but the interval quality might change. Thus, for instance, a minor third may move in parallel motion to a major third.

5.9

Top voice ascends by *minor* second from E to F . . . and bottom voice ascends by *major* second from C to D . . .

. . . nevertheless, both voices move up by a second and thus in parallel motion.

The first interval (C-E) is a major third; the second (D-F) is a minor third. The interval *size* stays the same but the *quality* changes.

MOTION BETWEEN PAIRS OF INTERVALS IN FOUR-PART HARMONY

The voice leading from one chord to another in four-part harmony can be understood as involving a number of simultaneous motions between pairs of voices.

5.10

In this chord progression:

The soprano and alto approach a fifth in oblique motion.

The soprano and bass approach a fifth in contrary motion.

The alto and bass approach an octave in oblique motion.

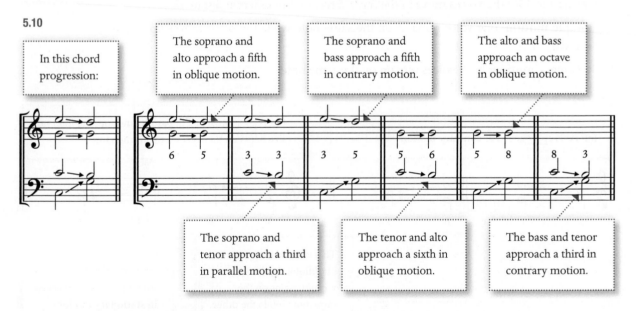

The soprano and tenor approach a third in parallel motion.

The tenor and alto approach a sixth in oblique motion.

The bass and tenor approach a third in contrary motion.

VOICE LEADING IN FOUR-PART HARMONY

The most important voice-leading rules involve (1) approaching perfect intervals and (2) treatment of tendency tones, such as leading tones and chordal sevenths.

PARALLEL OCTAVES AND FIFTHS

A perfect interval—such as a perfect octave, a perfect fifth, or a perfect unison—may *not* be approached in parallel motion. This prohibition applies to compound as well as to simple octaves and fifths. Approaching an octave in parallel motion produces **parallel octaves**; approaching a perfect fifth produces **parallel fifths**; approaching a unison produces **parallel unisons**.

5.11

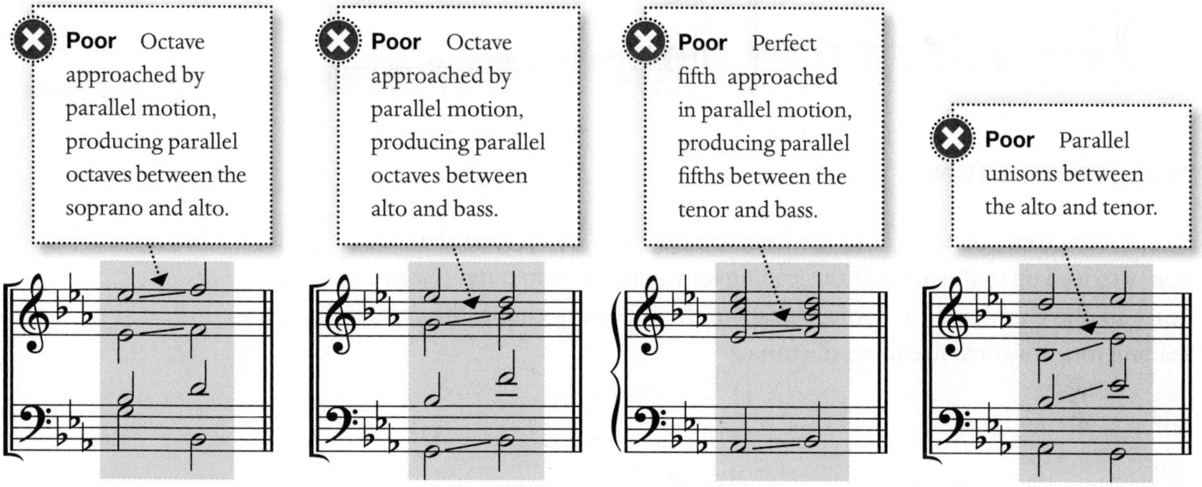

Poor Octave approached by parallel motion, producing parallel octaves between the soprano and alto.
Poor Octave approached by parallel motion, producing parallel octaves between alto and bass.
Poor Perfect fifth approached in parallel motion, producing parallel fifths between the tenor and bass.
Poor Parallel unisons between the alto and tenor.

At times something that at first looks like faulty parallel fifths or octaves actually arises between two *different* pairs of voices, and therefore is unproblematic. Also, octaves and fifths approached in stationary motion are always allowed.

5.12

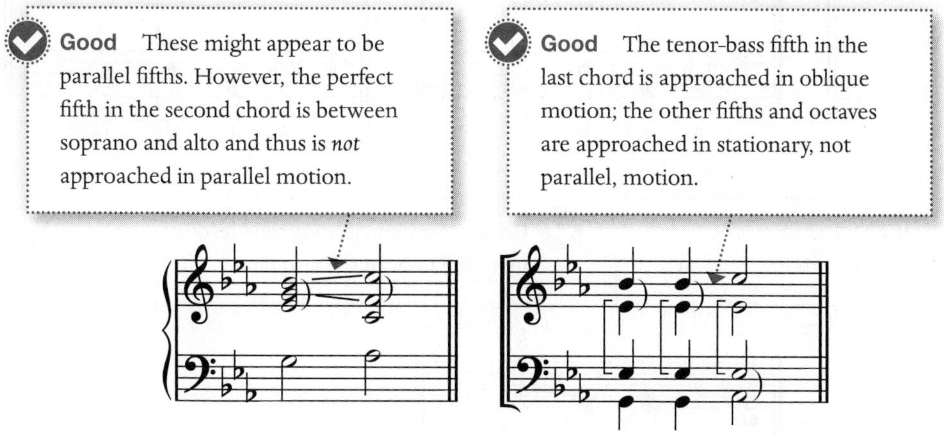

Good These might appear to be parallel fifths. However, the perfect fifth in the second chord is between soprano and alto and thus is *not* approached in parallel motion.
Good The tenor-bass fifth in the last chord is approached in oblique motion; the other fifths and octaves are approached in stationary, not parallel, motion.

You may move from a perfect fifth to a diminished fifth, since this does not entail approaching a *perfect* interval in parallel motion. On the other hand, you may not move from a diminished fifth to a perfect fifth (except in special cases that will be discussed in Chapter 13), since this would involve approaching a perfect interval in parallel motion.

5.13

Good Motion from P5 (E♭–B♭) to d5 (D–A♭)

Poor Motion from d5 (D–A♭) to P5 (E♭–B♭)

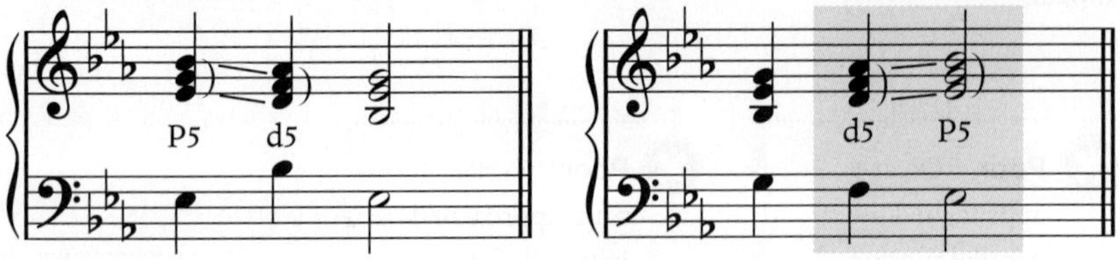

THE LEADING TONE

The leading tone (that is, $\hat{7}$ in major keys or raised $\hat{7}$ in minor keys) has a strong tendency to lead up to the tonic. If the leading tone appears in an outer (bass or soprano) voice in one chord and the tonic appears in the following chord, the voice with the leading tone must resolve up to the tonic.

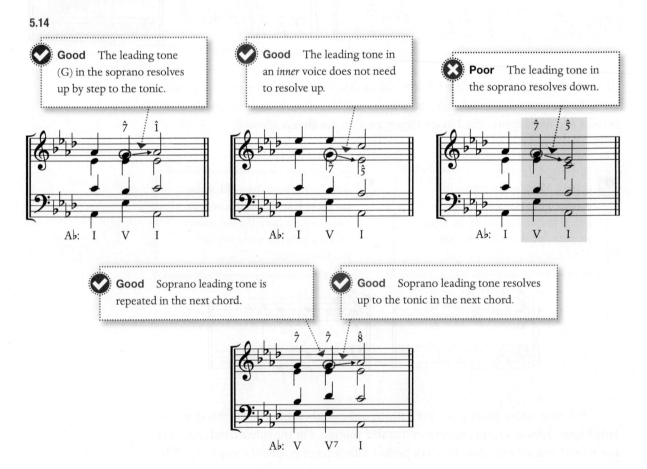

5.14

Good The leading tone (G) in the soprano resolves up by step to the tonic.

Good The leading tone in an *inner* voice does not need to resolve up.

Poor The leading tone in the soprano resolves down.

Good Soprano leading tone is repeated in the next chord.

Good Soprano leading tone resolves up to the tonic in the next chord.

5.15 **Church Hymnal of the Church of Ireland, no. 55**

Leading tone in an outer voice (bass) resolves up by step.

Leading tone in an inner voice (alto) need not resolve up by step.

CHORDAL SEVENTHS

Dissonant tones, including especially the **chordal seventh**, also have a strong melodic tendency to resolve *down* by step, even if they appear in an inner voice.

5.16

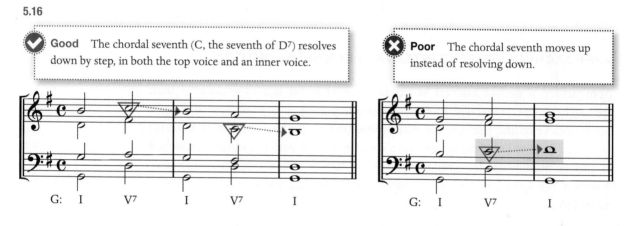

Good The chordal seventh (C, the seventh of D7) resolves down by step, in both the top voice and an inner voice.

Poor The chordal seventh moves up instead of resolving down.

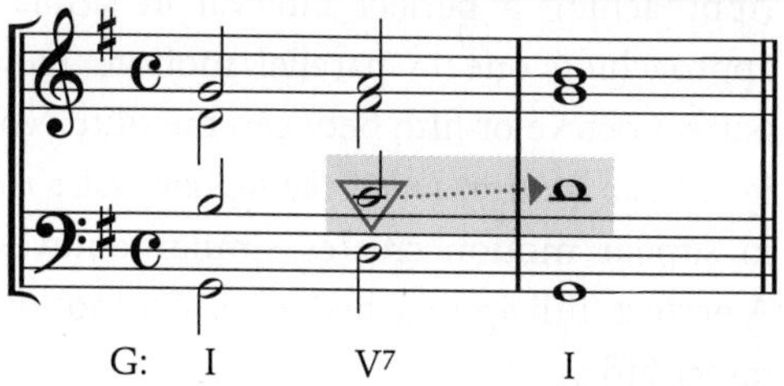

An exception arises when the chord that contains a chordal seventh is repeated. In such a case, the chordal seventh is repeated along with the other notes of the chords or shifted to another voice, so that its resolution is momentarily delayed until a new harmony enters.

5.17

Good The chord—along with the chordal seventh—repeats, then the seventh resolves down by step when the chord changes.

Good The chordal seventh is shifted to another voice and register, then resolves down by step.

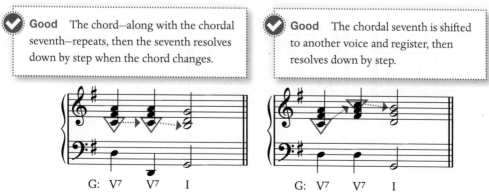

5.18 Bortniansky, "We praise Thee, the Lord"

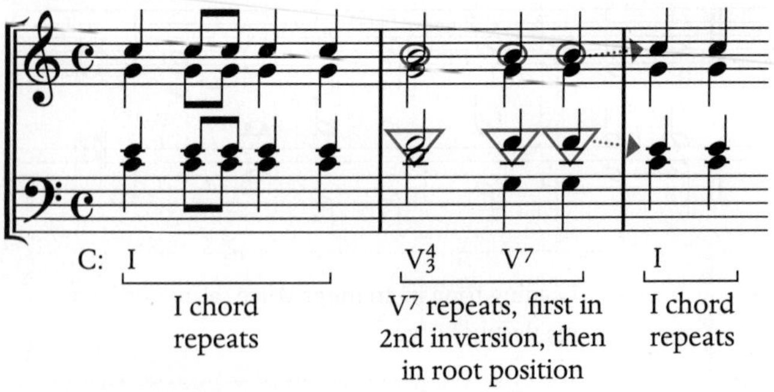

As is typical, the bass leaps, but the upper voices are smooth.

With repeated chords, there are no parallel fifths or octaves, but rather *stationary* fifths and octaves.

After V^7 repeats, the leading tone (B) resolves up and the chordal seventh (F) resolves down.

APPROACHING PERFECT INTERVALS IN SIMILAR MOTION

Approaching a perfect interval in similar motion is far less objectionable than approaching one in parallel motion. However, you should avoid approaching a perfect octave or fifth between the outer voices (that is, the bass and soprano voices) in similar motion *unless the soprano voice moves by step*. A perfect octave approached in similar motion creates **similar octaves** (or hidden octaves or direct octaves). A perfect fifth approached in similar motion creates **similar fifths** (or hidden fifths or direct fifths).

5.19

Good The octave D-D is approached in similar motion, with the soprano moving by step.

Poor Similar octaves: the octave D-D is approached in similar motion in the *outer* voices, with the soprano moving by *leap*.

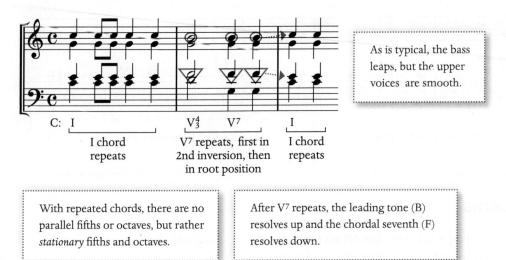

Good The fifth B–F♯ between the outer voices is approached in similar motion, with the soprano moving by step.

Poor Similar fifths: the fifth B–F♯ between the outer voices is approached in similar motion, with the soprano moving by *leap*.

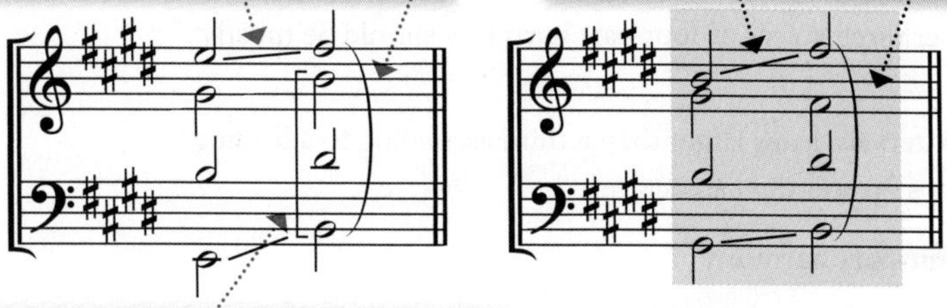

Good The octave B–B, approached in similar motion, is between the bass and an inner voice (alto).

Also, a perfect unison between any two voices should not be approached in similar motion.

5.20

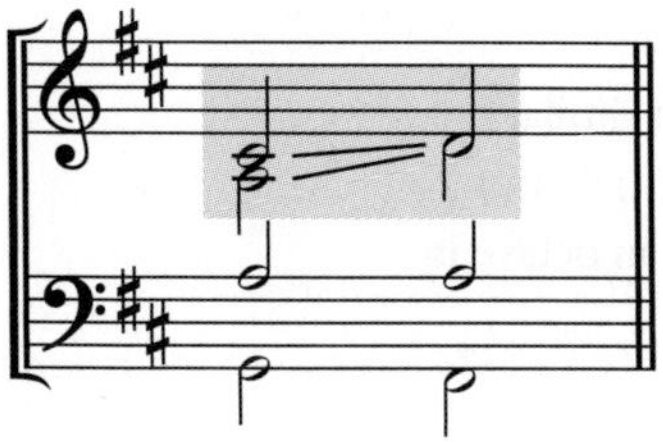

Poor The unison D–D is approached in similar motion.

Finally, an octave should not be approached in similar motion from a dissonant interval of a seventh or second.

5.21

Poor The octave F–F is approached in similar motion from a seventh (A–G).

Poor The octave F–F is approached in similar motion from a (compound) second (G–A).

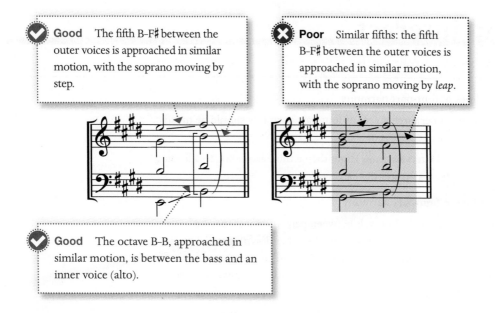

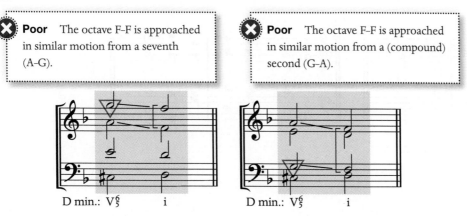

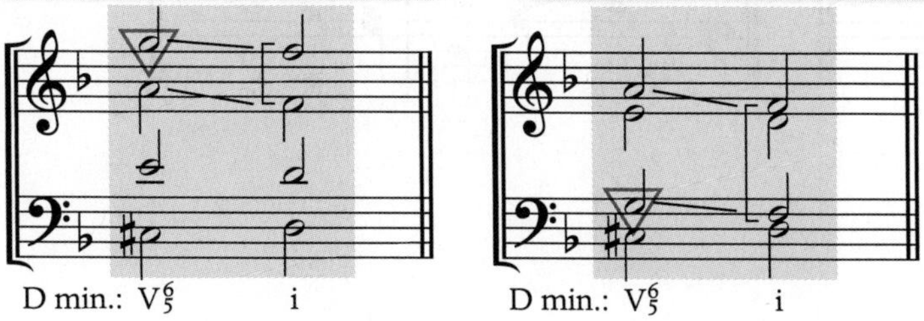

review and interact

POINTS FOR REVIEW

- **Guidelines for melodic lines in four-part harmony**
  - The melodic motion in the upper three voices of four-part harmony should be mostly smooth.
  - In all voices, avoid augmented intervals, leaps larger than a third ascending to a leading tone, leaps of a seventh, and leaps greater than an octave.
- **Guidelines for voice leading in four-part harmony**
  - **Types of motion between intervals**: Intervals between pairs of voices may be approached in contrary motion (one voice moves up, the other down), parallel motion (voices move in the same direction and the same distance), similar motion (voices move in the same direction but different distances), oblique motion (only one voice moves), or stationary motion (neither voice moves).
  - **Perfect intervals**: Do not approach a perfect octave, fifth, or unison in parallel motion.
  - **Leading tones**: A leading tone ($\hat{7}$) in the top voice must either repeat or resolve up to the tonic ($\hat{8}$).
  - **Chordal sevenths**: Chodal sevenths must resolve down by step, or be repeated from one chord to the next before resolving down by step.
  - **Similar motion to octaves and unisons**: (a) Do not approach an octave in similar motion between the bass and soprano unless the soprano moves by step; (b) do not approach a unison in similar motion; (c) do not lead from a dissonance to an octave in similar motion.

TEST YOURSELF

1. Which of these excerpts uses melodic lines that are more typical of standard four-part harmony, and why?

a.

b.

2. Label the type of motion in each pair of intervals below: contrary, parallel, similar, oblique, or stationary.

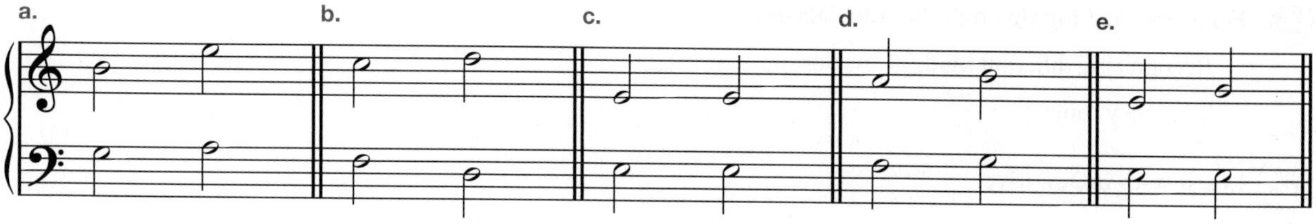

3. Which of the pairs of chords below involve faulty parallel motion?

4. Identify the leading tones in each of the two progressions below. Identify any chordal sevenths. Then fill in the missing notes.

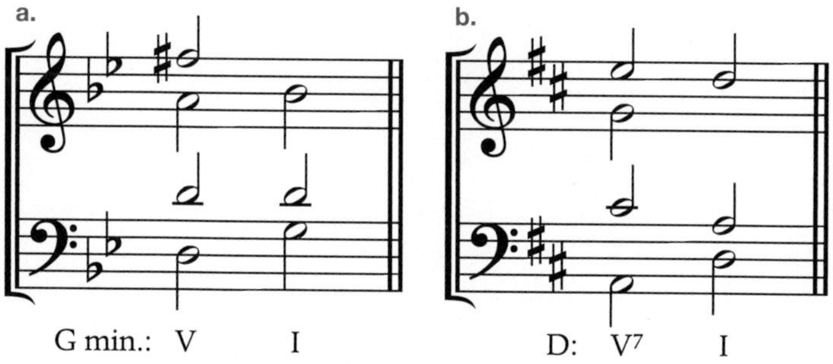

5. Mark the questionable instances of parallel or similar motion to a perfect interval, and explain the problem.

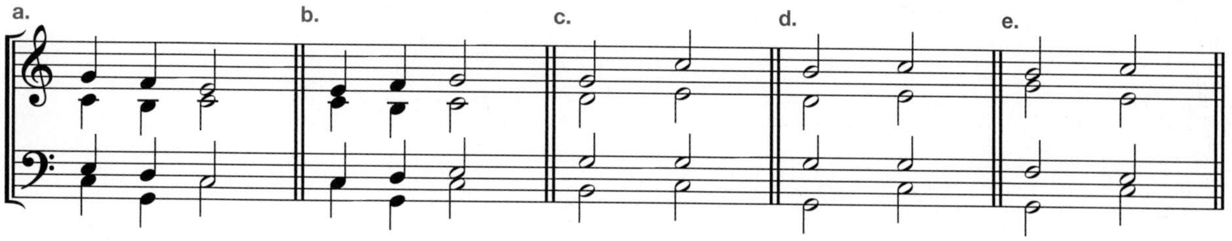

Know It? Show It!

Focus by working through the tutorials on:

- Recognizing different kinds of motion
- Tendency tones

Learn with inQuizitive.

Apply what you've learned to complete the assignments:

- Motion between Intervals
- Locating Perfect Octaves and Fifths within Chords
- Approaching Perfect Octaves and Fifths
- Smooth Voice Leading
- Resolving the Leading Tone and Chordal Sevenths
- Recognizing Errors Approaching Perfect Intervals
- Error Detection

chapter 6

Harmonic Progression

Harmonies in tonal music follow conventional progressions.

BEGINNING AND ENDING PHRASES

AUTHENTIC AND HALF CADENCES

A **phrase** is the basic unit of tonal music, akin to a sentence in language. Within a phrase, harmonies generally occur in conventional progressions. Typically, phrases begin with a root-position I triad. Even more standard is the harmony found at the end of the phrase, or the **cadence**. Phrases almost always conclude either with a root-position V or V^7 chord leading to root-position I (or i), or with a root-position V. A cadence consisting of V or V^7 moving to I (or i) is an **authentic cadence** (**AC**); a cadence ending with a V triad is a **half cadence** (**HC**). Because they end on a stable tonic harmony, authentic cadences generally sound more conclusive than half cadences.

6.1 Mozart, Clarinet Quintet in A, K. 581, IV

p
A: I
V
Half cadence (HC): The first phrase ends with root-position V.
I
V I
Authentic cadence (AC): The second phrase ends more conclusively with a V–I progression.
Both phrases begin with a root-position I triad.

PERFECT AND IMPERFECT AUTHENTIC CADENCES

Authentic cadences are further categorized by the final note in the melody. An authentic cadence that ends with $\hat{1}$ in the melody is a **perfect authentic cadence** (PAC). An authentic cadence that ends with $\hat{3}$ or $\hat{5}$ (the third or fifth of the I or i chord) in the melody is an **imperfect authentic cadence** (IAC). Perfect authentic cadences tend to sound more conclusive than imperfect authentic cadences.

6.2 Mozart, Variations on "La Belle Françoise," K. 353

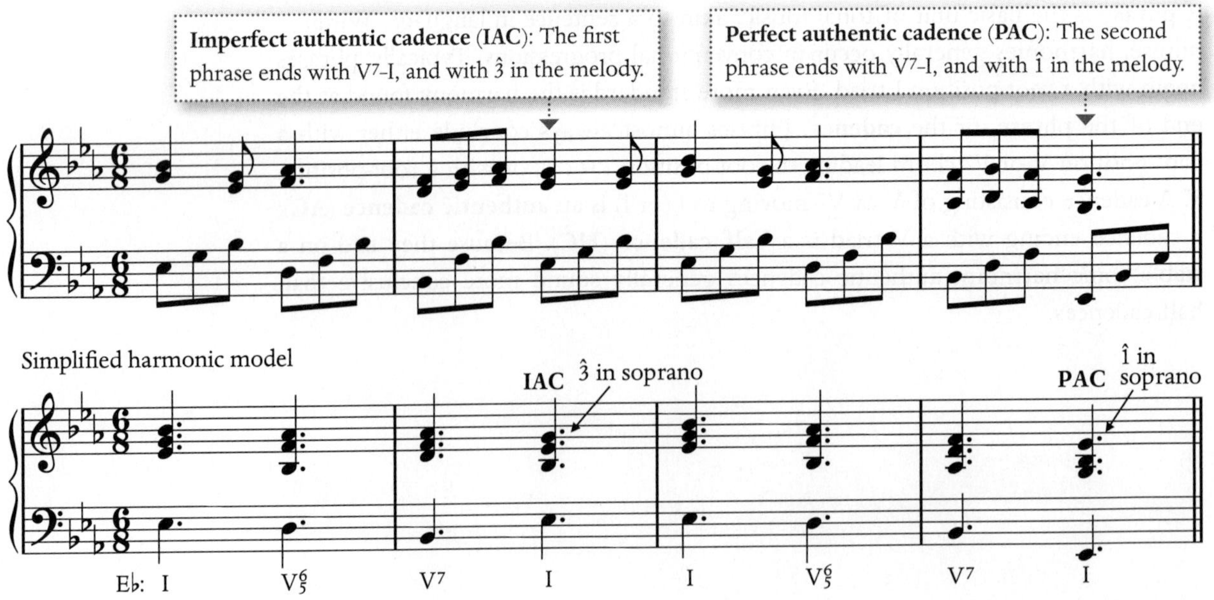
Imperfect authentic cadence (IAC): The first phrase ends with V7–I, and with 3̂ in the melody.
Perfect authentic cadence (PAC): The second phrase ends with V7–I, and with 1̂ in the melody.
Simplified harmonic model
IAC 3̂ in soprano
PAC 1̂ in soprano
E♭: I V6/5 V7 I I V6/5 V7 I

As you will see later, there are some other types of cadences; nevertheless, the HC, PAC, and IAC are by far the most common. Also, it should be noted that harmonies alone do not determine where cadences occur: cadences appear only at the ends of phrases, which are determined not only by the chords that are used, but also by the rhythm and melody.

FUNCTIONS AND HARMONIC PATTERNS

Compared to the beginning and end, the middle of a phrase offers a wider variety of harmonic possibilities. Choosing the proper order for chords in the middle of phrases can be challenging, and will be a primary focus of Parts 3 and 4. As you will see, each chord fits into one of a few **functions**, either **Tonic**, **Dominant**, or **Subdominant**. You already know the terms tonic, subdominant, and dominant to apply to I, IV, and V, but the *categories* of **T**onic, **D**ominant, and **S**ubdominant include more than these three chords, as you will see. These basic categories in turn help determine the order in which chords progress.

T–D–T (TONIC–DOMINANT–TONIC)

A particularly common pattern involves a stable **T**onic chord moving to an unstable **D**ominant and then back to a **T**onic (**T–D–T**). Different individual chords belong to the functional categories of **T**onic and **D**ominant. The **T**onic chord in the **T–D–T** progression must be a triad (not a seventh chord), and it can be in root position or (especially if it appears in the middle of a phrase) first inversion (I^6); it may *not* appear as a second-inversion chord (I^6_4), since I^6_4 is an unstable harmony. The **D**ominant chord may be V, V^7, or (especially if it appears in the middle of a phrase) an inversion (like V^6 or V^4_2), as well as other similar harmonies that will be discussed in Part 3.

6.3 The Tonic–Dominant–Tonic pattern

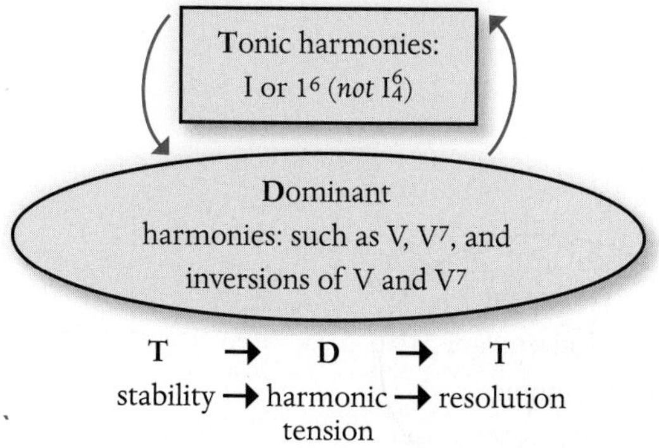

6.4

SOME EXAMPLES OF CHORD PROGRESSIONS THAT FOLLOW THE T-D-T PATTERN:			
I–V–I	I–V^7–I	I–V^6–I	I–V^4_3–I^6
T–D–T	**T–D–T**	**T–D–T**	**T–D–T**

Within the T–D–T pattern, a chord may repeat or move to another chord within the same category before progressing onward.

6.5

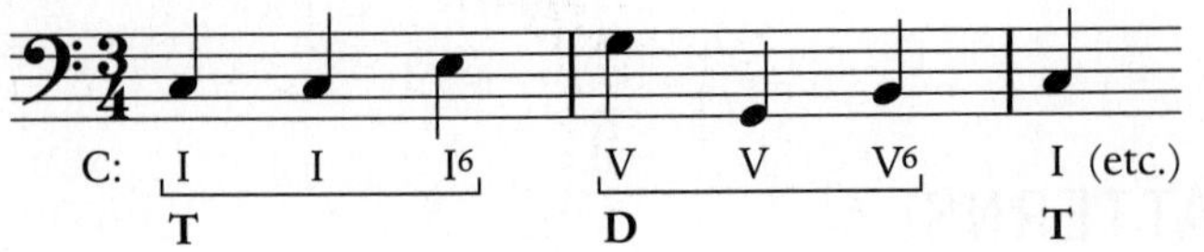

Two or more tonic chords may appear in a row; two or more dominant chords may appear in a row.

6.6 "Let all on Earth their voices raise" (from *Hymnal of the Episcopal Church*)

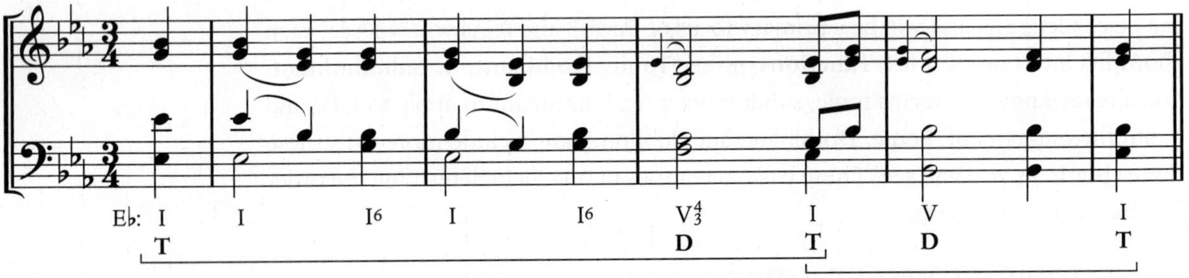

The chord progressions in this excerpt follow the standard **T**onic-**D**ominant-**T**onic pattern.

T–S–D–T (TONIC–SUBDOMINANT–DOMINANT–TONIC)

Another harmonic pattern involves a **T**onic chord that moves through a **S**ubdominant chord to a **D**ominant and back to a **T**onic (**T–S–D–T**). Like the **T**onic and **D**ominant categories, the **S**ubdominant category includes a number of chords: IV, ii6, and other chords to be discussed later.

6.7 The Tonic-Subdominant-Dominant-Tonic pattern

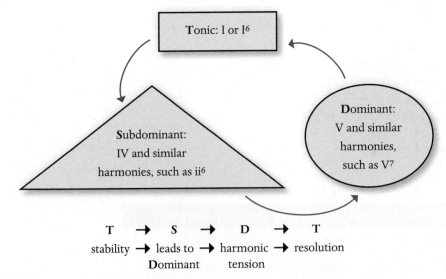

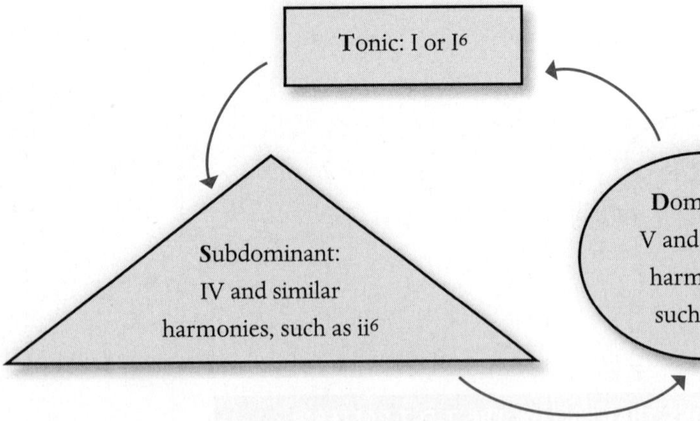

T → S → D → T

stability → leads to Dominant → harmonic tension → resolution

6.8

SOME EXAMPLES OF CHORD PROGRESSIONS THAT FOLLOW THE T-S-D-T PATTERN:				
I–IV–V–I	I–ii^6–V^7–I	I–IV–V^4_3–I	I–ii^6–V–I^6	I–ii^6–V^6–I
T–S–D–T	**T–S–D–T**	**T–S–D–T**	**T–S–D–T**	**T–S–D–T**

A **S**ubdominant chord may repeat or be followed by another **S**ubdominant chord before progressing to a **D**ominant.

6.9

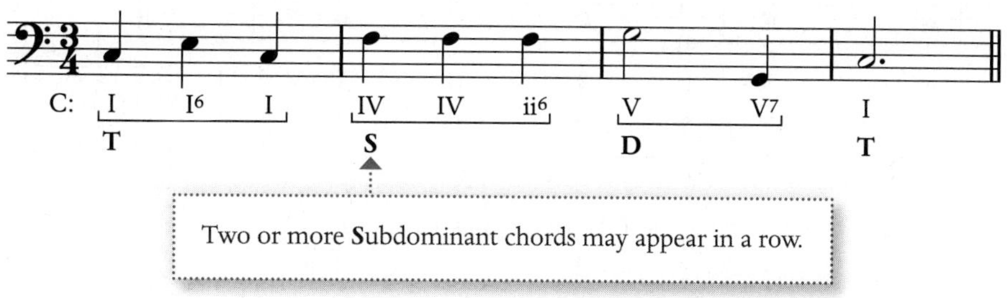
C: I I6 I IV IV ii6 V V7 I
T S D T
Two or more Subdominant chords may appear in a row.

Although a **S**ubdominant often leads to a **D**ominant, the reverse is *not* true: in four-part harmony, it is very unusual for a **D**ominant to move to a **S**ubdominant, as in I-V-IV-I or I-V^7-ii^6-I.

6.10

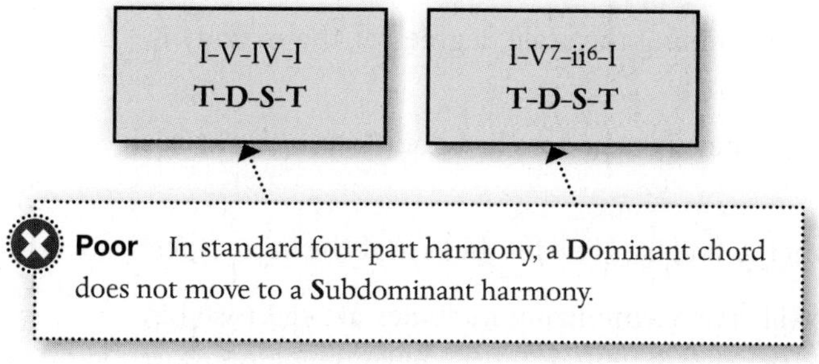
I-V-IV-I
T-D-S-T
I-V7-ii6-I
T-D-S-T
Poor In standard four-part harmony, a Dominant chord does not move to a Subdominant harmony.

T-D-T and **T-S-D-T** do not exhaust the possibilities for harmonic progressions. For instance, another particularly common chord progression is I-IV-I (**T**onic-**S**ubdominant-**T**onic, see Chapter 16). Nonetheless, the harmonic structure of most tonal music may be understood as a series of **T-D-T** and **T-S-D-T** patterns.

6.11 Beethoven, Variations in G, WoO 77

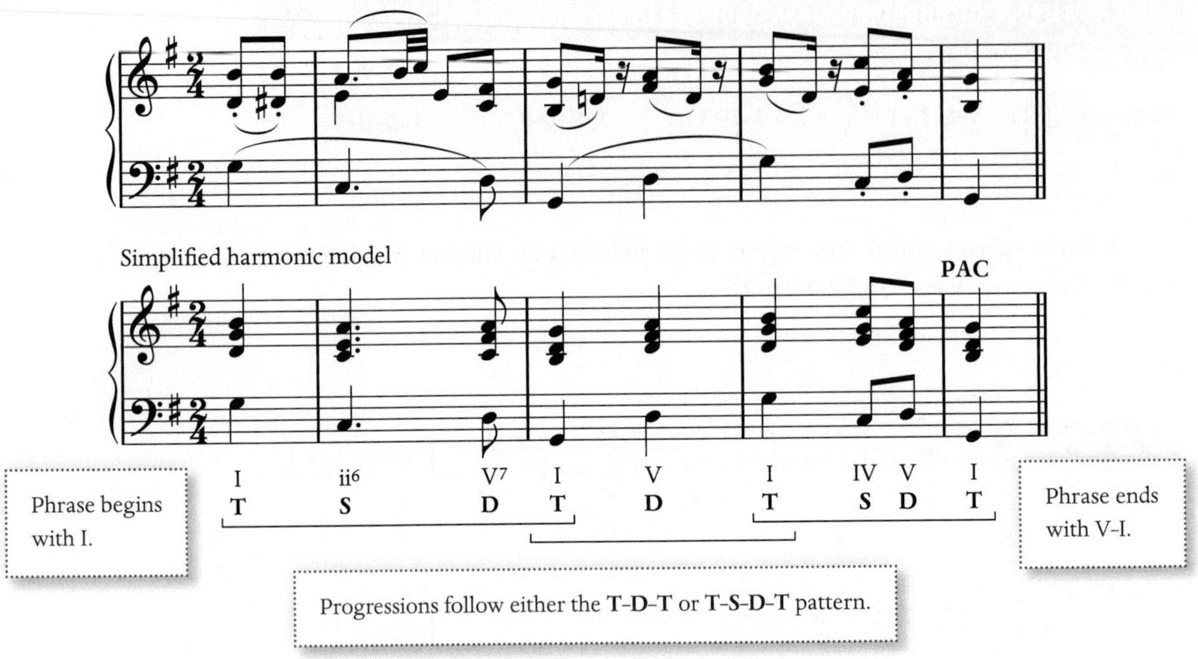
Simplified harmonic model
PAC
I ii6 V7 I V I IV V I
T S D T D T S D T
Phrase begins with I.
Phrase ends with V–I.
Progressions follow either the T–D–T or T–S–D–T pattern.

HARMONIZING MELODIES

One way to enhance your understanding of harmonic progressions is to **harmonize** melodies. When harmonizing a melody, you are given a melody with a simple rhythm and directed to supply a harmony for every note (or almost every note), using standard voice-leading and harmonic procedures.

- Begin by identifying the key and determining the scale degrees of the melody in that key.
- Then locate the cadences and determine a proper bass line and Roman numerals for the cadences.
- Finally, determine the Roman numerals and bass line for the rest of the harmonies.

Strategies for developing the skills for harmonizing melodies are discussed in detail starting in Part 3. In each case, the chords chosen for the harmonization must include the notes found in the melody, allowing for good voice leading and harmonic progressions.

6.12

***Task*: Harmonize this melody by providing a bass line and Roman numerals.**

MATCHING CHORDS TO THE MELODY

In harmonizing a melody, you must make sure that each note belongs to the chord chosen to harmonize it.

6.13

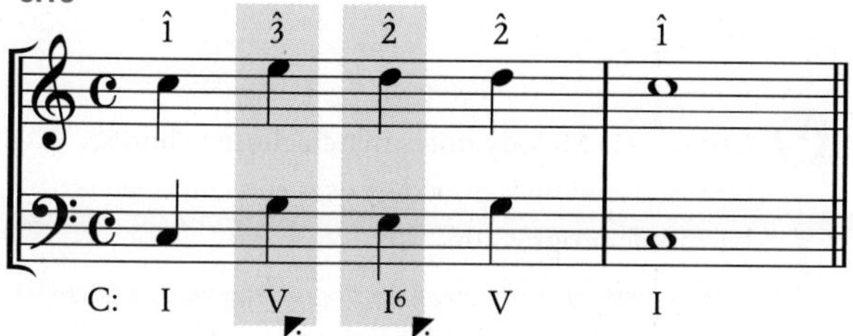

In C major, V = G-B-D; I^6 = C-E-G (with E in bass).

Poor The note E ($\hat{3}$) is not in V.

Poor The note D ($\hat{2}$) is not in I^6.

The note in the melody must be part of the chosen chord.

VOICE LEADING

In harmonizing a melody, you should follow voice-leading and chord construction guidelines, such as avoiding parallel fifths and avoiding doubled leading tones.

6.14

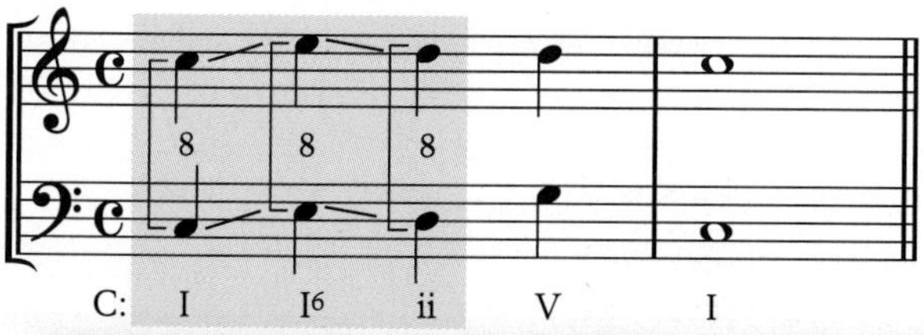

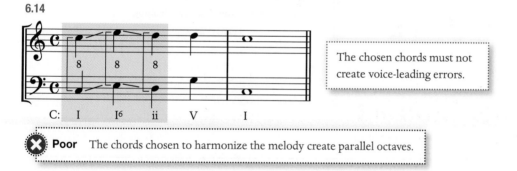

The chosen chords must not create voice-leading errors.

Poor The chords chosen to harmonize the melody create parallel octaves.

CONVENTIONAL HARMONIC PROGRESSIONS

Finally, the harmonization should follow conventional harmonic progressions, using patterns such as **T–D–T** or **T–S–D–T** and ending each phrase with a cadence.

6.15

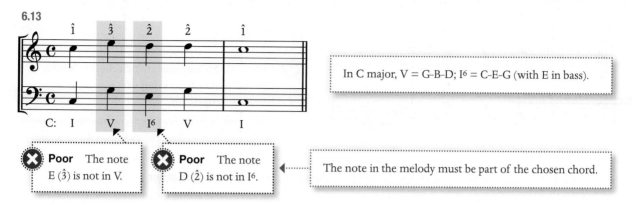

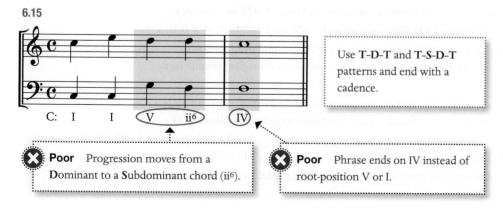

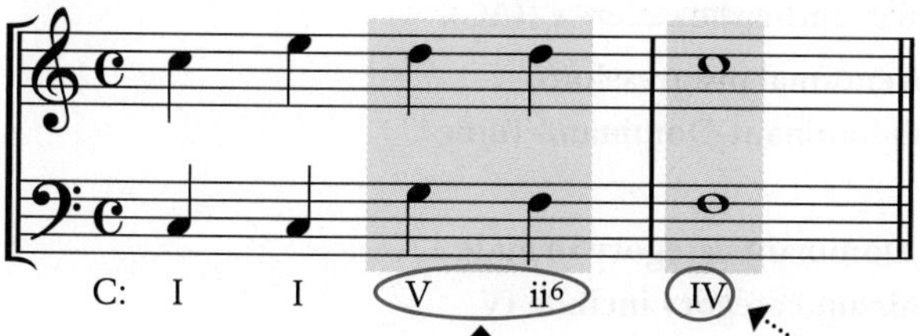

Use **T–D–T** and **T–S–D–T** patterns and end with a cadence.

Poor Progression moves from a Dominant to a Subdominant chord (ii^6).

Poor Phrase ends on IV instead of root-position V or I.

The following harmonization of the melody is good: the notes of the melody appear in each of the chords chosen to harmonize them, there are no voice-leading errors, and the chord progression follows conventional harmonic practice, with an appropriate chord progression at the cadence.

6.16

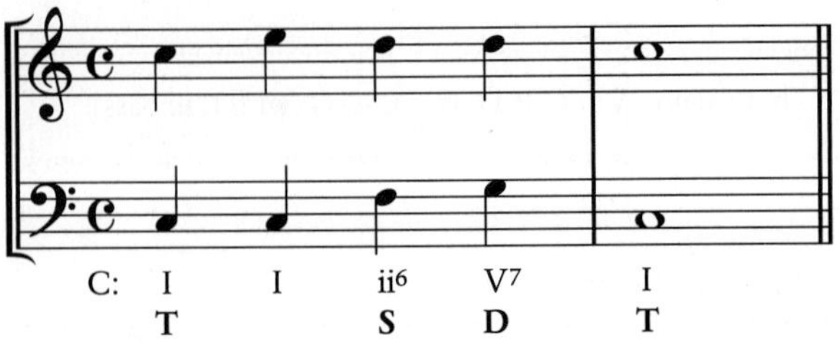

Good (1) Melody notes match chosen chords; (2) voice leading is good; (3) uses conventional harmonic progression.

After choosing the harmonies and writing the bass line, you can fill in the inner voices, paying attention to chord construction (see Chapter 4) and voice leading (see Chapter 5).

6.17

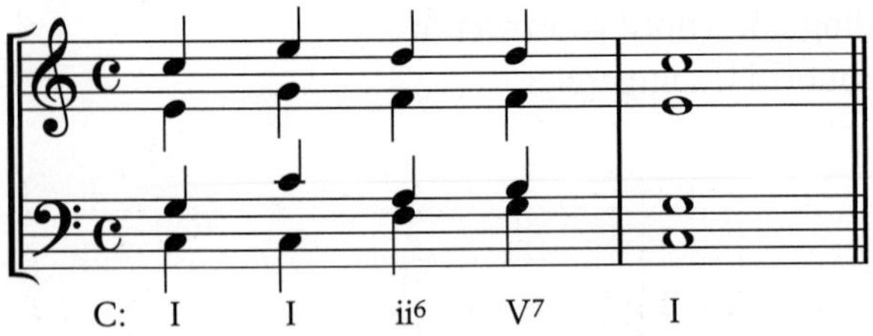

Good Realization follows proper chord construction and voice leading.

review and interact

POINTS FOR REVIEW

- **Phrases most often begin with a root-position I chord, and end either with a cadence on a root-position V, or with a cadence on a root-position I preceded by root-position V (or V^7).**
- **A cadence ending on a root-position V is a half cadence (HC).**
- **A cadence that ends V–I or V^7–I is an authentic cadence (AC). An authentic cadence that ends with $\hat{1}$ in the soprano is a perfect authentic cadence (PAC); an authentic cadence that ends with $\hat{3}$ or $\hat{5}$ in the melody is an imperfect authentic cadence (IAC).**
- **The ordering of harmonies within a phrase follows conventional progressions, including Tonic–Dominant–Tonic (T–D–T) and Tonic–Subdominant–Dominant–Tonic (T–S–D–T).**
- **Chords in the Tonic category are I and I^6; chords in the Dominant category include V, V^7, and inversions of V and V^7; chords in the Subdominant category include IV and ii^6.**
- **In a good melody harmonization, the chord chosen for each note of the melody should include the melody note, conform to voice-leading guidelines, and result in a chord progression that follows the conventions of harmony.**

TEST YOURSELF

1. In the examples below, do the phrases (each ending is marked by a fermata) end with a PAC, IAC, or HC?

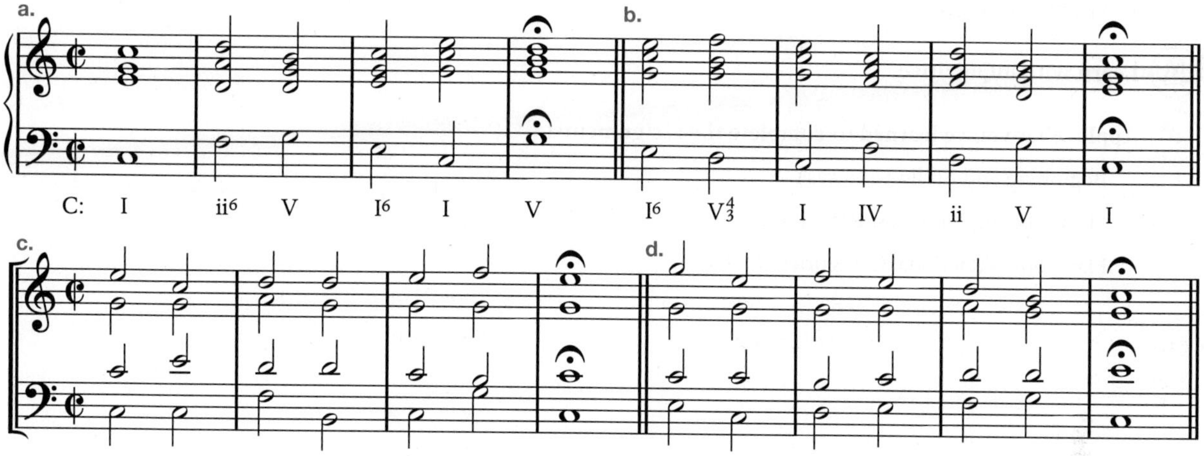

2. Why are the following phrase endings (indicated by fermatas) not conventional cadences?

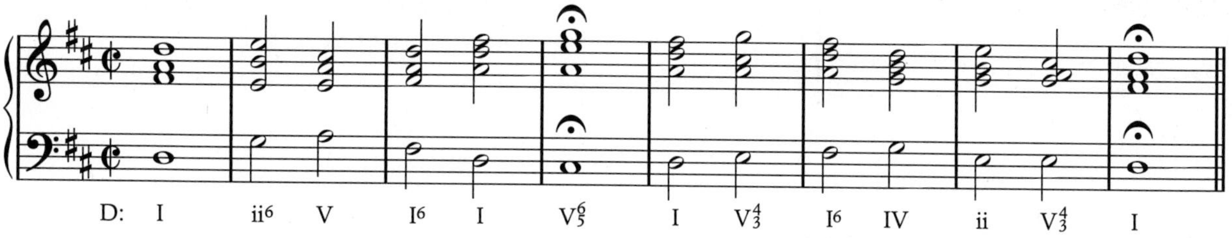

3. Which of the following are **T**onic-**D**ominant-**T**onic chord progressions, which are **T**onic-**S**ubdominant-**D**ominant-**T**onic progressions, and which are neither?

   a. I-V-I b. I-I-V-V6-I c. I-V-IV-I d. I-ii6-V-I

4. Which of the following are good harmonizations of the given melodies? If the harmonization is not good, what is the problem with it?

Know It? Show It!

Focus by working through the tutorials on:

- Cadences
- Harmonic progression

Learn with inQuizitive.

Apply what you've learned to complete the assignments:

- Beginning and Ending a Phrase
- Harmonizing Melodies: Preparatory Exercises
- Harmonic Functional Categories: **T**, **S**, **D**

chapter 7

Figuration and Embellishing Tones

Harmonies may be elaborated by figuration and embellishing tones, including arpeggiations, passing tones, and neighboring tones.

ARPEGGIATION

In four-part harmony, each chord has four different notes. However, four separate voices are not needed to imply four-voice harmony. For instance, instead of sounding at the same time, some (or all) of the chord tones may appear in succession, with **chord skips** (leaps from one chord tone to another), resulting in an **arpeggiation**. To determine the underlying harmony in such a case, imagine the notes as if they were played at the same time.

7.1 Fischer, *Clio* Suite (Suite 1 from *Musicalischer Parnassus*)

Simplified model in four-part harmony (with arpeggiations removed)

This passage can be understood in relation to a four-part model by imagining the notes of the arpeggiation played simultaneously.

OCTAVE DOUBLING

Any voice of a four-part texture may be **doubled** in parallel octaves throughout, resulting in what appears to be a five-voice texture. These octave doublings simply enrich the underlying four-part texture so as to create a fuller sound, however, and are thus not considered forbidden parallel octaves.

7.2 Schubert, *Moments musicaux*, op. 94, no. 2 ➔

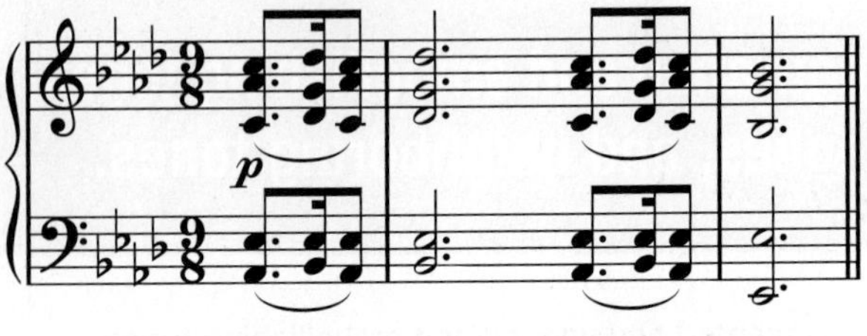

Though each chord uses five notes, this passage is *not* in five-part harmony, but rather four-part harmony with the outer notes of the treble-clef part doubled in octaves.

Simplified model in four-part harmony (with octave doubling removed)

EMBELLISHING TONES

Chord tones also may be decorated by notes that do not belong to the harmony. In identifying the underlying harmony, these **embellishing tones** may be ignored.

7.3 J. S. Bach, Chorale 330 ➔

Embellishing tones (highlighted by triangles) decorate the notes of the harmony.

Simplified harmonic model (with embellishing tones removed)

APPROACHING AND LEAVING AN EMBELLISHING TONE

Embellishing tones are classified by how they are approached and left—by step, leap, or common tone.

7.4

Approached by step and left by step | Approached by step and left by leap | Approached by common tone and left by step

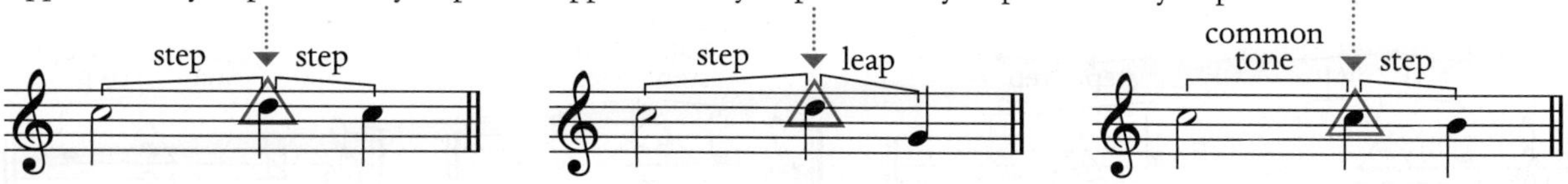

ACCENTED AND UNACCENTED EMBELLISHING TONES

Embellishing tones are also classified as either **accented** or **unaccented**. An unaccented embellishing tone appears after the arrival of the chord, on a weaker beat or part of the beat. In contrast, an accented embellishing tone appears at the very start of the chord.

7.5 J. S. Bach, Chorale 256

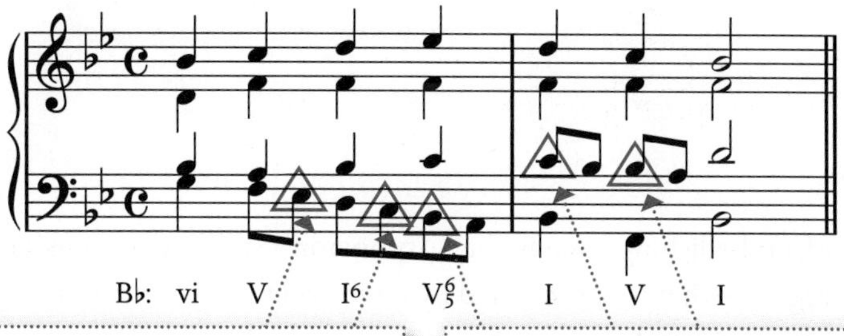

Unaccented embellishing tones appear after the start of the chord and on a weak part of the beat.

Accented embellishing tones appear at the onset of the chord.

PASSING TONES

The most common type of embellishing tone is a **passing tone** (PT). Passing tones fill in the space between two different chord tones with stepwise motion. A passing tone is thus always approached and left by step in the same direction.

7.6

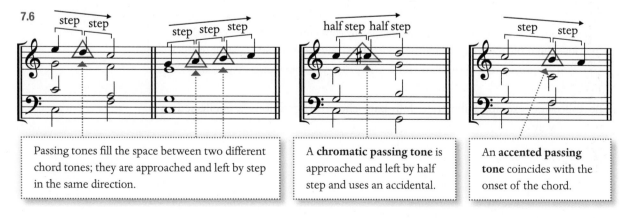

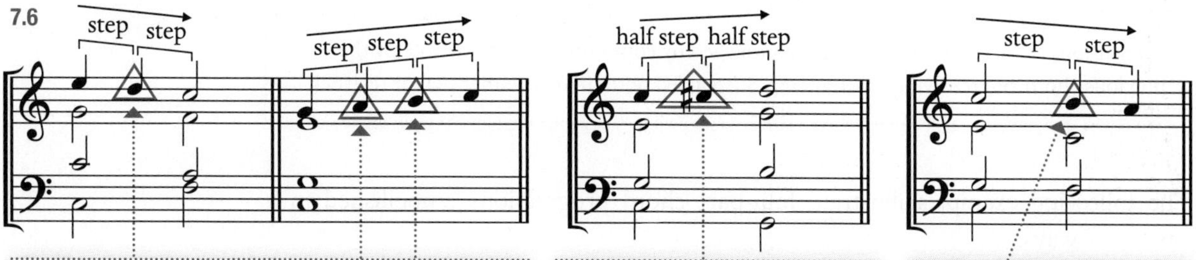

Passing tones fill the space between two different chord tones; they are approached and left by step in the same direction.

A **chromatic passing tone** is approached and left by half step and uses an accidental.

An **accented passing tone** coincides with the onset of the chord.

NEIGHBOR TONES

Unlike the passing tone, which moves between two different chord tones, the **neighbor tone** (NT) decorates a single tone. Accordingly, a neighbor tone departs from a chord tone by step and returns to the same tone by step in the opposite direction.

7.7

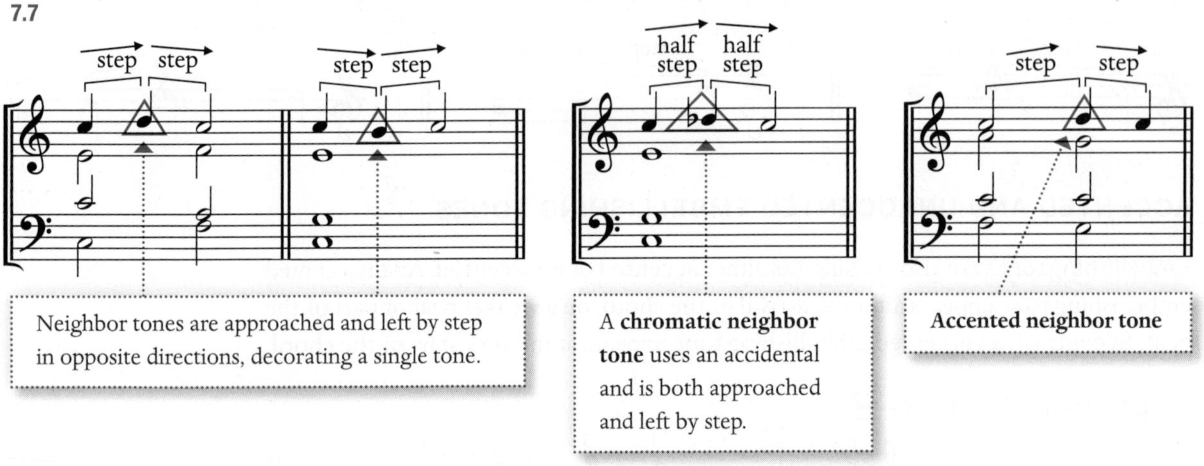

step step
step step
half step half step
step step
Neighbor tones are approached and left by step in opposite directions, decorating a single tone.
A **chromatic neighbor tone** uses an accidental and is both approached and left by step.
Accented neighbor tone

SUSPENSIONS

Another common type of embellishing tone is the **suspension** (SUS). A suspension is an accented embellishing tone that is approached by common tone from a note of the previous chord. A suspension resolves *down* by step.

7.8

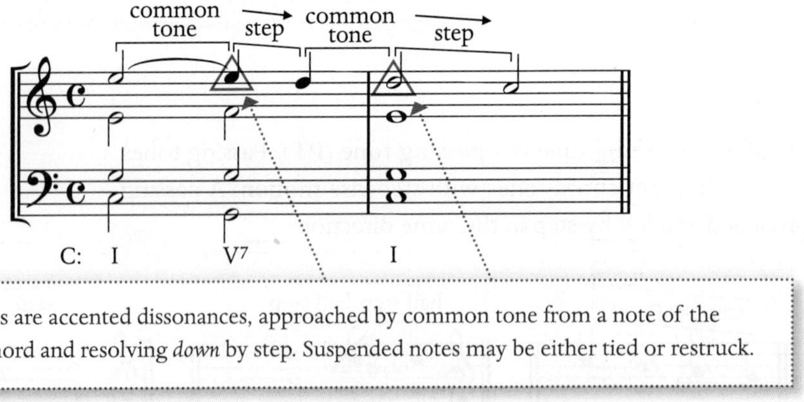

common tone
step
common tone
step
C: I V7 I
Suspensions are accented dissonances, approached by common tone from a note of the previous chord and resolving *down* by step. Suspended notes may be either tied or restruck.

The following examples illustrate four-part chord progressions embellished in a variety of ways.

7.9 J. S. Bach, Chorale 147

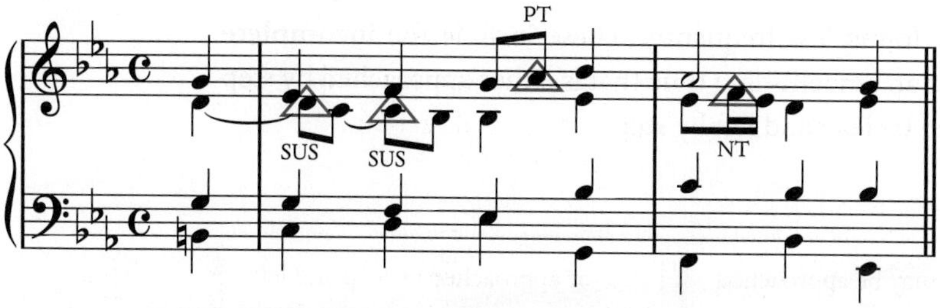

Simplified harmonic model (with embellishing tones removed)

7.10 L. Reichardt, "Poesie von Tieck" (Poem by Tieck)

Simplified harmonic model (with octave doublings, non-chord tones, arpeggiations, and repeated melodic tones removed)

Translation: Rest, sweet love, in the shade of the green twilight. The grass rustles in the meadow . . .

OTHER EMBELLISHMENTS

Other embellishing tones are found less frequently. These include the **incomplete neighbor tone** (INT), which is an embellishing tone that is either approached by step and left by leap, or approached by leap and left by step.

7.11

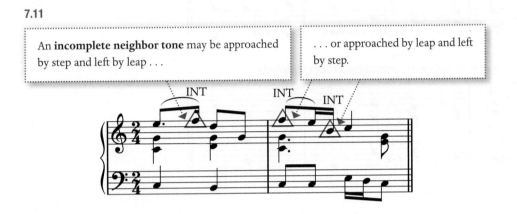

An **incomplete neighbor tone** may be approached by step and left by leap . . .

. . . or approached by leap and left by step.

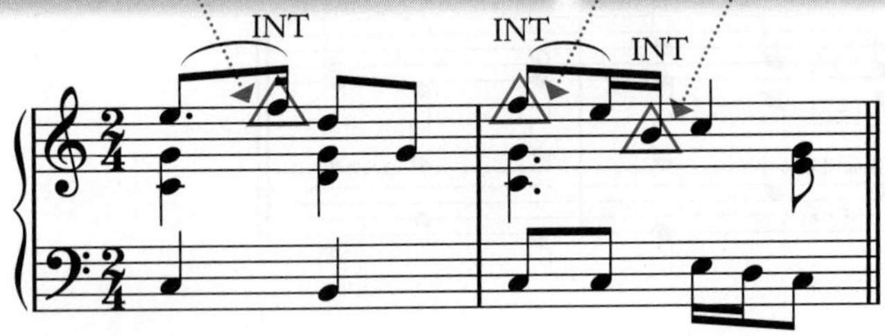

Still rarer are the **anticipation** (ANT), an unaccented non-chord tone that is approached by step and left by common tone; and the **retardation** (RET), an accented embellishing tone that is approached by common tone and resolves up by step.

7.12 Handel, Sonata for Violin and Continuo in E Major, III ➔

An anticipation is approached by step and left by common tone, so that a note of the upcoming chord arrives early.

7.13 Mozart, Sonata in F Major, K. 494 ➔

A retardation is like a suspension, except that it resolves *up* by step.

For more on neighbor tones, see A Closer Look.

review and interact

POINTS FOR REVIEW

- **Chord tones may appear successively, forming arpeggiations.**
- **One or more voices in a four-part texture may be doubled in parallel octaves. This is not considered a voice-leading error.**
- **Chord tones may be decorated by embellishing tones. These embellishing tones are classified by how they are approached and left (by step, leap, or common tone—up or down), as well as whether they are accented or unaccented.**
- **The most common embellishing tones are the passing tone (PT), neighbor tone (NT), and suspension (SUS).**

passing tone
- links two different tones
- approached and left by step in the same direction
- may be accented or unaccented

neighbor tone
- decorates a single tone
- approached and left by step in opposite directions
- may be accented or unaccented

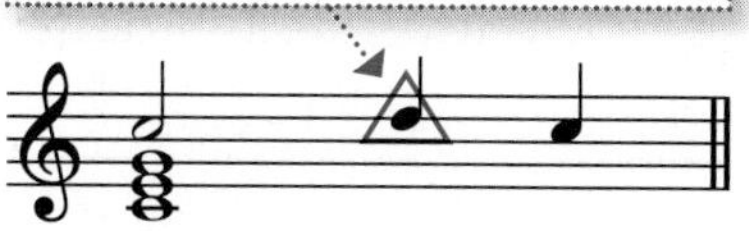

suspension
- must be accented
- approached by common tone, then resolves down by step
- may be either tied or restruck

- **Less common embellishing tones include the incomplete neighbor tone (INT), anticipation, and retardation.**

incomplete neighbor tone
- either approached by step and left by leap, or approached by leap and left by step

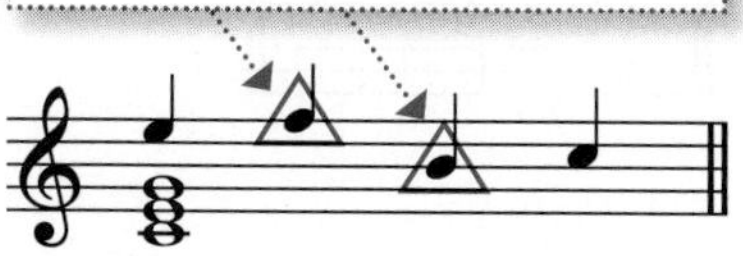

anticipation
- decorates a single tone
- approached and left by common tone
- must be unaccented

retardation
- must be accented
- approached by common tone, then resolves up by step

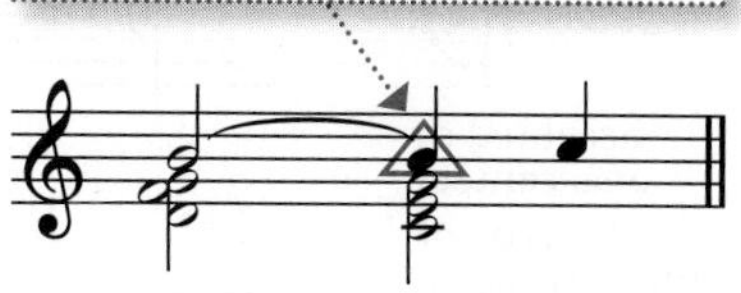

TEST YOURSELF

1. Complete a Roman numeral analysis of the excerpt below.

C: ____ ____ ____ ____

2. In the example below, how many notes are in each chord? How might the example be understood to represent four parts?

3. For the examples below, label how each embellishing tone (marked by a triangle) is approached and left: by step, leap, or common tone.

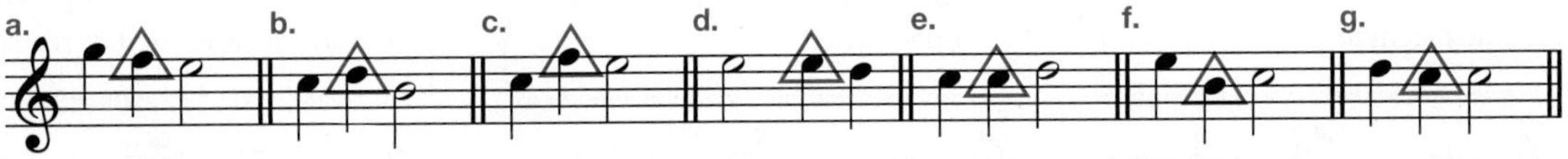

approached by: ____ ____ ____ ____ ____ ____ ____

left by: ____ ____ ____ ____ ____ ____ ____

4. For the examples below, label each embellishing tone (marked by a triangle) as either accented or unaccented. Then identify whether it is a PT (passing tone), NT (neighbor tone), SUS (suspension), ANT (anticipation), RET (retardation), or INT (incomplete neighbor tone).

accented or unaccented? ____ ____ ____ ____

type of embellishment: ____ ____ ____ ____

accented or unaccented? ________ ________ ________ ________

type of embellishment: ________ ________ ________ ________

Know It? Show It!

Focus by working through the tutorials on:

- Recognizing embellishing tones

Learn with inQuizitive.

Apply what you've learned to complete the assignments:

- Arpeggiation
- Identifying Embellishing Tones
- Analysis
- Writing Figuration
- Interpreting Figuration

chapter

8 Species Counterpoint

Species counterpoint involves writing a new melody to sound with a given melody.

Species counterpoint is a traditional way to learn voice leading, especially the use of dissonant embellishing tones and the treatment of perfect consonances. In species counterpoint, you are given a melody in whole notes, called a **cantus firmus**, and asked to write a melody to go with it. There are five *species* in this method, each defining the rhythmic values and embellishing tones you may use in the added melody:

- whole notes and no dissonance in first species;
- half notes and dissonant passing or neighboring notes in second species;
- quarter notes and dissonant passing or neighboring notes in third species;
- half notes tied across the barline and dissonant suspensions in fourth species;
- and a free combination of all the previous possibilities in fifth species.

In what follows, we will discuss only first, second, and fourth species, and we will be concerned only with melodies composed above the cantus firmus.

FIRST SPECIES

In **first-species counterpoint**, a new melody in whole notes is written against the cantus firmus, using only consonant intervals between the melodies. To help keep track of the intervals, label them between the staves, and put a box around any perfect intervals—they require special treatment.

8.1

Counterpoint starts on $\hat{1}$, an octave above the cantus.

Counterpoint moves mostly by step and has a single melodic high point in the middle.

Counterpoint ends $\hat{7}$-$\hat{8}$, while the cantus firmus ends $\hat{2}$-$\hat{1}$. Scale-degree $\hat{7}$ is raised to leading tone in minor.

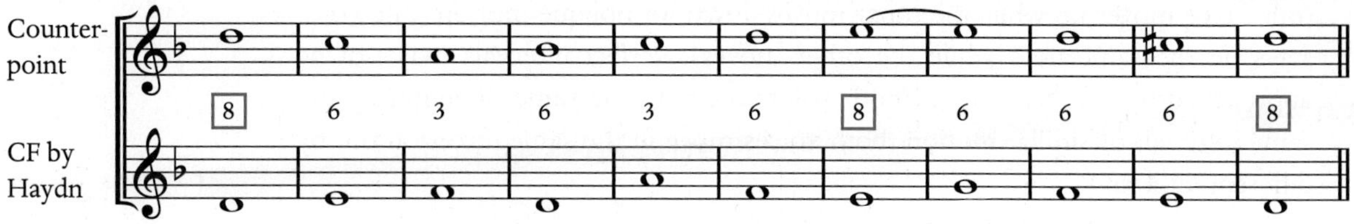

Only consonant intervals are used between the melodies, mostly imperfect consonances (thirds and sixths).

Perfect consonances (boxed) are approached in contrary or oblique motion, never in similar or parallel motion.

8.2

Counterpoint starts on $\hat{5}$, a fifth above the cantus.

Counterpoint moves mostly by step, with a large leap to the melodic high point followed by a long stepwise descent.

Counterpoint ends $\hat{7}$-$\hat{8}$, while the cantus firmus ends $\hat{2}$-$\hat{1}$. Scale-degree $\hat{7}$ is raised in minor.

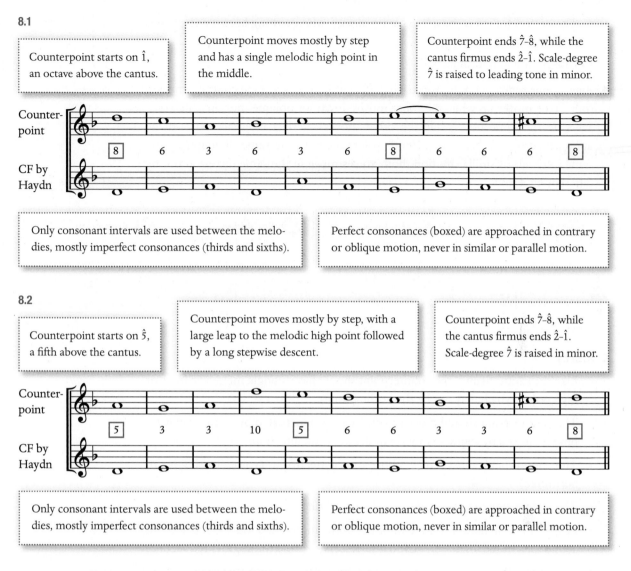

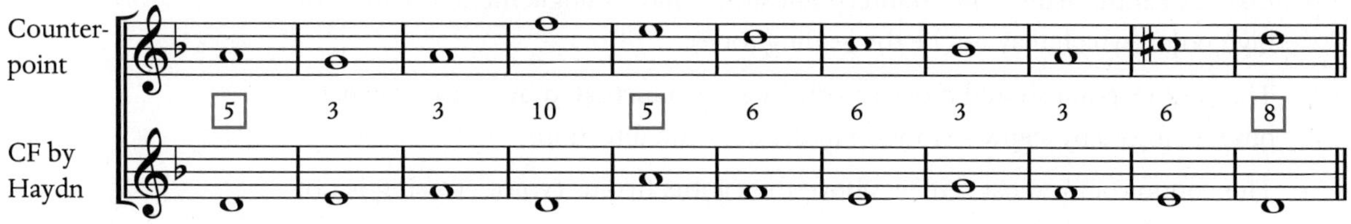

Only consonant intervals are used between the melodies, mostly imperfect consonances (thirds and sixths).

Perfect consonances (boxed) are approached in contrary or oblique motion, never in similar or parallel motion.

As you write first-species counterpoint, follow these guidelines:

1. *Rhythm*: Use whole notes only.
2. *Beginning and ending*: Start the counterpoint a fifth or an octave above the cantus; conclude it with $\hat{7}$-$\hat{8}$ (in minor, raising the supertonic to leading tone). The cantus firmus always ends $\hat{2}$-$\hat{1}$, so the last two intervals between the melodies will always be 6-8 (a sixth expanding to an octave).
3. *Harmonic intervals*:
   - Use only consonances.
   - Major or minor thirds and sixths should predominate; perfect fifths and octaves appear less frequently.
   - Dissonances, including seconds, sevenths, and augmented or diminished intervals, are forbidden. (Beware the diminished fifth between $\hat{7}$ and $\hat{4}$!)

- The perfect fourth is considered a dissonance when writing in two parts and is forbidden.
- Unisons are also forbidden.

4. *Approaching perfect intervals*: Approach perfect fifths and octaves in contrary motion (one voice moves up while the other moves down) or oblique motion (one voice stays on the same note while the other moves). Perfect intervals may not be approached by parallel motion (both voices move in the same direction by the same interval) or similar motion (both voices move in the same direction but by different intervals).

8.3

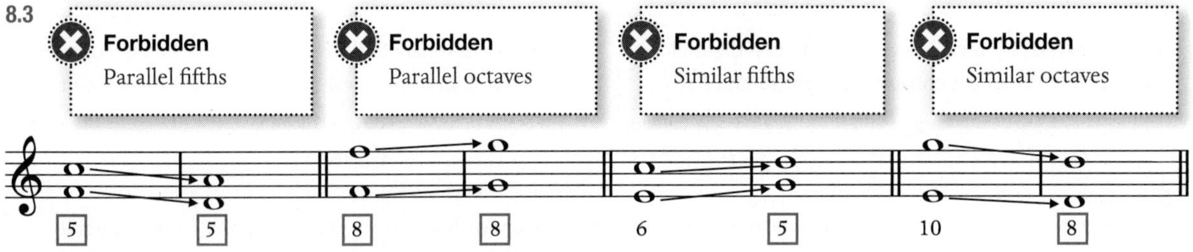

5. *Melody*:
   - Like the cantus firmus, the counterpoint should have a single melodic climax or high point (which may not be the leading tone).
   - The counterpoint should move mostly by step, punctuated by leaps, which are often followed by stepwise motion in the opposite direction.
   - The counterpoint must remain above the cantus firmus (voice crossing is not permitted).
   - The counterpoint may contain a single pair of tied notes.
   - Leaps by augmented second, diminished fifth, augmented fourth, and seventh are not permitted. In minor, raise $\hat{6}$ if necessary to avoid the augmented second.
   - Leaps up to the leading tone by intervals greater than a third are not permitted.
   - Do not use any accidentals, other than raised $\hat{7}$ or raised $\hat{6}$ and $\hat{7}$ at the very end of a minor-key counterpoint. Do not write chromatic semitones (like B♭–B♮).

8.4

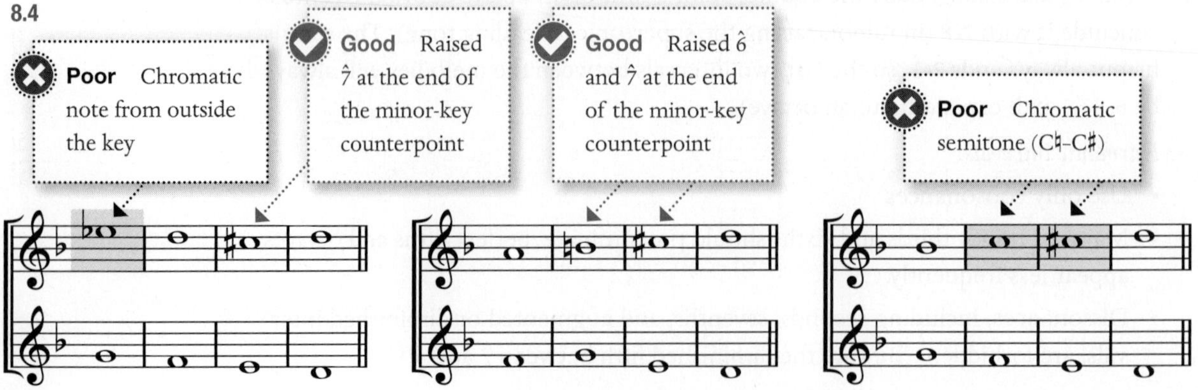

SECOND SPECIES

Second-species melodies are written in half notes, so there are two notes in the counterpoint for each whole note in the cantus firmus.

- Dissonant intervals may be used, but only on the unaccented second half of the measure and when the dissonant note is both approached and left by step: you may not leap into or out of a dissonance.
- As a result, every dissonance is either a passing tone (connecting two consonant tones a third apart) or a neighbor tone (stepping away from and back to a consonant tone).
- As in first species, fifths and octaves on the downbeats must be approached in contrary motion (never in similar or parallel motion).
- Perfect consonances on downbeats and all dissonances require special treatment (in exercises, place dissonant intervals in triangles and perfect consonances in boxes).
- Unisons are permitted on weak beats.

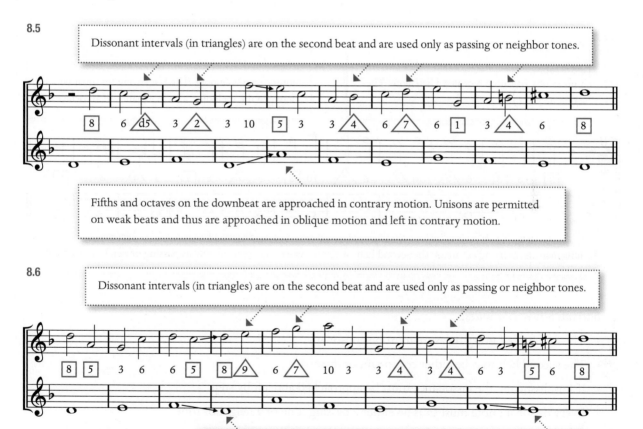

8.5

Dissonant intervals (in triangles) are on the second beat and are used only as passing or neighbor tones.

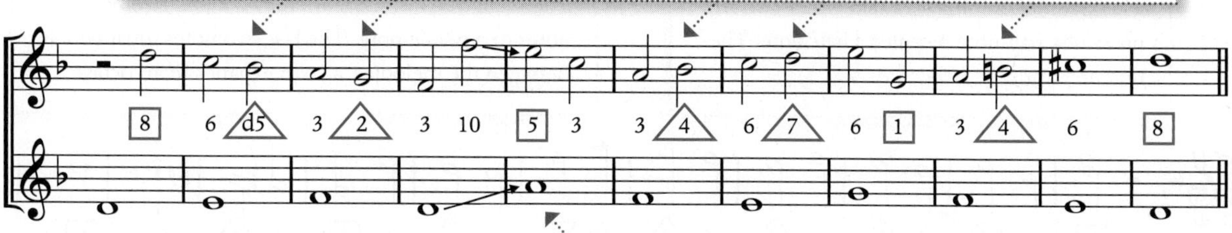

Fifths and octaves on the downbeat are approached in contrary motion. Unisons are permitted on weak beats and thus are approached in oblique motion and left in contrary motion.

8.6

Dissonant intervals (in triangles) are on the second beat and are used only as passing or neighbor tones.

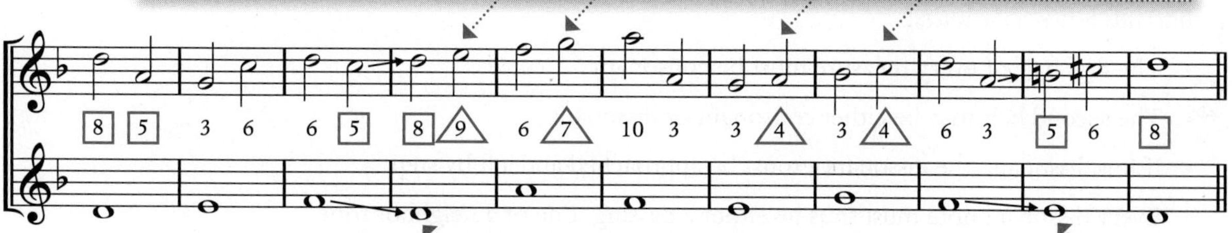

Fifths and octaves on the downbeat must be approached in contrary motion.

Here are guidelines for writing second-species counterpoint:

1. *Rhythm*: Use half notes throughout, with only these exceptions:
   - the first measure may begin with a half-note rest;
   - the second-to-last measure may contain a whole note;
   - the last measure must be a whole note;
   - do not repeat or tie notes.
2. *Beginning and ending*:
   - The first note must be $\hat{5}$ or $\hat{8}$ (a fifth or octave above the cantus firmus).
   - The second-to-last note must be $\hat{7}$ (raised in minor, and $\hat{6}$ may also have to be raised to avoid a melodic augmented second).
   - The final note must be an octave above the cantus.
   - As in first species, the last two intervals between the melodies will always be 6–8 (a sixth expanding to an octave).

8.7

The first measure may contain either two half notes or a half-note rest plus a half note. The first note must be either $\hat{5}$ or $\hat{8}$.

The second-to-last measure may contain two half notes or a whole note. The last two notes must be $\hat{7}$–$\hat{8}$. Between the melodies, a sixth expands to an octave.

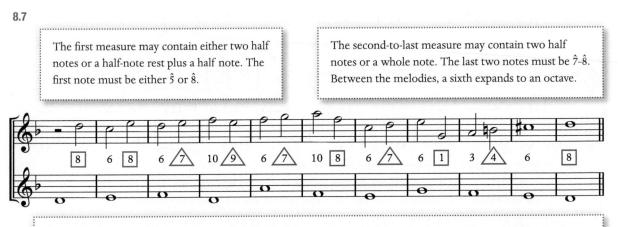

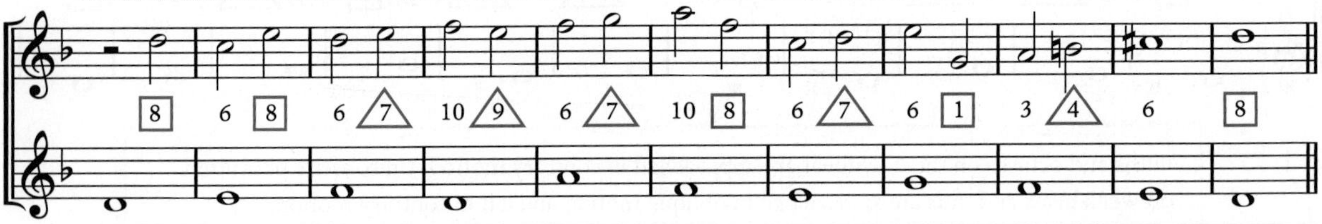

Dissonances (in triangles) are on the second half of the measure and are used only as passing or neighboring tones.

3. *Intervals between the voices*:
   - The first half of every measure must be consonant.
   - The second half may be either consonant or dissonant.
   - If it is dissonant, the dissonance must be approached and left by step.
   - Every dissonant note must thus be either a passing tone or a neighbor tone.
   - Unlike dissonant notes, consonant notes may be freely leapt to and away from.
   - Unisons may occur on the second beat, approached by leap and left by step.

4. *Approaching perfect fifths and octaves*: A fifth or octave that appears on the downbeat may not be approached by parallel or similar motion.

8.8

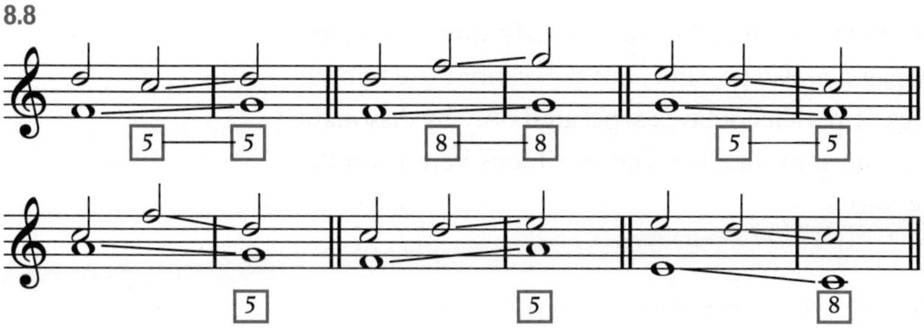

Forbidden Parallel fifths and octaves

Forbidden Similar motion to a fifth or octave

5. Avoid using the same perfect interval (fifth or octave) on two successive downbeats, even when the second one is approached in contrary motion.

8.9

Poor Fifths on successive downbeats

Poor Octaves on successive downbeats

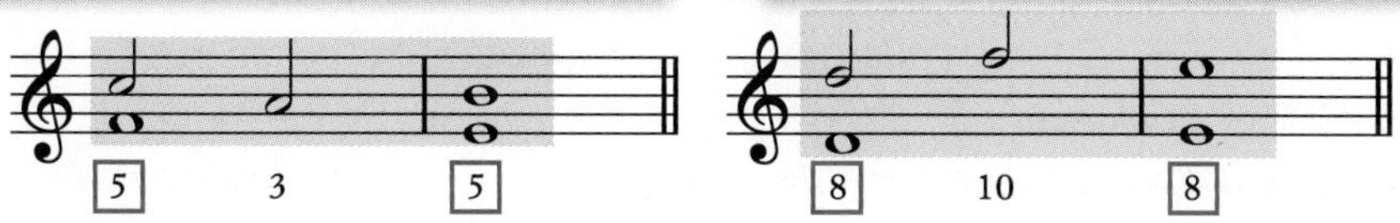

6. *Melody*:
   - As in first species, the counterpoint should have a single melodic high point (which must not be the leading tone).
   - As in first species, the counterpoint should move mostly by step, punctuated by leaps. Leaps larger than a third generally occur within the measure (from the first to the second half note), rather than across the barline, and are often followed by stepwise motion in the opposite direction from the leap.
   - As in first species, do not cross the voices (the melody has to be higher than the cantus); do not leap by diminished fifth, augmented fourth, or seventh; do not use any accidentals other than raised $\hat{7}$ or raised $\hat{6}$ and $\hat{7}$ at the very end of the counterpoint in a minor key; do not write chromatic semitones (like B♭–B♮).
   - Unlike first species, you may not repeat a note.

FOURTH SPECIES

Fourth-species counterpoint is mostly written in pairs of half notes that are tied across the barline. Dissonances may occur only on the *first* half of the measure (the second note of a tied pair) and only with a consonant preparation (the first note of a tied pair) and a resolution down by step to another consonant interval. A strong-beat dissonance like this, with a consonant preparation and a stepwise resolution down, is a **suspension**.

Suspensions are named by the intervals of the dissonant suspension and its resolution: 7-6, for example, refers to a suspended seventh resolving to a sixth. The best dissonant suspensions are 7-6 and 4-3. You may use two or more 7-6 or 4-3 suspensions in a row; in fact, chains of suspensions, pushing the melody downward, are typical of fourth species. A 9-8 suspension is also possible, but you cannot use two (or more) in a row, as that creates a series of parallel octaves separated only by dissonant ninths. (There are also consonant suspensions, like 6-5, but our focus here is on the proper treatment of dissonant suspensions.)

8.10

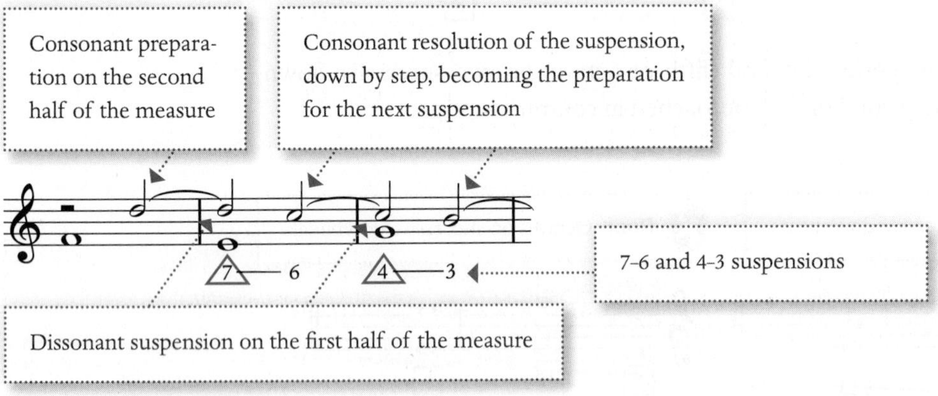

Consonant preparation on the second half of the measure
Consonant resolution of the suspension, down by step, becoming the preparation for the next suspension
7 6
4 3
7-6 and 4-3 suspensions
Dissonant suspension on the first half of the measure

8.11

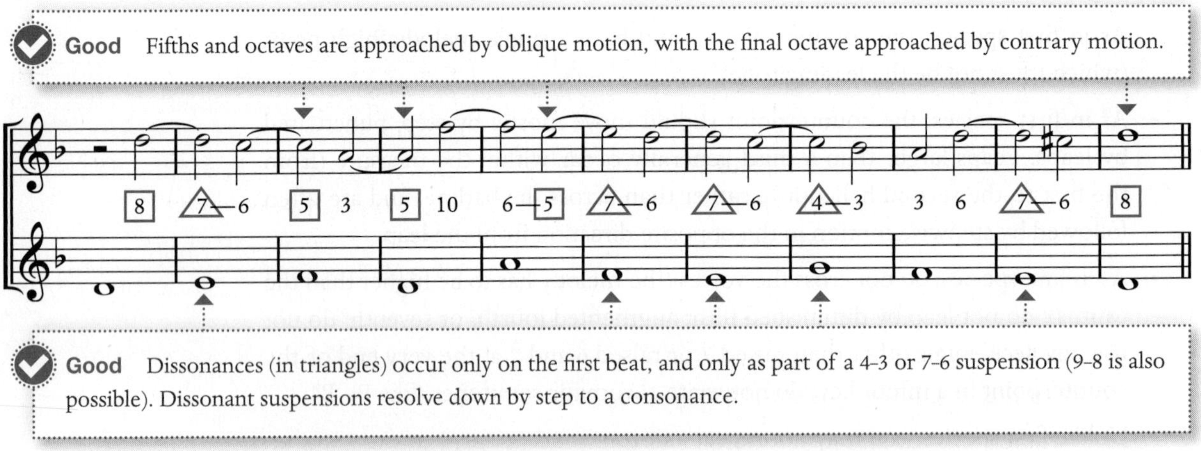

Good Fifths and octaves are approached by oblique motion, with the final octave approached by contrary motion.
8 7 6 5 3 5 10 6 5 7 6 7 6 4 3 3 6 7 6 8
Good Dissonances (in triangles) occur only on the first beat, and only as part of a 4-3 or 7-6 suspension (9-8 is also possible). Dissonant suspensions resolve down by step to a consonance.

Here are guidelines for writing fourth-species counterpoint:

1. *Rhythm*: Use only half notes, except in the first measure, which begins with a half-note rest, and the last measure, which should be a whole note. Generally, the second half note of each measure should be tied to the first half note of the next, but there may occasionally be pairs of non-tied half notes (as in second species).
2. *Beginning and ending*: The first note must be an octave or fifth above the cantus. In the second-to-last measure, a 7-6 suspension resolves to $\hat{7}$ (raised in minor), followed in the last measure by a whole note an octave above the cantus (the same sixth expanding to an octave that ends first and second species).

3. *Intervals between the voices*:
   - Dissonances may occur only on the first half of the measure and only as suspensions.
   - Consonances that occur on the first beat of the measure may be left either by step or by leap (to another consonance).
   - For untied half notes, the rules of second species apply: the second half of the measure may be a dissonant passing or neighbor tone, and the first half of the measure must be a consonance.
4. *Approaching fifths and octaves*: Because voices generally do not move at the same time, motion between them is oblique; there is no restriction on approaching a fifth or octave with oblique motion. If the first half note of a measure is not tied from the previous measure, however, fifths and octaves must be approached in contrary motion, not in similar or parallel motion (as in second species).

8.12

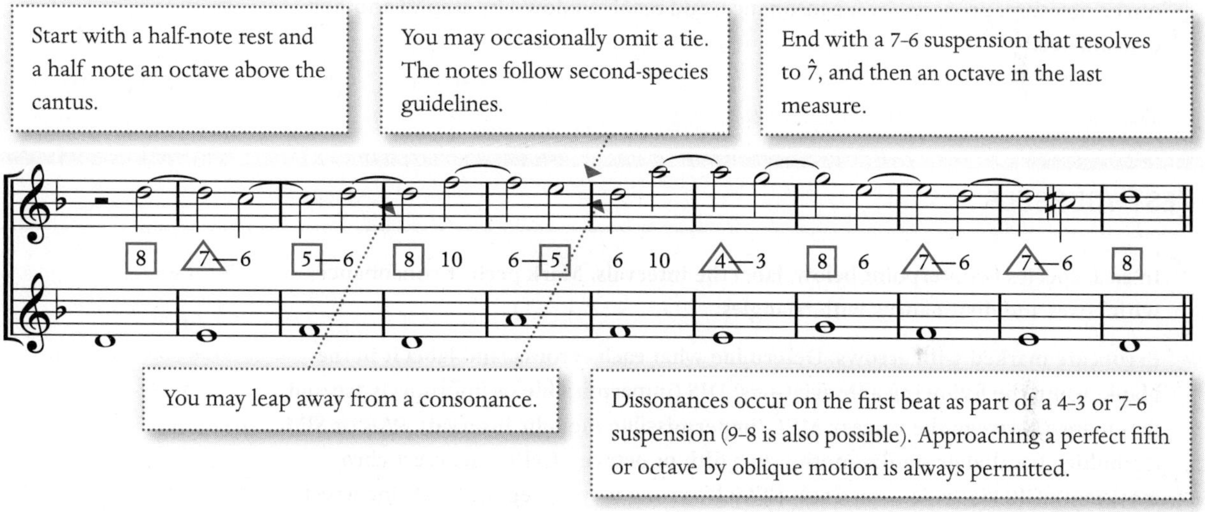
Start with a half-note rest and a half note an octave above the cantus.
You may occasionally omit a tie. The notes follow second-species guidelines.
End with a 7-6 suspension that resolves to $\hat{7}$, and then an octave in the last measure.
8
7–6
5–6
8
10
6–5
6
10
4–3
8
6
7–6
7–6
8
You may leap away from a consonance.
Dissonances occur on the first beat as part of a 4-3 or 7-6 suspension (9-8 is also possible). Approaching a perfect fifth or octave by oblique motion is always permitted.

5. *Melody*:
   - As with first and second species, the counterpoint should have a single melodic climax or high point (which should not be the leading tone).
   - The counterpoint should move mostly by step, punctuated by leaps. Because suspensions must resolve down by step, there is a tendency for fourth-species counterpoint to move continually downward. Look for opportunities to step or leap up, either by occasionally not tying the half notes across the barline or by placing a consonance on the first beat of the measure (you are always free to leap away from a consonance).
   - As in first species, do not cross the voices; do not leap by diminished fifth, augmented fourth, or seventh; do not use any accidentals other than raised $\hat{7}$ or raised $\hat{6}$ and $\hat{7}$ at the very end of the counterpoint in a minor key; do not write chromatic semitones (like B♭–B♮).

review and interact

POINTS FOR REVIEW

- **Species counterpoint is a traditional way of learning about tonal voice leading, especially the proper treatment of dissonance and approaches to perfect fifths and octaves.**
- **First-species counterpoint involves writing a melody in whole notes against the cantus firmus, also in whole notes. Only consonant intervals are permitted between the parts. Parallel and similar fifths and octaves are prohibited.**
- **Second-species counterpoint involves writing a melody in half notes against the cantus firmus in whole notes. Dissonant passing and neighbor tones are permitted on the second half of the measure.**
- **Fourth-species counterpoint involves writing a melody consisting mostly of pairs of half notes tied across the measure. Dissonant suspensions occur on the first half of the measure, prepared by a consonance, and resolved down by step to another consonance.**

TEST YOURSELF

- **In each species counterpoint below, label the intervals. Mark perfect consonances with boxes and dissonances with triangles.**
- **Errors are marked with arrows. Determine what each error is, and label it in the blank, using the following abbreviations: DIS (impermissible or improperly treated dissonance between the voices); MEL (impermissible melodic interval); PAR or SIM (forbidden parallel or similar motion to a fifth or octave); CHR (incorrect chromaticism); CROSS (voice crossing); START (wrong way to begin); CAD (incorrect cadence).**

1. First species

2. Second species

3. Fourth species

Know It? Show It!

Focus by working through the tutorials on:

- First-species counterpoint
- Passing tones and neighbor tones in second-species counterpoint
- Writing suspensions in fourth-species counterpoint

Learn with inQuizitive.

Apply what you've learned to complete the assignments:

- First Species
- Second Species
- Fourth Species

part three

Diatonic Harmony

chapter 9 I and V

The relationship between the I and V triads is central to tonal harmony, with the stability of I contrasted with the tension of V.

THE TONIC AND DOMINANT TRIADS

The I and V triads in root position are among the most important chords of tonal harmony. The I chord has a **T**onic function and establishes tonal repose. The V chord has a **D**ominant function. It creates a sense of tension, released only when V progresses to I. I and V triads may appear anywhere within a phrase, especially as part of a cadence.

9.1 Theme by Salieri, arr. Beethoven, WoO 73

Mm. 3–4 echo 1–2, now moving from V to I.

Simplified model in four-part harmony

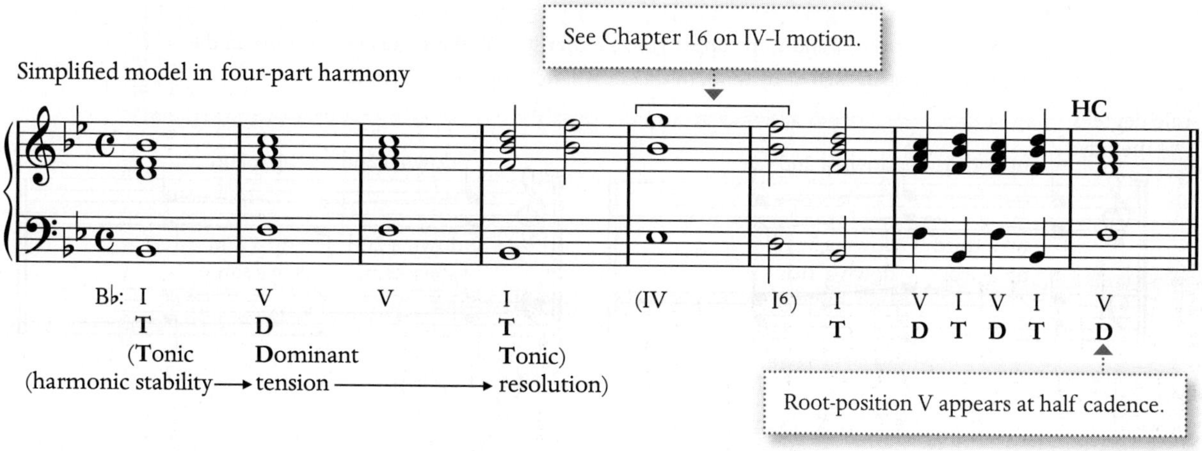

9.2 Morley, "Nancie"

Simplified model in four-part harmony

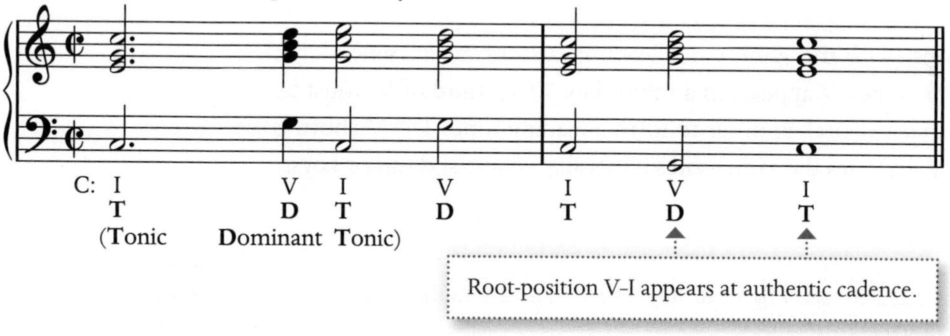

VOICE-LEADING IN FOUR-PART HARMONY

In four-part harmony, it is generally best to double the root of a root-position I or V chord. When progressing between I and V, the upper parts (soprano, alto, and tenor) usually either stay on the same note or move to the nearest chord tone.

9.3

In moving between I and V, the upper voices either stay on the same note or move in the same direction, by step or by third, to the nearest note of the next chord.

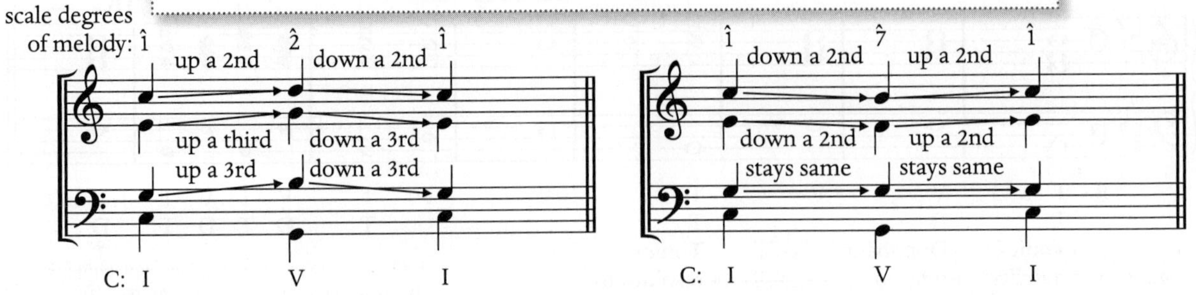

9.4 Beethoven, Piano Concerto in E♭, I

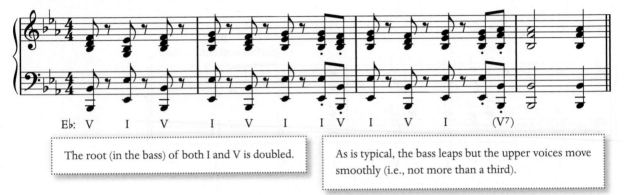

The root (in the bass) of both I and V is doubled.

As is typical, the bass leaps but the upper voices move smoothly (i.e., not more than a third).

Similar progressions—with the same voice leading—also occur in minor keys, with a minor tonic chord. When V appears in a minor key, $\hat{7}$ (the third of V) must be raised a half step with an accidental, in order to form a leading tone. The V chord is thus always a major triad and uses the same notes in parallel major and minor keys.

9.5

In minor keys, use an accidental to raise $\hat{7}$ by a half step. The V chord is thus the same as it would be in the parallel major.

In a minor key, the tonic triad (i) is minor and the dominant triad (V) is major.

THE LEADING TONE WITHIN THE V CHORD

The V chord includes the leading tone ($\hat{7}$). As noted in Chapter 4, the leading tone is a tendency tone that strives upward. As a result, the leading tone may not be doubled, and if it appears in an outer voice, it must resolve *up* by step to the tonic when V progresses to I.

9.6 J. S. Bach, Chorale 58

9.7

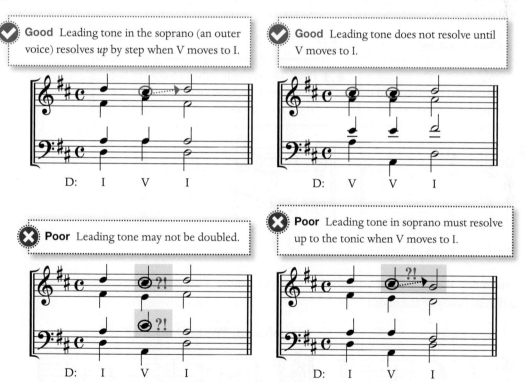

Good Leading tone in the soprano (an outer voice) resolves *up* by step when V moves to I.

Good Leading tone does not resolve until V moves to I.

Poor Leading tone may not be doubled.

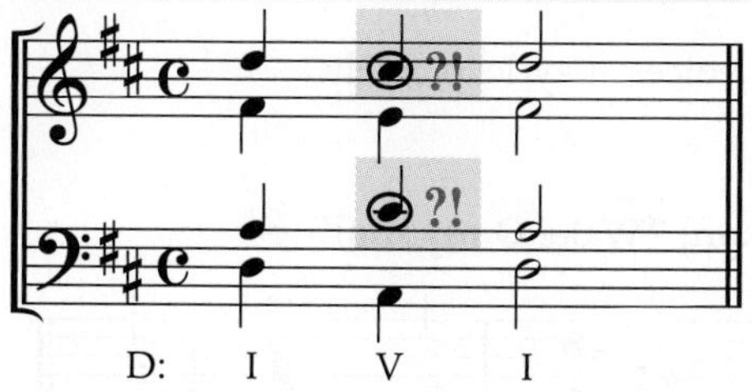

Poor Leading tone in soprano must resolve up to the tonic when V moves to I.

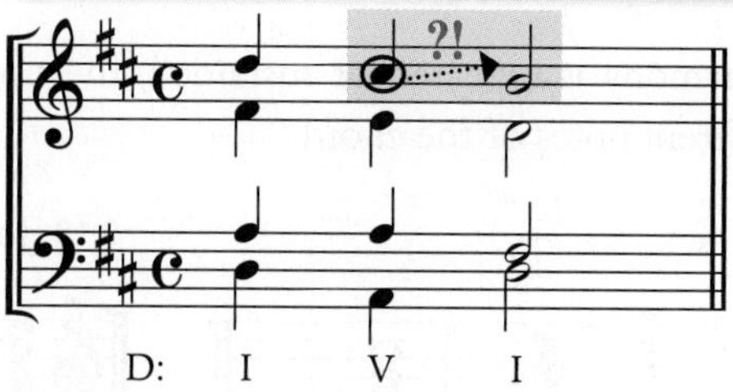

However, when it appears in an inner voice (the tenor or alto)—where it is less prominent—the leading tone does not need to resolve up by step.

9.8

9.9 J. S. Bach, Chorale 250 ➔

Good When it appears in an inner voice, the leading tone does not necessarily resolve up by step.

LEAPS IN UPPER VOICES

Although the upper voices usually move smoothly when one chord moves to another, they may *occasionally* leap. If you use leaps in the upper voices to progress between I and V, be careful to avoid voice-leading errors, such as parallel octaves and fifths.

9.10 J. S. Bach, Chorale 64 ➔

Good Bach's tenor part leaps between I and V, with no parallel fifths or octaves.

9.11

Poor This example includes too many leaps in the upper voices when I moves to V. The leaps create parallel octaves and fifths.

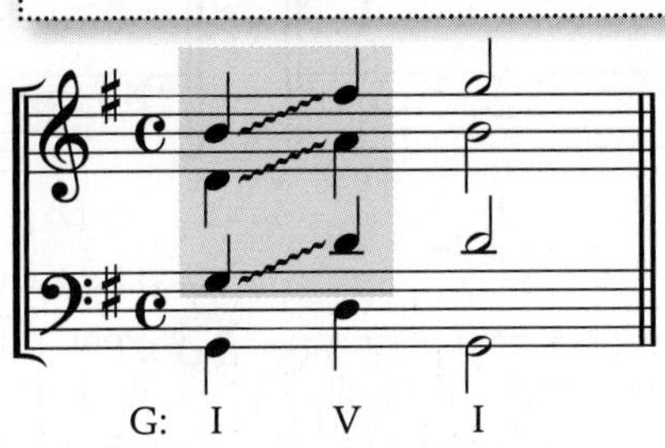

Also, when a harmony is repeated or sustained, the upper voices may leap freely between the different notes of the chord.

9.12

9.13 Johnson, "Wake O my soul" ➔

Leaps of a fourth or more in upper voices are common when a chord is sustained or repeats.

MELODIC PATTERNS

Certain melodic patterns may be harmonized with a I–V–I progression. Memorizing some of the more common of these patterns will be helpful in harmonizing melodies.

9.14

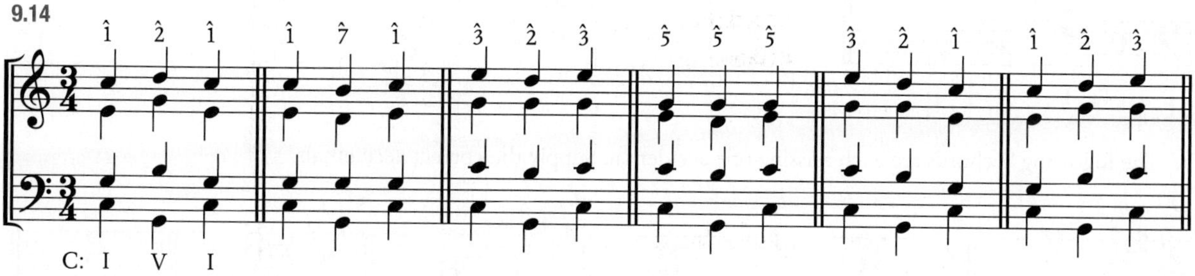

review and interact

POINTS FOR REVIEW

- **The I triad establishes harmonic stability, and the V triad creates harmonic tension. V moving to I creates a sense of resolution.**
- **In four-part harmony, the root (bass) of root-position I and V triads typically is doubled.**
- **In I–V and V–I progressions, the upper voices usually move smoothly, with melodic intervals of a third or smaller.**
- **Do not double the leading tone. When the leading tone is in the soprano, it must resolve up by step when V progresses to I.**
- **In minor keys, $\hat{7}$ must be raised by a half step with an accidental in order to form a leading tone.**
- **Upper voices may leap freely when a chord repeats.**

TEST YOURSELF

1. Spell the I and V chords in (a) E♭ major, (b) E major, and (c) E minor.
2. Compare the voice leading in each of the following pairs. Is the voice leading better in (a) or (b)? In (c) or (d)?

3. In the excerpt below, complete the chords by filling in the missing notes.

4. The following V chords are each missing one accidental. Supply the correct accidentals.

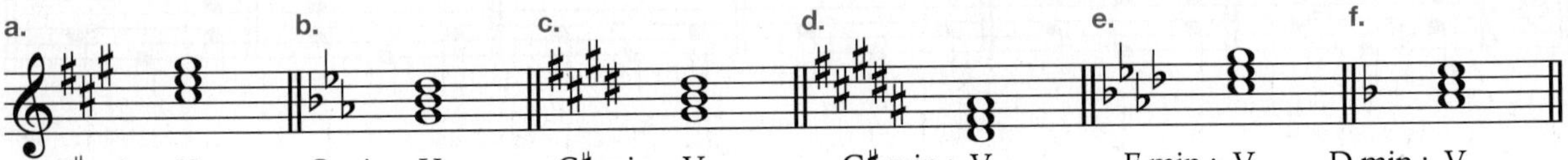

5. Find the errors in the progressions below.

Know It? Show It!

Focus by working through the tutorials on:

- Writing I and V triads
- Harmonizing with I and V

Learn with inQuizitive.

Apply what you've learned to complete the assignments:

- Spelling I and V
- Realizing Roman Numerals
- Realizing Figured Bass
- Harmonizing Melodies
- Composition
- Analysis

chapter

10 The Dominant Seventh Chord: V7

V7 is a Dominant harmony whose instability is intensified by a dissonant chordal seventh.

- V7 and Tendency Tones
- Omitting the Fifth of V7 or I in Four-Part Harmony
- V to V7 (V8–7)
- V7 at Cadences
- Melodic Patterns

V7 AND TENDENCY TONES

The root-position V7 (the **dominant seventh chord**) functions much like V (the dominant triad), except that V7 is less stable and thus resolves more emphatically to I.

10.1 Haydn, Divertimento, Hob. XVI:1, III

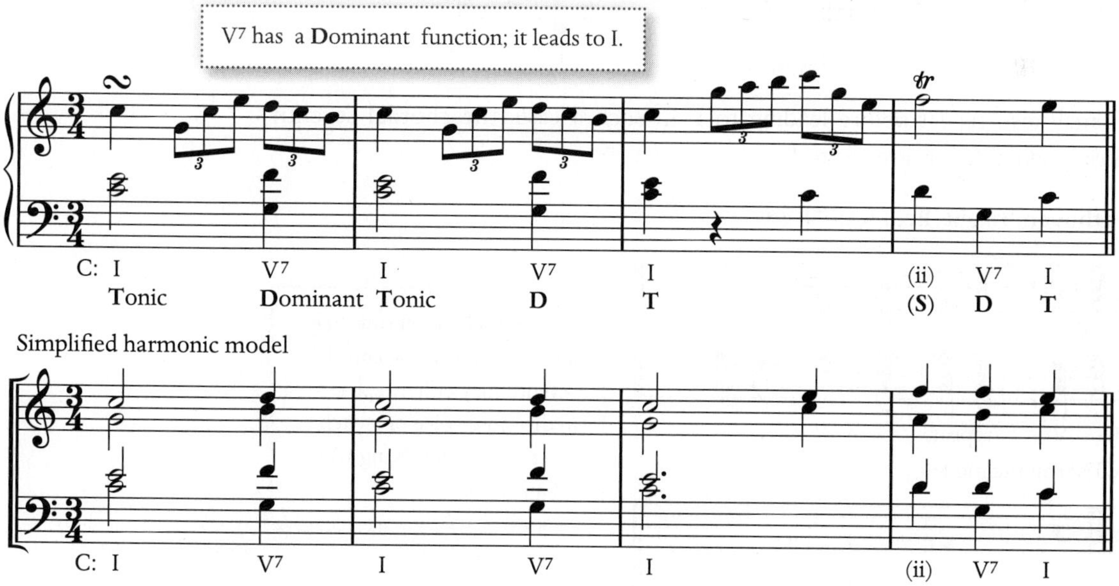

V7 contains two tendency tones that pull in opposite directions: the chordal seventh and the leading tone. Do not confuse these two. The chordal seventh (the seventh of the *chord*) must resolve *down* by step when V7 moves to I (even if it appears in an inner voice). The leading tone (the seventh degree of the *scale*) tends to resolve *up* by step (though it need not do so if it appears in an inner voice). These two tendency tones are separated by a dissonant diminished fifth or augmented fourth.

10.2

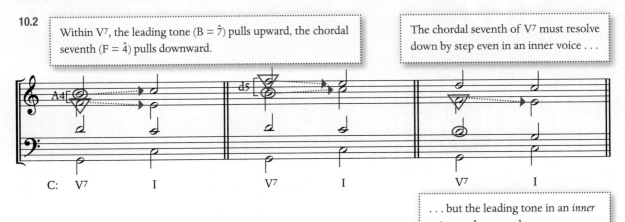

Within V7, the leading tone (B = $\hat{7}$) pulls upward, the chordal seventh (F = $\hat{4}$) pulls downward.

The chordal seventh of V7 must resolve down by step even in an inner voice . . .

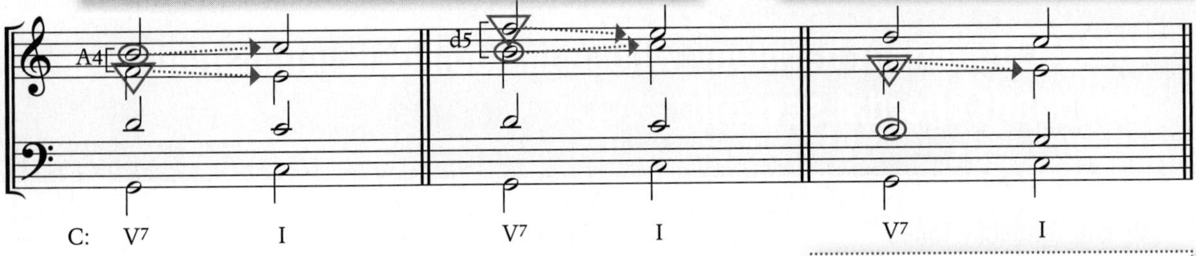

. . . but the leading tone in an *inner voice* need not resolve up.

10.3 Mozart, Sonata for Violin and Piano in E Minor, K. 304, I

The seventh of V7 (A) must resolve down by step; the leading tone (D♯) must resolve up by step when it occurs in an outer voice.

V7 may also repeat before leading to I. In such a case, the chordal seventh resolves only when V7 progresses to I.

10.4 Beethoven, Bagatelle, Hess 74

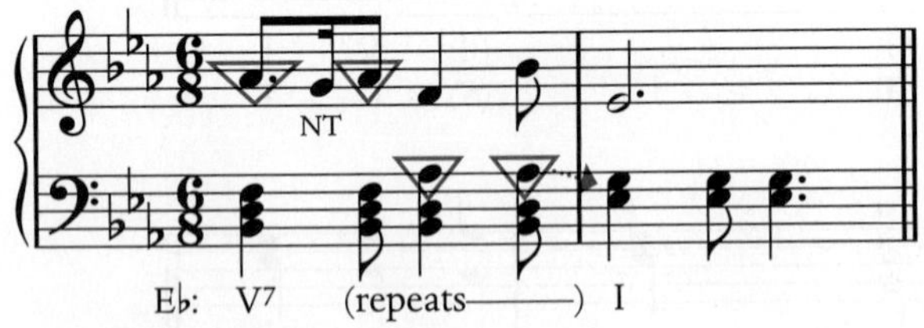

Simplified harmonic model

Two or more V7 chords may appear in a row; the chordal seventh may either repeat in the same voice or switch voices before resolving when V7 moves to I.

OMITTING THE FIFTH OF V7 OR I IN FOUR-PART HARMONY

In four-part harmony, you may omit the fifth of the chord of either V7 or I. Indeed, to avoid voice-leading errors, the fifth must be omitted from one of the chords of a V7–I progression when the leading tone appears in the top voice of V7.

10.5

Good When $\hat{7}$ appears in the top voice, the fifth must be omitted from one of the chords in a V7–I progression.

Poor The fifths are not omitted in any of the chords in these V7–I progressions, creating voice-leading problems.

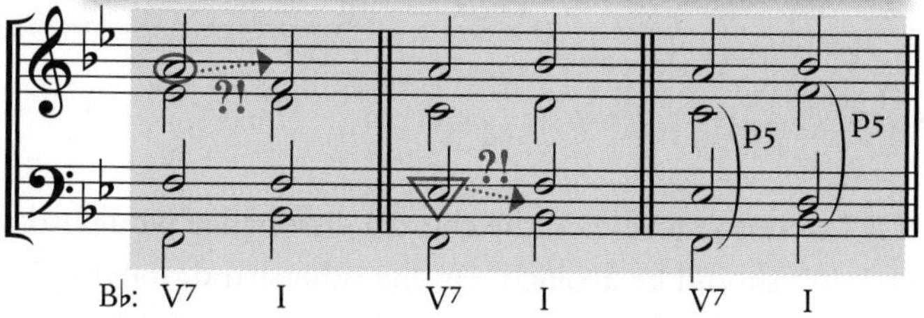

The fifth of I (F) is omitted and the root (B♭) is tripled.

The fifth of the V7 chord (C) is omitted and the root (F) is doubled.

When the fifth is omitted from V7, you should double the root of the chord (you may *not* double the leading tone or chordal seventh). When the fifth is omitted from I, you should *triple* the root of the chord.

10.6 Brahms, "Marias Wallfahrt" (Mary's Pilgrimage) ➔

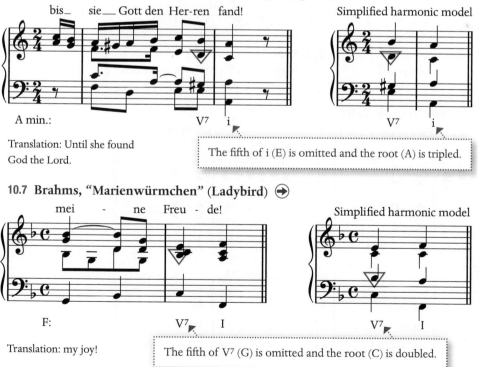

Simplified harmonic model

Translation: Until she found God the Lord.

The fifth of i (E) is omitted and the root (A) is tripled.

10.7 Brahms, "Marienwürmchen" (Ladybird) ➔

Simplified harmonic model

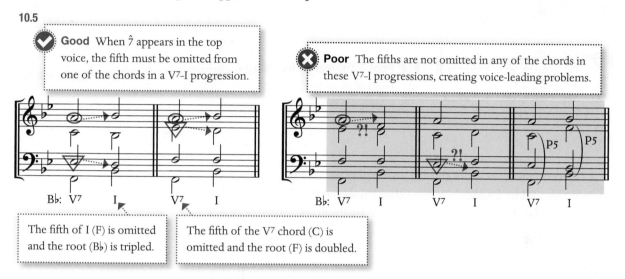

Translation: my joy!

The fifth of V7 (G) is omitted and the root (C) is doubled.

Although you may omit the fifth of a chord, you should not omit the third, since this creates a hollow-sounding sonority.

10.8

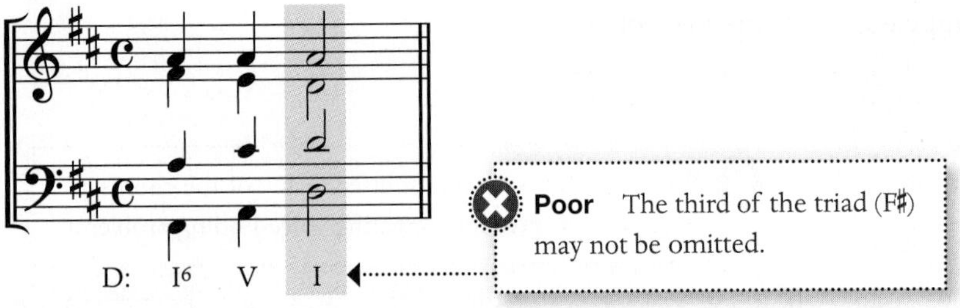

V TO V7 (V8-7)

If V^7 were to move to V, the chordal dissonance would not resolve; thus a V^7–V progression should be avoided. On the other hand, moving from V to V^7 increases the urgency of the dominant's need to resolve to the tonic. For this reason, the V–V^7 progression is extremely common.

10.9

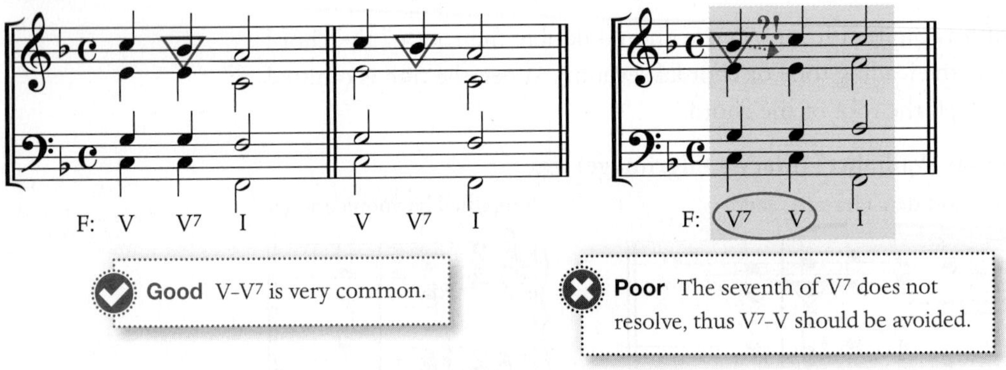

10.10 Beethoven, Piano Sonata in C, op. 2, no. 3, I

Simplified harmonic model

The succession V–V^7 is usually labeled simply as a V$^{8-7}$. V$^{8-7}$–I almost always results from a V–I progression decorated by an embellishing tone in an upper voice.

10.11 J. S. Bach, Chorale 90

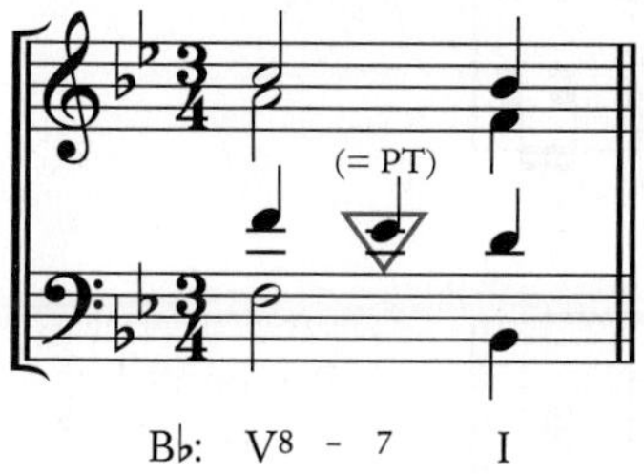

10.12 J. S. Bach, Chorale 176

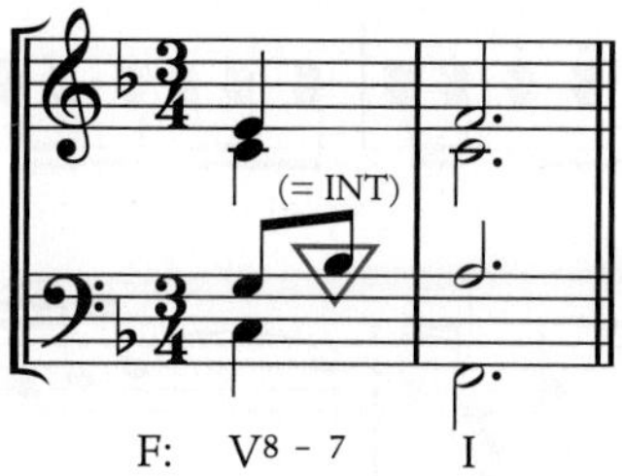

In each of these progressions, V$^{8-7}$–I results when the tenor voice in a V–I progression is decorated by an embellishing tone. (V$^{8-7}$ means the same thing as V–V^7.)

In figured bass, the figures $^{8-7}$ underneath a single bass note designate a root-position triad followed by a root-position seventh chord. An accidental sign below the figures $^{8-7}$ applies to the third above the bass.

10.13

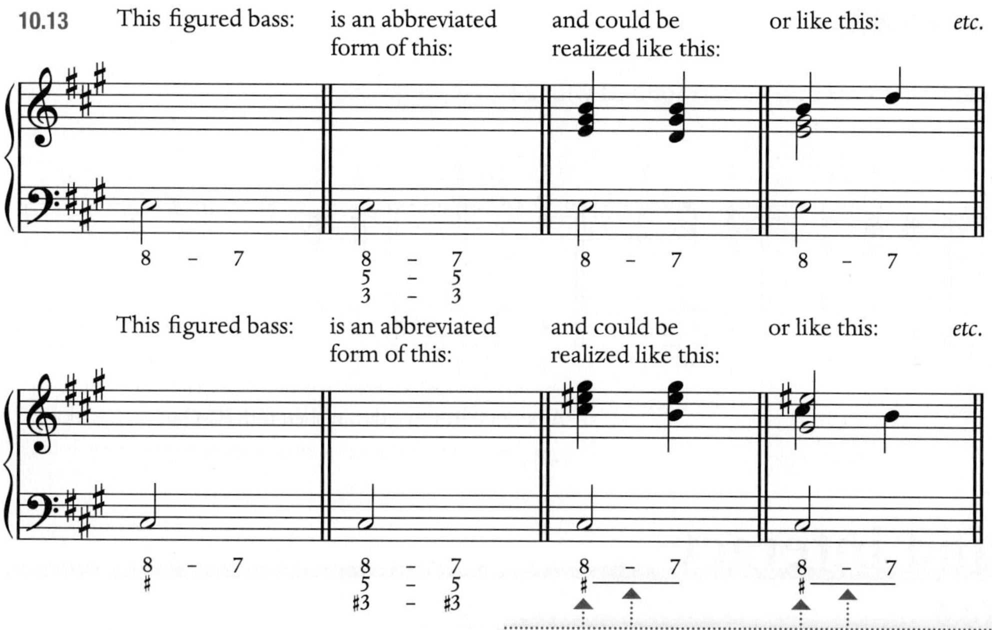

This ♯ sign indicates that the third above the bass (E) is to be sharped. The dash indicates that the E♯ is sustained as the seventh enters.

V^7 AT CADENCES

Much like V–I, either V^7–I or V$^{8-7}$–I may appear at a perfect authentic cadence (PAC) or an imperfect authentic cadence (IAC). The instability of V^7 makes it less well suited to serve as a resting point at a *half cadence* (HC), however. Accordingly, in basic four-part harmony a half cadence should arrive on V, *not* on V^7.

10.14 Rossini, *William Tell* Overture

HC on V (*not* V^7)

PAC on V^7–I

MELODIC PATTERNS

Certain standard melodic patterns may be harmonized with a I–V^7–I progression.

10.15

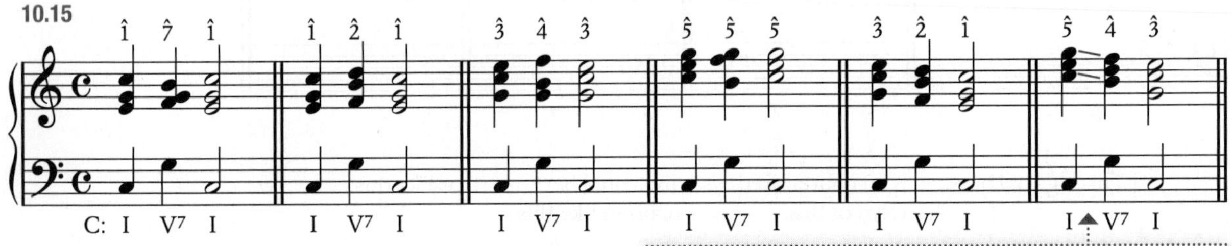

A perfect fifth to a diminished fifth (C–G to B–F) is okay.

review and interact

POINTS FOR REVIEW

- **V^7 functions like V—both chords function as Dominants and lead to I.**
- **The chordal dissonance within V^7 must resolve down by step when V^7 moves to I, even if the seventh appears in an inner voice.**
- **The leading tone tends to resolve up by step, but need not do so if it appears in an inner voice.**
- **When V^7 resolves to I, you may omit the fifth and double the root of V^7, or you may omit the fifth and triple the root of I. Do not omit the third of a chord.**
- **V may not follow V^7, but V^7 may follow V. V–V^7 is labeled V^{8-7}.**
- **V^7 often comes before I in an authentic cadence (AC), but avoid V^7 at a half cadence (HC).**

TEST YOURSELF

1. Spell V7 **a.** in the key of G; **b.** in E; **c.** in E♭; **d.** in D♭.

2. Below are various V7 chords in minor keys. What is the key of each, and what is the missing accidental?

3. In the excerpts below, some chords are missing one or two notes. What are the missing notes? Complete excerpts (a) and (b) in different ways, and also complete (c) and (d) in different ways.

4. Identify the chords below with Roman numerals, in two different ways.

5. Some of the following I–V7–I progressions contain voice-leading errors. Identify the key of each. Then identify any errors (such as faulty parallel fifths or octaves or incorrectly omitted tones).

6. Below are a series of pairs of V^{8-7}–I progressions notated in different way. Which of each pair is notated incorrectly? What is incorrect about it?

a. (i) (ii) b. (i) (ii) c. (i) (ii)

Know It? Show It!

Focus by working through the tutorials on:

- Resolving V^7 to I

Learn with inQuizitive.

Apply what you've learned to complete the assignments:

- Spelling Chords
- Realizing Roman Numerals
- Realizing Figured Bass
- Harmonizing Melodies
- Composition
- Analysis

chapter

11 I^6 and V^6

I^6 and V^6—first-inversion tonic and dominant triads—can appear anywhere except at the end of a phrase.

I^6

HARMONIC PROGRESSION

The I^6 chord—a first-inversion tonic triad—functions like I in root position. It is somewhat less stable, however, because its bass is $\hat{3}$ rather than $\hat{1}$. I^6 appears toward the beginning or middle of a phrase, rather than at its end; it allows for an active bass line by extending, alternating with, or substituting for I (tonic triad in root position).

11.1

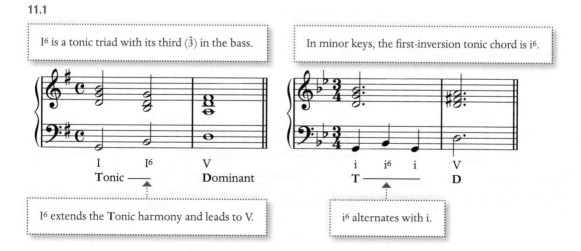

I^6 is a tonic triad with its third ($\hat{3}$) in the bass.

In minor keys, the first-inversion tonic chord is i^6.

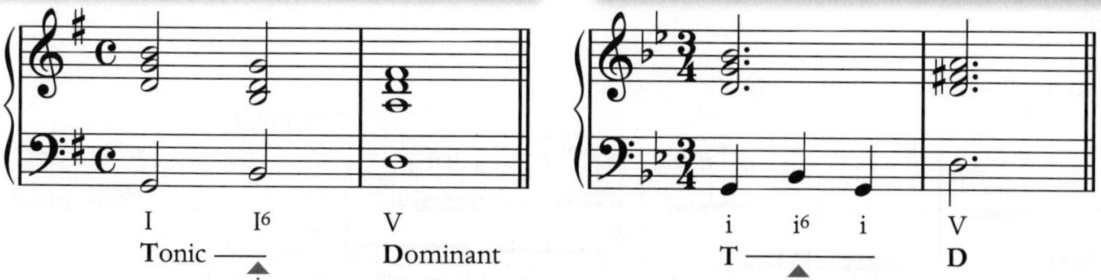

I^6 extends the Tonic harmony and leads to V.

i^6 alternates with i.

11.2 Haydn, Symphony no. 45 ("Farewell"), IV

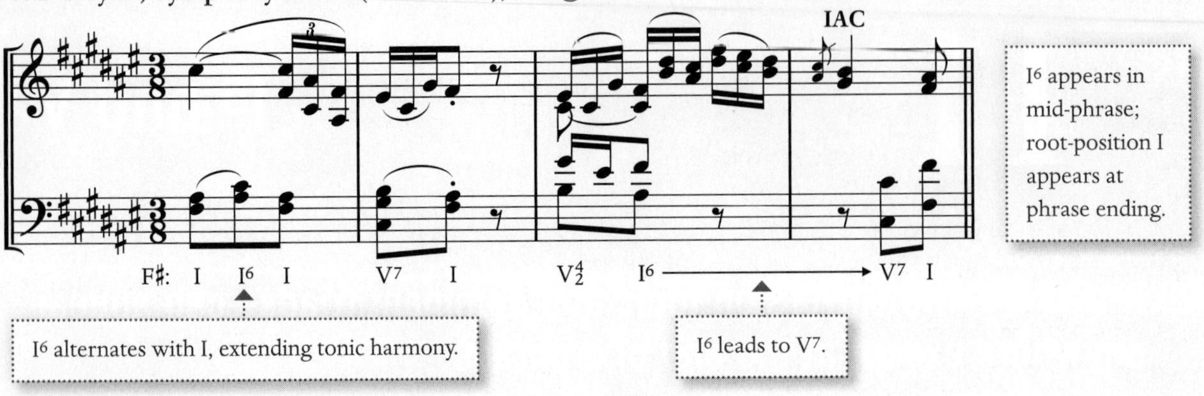
IAC
F♯: I I6 I V7 I V4/2 I6 V7 I
I6 appears in mid-phrase; root-position I appears at phrase ending.
I6 alternates with I, extending tonic harmony.
I6 leads to V7.

Like I, I6 may be followed by any harmony. In particular, I6 frequently leads to V (in root position) in a half or an authentic cadence. However, I—*not* I6—must serve as the final harmony of an authentic cadence.

11.3 Beethoven, Symphony no. 2, II

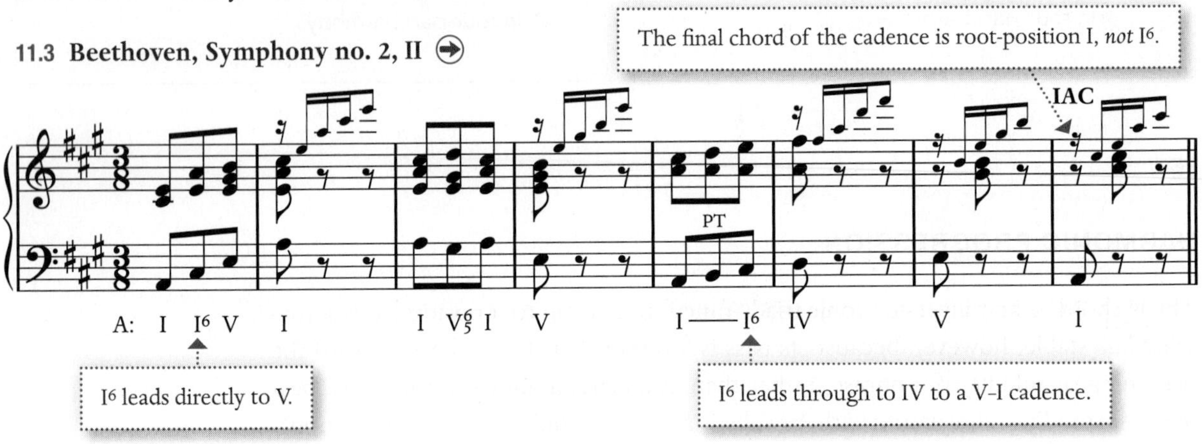
The final chord of the cadence is root-position I, *not* I6.
IAC
PT
A: I I6 V I I V6/5 I V I—I6 IV V I
I6 leads directly to V.
I6 leads through to IV to a V–I cadence.

Sometimes a perfect authentic cadence (PAC) is surprisingly averted when the expected appearance of I toward the end of a phrase is replaced with I6. This creates what is known as an **evaded cadence**, which often also involves a sudden shift or break in the melody.

11.4 Mozart, Sonata in C Major, K. 309, I

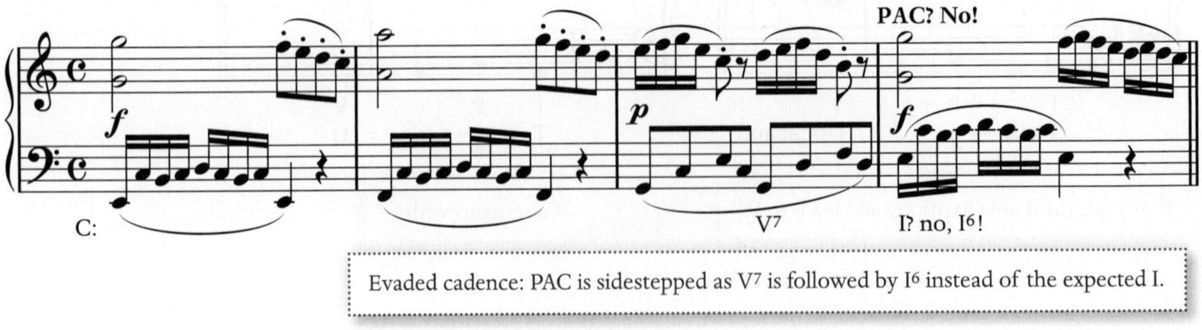
PAC? No!
f
p
f
C: V7 I? no, I6!
Evaded cadence: PAC is sidestepped as V7 is followed by I6 instead of the expected I.

I^6 IN FOUR-PART HARMONY

In four-part harmony, you may double any note of I^6: root, third, or fifth. When moving between I and I^6 the upper voices may remain on the same notes or may leap to other notes of the tonic harmony. I and I^6 may also participate in a **voice exchange**, when $\hat{1}$ and $\hat{3}$ are traded between two voices.

11.5 J. S. Bach, Chorale 192

The upper voice moves in contrary motion with the bass; the root of I^6 is doubled.

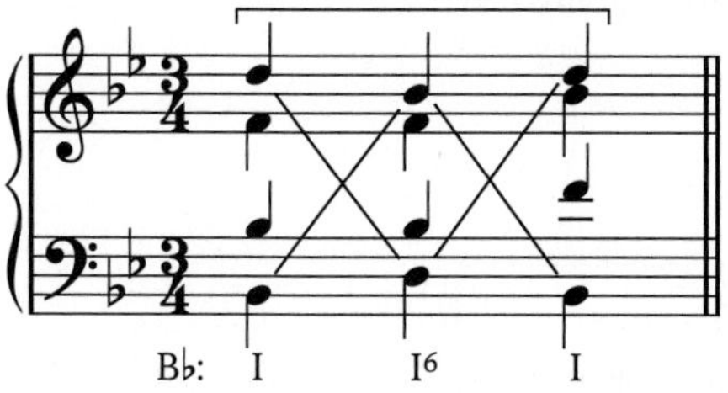

Diagonal lines trace two voice exchanges as B♭ ($\hat{1}$) and D ($\hat{3}$) swap places.

11.6 J. S. Bach, Chorale 108

The upper voice leaps; the fifth of I^6 is doubled.

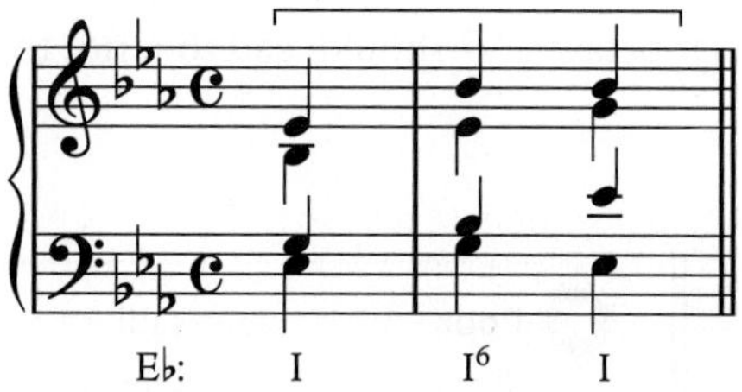

I may move to I^6, and vice versa.

In progressing between I^6 and V, the upper voices tend to stay on the same notes or move smoothly up or down, just as they do in moving between I and V.

11.7 J. S. Bach, Chorale 195

The upper voices stay the same between I and I^6; they move smoothly between I^6 and V. The third of I^6 is doubled.

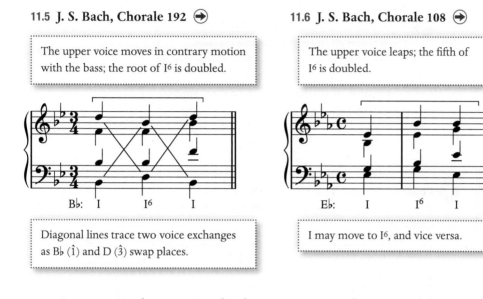

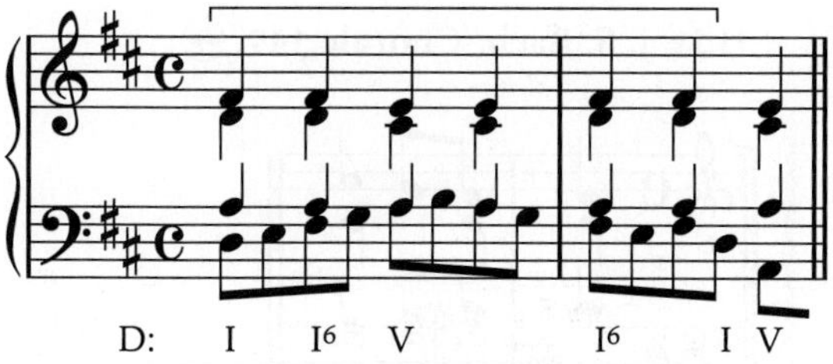

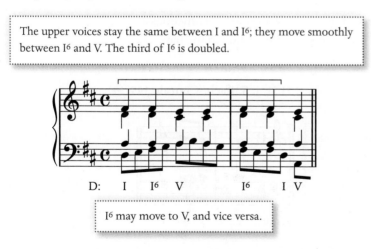

I^6 may move to V, and vice versa.

When using I^6 in four-part harmony, be careful to avoid **parallel octaves**, which are far more likely to arise than when dealing with root-position I.

11.8

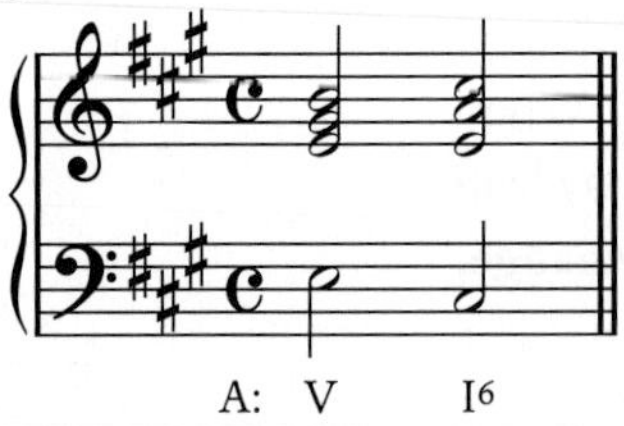

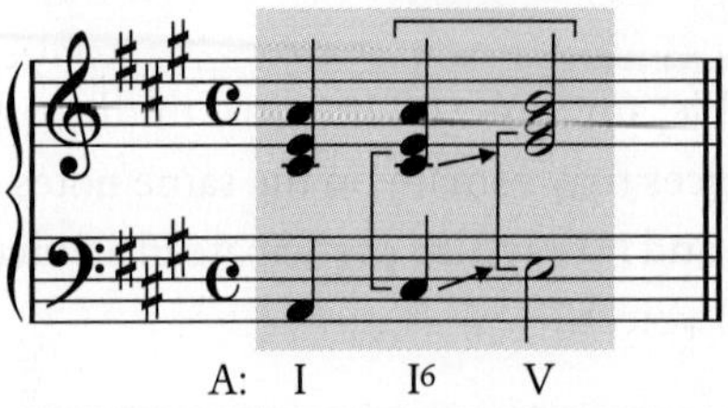

Poor Faulty parallel octaves: C♯–E

Good V to I6 with no parallel octaves

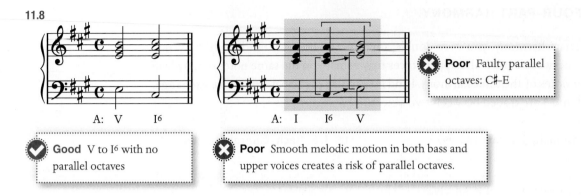

Poor Smooth melodic motion in both bass and upper voices creates a risk of parallel octaves.

I6 may also lead to V7. A V7–I6 progression is problematic, however, since it often creates faulty similar octaves. V7 should lead to I, not to I6.

11.9

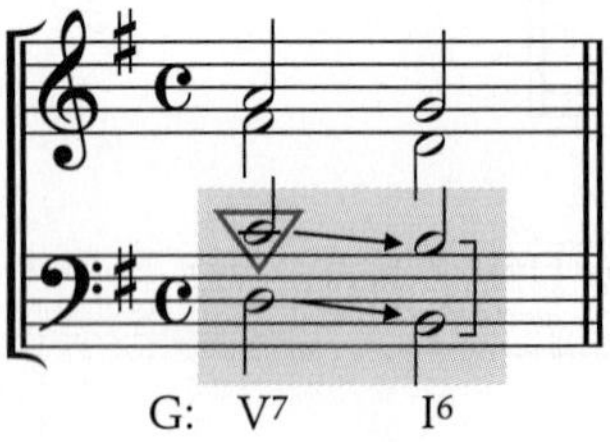

Poor V7–I6 creates faulty similar octaves, with a dissonance (D–C) leading in similar motion to an octave (B–B).

V6

HARMONIC PROGRESSION

V6 is a dominant triad in first inversion; the leading tone is in the bass. V6 functions as a **D**ominant (like V). In moving to I, there is usually stepwise motion in the bass and smooth motion in the upper voices.

11.10 J. S. Bach, Chorale 148

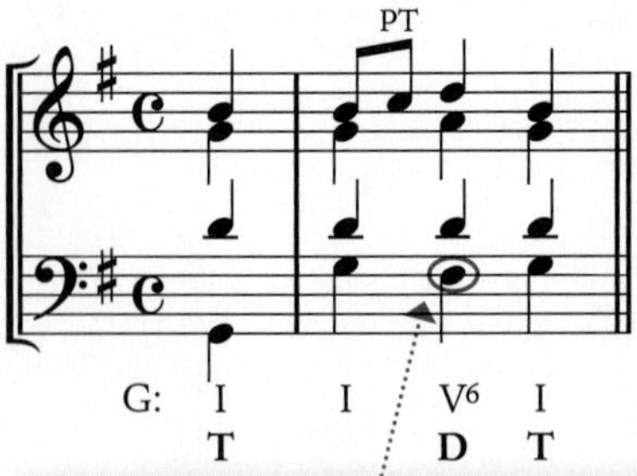

V6 leads to I with smooth melodic motion in bass and upper voices.

V6 = dominant triad in first inversion, with the leading tone in the bass.

11.11 J. S. Bach, Chorale 145

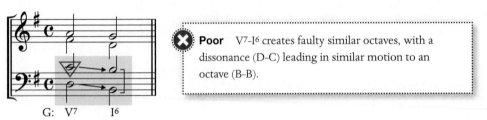

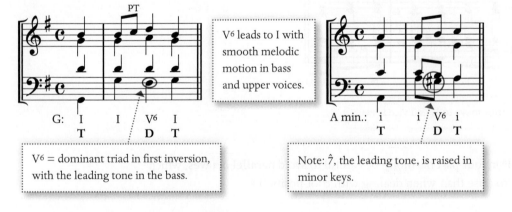

Note: $\hat{7}$, the leading tone, is raised in minor keys.

V^6 also frequently alternates with other V chords; it is particularly common for V^6 to be followed by V or V^7, or for V to be followed by V^6. However, V^6 should not follow V^7, since the chordal dissonance within V^7 would not resolve properly.

11.12

E♭: V^6 V I | V V^6 I | V^6 V^7 I
D T | D T | D T

Good V^6–V, V–V^6, and V^6–V^7 are common progressions.

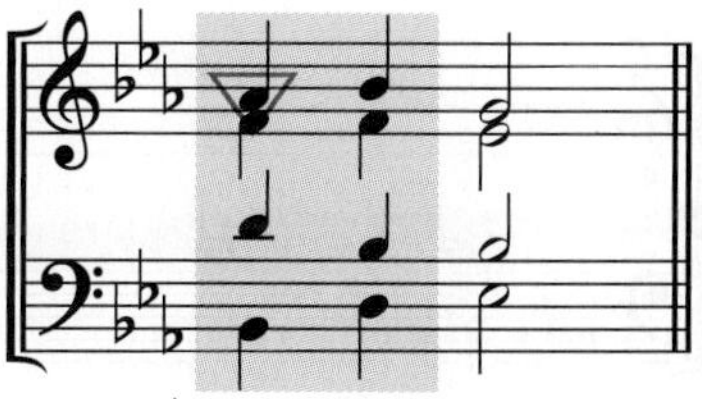

E♭: V^7 V^6 I

Poor Since the chordal dissonance does not resolve, V^7 should not move to V^6.

11.13 Praetorius, Courante

C: I [V V^6] I [V V^6] I

V can move to V^6, and V^6 can move to V or V^7.

11.14 Handel, Air

E: I [V^6 V] I V^6

V can move to V^6, and V^6 can move to V or V^7.

11.15 Vivaldi, Violin Concerto, op. 7, no. 2, RV 299, II

E min.: i [V^6 V^7] i

Simplified harmonic model

E min.: i [V^6 V^7] i

V^6 moves to V^7 (but not vice versa).

Since a leading tone in an outer voice should resolve to the tonic, V^6 does not typically progress to I^6. On the other hand, a I^6–V^6 progression is common, providing that the bass leaps down.

11.16

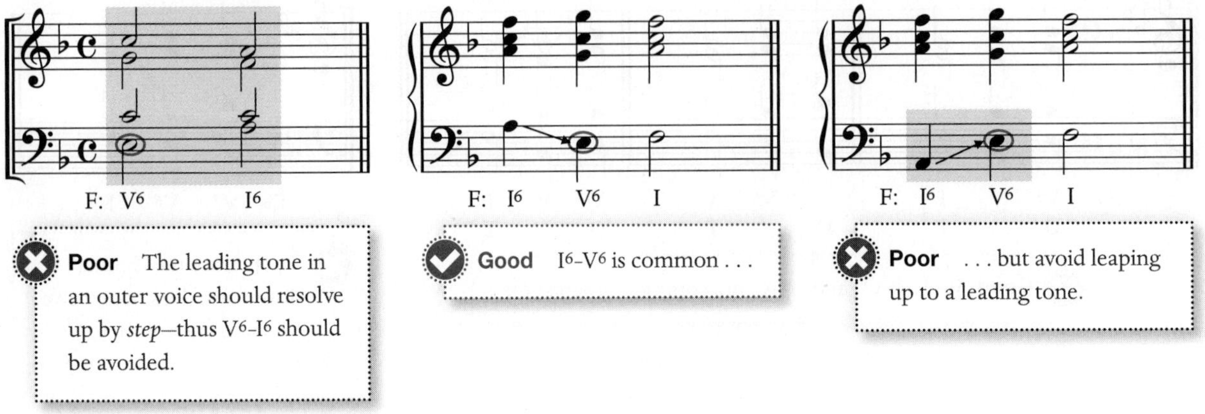

F: V6 I6
Poor The leading tone in an outer voice should resolve up by *step*—thus V6–I6 should be avoided.
F: I6 V6 I
Good I6–V6 is common . . .
F: I6 V6 I
Poor . . . but avoid leaping up to a leading tone.

11.17 F. Couperin, *Les Brinborions*

HC
A: I V6 V7 I V4/3 I6 V6 I V

Simplified harmonic model

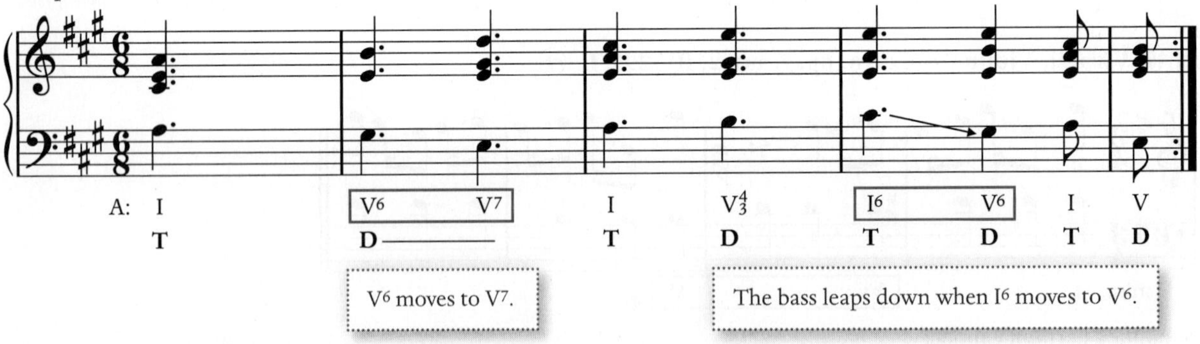

A: I V6 V7 I V4/3 I6 V6 I V
T D T D T D T D
V6 moves to V7.
The bass leaps down when I6 moves to V6.

Like I^6, V^6 typically appears at the beginning or middle of a phrase. V^6 should not be the final chord of a half cadence (HC) or the dominant chord in a perfect authentic cadence (PAC). At a cadence, the dominant chord must be in root position. Furthermore, V^6 usually does not immediately precede the root-position dominant of a PAC or HC.

11.18 Handel, Sonata in E for Violin, III

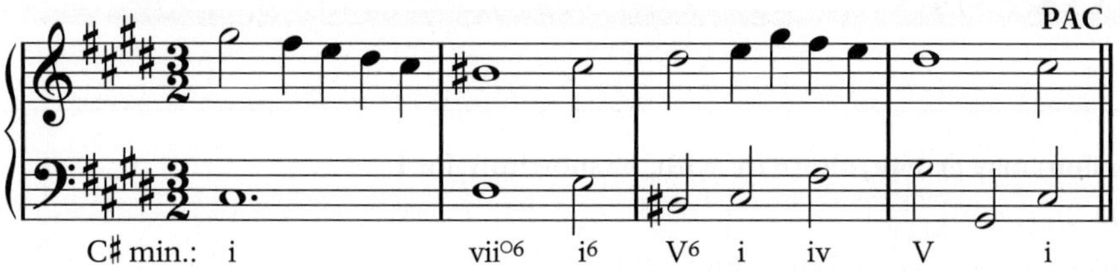

At a cadence, it is normal for V to be in root position, *not* in inversion or immediately preceded by V in inversion.

11.19 J. S. Bach, Chorale "Herr, nicht schicke deine Rache"

The tonic chord at the cadence is in root position, *not* in first inversion; i6 and V6 chords appear in the middle of the phrase.

V6 IN FOUR-PART HARMONY

In four-part harmony, you may double any note of V6 *except* the bass—the third of the chord, which is the leading tone within the key. When moving between I and V6, the upper voices usually stay on the same notes or move smoothly by step or third.

11.20

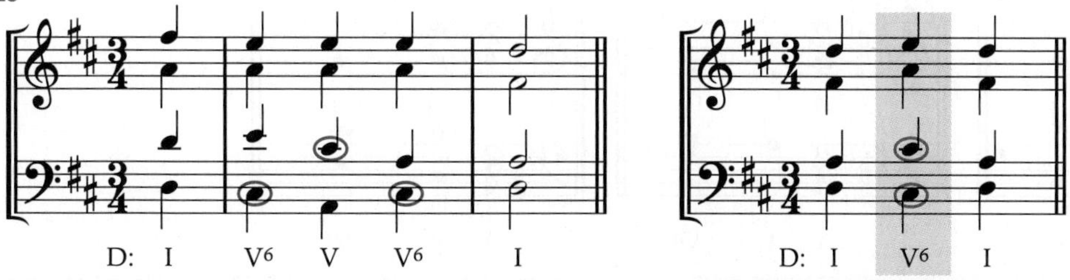

Good Double either the root or the fifth of V6—*not* the third of the chord, which is the leading tone.

Poor Do not double the bass of V6 (= leading tone).

Various standard melodic patterns may be harmonized I-V6-I.

11.21

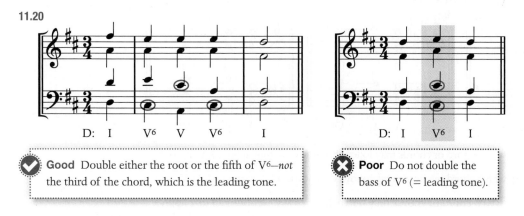

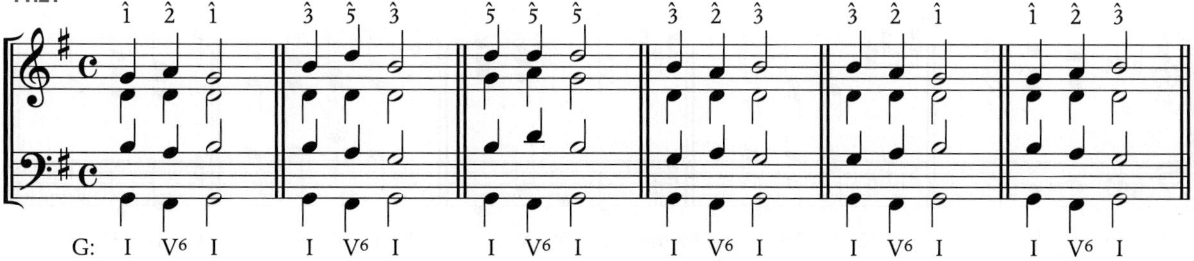

Upper voices move smoothly when V6 moves to I.

review and interact

POINTS FOR REVIEW

- **I^6 (the tonic chord in first inversion) may extend, alternate with, or substitute for I (the root-position tonic chord).**
  - Phrases that end with an authentic cadence should end with I, *not* I^6.
  - Any tone of I^6 may be doubled.
- **V^6 may extend, alternate with, or substitute for V (the root-position dominant chord).**
  - V^6 often leads directly to I, with smooth motion in all voices.
  - V^6 may move to V or V^7, but V^6 may not follow V^7.
  - Any tone of V^6 may be doubled except the bass (the third of the chord, which is the leading tone).
  - Use V—not V^6—in a cadence.

TEST YOURSELF

1. In each of the following, the soprano is missing from the second chord. What note(s) could be used to complete the chord?

a. b. c.

G min.: i i^6 A: I V^6 F: V V^6

2. Of the following, which chord or chords may follow I^6 (choose all that apply): I, V, V^6, or V^7?
3. Of the following, which chord or chords may follow V^6 (choose all that apply): I, I^6, V, or V^7?
4. Of the following, which chord or chords may normally follow V^7 (choose all that apply): I, I^6, V, or V^6?
5. Identify the errors in each of these harmonic fragments.

a. b. c. d. e.

D min.: i V^6 i E: I^6 V^6 I F♯ min.: i i^6 V i B♭: I V^7 V^6 I G: I V^6 I^6

Know It? Show It!

Focus by working through the tutorials on:

- Figured bass with I^6 and V^6
- Harmonizing with I, I^6, V, V^6, and V^7

Learn with inQuizitive.

Apply what you've learned to complete the assignments:

- I^6
- V^6
- Realizing Roman Numerals
- Realizing Figured Bass
- Identifying Voice-Leading Errors
- Harmonizing Melodies
- Composition
- Analysis

chapter

12 V^6_5 and V^4_2

V^6_5 and V^4_2 are inversions of V^7 that embellish Tonic harmony: V^6_5 leads to I, V^4_2 leads to I^6.

Harmonic Progressions

V^6_5 and V^4_2 as Embellishing Harmonies

Voice Leading in Four-Part Harmony

Figured Bass

HARMONIC PROGRESSIONS

V^6_5 and V^4_2 are the first and third inversions of V^7, respectively.

12.1

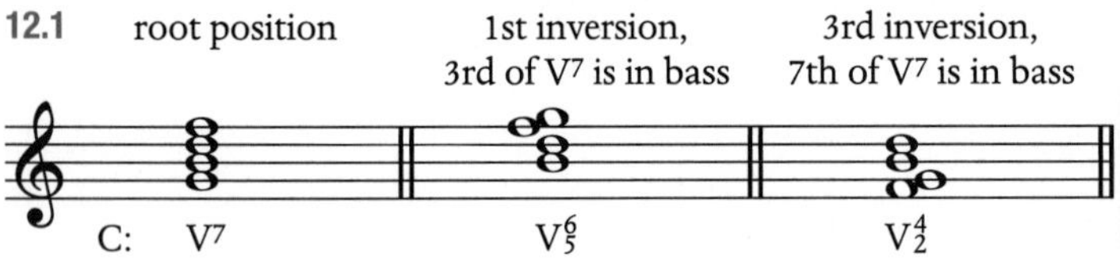

V^6_5 and V^4_2 are inversions of V^7.

Like other **D**ominant harmonies, V^6_5 and V^4_2 lead toward the tonic chord. Since the leading tone is in the bass of V^6_5 and must resolve *up by step*, V^6_5 resolves to I in root position (I), *not* first inversion (I^6). Similarly, since the chordal seventh in the bass of V^4_2 must resolve *down by step*, V^4_2 resolves to I^6, *not* to I in root position.

12.2 Haydn, Sonata in C, Hob. XVI:35, I

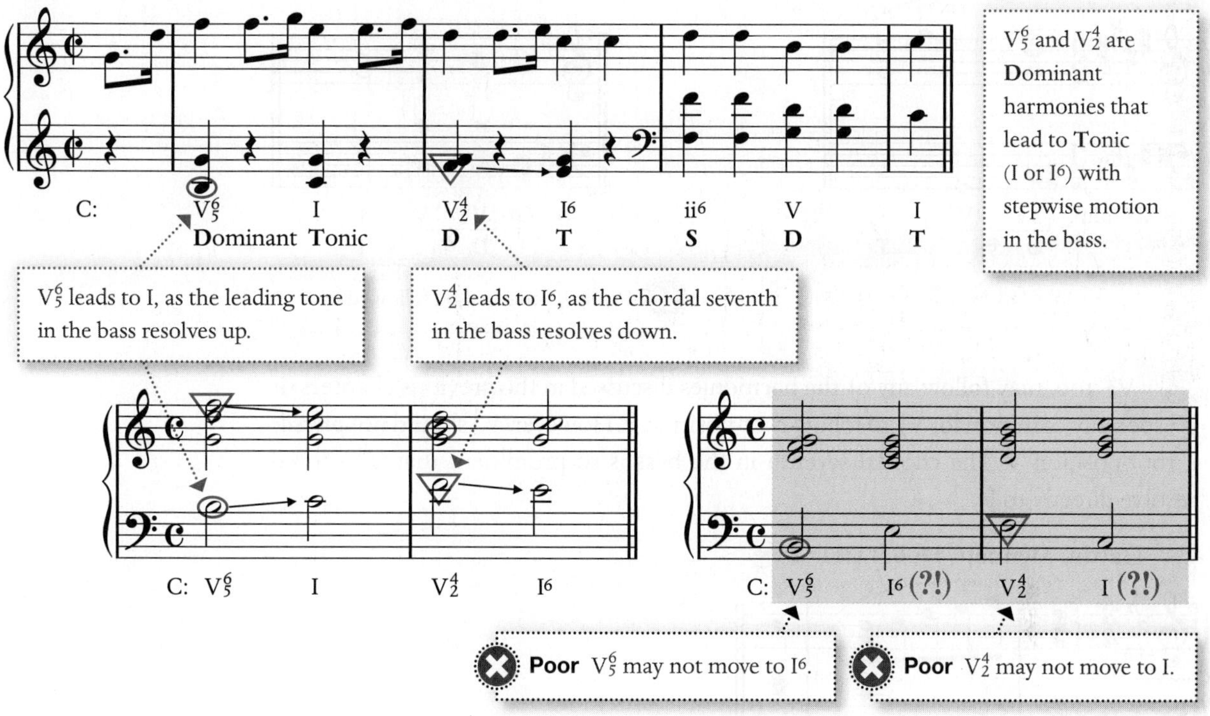

C: V^6_5 I V^4_2 I^6 ii^6 V I
Dominant Tonic D T S D T
V^6_5 and V^4_2 are **Dominant** harmonies that lead to **Tonic** (I or I^6) with stepwise motion in the bass.
V^6_5 leads to I, as the leading tone in the bass resolves up.
V^4_2 leads to I^6, as the chordal seventh in the bass resolves down.
C: V^6_5 I V^4_2 I^6
C: V^6_5 I^6 (?!) V^4_2 I (?!)
Poor V^6_5 may not move to I^6.
Poor V^4_2 may not move to I.

V^6_5 may follow any of the harmonies discussed in the previous chapters (I, I^6, V, V^7, and V^6).

12.3 Beethoven, Symphony no. 9, III

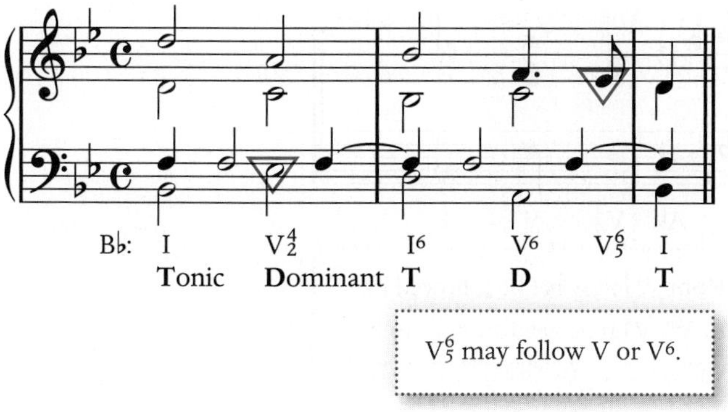

B♭: I V^4_2 I^6 V^6 V^6_5 I
Tonic Dominant T D T
V^6_5 may follow V or V^6.

V^6_5 also may lead to V^7 in root position or in inversion. V^6_5 may not be directly followed by V or V^6, however, since if it did its chordal seventh would not be able to resolve down by step.

12.4 Handel, Violin Sonata in E, HWV 373, III ➔ **12.5**

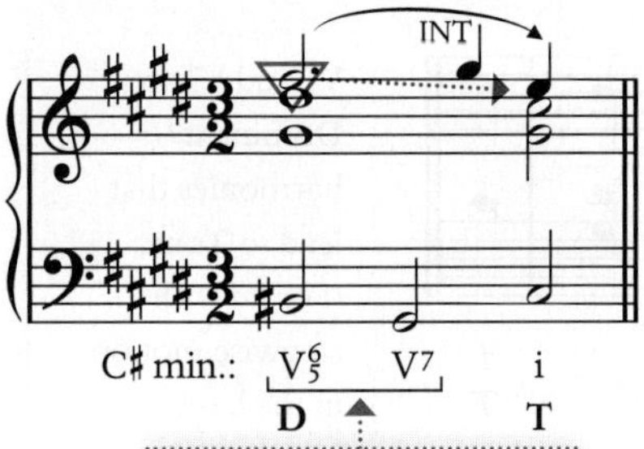

V_5^6 may followed by V^7.

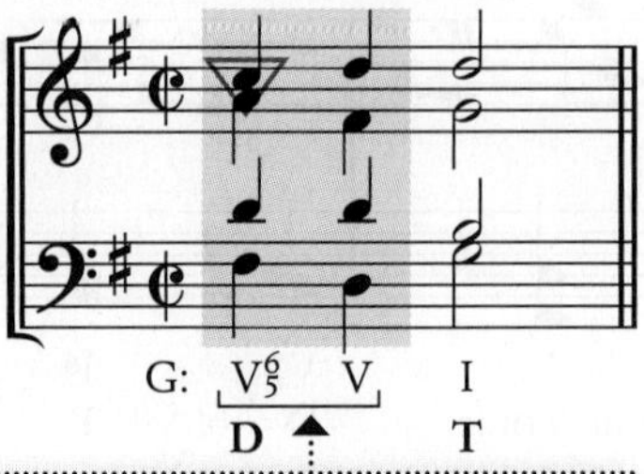

Poor V_5^6 may *not* be followed by V.

V_2^4, too, may follow any of the harmonies discussed in the previous chapters. It is especially common for V_2^4 to follow root-position V. However, V_2^4 should not *precede* a root-position V. The chordal seventh in the bass is so prominent that V_2^4 should resolve directly to I^6.

12.6 Haydn, Menuett, Hob. IX:11/2 ➔

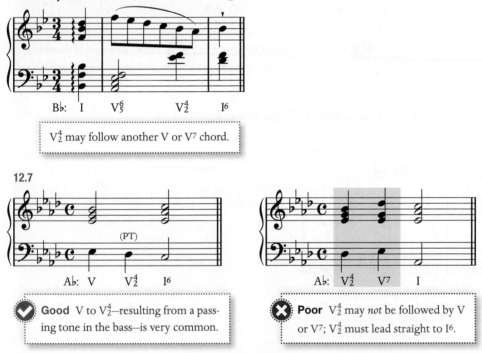

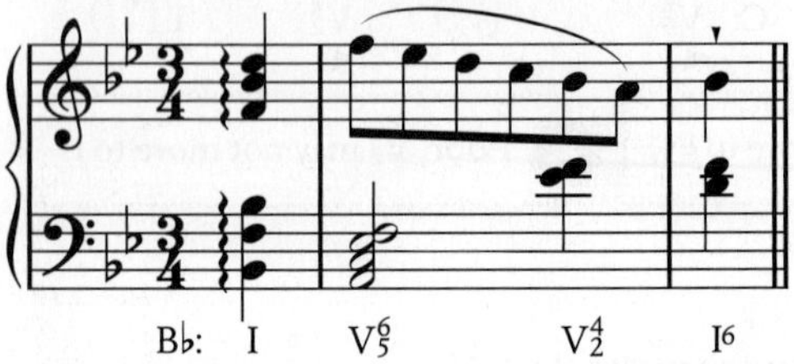

V_2^4 may follow another V or V^7 chord.

12.7

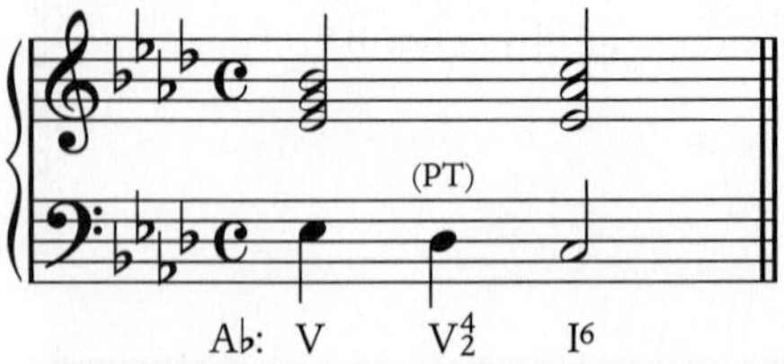

Good V to V_2^4—resulting from a passing tone in the bass—is very common.

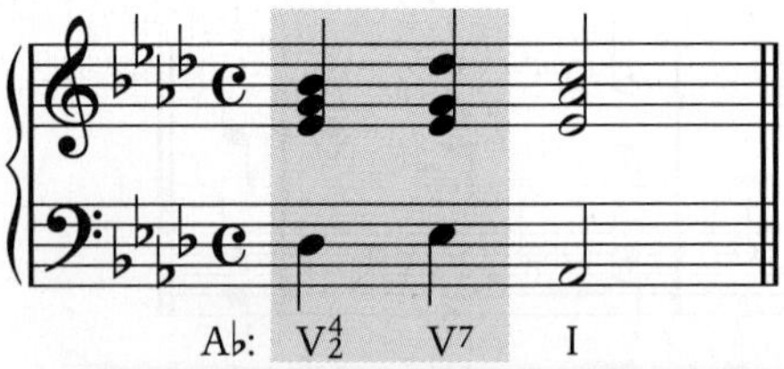

Poor V_2^4 may *not* be followed by V or V^7; V_2^4 must lead straight to I^6.

V_5^6 AND V_2^4 AS EMBELLISHING HARMONIES

The bass motions involving V_5^6–I and V_2^4–I^6 often resemble neighbor-tone or incomplete neighbor-tone motions. This is because V_5^6 and V_2^4 are relatively unstable tonally and their basses resolve by step to notes of the tonic triad. Thus, much as neighbor or incomplete neighbor tones embellish a given note, so V_5^6 and V_2^4 may be regarded as embellishing a Tonic harmony.

12.8

These neighbor and incomplete neighbor tones embellish the notes C and E, to which they resolve by step.

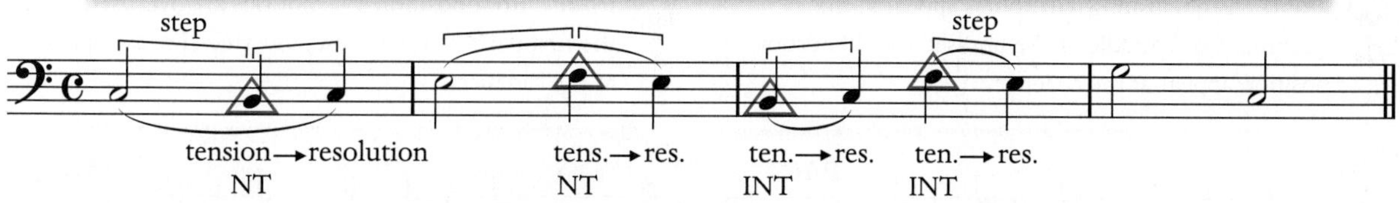

Similarly, these V^6_5 and V^4_2 chords embellish the I and I^6, to which they resolve by step in the bass.

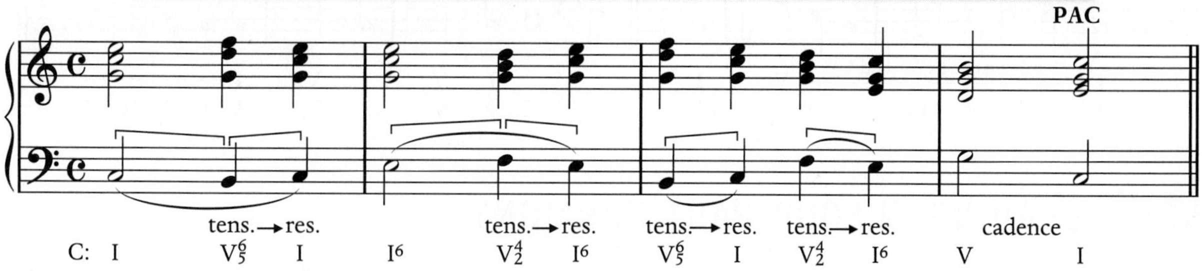

12.9 Haydn, *Variations faciles*

Simplified harmonic model

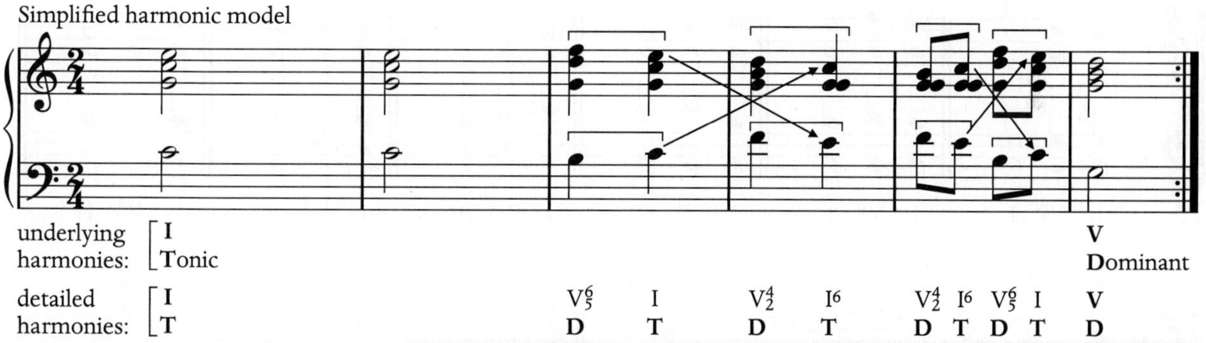

The stepwise motions in the bass of V^6_5–I and V^4_2–I^6 embellish Tonic harmony.

Like other inversions of V, V^6_5 and V^4_2 may be used anywhere within the phrase except for the cadence, where V or I is required. Indeed, since a cadence must involve root-position V or V–I, inversions earlier within the phrase are extremely helpful in promoting variety and providing an interesting bass line.

12.10

Good Embellishing harmonies appear at the beginning and middle of the phrase; V and I in root position appear at the cadence.

Poor Root-position V–I motions are overused in the first parts of the phrase; inverted chords appear at the cadence.

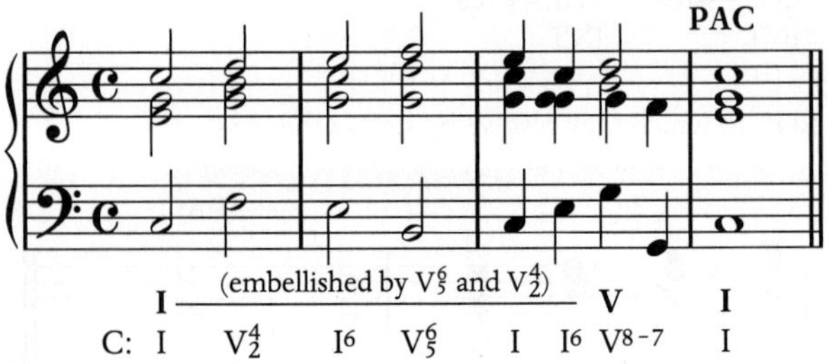

VOICE LEADING IN FOUR-PART HARMONY

In four-part harmony the upper voices typically move smoothly within V^6_5–I and V^4_2–I^6 progressions, with the chordal seventh resolving down by step and the leading tone resolving up by step. Usually none of the notes (not even the chordal fifth) of V^6_5 or V^4_2 is omitted in four-part harmony, and thus usually none of the notes in the chord is doubled.

12.11

Upper voices usually move by step or common tone in V^6_5–I and V^4_2–I^6 progressions.

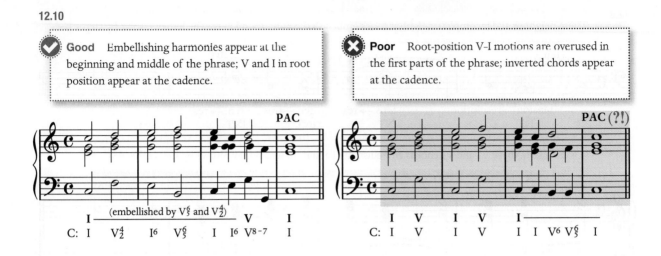

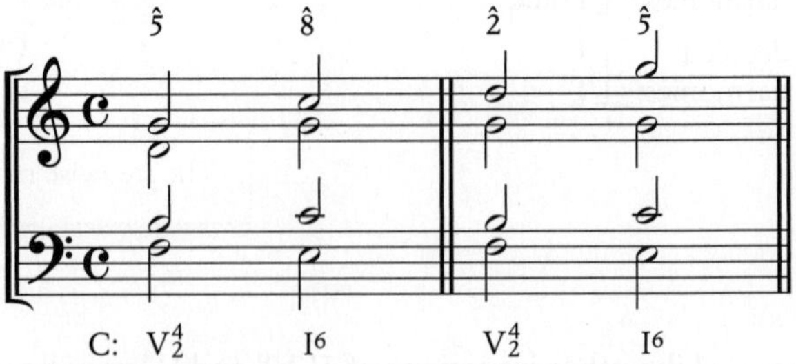

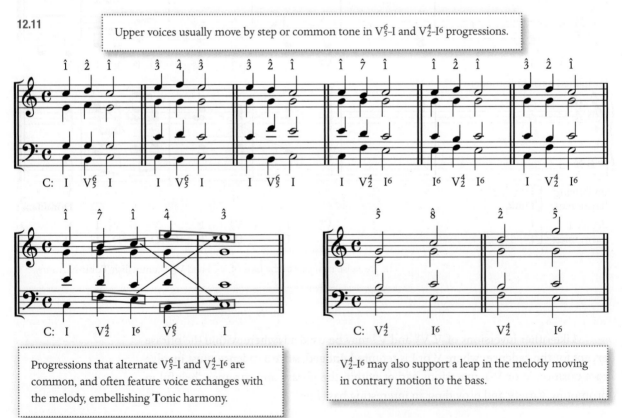

Progressions that alternate V^6_5–I and V^4_2–I^6 are common, and often feature voice exchanges with the melody, embellishing Tonic harmony.

V^4_2–I^6 may also support a leap in the melody moving in contrary motion to the bass.

FIGURED BASS

In figured bass, V^{6}_{5} is indicated either with the numbers $\begin{smallmatrix}6\\5\\3\end{smallmatrix}$ or (more commonly) $\begin{smallmatrix}6\\5\end{smallmatrix}$ placed below the leading tone in the bass. Note that the fifth above the bass in this case is diminished, not perfect. However, as always, you should assume that a note needs no accidental unless an accidental is expressly indicated by the figures.

12.12

These figures . . . may be realized like this . . .

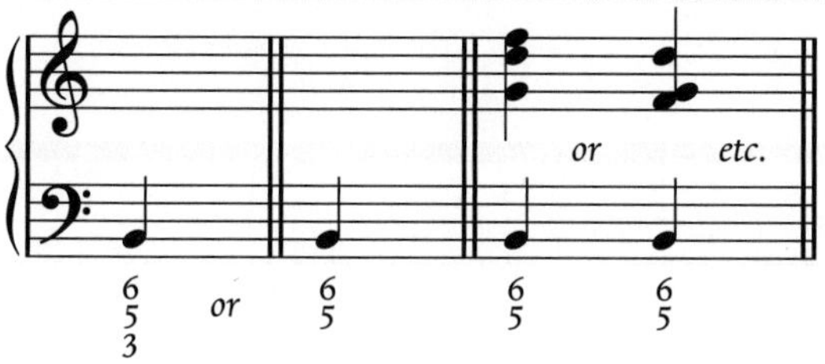

. . . but not like this!

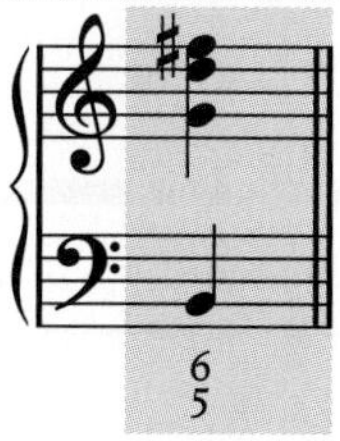

Poor Unless indicated by the figures, do not raise 5 above the bass to create a perfect fifth.

V^{4}_{2} in figured bass is indicated either with the figures $\begin{smallmatrix}6\\4\\2\end{smallmatrix}$ or (more commonly) $\begin{smallmatrix}4\\2\end{smallmatrix}$ placed below $\hat{4}$ in the bass. The fourth above the bass of V^{4}_{2} is a leading tone and thus must be raised in minor keys. In figured bass, this raising of the fourth above the bass is indicated by placing a sharp or natural next to the number 4, or shown with a diagonal slash through or plus sign attached to the number 4.

12.13

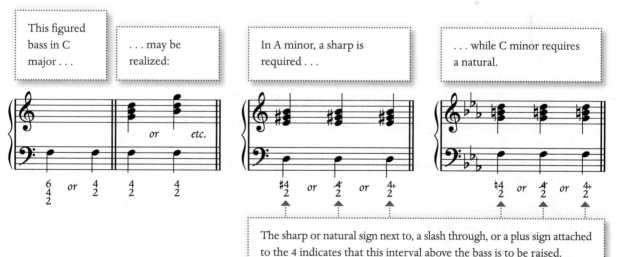

This figured bass in C major . . .

. . . may be realized:

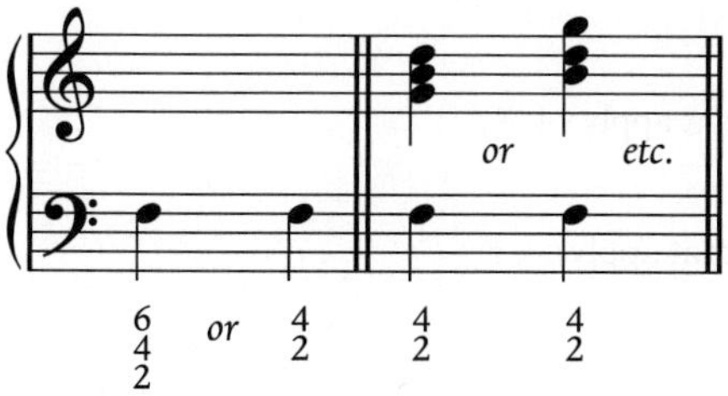

In A minor, a sharp is required . . .

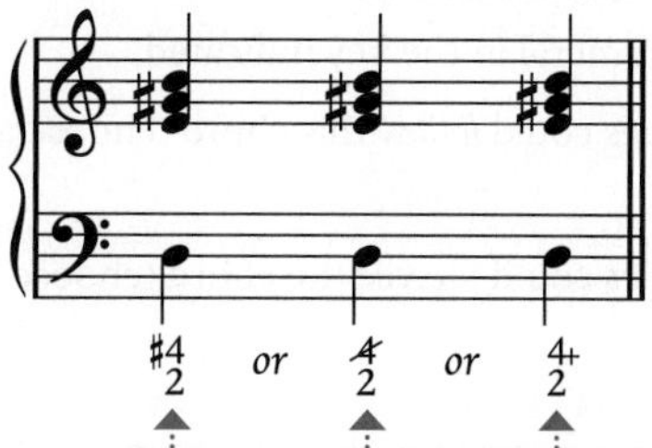

. . . while C minor requires a natural.

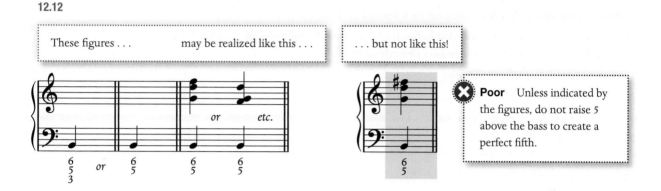

The sharp or natural sign next to, a slash through, or a plus sign attached to the 4 indicates that this interval above the bass is to be raised.

review and interact

POINTS FOR REVIEW

- V^6_5 and V^4_2 are inversions of V^7; they are Dominant harmonies.
- V^6_5 resolves to I; V^4_2 resolves to I^6.
- V^6_5 may follow another Dominant harmony. V^6_5 may also be followed directly by V^7 or an inversion of V^7, but it may *not* be followed by V or V^6.
- V^4_2 may follow another Dominant harmony. V^4_2 may *not* be followed by another V or V^7, however, but rather must resolve directly to I^6.
- Do not use V^6_5 or V^4_2 at cadences.

TEST YOURSELF

1. In the example below:
   a. Label the chord with a Roman numeral in the key indicated.
   b. Which of the following Tonic harmonies could *follow* this chord: I or I^6? Which of the following Dominant harmonies could *follow* this chord (choose all that apply): V, V^6, V^7, or V^4_2?
   c. Which of the following harmonies could *precede* the chord (choose all that apply): I, I^6, V, V^7, or V^4_2?

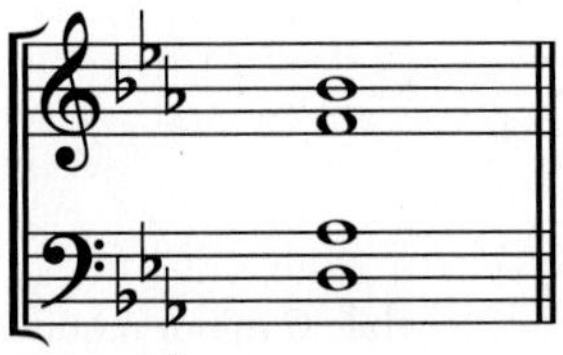

E♭:

2. In the example below:
   a. Label the chord with a Roman numeral in the key indicated.
   b. Which of the following harmonies could *follow* this chord (choose all that apply): i, i^6, V, V^6, or V^7?
   c. Which of the following harmonies could *precede* the chord (choose all that apply): i, i^6, V, V^7, or V^6_5?

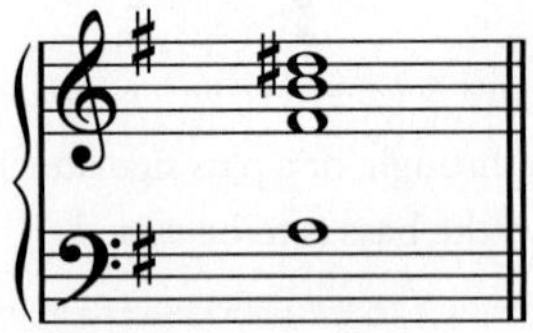

E min.:

3. Below is a melodic phrase in D major.
   a. Which of the notes with an asterisk could be harmonized with V^6_5? Which of the notes with an asterisk could be harmonized with V^4_2? (Hint: the chord chosen should not create a poor doubling.)
   b. What harmonies should you use in measure 4?
   c. In which measure could you place a voice exchange between the bass and melody?

4. What notes are in the following chords, as indicated by the figured basses?

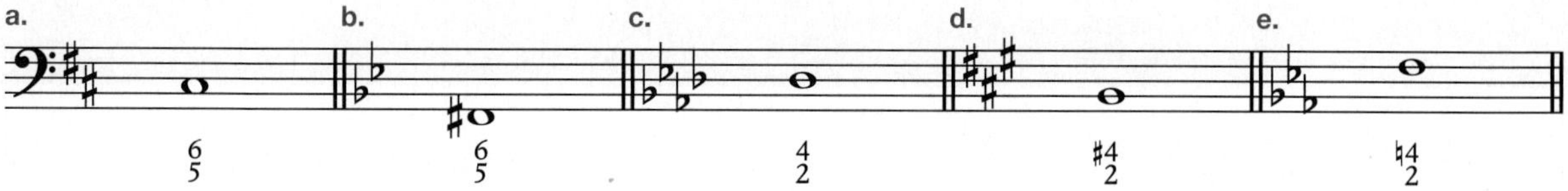

Know It? Show It!

Focus by working through the tutorials on:

- Writing V^6_5 and V^4_2 chords

Learn with inQuizitive.

Apply what you've learned to complete the assignments:

- Spelling Chords
- Realizing Roman Numerals
- Realizing Figured Bass
- Identifying Voice-Leading Errors
- Harmonizing Melodies
- Composition
- Analysis

chapter

13 V^4_3 and vii$^{\circ 6}$

V^4_3 and vii$^{\circ 6}$ are Dominant harmonies that embellish the tonic, usually with passing or neighbor motion in the bass leading to I or I^6.

Harmonic Progressions
- V^4_3 and vii$^{\circ 6}$ as passing chords between I and I^6
- V^4_3 and vii$^{\circ 6}$ as neighbor chords to I

Alternating with Other Dominant-to-Tonic Progressions
- Moving from V^4_3 or vii$^{\circ 6}$ to other Dominant harmonies

Voice-Leading in Four-Part Harmony
- V^4_3 or vii$^{\circ 6}$ to I
- Harmonizing $\hat{3}$-$\hat{4}$-$\hat{5}$: special exceptions involving V^4_3 or vii$^{\circ 6}$

Figured Bass

HARMONIC PROGRESSIONS

V^4_3 is the second inversion of V^7; vii$^{\circ 6}$ is a first-inversion diminished triad whose root is the leading tone. V^4_3 and vii$^{\circ 6}$ are extremely similar, since they share the same bass ($\hat{2}$) and most of the same tones ($\hat{7}$, $\hat{2}$, and $\hat{4}$ are in both).

13.1

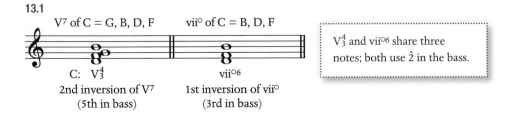

V^7 of C = G, B, D, F　　vii$^\circ$ of C = B, D, F

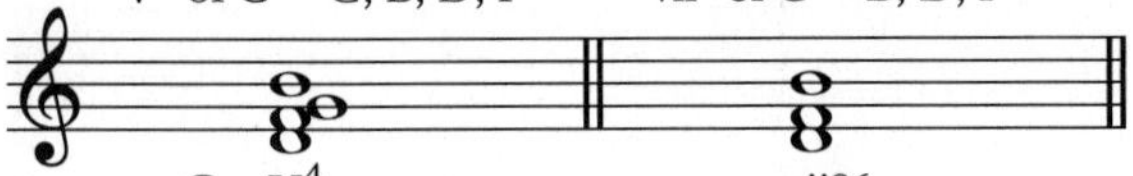

C: V^4_3　　vii$^{\circ 6}$

2nd inversion of V^7 (5th in bass)　　1st inversion of vii$^\circ$ (3rd in bass)

V^4_3 and vii$^{\circ 6}$ share three notes; both use $\hat{2}$ in the bass.

V^4_3 and vii$^{\circ 6}$ function similarly as well. They both are **D**ominant chords, leading to I or I^6 with stepwise motion in the bass. Because they usually lead to a tonic chord with smooth motion in all voices, V^4_3 and vii$^{\circ 6}$ are used to embellish the tonic harmony, and thus they do not appear at cadences.

V$^4_3$ AND vii$^{\circ 6}$ AS PASSING CHORDS BETWEEN I AND I^6

V$^4_3$ and vii$^{\circ 6}$ often lead between I and I^6 with **passing motion** in the bass.

13.2

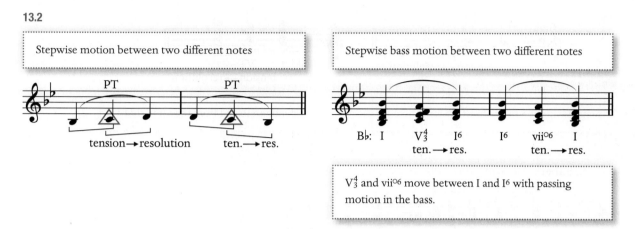

Stepwise motion between two different notes

Stepwise bass motion between two different notes

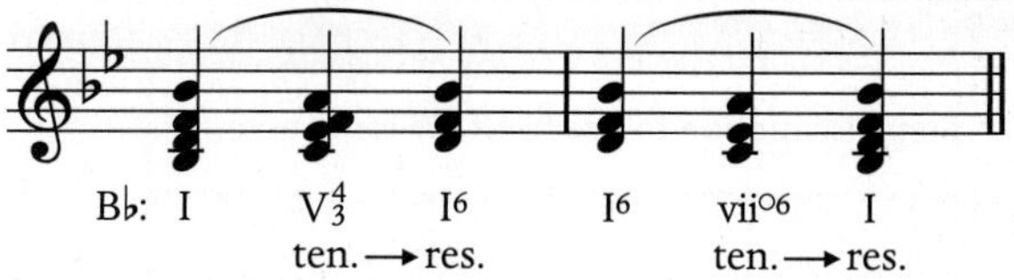

V$^4_3$ and vii$^{\circ 6}$ move between I and I^6 with passing motion in the bass.

13.3 Haydn, Menuet, Hob. XI:11/2

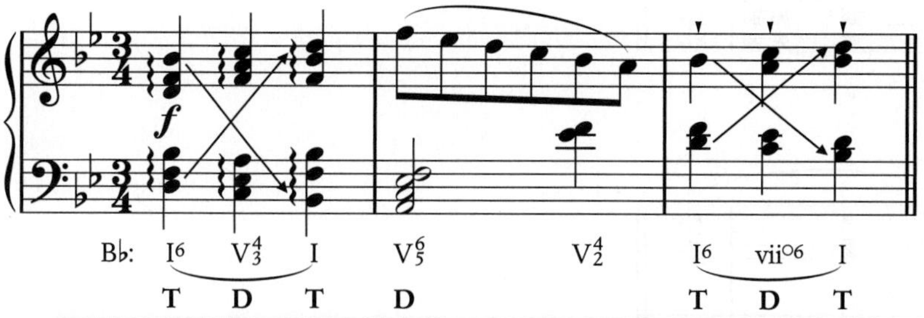

Passing motions in the bass and melody can give rise to voice exchanges.

13.4 J. S. Bach, Chorale 144 **13.5 J. S. Bach, Chorale 269**

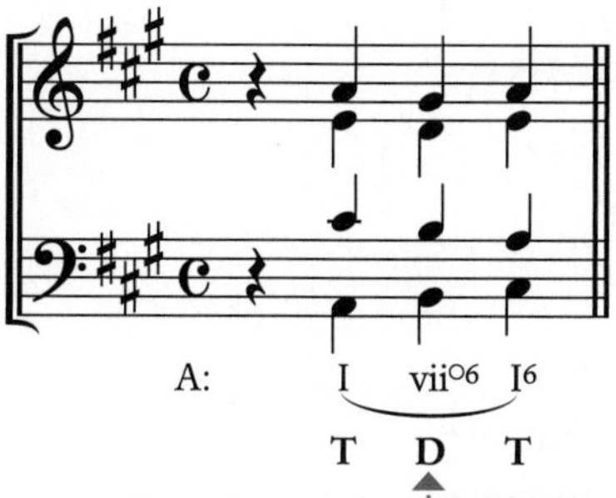

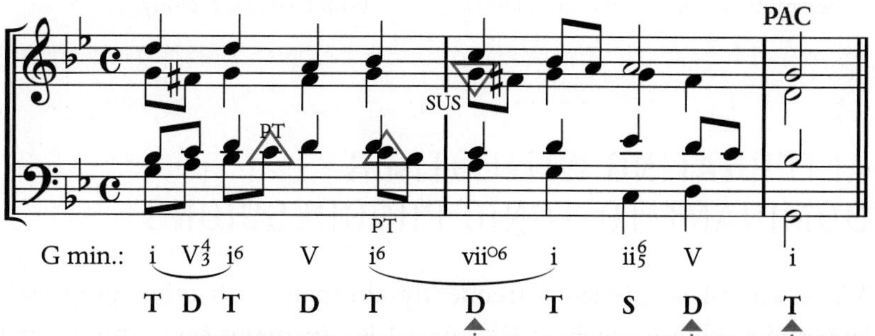

I passes through vii$^{\circ 6}$ to I^6.

i^6 passes through vii$^{\circ 6}$ to i.

Root-position V–i appears in the cadence.

V^4_3 AND vii$^{\circ6}$ AS NEIGHBOR CHORDS TO I

V^4_3 or vii$^{\circ6}$ may also appear between two I chords with **neighbor motion** in the bass.

13.6

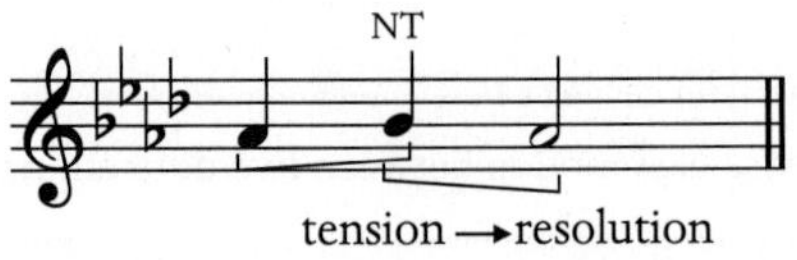

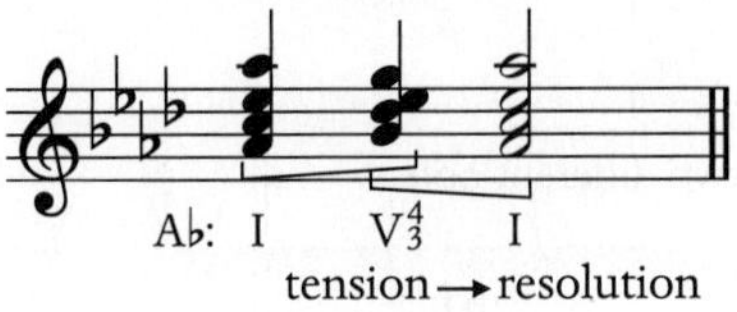

Stepwise motion to and from the same note

Stepwise motion to and from the same chord

13.7 **Schubert, *Moments Musicaux*, op. 94, no. 2**

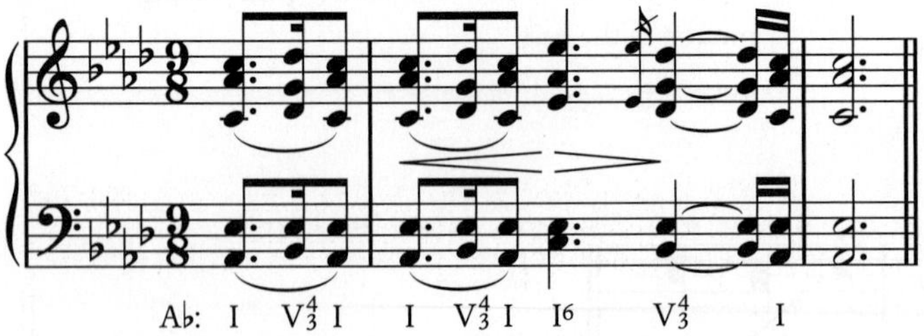

Simplified harmonic model

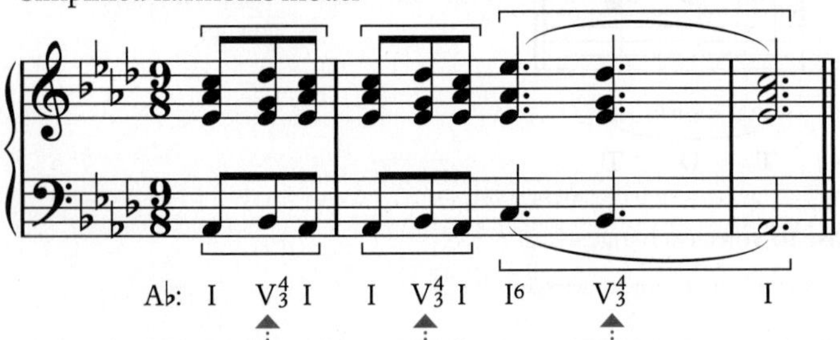

I moves to and from V^4_3, with neighbor motion in both bass and melody.

V^4_3 between I and I^6, with passing motion in both bass and melody

ALTERNATING WITH OTHER DOMINANT-TO-TONIC PROGRESSIONS

V^4_3 or vii$^{\circ6}$–I progressions frequently alternate with other progressions that use inverted V chords (such as V^6_5–I or V^4_2–I^6). In many cases this gives rise to voice exchanges that involve pairs of notes in the outer voices and that embellish tonic harmony.

13.8 Beethoven, Piano Sonata in G, op. 14, no. 2, II

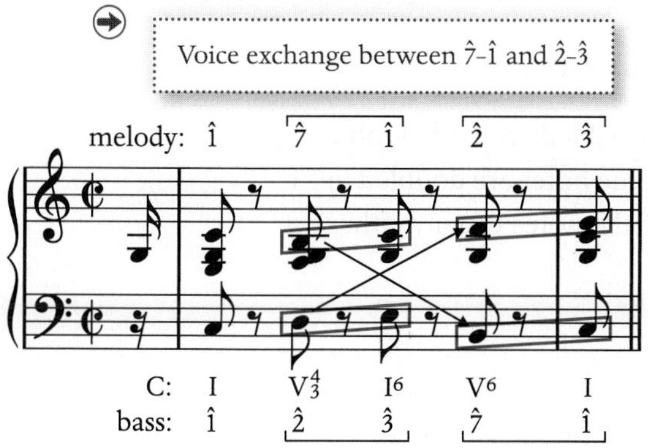

13.9 Handel, Violin Sonata in E, HWV 373, III

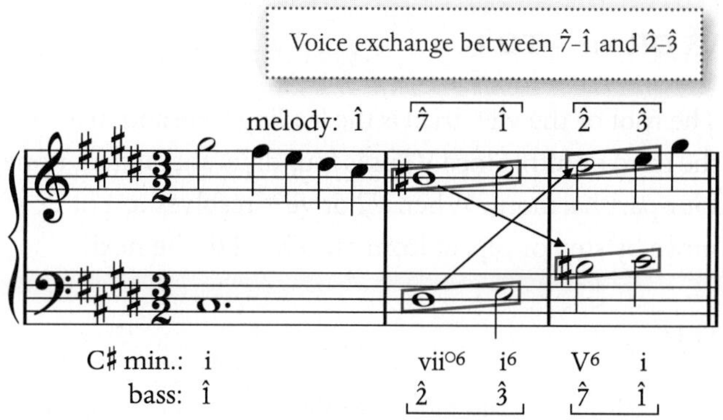

13.10 Mozart, Piano Sonata in F, K. 280, III

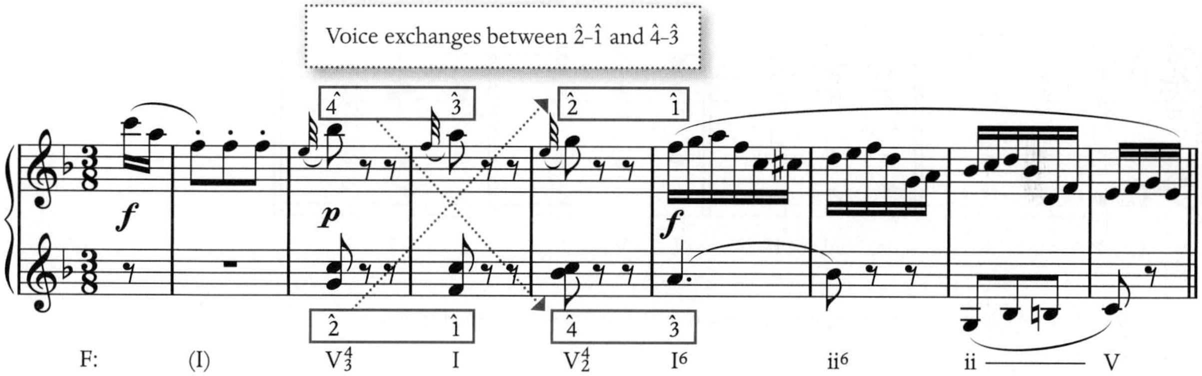

MOVING FROM V$^4_3$ OR vii^{o6} TO OTHER DOMINANT HARMONIES

At times V$^4_3$ moves to another inversion of V^7 before resolving to I or I^6.

13.11 Beethoven, Piano Sonata in A♭, op. 110, I

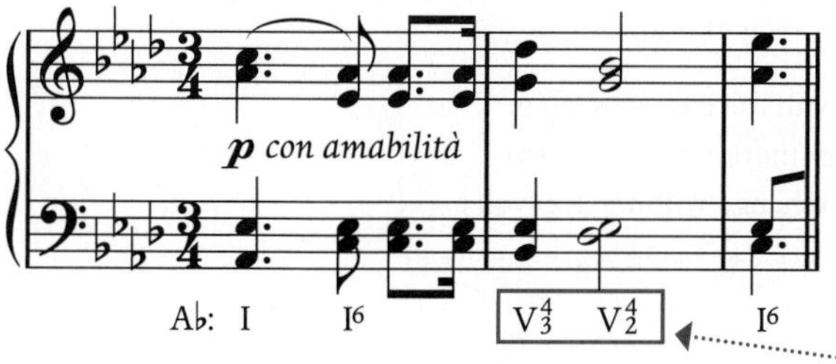

V$^4_3$ may move to or from other inversions of V^7.

13.12 Mozart, Piano Sonata in G, K. 283, I

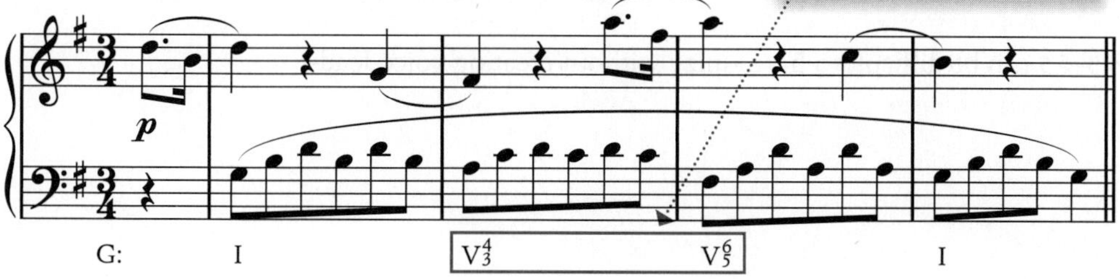

VOICE LEADING IN FOUR-PART HARMONY

V^4_3 OR vii$^{\circ 6}$ TO I

The root of the vii$^{\circ 6}$ triad is the leading tone and may not be doubled; instead, double the third or fifth. Since V^4_3 uses four different pitches, none of the notes are doubled in four-part harmony. When V^4_3 or vii$^{\circ 6}$ resolves to I or I^6, all of the notes usually either move by step or repeat from one chord to the next.

13.13

All notes usually move smoothly when V^4_3 or vii$^{\circ 6}$ moves to I or I^6. Do not double the root (= leading tone) of vii$^{\circ 6}$.

V^4_3 and vii$^{\circ 6}$ can harmonize neighbor motion or a stationary tone in the top voice.

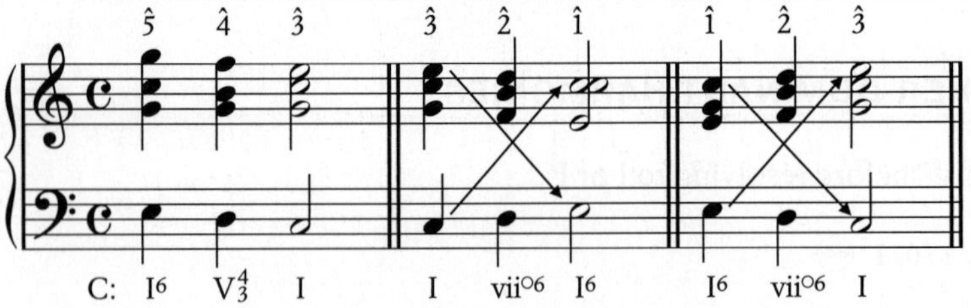

Augmented fourth to perfect fourth (F–B to G–C) is okay between upper voices when vii$^{\circ 6}$ moves to I or I^6.

These harmonies can also be used with passing motion in the top voice, either with the bass moving in parallel motion with the top voice . . .

. . . or with the bass moving in contrary motion so as to form a voice exchange with the top voice.

HARMONIZING $\hat{3}$-$\hat{4}$-$\hat{5}$: SPECIAL EXCEPTIONS INVOLVING V^4_3 OR vii$^{\circ 6}$

The melodic pattern $\hat{3}$-$\hat{4}$-$\hat{5}$ can be difficult to harmonize without creating voice-leading problems.

13.14

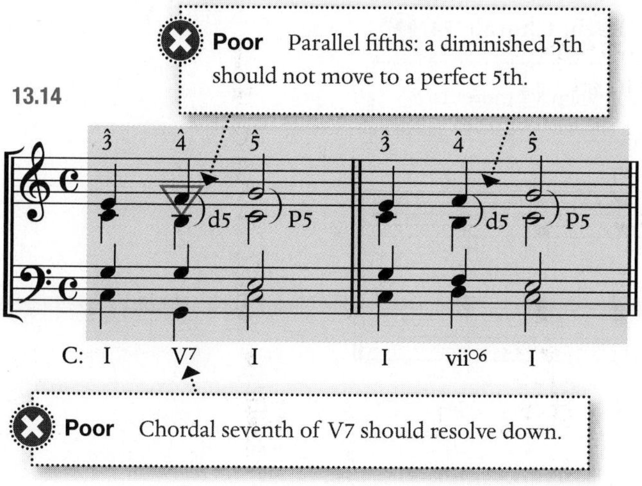

Poor Parallel fifths: a diminished 5th should not move to a perfect 5th.
$\hat{3}$ $\hat{4}$ $\hat{5}$ $\hat{3}$ $\hat{4}$ $\hat{5}$
d5 P5 d5 P5
C: I V7 I I vii°6 I
Poor Chordal seventh of V7 should resolve down.

However, special exceptions to standard voice-leading guidelines allow you to harmonize the melodic pattern $\hat{3}$-$\hat{4}$-$\hat{5}$ with either I-V$^4_3$-I^6 or I-vii$^{\circ 6}$-I^6. In these situations, the bass moves in parallel tenths (i.e., compound thirds) with the top voice. One of the special exceptions is that in these progressions a diminished fifth may move to a perfect fifth when V$^4_3$ or vii$^{\circ 6}$ moves to I^6.

13.15

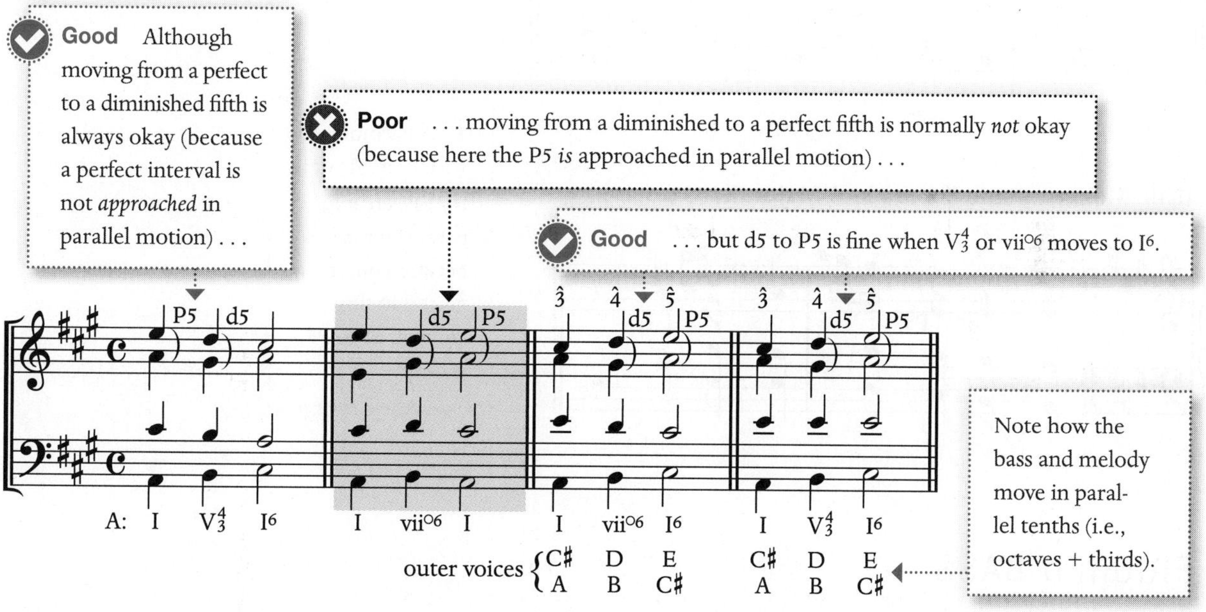

Good Although moving from a perfect to a diminished fifth is always okay (because a perfect interval is not *approached* in parallel motion) . . .
Poor . . . moving from a diminished to a perfect fifth is normally *not* okay (because here the P5 *is* approached in parallel motion) . . .
Good . . . but d5 to P5 is fine when V$^4_3$ or vii$^{\circ 6}$ moves to I^6.
P5 d5 d5 P5 d5 P5 d5 P5
$\hat{3}$ $\hat{4}$ $\hat{5}$ $\hat{3}$ $\hat{4}$ $\hat{5}$
A: I V$^4_3$ I^6 I vii$^{\circ 6}$ I I vii$^{\circ 6}$ I^6 I V$^4_3$ I^6
outer voices C♯ D E C♯ D E
A B C♯ A B C♯
Note how the bass and melody move in parallel tenths (i.e., octaves + thirds).

Likewise, although normally the chordal seventh of V^7 must resolve down, a special exception arises when V$^4_3$ moves to I^6. In such a case, the chordal seventh of V$^4_3$ may move up by step, in parallel motion with the bass.

13.16

Good — Chordal seventh of V7 need not resolve down when V^4_3 moves to I6.

G: I V^4_3 I6

Bass and soprano move in parallel tenths, harmonizing 3̂–4̂–5̂ in melody.

13.17 J. S. Bach, Chorale 54

G: I V^4_3 I6

Bass and tenor move in parallel thirds, with 3̂–4̂–5̂ in the tenor.

13.18 J. S. Bach, Chorale 26

F: I I vii6 I6 I

13.19 Mozart, Piano Sonata in A Major, K. 331, I

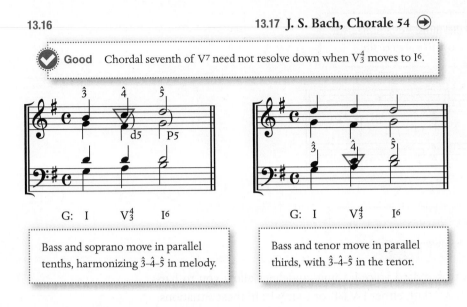

A: I V^4_3 I6

3̂–4̂–5̂ harmonized with I–viio6–I6 or I–V^4_3–I6, creating parallel tenths between outer voices. In this context, d5 to P5 is okay.

FIGURED BASS

In figured bass, V^4_3 is indicated with either $\begin{smallmatrix}6\\4\\3\end{smallmatrix}$ or $\begin{smallmatrix}4\\3\end{smallmatrix}$ below 2̂; viio6 is indicated with either $\begin{smallmatrix}6\\3\end{smallmatrix}$ or 6. In minor keys, the sixth above the bass is the leading tone, and thus must be raised. This is indicated either as ♯6 or ♮6, or else by 6̸.

13.20 The sharp or natural next to (or slash through) the figure 6 indicates that the sixth above the bass should be raised.

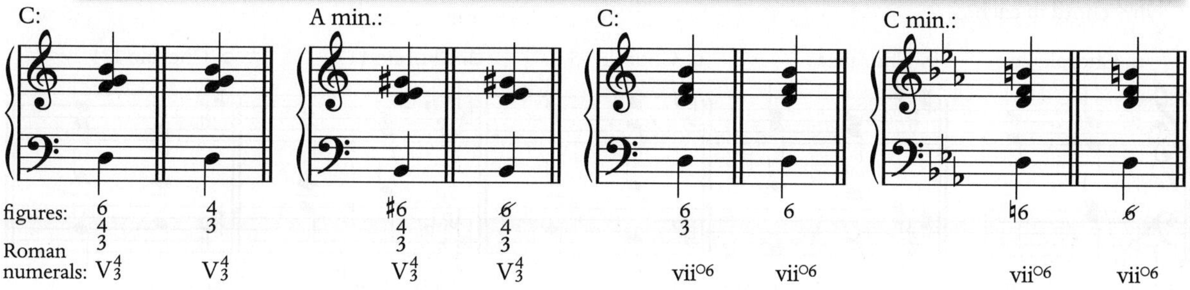

review and interact

POINTS FOR REVIEW

- **V$^4_3$ and vii°6 are both Dominant harmonies built on $\hat{2}$ in the bass.**
- **V$^4_3$ and vii°6 share most of the same notes, including the bass, and both move with stepwise motion in the bass to I or I6.**
- **V$^4_3$ and vii°6 are sometimes used between I and I6 (passing motion) or between two I chords (neighbor motion).**
- **The root of the vii°6 triad is the leading tone and may not be doubled in four-part harmony; double the third or fifth.**
- **The progression I–V$^4_3$–I6 (or I–vii°6–I6) frequently is used to harmonize the melodic progression $\hat{3}$-$\hat{4}$-$\hat{5}$ (with parallel tenths in the outer voices), owing to special voice-leading exceptions involving these progressions:**
  - When V$^4_3$ or vii°6 moves to I6, a diminished fifth may move to a perfect fifth.
  - When V$^4_3$ moves to I6, the seventh of the chord may move up by step.

TEST YOURSELF

1. Name the notes of both V$^4_3$ and vii°6 in the following keys, and identify the bass note for each: **a.** G major **b.** B♭ major **c.** E major **d.** E minor

2. In the example below, determine whether each of the labeled chords (a, b, c, d) is a V$^4_3$, vii°6, V$^6_5$, or V$^4_2$.

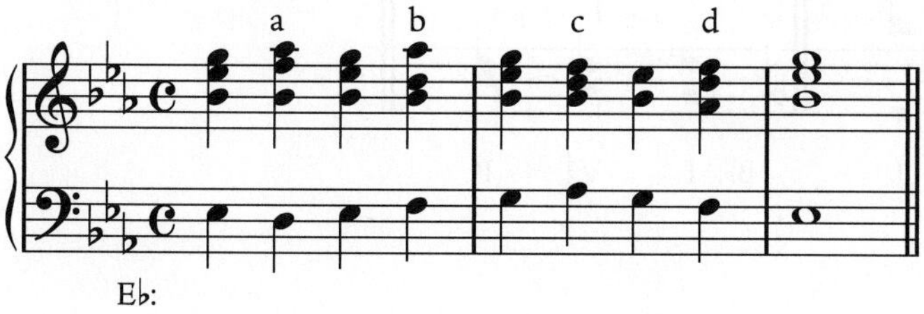

3. Below are some two-chord excerpts from chorales by J. S. Bach (some with embellishing tones omitted and the rhythm simplified). What note (root, third, fifth) is doubled in the vii$^{\circ 6}$ chord in each?

a. Chorale 26 **b.** Chorale 43 **c.** Chorale 95 **d.** Chorale 117 **e.** Chorale 135

F: vii$^{\circ 6}$ I^{6} A: vii$^{\circ 6}$ I B♭: vii$^{\circ 6}$ I^{6} A♭: vii$^{\circ 6}$ I D: vii$^{\circ 6}$ I

4. Below are some three-chord excerpts from chorales by J. S. Bach (some with embellishing tones omitted and with the rhythm simplified), each of which involves a vii$^{\circ 6}$ or V$^{4}_{3}$ that appears between I and I^{6}.

- What type of melody is in the soprano: neighbor motion, passing motion, or a stationary tone?
- In which of these do the outer voices move in parallel motion?
- In which, contrary motion?
- Which involves a voice exchange between the outer voices?
- In which of these is there an augmented fourth moving to perfect fourth between a pair of upper voices?

a. Chorale 144 **b.** Chorale 178 **c.** Chorale 258 **d.** Chorale 269 **e.** Chorale 321

A: I vii$^{\circ 6}$ I^{6} G min.: i^{6} vii$^{\circ 6}$ i G: I vii$^{\circ 6}$ I^{6} G min.: i V$^{4}_{3}$ i^{6} G min.: i^{6} vii$^{\circ 6}$ i

5. In each of the following, determine if there is a faulty approach to a perfect fifth and/or an improper treatment of a chordal seventh, and explain why or why not.

a. **b.** **c.**

E♭: I^{6} V$^{4}_{3}$ I G: I V^{7} I B♭: I V$^{4}_{3}$ I^{6}

Know It? Show It!

Focus by working through the tutorials on:

- Writing vii^{o6}
- Writing V^4_3

Learn with inQuizitive.

Apply what you've learned to complete the assignments:

- Preliminary Exercises
- Realizing Roman Numerals
- Realizing Figured Bass
- Harmonizing Melodies
- Composition
- Analysis

chapter 14

Approaching the Dominant: IV, ii^6, and ii$^6_5$

IV, ii^6, and ii$^6_5$ are Subdominant harmonies that lead toward the Dominant.

Moving toward **D**ominant Harmonies
- Subdominant harmonies
- Leading to **D**ominant harmonies
- **S**ubdominant harmonies do not follow **D**ominant harmonies
- Moving between **S**ubdominant harmonies

Voice Leading in Four-Part Harmony
- Subdominant to **D**ominant: IV and ii^6
- Subdominant to **D**ominant: ii$^6_5$
- Subdominant to **D**ominant: iv, ii$^{\circ 6}$, and ii$^{\varnothing 6}_{5}$ in minor keys

MOVING TOWARD **D**OMINANT HARMONIES

SUBDOMINANT HARMONIES

IV, ii^6, and ii$^6_5$ all function as **S**ubdominant harmonies. They use $\hat{4}$ in the bass, share most of the same notes, and function similarly.

14.1 major (B♭, D, F) | minor 1st inversion (G, B♭, D) | minor 7th 1st inversion (G, B♭, D, F)

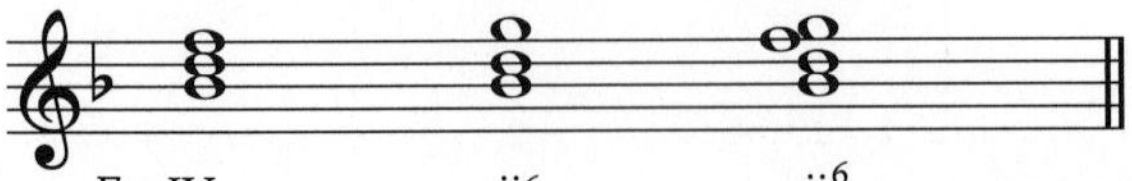

F: IV | ii^6 | ii$^6_5$

IV, ii^6, and ii$^6_5$ are **S**ubdominant harmonies.

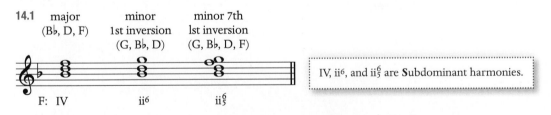

Each **S**ubdominant harmony contains $\hat{6}$. In minor keys, $\hat{6}$ is a semitone lower than in major keys. As a result, iv, ii$^{\circ 6}$, and ii$^{\varnothing 6}_{5}$ have different qualities in minor keys than the analogous chords in major keys, though their function is the same:

14.2 minor (B♭, **D**♭, F) | diminished 1st inversion (G, B♭, **D**♭) | half-diminished 7th 1st inversion (G, B♭, **D**♭, F)

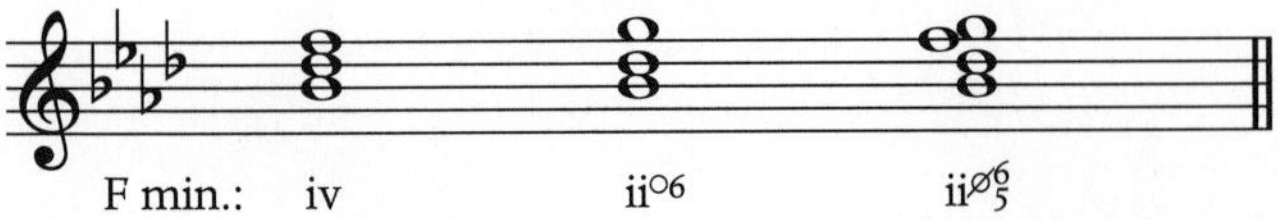

F min.: iv | ii$^{\circ 6}$ | ii$^{\varnothing 6}_{5}$

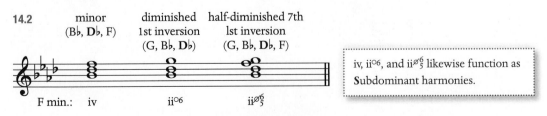

iv, ii$^{\circ 6}$, and ii$^{\varnothing 6}_{5}$ likewise function as **S**ubdominant harmonies.

LEADING TO DOMINANT HARMONIES

Most commonly, IV, ii^6, and ii$^6_5$ lead to **D**ominant harmonies, such as V or V^7 (in root position or inversion) or vii$^{\circ 6}$. The **T**onic-**S**ubdominant-**D**ominant-**T**onic pattern (**T**-**S**-**D**-**T**) includes all of the notes within the key, and thus typically allows for more-secure establishment of the key than the simpler **T**onic-**D**ominant-**T**onic pattern discussed in Chapters 9-13.

14.3

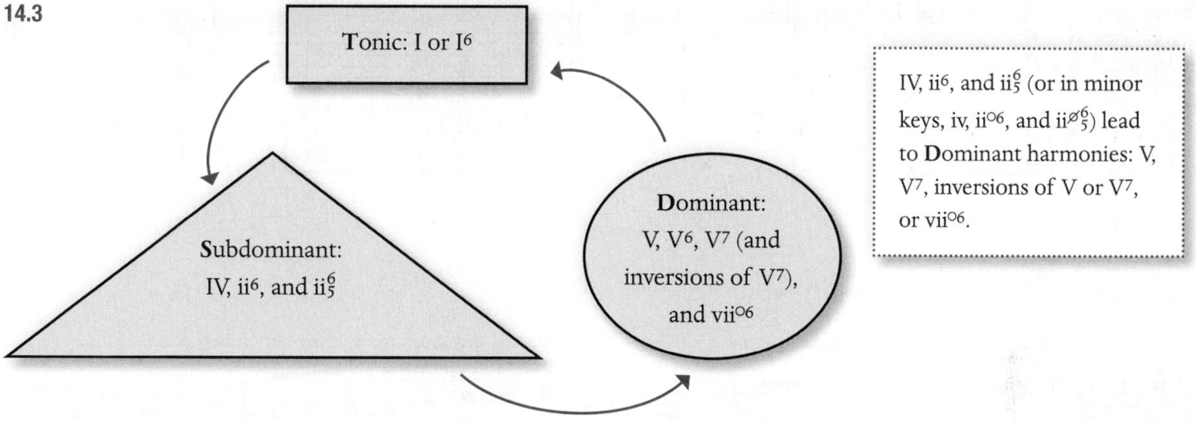

14.4 Beethoven, Cello Sonata, op. 5, no. 2, III

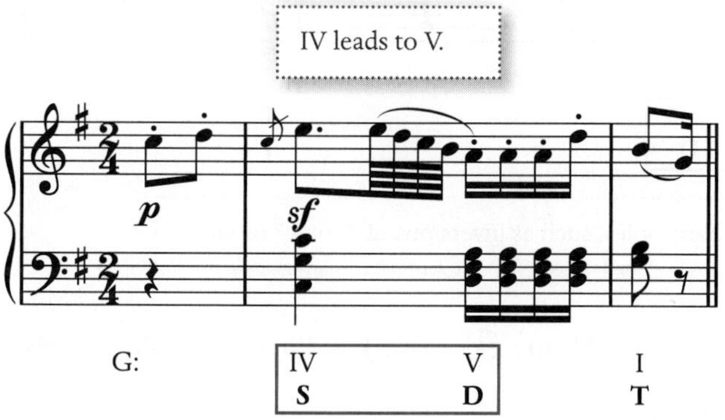

14.5 Dussek, Harp Sonata no. 3, II

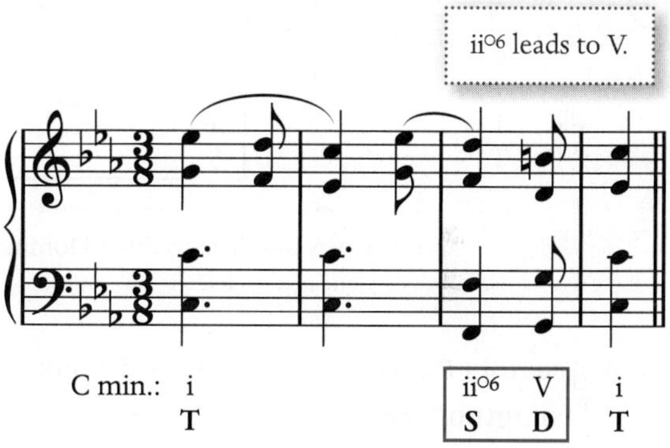

14.6 ***Congregational Hymnal*, no. 26**

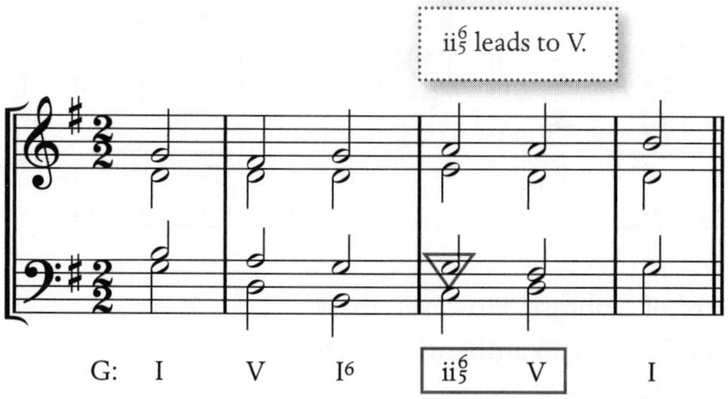

14.7 Purcell, "Dido's Lament," from *Dido and Aeneas*

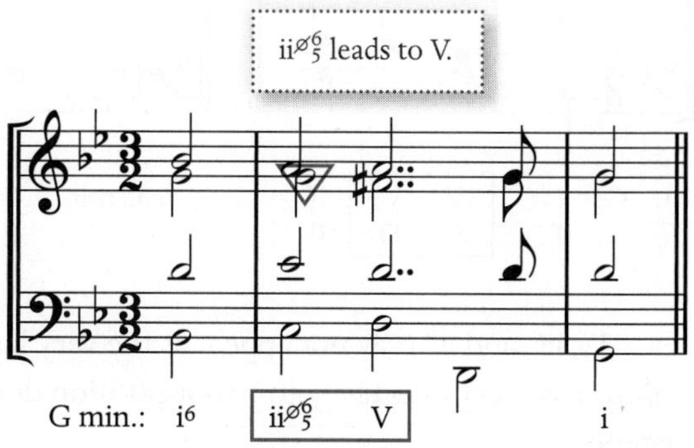

14.8 Brahms, "Die Wollust in den Maien" (The Merry Month of May)

IV, ii^6, and ii$^6_5$ may also lead to V^7 in root position . . .

choral version

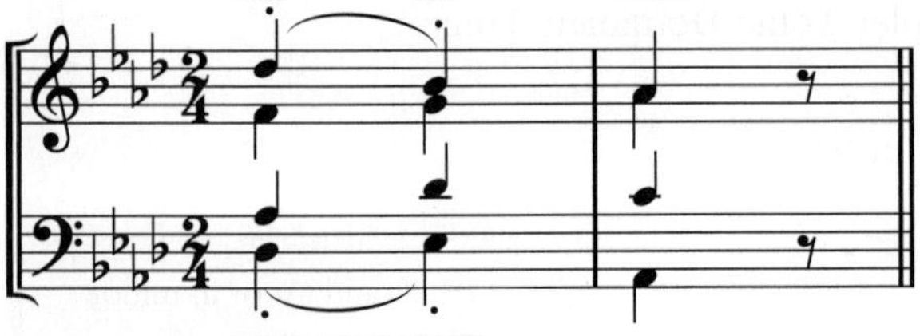

A♭: IV V^7 I
S D T

piano–voice version

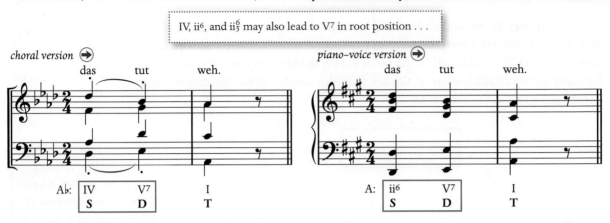

A: ii^6 V^7 I
S D T

Translation: That's what hurts.

14.9 Foster, "Beautiful Dreamer"

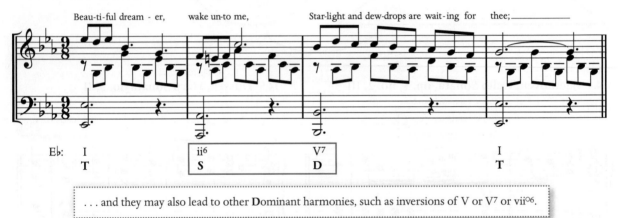

E♭: I ii^6 V^7 I
T S D T

. . . and they may also lead to other Dominant harmonies, such as inversions of V or V^7 or vii^{o6}.

14.10 *American Psalmody*, "Islington"

C: I IV V$^4_2$ I^6
T S D T

14.11 Chopin, Prelude in C Minor

C min.: i^6 iv V^6 i
T S D T

14.12 J. S. Bach, Chorale 103

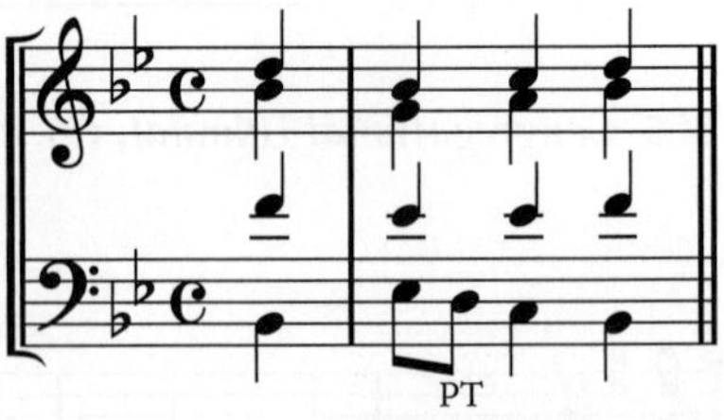

B♭: I IV vii^{o6} I
T S D T

IV, ii^6, and ii$^6_5$ may not appear as the very last chord of a phrase. However, these chords lead very effectively to a root-position dominant chord in an authentic or half cadence.

14.13 Mozart, Sonata for Piano and Violin, K. 377

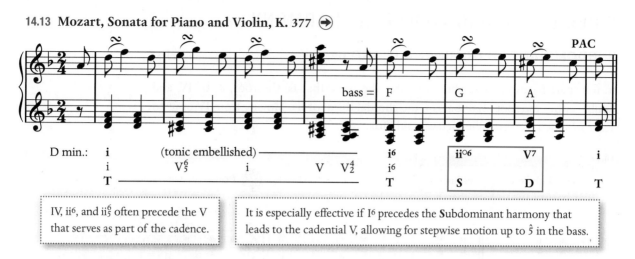

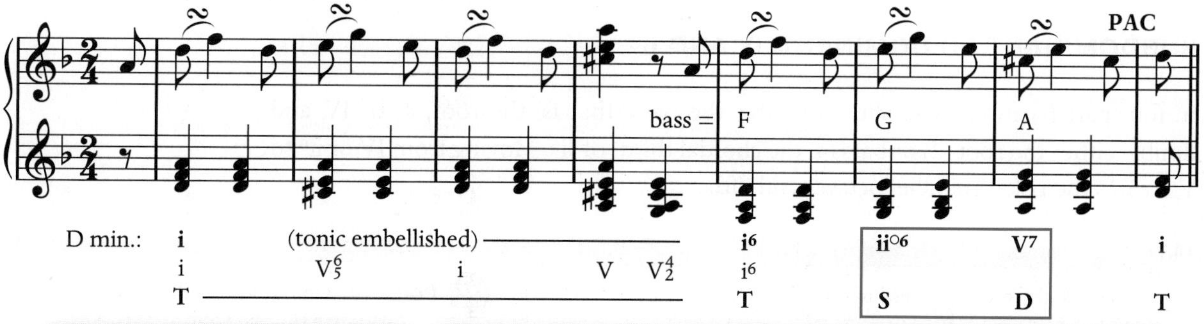

IV, ii6, and ii6 5 often precede the V that serves as part of the cadence.

It is especially effective if I6 precedes the **S**ubdominant harmony that leads to the cadential V, allowing for stepwise motion up to $\hat{5}$ in the bass.

SUBDOMINANT HARMONIES DO NOT FOLLOW DOMINANT HARMONIES

Except in very special circumstances (to be discussed in later chapters) IV, ii6, and ii6 5 should not follow a **D**ominant harmony.

14.14

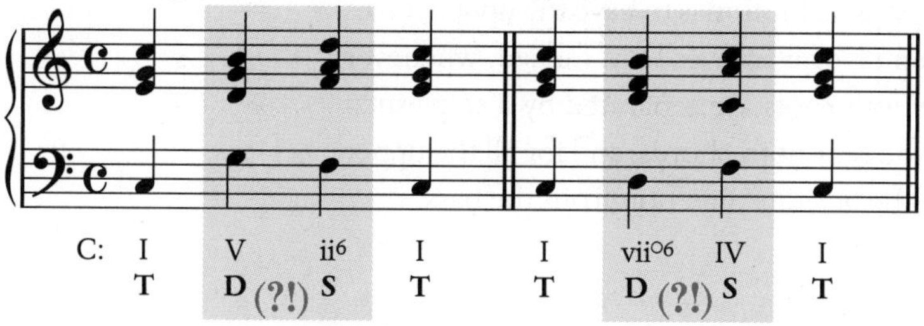

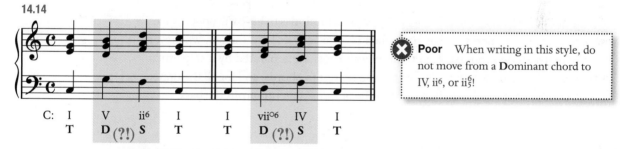

Poor When writing in this style, do not move from a **D**ominant chord to IV, ii6, or ii6 5!

MOVING BETWEEN SUBDOMINANT HARMONIES

Before proceeding to V, IV may be followed by ii6 (the reverse—ii6 followed by IV—is far less common). Since the two chords function so similarly, the resulting IV–ii6 succession essentially represents an elaboration of a single harmony by means of an embellishing motion in the upper voice.

14.15

14.16 Handel, Chaconne in G

Good IV may move to ii6 before progressing to V.

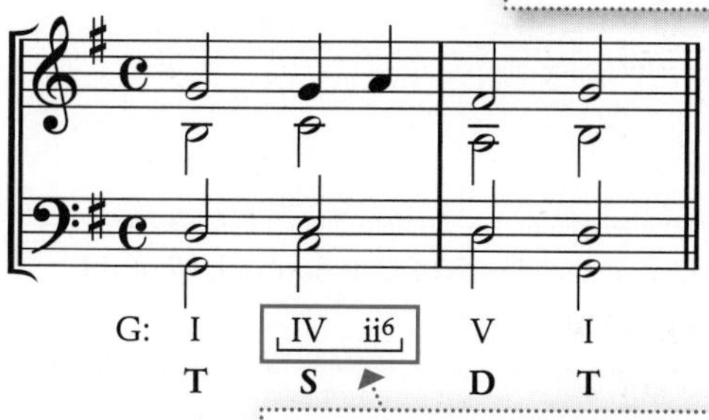

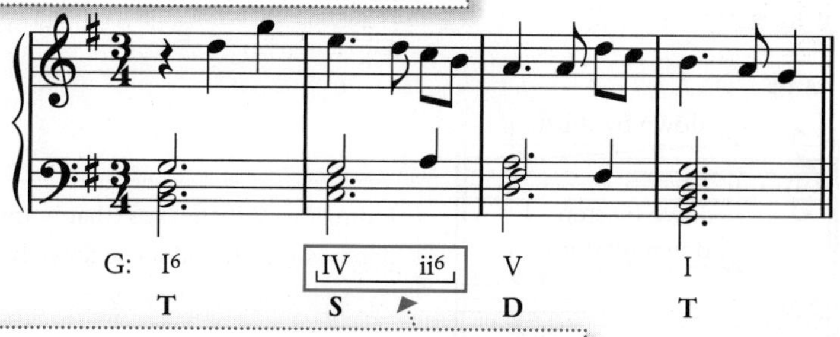

As the 5th (G) above the bass moves to a 6th (A), IV (C-E-G) moves to ii6 (C-E-*A*).

VOICE LEADING IN FOUR-PART HARMONY

SUBDOMINANT TO DOMINANT: IV AND ii6

In four-part harmony, you should double the bass (that is, the root, $\hat{4}$) of IV, and double either the root ($\hat{2}$) or bass ($\hat{4}$, the chordal third) of ii6. Moving from IV or ii6 to V creates the risk of parallel octaves and fifths.

14.17

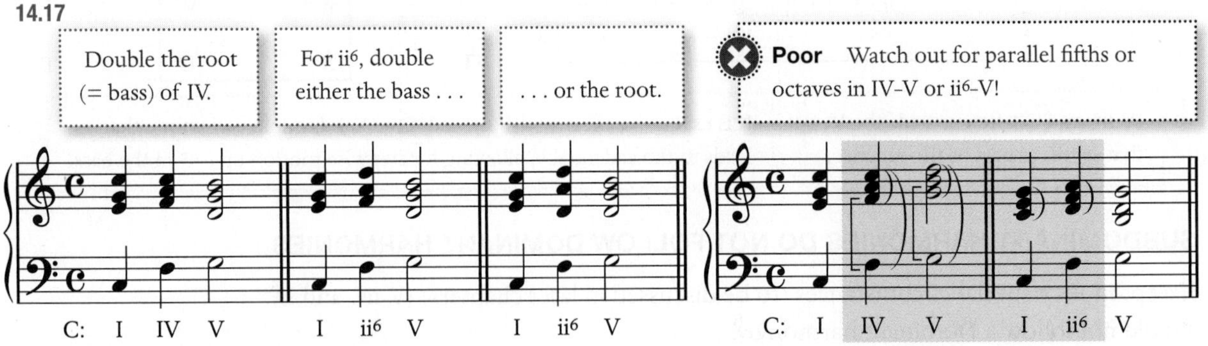

A standard strategy for avoiding faulty parallel motion is to have the upper voices move in contrary motion with the bass when IV or ii6 moves to V. Indeed, whenever moving between two root-position triads whose roots are separated by a step—such as IV and V—it is usually best to double the roots of both chords, and for all the upper voices to move to the nearest chord tone in the *opposite* direction from the bass.

14.18

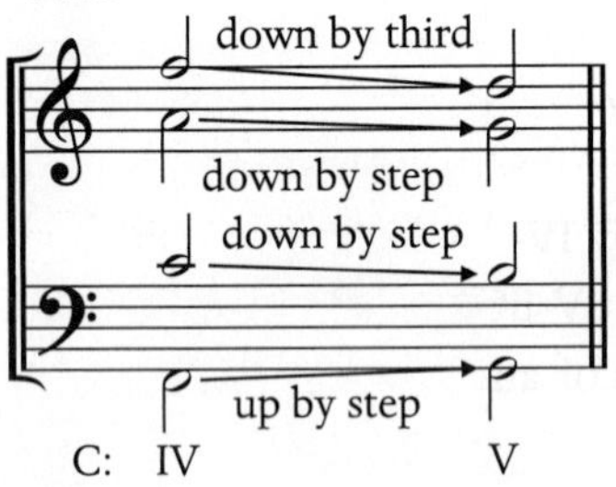

From IV to V, the bass moves up by step, the upper voices *all* move down by step or third.

In general, when moving between two $\substack{5\\3}$ chords separated by a step, (a) double the root in both chords and (b) move all the upper voices in opposite direction of the bass.

Similarly, when the bass of ii6 is doubled (as it often is), all of its voices should move down to the nearest chord tone—in the *opposite* direction from the bass—when ii6 progresses to V.

14.19

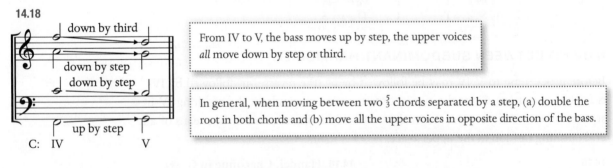

From ii6 to V, if the bass (that is, the third of the chord) of ii6 is doubled, *all* of the upper voices should move down by step or third.

Other voice-leading possibilities arise when the root of ii^6 is doubled, or when ii^6 or IV progresses to V^7 (or an inversion of V or V^7). Although contrary motion between the bass and upper voices remains the norm, in these situations one or more of the upper voices may remain on a common tone or move in the same direction as the bass—providing that special care is taken to avoid parallel fifths or octaves.

14.20

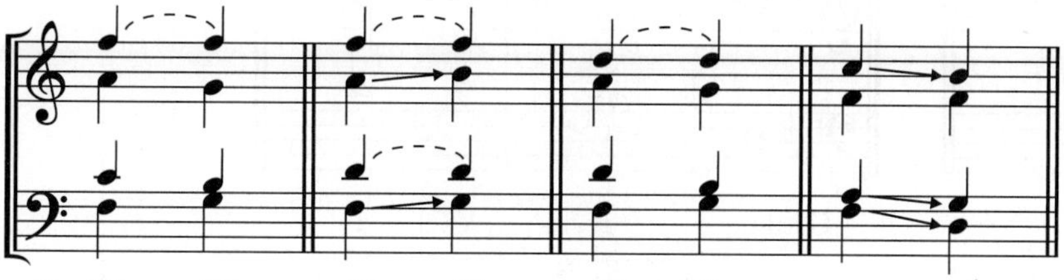

The upper voices may remain on the same note or move in the same direction as the bass if IV or ii^6 moves to V^7 or an inversion of V, or if the root of ii^6 is doubled.

SUBDOMINANT TO DOMINANT: ii$^6_5$

Because it is a seventh chord, normally none of the notes of ii$^6_5$ is doubled. The chordal seventh of ii$^6_5$—which is $\hat{1}$—should be prepared by common tone: in other words, the chordal seventh of ii$^6_5$ should be held over from the previous chord. Like all chordal sevenths, it must resolve down by step when ii$^6_5$ moves to V.

14.21 **R. Schumann, "Ein Choral" (A Chorale)**

The chordal seventh of ii$^6_5$ (G, $\hat{1}$) is prepared by common tone (notice the alto G in the previous chord) and resolves down by step.

SUBDOMINANT TO DOMINANT: iv, ii$^{\circ 6}$, AND ii$^{\varnothing 6}_{\ 5}$ IN MINOR KEYS

In minor keys, the minor form of $\hat{6}$ (that is, $\hat{6}$ as it appears in the natural minor, harmonic minor, or descending melodic minor scales) is a tendency tone that pulls strongly *down* toward $\hat{5}$. The minor form of $\hat{6}$ should not move up to the leading tone, since that would create a melodic **augmented second**, which sounds too exotic for basic four-part harmony. As with other tendency tones, avoid doubling the minor form of $\hat{6}$.

14.22

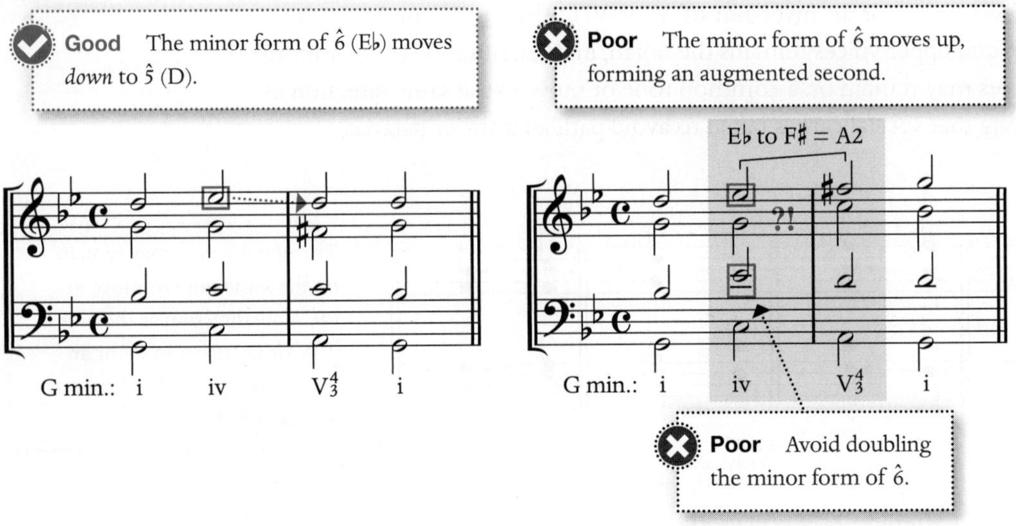
Good The minor form of $\hat{6}$ (E♭) moves *down* to $\hat{5}$ (D).
Poor The minor form of $\hat{6}$ moves up, forming an augmented second.
E♭ to F♯ = A2
?!
G min.: i iv V$^4_3$ i
G min.: i iv V$^4_3$ i
Poor Avoid doubling the minor form of $\hat{6}$.

14.23 Schubert, "Lied," D. 373

G min.: i vii^{o6} i^6 iv V i

It is also possible to raise $\hat{6}$ in minor keys, as in the ascending melodic minor scale, thereby changing the quality of iv, ii^{o6}, or ii$^{ø6}_{5}$ to IV, ii^6, or ii$^6_5$. Raised $\hat{6}$ moves up to the leading tone without creating an augmented second.

14.24 J. S. Bach, Chorale 111

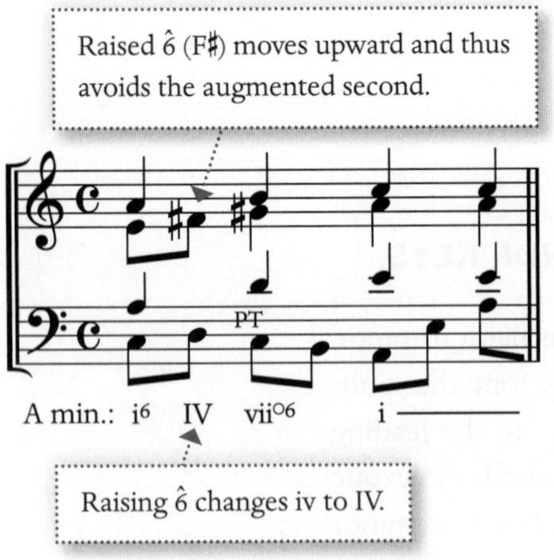
Raised $\hat{6}$ (F♯) moves upward and thus avoids the augmented second.
PT
A min.: i^6 IV vii^{o6} i
Raising $\hat{6}$ changes iv to IV.

review and interact

POINTS FOR REVIEW

- **IV, ii^6, and ii$^6_5$ (and iv, ii^{o6}, and ii$^{ø6}_5$ in minor keys) are Subdominant harmonies that share the same bass tone and most of the same notes. These chords function similarly.**
- **IV, ii^6, and ii$^6_5$ lead toward Dominant harmonies such as V or V^7 (in root position or inversion) or vii^{o6}.**
- **IV, ii^6, and ii$^6_5$ may not follow a Dominant harmony.**
- **Double the bass (= root, $\hat{4}$) of IV; double either the bass (= third of chord, $\hat{4}$) or root ($\hat{2}$) of ii^6.**
- **In IV–V progressions (or in ii^6–V progressions in which the bass of ii^6 is doubled), the upper voices of IV or ii^6 move down to the nearest note of the V triad.**
- **IV may move to ii^6.**
- **The seventh of ii$^6_5$ is a chordal dissonance that should be prepared by common tone and resolve down by step.**
- **In minor keys, the minor form of $\hat{6}$ should move down, not up to the leading tone (which would create an augmented second). If $\hat{6}$ is raised in minor, however, it may move up to the leading tone.**

TEST YOURSELF

1. Which of the following chord progressions are stylistically correct in standard four-part harmony?

   a. I–V–I
   b. I–IV–V–I^6
   c. I–ii^6–vii^{o6}–I
   d. I–V^6–ii$^6_5$–I
   e. I–IV–V–ii^6–I
   f. I^6–ii$^6_5$–V$^4_2$–I^6
   g. I–vii^{o6}–IV–I
   h. I–IV–ii^6–V^7–I
   i. I–IV–ii^6–V–V^6–I–V–I

2. Below are the Roman numerals of chords and their qualities in major keys. What are the analogous chords and qualities in minor keys (using the notes in the natural minor scale)?

major key	**minor key**
I, quality = major	i, quality = minor
a. IV, quality = major	_____, quality = ______________
b. ii^6, quality = minor	_____, quality = ______________
c. ii$^6_5$, quality = minor 7th	_____, quality = ______________

3. What notes of the chord (root, third, or fifth) and scale degrees are best to double in the following triads? For some of these there is more than one answer.

   a. I
   b. I^6
   c. V
   d. V^6
   e. IV
   f. ii^6

4. Below are a series of ii$^6_5$ chords and V^7 chords in various keys. Identify the note and scale degree of the chordal seventh in each:

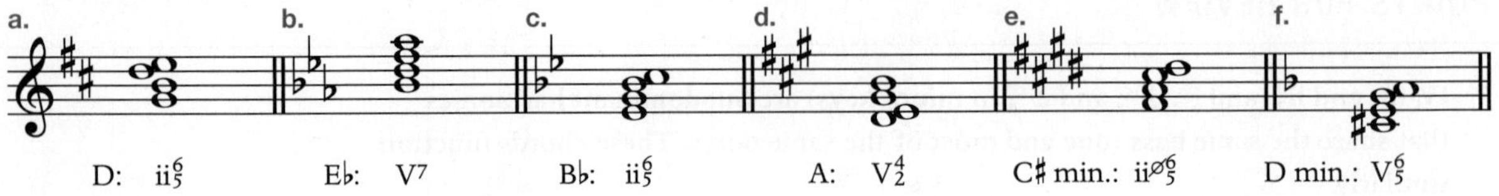

5. Which of the following statements are true in standard four-part harmony?
   a. A chordal seventh must resolve down by step.
   b. $\hat{4}$ must resolve down by step.
   c. $\hat{4}$ must resolve down by step if it is the seventh of V^7.
   d. $\hat{1}$ must resolve down by step if it is the seventh of ii$^6_5$.

6. Identify the errors in the following fragments:

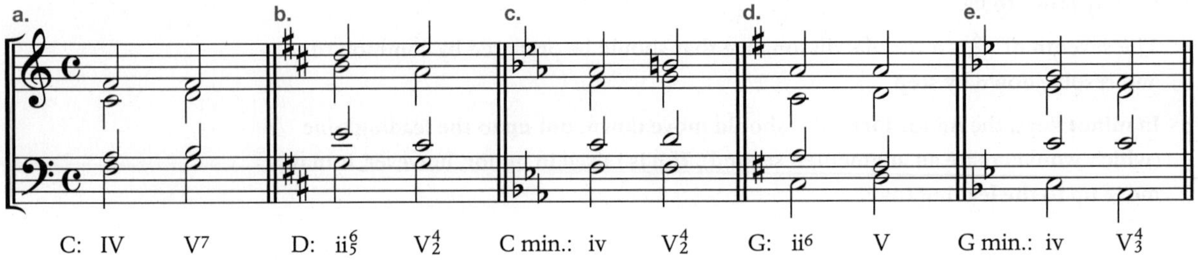

Know It? Show It!

Focus by working through the tutorials on:

- IV–V and ii^6–V
- Writing ii$^6_5$–V
- Harmonizing with Subdominant chords

Learn with inQuizitive.

Apply what you've learned to complete the assignments:

- Realizing Roman Numerals
- Realizing Figured Bass
- Harmonizing Melodies
- Composition
- Analysis

chapter

15 Embellishing V: Cadential $^6_4$

The cadential $^6_4$ consists of accented embellishing tones that resolve down by step to the upper notes of a root-position V chord.

EMBELLISHING V

Root-position dominant chords frequently are embellished by the intervals of a sixth and fourth above $\hat{5}$ in the bass. These embellishing tones are metrically accented and they delay the arrival of the dominant chord's third and fifth. The sonority that embellishes V is known as a **cadential $^6_4$**. Notice that the scale degrees of the cadential $^6_4$ ($\hat{5}$, $\hat{1}$, and $\hat{3}$) are the same as those of the tonic triad, but here are used to embellish V: this is a **D**ominant harmony, not a **T**onic harmony.

15.1

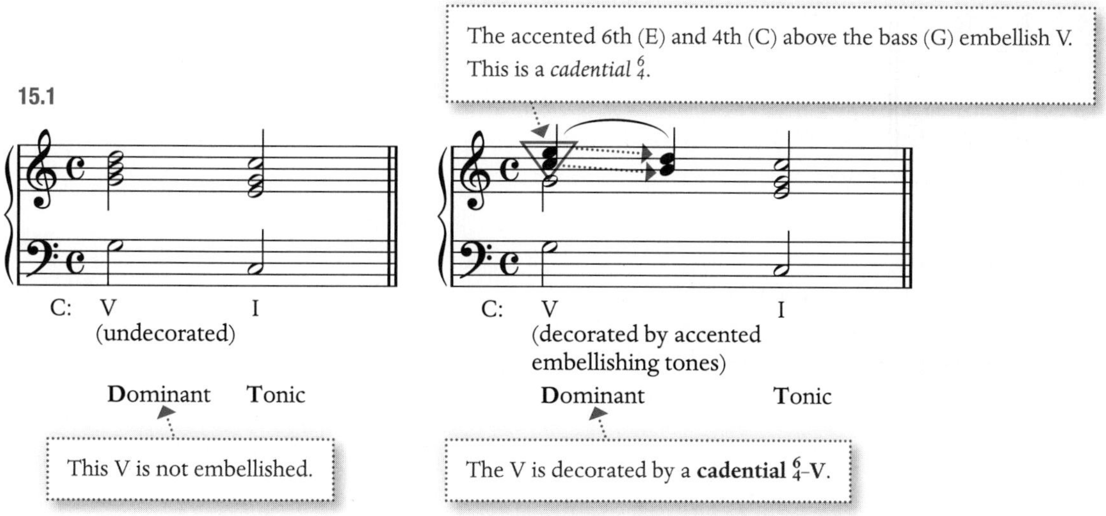

The accented 6th (E) and 4th (C) above the bass (G) embellish V. This is a *cadential* $^6_4$.
C: V I
(undecorated)
Dominant Tonic
This V is not embellished.
C: V I
(decorated by accented embellishing tones)
Dominant Tonic
The V is decorated by a **cadential** $^6_4$–**V**.

15.2

Cadential $^6_4$ chords are usually formed by suspensions or accented passing tones that embellish V.

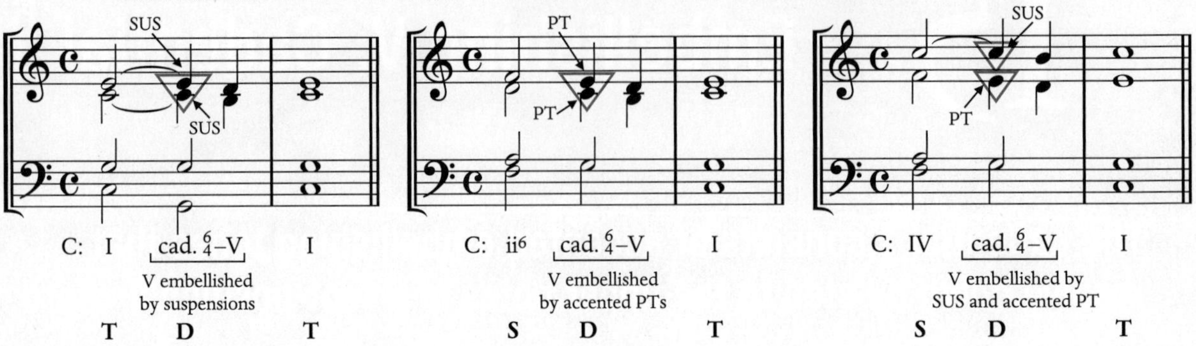

The cadential $^6_4$ should be directly followed by *root-position* V or V7 (not by an inversion of V or V7).

15.3

The cadential $^6_4$ should be followed directly by a *root-position* V or V7.

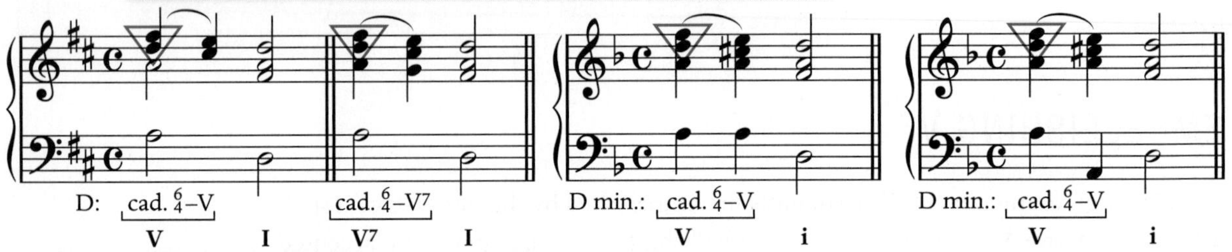

Good When a cadential $^6_4$ moves to root-position V or V7, the bass may be sustained . . .

. . . or repeated . . .

. . . or leap an octave.

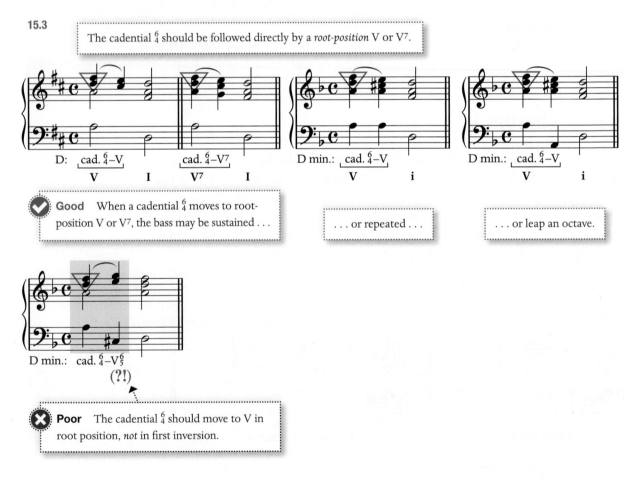

Poor The cadential $^6_4$ should move to V in root position, *not* in first inversion.

15.4 Carulli, Larghetto for Guitar

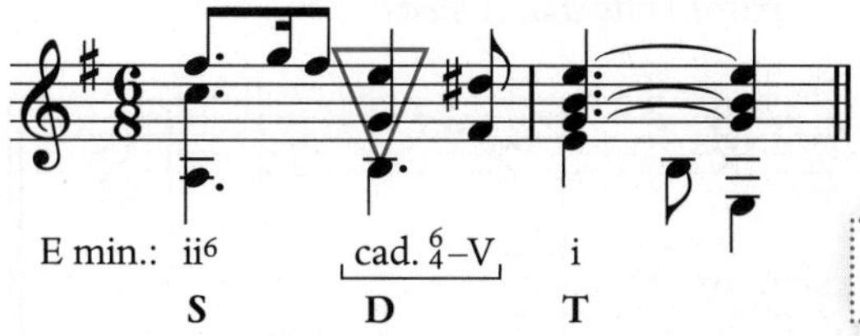

The cadential $^6_4$ is immediately followed by a *root-position* V or V7.

15.5 Excerpt from *American Psalmody*

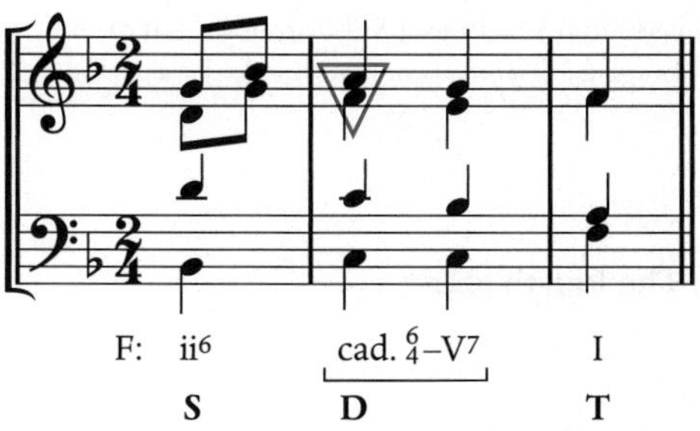

15.6 Foster, "Annie, my own love"

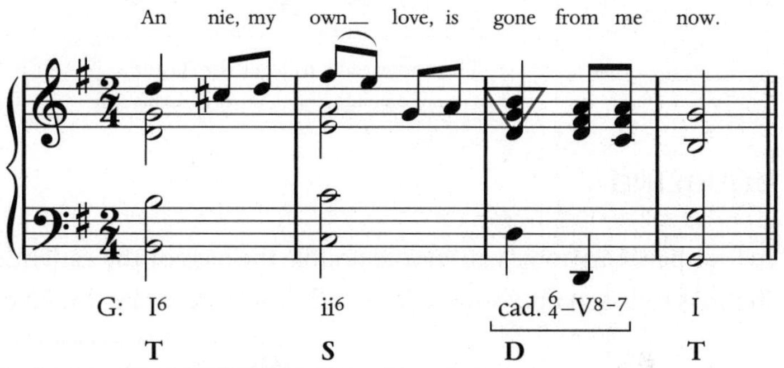

The cadential $^6_4$ is immediately followed by a *root-position* V or V7.

HARMONIC PROGRESSION AND VOICE LEADING

A cadential $^6_4$ may be preceded by any **T**onic or **S**ubdominant chord. Since a cadential $^6_4$ delays the arrival of V, however, it may *not* follow a **D**ominant harmony, such as V, V7, or vii°6.

15.7

Good A cadential $^6_4$ may follow a **T**onic or **S**ubdominant harmony.

Poor A cadential $^6_4$ may *not* follow a **D**ominant harmony.

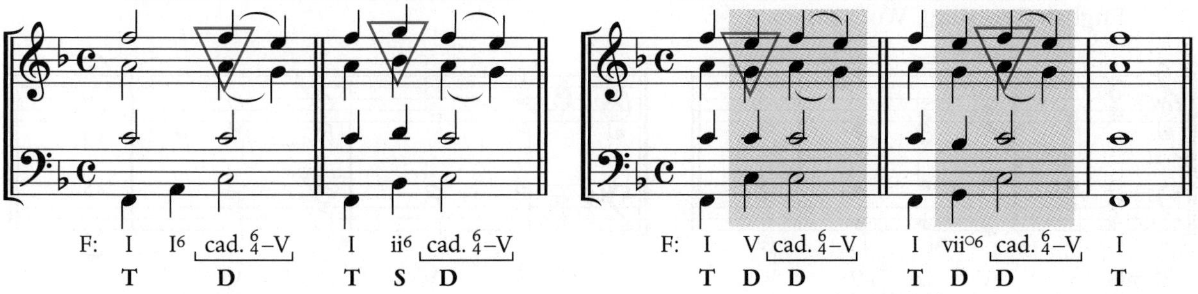

15.8 Beethoven, Piano Sonata in E, op. 14, no. 1, II ➔

E min.: i cad. $^6_4$–V7 i

T D T

The cadential $^6_4$ follows the Tonic.

15.9 Purcell, "Dido's Lament," from *Dido and Aeneas* ➔

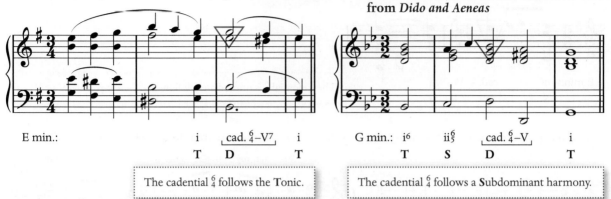

G min.: i6 ii$^6_5$ cad. $^6_4$–V i

T S D T

The cadential $^6_4$ follows a **S**ubdominant harmony.

DOUBLING

In four-part harmony, you should double the bass of the cadential $^6_4$. The fourth above the bass is dissonant with the bass and should never be doubled.

15.10

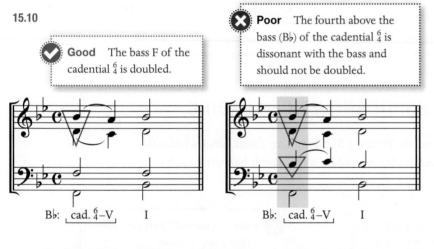

Good The bass F of the cadential $^6_4$ is doubled.

B♭: cad. $^6_4$–V I

Poor The fourth above the bass (B♭) of the cadential $^6_4$ is dissonant with the bass and should not be doubled.

B♭: cad. $^6_4$–V I

15.11 Brahms, "Der englische Gruß" (The English Greeting), WoO 32, no. 8 ➔

dar - in - nen sie rang.

D min.: i iv cad. $^6_4$–V7 i

The bass (A) is doubled in the cadential $^6_4$.

Translation: . . . as she struggled [in prayer].

15.12 R. Schumann, "Ein Choral" (A Chorale) ➔

G: I IV6 cad. $^6_4$ – V8 - 7 I

The bass (D) is doubled in the cadential $^6_4$.

RESOLVING THE CADENTIAL $^6_4$

The fourth of the cadential $^6_4$ is a dissonance and should resolve down by step. The sixth, though also an embellishment, does not form a dissonance, and thus may move in either direction—though it, too, usually moves downward.

15.13

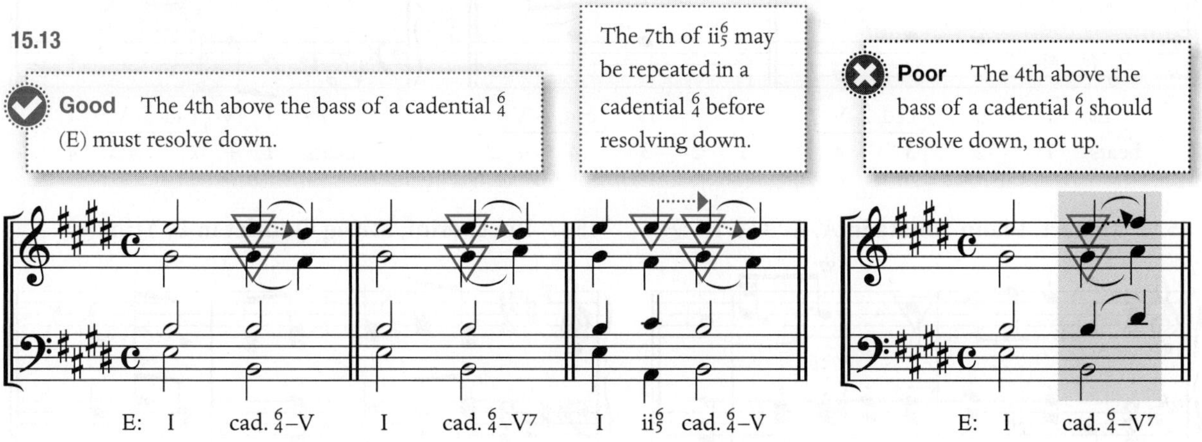
Good The 4th above the bass of a cadential $^6_4$ (E) must resolve down.
The 7th of ii^6_5 may be repeated in a cadential $^6_4$ before resolving down.
Poor The 4th above the bass of a cadential $^6_4$ should resolve down, not up.
E: I cad. $^6_4$–V I cad. $^6_4$–V^7 I ii^6_5 cad. $^6_4$–V
E: I cad. $^6_4$–V^7

15.14 Haydn, String Quartet, op. 33, no. 4, II

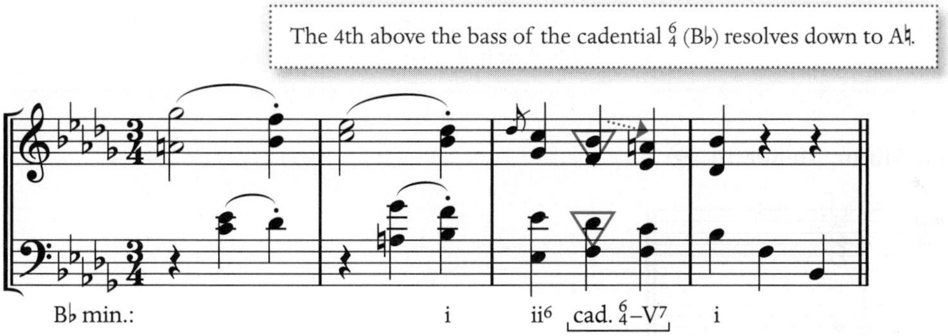
The 4th above the bass of the cadential $^6_4$ (B♭) resolves down to A♮.
B♭ min.: i ii^6 cad. $^6_4$–V^7 i

RHYTHMIC POSITION

Since it derives from suspensions or other accented embellishing tones that decorate a **D**ominant harmony, a cadential $^6_4$ must appear on a *stronger* beat (or stronger part of the beat) than the V or V^7 to which it resolves.

15.15

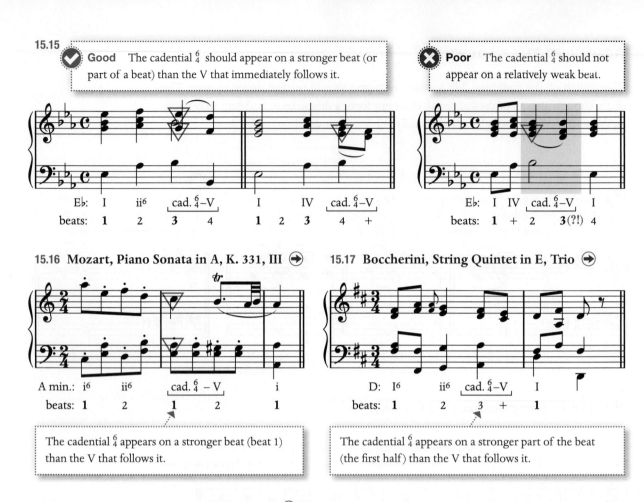

Good The cadential $^6_4$ should appear on a stronger beat (or part of a beat) than the V that immediately follows it.

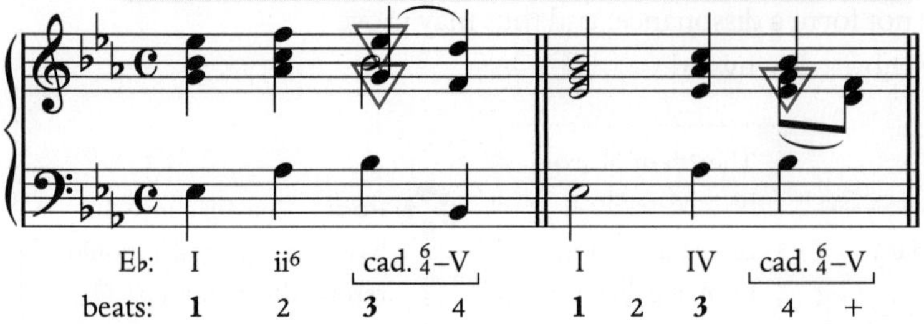

Poor The cadential $^6_4$ should not appear on a relatively weak beat.

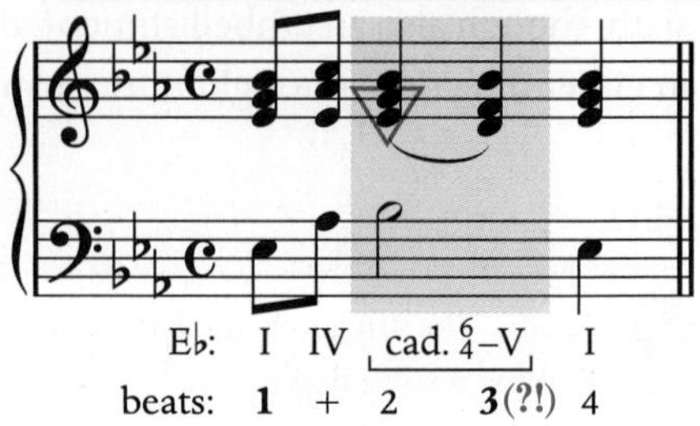

15.16 Mozart, Piano Sonata in A, K. 331, III

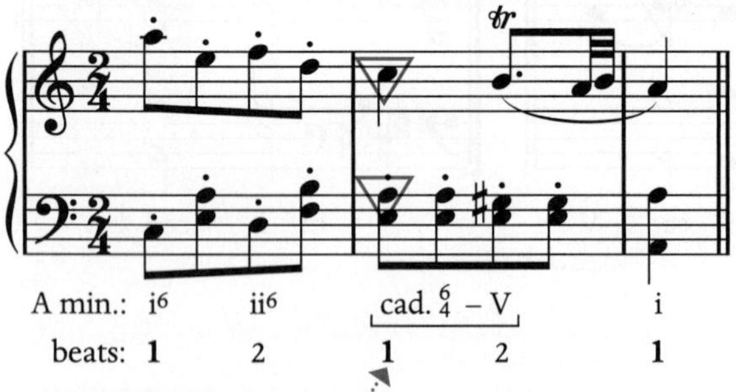

The cadential $^6_4$ appears on a stronger beat (beat 1) than the V that follows it.

15.17 Boccherini, String Quintet in E, Trio

The cadential $^6_4$ appears on a stronger part of the beat (the first half) than the V that follows it.

15.18 Handel, Suite in D Minor, Menuetto

Good In $^3_4$ time, beat 2 is sometimes stronger than beat 3, especially if a cadential $^6_4$ appears on beat 2.

LABELING THE CADENTIAL $^6_4$

FIGURED BASS

In figured bass, a dominant harmony embellished by a cadential $^6_4$ is indicated with two sets of figures ($^{6-5}_{4-3}$) below a single bass tone (or one that repeats or leaps an octave). If the third of V needs to be raised by a half step (as is the case in minor keys), then write the accidental by itself (the 3 is implied).

15.19

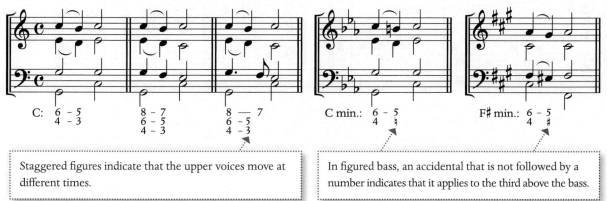

Staggered figures indicate that the upper voices move at different times.

In figured bass, an accidental that is not followed by a number indicates that it applies to the third above the bass.

ROMAN NUMERALS

Since it embellishes an underlying V chord, the cadential $^6_4$ generally is not labeled with its own Roman numeral. Rather, a **D**ominant harmony decorated by a cadential $^6_4$ is labeled with V followed by figured bass symbols indicating the intervals above the bass. Thus cadential $^6_4$-V is labeled as V^{6-5}_{4-3}, and cadential $^6_4$-V^7 is labeled as $V^{8-7}_{\substack{6-5\\4-3}}$. The "$^6_4$" within the label V^{6-5}_{4-3} does *not* refer to a second inversion of a V triad (an uncommon chord with $\hat{2}$ in the bass). Instead, these figures indicate that a sixth and fourth move to a fifth and third above $\hat{5}$ in the bass.

15.20

***Task*: Write V^{6-5}_{4-3} in F major.**

1. Find $\hat{5}$; this note should be in the bass and be doubled: *in the key of F, $\hat{5}$ = C.*
2. Then find the intervals of a sixth and a fourth above $\hat{5}$: *6th above $\hat{5}$ = A; 4th above $\hat{5}$ = F.*
3. 6 and 4 above the bass should move down to 5 and 3 above the bass, while the bass remains on $\hat{5}$: *A and F should move to E and G, respectively, while the bass remains on C.*

Some possible solutions:

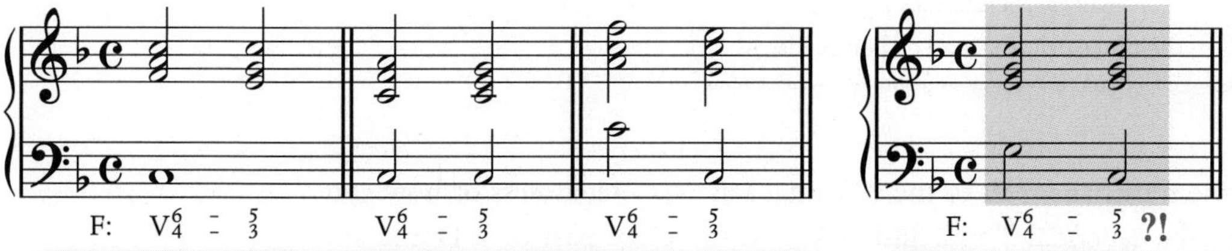

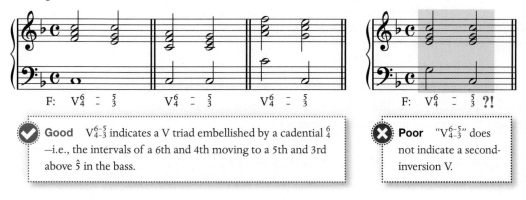

Good V^{6-5}_{4-3} indicates a V triad embellished by a cadential $^6_4$ —i.e., the intervals of a 6th and 4th moving to a 5th and 3rd above $\hat{5}$ in the bass.

Poor "V^{6-5}_{4-3}" does not indicate a second-inversion V.

15.21 Mozart, Piano Sonata in C, K. 330, III ➔

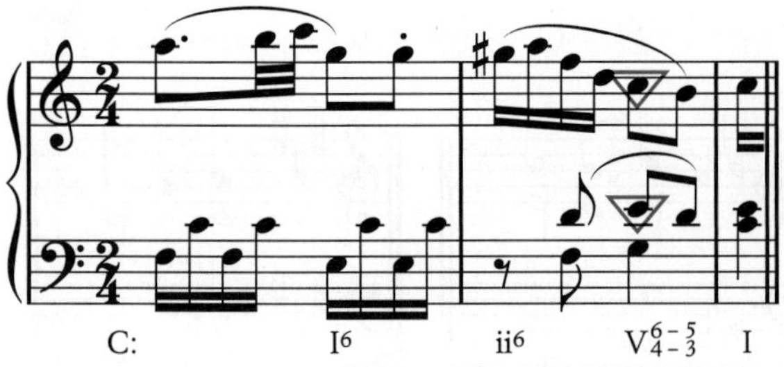

Cadential $^6_4$–V is labeled V^{6-5}_{4-3}.

15.22 Mozart, String Quartet in E♭, K. 171, II ➔

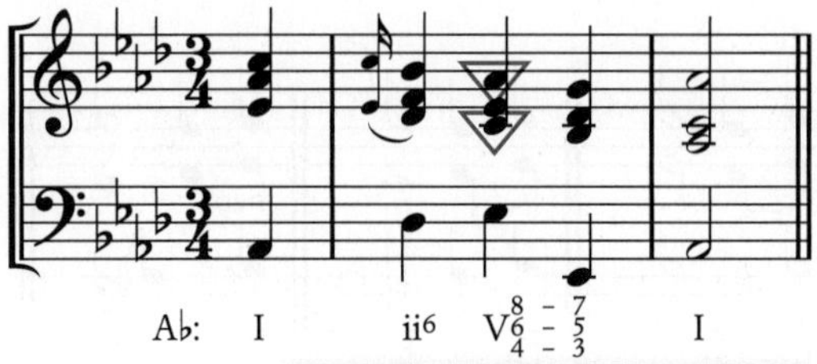

Cadential $^6_4$–V7 is labeled $V^{8-7}_{\substack{6-5\\4-3}}$.

I^6_4

Notice that the cadential $^6_4$ uses the notes of a tonic triad in second inversion—that is, I^6_4. Thus you can also spell a cadential $^6_4$ by thinking of a tonic triad in second inversion.

15.23

***Task*: Determine the notes in V^{6-5}_{4-3} in F major, thinking of it as a tonic triad in second inversion.**

1. Find the notes of I^6_4, and double the bass: *in the key of F, I^6_4 = C-F-A, and the bass note C should be doubled.*
2. The notes of I^6_4 should move to the notes of V: *C-F-A (I^6_4) should move to C-E-G (V).*

Some possible solutions:

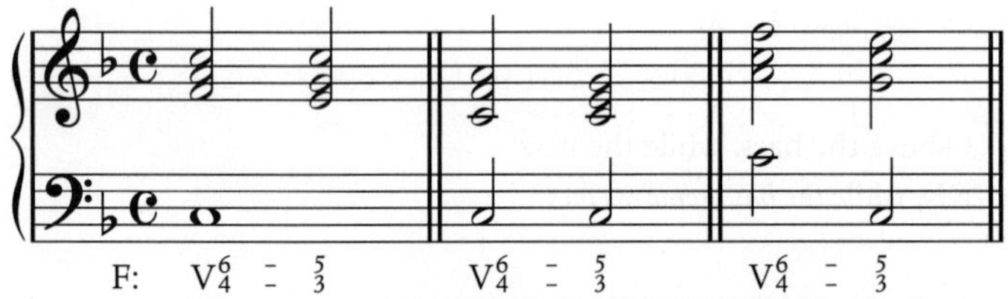

With V^{6-5}_{4-3}, the notes of an accented I^6_4 embellish V.

This method of determining the notes of V^{6-5}_{4-3} in F major yields the same results as the method shown in 15.20.

Indeed, some musicians refer to the cadential $^6_4$ as "I^6_4." Regardless of how you label it, however, the cadential $^6_4$ embellishes V. It is therefore part of a **Dominant** harmony, unlike I and I6, which are always **Tonic** harmonies.

15.24

TONIC CHORD (I OR I^6)	CADENTIAL $^6_4$ (SAME NOTES AS I OR I^6, BUT WITH THE FIFTH IN THE BASS)
Very stable chord.	Very *unstable*, dissonant chord.
Usually follows dominant chord.	*Never* follows a dominant chord.
May be followed by any chord.	Must be followed by V or V^7.
Usually its root is doubled (in I^6, any note may be doubled).	Its root (the note that lies a fourth above the bass) is a dissonance that must *never* be doubled.
May appear on any beat of a measure.	Must appear on a relatively stronger beat than the V or V^7 that follows it.

THE CADENTIAL $^6_4$ WITHIN PHRASES

The cadential $^6_4$ often embellishes V or V^7, which appears as part of a half cadence or authentic cadence.

15.25 Mozart, Sonata for Piano in A, K. 331, I

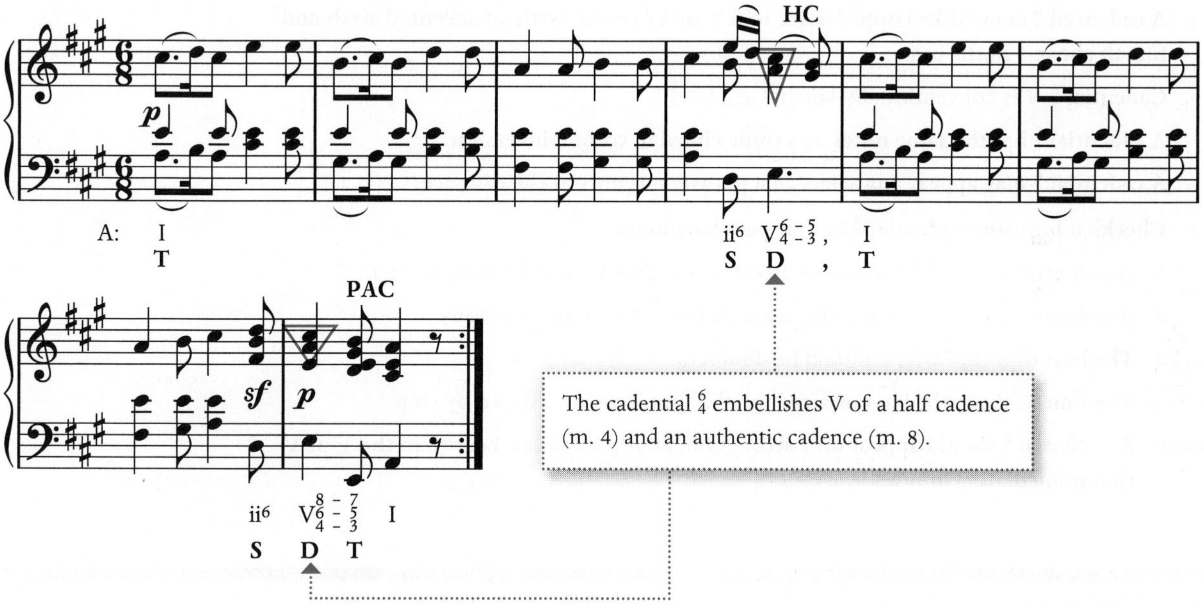

However, the cadential $^6_4$ is not restricted to appearing at cadences: despite its name, a cadential $^6_4$ may appear anywhere within a phrase.

15.26 Schubert, "Die liebe Farbe" (The Favorite Color)

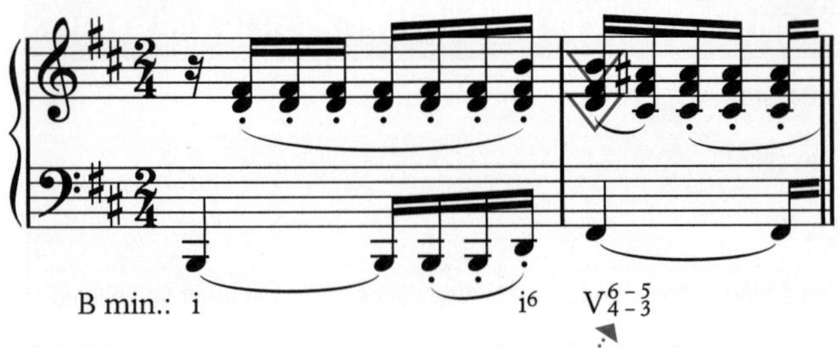

15.27 J. S. Bach, Prelude in F Minor, WTC II

A cadential $^6_4$ may decorate a non-cadential dominant harmony that appears in the beginning or the middle of a phrase.

For more on the resolution of the cadential $^6_4$, see A Closer Look.

review and interact

POINTS FOR REVIEW

- **A cadential $^6_4$ embellishes upper notes of a V or V7 chord, with an accented sixth and fourth above $\hat{5}$ in the bass.**
- **Cadential $^6_4$-V is conventionally labeled as "V^{6-5}_{4-3}."**
- **A cadential $^6_4$ has the same notes as a tonic chord in second inversion.**
- **A cadential $^6_4$ may appear anywhere in a phrase, not only at the cadence.**
- **Checklist for using cadential $^6_4$ in four-part harmony:**
  1. **A cadential $^6_4$ should be followed directly by either V or V7 in *root position*.**
  2. **A cadential $^6_4$ can follow any chord *except* for a Dominant harmony.**
  3. **The bass of a cadential $^6_4$ should be doubled.**
  4. **The fourth above the bass of a cadential $^6_4$ should resolve down by step.**
  5. **A cadential $^6_4$ should appear on a stronger beat or part of the beat than the V or V7 that immediately follows it.**

TEST YOURSELF

1. Identify the following scale degrees and intervals above the bass.
   a. In G major, $\hat{5}$ is D. What notes are a sixth and fourth above? _____ and _____.
   b. In E♭ major, $\hat{5}$ is _____. A sixth and fourth above this are _____ and _____.
   c. In D minor, $\hat{5}$ is _____. A sixth and fourth above this are _____ and _____.
   d. In E minor, $\hat{5}$ is _____. A sixth and fourth above this are _____ and _____.

2. Spell a cadential $^6_4$, starting with the bass, in the following keys.

   a. F major
   b. B major
   c. G minor
   d. A minor

3. Complete the progressions by filling in the missing note(s).

4. Which of the excerpts use cadential $^6_4$–V (i.e., V$^{6-5}_{4-3}$) incorrectly? Identify the errors.

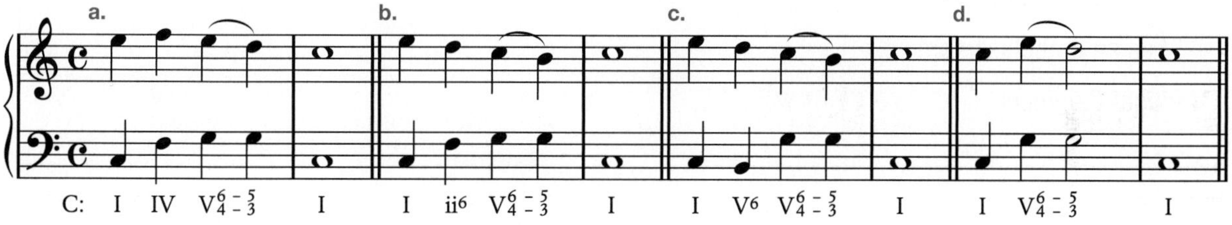

Know It? Show It!

Focus by working through the tutorials on:

- Recognizing cadential $^6_4$ chords
- Writing cadential $^6_4$ chords

Learn with inQuizitive.

Apply what you've learned to complete the assignments:

- Realizing Roman Numerals
- Realizing Figured Bass
- Harmonizing Melodies
- Composition
- Analysis

chapter

16 Leading to the Tonic: IV

IV may embellish the tonic harmony by appearing between two I chords.

Harmonic Progression

IV as an Embellishment

Plagal Cadence

HARMONIC PROGRESSION

IV typically progresses to V or a similar **D**ominant harmony (see Chapter 13). However, IV can also be followed directly by I or I6. When IV is sandwiched between two tonic chords, it forms a **T**onic-**S**ubdominant-**T**onic pattern. Since IV lacks a leading tone, IV–I motion tends to confirm the tonic less strongly than V–I.

16.1

I–IV–I progressions are common.

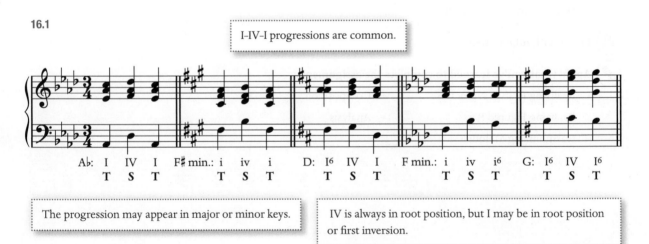

The progression may appear in major or minor keys.

IV is always in root position, but I may be in root position or first inversion.

16.2 Chopin, Mazurka in B♭, op. 17, no. 1

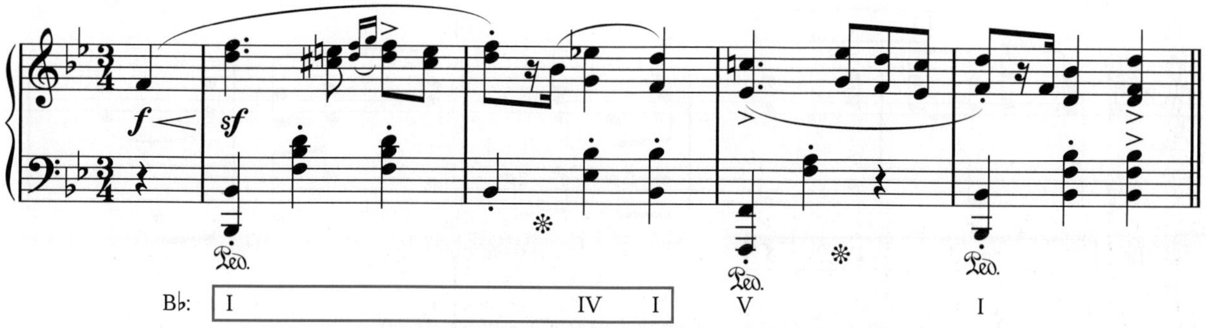

In each example, root-position IV comes from and returns to I or I6.

16.3 Handel, Suite in E, Air, HWV 430

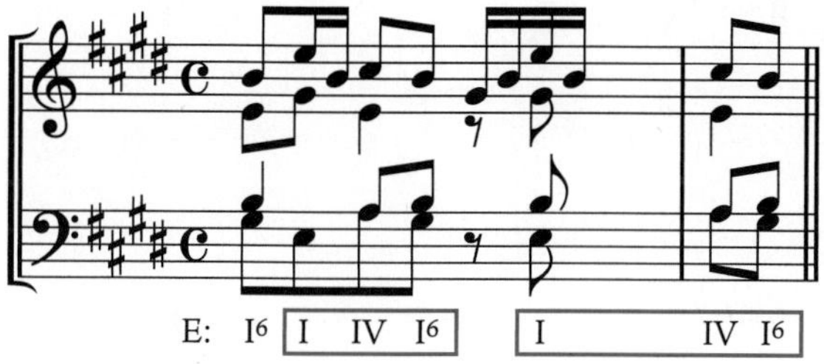

16.4 Tchaikovsky, "The Witch"

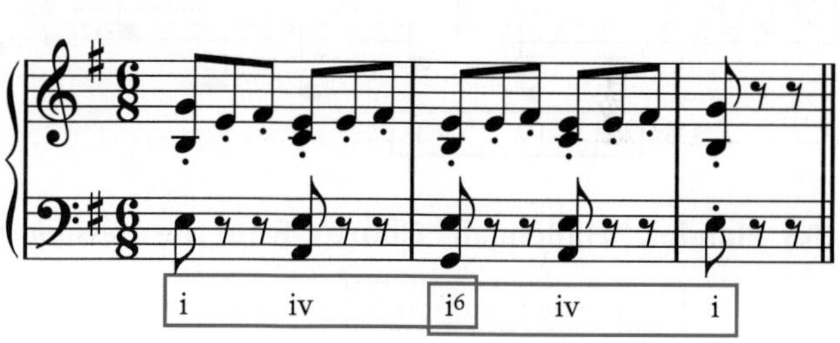

IV AS AN EMBELLISHMENT

Typically, in the progression I-IV-I, one upper voice sustains $\hat{1}$, while the others employ neighboring motion, as the I-IV-I progression embellishes tonic harmony.

16.5

Much as its upper voices embellish notes of the tonic triad with sustained tones or neighbor motions . . .

. . . so I-IV-I often embellishes the tonic harmony.

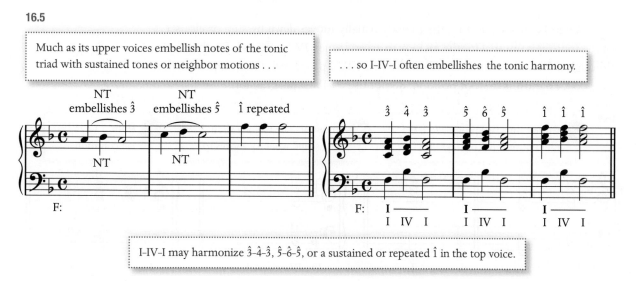

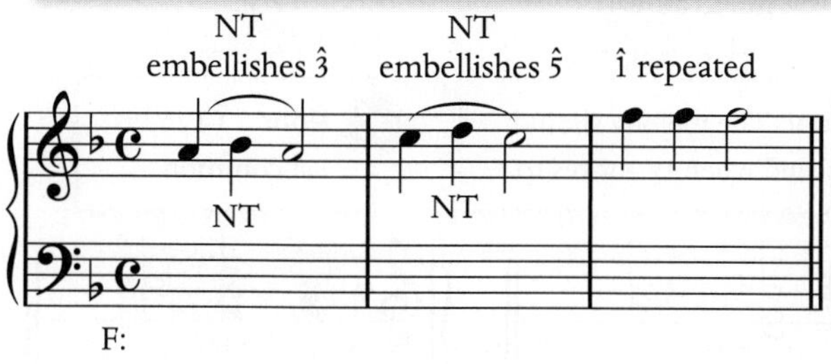

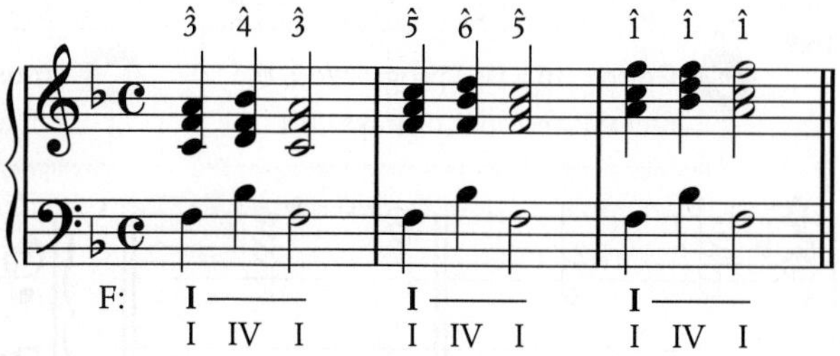

I-IV-I may harmonize $\hat{3}$-$\hat{4}$-$\hat{3}$, $\hat{5}$-$\hat{6}$-$\hat{5}$, or a sustained or repeated $\hat{1}$ in the top voice.

16.6 Brahms, *Variations on a Theme by Haydn*

16.7 Beethoven, Piano Sonata in F Minor ("Appassionata"), op. 57, II

16.8 Handel, "Hallelujah" Chorus, from the *Messiah*

When IV progresses to I, the melody usually moves *down* by step or else stays on the tonic; it is unusual for the melody to ascend when IV moves to I. Furthermore, although either of the tonic chords within the I–IV–I progression may appear in first inversion, IV must be in root position: do not use a I–IV⁶–I progression.

16.9

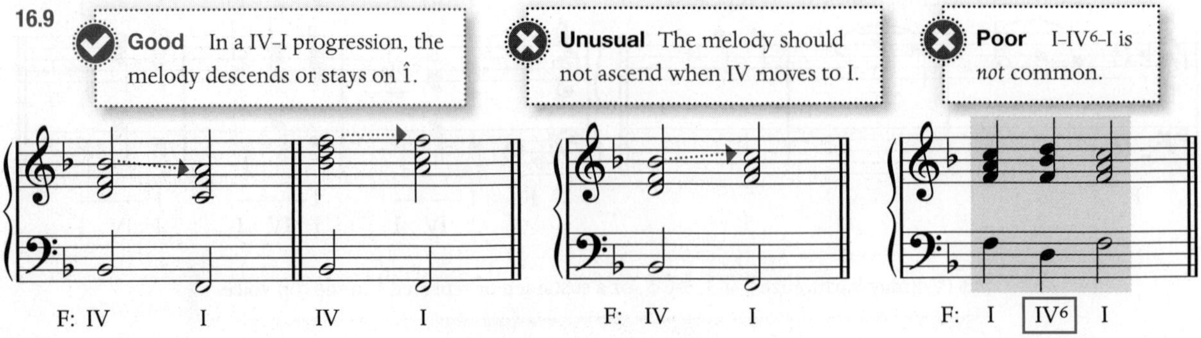

PLAGAL CADENCE

IV–I motion typically appears toward the beginning of a phrase as it embellishes the tonic harmony. However, IV–I sometimes appears immediately after a strong perfect authentic cadence, as though to provide added confirmation of the phrase's ending. IV–I at the end of a phrase forms a **plagal cadence**.

16.10 ***Church of Ireland Hymnal*****, Hymn 82**

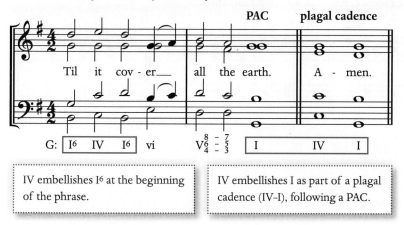

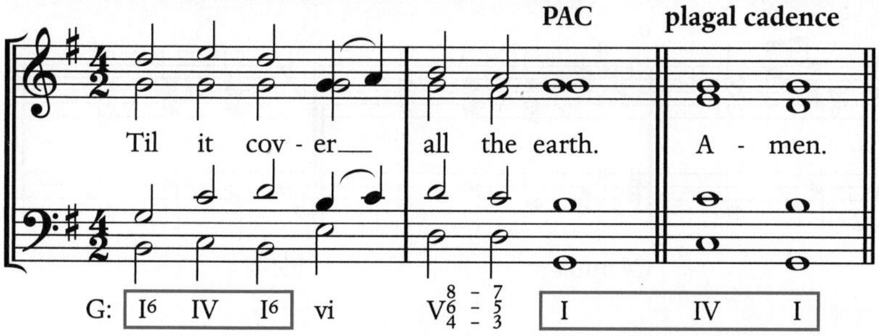

IV embellishes I6 at the beginning of the phrase.

IV embellishes I as part of a plagal cadence (IV–I), following a PAC.

For more on embellishing the tonic with IV, see A Closer Look.

review and interact

POINTS FOR REVIEW

- **IV may appear between two tonic chords (I or I6).**
- **I–IV–I often supports $\hat{3}$-$\hat{4}$-$\hat{3}$, $\hat{5}$-$\hat{6}$-$\hat{5}$, or $\hat{1}$-$\hat{1}$-$\hat{1}$ in the upper voice, embellishing the tonic harmony. When IV moves to I, the upper voices should descend.**
- **Avoid the progression I–IV6–I.**
- **A IV–I progression that appears at the end of a phrase (usually following a perfect authentic cadence) forms a *plagal cadence.***

TEST YOURSELF

1. Which of these progressions commonly occur?

   a. I–IV–I b. I–IV–I6 c. I6–IV–I d. I–IV6–I e. I6–IV–I6

2. What are scale degrees of the three-note melodic patterns that often are harmonized with I–IV–I?

3. Which of these melodies (all in major keys) could be harmonized with I-IV-I?

4. What are the Roman numerals of the following chord progressions? If they appeared at the very end of a phrase, what type of cadence would be formed by each: a perfect authentic cadence, imperfect authentic cadence, half cadence, or plagal cadence?

Know It? Show It!

Focus by working through the tutorials on:

- Writing I-IV-I
- Plagal cadence

Learn with inQuizitive.

Apply what you've learned to complete the assignments:

- Realizing Roman Numerals
- Realizing Figured Bass
- Harmonizing Melodies
- Composition
- Analysis

chapter

17 The Leading-Tone Seventh Chord: vii°7 and viiø7

Leading-tone seventh chords (vii°7, viiø7, and their inversions) function as Dominants, leading to Tonic (I and I6).

vii°7

HARMONIC PROGRESSIONS

The vii°7 is a diminished seventh chord whose root is the leading tone. Like V7, with which it shares three notes, vii°7 functions as a **D**ominant. However, since it contains two tritones (augmented fourths or diminished fifths), vii°7 sounds somewhat more dissonant than V7, and it always requires an accidental.

17.1

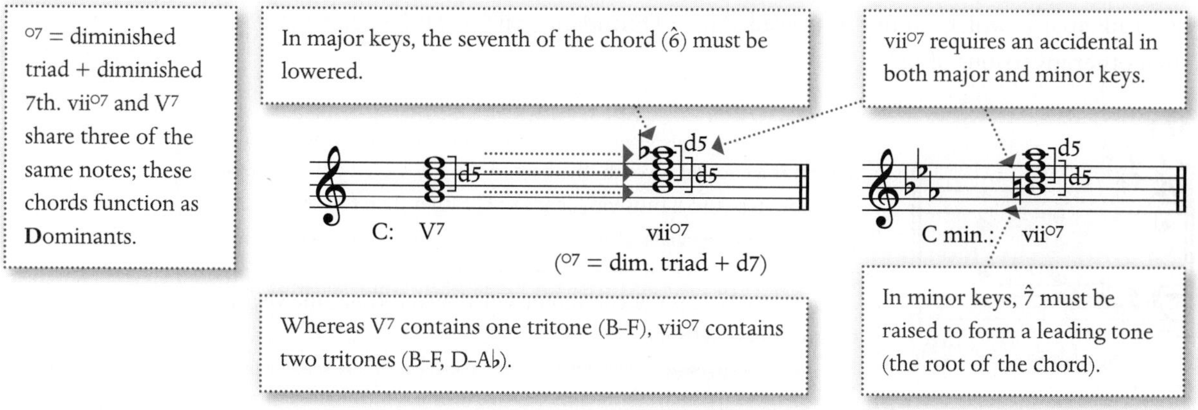

°7 = diminished triad + diminished 7th. vii°7 and V7 share three of the same notes; these chords function as **D**ominants.
In major keys, the seventh of the chord ($\hat{6}$) must be lowered.
vii°7 requires an accidental in both major and minor keys.
d5
d5
d5
d5
d5
C: V7
vii°7
(°7 = dim. triad + d7)
C min.: vii°7
Whereas V7 contains one tritone (B–F), vii°7 contains two tritones (B–F, D–A♭).
In minor keys, $\hat{7}$ must be raised to form a leading tone (the root of the chord).

Unlike the vii° triad, which is *not* used in root position, $\text{vii}^{\circ 7}$ may appear in root position or inversion. In each case, it is treated like the inversion of V^7 that has the same bass tone, leading to either I or I^6.

17.2

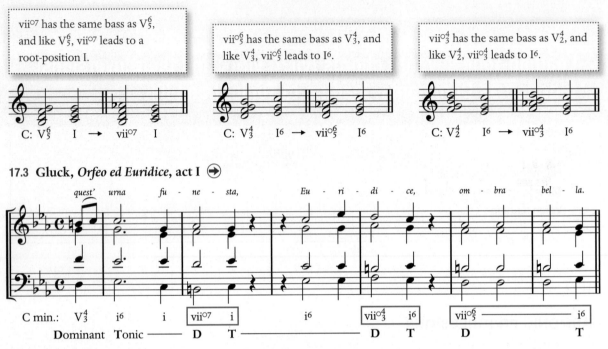

$\text{vii}^{\circ 7}$ has the same bass as V^6_5, and like V^6_5, $\text{vii}^{\circ 7}$ leads to a root-position I.

$\text{vii}^{\circ 6}_5$ has the same bass as V^4_3, and like V^4_3, $\text{vii}^{\circ 6}_5$ leads to I^6.

$\text{vii}^{\circ 4}_3$ has the same bass as V^4_2, and like V^4_2, $\text{vii}^{\circ 4}_3$ leads to I^6.

17.3 Gluck, *Orfeo ed Euridice*, act I

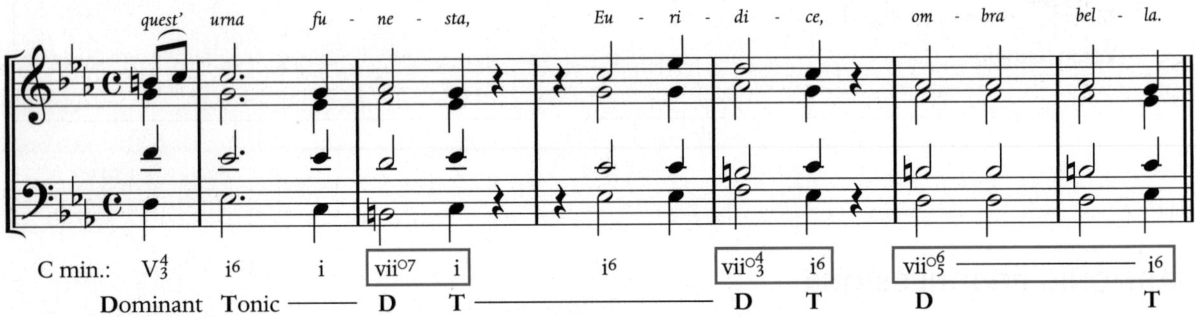

Translation: [You hover around] this funeral urn, Eurydice, sweet spirit.

The $\text{vii}^{\circ 4}_2$ is the only inversion of $\text{vii}^{\circ 7}$ that does not share a bass note with an inversion of V^7, and it is the only one that does not lead to I or I^6. Since its bass is the chordal seventh—which must resolve down by step—$\text{vii}^{\circ 4}_2$ instead leads to a tonic triad in second inversion. However, since a I chord in second inversion usually functions as a cadential $^6_4$ (which cannot be preceded by a **Dominant**), $\text{vii}^{\circ 4}_2$ is far less common than other inversions of $\text{vii}^{\circ 7}$.

17.4

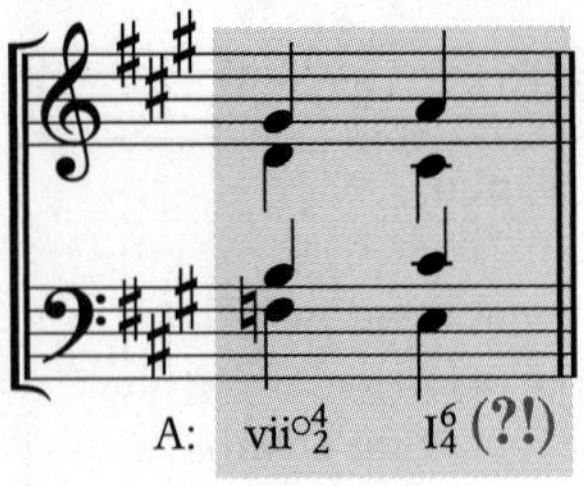

Since it is a chordal seventh, the bass of $\text{vii}^{\circ 4}_2$ (lowered $\hat{6}$) must resolve down by step (to $\hat{5}$); thus $\text{vii}^{\circ 4}_2$ leads to I^6_4 rather than to I or I^6 . . .

. . . but since I^6_4 does not commonly function as a Tonic, the $\text{vii}^{\circ 4}_2$–I^6_4 progression is unusual.

MOVING BETWEEN vii$^{\circ 7}$ AND V^7

The vii$^{\circ 7}$ and all of its inversions—including vii$^{\circ 4}_{2}$ —may follow or be followed by an inversion of V^7 before resolving to I. Since vii$^{\circ 7}$ and V^7 share three notes, only one note of the chord needs to change when moving between them. Consequently, motions between vii$^{\circ 7}$ and V^7 usually result from neighbor motion in one of the voices.

17.5

vii$^{\circ 7}$ may move to V^7, and vice versa.

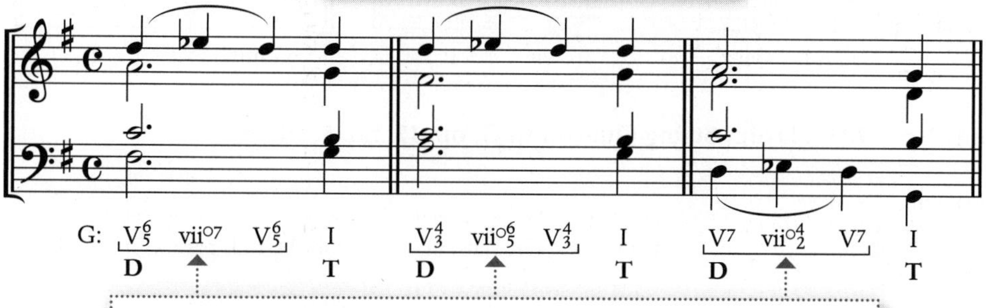

vii$^{\circ 7}$ results from embellishing a dominant seventh chord with neighbor motion in one of the voices.

17.6 Beethoven, String Quartet in C, op. 59, no. 3, I

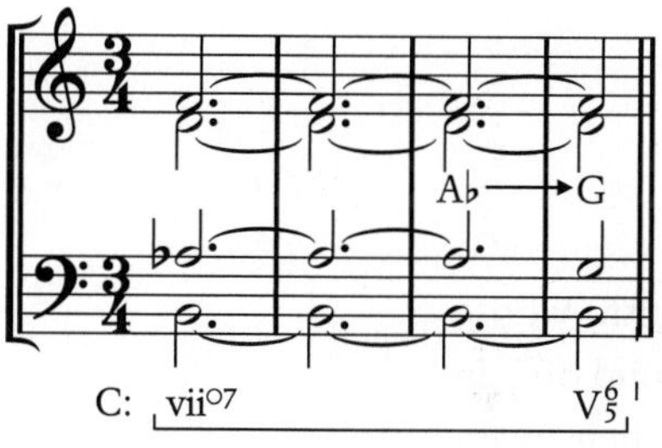

17.7 Mozart, Piano Sonata in C Minor, K. 457, I

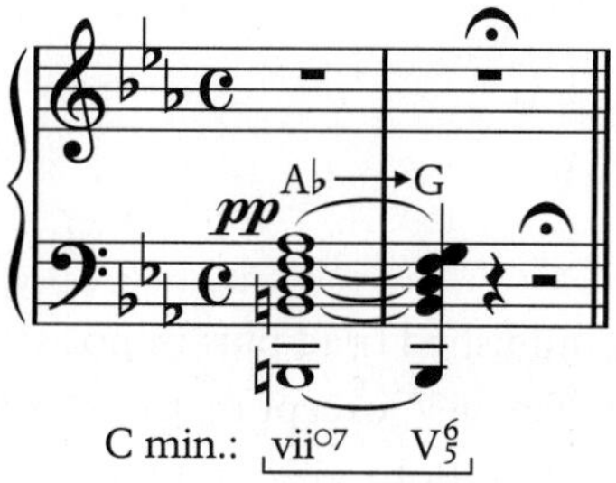

17.8 Mozart, Rondo in D, K. 485

Only one note needs to move (by half step) in a progression between vii$^{\circ 7}$ and V^7.

VOICE LEADING

When vii$^{\circ 7}$ or one of its inversions resolves to I or I^6, the chordal seventh of vii$^{\circ 7}$ must resolve down by step, and the root of vii$^{\circ 7}$—the leading tone—must resolve up by step. When resolving vii$^{\circ 7}$, be careful to avoid having a diminished fifth move to a perfect fifth. To avoid this parallel motion to a perfect fifth, you may need to double the third of the tonic chord, rather than its root.

17.9

Good The seventh of the vii^{o7} chord resolves down; the leading tone resolves up.

Poor A diminished 5th (A-E♭ or F♯-C) may *not* move to a perfect 5th (G-D).

Good To avoid parallel fifths, the third of the tonic chord may be doubled: here, both A ($\hat{2}$) and C ($\hat{4}$) converge on B♭ ($\hat{3}$).

17.10 J. S. Bach, Chorale 160 ➔ **17.11 Haydn, String Quartet in G, op. 17, no. 5, III** ➔

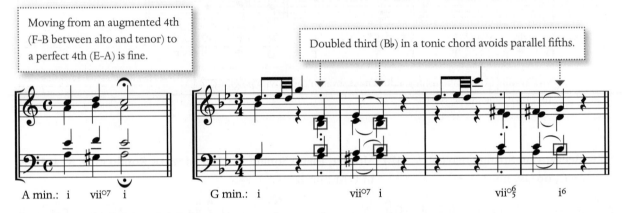

Moving from an augmented 4th (F-B between alto and tenor) to a perfect 4th (E-A) is fine.

Doubled third (B♭) in a tonic chord avoids parallel fifths.

vii^{ø7}

vii^{ø7} is a half-diminished seventh chord (diminished triad plus minor seventh) whose root is the leading tone. It is treated much like vii^{o7}, except that vii^{ø7} is found only in major keys and does not require an accidental. Both vii^{o7} and vii^{ø7} and their inversions function as **D**ominants: they lead to I or I^6.

17.12

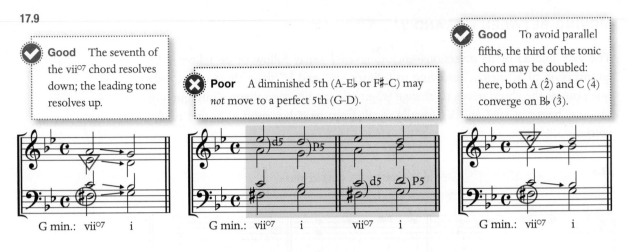

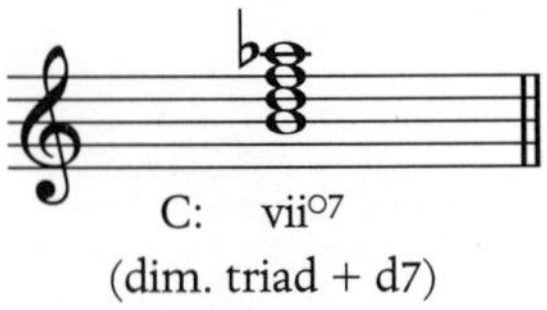

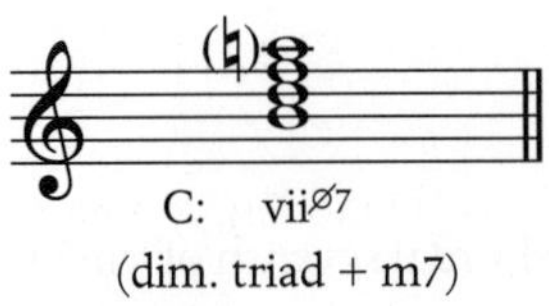

vii^{ø7} is used only in *major* keys.

As with vii^{o7}, in progressing from vii^{ø7} to I the chordal seventh resolves down by step, and the leading tone resolves up by step. Often special care must be taken in order to avoid parallel fifths in moving from vii^{ø7} to I.

17.13

Good When $\text{vii}^{\varnothing 7}$ moves to I, the tendency tones must resolve properly.

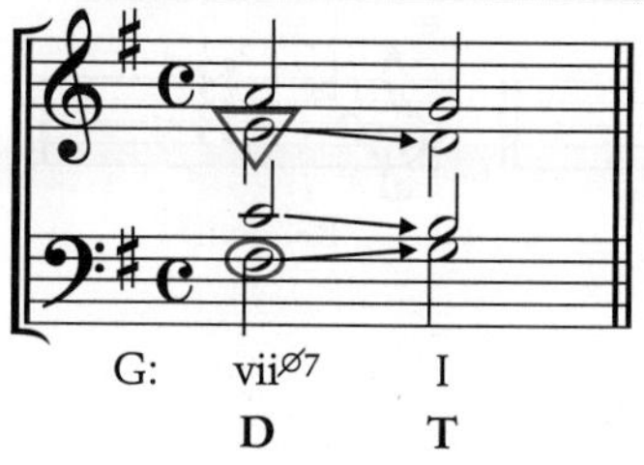

Poor Watch out for parallel fifths (A–E, G–D) when $\text{vii}^{\varnothing 7}$ moves to I!

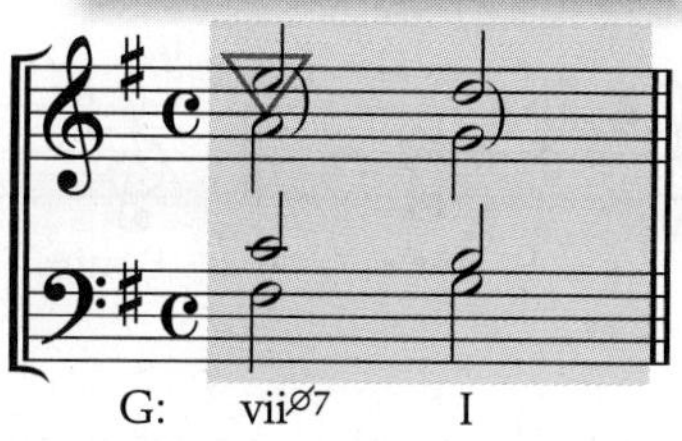

17.14 Schubert, Piano Sonata in A Minor, D. 845, III

17.15 Webbe, Psalm Tune, no. 17

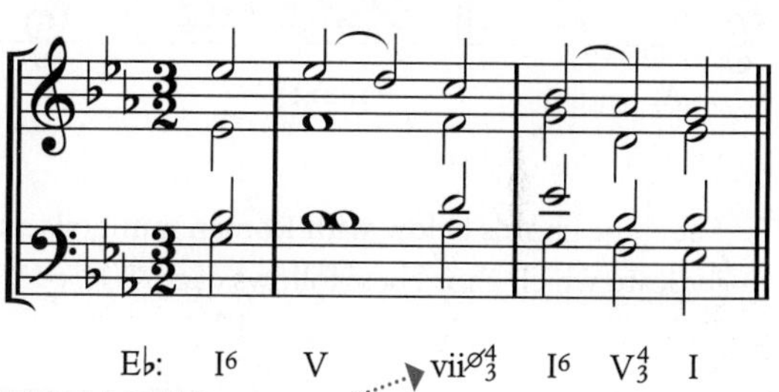

$\text{vii}^{\varnothing 7}$ may appear in root position or inversion.

review and interact

POINTS FOR REVIEW

- **$\text{vii}^{\circ 7}$ functions as a Dominant: it leads to Tonic.**
- **$\text{vii}^{\circ 7}$ may be used in major or minor keys, always requires an accidental, and may appear in root position or inversion.**
- **When $\text{vii}^{\circ 7}$ resolves to I or I^6, the chordal seventh of $\text{vii}^{\circ 7}$ must resolve down by step and the leading tone must resolve up by step.**
- **Before leading to the Tonic, $\text{vii}^{\circ 7}$ may follow or be followed directly by an inversion of V^7.**
- **In the $\text{vii}^{\circ 7}$–I progression, be careful to avoid a diminished fifth moving to a perfect fifth.**
- **$\text{vii}^{\varnothing 7}$ is used only in major keys and does not require an accidental; it is treated like $\text{vii}^{\circ 7}$.**

TEST YOURSELF

1. Add accidentals to the chords below (as needed) to create the specified harmonies. Some chords may not require an accidental.

2. Label the chords below with Roman numerals and figures in the keys indicated. Then indicate the chordal seventh and the leading tone in each.

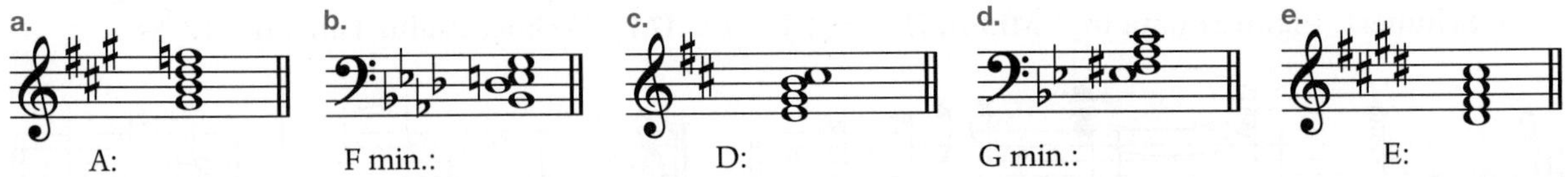

3. Label the chords below with Roman numerals and figures in the keys indicated. Then indicate which chord best follows each: I, I^6, or V^7.

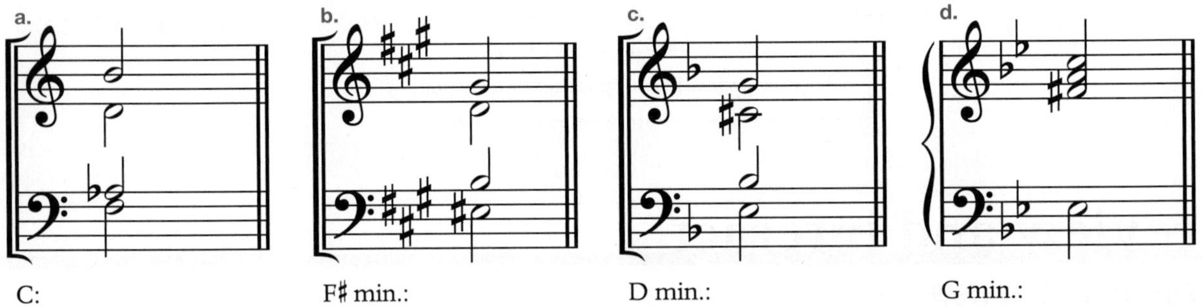

4. Fill in the missing note in the following chord progressions; explain your choice.

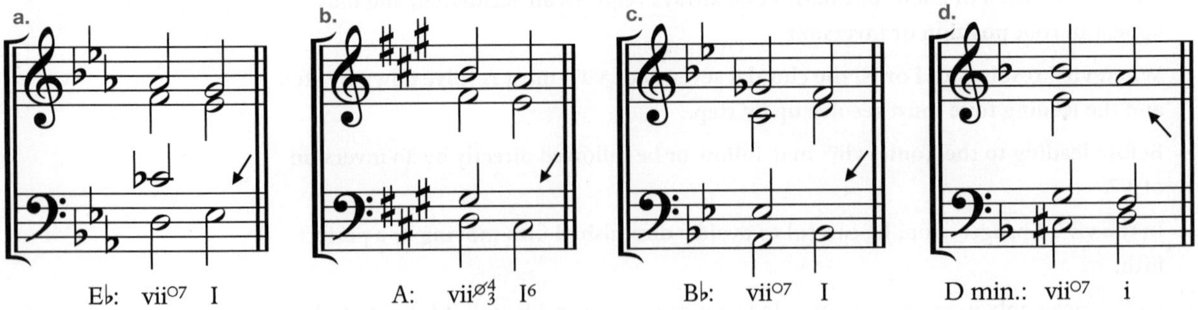

Know It? Show It!

Focus by working through the tutorials on:

- Writing vii^{o7}

Learn with inQuizitive.

Apply what you've learned to complete the assignments:

- Spelling Chords
- Realizing Roman Numerals
- Realizing Figured Bass
- Harmonizing Melodies
- Analysis

chapter

18 Approaching V: IV^6, ii, ii^7, and IV^7

IV^6, ii, ii^7, and IV^7 appear in a variety of positions as Subdominant harmonies that lead to V.

IV^6

IV^6 is a first-inversion **S**ubdominant chord that leads to V or V^7 in root position or first inversion with stepwise motion in the bass.

18.1 **18.2 Rossini, *Barber of Seville*** **18.3 J. S. Bach, Chorale 42**

Like IV, IV^6 (or iv^6 in minor keys) leads to a **D**ominant harmony.

Translation: From my lips hear me say my name.

In minor keys, iv^6 often precedes the V of a half cadence. A half cadence that concludes with a iv^6–V progression is called a **Phrygian cadence**.

18.4

18.5 Dowland, "Fine knacks for the ladies"

A Phrygian cadence ends iv6–V.

DOUBLING AND VOICE LEADING

In major keys, you can double any note of IV6.

18.6 R. Schumann, "Ein Choral"

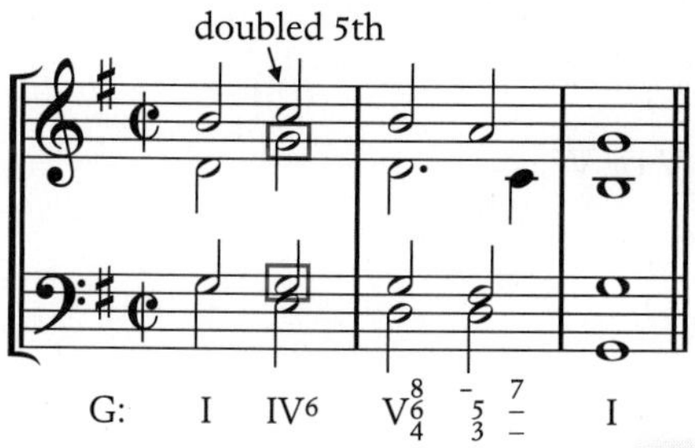

18.7 J. S. Bach, Chorale 215

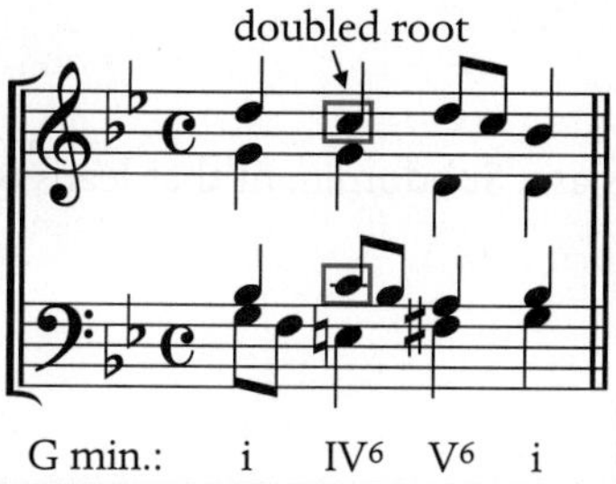

18.8 J. S. Bach, Chorale 80

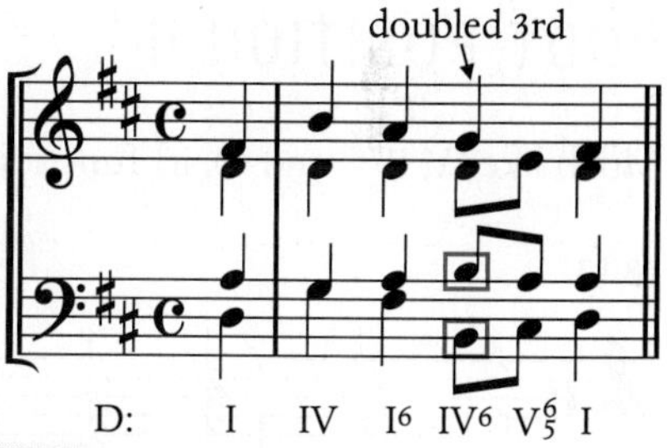

Any note of a (major) IV6 may be doubled.

In minor keys, however, you usually should not double the third (the bass) of iv6. This is because the third of iv6 is the minor form of $\hat{6}$, a tendency tone that pulls down to $\hat{5}$ (as in the descending melodic minor scale).

18.9

Good It is often helpful to double the fifth of iv6 (= $\hat{1}$).

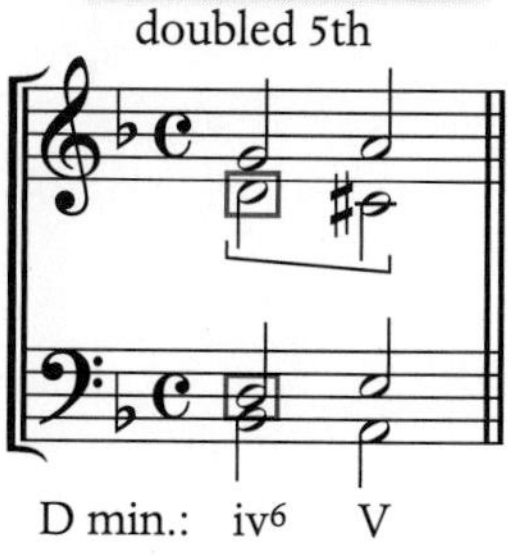

Poor The third of (minor) iv6 should not be doubled, as it creates voice-leading problems.

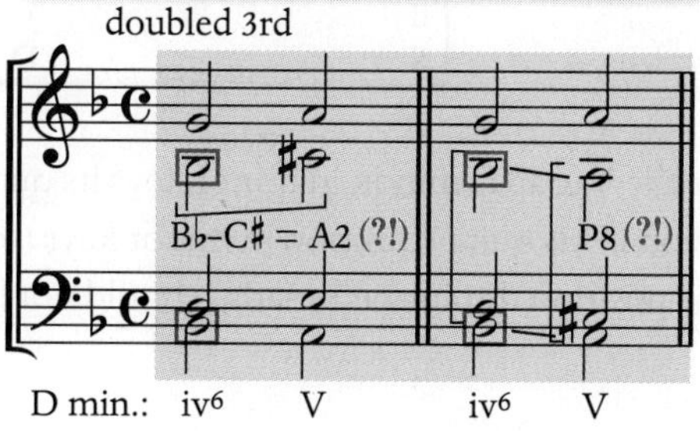

18.10 Corelli, Concerto Grosso, op. 6, no. 6, III

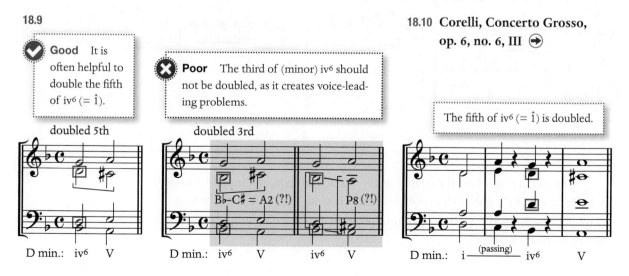

The fifth of iv6 (= $\hat{1}$) is doubled.

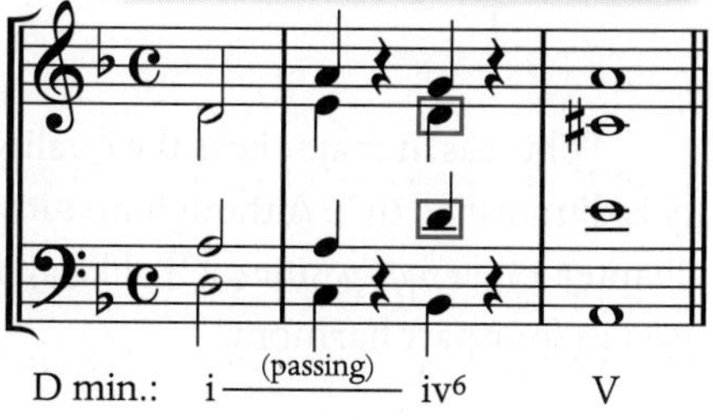

If the bass in a minor key ascends from $\hat{6}$ to $\hat{7}$, you should use the raised form of $\hat{6}$ (as in the ascending melodic minor scale), turning iv^6 into IV^6.

18.11

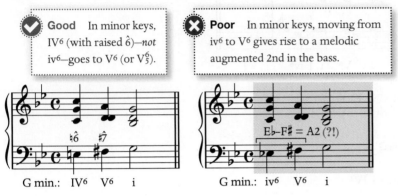

Good In minor keys, IV^6 (with raised $\hat{6}$)—*not* iv^6—goes to V^6 (or V^6_5).

Poor In minor keys, moving from iv^6 to V^6 gives rise to a melodic augmented 2nd in the bass.

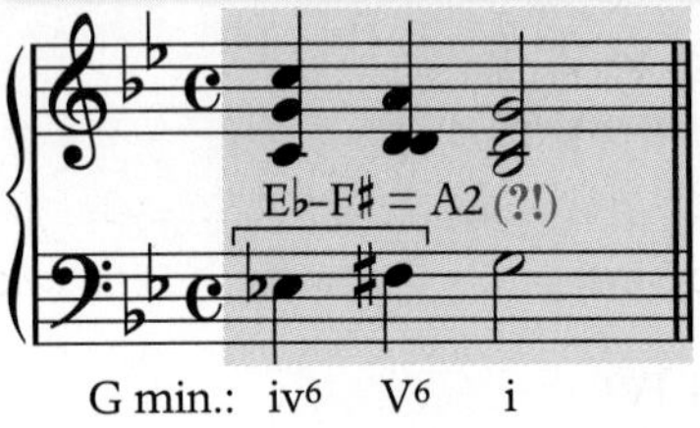

ROOT-POSITION ii

Much like IV, IV^6, and ii^6, ii^5_3 functions as a **S**ubdominant that leads to V or V^7.

18.12

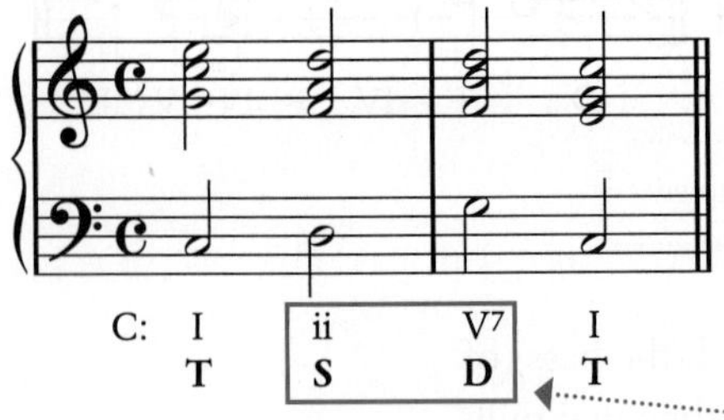

Root-position ii leads to a **D**ominant harmony.

18.13 Cimarosa, Overture to *Il matrimonio segreto*

Whereas in major keys the quality of the ii triad is minor, in minor keys its quality is diminished (ii°). Although first-inversion $ii^{\circ 6}$ is quite common in minor keys (see Chapter 13), a *root-position* $ii^{\circ 5}_{3}$—like all root-position diminished triads—should not be used in four-part harmony.

18.14

Good In minor keys, ii$^{\circ 6}$ is common . . .

G min.: i ii$^{\circ 6}$ V i

Poor . . . but a *root-position* ii$^{\circ}$ triad should be avoided.

G min.: i ii$^{\circ}$(?!) V i

DOUBLING AND VOICE LEADING

In four-part harmony you should double the root of a ii$^5_3$ triad. To avoid parallel fifths and octaves, usually all of the upper voices move in contrary motion with the bass when I progresses to ii.

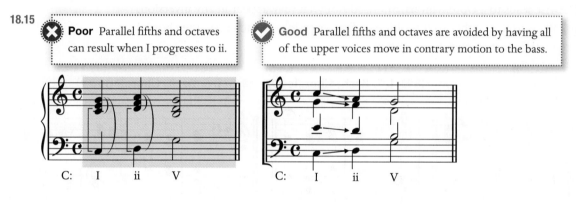

18.15

Poor Parallel fifths and octaves can result when I progresses to ii.

C: I ii V

Good Parallel fifths and octaves are avoided by having all of the upper voices move in contrary motion to the bass.

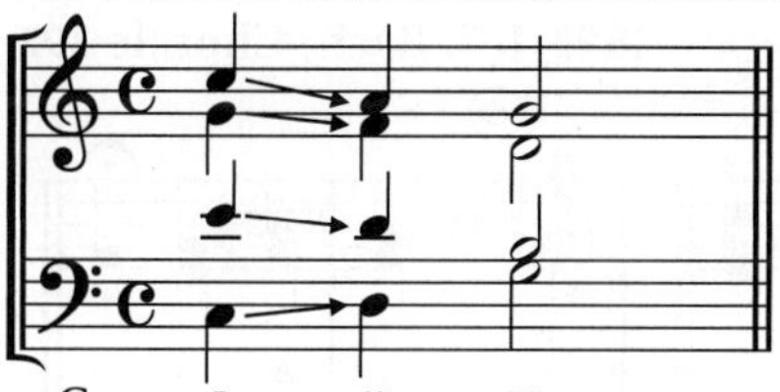

C: I ii V

ii^7 and IV^7

ii^7

The ii^7 also functions as a **S**ubdominant that leads to the **D**ominant. ii^7 usually appears in first inversion, as ii$^6_5$ (see Chapter 13). However, ii^7 also may appear in root position or in second or third inversion. When it progresses to V, the chordal seventh of ii^7 must resolve down by step.

18.16

ii^7—in root position or inversion—leads to a **D**ominant harmony, with its chordal seventh resolving down by step.

ii$^6_5$ extremely common (see Chapter 13) | **ii^7** usually leads to root-position V or V^7 | **ii$^4_2$** leads to V^6 or V$^6_5$ | **ii$^4_3$** less common; leads to root-position V or V^7

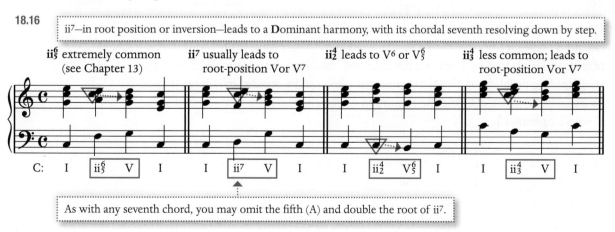

C: I [ii$^6_5$ V] I | I [ii^7 V] I | I [ii$^4_2$ V$^6_5$] I | I [ii$^4_3$ V] I

As with any seventh chord, you may omit the fifth (A) and double the root of ii^7.

18.17 Grieg, *Holberg Suite*, Gavotte

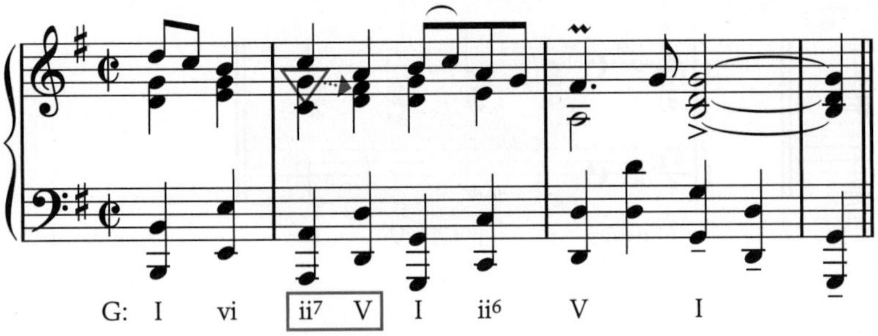

18.18 Corelli, Concerto Grosso, op. 6, no. 6, III

IV^7

IV^7 likewise leads to a **D**ominant harmony. Although it may appear in any inversion, IV^7 usually is used in either root position or first inversion. In each case, the chordal seventh of IV^7 must resolve down by step.

18.19

18.20 J. S. Bach, Chorale 292

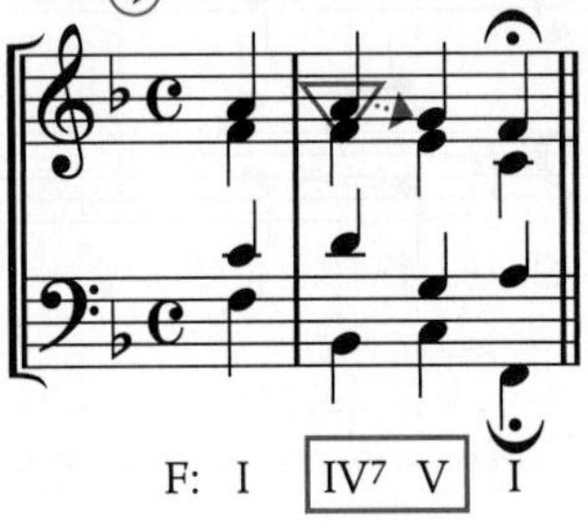

18.21 J. S. Bach, Chorale 50

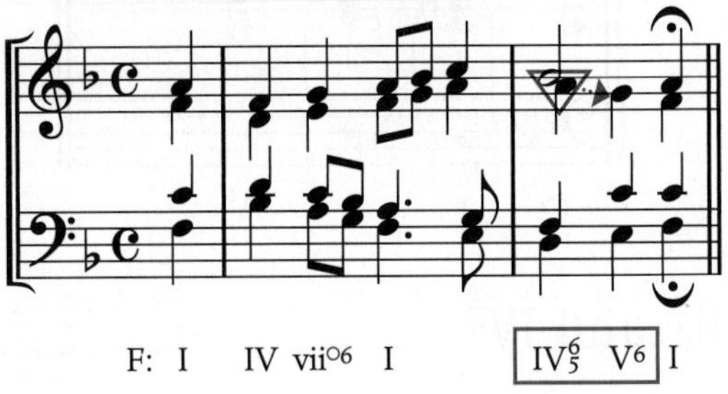

> IV^7 leads to a **D**ominant harmony, its chordal seventh resolving down by step.

FOUR-PART HARMONY AND VOICE LEADING

Special care must be taken to avoid parallel fifths when using ii^7 or IV^7 in four-part harmony. Voice-leading problems that may arise in progressing from I to ii^7 sometimes can be averted by omitting the fifth and doubling the root of ii^7. Likewise, voice-leading problems in IV^7–V progressions often can be avoided by a large leap in an inner voice, or by delaying the resolution of the chordal seventh by embellishing V with a cadential $^6_4$.

18.22

Poor Parallel fifths!

Poor Parallel fifths!

Good Parallel fifths are avoided by omitting the fifth (A) from ii⁷.

Good Parallel fifths are avoided by the leap in the tenor.

Good Parallel fifths are avoided by inserting a cadential $^6_4$ between IV⁷ and V.

ALTERNATING BETWEEN SUBDOMINANT HARMONIES

Subdominant chords may alternate with one another before progressing to V.

18.23 Beethoven, Bagatelle, op. 126, no. 1

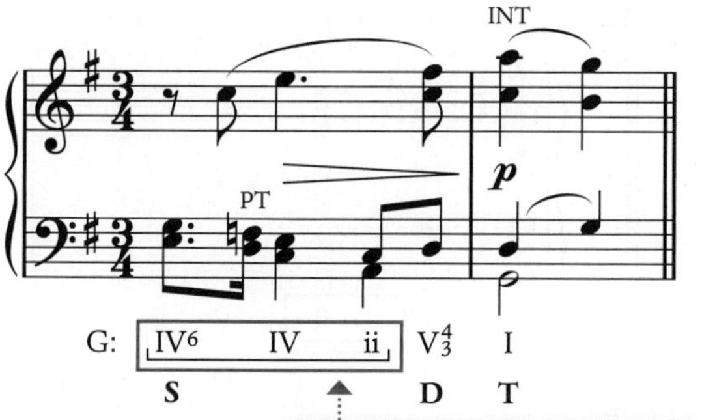

18.24 J. S. Bach, Chorale 269

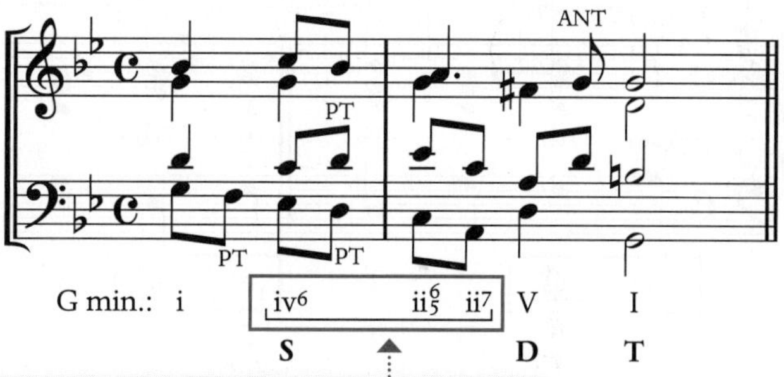

Good It is fine to move from IV to ii or between different positions of ii or IV.

When moving between **S**ubdominant harmonies, the bass typically moves down by a third, rather than up by a third. Thus, for instance, IV–ii is far more common than ii–IV.

18.25

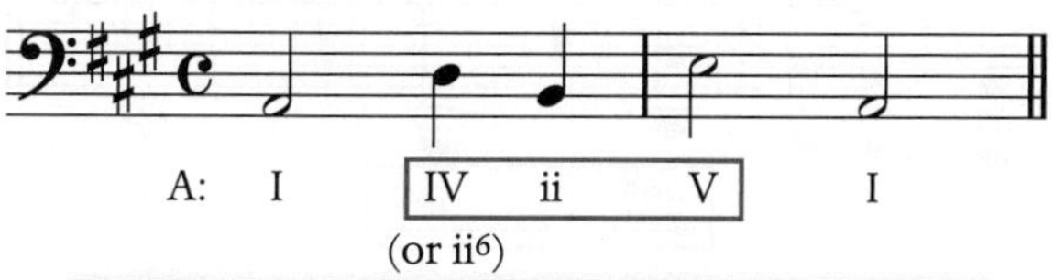

IV–ii–V and ii⁶–ii–V are more common than I–ii–V.

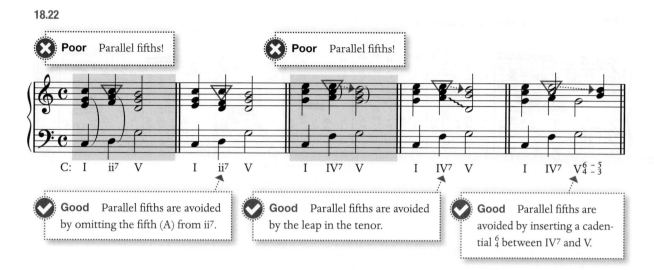

Bass motion *up* by a third between two root-position chords is uncommon.

18.26 Berlioz, *Symphony fantastique* (arr. by Liszt), II

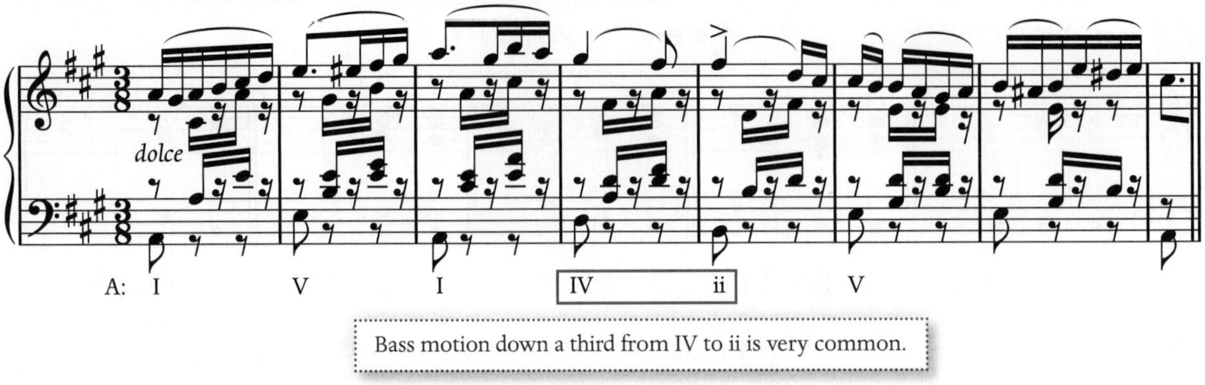
dolce
A: I V I IV ii V
Bass motion down a third from IV to ii is very common.

Just as V may lead to but not follow V^7, ii or IV may lead to—but *not* follow—ii^7 or IV^7. If ii^7 or IV^7 did move to a ii or IV triad, the chordal seventh in these harmonies would not be able to resolve properly.

18.27

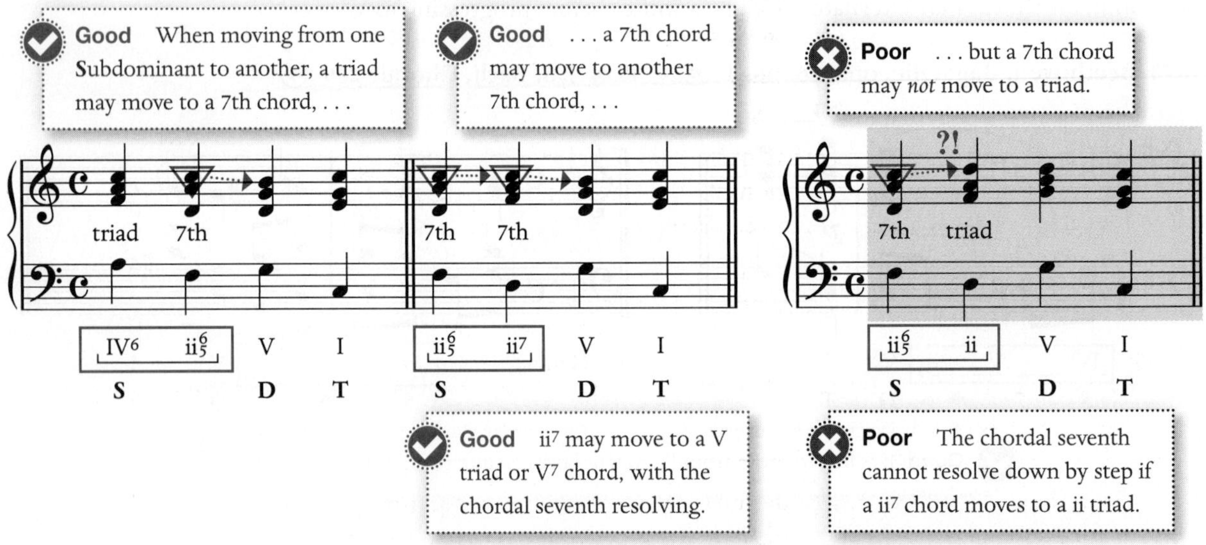
Good When moving from one Subdominant to another, a triad may move to a 7th chord, . . .
Good . . . a 7th chord may move to another 7th chord, . . .
Poor . . . but a 7th chord may *not* move to a triad.
triad 7th
7th 7th
?!
7th triad
IV^6 ii$^6_5$ V I
S D T
ii$^6_5$ ii^7 V I
S D T
ii$^6_5$ ii V I
S D T
Good ii^7 may move to a V triad or V^7 chord, with the chordal seventh resolving.
Poor The chordal seventh cannot resolve down by step if a ii^7 chord moves to a ii triad.

18.28 J. S. Bach, Chorale 118

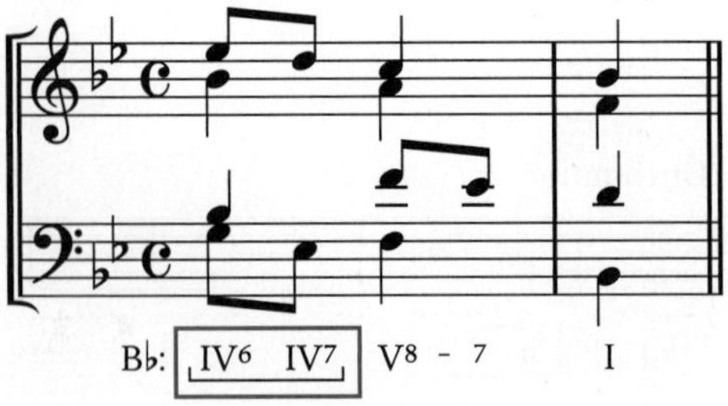
B♭: IV^6 IV^7 V$^{8-7}$ I

Good IV^6 moves to IV^7 before progressing to V.

18.29 Berlioz, *Symphony fantastique*, IV

G min.: i ii$^{ø6}_5$ ii^{ø7} V

Good ii$^{ø6}_5$ moves to ii^{ø7}.

18.30

> Before moving to a **D**ominant, a **S**ubdominant chord may move to another **S**ubdominant, usually with the bass moving down by a third.

bass moves down by third ↓

SUBDOMINANT ⟶	**DOMINANT** ⟶	**TONIC**
IV^6 (bass = $\hat{6}$) ↘		
IV, ii^6 (bass = $\hat{4}$) ⟶	**V** and similar chords ⟶	**I** and **I^6**
ii (bass = $\hat{2}$) ↗	(V, V^7, V^6, vii^{o7}, cad. $^6_4$–V, etc.)	
triad ⟶ seventh chord	triad ⟶ seventh chord	

> A **S**ubdominant triad may move to a **S**ubdominant seventh chord, but not vice versa.

review and interact

POINTS FOR REVIEW

- **IV^6, root-position ii, ii^7 (in root position and inversions), and IV^7 (in root position and inversions) are Subdominant chords that lead to Dominant harmonies.**
- **The ii^o triad, which occurs in minor keys, should not be used in root position.**
- **The sevenths of ii^7 and IV^7 (and the inversions of these chords) are chordal dissonances that must resolve down by step.**
- **Subdominant harmonies may move to or from one another before progressing to a Dominant harmony. In moving between Subdominant harmonies, the bass typically moves down—rather than up—by a third. Also, ii^7 and IV^7 chords may not move to IV or ii triads.**
- **A Phrygian cadence ends with the progression iv^6–V in a minor key.**

TEST YOURSELF

1. Compare the progressions in each of the following pairs. Which (if either) contains errors, and what are the errors? (Note that both progressions may be good.) Which of the two progressions in the pair is more typical?

   a. I -ii–V–I; I–V–ii–I
   b. I–IV–ii–V; I–ii–IV–V
   c. I–ii^7–V$^{6\ 5}_{4\ 3}$–I; I–IV^7–V$^{6\ 5}_{4\ 3}$–I
   d. I–ii–ii^7–V–I; I–ii^7–ii–V–I
   e. i–iv^6–V; I–ii^7–V^7–I
   f. I–ii$^6_5$–ii^7–V–I; I–ii^6–ii–vii^{o6}–I

2. Which of each of the following pairs of progressions has voice-leading problems? What is the error?

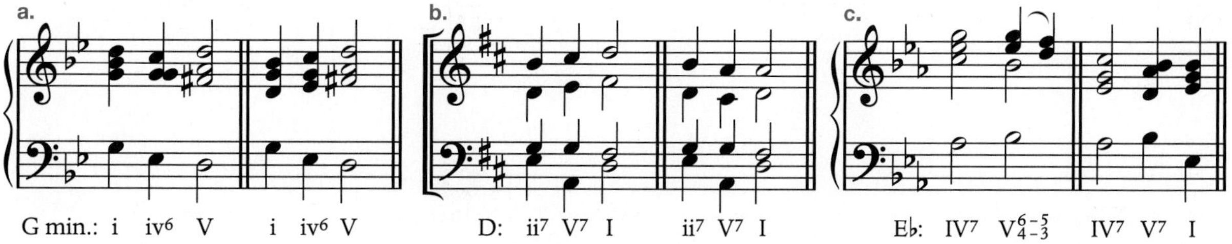

3. Which of the following statements is true?
   a. In a iv^6 chord, you should always double the bass.
   b. A Phrygian cadence consists of the progression iv^6–V in a minor key.
   c. A root-position ii[°] may appear in minor keys.
   d. The chordal seventh of both ii^7 and IV^7 must resolve down by step, whether the chord appears in root position or in inversion.
   e. It is normal for IV^7 to be followed by a IV triad.
   f. It is normal for ii^7 to be followed by a V triad.

Know It? Show It!

Focus by working through the tutorials on:

- Writing iv^6 chords in minor
- Writing I–ii–V^7–I
- ii^7 and IV^7

Learn with inQuizitive.

Apply what you've learned to complete the assignments:

- Spelling Chords
- Realizing Roman Numerals
- Realizing Figured Bass
- Harmonizing Melodies
- Analysis

chapter 19 Multiple Functions: VI

VI has several different functions: it may follow either I or V and lead to a variety of harmonies.

HARMONIES THAT FOLLOW VI

LEADING TO SUBDOMINANT HARMONIES

The vi (or in minor keys, VI) frequently leads to a **S**ubdominant harmony. For instance, it may lead to IV, ii^6, or ii^6_5, with a descending third motion in the bass.

19.1

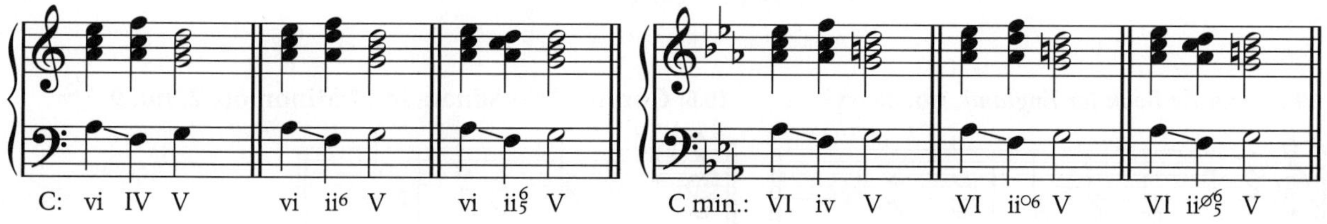

19.2 **Hymn from *The Boston Handel and Haydn Society Collection of Church Music***

19.3 **Hymn from *The Boston Handel and Haydn Society Collection of Church Music***

Note the characteristic descending 3rd motion in the bass as vi leads from the tonic to IV, ii^6, or ii$^{ø6}_{5}$.

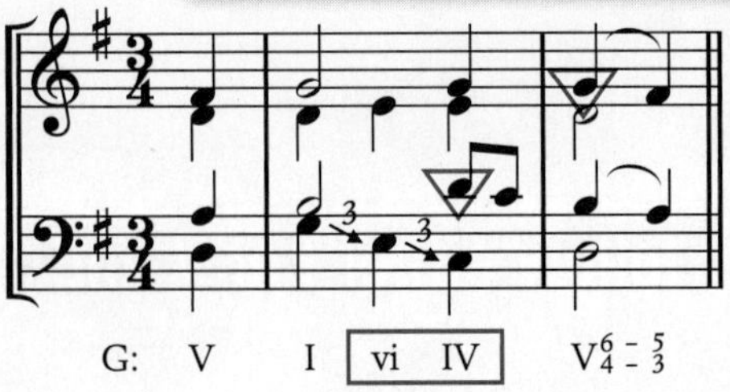

19.4 **Schubert, "Ständchen" (Serenade)**

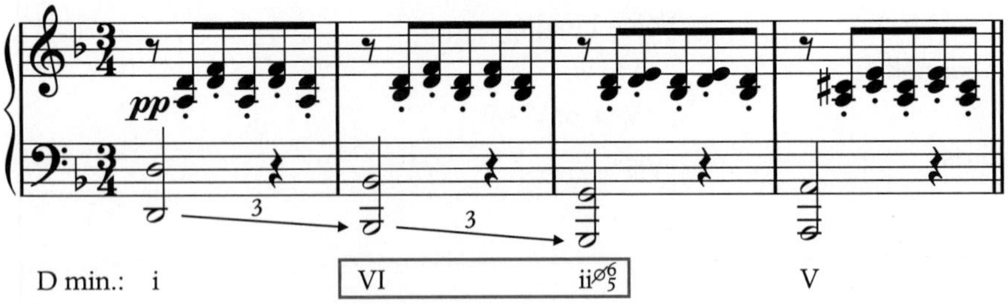

A vi may lead to root-position ii or to IV^6.

19.5 ***Chorale Book for England*, no. 29**

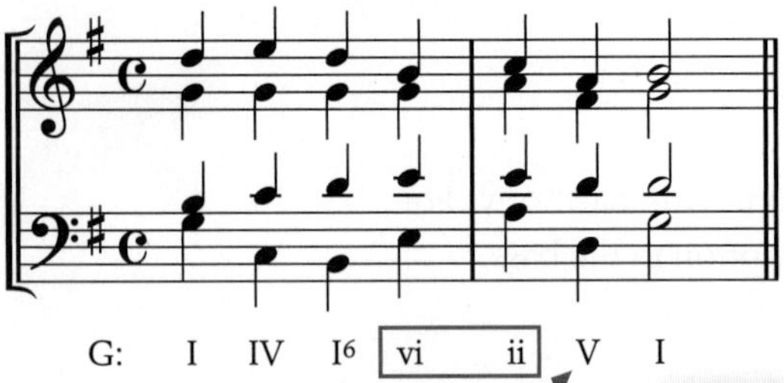

19.6 **Grieg, *Holberg Suite*, Sarabande**

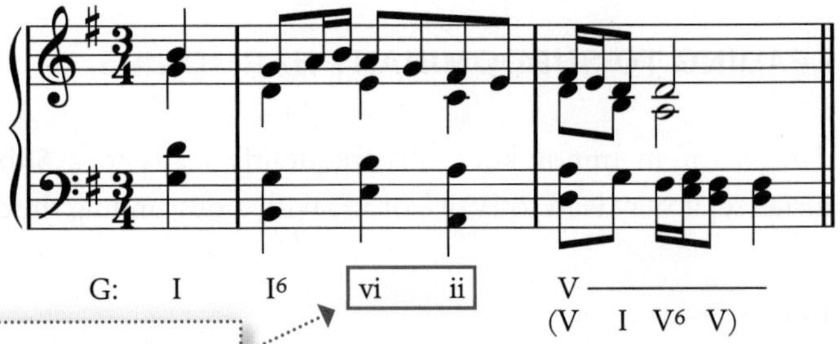

vi leads to root-position ii.

19.7 ***Chorale Book for England*, no. 28**

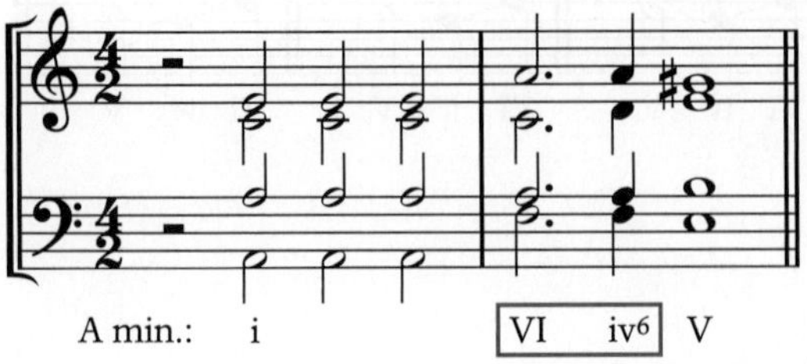

19.8 **Corelli, Trio Sonata in F♯ Minor, op. 2, no. 9**

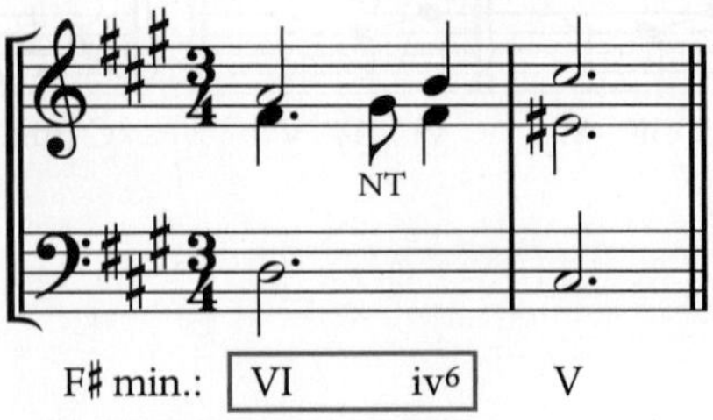

The bass remains stationary as VI moves to iv^6.

LEADING TO I6

A vi also frequently progresses to I6, with the bass moving down by a fourth.

19.9 J. S. Bach, Chorale 2

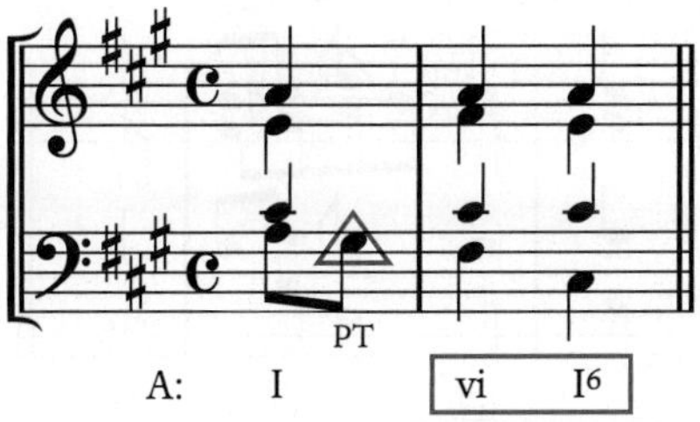

vi leads to I6.

19.10 Schubert, "Auf dem Flusse" (On the River)

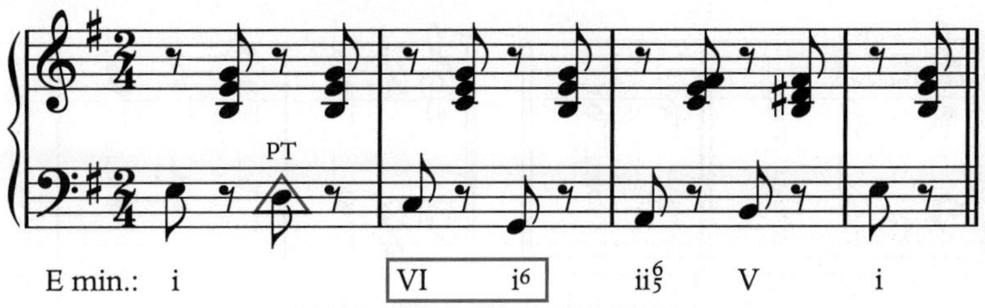

VI leads to i6 in a minor key.

LEADING TO DOMINANT CHORDS

A V triad or seventh chord in root position or first inversion may sometimes directly follow vi. This is a less common option, however: it is much more normal for vi to lead to a **S**ubdominant harmony than to a **D**ominant harmony.

19.11 R. Schumann, "Ein Choral" (A Chorale)

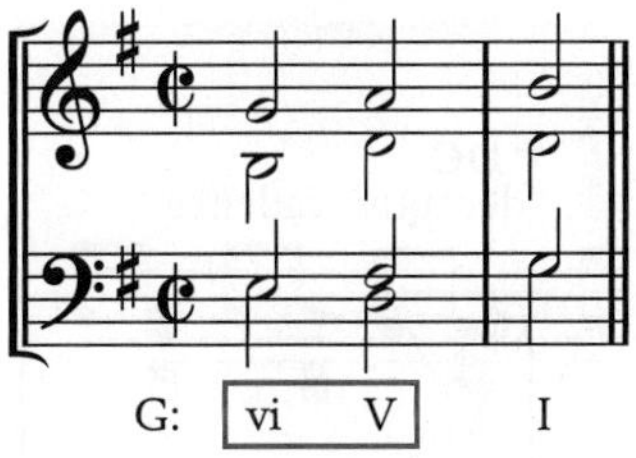

19.12 J. S. Bach, Chorale 103

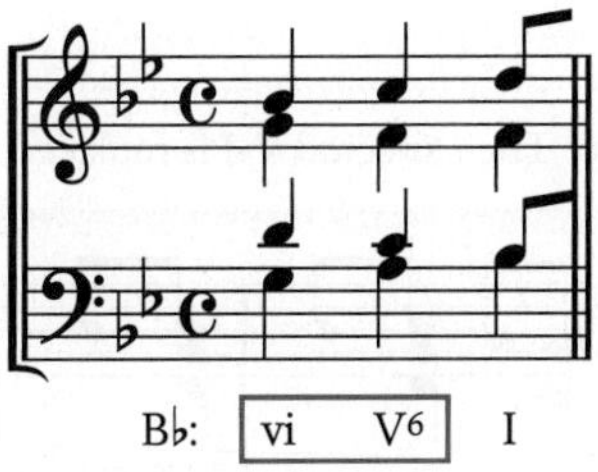

It is possible—though less common—for vi to lead directly to V or V6.

HARMONIES THAT LEAD TO VI

As with all other harmonies, vi may directly follow I.

19.13 Bortniansky, Hymn

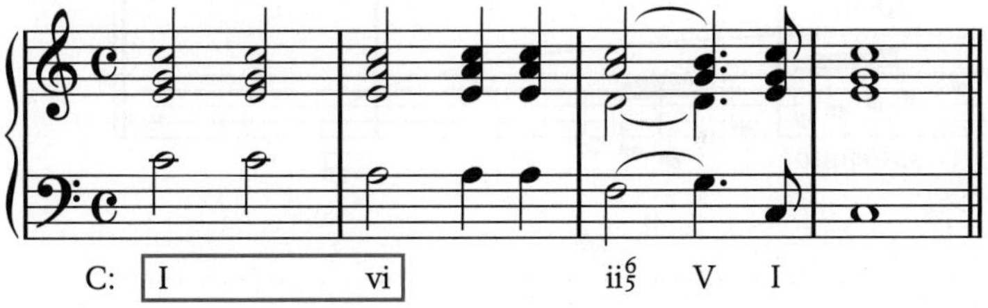

vi may follow I.

A vi may also follow root-position V or V7. In such a case the resulting V–vi substitutes for the more typical V–I progression.

19.14

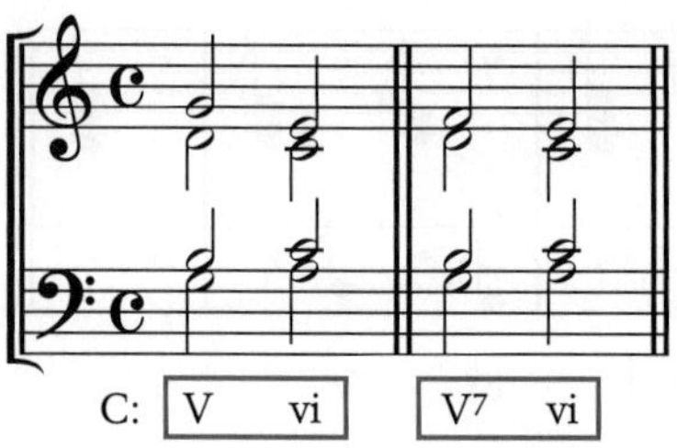

19.15 Purcell, "To the hills and the vale," from *Dido and Aeneas*

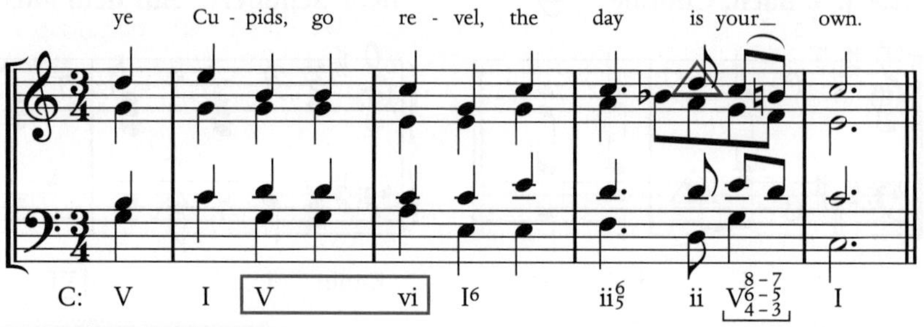

vi may follow root-position V or V7.

DECEPTIVE CADENCE

At times an expected authentic cadence is thwarted when a root-position V or V7 moves to vi instead of to I. This is known as a **deceptive cadence** (**DC**).

19.16 Chopin, Prelude in B Minor, op. 28

A deceptive cadence must involve a *root-position* V or V7 (*not* an inverted V).

PAC here? No! The expected V–I is replaced with V–VI!

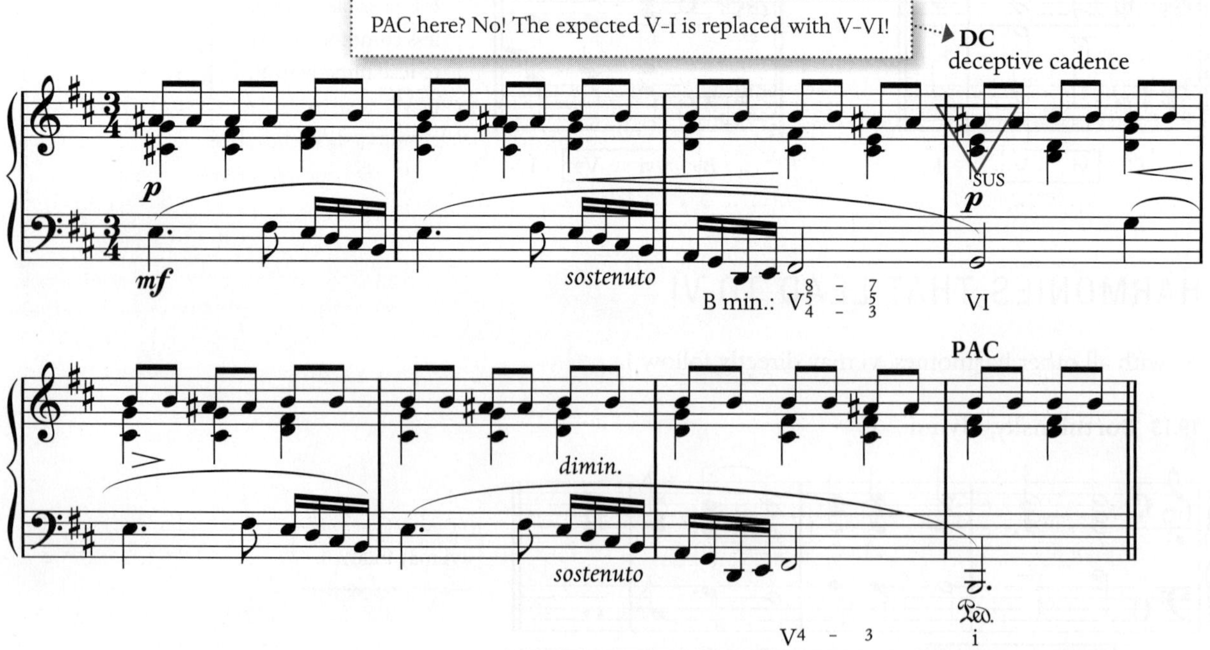

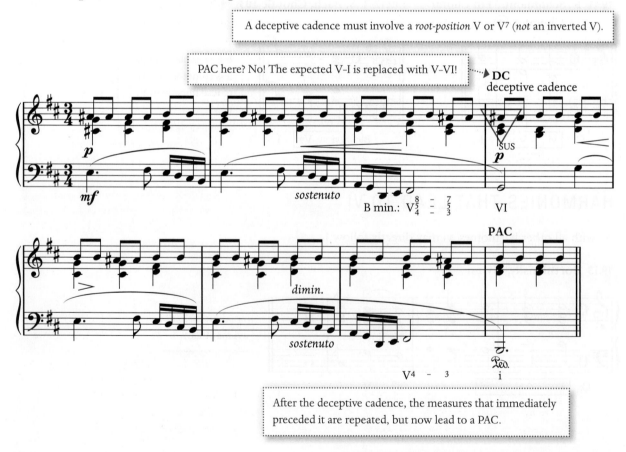

After the deceptive cadence, the measures that immediately preceded it are repeated, but now lead to a PAC.

The following chart summarizes chords that lead to or from vi:

19.17

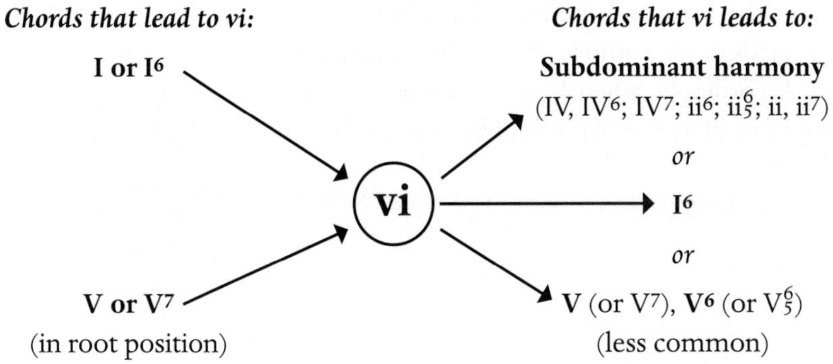

VOICE LEADING

I to vi

When I moves to vi in four-part harmony, usually the root of vi is doubled. Like other chords whose roots are a third apart, I and vi share two tones in common. Accordingly, when moving between root-position triads whose roots are separated by a third, the two common tones repeat in the upper voices, and a third upper voice moves by step in contrary motion to the bass.

19.18

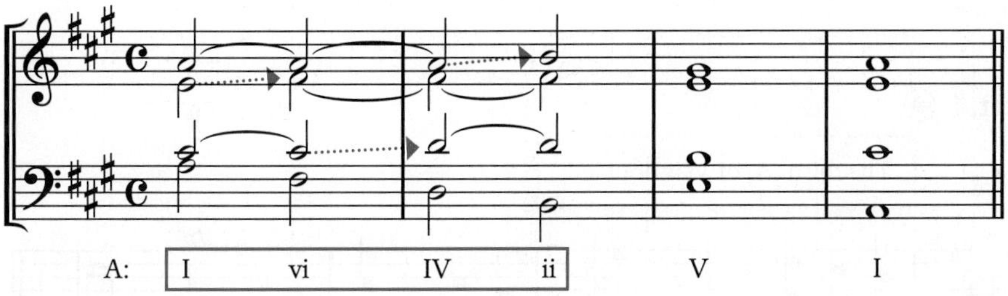

When root-position chords progress down by thirds, the two shared tones in the upper voices repeat (see tied notes) while the other upper voice moves in contrary motion to the bass.

Incidentally, although descending root motion by third occurs frequently, ascending motion by third is far less common.

19.19

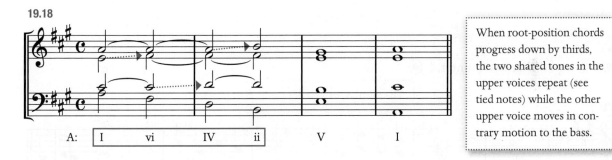

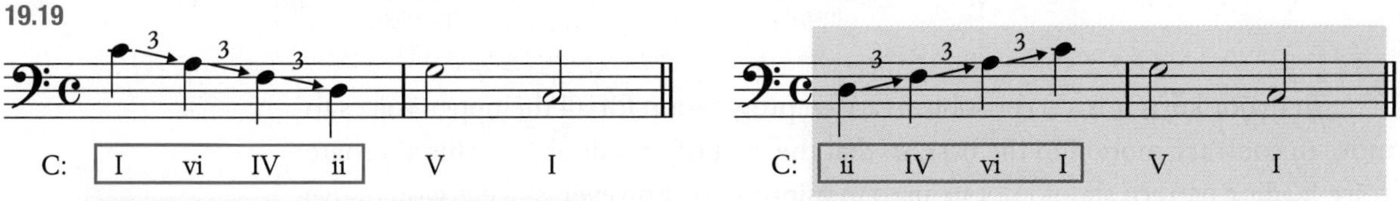

Good Motion of root-position triads *down* by a third is common.

Odd Motion of root-position triads *up* by a third is *not* common.

V-vi (or V7-vi)

When one root-position chord moves up by step to another, the upper voices usually all move down, in contrary motion with the bass, and the root is doubled in both chords. With V-vi (or V7-vi), however, matters are complicated by the leading tone within V, which leads up to the tonic. Accordingly, when V or V7 moves to vi, the leading tone moves up by step, and the third of vi (i.e., $\hat{1}$) is doubled, rather than its root.

19.20

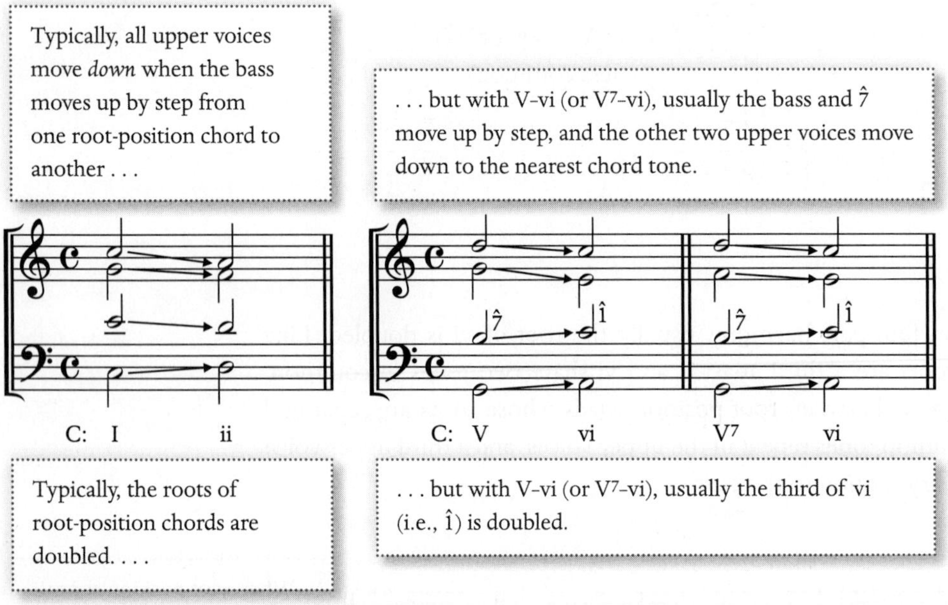

Typically, all upper voices move *down* when the bass moves up by step from one root-position chord to another . . .
. . . but with V-vi (or V7-vi), usually the bass and $\hat{7}$ move up by step, and the other two upper voices move down to the nearest chord tone.
$\hat{7}$ $\hat{1}$ $\hat{7}$ $\hat{1}$
C: I ii
C: V vi V7 vi
Typically, the roots of root-position chords are doubled. . . .
. . . but with V-vi (or V7-vi), usually the third of vi (i.e., $\hat{1}$) is doubled.

19.21 Mozart, Clarinet Quintet, I

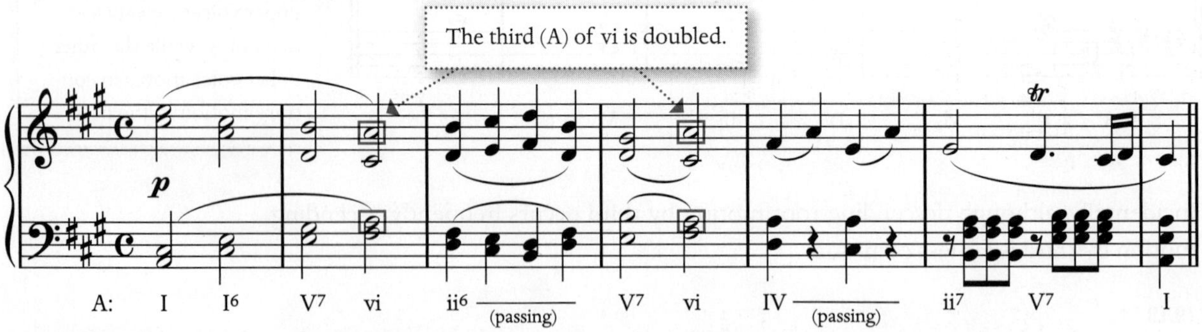

The third (A) of vi is doubled.
p
tr
A: I I6 V7 vi ii6 (passing) V7 vi IV (passing) ii7 V7 I

In major keys, it is also possible in a V-vi progression for all the upper voices to move in contrary motion to the bass, so that the root of vi is doubled. This alternate voice-leading pattern should not be used in minor keys, however, since it would give rise to a melodic augmented second between $\hat{7}$ and $\hat{6}$.

19.22

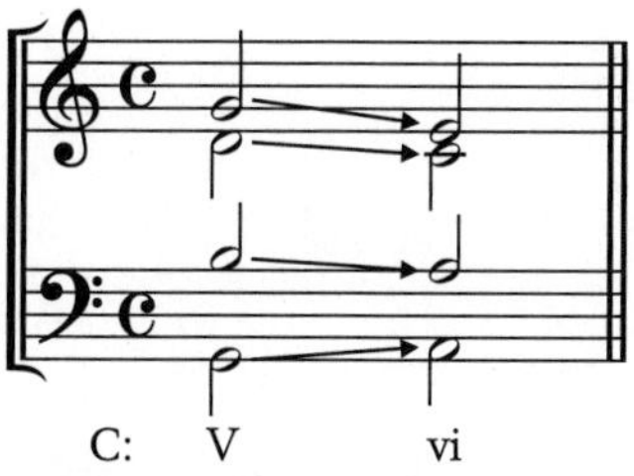

19.23 J. S. Bach, Chorale 22

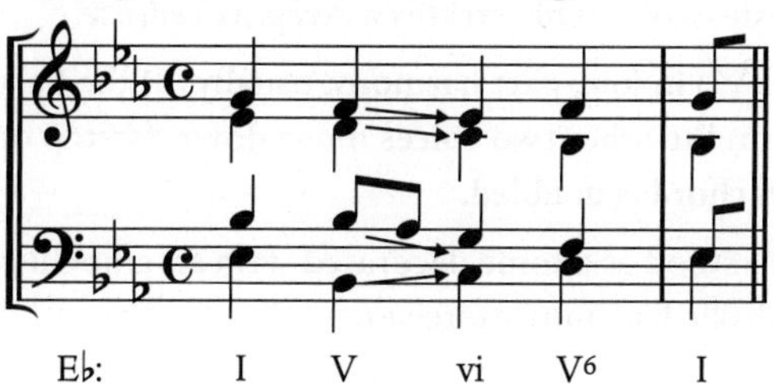

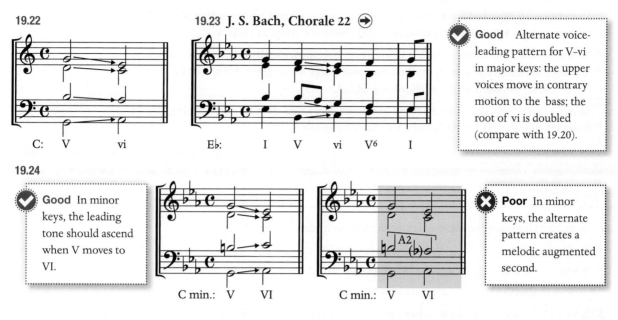

Good Alternate voice-leading pattern for V–vi in major keys: the upper voices move in contrary motion to the bass; the root of vi is doubled (compare with 19.20).

19.24

Good In minor keys, the leading tone should ascend when V moves to VI.

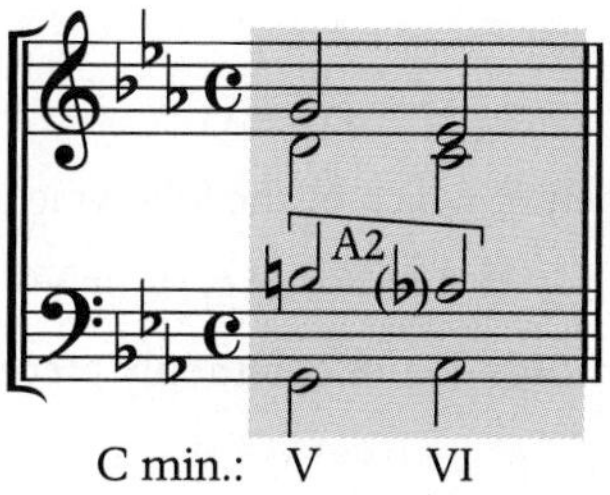

Poor In minor keys, the alternate pattern creates a melodic augmented second.

"VI6"

Sometimes neighbor tones, passing tones, or other embellishments in an upper voice give rise to what is literally vi6. In identifying harmonies, this chord is usually understood as a Tonic chord decorated with an embellishing tone. A "vi6" should *not* be used in basic four-part harmony exercises.

19.25 Schubert, Piano Sonata in A, D. 664, II

The embellishing tone B in measure 2 creates what is literally a vi6 (D-F♯-B) . . .

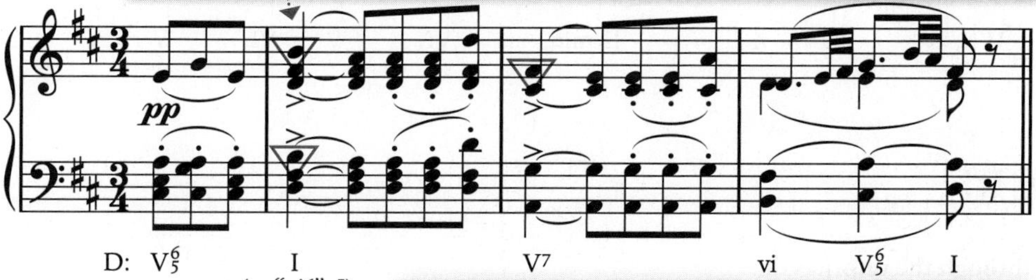

(= "vi6"–I) . . . but the chord nonetheless is essentially a decorated I.

review and interact

POINTS FOR REVIEW

- vi (or VI in minor) often leads to a Subdominant harmony, such as IV, IV6, IV7, ii6, ii6/5, ii or ii7. It also often leads to I6. Less commonly, it may lead directly to V or V6.
- vi (or VI in minor) may follow tonic harmony; it may also follow V or V7 in root position.

- **Sometimes an expected authentic cadence is thwarted when a root-position V (or V^7) moves to vi (or VI in minor) instead of I. This creates a *deceptive cadence*.**
- **When V (or V^7) moves to vi (or VI) in four-part harmony, usually (a) the bass and leading tone move up by step, (b) the other two voices move down by step or by third, and (c) the third of the vi chord is doubled.**
- **In most cases "vi^6" is best understood as a tonic decorated with an embellishing tone; vi^6 should *not* be used in basic harmony exercises.**

TEST YOURSELF

1. In standard harmonic practice, which of the following chords may follow vi?

   a. IV, ii^6, ii^6_5, iv^6, ii, or ii^7 b. I or I^6 c. V or V^6

2. Which of the following chords do not commonly precede vi?

   I; I^6; V; V^7; IV; ii^6

3. Which of the following chord progressions may be found at a deceptive cadence?

   a. V–vi b. V^7–vi c. V^6_5–vi d. V–vi^6 e. I–vi

4. Which of the following chord progressions contain a voice-leading error? What is the error, and how should it be fixed?

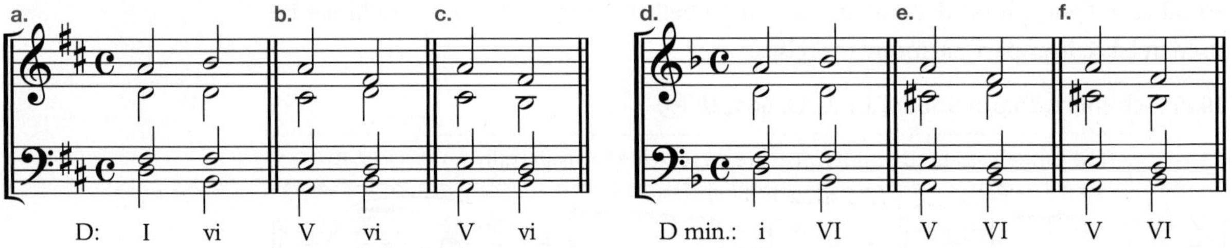

Know It? Show It!

Focus by working through the tutorials on:

- Writing I–vi–IV–ii
- Writing V–vi

Learn with inQuizitive.

Apply what you've learned to complete the assignments:

- Realizing Roman Numerals
- Realizing Figured Bass
- Harmonizing Melodies
- Composition
- Analysis

chapter 20 Embellishing Tones in Four-Part Harmony

Embellishing tones elaborate harmonies, but can also create or solve voice-leading problems.

VOICE LEADING (CREATING AND REMOVING PARALLELS)

When using embellishing tones (such as passing tones) in four-part harmony, you must be careful that they do not result in parallel fifths and octaves. Such faulty parallels might arise when using two embellishing tones at the same time.

20.1

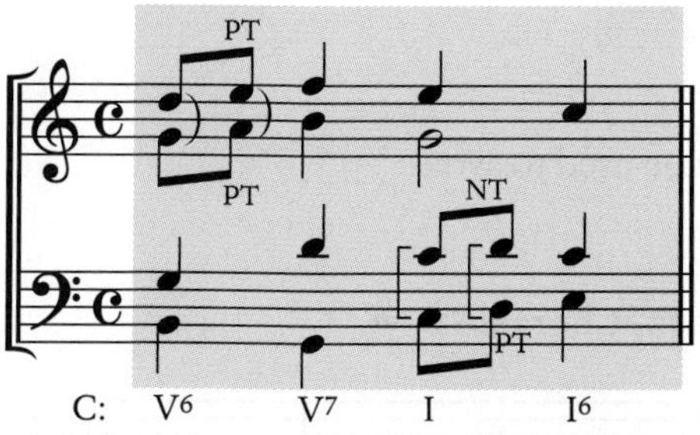

Poor Passing and neighbor tones form parallel fifths and octaves.

20.2 J. S. Bach, Chorale 117

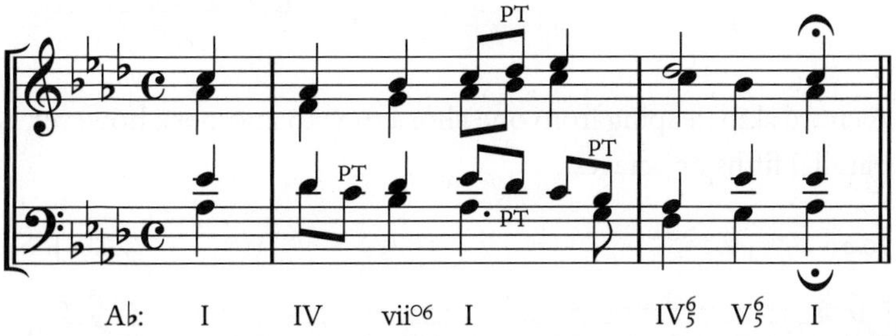

Good Passing tones do not create parallel fifths or octaves.

Parallel octaves and fifths may also arise between a single embellishing tone and a chord tone. As a result, adding embellishing tones to a passage with good voice leading might give rise to faulty parallels.

20.3

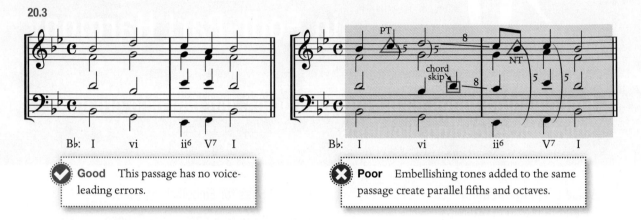

Good This passage has no voice-leading errors.

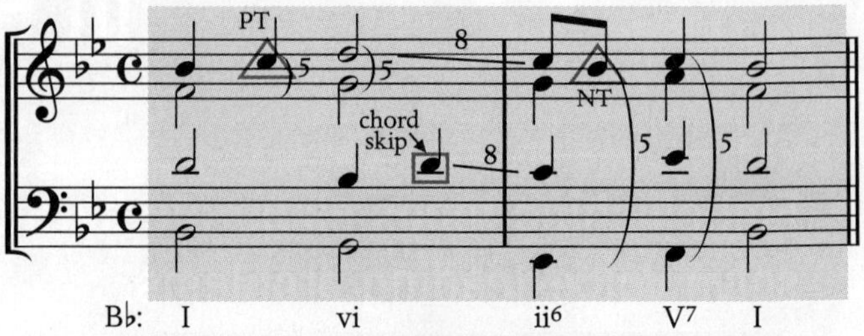

Poor Embellishing tones added to the same passage create parallel fifths and octaves.

Although they can create parallel fifths and octaves, dissonant embellishing tones added to a passage cannot correct a voice-leading error. For instance, if there are parallel octaves between a pair of voices, then the voice leading would be considered faulty even if a dissonant passing tone were added in one of the voices.

20.4

Poor Parallel octaves between bass and soprano.

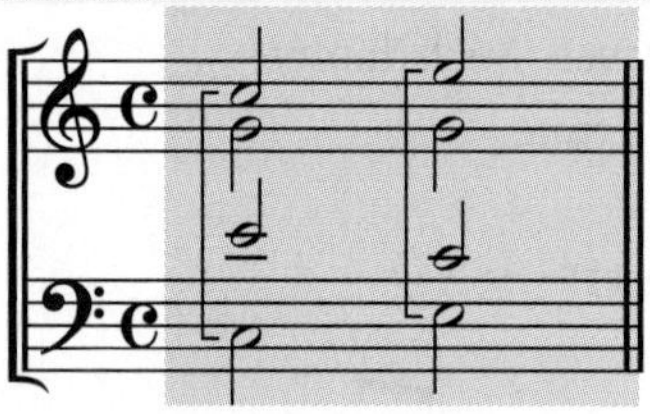

Poor Adding a passing tone doesn't fix the parallel octaves.

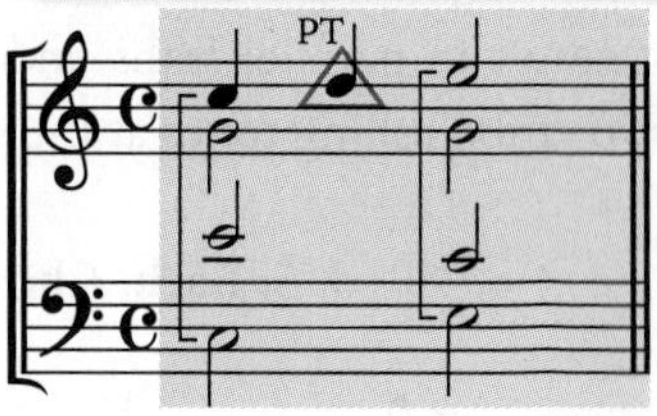

A chord skip (leaping from one chord tone to another), however, can be used to avoid parallel fifths or octaves.

20.5

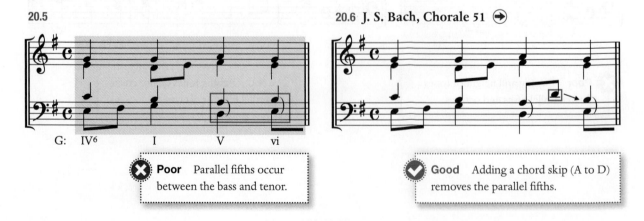

Poor Parallel fifths occur between the bass and tenor.

20.6 J. S. Bach, Chorale 51

Good Adding a chord skip (A to D) removes the parallel fifths.

ACCENTED DISSONANCES IN FOUR-PART HARMONY

At times an accented embellishing tone may delay the full arrival of a harmony. That is, when a chord is decorated by a suspension, accented passing tone, or accented neighbor tone, the complete harmony might appear only when the embellishment resolves to the chord tone.

20.7

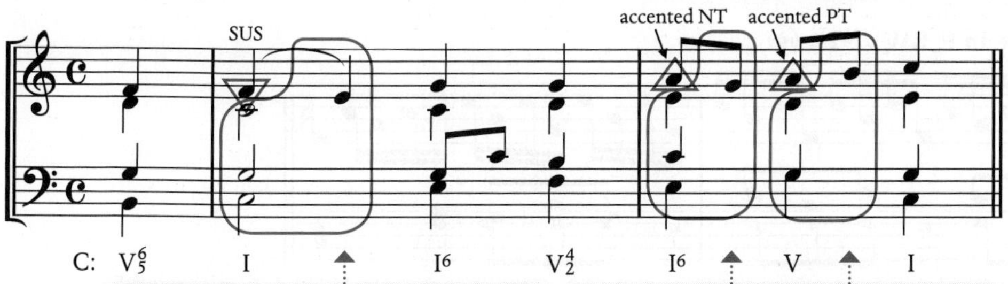

The third of I (E) doesn't appear until after the suspension resolves.

All the notes of I6 and V don't appear until after the accented neighbor tone and passing tone resolve.

Indeed, when it is decorated by an accented dissonance, the third of a chord should not appear in any voice until the dissonance resolves.

20.8

The thirds of both I and V are decorated by accented, dissonant embellishing tones.

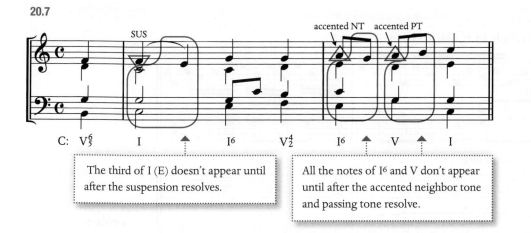

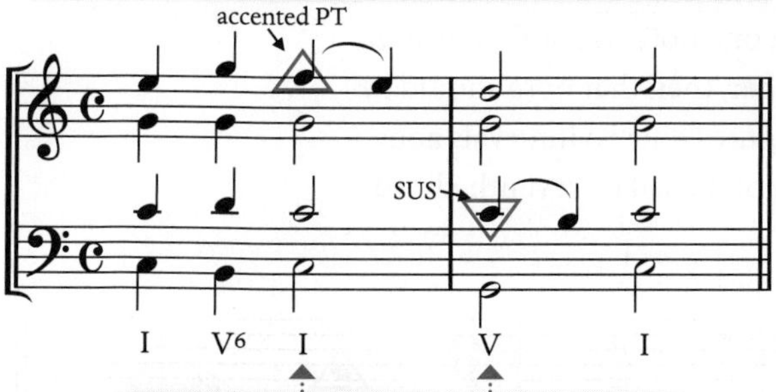

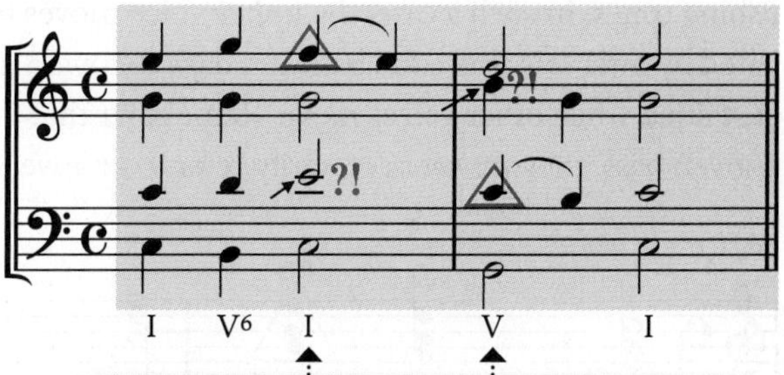

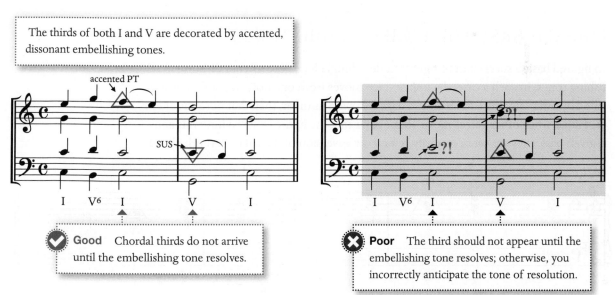

Good Chordal thirds do not arrive until the embellishing tone resolves.

Poor The third should not appear until the embellishing tone resolves; otherwise, you incorrectly anticipate the tone of resolution.

PEDAL POINT

A **pedal point** arises when a single tone is sustained—usually in the bass—as the chords around it change. Unlike most embellishing tones, which decorate the underlying chord, a pedal point is itself decorated by chords that sound above it. Pedal points usually appear toward the start or conclusion of a piece or large section of a piece, embellishing either a tonic or dominant chord that appears at both the start and end of the pedal point.

20.9 J. S. Bach, Prelude in F, BWV 927 ➔

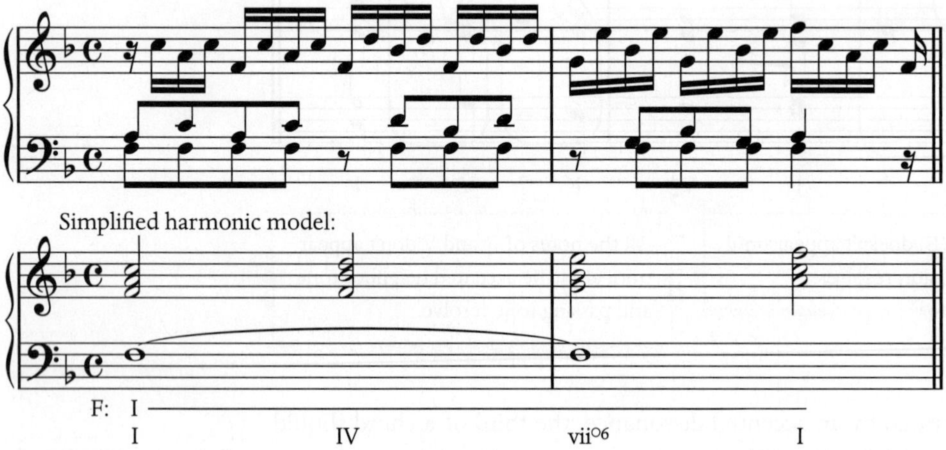

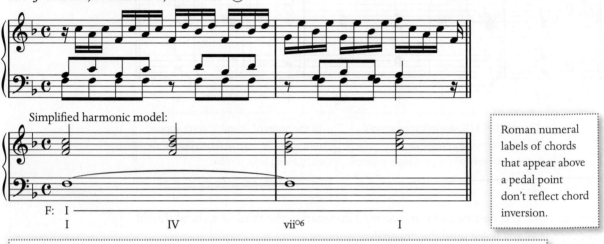

Roman numeral labels of chords that appear above a pedal point don't reflect chord inversion.

A *pedal point* is a note that is sustained in one voice, embellished by a chord progression that appears above it.

FIGURED BASS FOR EMBELLISHING TONES

In figured bass, a succession of figures under a single bass note often indicates embellishing tones. In such a case, the upper voice moves from one note to another as indicated by intervals above the bass. If a dash follows a number, then that note should be sustained while other voices move. Remember that the figures refer to intervals above a given bass: they do *not* necessarily refer to an inversion of a triad or seventh chord.

20.10

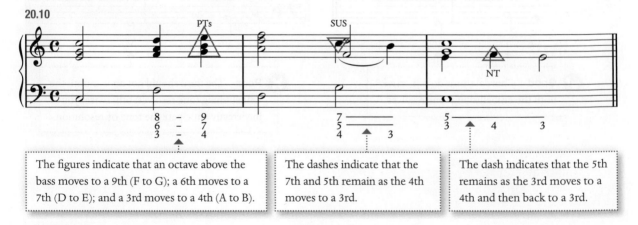

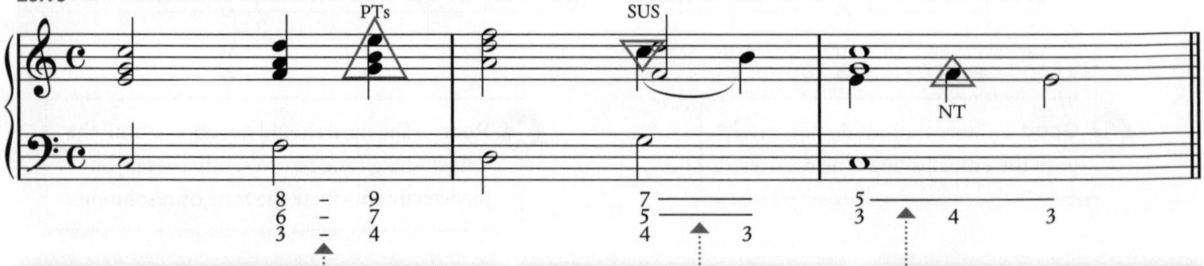

The figures indicate that an octave above the bass moves to a 9th (F to G); a 6th moves to a 7th (D to E); and a 3rd moves to a 4th (A to B).

The dashes indicate that the 7th and 5th remain as the 4th moves to a 3rd.

The dash indicates that the 5th remains as the 3rd moves to a 4th and then back to a 3rd.

A particularly common figured bass that involves an embellishing tone occurs when the third of a root-position triad is decorated by an accented dissonant fourth above $\hat{5}$ in the bass. The figured bass for this is "$^{5-}_{4-3}$," which may be abbreviated as either "4 3" or—if the third above the bass is raised by means of an accidental—as "4 ♯" or "4 ♮." In such cases, the bass should be doubled, not the fourth above the bass (which is a dissonance). The resulting harmony is labeled with Roman numerals as "V4-3."

20.11

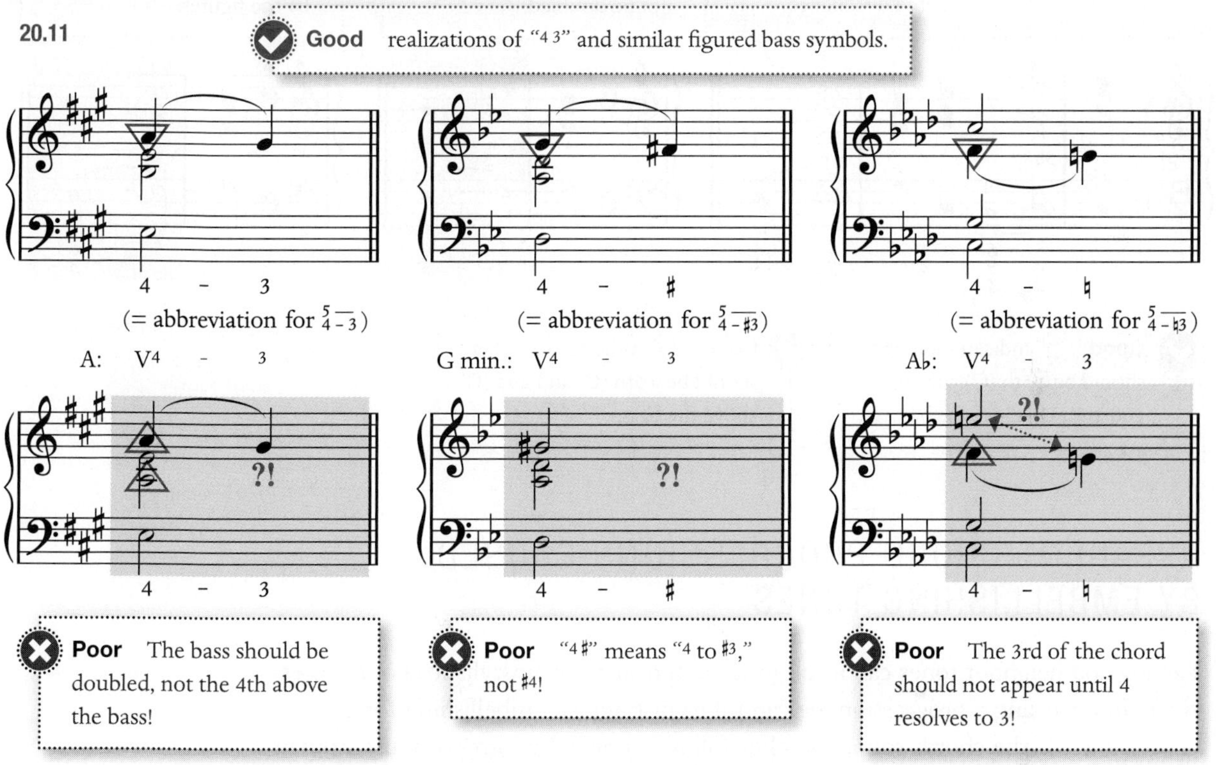

Good realizations of "4 3" and similar figured bass symbols.
4 – 3
(= abbreviation for $^{5-}_{4-3}$)
A: V4 – 3
4 – ♯
(= abbreviation for $^{5-}_{4-\sharp3}$)
G min.: V4 – 3
4 – ♮
(= abbreviation for $^{5-}_{4-\natural3}$)
A♭: V4 – 3
?!
4 – 3
?!
4 – ♯
?!
4 – ♮
Poor The bass should be doubled, not the 4th above the bass!
Poor "4 ♯" means "4 to ♯3," not ♯4!
Poor The 3rd of the chord should not appear until 4 resolves to 3!

Sometimes an embellishing tone is found in the bass while the upper voices remain stationary. This is indicated in the figured bass with a dash below the embellishing bass note. When the only symbol below a bass note is a dash, the upper voices should stay on the same notes while only the bass voice moves.

20.12

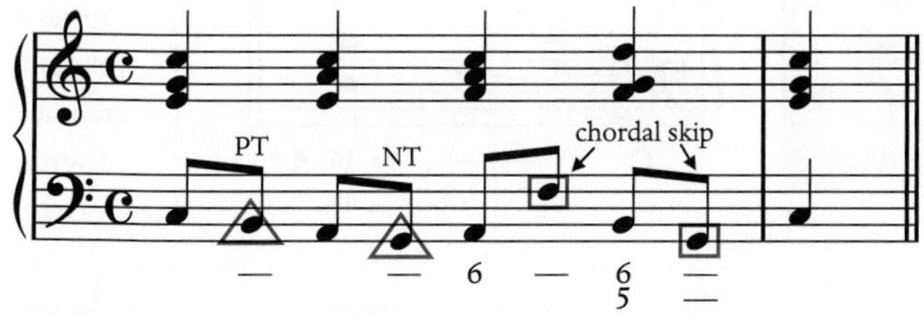

PT
NT
chordal skip
— — 6 — 6/5 —/—

If the only figured bass symbol below a bass note is a dash, only the bass moves.

While most dissonances indicated by figures (such as sevenths) relate to an upper voice that then must resolve, the figure "2" indicates that the bass is dissonant. In such a case the bass should not be doubled.

20.13

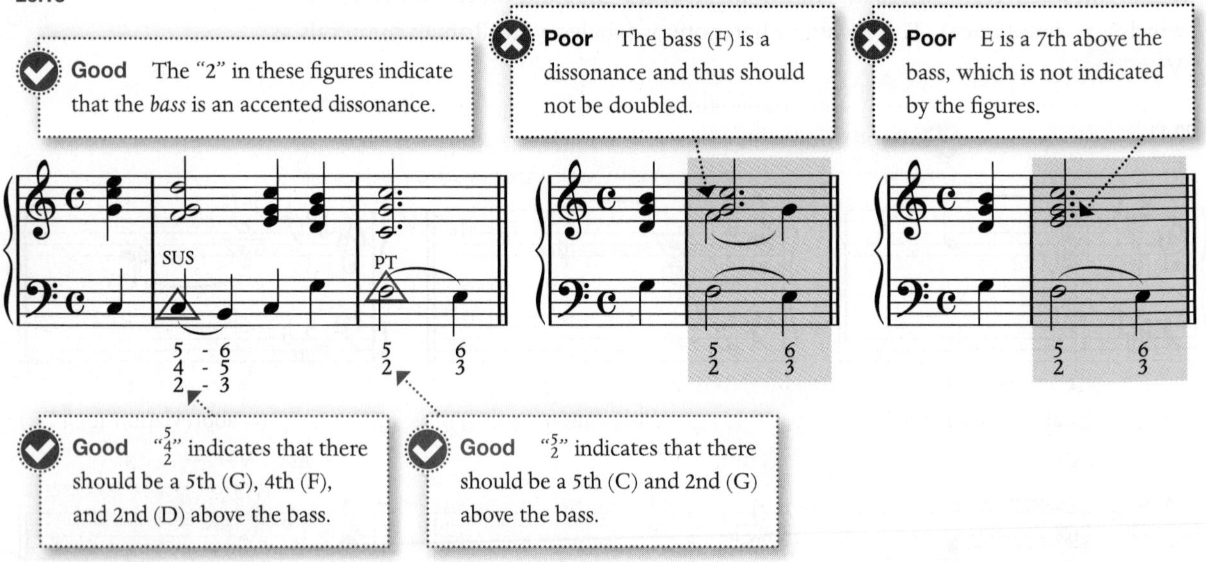
Good The "2" in these figures indicate that the *bass* is an accented dissonance.
Poor The bass (F) is a dissonance and thus should not be doubled.
Poor E is a 7th above the bass, which is not indicated by the figures.
SUS
PT
5 - 6
4 - 5
2 - 3
5
2
6
3
Good "$\begin{smallmatrix}5\\4\\2\end{smallmatrix}$" indicates that there should be a 5th (G), 4th (F), and 2nd (D) above the bass.
Good "$\begin{smallmatrix}5\\2\end{smallmatrix}$" indicates that there should be a 5th (C) and 2nd (G) above the bass.

APPARENT CHORD PROGRESSIONS CAUSED BY EMBELLISHING TONES

Passing and neighbor tones can result in what appear to be unstylistic chord successions. In analyzing a progression, be careful to distinguish embellishing tones from chord tones. If the chords sound like they follow a normal progression, the Roman numeral analysis should reflect this.

20.14

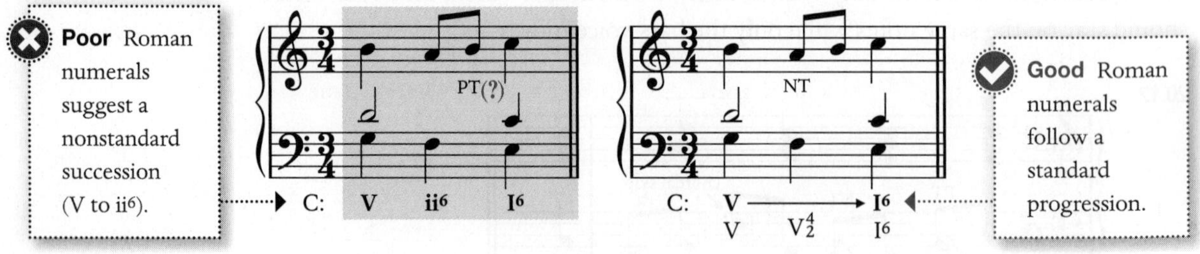
Poor Roman numerals suggest a nonstandard succession (V to ii6).
PT(?)
C: V ii6 I6
NT
C: V I6
V V^4_2 I6
Good Roman numerals follow a standard progression.

review and interact

POINTS FOR REVIEW

- The addition of embellishing tones might create parallel fifths or octaves, either between the embellishing tones themselves or between the embellishing tones and the chord tones.
- Adding an embellishing tone to a passage cannot fix parallel octaves or fifths.
- Suspensions, accented passing tones, and accented neighbor tones can delay the appearance of chord tones.
- A *pedal point* occurs when a note is sustained in one voice (usually the bass) while there is a chord progression in the other voices.
- Figured bass symbols may indicate the presence of embellishing tones in the upper voices by using successive sets of numerals under a single bass tone.
- The figured bass symbol "4 3" is an abbreviation for "$^{5—}_{4-3}$."
- A dash under a bass tone in the figured bass indicates that the bass moves while the upper voices remain on the same notes.
- When embellishing tones create an apparent chord, be sure the chord is part of a stylistically normal progression before you assign a Roman numeral to it.

TEST YOURSELF

1. Which of the following include parallel fifths or octaves?

a. b. c. d. e.

2. In four-part harmony, what are the notes in the upper voices of the following chords? If the chords use only three different pitches, make sure to indicate which tone(s) can be doubled in four-part harmony.

a. b. c. d. e.

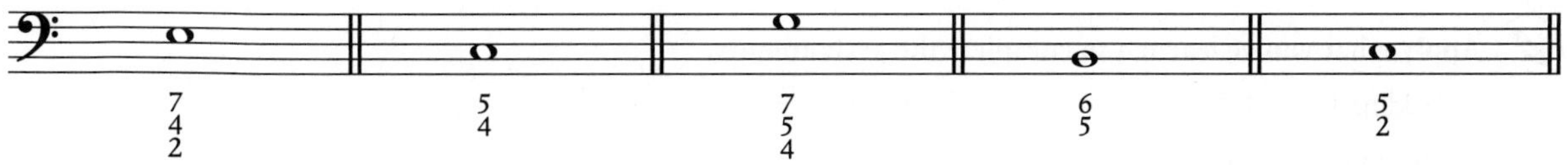

3. What notes are found in the upper voices on the first and second beats of the following chords?

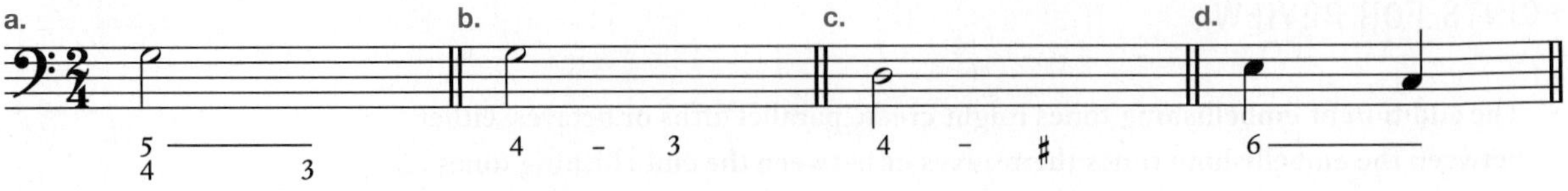

4. Complete a Roman numeral analysis of the passage below; identify the embellishing tones as (accented or unaccented) neighbor tones, incomplete neighbor tones, passing tones; suspensions, anticipations, retardations, or chord skips.

5. Below are three figured bass fragments, each with two proposed realizations. For each, which realization is correct, and why?

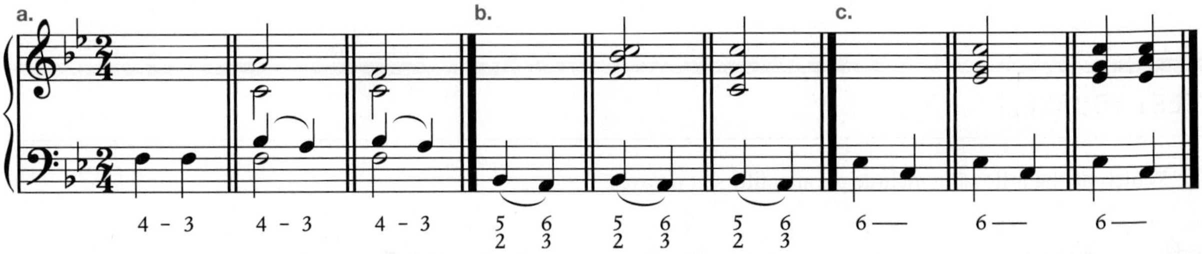

Know It? Show It!

Focus by working through the tutorials on:

- Adding passing tones and neighbor tones to four-part harmony
- Writing suspensions from figures

Learn with inQuizitive.

Apply what you've learned to complete the assignments:

- Adding Embellishments
- Reading Figured Bass
- Realizing Figured Bass
- Harmonizing Melodies
- Composition
- Analysis

chapter

21 III and VII

The III and VII chords are rarely used in simple diatonic settings, but occasionally can substitute for more-common harmonies, lead to a Dominant harmony, or both.

- Root-Position III
- "III6"
- VII°$^{5}_{3}$
- Subtonic VII and VII7

ROOT-POSITION III

A root-position mediant chord—iii in major keys or III in minor keys— shares the same bass and two of the same notes as I6. Occasionally, iii substitutes for I6—that is, it is found in situations similar to those in which I6 appears.

21.1

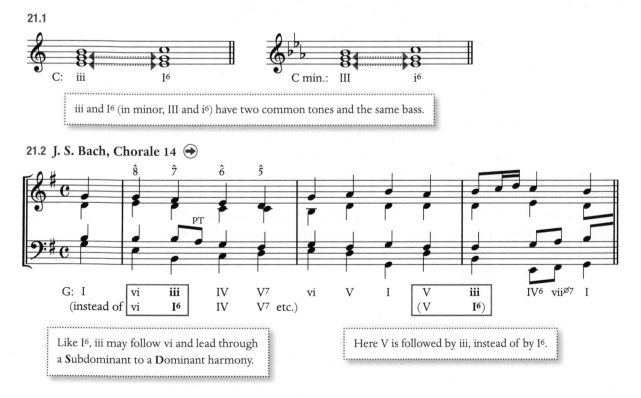

iii and I6 (in minor, III and i6) have two common tones and the same bass.

21.2 J. S. Bach, Chorale 14

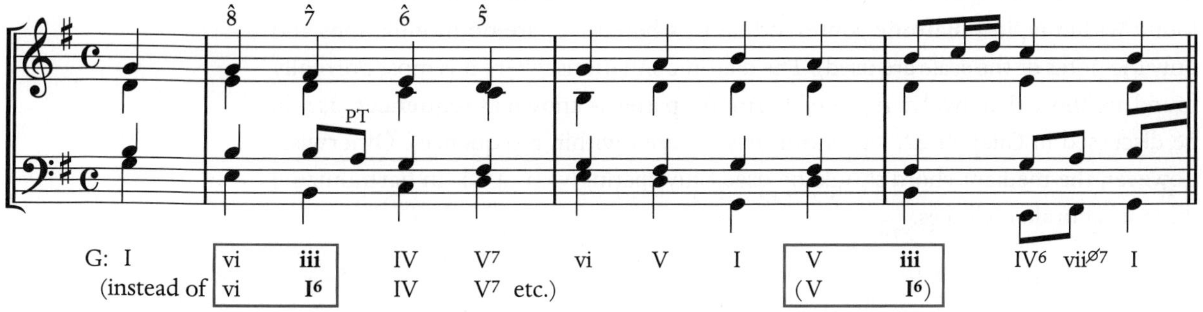

Like I6, iii may follow vi and lead through a **S**ubdominant to a **D**ominant harmony.

Here V is followed by iii, instead of by I6.

The $\hat{7}$ within the iii chord does not need to ascend to tonic. Accordingly, iii is sometimes used to harmonize melodies in which $\hat{7}$ descends to $\hat{6}$. And since it does not lead up to the tonic, $\hat{7}$ within III is not raised in minor keys.

21.3 Schubert, "Im Frühling" (In Springtime)

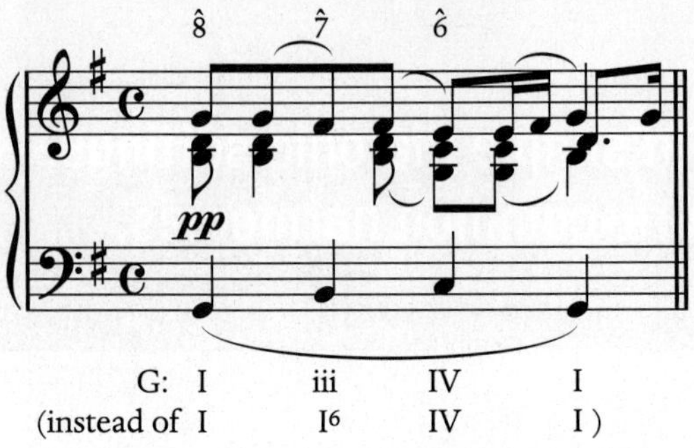

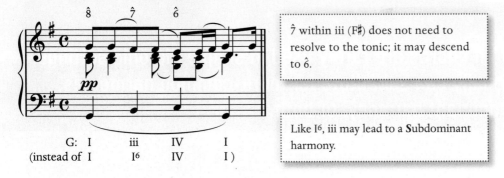

$\hat{7}$ within iii (F♯) does not need to resolve to the tonic; it may descend to $\hat{6}$.

Like I^6, iii may lead to a **S**ubdominant harmony.

21.4 Beethoven, Piano Sonata in C♯ Minor, op. 27, no. 2, I ("Moonlight")

$\hat{7}$ (B) within III in minor keys is *not* raised.

Like i^6, III may lead directly to a **D**ominant.

The mediant chord is most often found in passages where there are **modulations** (that is, changes of key), chromatic alterations, or both (see Part 4). Compared to harmonies discussed in the previous chapters, however, the mediant triad is seldom found within typical **diatonic** contexts (that is, where there are no modulations and only the notes of the scale are used). The diatonic situations where it is most normally found are those that involve repeated harmonic patterns known as **sequences** (as will be discussed in Chapter 22, *any* chord may be used within a sequence). Otherwise, however, the mediant chord should be used only sparingly—if at all—in harmonizing diatonic chorale melodies.

"III6"

The "iii⁶" in major keys and "III+⁶" in minor keys each function like a root-position V in which the fifth of the chord is replaced with a sixth above the bass. Indeed, a chord that literally forms "iii⁶" is usually simply labeled as a V that is decorated with an embellishing tone.

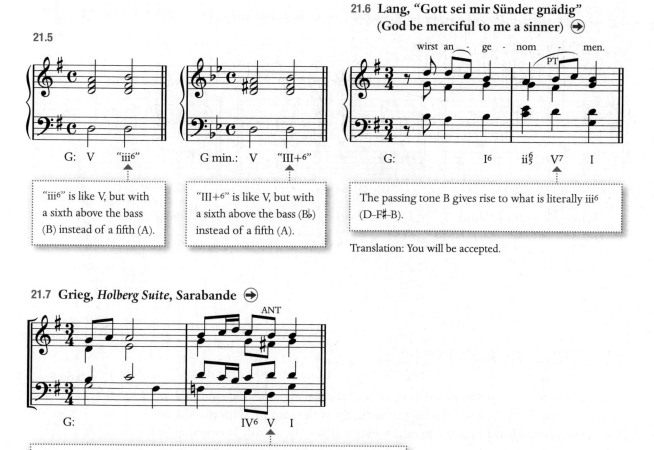

21.5

"iii6" is like V, but with a sixth above the bass (B) instead of a fifth (A).

"III+6" is like V, but with a sixth above the bass (B♭) instead of a fifth (A).

21.6 Lang, "Gott sei mir Sünder gnädig" (God be merciful to me a sinner)

The passing tone B gives rise to what is literally iii6 (D–F♯–B).

Translation: You will be accepted.

21.7 Grieg, *Holberg Suite*, Sarabande

Though D–F♯–B is literally "iii6," this is labeled as a V (with B instead of A).

Especially in later nineteenth-century music, "iii⁶" often substitutes for V. However, this chord is not suited for simple chorale contexts. Accordingly, you should *not* use "iii⁶" in four-part harmony exercises.

VII$^{\circ}{}^{5}_{3}$

Whereas vii$^{\circ 6}$ is extremely common in four-part harmony, the root-position vii$^{\circ}$ triad is *not*. Indeed, even when it appears in textures with three voices, what appears to be a vii$^{\circ}{}^{5}_{3}$ triad is to be understood as a V$^{6}_{5}$ in which the root is omitted. Except within sequences (see Chapter 22), do *not* use a root-position vii$^{\circ}$ triad in four-part harmony exercises.

21.8 Haydn, Symphony no. 47, III

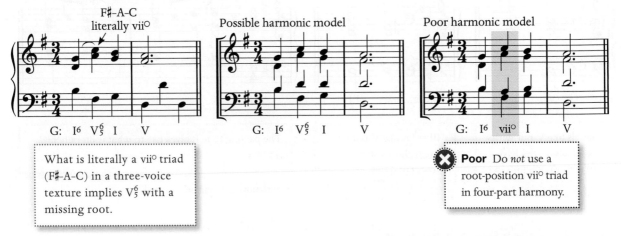

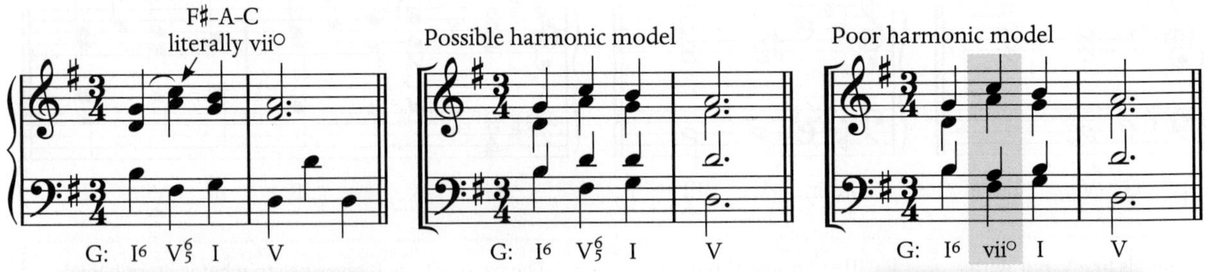

What is literally a vii$^{\circ}$ triad (F♯-A-C) in a three-voice texture implies V$^{6}_{5}$ with a missing root.

Poor Do *not* use a root-position vii$^{\circ}$ triad in four-part harmony.

SUBTONIC VII AND VII^{7}

While $\hat{7}$ is regularly raised in minor keys to form the leading tone, the **subtonic** or unaltered form of $\hat{7}$ can also be used harmonically as the root of **subtonic VII** or **VII^{7}**. Since raised $\hat{7}$ is so important in establishing a minor key, a strongly emphasized subtonic VII can undermine a minor key tonality. Accordingly, subtonic VII is most often used to move to the relative major, either briefly or in a more extended way (see Chapters 26 and 28). It is also possible for the subtonic VII or VII^{7} to lead directly to V or V^{7}, though even in such cases the subtonic VII usually hints at a change of key.

21.9 Schubert, "Der Schatzgräber" (The Treasure Hunter)

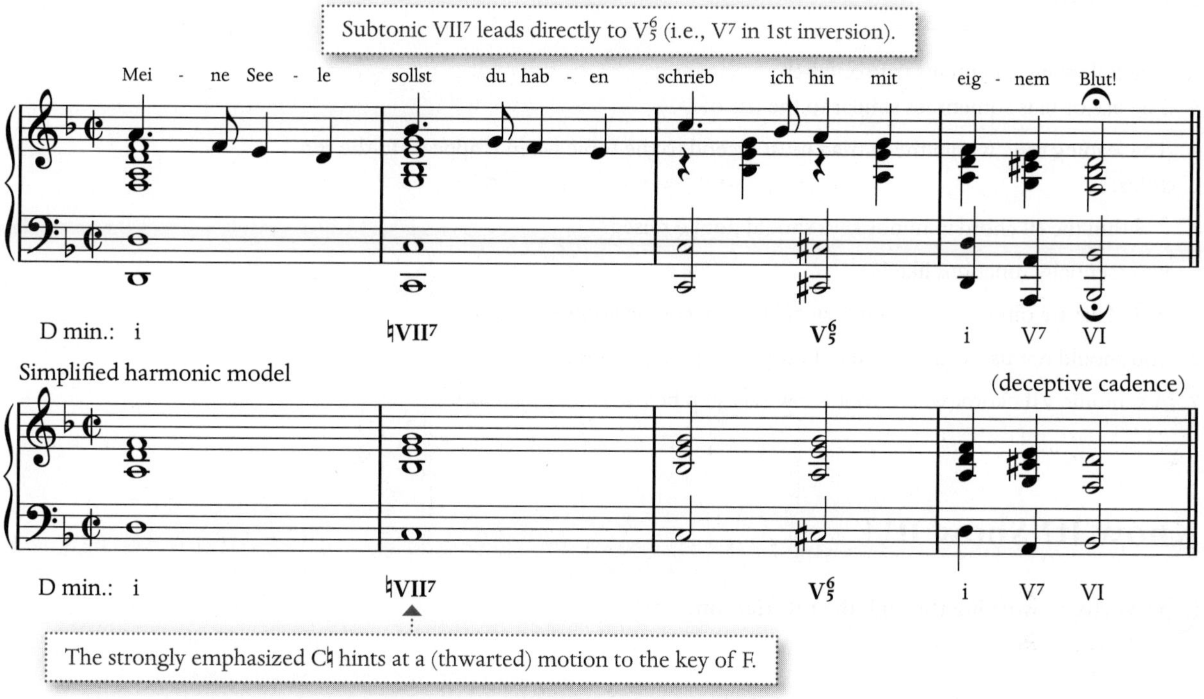
Subtonic VII⁷ leads directly to V$^6_5$ (i.e., V⁷ in 1st inversion).
Mei - ne See - le sollst du hab - en schrieb ich hin mit eig - nem Blut!
D min.: i ♮VII⁷ V$^6_5$ i V⁷ VI
Simplified harmonic model
(deceptive cadence)
D min.: i ♮VII⁷ V$^6_5$ i V⁷ VI
The strongly emphasized C♮ hints at a (thwarted) motion to the key of F.

Translation: "My soul you shall have," I wrote in my own blood!

As a result of these complications, except within sequences (see Chapter 22) you should *not* use the subtonic VII in diatonic four-part harmony exercises.

To learn about vii°$^6_4$, and V$^7_6$ see, A Closer Look.

review and interact

POINTS FOR REVIEW

- **The root-position mediant (iii in major keys and III in minor keys) occasionally substitutes for I⁶.**
- **$\hat{7}$ within the root-position mediant triad does not need to resolve up to the tonic, and thus iii is sometimes used to harmonize melodic motions from $\hat{7}$ to $\hat{6}$.**
- **In minor keys, do not raise $\hat{7}$ within III$^5_3$.**
- **"iii⁶" (in minor keys, "III+⁶") is essentially a V triad with a sixth above the bass replacing the fifth of the chord; "iii⁶" should *not* be used in basic harmony exercises.**
- **When they appear in three-voice textures, root-position vii° triads suggest V$^6_5$ with an implied root; they should *not* be used in four-part harmony.**
- **The subtonic VII and VII⁷ are chords whose root is natural-minor $\hat{7}$. Occasionally, the subtonic VII or VII⁷ may lead to V or V⁷.**

TEST YOURSELF

Are the following statements true or false?

1. The use of iii is sometimes similar to the use of I^6.
2. The leading tone within the iii triad must ascend to the tonic when it appears in the top voice.
3. $\hat{7}$ within the III chord in minor keys should not be raised.
4. iii^6 essentially functions like V.
5. iii and iii^6 are often used within basic melody harmonization exercises.
6. You should not use a vii^{o6} chord in four-part harmony exercises.
7. A subtonic VII chord (whose root is a whole step below $\hat{1}$) may lead to V^6.

Know It? Show It!

Focus by working through the tutorials on:

- Writing I-iii-IV-V-I

Learn with inQuizitive.

Apply what you've learned to complete the assignments:

- Realizing Roman Numerals
- Realizing Figured Bass
- Composition
- Analysis

chapter

22 Sequences

Sequences are repeated musical segments that are transposed in a regular pattern.

REPEATED PATTERNS

A **sequence** occurs when a segment of music repeats one or more times in succession, transposed in a regular pattern. The segment that forms the basis of the sequence can be as brief as a single beat and consist of only a single harmony, or as long as several measures and involve a melody (**melodic sequence**), a progression of several harmonies (**harmonic sequence**), or both. Sequences usually occur in the middle of a phrase, and they are particularly common in the middle section of a composition.

22.1 C. P. E. Bach, Sonata in A Minor for Solo Flute, III ➔

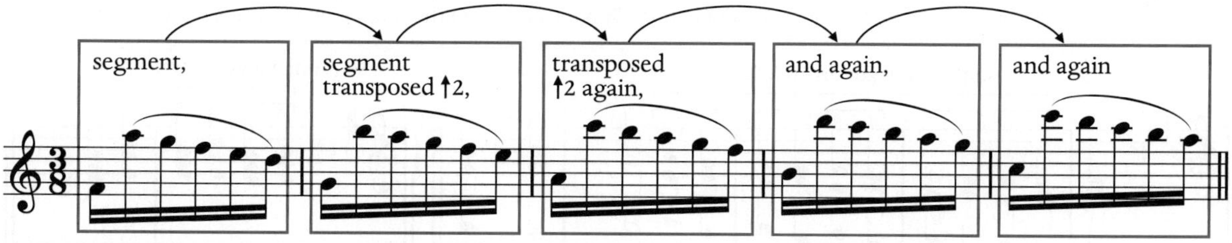

In this *melodic sequence*, the segment repeats, transposed up a second each time.

22.2 J. S. Bach, C Major Invention ➔

In this sequence involving two melodies, a segment is repeated twice, transposed down a third each time.

Typically, a *harmonic sequence* involves a repeated two-chord pattern in which every pair of chords is transposed up or down in a systematic fashion.

22.3

As a result of the sequential pattern, every pair of chords here (indicated by brackets above staff) is systematically transposed up by step.

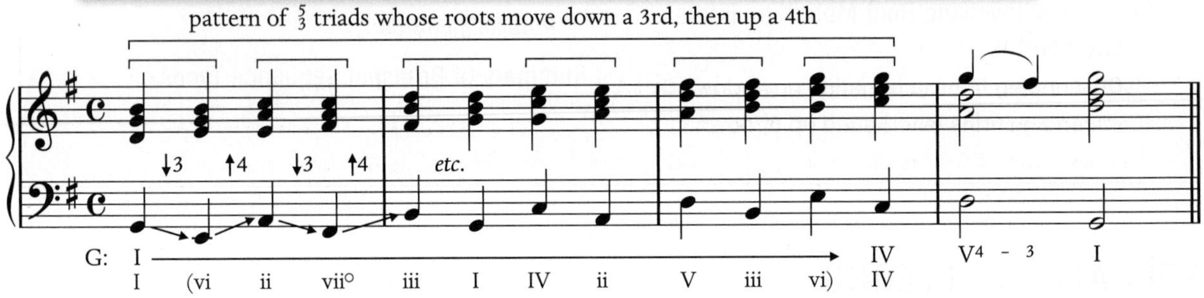

The harmonies of a sequence lead from the sequence's first chord to its last. Once a sequence starts, there is an expectation that the pattern of transposition will continue. As a result, the logic of chord successions within the middle of a sequence derives from the harmonic pattern, not from the functional categories (**T**onic, **D**ominant, or **S**ubdominant) of the individual chords. Accordingly, in the middle of a sequence you may find chords or harmonic successions that in other contexts would be unusual.

22.4

Good Although in a standard functional progression you avoid chords such as iii^6, vi^6, and vii°$^5_3$, or chord progressions such as V (**D**ominant) moving to ii (**S**ubdominant), in the middle of a sequence they are fine!

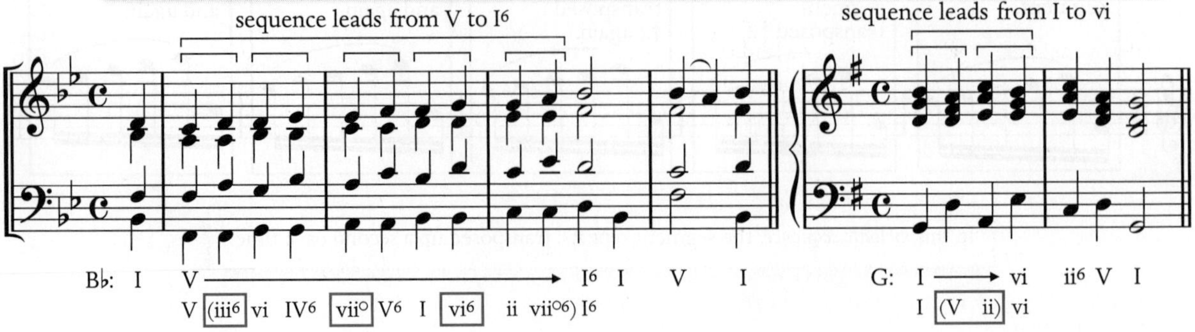

VOICE LEADING IN SEQUENCES

As in standard functional progressions, parallel perfect intervals and unresolved chordal sevenths are *not* allowed within sequential progressions.

22.5

Good There are no parallel fifths or octaves, and all chordal sevenths resolve down by step.

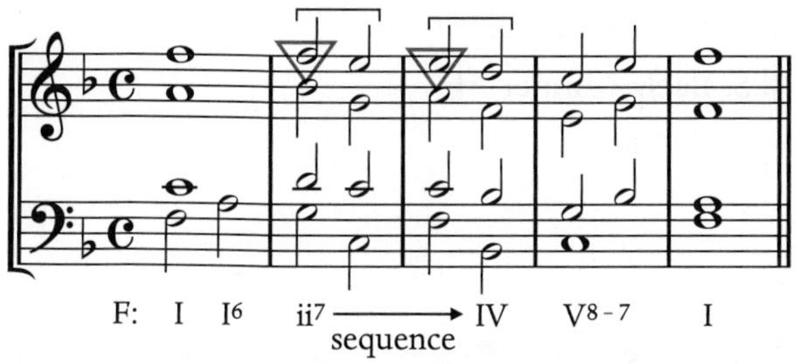

Poor Parallel fifths and unresolved chordal dissonances are *not* allowed within a sequence.

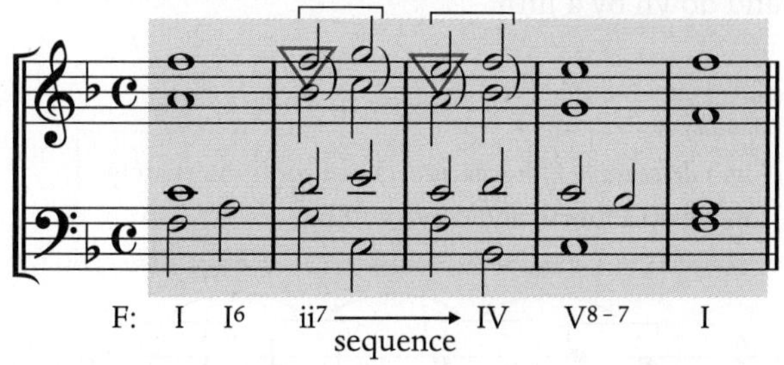

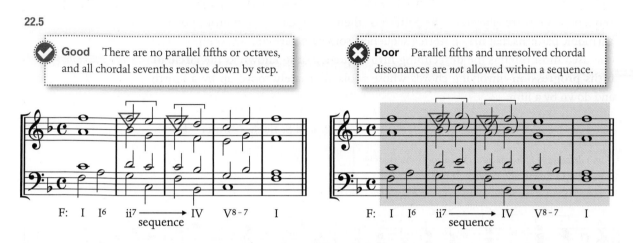

On the other hand, the leading tone may be doubled in the middle of a sequence, where the momentum created by the repetition of the sequential pattern is stronger than the leading tone's need to ascend. Likewise, in the middle of a minor-key sequence, $\hat{7}$ need not be raised.

22.6

Good The leading tone (B) may be doubled in the middle of a sequence.

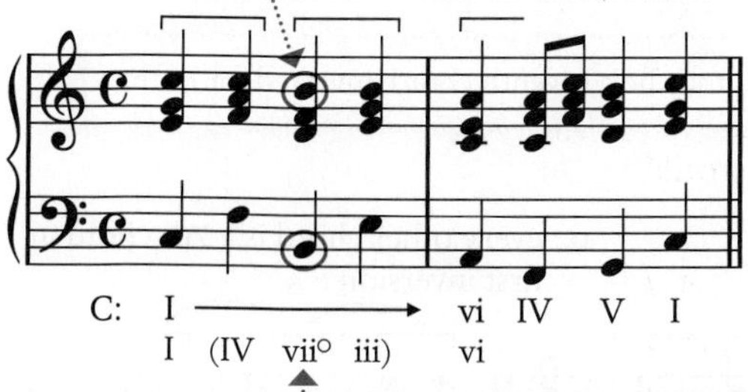

Good $\hat{7}$ need not be raised in the middle of a sequence.

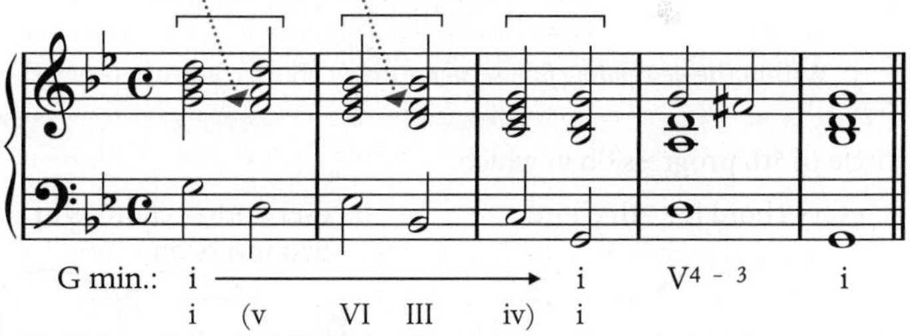

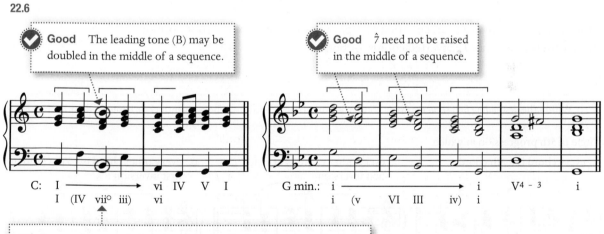

Whereas under normal circumstances a leading tone is expected to lead up to the tonic, in mid-sequence one expects the pattern to continue.

SEQUENCES INVOLVING ROOT MOTION BY FIFTHS AND FOURTHS

DESCENDING FIFTHS (ALTERNATING UP 4, DOWN 5)

Sequences often are labeled by the pattern of their roots. Of the numerous possible harmonic patterns that may govern a sequence, some are particularly common. The one used most often is the **descending fifth sequence**–also known as the **circle of fifths progression**–involving chords whose roots alternately move up by a fourth and down by a fifth.

22.7

In a *descending fifth sequence*, chord roots alternately move up a fourth and down a fifth.

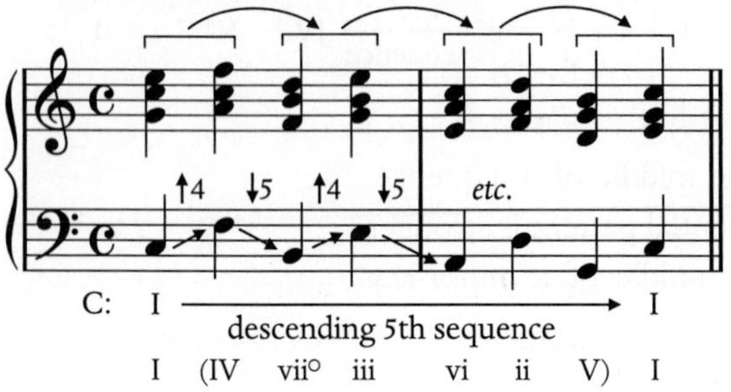

22.8 J. S. Bach, Minuet

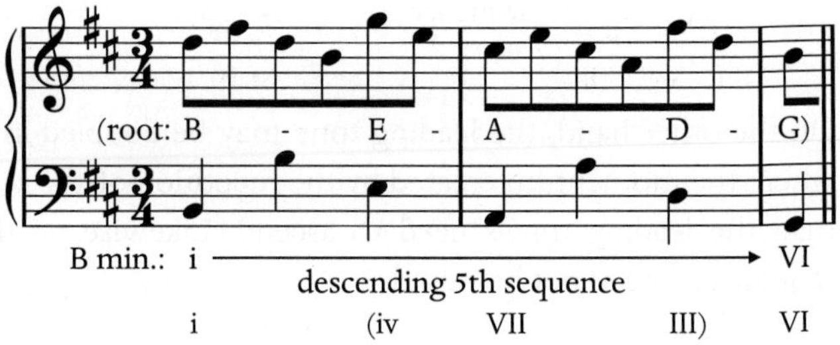

Descending fifth sequences can be varied by replacing some or all of the root-position triads with seventh chords, inverted chords, or both.

22.9

Within the *descending fifth sequence* every chord (or every other chord) may be a seventh chord, inverted, or both.

Circle of 5th progression in which:

a. every chord is a 7th chord

b. every other chord is in first inversion

c. every other chord is a 7th chord in first inversion

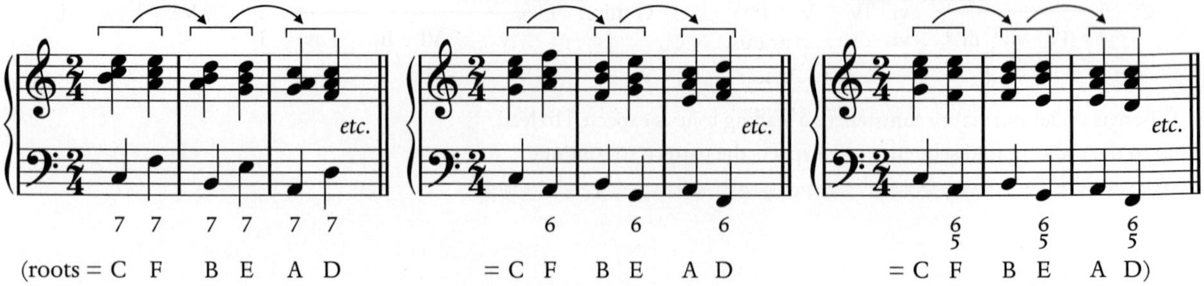

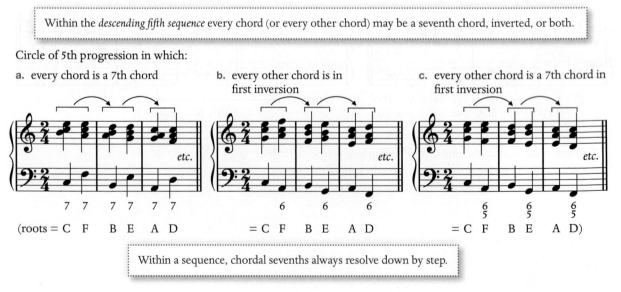

Within a sequence, chordal sevenths always resolve down by step.

22.10 Handel, Violin Sonata in E, HWV 373, III

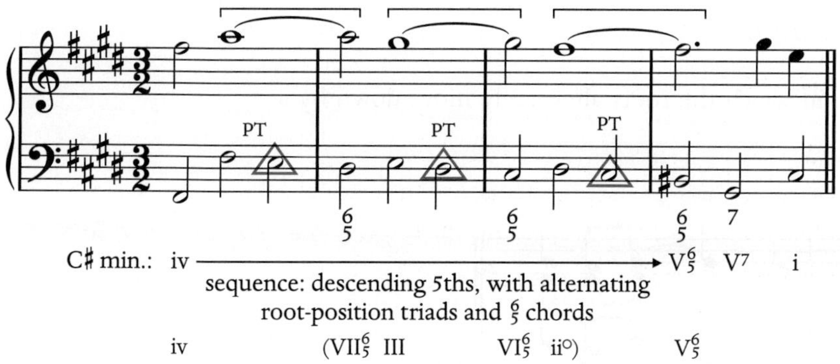

ASCENDING FIFTHS (ALTERNATING UP 5, DOWN 4)

Another common pattern is the **ascending fifth sequence**, which involves chords whose roots alternately move up by a fifth and down by a fourth. All the triads used within an ascending fifth sequence must be either major or minor; diminished triads sound too harsh within this sequence.

22.11

22.12 Beethoven, Piano Sonata in C, op. 53 ("Waldstein"), III

In an *ascending fifth sequence*, chord roots alternately move up a fifth and down a fourth.

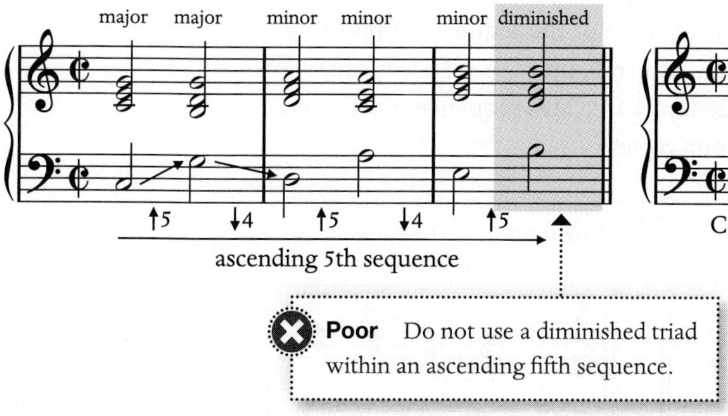

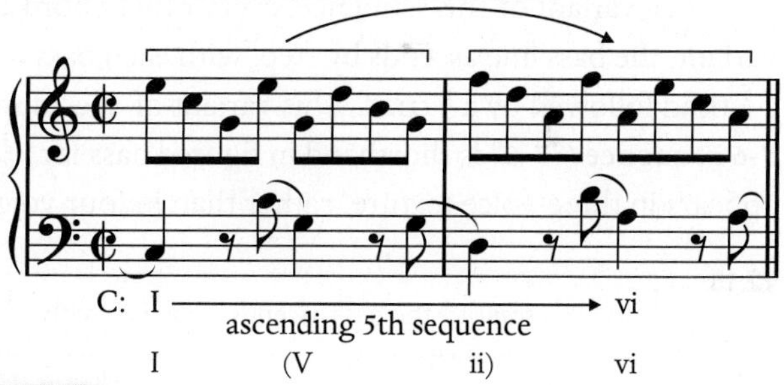

OTHER COMMON SEQUENCES

ROOTS ALTERNATE DOWN 3, UP 4

Another common sequence is one in which the roots alternately move down by a third, then up by a fourth.

22.13

B♭: I —— sequence ——→ IV V I

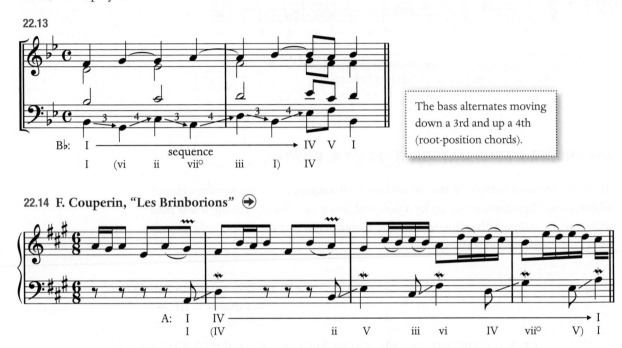

I (vi ii vii° iii I) IV

The bass alternates moving down a 3rd and up a 4th (root-position chords).

22.14 F. Couperin, "Les Brinborions" ➔

A: I IV ——————→ I

I (IV ii V iii vi IV vii° V) I

In a variant of this sequence, every other chord appears in first inversion. In this variant, the bass line ascends by step, with each bass note of the sequence supporting a $^5_3$ triad followed by a $^6_3$ triad. This variant of the "down 3, up 4" sequence is called a **5-6 sequence** ("5-6" is shorthand in figured bass for "$^{5-6}_{3-3}$"). This sequence most often appears in three-voice texture, rather than in four voices.

22.15

In a *5-6 sequence* the bass ascends stepwise, with a $^5_3$ to $^6_3$ triad over each bass note.

5 - 6 5 - 6 5 - 6

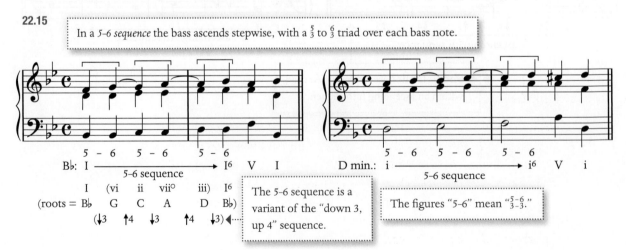

B♭: I —— 5-6 sequence ——→ I⁶ V I

I (vi ii vii° iii) I⁶

(roots = B♭ G C A D B♭)

(↓3 ↑4 ↓3 ↑4 ↓3)

The 5-6 sequence is a variant of the "down 3, up 4" sequence.

5 - 6 5 - 6 5 - 6

D min.: i —— 5-6 sequence ——→ i⁶ V i

The figures "5-6" mean "$^{5-6}_{3-3}$."

ROOTS ALTERNATE DOWN 4, UP 2

In another common sequence, the roots of the chords move alternately down by a fourth then up by step. This sequence is sometimes referred to as a **Romanesca**.

22.16

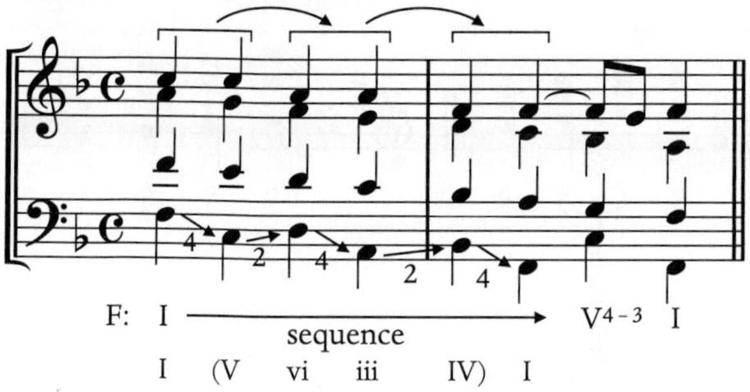

22.17 Pachelbel, Canon in D

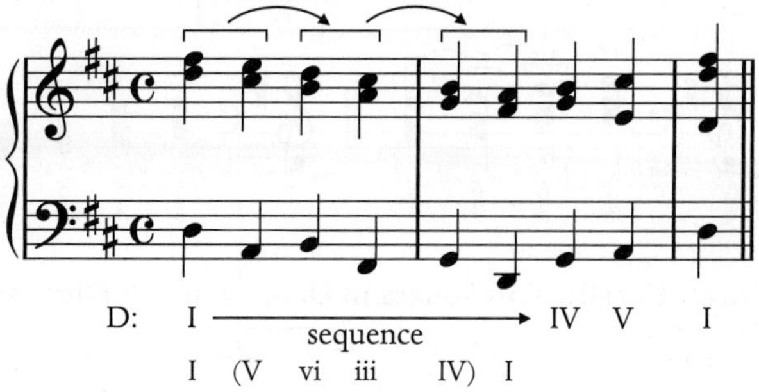

The bass alternately moves down a fourth, then up a step.

A variant of this arises when every other chord is in first inversion, so that the bass descends by step.

22.18

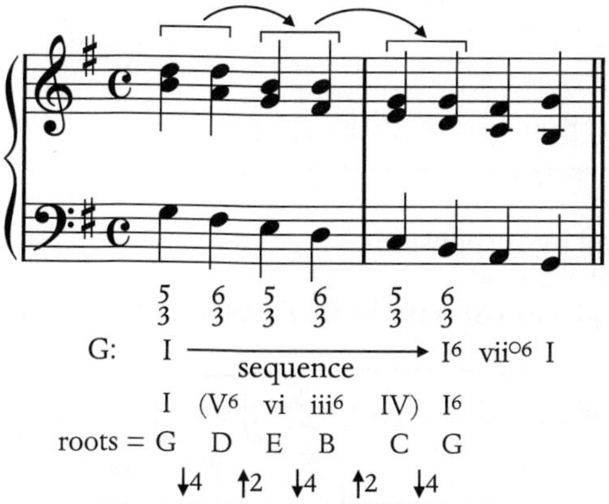

22.19 Beethoven, Piano Sonata in G, op. 79, III

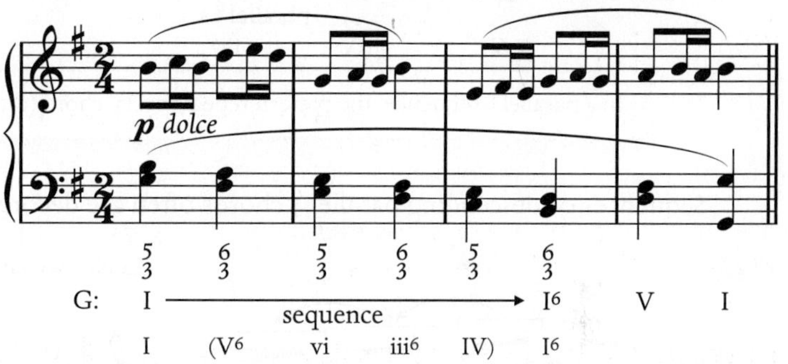

In a variant of the "down 4, up 2" sequence, the bass descends by step, alternately supporting $^5_3$ and $^6_3$ chords.

PARALLEL $^6_3$ CHORDS

Another common sequence involves descending **parallel $^6_3$ chords**, in which a first-inversion chord is repeatedly transposed down by step. Only first-inversion triads can move in parallel motion without producing voice-leading errors: parallel $^5_3$ chords result in parallel fifths, and parallel $^6_4$ chords involve dissonances that do not resolve. In order to avoid voice-leading errors, however, the two upper voices of parallel $^6_3$ chords must move in parallel fourths, not fifths. Parallel $^6_3$ chords most often appear in three-part rather than four-part textures.

22.20

Good Descending parallel $\substack{6\\3}$ chords: Parallel perfect fourths between the two top voices (unlike perfect fifths) are fine.

Poor Parallel $\substack{5\\3}$ or parallel $\substack{6\\4}$ chords would create parallel fifths or unresolved dissonances.

Poor Parallel $\substack{6\\3}$ chords can use parallel perfect fourths in the top voices, but not perfect fifths.

22.21 Corelli, Trio Sonata in D, op. 4, no. 4, Giga

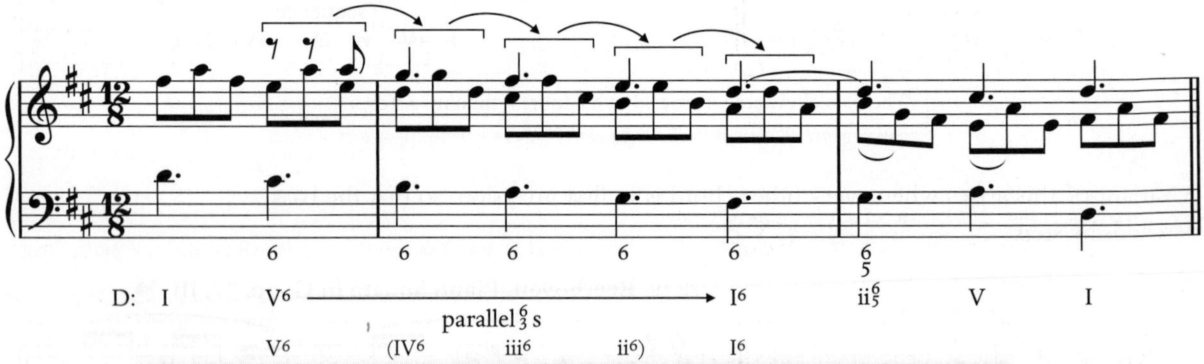

In a parallel $\substack{6\\3}$ sequence, the pattern repeats every chord (rather than every other chord).

Sequences of descending parallel $\substack{6\\3}$ chords often are decorated by suspensions.

22.22

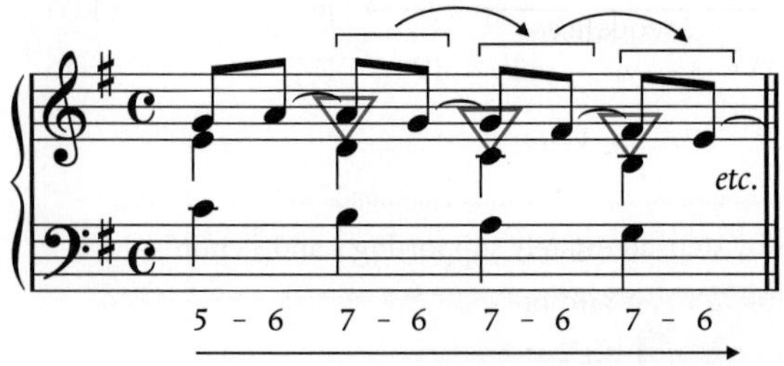

22.23 Mozart, Piano Sonata in G, K. 283, I

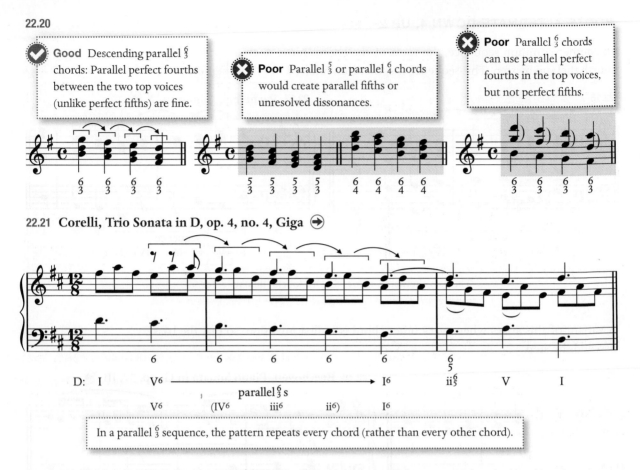

Descending parallel $\substack{6\\3}$ chords decorated by a series of 7-6 suspensions.

SUMMARY OF PRINCIPAL SEQUENCE TYPES

The sequential patterns discussed here are only some of the possibilities. There are many other types of possible sequential patterns, including other variants of the ones discussed above, as well as sequences that involve chromaticism; some of these other sequences are discussed in Chapter 32.

22.24

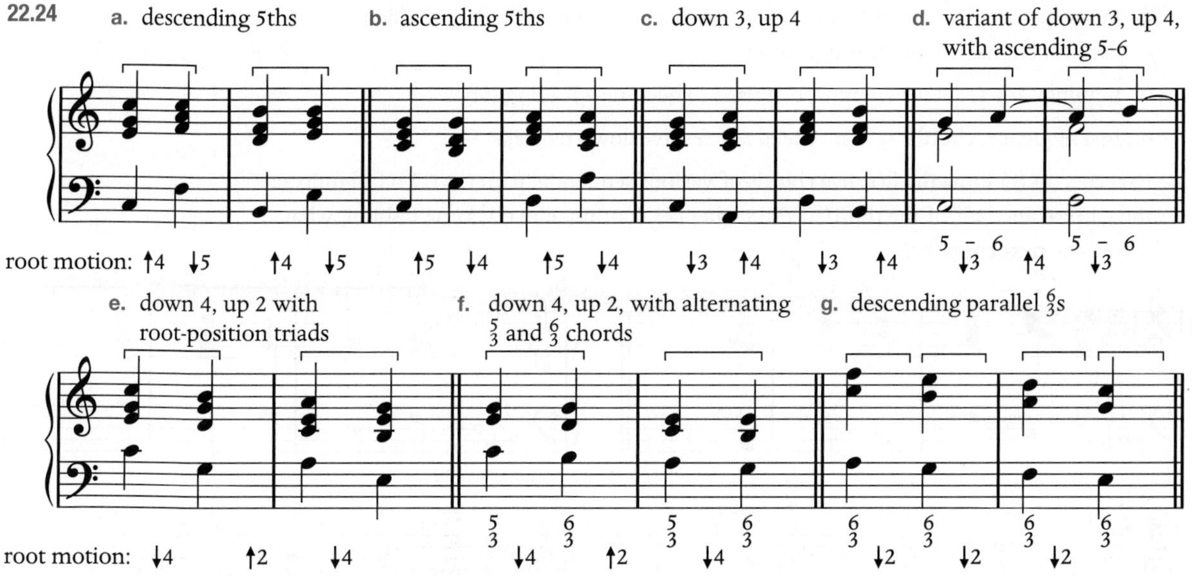

review and interact

POINTS FOR REVIEW

- **In a sequence, a musical segment or a harmonic progression is transposed following a recurring pattern.**
- **A sequence typically appears in the middle of a phrase or the middle section of a composition.**
- **The logic of the chord progression in the middle of a sequence is determined by the sequential pattern, rather than by the functional categories of the chords.**
- **Within a sequence, parallel fifths and octaves are not allowed, and chordal sevenths must resolve down by step.**
- **The leading tone may be doubled in the middle of a sequence; in minor keys, $\hat{7}$ need not be raised in the middle of a sequence.**
- **Some common sequence patterns include those that involve root motions by descending or ascending fifths; root motions alternating down a third and up a fourth; root motions alternating down a fourth and up a second; and variants of these involving inverted chords and seventh chords.**
- **In parallel $^6_3$ sequences, parallel fourths between the upper voices are fine, but parallel fifths are not.**

TEST YOURSELF

1. Which of the following statements are true?
   a. In a sequence, doubled leading tones are permissible.
   b. In a sequence, parallel fifths and octaves are permissible.

c. In a sequence, you might find chord successions that are normally forbidden in standard functional harmonic progressions.

d. In minor-key sequences, $\hat{7}$ must be raised to become a leading tone.

e. In a sequence, chordal sevenths need not resolve down by step.

2. Excerpts (a)–(f) show the first five chords of various sequential patterns (two full units of the pattern and half of the third). If the sequences continued in the same fashion, what would the next chord be?

a.

b.

c.

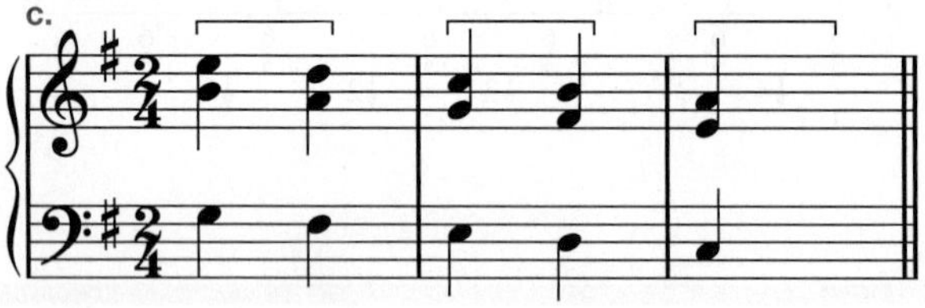

d.

e.

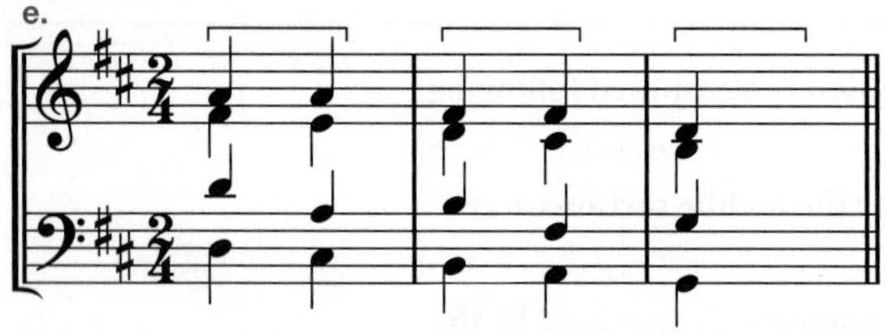

f.

Know It? Show It!

Focus by working through the tutorials on:

- Writing a descending fifth sequence
- Ascending fifth sequence
- Sequence with roots moving down by a third, up by a fourth
- Romanesca sequence

Learn with inQuizitive.

Apply what you've learned to complete the assignments:

- Melodic Sequences
- Descending Fifth Sequences
- Other Sequences
- Realizing Figured Bass
- Sequences with Figuration in Multiple Voices
- Composition
- Analysis

chapter 23 Other $^6_4$ Chords

Because they include a dissonant fourth between the bass and an upper voice, $^6_4$ chords embellish other more-stable harmonies in a variety of contexts.

$^6_4$ CHORDS AS EMBELLISHING HARMONIES

Because $^6_4$ chords contain a dissonant fourth above the bass, they generally do not function like the $^5_3$ or $^6_3$ chords with the same root. For instance, I and I^6 function similarly, as do ii and ii^6. In contrast, I$^6_4$ does *not* function like I or I^6, and ii$^6_4$ is *not* interchangeable with ii or ii^6.

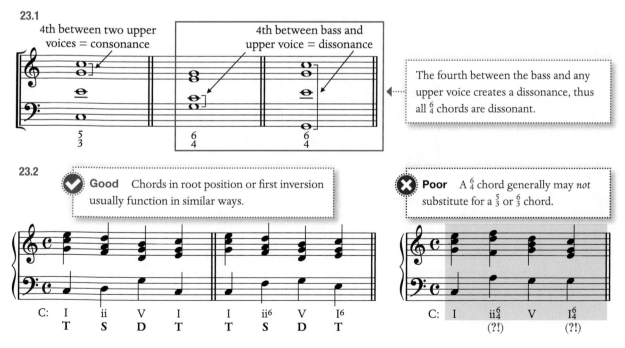

23.1

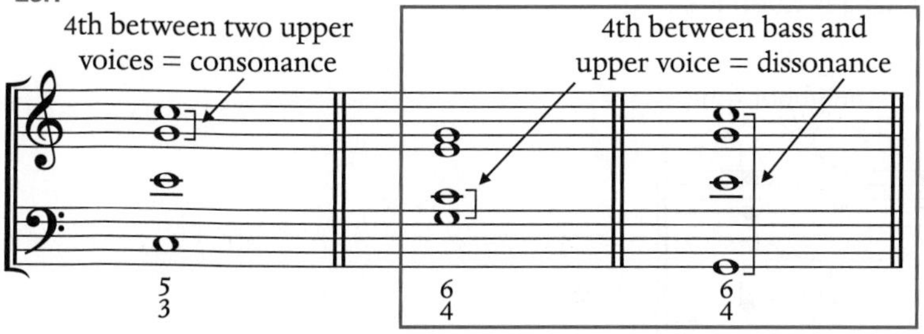

The fourth between the bass and any upper voice creates a dissonance, thus all $^6_4$ chords are dissonant.

23.2

Good Chords in root position or first inversion usually function in similar ways.

Poor A $^6_4$ chord generally may *not* substitute for a $^5_3$ or $^6_3$ chord.

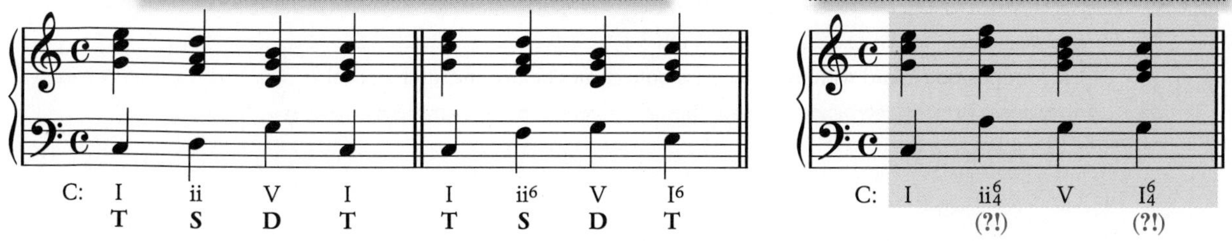

$^6_4$ chords usually embellish other harmonies. In Chapter 15, we discussed the most important type of $^6_4$ chord, namely the **cadential $^6_4$**. Other $^6_4$ chords include the **pedal $^6_4$**, the **passing $^6_4$**, and the **arpeggiated $^6_4$**. Unlike the cadential $^6_4$, these other $^6_4$ chords often appear in metrically weak positions. Because they act as embellishments, the specific function of each of these $^6_4$ chords is determined by how it is approached and left, rather than by its root. Accordingly, they are usually labeled by their specific function in addition to their Roman numeral.

23.3

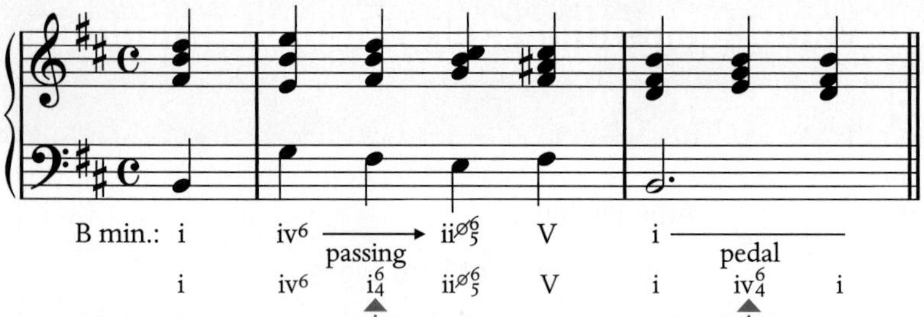

To clarify their function, these $^6_4$ chords are labeled as passing or pedal as well as with a Roman numeral.

PEDAL $^6_4$

A *pedal* $^6_4$ chord results when the bass of a root-position chord is sustained while the upper voices are decorated with embellishing tones that form a $^6_4$ chord. A pedal $^6_4$ is both preceded and followed by a root-position chord that uses the same bass note. In four-part harmony, usually the bass of a pedal $^6_4$ is doubled.

23.4

Neighbor tones in the upper voices give rise to a pedal $^6_4$ over a stationary bass.

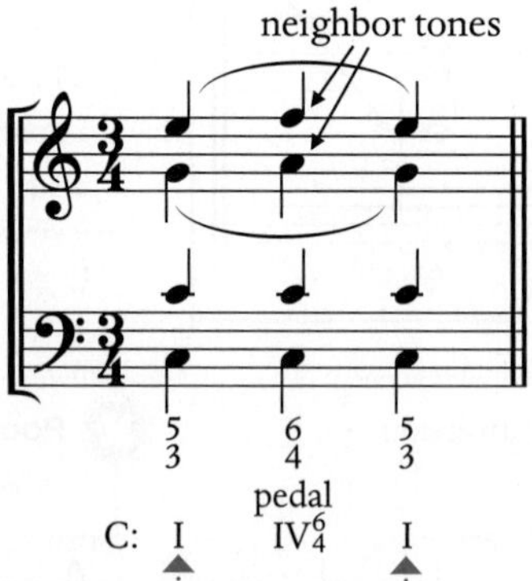

A root-position chord with the same bass note comes before and after a pedal $^6_4$.

23.5 Handel, "La Paix," from *Royal Fireworks Music*

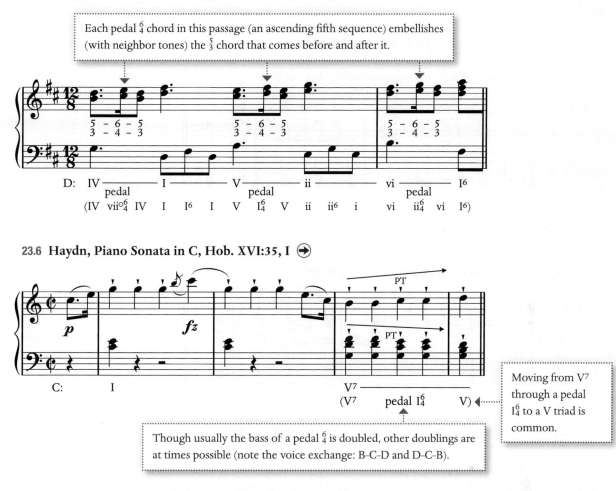

Each pedal $^6_4$ chord in this passage (an ascending fifth sequence) embellishes (with neighbor tones) the $^5_3$ chord that comes before and after it.

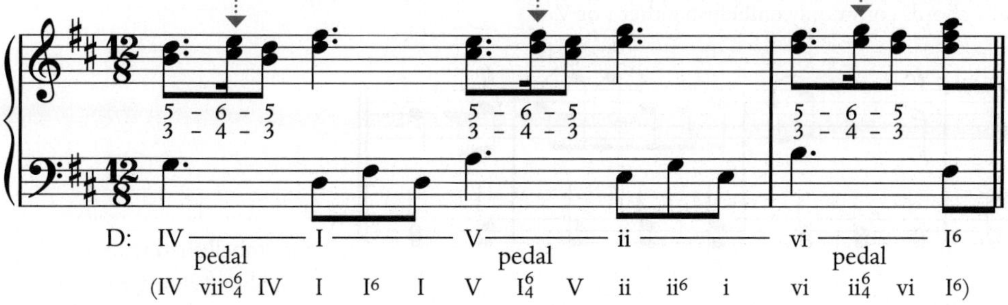

23.6 Haydn, Piano Sonata in C, Hob. XVI:35, I

Moving from V7 through a pedal I$^6_4$ to a V triad is common.

Though usually the bass of a pedal $^6_4$ is doubled, other doublings are at times possible (note the voice exchange: B-C-D and D-C-B).

23.7 Cadenza doppia (standard 18th-century cadential formula)

A combination of passing and neighbor tones in the upper voices here produces a pedal $^6_4$ chord that embellishes the **D**ominant harmony.

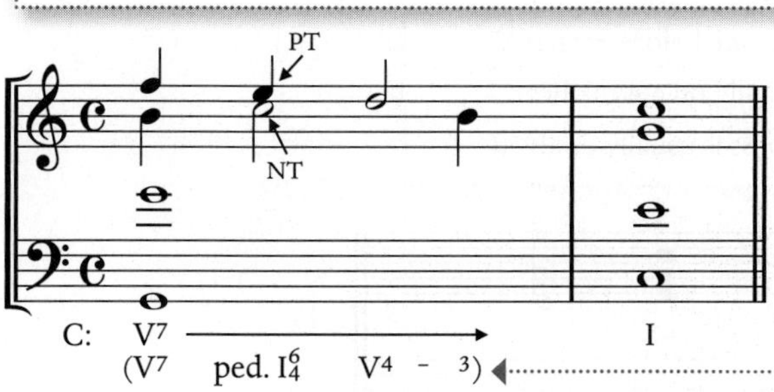

Moving from V7 through a pedal I$^6_4$ to a V triad is common.

Although they may decorate any root-position chord, pedal $^6_4$ chords most often embellish either I or V.

23.8 Haydn, Divertimento in E, Hob. XVI:13, II

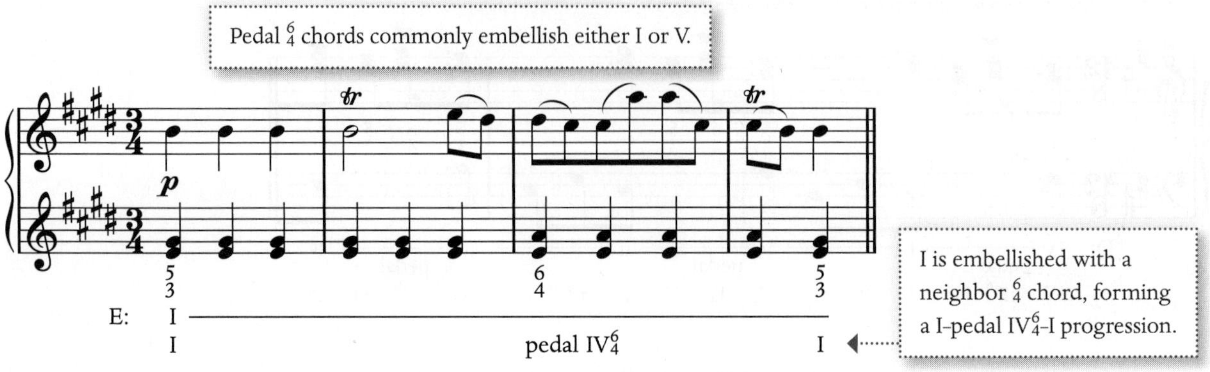

Pedal $^6_4$ chords commonly embellish either I or V.
p
$^5_3$ $^6_4$ $^5_3$
E: I
I pedal IV^6_4 I
I is embellished with a neighbor $^6_4$ chord, forming a I-pedal IV^6_4-I progression.

23.9 Schubert, Piano Sonata in A minor, D. 845, II

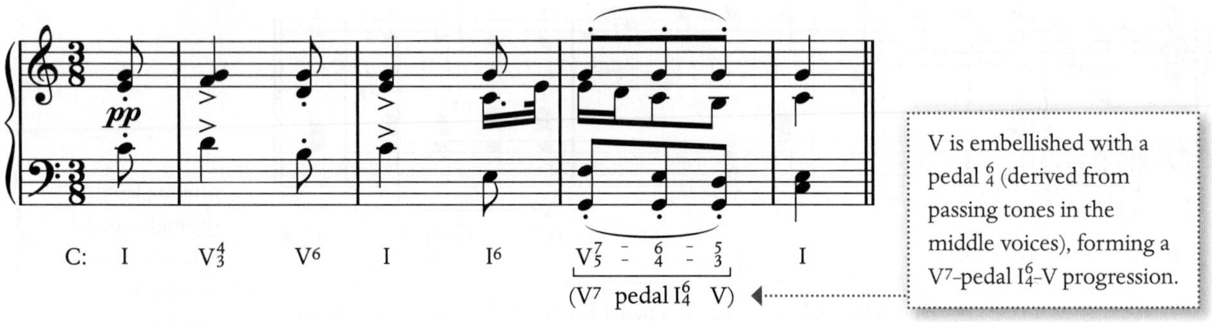

pp
C: I V^4_3 V^6 I I^6 V^7_5 - $^6_4$ - $^5_3$ I
(V^7 pedal I^6_4 V)
V is embellished with a pedal $^6_4$ (derived from passing tones in the middle voices), forming a V^7-pedal I^6_4-V progression.

Note that both the cadential $^6_4$ and the pedal $^6_4$ are followed immediately by a root-position chord over the same note in the bass. A cadential $^6_4$, however, cannot be *preceded* by V, and it has other restrictions as well that differentiate it from the pedal $^6_4$.

23.10

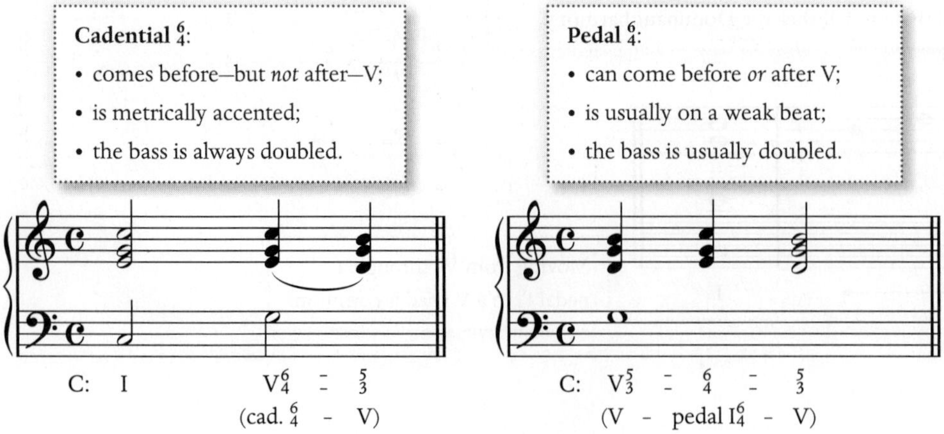

Cadential $^6_4$:
• comes before—but *not* after—V;
• is metrically accented;
• the bass is always doubled.
Pedal $^6_4$:
• can come before *or* after V;
• is usually on a weak beat;
• the bass is usually doubled.
C: I V^6_4 - $^5_3$
(cad. $^6_4$ - V)
C: V^5_3 - $^6_4$ - $^5_3$
(V - pedal I^6_4 - V)

PASSING $^6_4$

A *passing* $^6_4$ chord is a second-inversion triad whose bass is a passing tone. In four-part harmony the bass of a passing $^6_4$ is usually doubled.

23.11

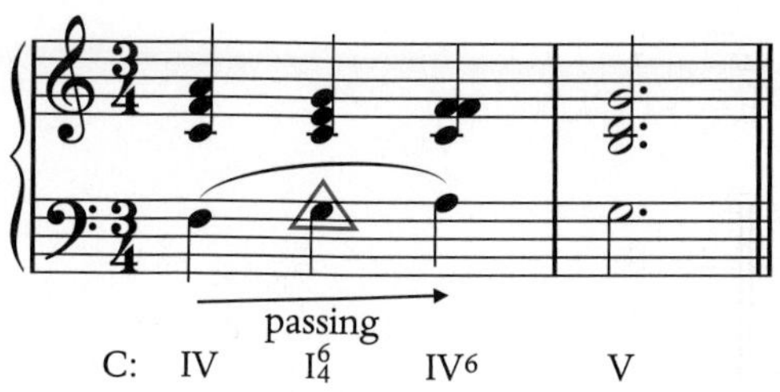

Passing $^6_4$: The passing tone G in the bass (part of the F–G–A passing motion) supports a $^6_4$ chord (G–C–E), with the bass doubled.

23.12 Beethoven, Piano Sonata op. 27, no. 2, I ("Moonlight")

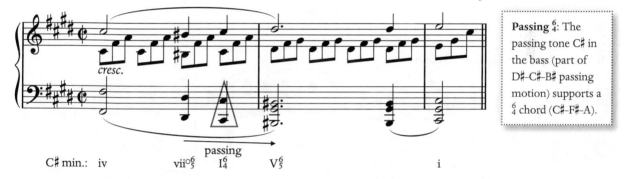

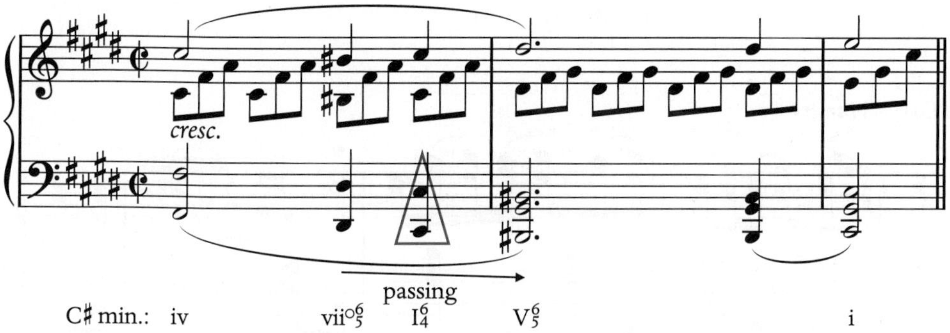

Passing $^6_4$: The passing tone C♯ in the bass (part of D♯–C♯–B♯ passing motion) supports a $^6_4$ chord (C♯–F♯–A).

Although a passing $^6_4$ may appear over any scale degree in the bass, it most commonly appears over $\hat{5}$.

23.13 Mozart, Piano Sonata in D, K. 311, II

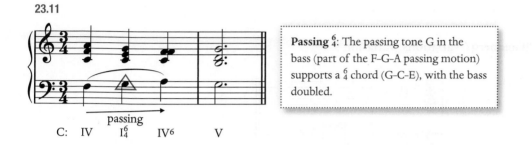

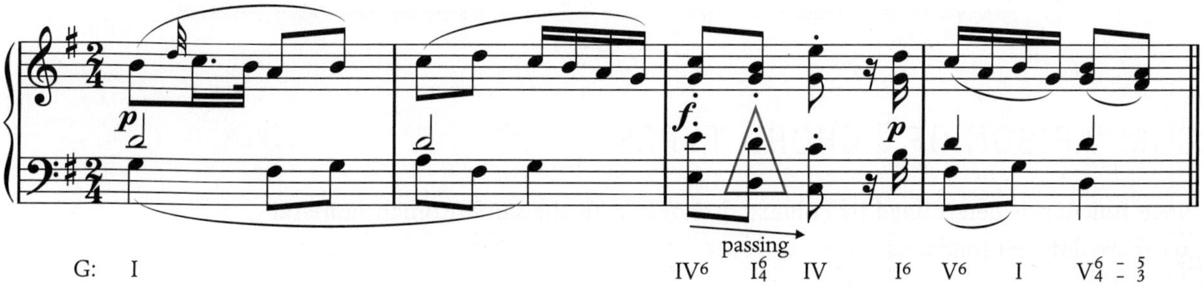

A passing I$^6_4$ chord (i.e., one whose bass is $\hat{5}$) is particularly common.

ARPEGGIATED $^6_4$

An *arpeggiated* $^6_4$ arises when a chord is sustained in the upper voices as the bass voice either arpeggiates the entire triad or oscillates between the root and fifth of the chord. Arpeggiated $^6_4$ chords are found mostly in instrumental genres rather than in four-part chorale settings.

23.14 J. S. Bach, "Goldberg" Variations, variation 9

The fifth appears in the bass during an arpeggio, resulting in a brief *arpeggiated* $^6_4$ chord.

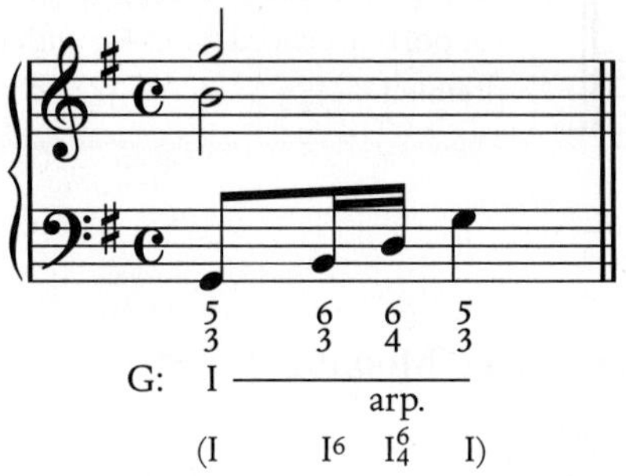

23.15 Scott Joplin, *The Easy Winners*

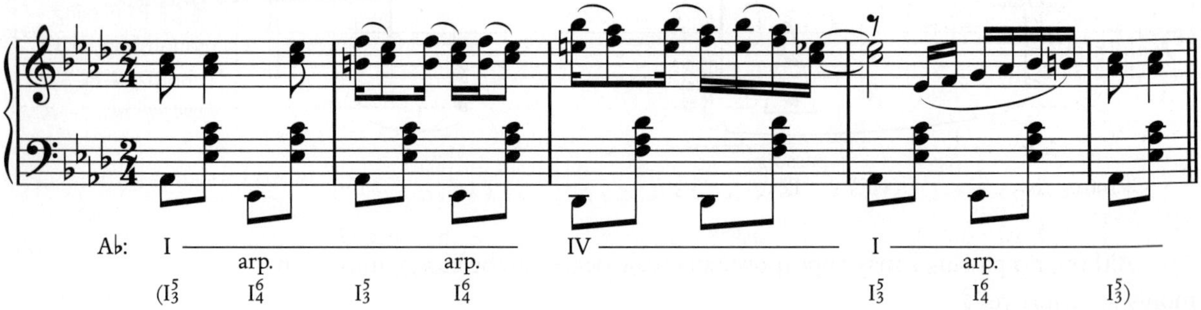

The bass oscillates between the root and fifth of I, resulting in arpeggiated $^6_4$ chords.

COMPARISON OF $^6_4$ CHORD TYPES

Since function is determined by context, $^6_4$ chords with the same Roman numeral may have different functions.

23.16

Cadential $^6_4$:
- is accented
- leads directly to V^5_3
- doesn't follow V.

Pedal $^6_4$:
- $^6_4$ is formed by PT and/or NT above a stationary bass.

Passing $^6_4$:
- is formed by $^6_4$ chord above PT in the bass.

Arpeggiated $^6_4$:
- $^6_4$ is formed by a chordal skip in the bass.

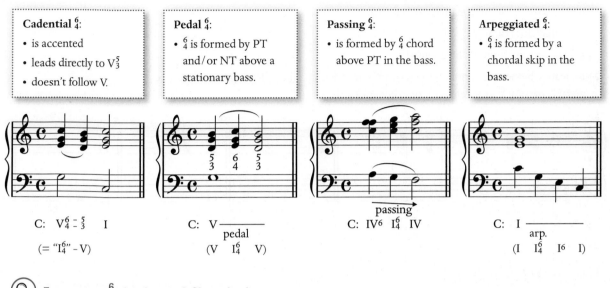

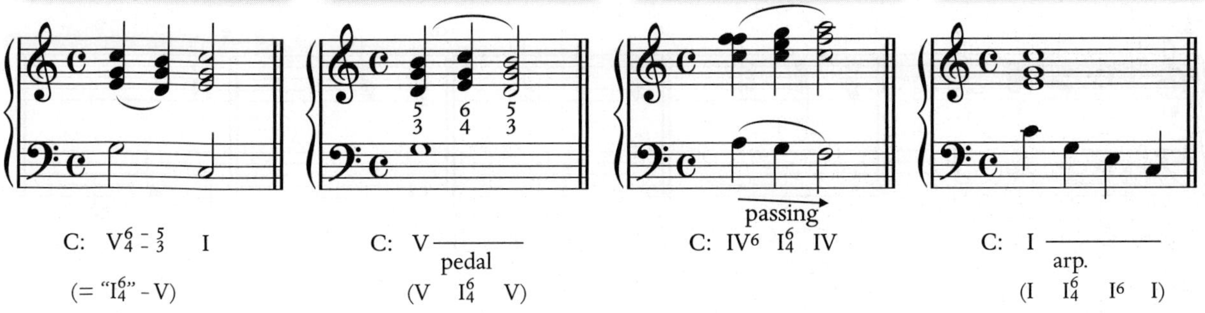

For more on $^6_4$ chords, see A Closer Look.

review and interact

POINTS FOR REVIEW

- **The function of a $^6_4$ chord differs from that of the $^6_3$ and $^5_3$ chords with the same root.**
- **The most important type of $^6_4$ chord is the cadential $^6_4$ (discussed in Chapter 15).**
- **A pedal $^6_4$ chord results when a root-position chord is decorated with embellishing tones in the *upper* voices so as to form a second-inversion triad, while the bass remains stationary.**
- **A passing $^6_4$ chord results when a passing tone in the *bass* voice supports a second-inversion triad.**
- **An arpeggiated $^6_4$ results when an arpeggio or partial arpeggio in the bass gives rise to a second-inversion triad.**
- **While a cadential $^6_4$ is metrically accented, occurring on a relatively strong beat or part of a beat, other $^6_4$ chords usually appear in metrically unaccented positions.**
- **In four-part harmony, the bass is usually doubled in all types of $^6_4$ chords.**

TEST YOURSELF

1. Which of the following statements are true?
   a. The interval of a fourth between the bass and an upper voice creates a dissonance.
   b. I^6_4 may be used in situations that are similar to those in which one may find I or I^6.

c. I^6_4 must be followed by V or V^7.

d. I^6_4 must appear on a relatively strong beat.

e. I^6_4 may not follow V or V^7.

f. The bass of I^6_4 should be doubled.

2. Indicate whether the chord on the second beat of each of the following fragments is a pedal $^6_4$, passing $^6_4$, arpeggiated $^6_4$, or cadential $^6_4$.

Know It? Show It!

Focus by working through the tutorials on:

- Pedal $^6_4$ chords
- Passing $^6_4$ chords

Learn with inQuizitive.

Apply what you've learned to complete the assignments:

- Realizing Roman Numerals
- Realizing Figured Bass
- Analysis

chapter 24

Other Embellishing Chords

Combinations of neighboring or passing tones can create a nonfunctional embellishing chord.

PASSING AND NEIGHBOR CHORDS

As we have already seen, at times an apparent chord might appear as a result of neighbor tones or passing tones in one or more of the voices.

24.1 Mozart, Piano Sonata in C, K. 279, III

Passing tones above a sustained bass form the notes of "IV" (F-A-C), which embellishes V^4_2.

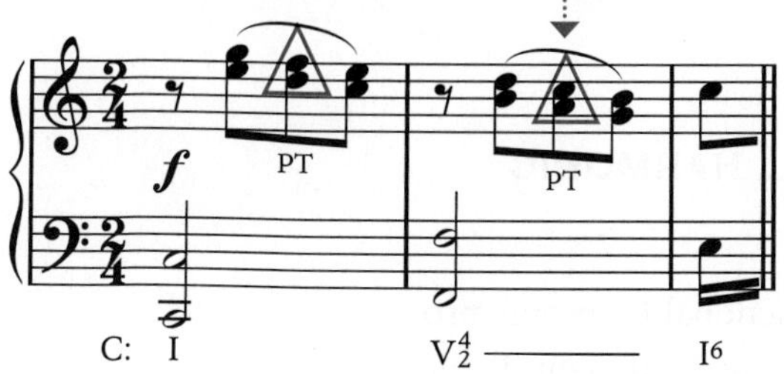

24.2 Bruckner, "Ave Maria," WAB6

A neighbor tone above a sustained bass forms the notes of "vi6" (F-A-D), which embellishes I.

Particularly notable are embellishing sonorities that involve a passing or neighbor tone in the bass (perhaps along with other embellishing tones in the upper voices), forming what are known as **passing chords** or **neighbor chords**.

24.3 Mendelssohn, *Songs without Words*, op. 102, no. 6

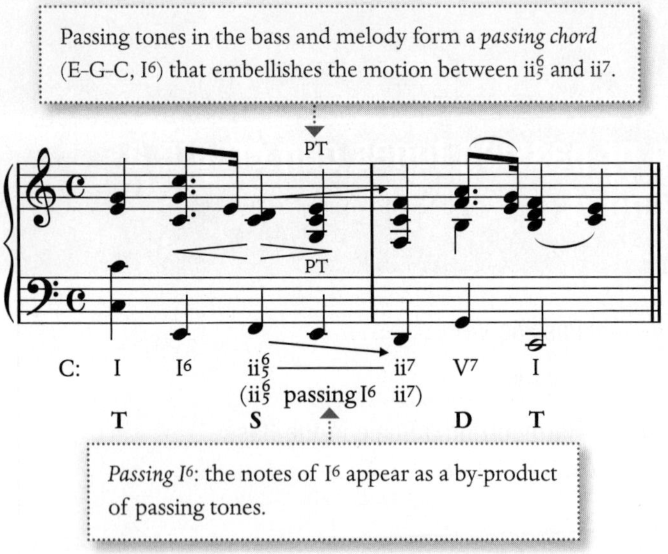
Passing tones in the bass and melody form a *passing chord* (E–G–C, I6) that embellishes the motion between ii6/5 and ii7.
PT
PT
C: I I6 ii6/5 ii7 V7 I
(ii6/5 passing I6 ii7)
T S D T
Passing I6: the notes of I6 appear as a by-product of passing tones.

24.4 Chopin, Prelude in A♭, op. 28

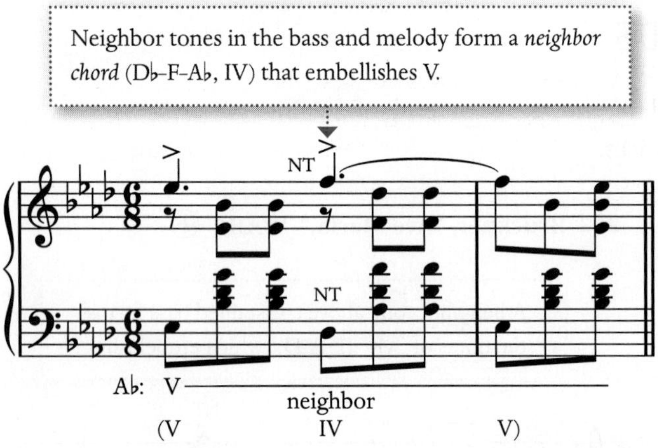
Neighbor tones in the bass and melody form a *neighbor chord* (D♭–F–A♭, IV) that embellishes V.
NT
NT
A♭: V
neighbor
(V IV V)

EMBELLISHING HARMONIES WITHIN FUNCTIONAL HARMONIC PROGRESSIONS

Passing and neighbor chords often form part of standard functional harmonic progressions, such as Tonic-Dominant-Tonic or Tonic-Subdominant-Dominant-Tonic. In analyzing passages that include such harmonies, one may choose to label the Roman numerals of all the chords—including the passing and neighbor chords—or to label just the underlying harmonies, depending on the level of detail desired.

24.5 J. S. Bach, Chorale 3

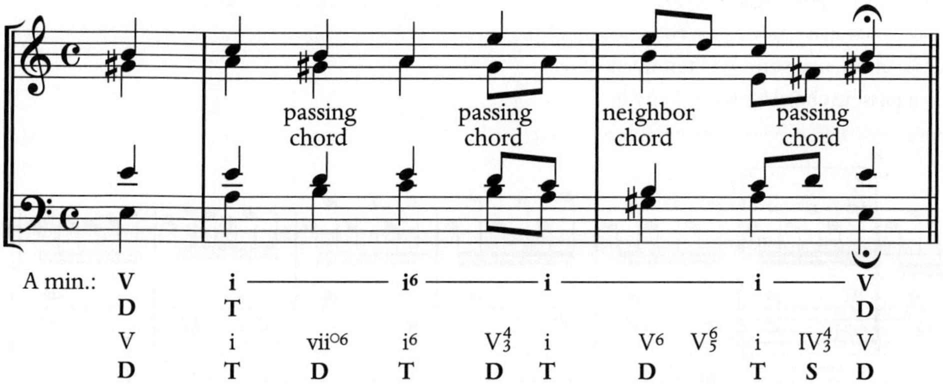

The top line of Roman numerals labels only the underlying harmonies. A detailed analysis (the bottom line of Roman numerals) indicates how the passing and neighbor chords form parts of standard harmonic progressions.

EMBELLISHING HARMONIES WITHIN NONFUNCTIONAL HARMONIC SUCCESSIONS

Passing and neighbor chords do not always form parts of functional harmonic progressions, however. For instance, in the following two excerpts, notice how passing tones along with the sustained tonic in an inner voice combine to spell ii7. Unlike the IV and vii°6 chords of these passages (which also result from embellishing tones), however, this "ii7" is not part of a functional progression: that is, it does not lead to V, and its chordal seventh does not resolve down by step. Accordingly, if this chord is labeled at all, its passing function should be explicitly noted.

24.6 Schumann, "Soldatenmarsch" (Soldier's March)

Passing tones produce what looks like ii7: A-C-(E)-G. But this is part of a *non*functional progression: I-"ii7"-I6. If labeled at all, the resulting sonority should be called a *passing ii7*.

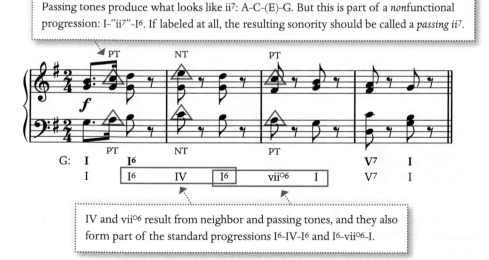

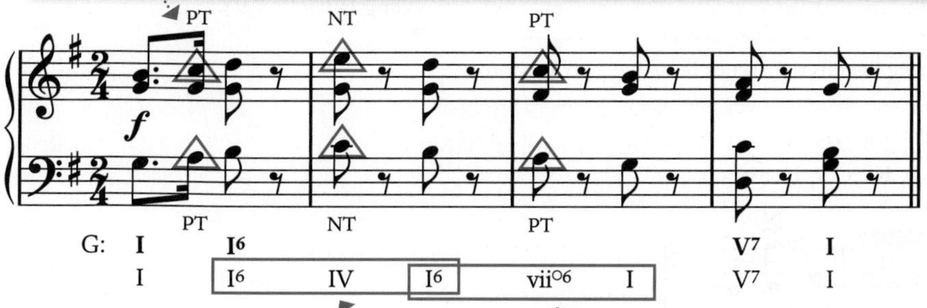

IV and vii°6 result from neighbor and passing tones, and they also form part of the standard progressions I6–IV–I6 and I6–vii°6–I.

24.7 J. S. Bach, Prelude in C♯ Major, WTC I

Though D♯-F♯-C♯ lasts for an entire measure and literally produces ii^7, it nonetheless serves as a passing chord between I and I^6.

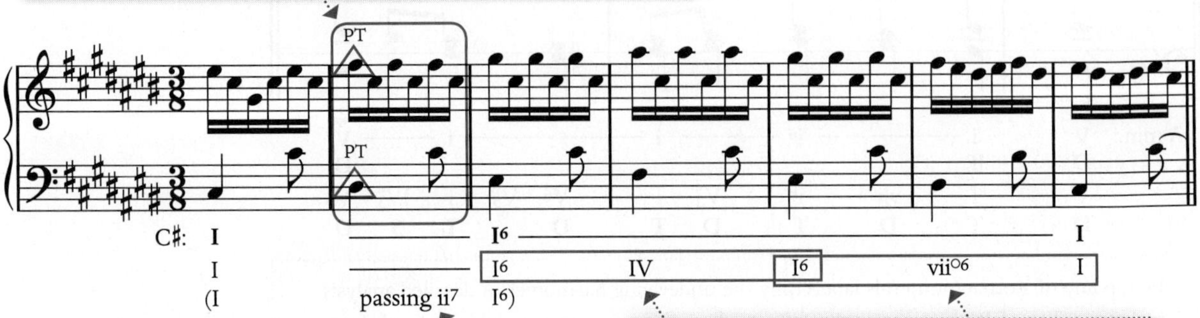

If labeled at all, this sonority should be called a *passing ii^7*.

These embellishing harmonies, on the other hand, are part of functional progressions.

PASSING IV^6

An embellishing chord that is particularly common is the **passing IV^6**, which appears in the middle of stepwise ascent in the bass that leads between V (or V^7) and V^6 (or V$^6_5$).

24.8

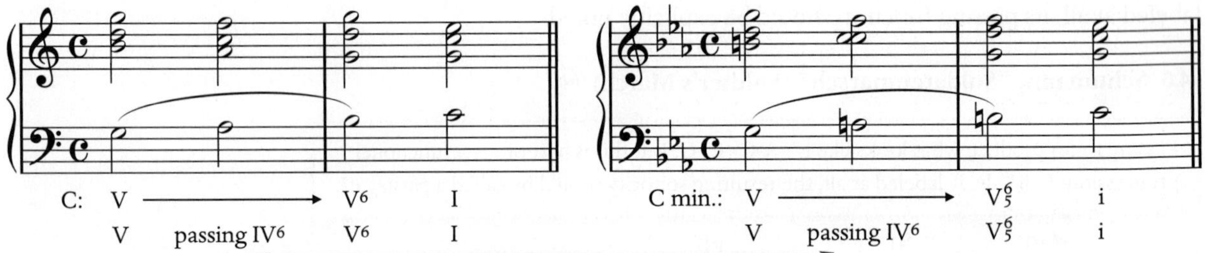

A *passing IV^6* fills the ascent between two V chords.

24.9 Mozart, Piano Sonata in F, K. 533, II

A passing IV^6 leads from V to V^6.

Note that under most circumstances, a V–IV^6 progression would be considered poor, since it creates a **D**ominant–**S**ubdominant progression. With a passing IV^6, however, V does not move to IV^6, but rather V moves through IV^6 to V^6 or V^6_5.

24.10

Poor V–IV^6 is an unidiomatic **D–S** progression.

Good V may move *through* a passing IV^6 to V^6_5.

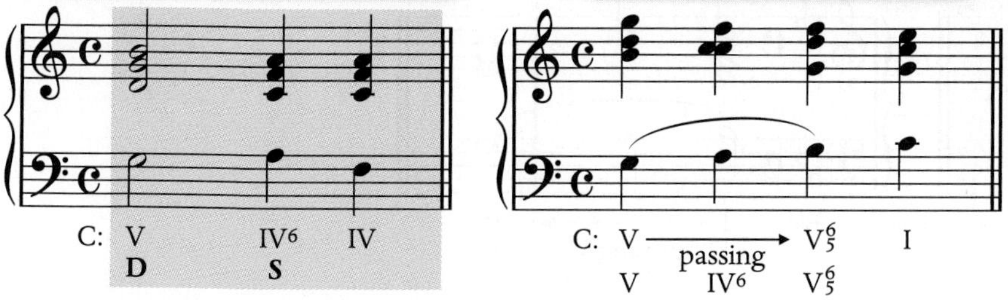

PASSING V6

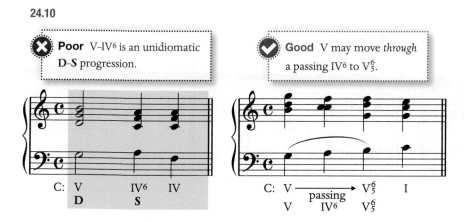

Another common passing chord is the **passing V^6**, which arises when the bass moves down in stepwise motion from I to vi or IV^6.

24.11

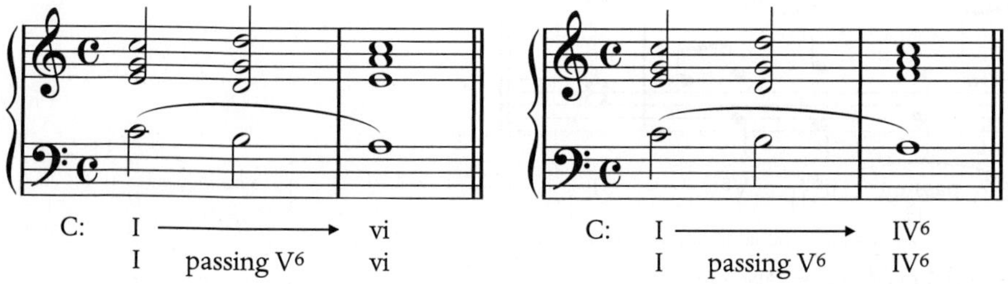

24.12 Vivaldi, from "Dopo i nembi," from *Giustino*, RV 717

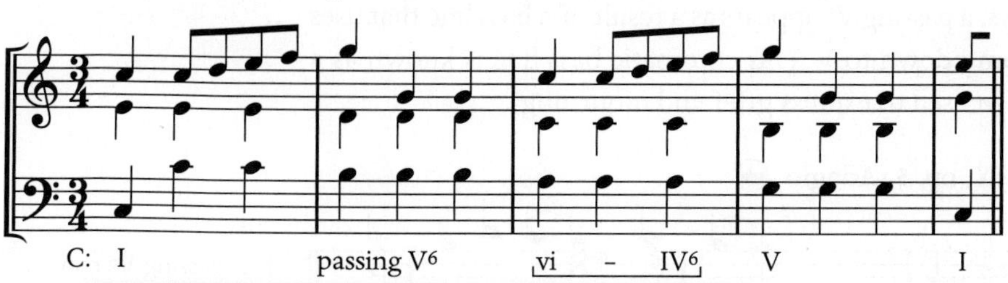

A *passing V^6* may be used in motion leading downward between I and vi or IV^6.

Under most circumstances, a V6–IV6 or V6–vi progression would be considered an improper **D–S** progression. A passing V6, however, does not function as a **D**ominant harmony that leads to I, but rather as part of a passing motion in the bass.

24.13

Poor V6–IV6 is an unidiomatic **D–S** progression.

Good V6 may serve as a passing chord between I and IV6.

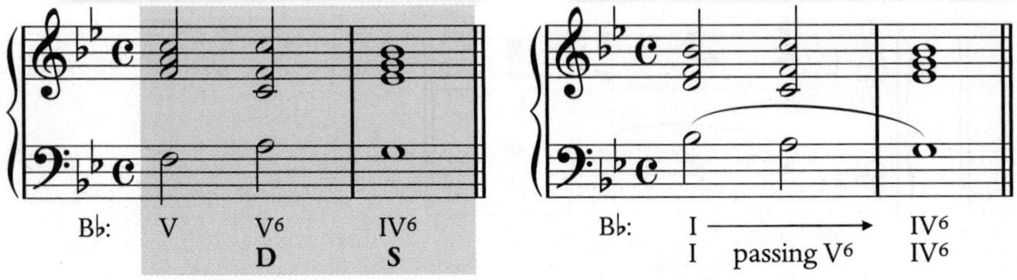

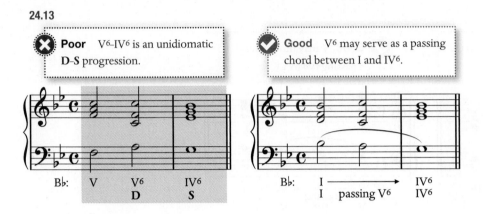

Since it does not function in the manner of a **D**ominant, in minor keys the $\hat{7}$ in the bass of this passing chord need not be raised. As a result, in minor keys this passing chord usually appears as a minor v6 triad.

24.14 J. S. Bach, Chorale 263

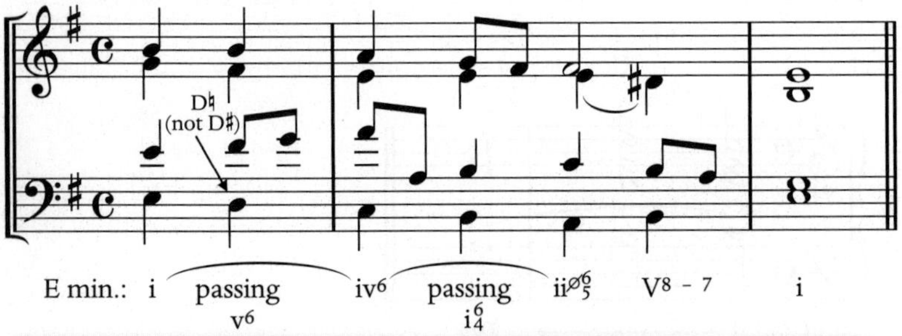

Since it does not lead up to the tonic, $\hat{7}$ need not be raised in a passing v6.

Sometimes in minor keys, a passing V6 appears as a result of a bass line that uses only half steps in moving from i down to V. This chromatic bass line is known as a **lament bass** (because it is often used to express grief and mourning).

24.15 Corelli, Violin Sonata IX, op. 5, Adagio

A passing V6 may be part of a *lament bass*, in which the bass line moves in half steps from i to V.

I–IV6–I6

A harmony also may function as an embellishment if it supports a passing or neighbor motion in the melody. A noteworthy instance of this arises when the melodic passing motion $\hat{3}$-$\hat{4}$-$\hat{5}$ is harmonized by the progression I–IV6–I6. As noted in Chapter 19, IV6 rarely moves directly to I; thus a I–IV6–I6 progression presents an important exception in which IV6 does embellish Tonic harmony.

24.16

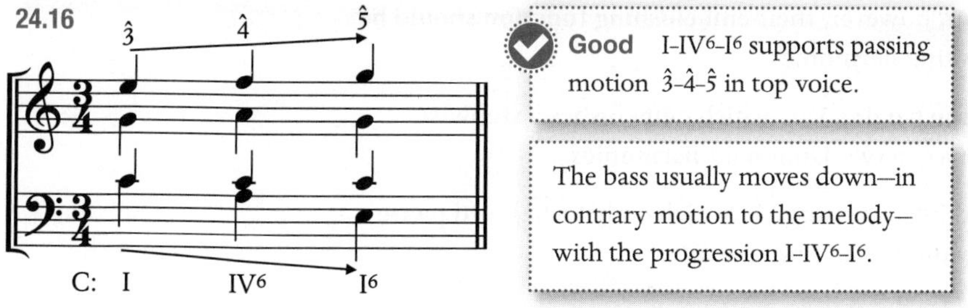

24.17 Beethoven, Piano Sonata in G, op. 31, no. 1, II

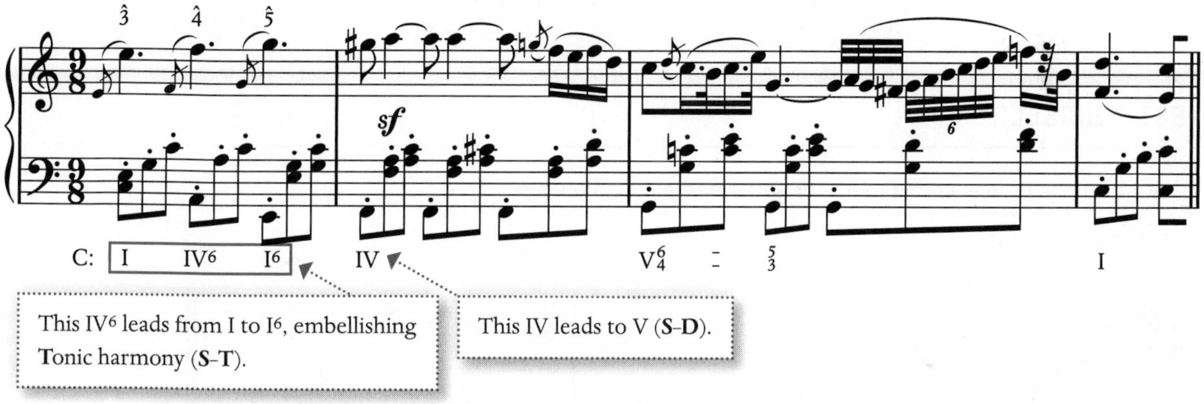

HARMONIZING A SCALE IN THE BASS

By using the passing IV6 and passing V6, along with progressions discussed in previous chapters, you can harmonize ascending and descending major and minor scales that appear in the bass voice.

24.18

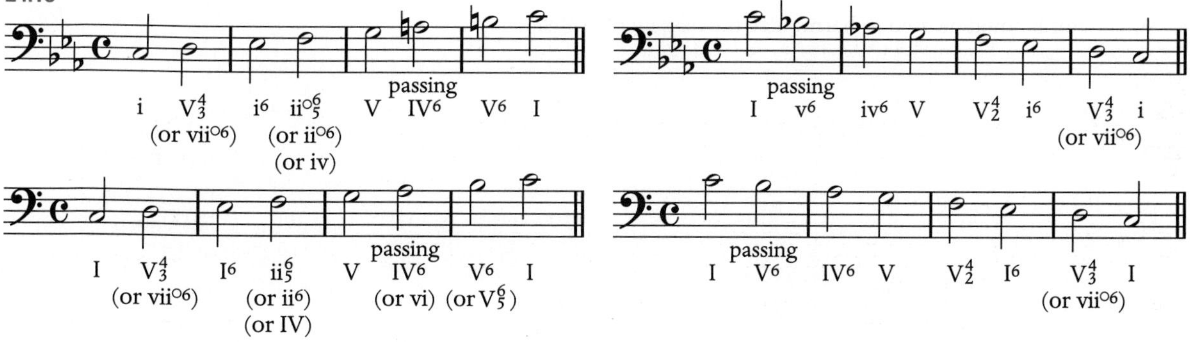

review and interact

POINTS FOR REVIEW

- **Passing and neighbor chords result when a chord is created by tones that embellish an underlying harmony.**
- **Sometimes, passing and neighbor chords form parts of standard harmonic progressions. Where they do not, however, their embellishing function should be noted in labeling these embellishing harmonies.**
- **An important passing chord is the passing IV6, which embellishes a stepwise *ascending* motion in the bass between two Dominant harmonies.**
- **Another common passing chord is the passing V6, which embellishes a stepwise *descending* motion in the bass leading from I to vi or IV6.**
- **I–IV6–I6 often supports the melodic line $\hat{3}$–$\hat{4}$–$\hat{5}$.**
- **Both the passing IV6 and passing V6 may be used in harmonizing a scale in the bass.**

TEST YOURSELF

1. What are the Roman numerals for the sonorities in the following?

J. S. Bach, Chorale 79

C: ____ ____ ____ ____ ____ ____ ____ ____ ____

2. Which of the above chord successions is not standard, and should be avoided in a four-part harmony exercise? What is the rationale for this odd chord succession?
3. What chords could be used to harmonize the bass line $\hat{8}$–$\hat{7}$–$\hat{6}$–$\hat{5}$?
4. What chords could be used to harmonize the bass line $\hat{5}$–$\hat{6}$–$\hat{7}$–$\hat{8}$?

5. Which chord in the following hymn passage has a primarily passing function?

Hymn from *The Boston Handel and Haydn Society Collection of Church Music*

Know It? Show It!

Focus by working through the tutorials on:

- Passing and neighbor chords
- Writing the passing IV^6
- Passing V^6

Learn with inQuizitive.

Apply what you've learned to complete the assignments:

- Realizing Roman Numerals
- Realizing Figured Bass
- $I–IV^6–I^6$
- Analysis

part four

Chromatic Harmony

chapter 25 Applied Dominants of V

V of V, or V/V, is an applied dominant chord—the dominant of the dominant—that leads to V.

TONICIZATION AND APPLIED DOMINANTS

In the middle of a composition it is possible to momentarily treat a note other than $\hat{1}$ as though it were the tonic. Such a momentary change of key, known as a **tonicization**, almost always requires the use of an accidental.

25.1 Chorale melody, "Jesu Leiden, Pein und Tod" (**Jesus' suffering, pain and death**)

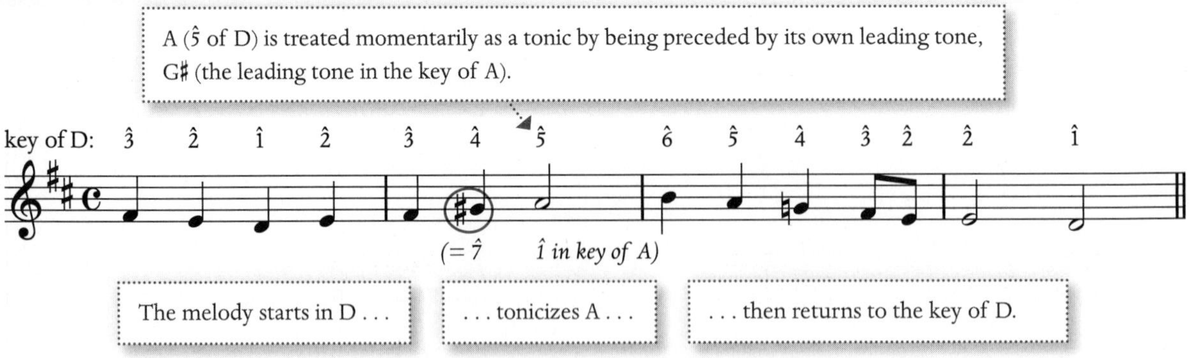

A ($\hat{5}$ of D) is treated momentarily as a tonic by being preceded by its own leading tone, G♯ (the leading tone in the key of A).
key of D: $\hat{3}$ $\hat{2}$ $\hat{1}$ $\hat{2}$ $\hat{3}$ $\hat{4}$ $\hat{5}$ $\hat{6}$ $\hat{5}$ $\hat{4}$ $\hat{3}$ $\hat{2}$ $\hat{2}$ $\hat{1}$
(= $\hat{7}$ $\hat{1}$ in key of A)
The melody starts in D . . .
. . . tonicizes A . . .
. . . then returns to the key of D.

Just as a *note* can be tonicized, any major or minor *triad* can be tonicized if it is preceded by an **applied dominant** (also known as a **secondary dominant**). An applied dominant contains a chromatic note and functions as a **D**ominant of a harmony other than I.

V/V

The most common applied dominant is **V of V**, notated as **V/V**. Just as V is a major triad whose root is a perfect fifth above I, V/V is a major triad whose root is a perfect fifth above V.

25.2

***Task*: Find V/V in the key of D.**

1. The root of V in the key of D = A
2. V in the key of A= E-G♯-B
3. Thus V/V in the key of D = E-G♯-B.

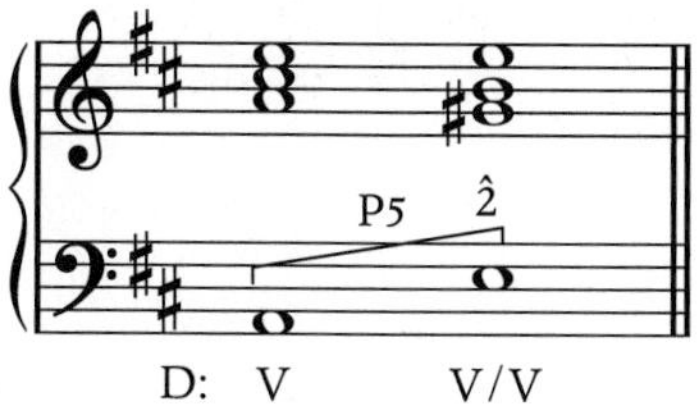

The root of V/V (E) is a perfect 5th above the root of V (A).

V/V must be a major triad; its third must be raised with an accidental (G♯ = leading tone of A).

Just as V leads to I, V/V leads to V.

25.3

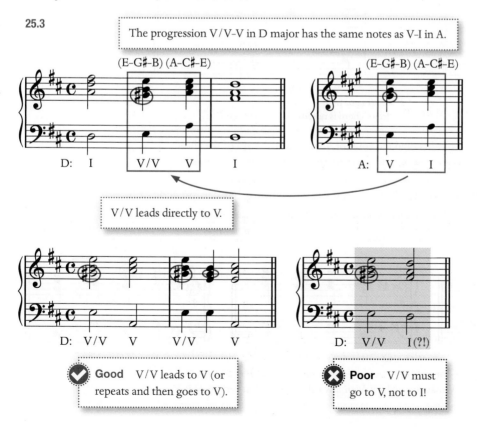

The progression V/V-V in D major has the same notes as V-I in A.

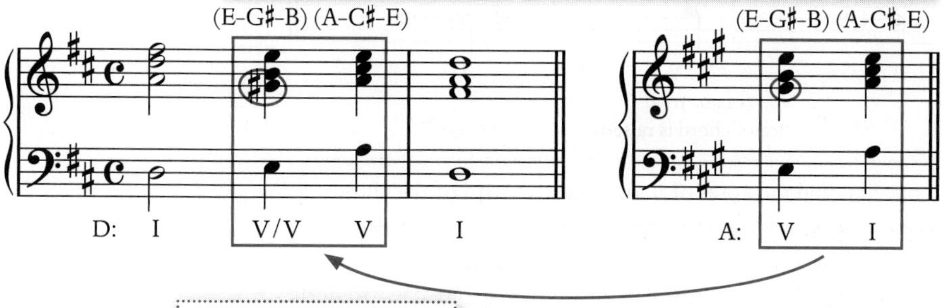

V/V leads directly to V.

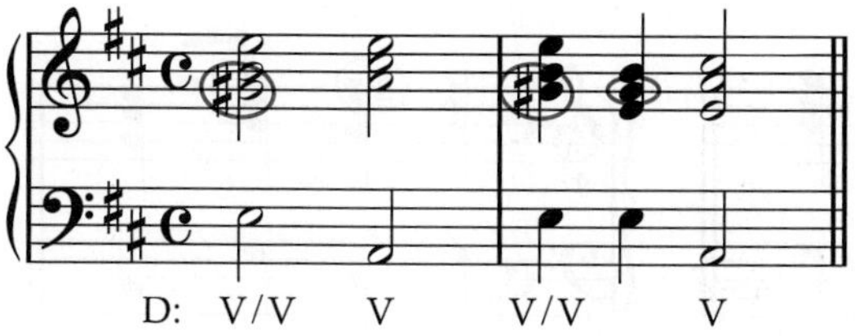

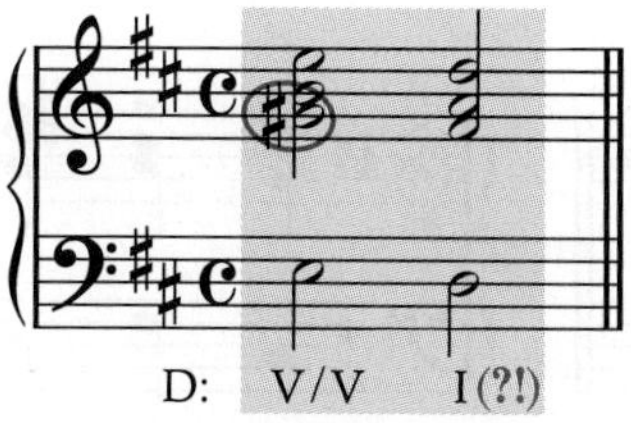

Good V/V leads to V (or repeats and then goes to V).

Poor V/V must go to V, not to I!

25.4 Advent Chorale, from *The English Hymnal*

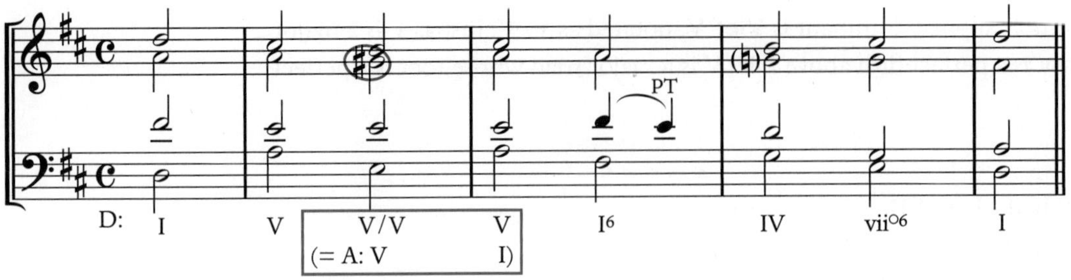

Notice that the root of V/V is $\hat{2}$. It thus has the same notes as a ii chord with the third raised by a half step.

25.5

***Task*: Find V/V in D (alternative method).**

1. ii in D= E–G–B.
2. Thus V/V in D = E–G♯–B.

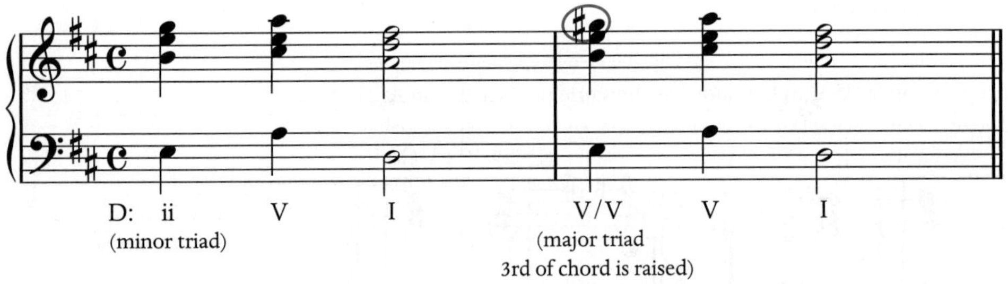

To find the notes of V/V you may first find the notes of ii, then raise the 3rd of the chord.

Since V/V points directly to the V that follows it, any chord that can precede V—such as a **T**onic or **S**ubdominant triad, or another V triad—may also precede V/V.

25.6

V/V may follow I, IV, V, or any other chord that can precede V.

THE SECONDARY LEADING TONE

Notice that the third of V/V is raised $\hat{4}$, which is the leading tone in the key of V (i.e., the key in which the V chord would be the tonic). This raised tone requires an accidental.

25.7

Raised $\hat{4}$ of B♭ (E♮) = leading tone of F

Raised $\hat{4}$ of E (A♯) = leading tone of B

The raised tone in V/V should be treated as a leading tone: it may not be doubled, and if it appears in an outer voice it resolves up by step when V/V moves to V.

25.8

Poor The raised 3rd within V/V functions as the leading tone to V and thus should not be doubled.

Poor Since it functions as the leading tone to V, the raised 3rd within V/V must resolve up when in the soprano.

Good The raised 3rd within V/V is not doubled and resolves up in the soprano.

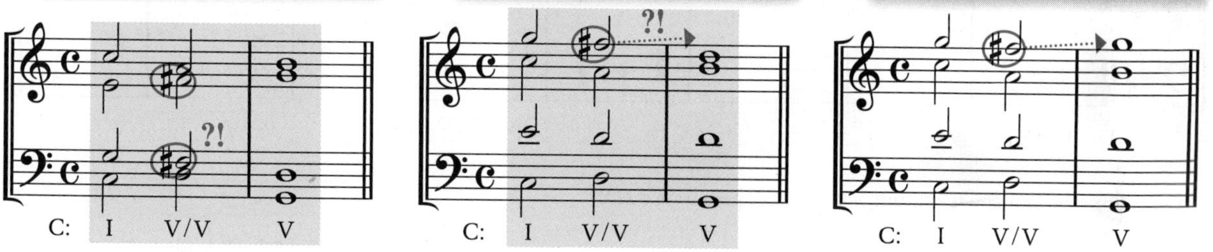

V6/V

V/V may also appear in first inversion—notated as **V6/V**. Just as V6 leads to a root-position I, V6/V leads to a root-position V.

25.9

25.10 Leonarda, *Magnificat*

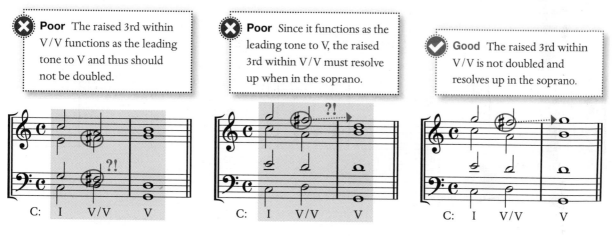

V6/V leads to root-position V.

V7/V IN ROOT POSITION AND INVERSIONS

A dominant seventh chord (a major triad plus a minor seventh) may also be used as an applied dominant of V (as **V7/V**). Just as with a V7, you may use all four notes of V7/V in four-part harmony, or you may omit the fifth and double the root.

25.11

V7/V is a dominant 7th chord; it has the same notes as V/V, plus a minor 7th above its root.

The 3rd of V7/V (B♭) must be raised by a half step with an accidental (to B♮). The chordal seventh of V7/V (F, 1̂) resolves down by step.

V7/V—G-B♮-F, with fifth (D) omitted—leads to V.

25.12 Rossini, *Il Turco in Italia*, act I, scene 8

Translation: The past and the future, who seeks to penetrate them?

V7/V (E-G♯-B-D) leads to V.

25.13 A. Sullivan, "A Wandering Minstrel," from *The Mikado*

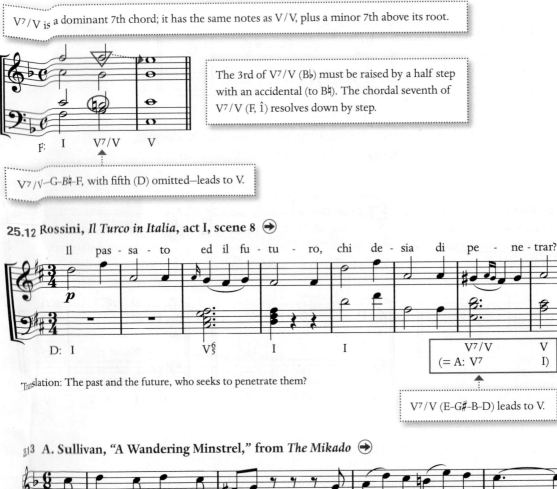

V7/V (G-B♮-D-F) leads to V.

V^7/ V may appear either in root position or in any inversion. In each case, the inversion of V^7/ V functions like the analogous inverted V^7 chord, except that it leads to a **D**ominant instead of a **T**onic. For instance, just as V^4_2 leads to I^6 (not to I), V^4_2/V leads to V^6 (not V).

25.14

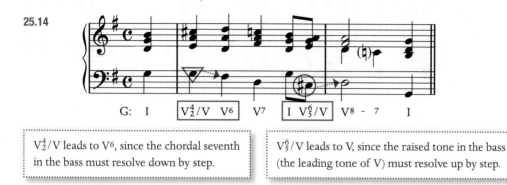

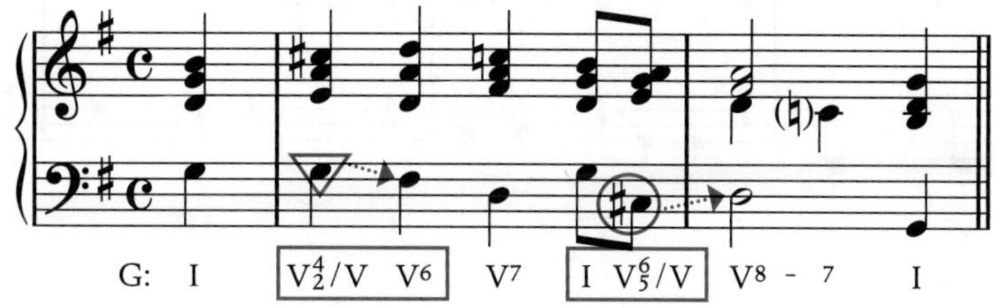

V^4_2/V leads to V^6, since the chordal seventh in the bass must resolve down by step.

V^6_5/V leads to V, since the raised tone in the bass (the leading tone of V) must resolve up by step.

25.15 Mendelssohn, *Songs without Words*, op. 19, no. 1

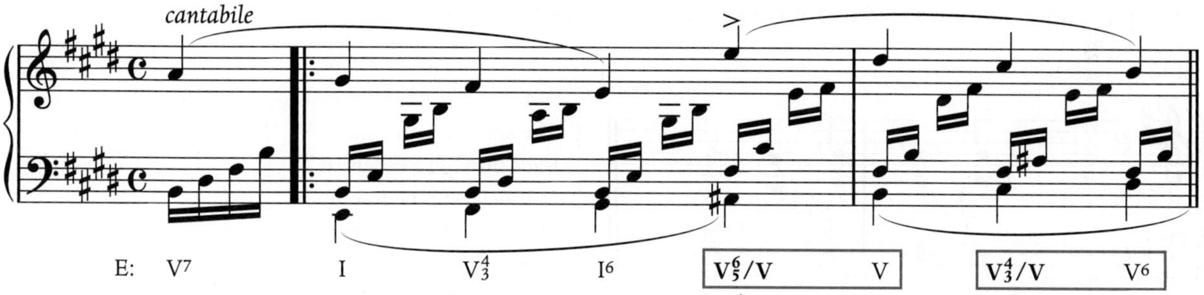

V^7/V may appear in any inversion.

V/V IN MINOR KEYS

Applied dominants of V also may be found in minor keys. In minor keys V / V requires *two* accidentals, raised $\hat{4}$ and raised $\hat{6}$.

25.16

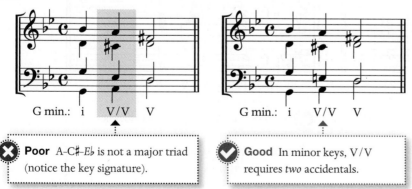

Poor A-C♯-*E♭* is not a major triad (notice the key signature).

Good In minor keys, V / V requires *two* accidentals.

25.17 Chopin, Ballade no. 1 in G Minor, op. 23

ii∅7 in G minor is A-C-E♭-G.

V7/V in G minor is A-C♯-E♮-G.

OTHER RESOLUTIONS OF V/V AND V7/V

An applied dominant may lead to a V chord that is decorated by a cadential $\begin{smallmatrix}6\\4\end{smallmatrix}$.

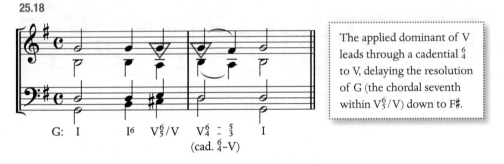

25.18

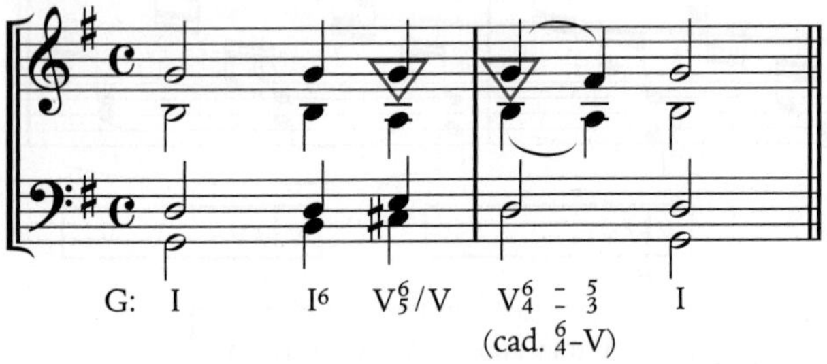

The applied dominant of V leads through a cadential $\begin{smallmatrix}6\\4\end{smallmatrix}$ to V, delaying the resolution of G (the chordal seventh within V^6_5/V) down to F♯.

An applied dominant at times may also lead to a V7 chord, instead of leading to a V triad. In such a case, a particularly beautiful voice leading can sometimes be used. Usually, raised $\hat{4}$, a leading tone directed up to $\hat{5}$, ascends to $\hat{5}$. When V7/V moves to V7, however, raised $\hat{4}$ may instead slide down by a half step, canceling the chromatic alteration to $\hat{4}$. This is possible even if the raised $\hat{4}$ appears in the top voice.

25.19

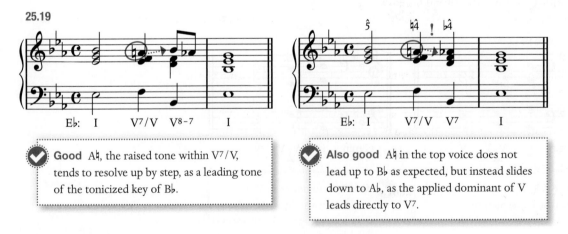

Good A♮, the raised tone within V7/V, tends to resolve up by step, as a leading tone of the tonicized key of B♭.

Also good A♮ in the top voice does not lead up to B♭ as expected, but instead slides down to A♭, as the applied dominant of V leads directly to V7.

25.20 Cherubini, *Lodoïska*, act I, scene 1

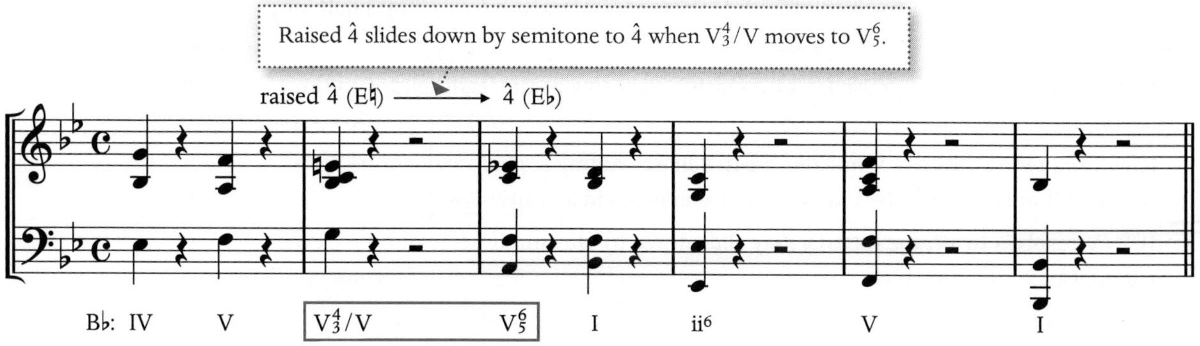

25.21 Schubert, "Lied" (Song), D. 284

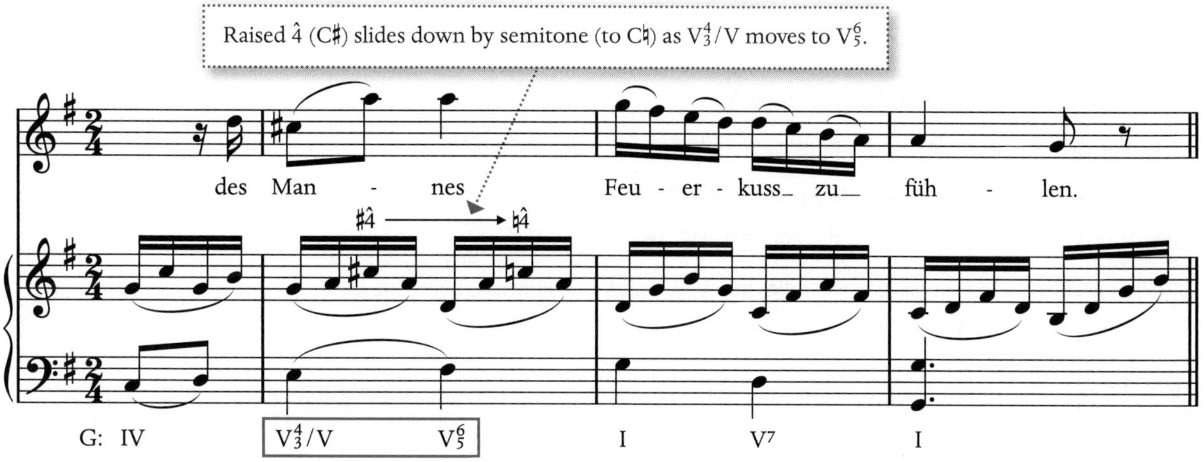

Translation: To feel a man's fiery kiss.

To learn about cross relations, see A Closer Look.

review and interact

POINTS FOR REVIEW

- **An applied dominant is a chord that functions as a dominant of a harmony other than the tonic.**
- **The most common applied dominants are V/V and V^7/V (read "V of V" and "V^7 of V"), which may appear in root position or inversion.**
- **V/V leads to a Dominant (V, V^7, inversions of V or V^7, or a cadential $^6_4$ followed by V); it may follow any chord that can precede V (any Tonic or Subdominant chord).**
- **The root of V/V is $\hat{2}$ (a perfect fifth above $\hat{5}$).**

- **V/V must be a major triad; V7/V is a dominant-seventh-type chord (a major triad with a minor seventh). The third of both V/V and V7/V must be raised by a half step with an accidental.**
- **The raised tone in V/V is raised $\hat{4}$ (♯$\hat{4}$), which is the same as the leading tone in the key of V.**
- **The raised tone within V/V must be treated like a leading tone: it may not be doubled, and it normally resolves up by step if it appears in an outer voice.**
- **If V/V resolves to V7, the raised $\hat{4}$ may slide down by chromatic semitone to $\hat{4}$, even if it appears in the top voice.**
- **In minor keys, two notes within V/V must be raised with accidentals, $\hat{4}$ and $\hat{6}$.**

TEST YOURSELF

1. Which of the following chords may follow V/V?

   a. V or V6 b. I c. IV or ii6 d. V7 e. cadential $^6_4$–V f. another V/V

2. Which of the following chords may precede V/V?

   a. V or V6 b. I c. IV or ii6 d. cadential $^6_4$–V e. another V/V

3. What accidentals are missing in the following V/V and V7/V chords? (Each one is missing one or two accidentals.)

4. What is the root of V/V in these keys?

   a. F major b. D major c. E major d. E minor e. A♭ major f. A♭ minor

5. What are the notes in V/V in these keys? Specify which notes need accidentals.

   a. F major b. D major c. E major d. C♯ major

6. What are the notes in V7/V in these keys? Specify which notes need accidentals.

   a. F minor b. D minor c. E minor d. C♯ major

7. In which of these situations does the third of the V/V chord *not* need to resolve upward?

   a. If it appears in an outer voice.

   b. If it appears in an inner voice.

   c. If the chord in which it appears is followed by another V/V.

   d. If it moves to the seventh of V7.

8. In four-part harmony, when may the third of V/V or V7/V be doubled?

   a. If it appears in an inner voice. b. If it appears at a cadence. c. Never.

Know It? Show It!

Focus by working through the tutorials on:

- Recognizing V of V
- Writing applied dominants

Learn with inQuizitive.

Apply what you've learned to complete the assignments:

- Realizing Roman Numerals
- Realizing Figured Bass
- Harmonizing Melodies
- Composition
- Analysis

chapter

26 Other Applied Chords

An applied chord functions like a Dominant, but leads to a harmony other than I.

APPLIED V AND V7

As discussed in the previous chapter, an *applied dominant* chord functions as a **D**ominant, but leads to a harmony other than I. An applied dominant can lead (or be applied) not only to V, but also to any major or minor triad. Thus V/ii leads to ii, V/vi leads to vi, and so on. In each case, the applied dominant may be a triad or seventh chord in root position or inversion. All applied chords *tonicize* the chord to which they are applied, momentarily treating the goal chord as tonic. The resolution of an applied dominant creates a **D**ominant-to-**T**onic progression within the key of the tonicized chord.

26.1

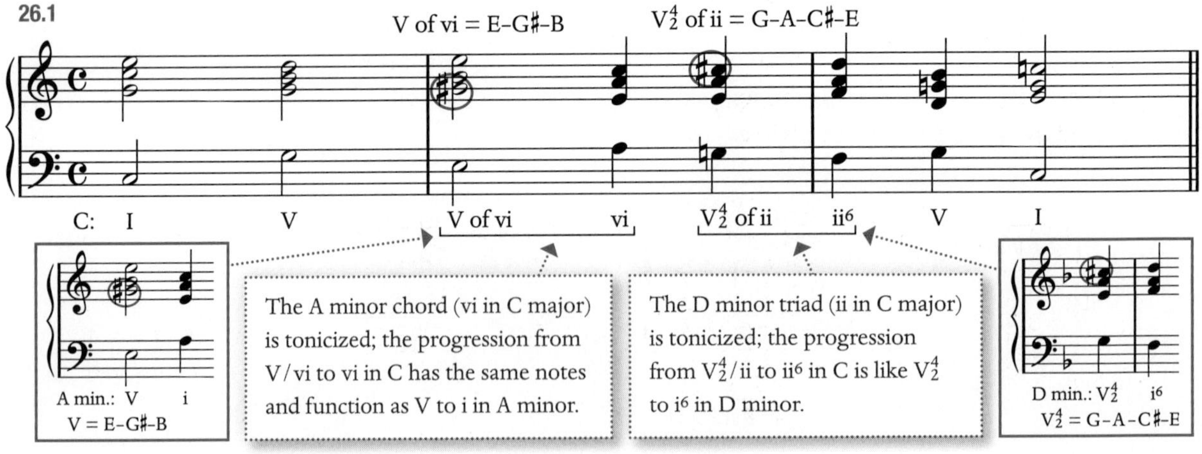

Since they lead to harmonies other than the tonic, applied dominant chords momentarily depart from the main key. As a result, almost all applied chords use at least one accidental. To spell an applied V triad, build a major triad whose root is a perfect fifth above the root of the goal chord (the tonicized harmony), making sure to use accidentals where needed. Thus V/vi is a major triad whose root is a perfect fifth above $\hat{6}$, V/ii is major triad whose root is a perfect fifth above $\hat{2}$, and so on.

26.2

***Task*: Spell V/vi in the key of F.**

1. In the key of F, the root of vi (the goal chord), $\hat{6}$, is D.
2. A perfect 5th above D = A.
3. A major triad = A-*C♯*-E

P5
F: V of vi
(accidental is needed for C♯)

26.3

***Task*: Spell V/ii in the key of B♭.**

1. In B♭, the root of ii (the goal chord), $\hat{2}$, is C.
2. A perfect 5th above C = G.
3. G major triad = G-*B♮*-D

P5
B♭: V of ii
(accidental is needed for B♮)

The procedure for spelling an applied V^7 is similar: build a dominant seventh chord (a major triad plus a minor seventh) on the note a perfect fifth above the root of the goal chord, using the correct accidentals. Thus V^7/IV is a dominant seventh chord whose root is a perfect fifth above $\hat{4}$, V^7/ii is a dominant seventh chord whose root is a perfect fifth above $\hat{2}$, and so on.

26.4

***Task*: Spell V^7/IV in the key of G.**

1. In the key of G, the root of IV, $\hat{4}$, is C.
2. A perfect 5th above C = G.
3. G dominant seventh chord = G-B-D-*F♮*.

P5
G: V7 of IV
(accidental is needed for F♮)

26.5

***Task*: Spell V^7/ii in the key of A.**

1. In the key of A, the root of ii, $\hat{2}$, is B.
2. A perfect 5th above B = F♯.
3. F♯ dominant seventh chord = F♯-*A♯*-C♯-E

P5
A: V7 of ii
(accidental is needed for A♯)

Since an applied chord functions as a **D**ominant, its third acts as the leading tone to the goal chord (it is a secondary leading tone). Accordingly, just like the primary leading tone within V, the third of an applied dominant cannot be doubled, and it must ascend by half step if it appears in an outer voice.

26.6

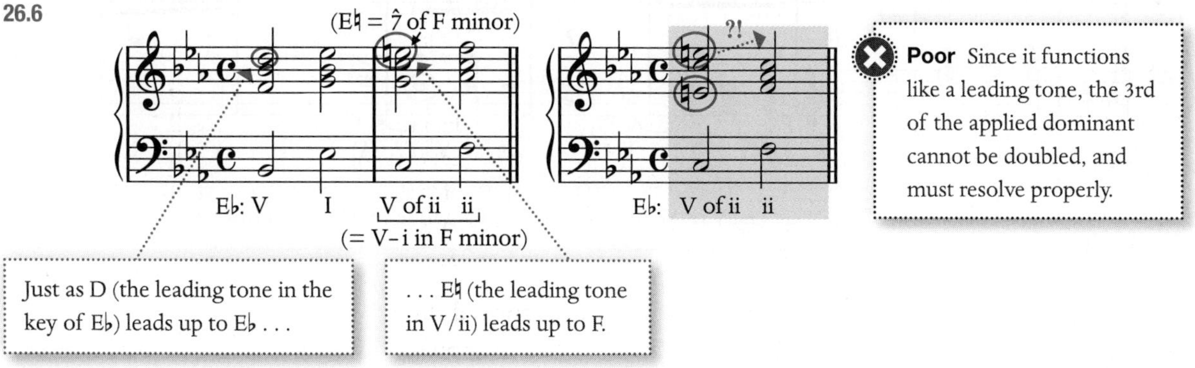

(E♮ = 7̂ of F minor)
E♭: V I V of ii ii
(= V–i in F minor)
?!
E♭: V of ii ii
Poor Since it functions like a leading tone, the 3rd of the applied dominant cannot be doubled, and must resolve properly.
Just as D (the leading tone in the key of E♭) leads up to E♭ . . .
. . . E♮ (the leading tone in V/ii) leads up to F.

IN MAJOR KEYS

In major keys, ii, iii, IV, V, or vi may be preceded by an applied dominant. Because a diminished triad cannot be the tonic of a key, vii° cannot be tonicized by an applied dominant. Like V/V, all applied dominant triads may appear in root position or first inversion, and applied dominant seventh chords may appear in any inversion.

26.7

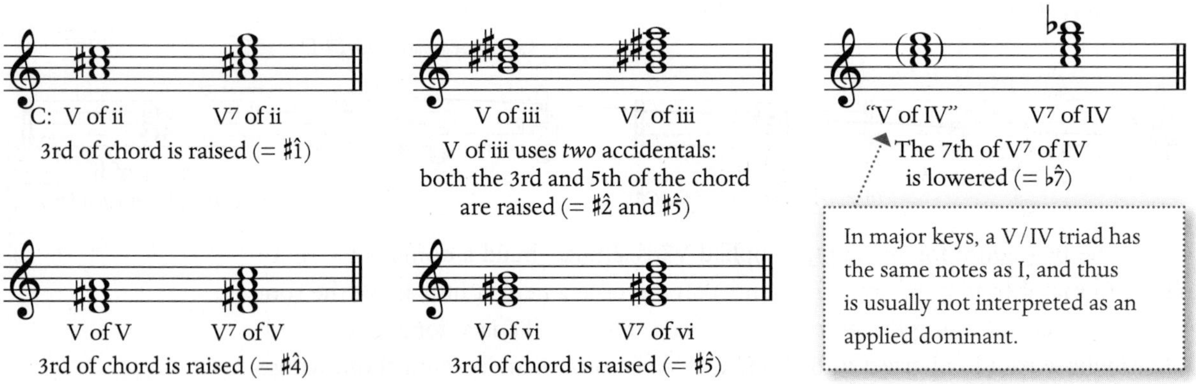

Any major or minor triad may be tonicized with an applied V or V7 in root position or inversion.

26.8 **Haydn, German Dance, Hob. IX:12/4**

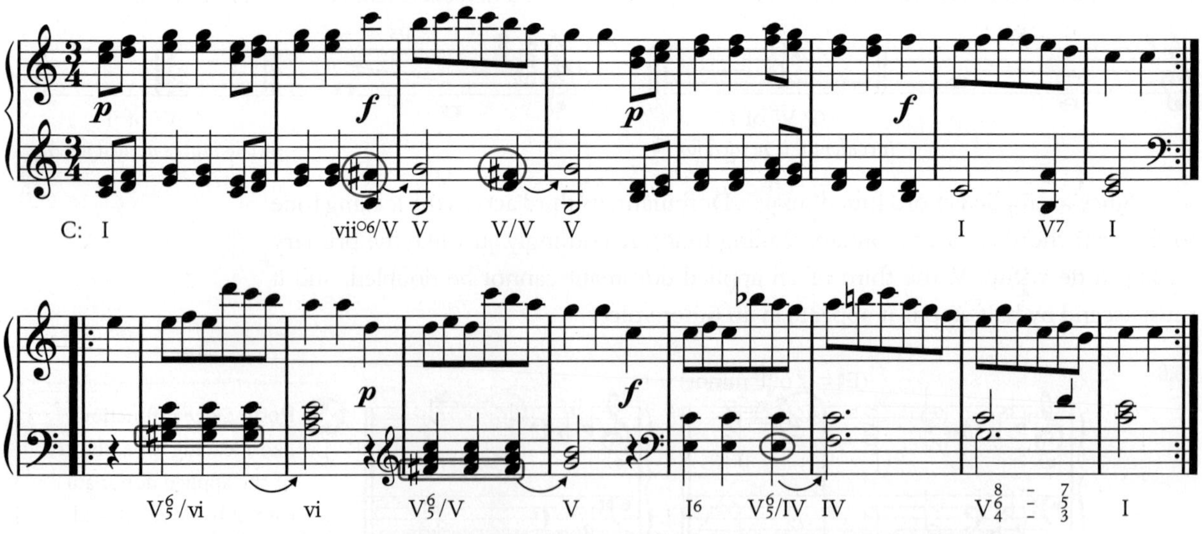

The third of every applied V or V7 functions as a leading tone to the goal chord.

26.9 Beethoven, Piano Sonata in G, op. 14, no. 2, II, excerpts ➔

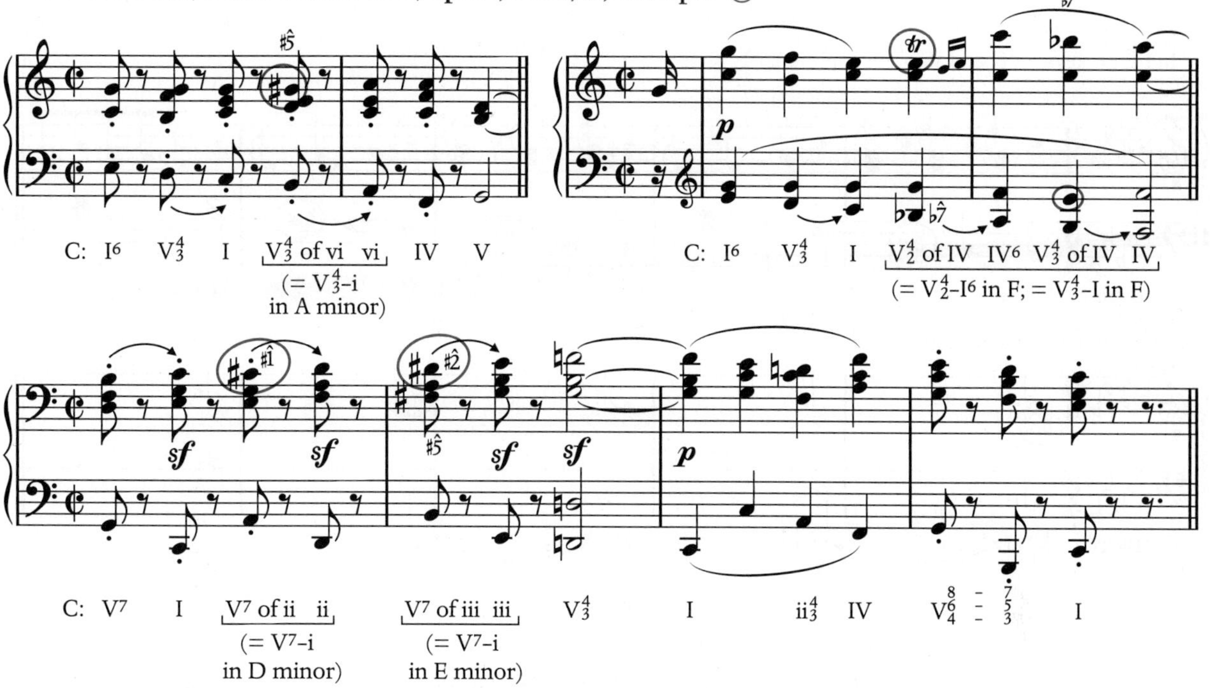

IN MINOR KEYS

In minor keys, too, five triads can be preceded by an applied dominant: III, iv, V, VI, and VII; ii° cannot, since it is diminished.

26.10

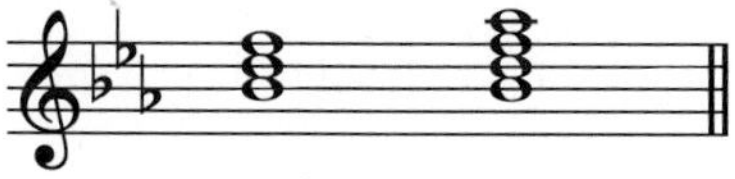

C min.: V of III V7 of III
no accidentals

> Although it uses the same notes as (the relatively rare) subtonic VII, this chord more often functions as V/III, leading to III.

C min.: V of iv V7 of iv
3rd of chord is raised

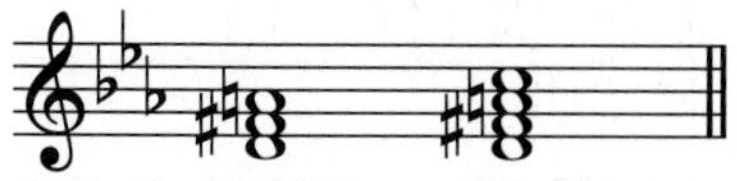

C min.: V of V V7 of V
V of V in a minor key needs *two* accidentals: 3rd and 5th of chord are raised

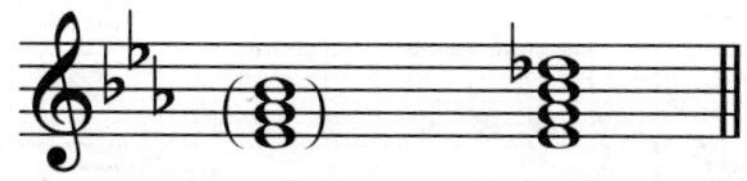

C min.: V of VI V7 of VI
no accidentals 7th of chord is lowered

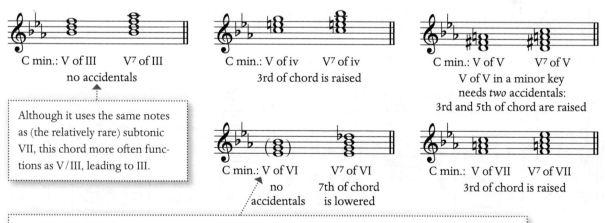

C min.: V of VII V7 of VII
3rd of chord is raised

> Since the V/VI triad has the same notes as III, this triad is usually not interpreted as an applied dominant.

26.11 Haydn, Keyboard Sonata in B♭, Hob. XVI:2/III

In minor keys, V/iv and V/V are common.

Simplified harmonic model

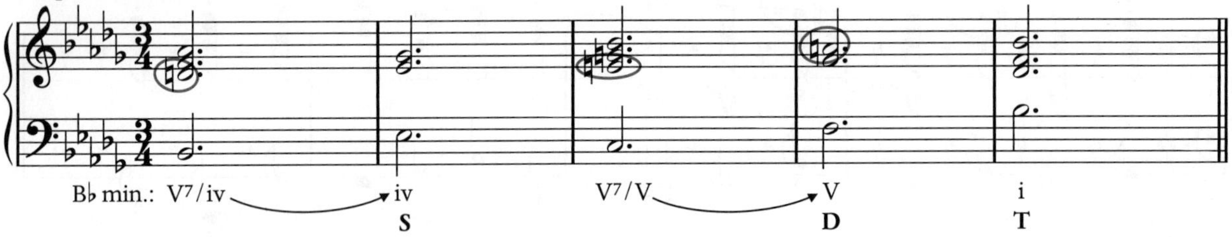

26.12 J. S. Bach, Chorale 48

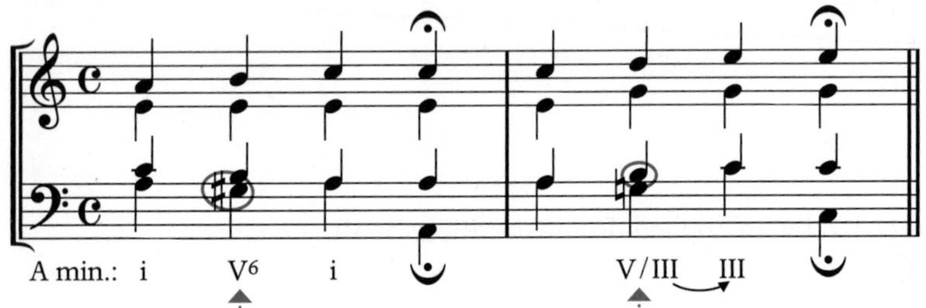

Though III is less common in simple diatonic passages, it often appears in minor-key passages that use applied dominants.

$\hat{7}$ is usually raised in minor keys, to form a leading tone . . .

. . . but when III is tonicized with V/III, $\hat{7}$ (G) is *not* raised.

26.13 Haydn, Symphony no. 19, II

In minor keys, V/VI and V/VII are also possible, though less common than other applied dominants.

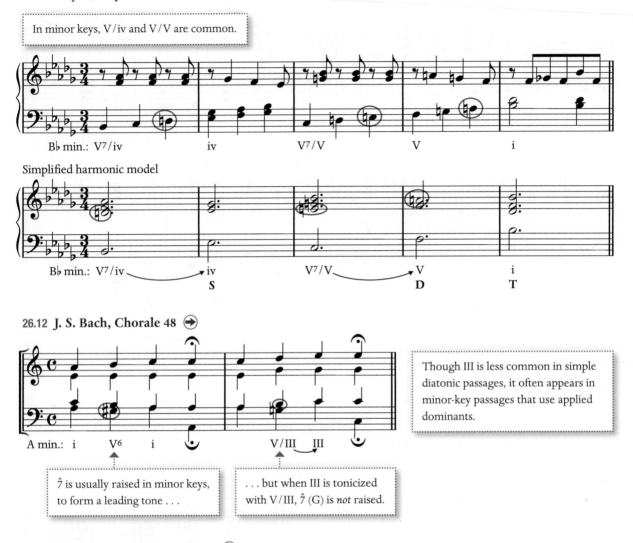

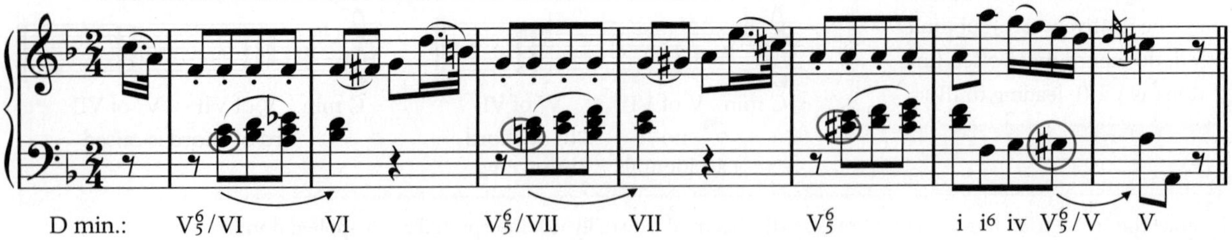

APPLIED vii°6 AND vii°7

Since vii°6 and vii°7 are **D**ominant harmonies, they too may serve as applied chords to any major or minor triad. The roots of applied vii°6 and applied vii°7 chords are the leading tones of the harmonies they tonicize. Accordingly, the root of an applied diminished chord must be a minor second (*not* a major second!) below the root of the goal chord. Furthermore, the root of an applied vii° triad or seventh chord must be treated as a leading tone: it cannot be doubled, and it must resolve up by step when in an outer voice.

26.14

Task: Spell vii°7/V in D.

1. In the key of D, the root of V (the goal chord), $\hat{5}$, is A.
2. The leading tone of A is G♯ (not G♮).
3. G♯ diminished seventh chord (diminished triad plus d7) = G♯–B–D–*F*♮.

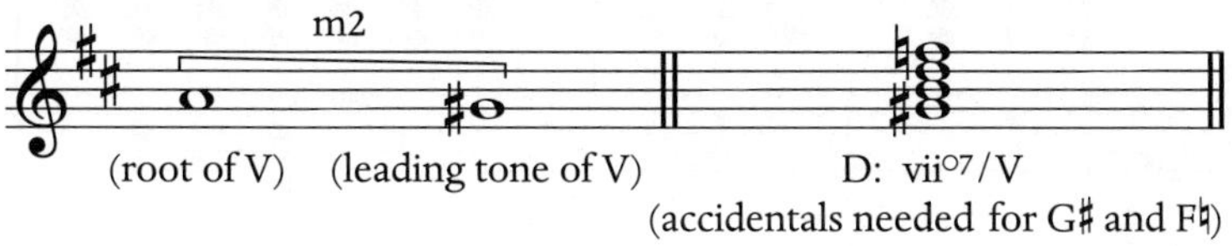

26.15 Beethoven, Piano Sonata in G, op. 14, no. 2, II

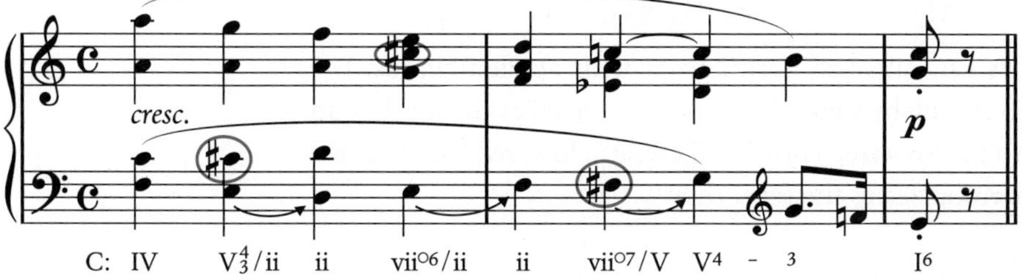

Just as vii°6 and vii°7 lead to a tonic chord, vii°6/ii leads to ii, vii°7/V leads to V, and so on.

26.16 Mozart, Piano Sonata in F, K. 280, II

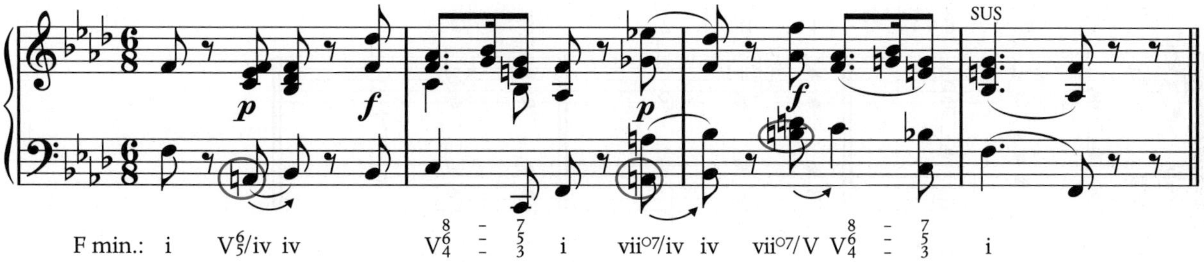

The vii^{ø7} (a half-diminished seventh chord) may also serve as an applied dominant. However, just as vii^{ø7} occurs only in major keys (not in minor keys), an applied vii^{ø7} should lead to a major chord (not a minor chord).

26.17

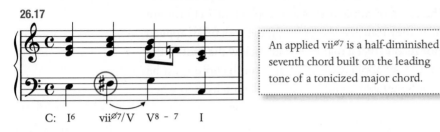

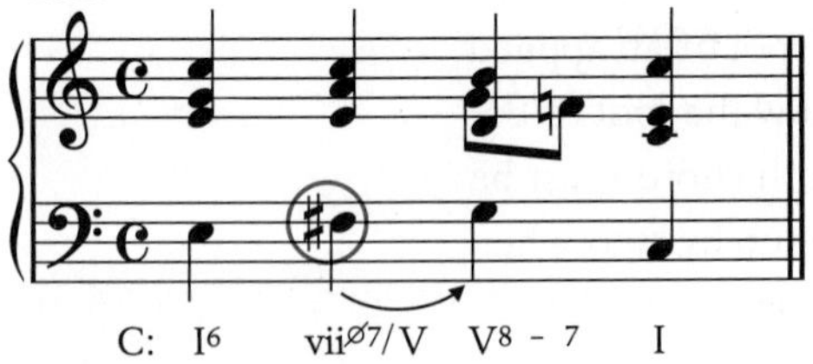

An applied vii^{ø7} is a half-diminished seventh chord built on the leading tone of a tonicized major chord.

26.18 Schubert, "An die Musik" (To Music)

Translation: In how many gray hours?

USING APPLIED CHORDS IN HARMONIZING MELODIES

Chromatic tones in melodies can often be harmonized with applied chords. For instance, a raised tone that moves up by step might be harmonized as the third of an applied V (the leading tone to the tonicized chord). Likewise, a lowered $\hat{7}$ that moves down by step can often be harmonized as the seventh of V^7/IV.

26.19

***Task*: Harmonize the following melodic fragments using applied dominants.**

Some possible solutions:

Raised notes are harmonized as thirds of applied V.

Lowered $\hat{7}$ is harmonized with V^7/IV.

review and interact

POINTS FOR REVIEW

- **An applied dominant functions as the dominant to a harmony other than the tonic.**
- **An applied dominant may be a triad or a dominant seventh chord, and it may appear in root position or inversion.**
- **An applied V is a major triad whose root is a perfect fifth above the root of the chord to which it is applied; an applied V^7 is a dominant seventh chord whose root is a perfect fifth above the root of the chord to which it is applied. Applied chords usually require the use of accidentals.**
- **Applied $\text{vii}^{\circ 6}$, applied $\text{vii}^{\circ 7}$, and applied $\text{vii}^{\varnothing 7}$ chords are diminished chords whose roots are the leading tone of the harmony that they tonicize.**
- **The third of an applied V chord—and the root of an applied vii° triad or seventh chord—is a leading tone: it may not be doubled, and it should resolve up by step if it appears in an outer voice.**
- **Only major and minor triads (not diminished triads) may be preceded by applied dominants, because only major and minor triads may be tonicized (treated like a tonic).**

TEST YOURSELF

1. Which of these chords typically follow a V/ii?

   a. ii b. ii^6 c. I d. another V/ii

2. Which accidentals (if any) are missing in these chords (in major keys)?

C: V/vi | B♭: V/ii | E: $\text{vii}^{\circ 7}$/vi | F: V^7/iii | B♭: $\text{vii}^{\circ 7}$/ii | G: V^7/IV

3. Which accidentals (if any) are missing in these chords (in minor keys)?

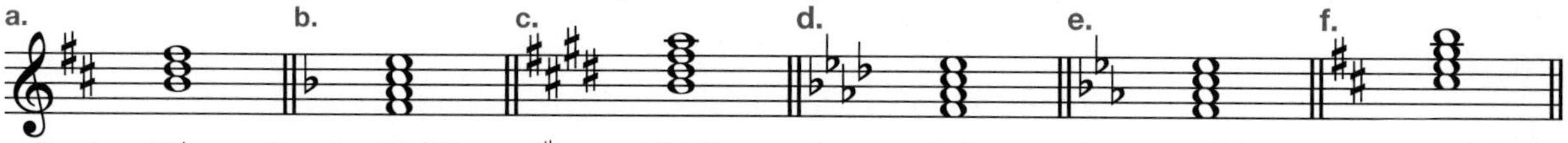

B min.: V/iv | D min.: V^7/VI | C♯ min.: V^7/III | F min.: V^7/iv | G min.: $\text{vii}^{\circ 7}$/V | B min.: $\text{vii}^{\varnothing 7}$/III

4. Which notes of the following triads may not be doubled?

F: V^6/vi | A: V/ii | D: $\text{vii}^{\circ 6}$/V | B♭: $\text{vii}^{\circ 6}$/IV | C♯ min.: V/III | E min.: $\text{vii}^{\circ 6}$/VI

5. Complete the following for the indicated applied chords.

a. G major, V/ii: root of goal chord = ____; root of applied chord = ____
notes in applied chord = ____, ____, ____; note(s) needing accidental = ____
leading tone in applied chord = ____

b. A♭ major, V^7/IV: root of goal chord = ____; root of applied chord = ____
notes in applied chord = ____, ____, ____, ____; note(s) needing accidental = ____
leading tone in applied chord = ____

c. E major, V/iii: root of goal chord = ____; root of applied chord = ____
notes in applied chord = ____, ____, ____; note(s) needing accidental = ____
leading tone in applied chord = ____

d. D minor, V/III: root of goal chord = ____; root of applied chord = ____
notes in applied chord = ____, ____, ____; note(s) needing accidental = ____
leading tone in applied chord = ____

Know It? Show It!

Focus by working through the tutorials on:

- Recognizing applied diminished chords
- Resolving applied diminished chords

Learn with inQuizitive.

Apply what you've learned to complete the assignments:

- Spelling Applied Dominants
- Realizing Roman Numerals
- Realizing Figured Bass
- Harmonizing Melodies
- Composition
- Analysis

chapter 27

Modulation to the Dominant Key

A modulation occurs when the key changes temporarily; the most common modulation is to the dominant key.

MODULATION

Pieces usually begin and end in the same key, known as the **main key** (or **home key** or **tonic key**). Within the course of the composition, however, the key may change, so that a harmony other than the original I chord is temporarily treated as though it were the tonic. Chapters 25 and 26 discussed how applied chords can create brief changes of key, known as *tonicizations*. A change of key that is lengthier and more substantial, and whose tonic is confirmed by a cadence, is known as a **modulation**. In the vast majority of cases, a modulation is not notated with a new key signature; rather, the modulation is indicated by the use of accidentals.

27.1 Sor, Leçons progressives, no. 5

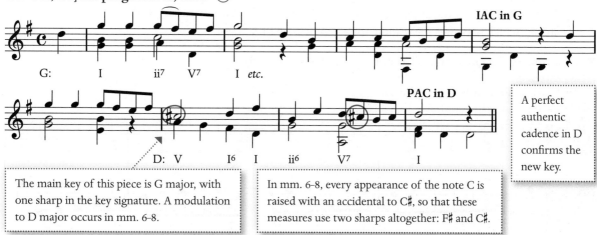

The main key of this piece is G major, with one sharp in the key signature. A modulation to D major occurs in mm. 6–8.

In mm. 6–8, every appearance of the note C is raised with an accidental to C♯, so that these measures use two sharps altogether: F♯ and C♯.

A perfect authentic cadence in D confirms the new key.

Once a modulation has begun, all the harmonies, scale degrees, and cadences are to be understood to function in the new key, and they should be labeled within the new key as well.

27.2 Filitz, "Blessed Night," from *Church of Ireland Hymnal*

The music starts in D (2♯s), and modulates in mm. 3–4 to A (3♯s), and ends by returning to the main key of D (2♯s).

After the modulation has begun, the cadence, scale degrees, and chords all function within the key of A (G♯, for example, is the leading tone of A).

♯s = F♯, C♯ (in key signature)

all Gs are ♯ here, so along with ♯s in the key signature, ♯s now = F♯, C♯, G♯

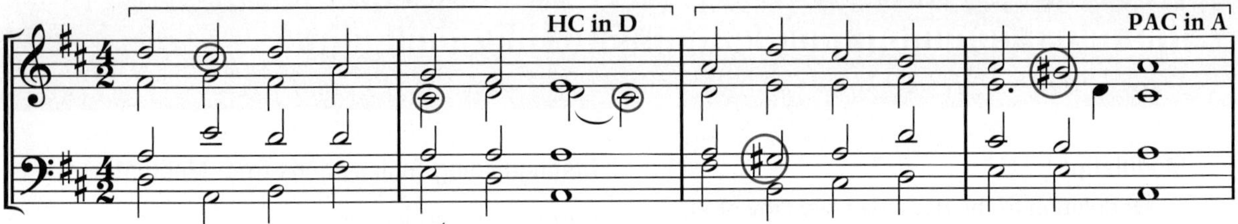

F♯ and C♯ (all Gs are natural)

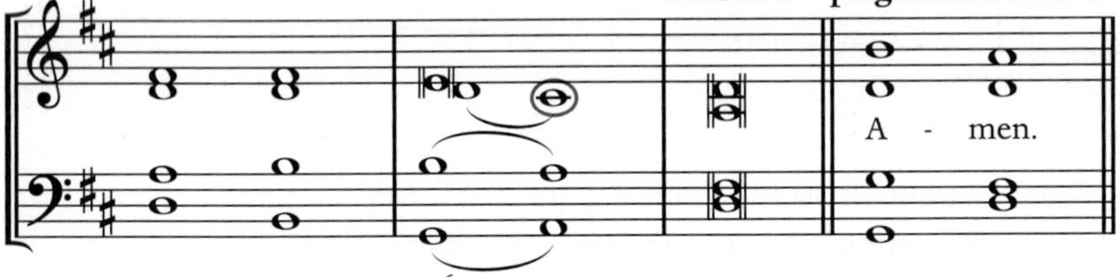

The main key (D major) returns in the last phrase, as the scale degrees, chords, and cadences once again function within this key.

MODULATION TO THE DOMINANT KEY (KEY OF V)

A new key that is established by a modulation is identified by its relationship with the main key—that is, by the position of its tonic within the scale of the main key. The most common modulation, particularly in major keys, is to the **dominant key** (or **key of V**). For instance, D-major compositions generally modulate to A major, A major being the dominant (V) in the key of D. Moving to the dominant involves raising $\hat{4}$ of the main key, which becomes the leading tone $\hat{7}$ in the key of V.

27.3 Haydn, String Quartet in D Major, op. 20, no. 4, Trio

The main key of this movement is D major.

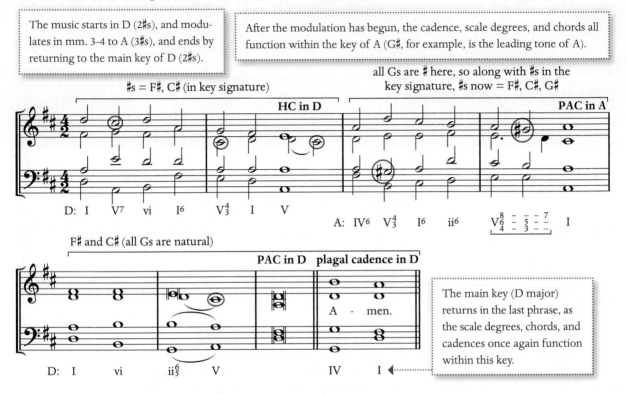

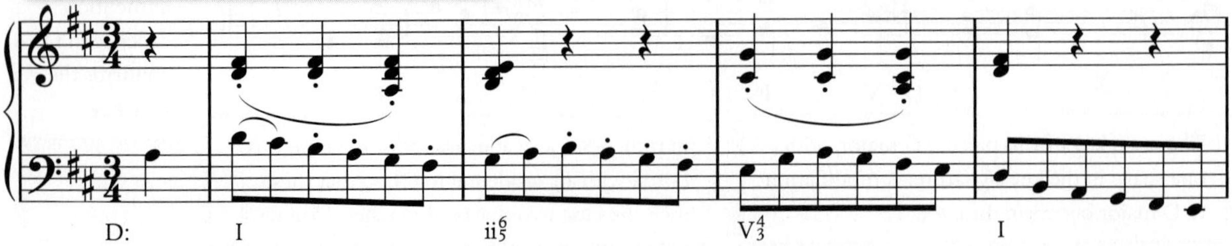

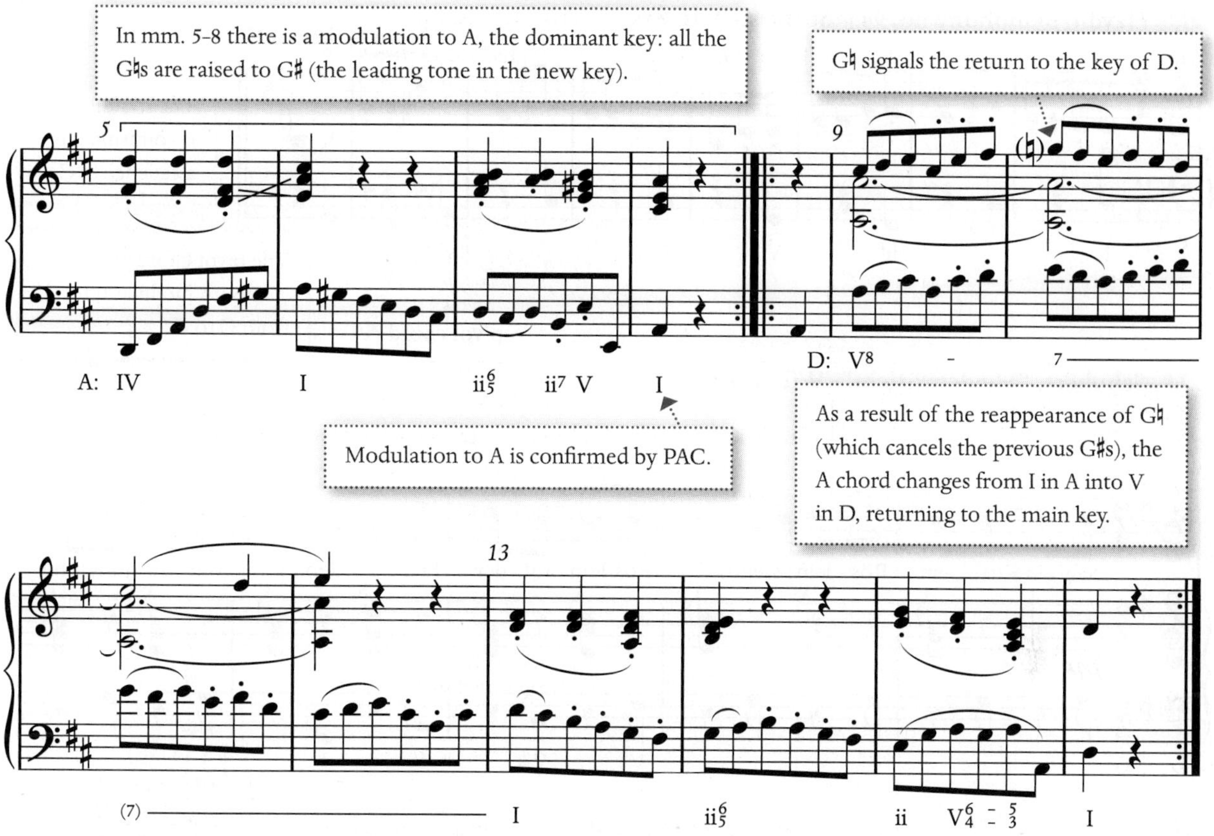
In mm. 5-8 there is a modulation to A, the dominant key: all the G♮s are raised to G♯ (the leading tone in the new key).
G♮ signals the return to the key of D.
A: IV I ii$^6_5$ ii^7 V I
D: V^8 - 7
Modulation to A is confirmed by PAC.
As a result of the reappearance of G♮ (which cancels the previous G♯s), the A chord changes from I in A into V in D, returning to the main key.
(7) I ii$^6_5$ ii V$^6_4$ - $^5_3$ I

PIVOT CHORDS

In a modulation from one key to another, in many cases the first chord in the new key is also a chord in the main key. Thus a harmony originally heard within the first key is subsequently reinterpreted in the new key, allowing for smooth motion from one key to the other. The shared harmony is known as a **pivot chord**. Pivot chords must be diatonic in both keys—that is, they should not require any accidentals in either key.

27.4

Modulation from C to G using pivot chord:

Progression that does not use pivot chord:

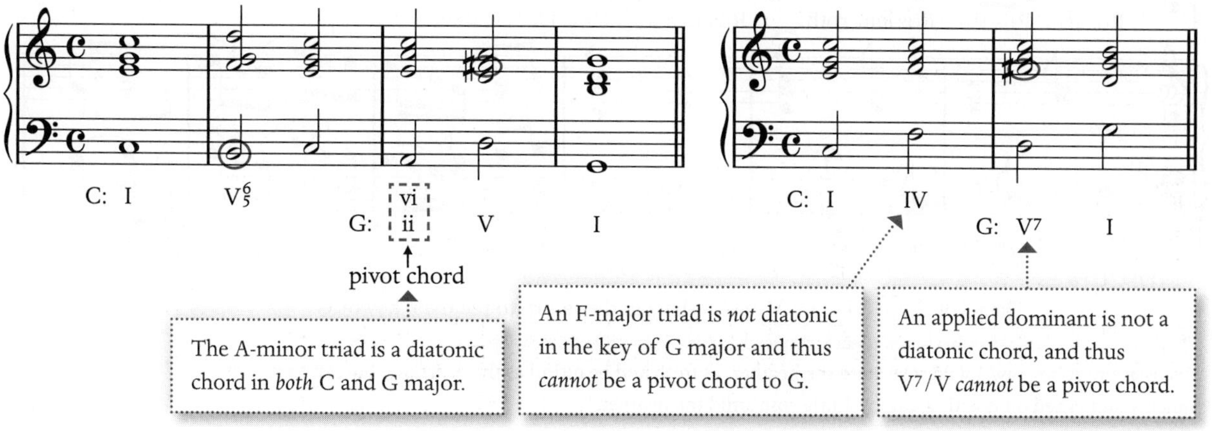
C: I V$^6_5$ vi
G: ii V I
pivot chord
C: I IV
G: V^7 I
The A-minor triad is a diatonic chord in *both* C and G major.
An F-major triad is *not* diatonic in the key of G major and thus *cannot* be a pivot chord to G.
An applied dominant is not a diatonic chord, and thus V^7/V *cannot* be a pivot chord.

27.5 Haydn, Symphony no. 94 ("Surprise"), II

PAC in G (key of V)
ten.
ten.
ten.
p
C: I ii6 V I
vi
G: ii V I
pivot chord
The modulation is confirmed by a cadence in G.
The pivot chord provides a smooth modulation from C to G.

27.6 Schubert, "Heidenröslein" (Wild Rose)

The pivot chord (I in G = IV in D) introduces the modulation to the dominant key.
Sah ein Knab' ein Rös - lein_stehn, Rös-lein auf der Hei - den, war so jung und
pp
G: I ii4/2 V6/5 V4/2 I6 I
I
D: IV
mor - gen_schön, lief er schnell es nah'_ zu_ sehn, sah's_ mit_ vie - len_ Freu - den.
cresc.
D: V4/2 I6 ii6 V7 vi I6 ii6 V7 I
Rös-lein, Rös-lein, Rös-lein roth, Rös-lein auf der Hei - den.
pp
G: V V4/2 I6 I IV IV6 V8-7/6-5/4-3 I IV ii V7/6-5/4-3 I
D: I
The pivot chord (I in D = V in G) ushers in the return to the main key of G.

Translation: A boy saw a wild rose amid the heather, as fresh and beautiful as the morning. He ran to it quickly and gazed on it with great joy. Little rose amid the heather.

To determine what harmonies may be used as pivot chords in modulating from one key to another, find the chords that are in both keys. In modulating from I to V, here are the possibilities:

Key of I		**Key of V**	**Key of I**		**Key of V**
I	*becomes*	IV	V	*becomes*	I
iii	*becomes*	vi	vi	*becomes*	ii

27.7

The four boxed harmonies could be pivot chords in a modulation between D and A major: I of D = IV of A, iii of D = vi of A, V of D = I of A, and vi of D = ii of A.

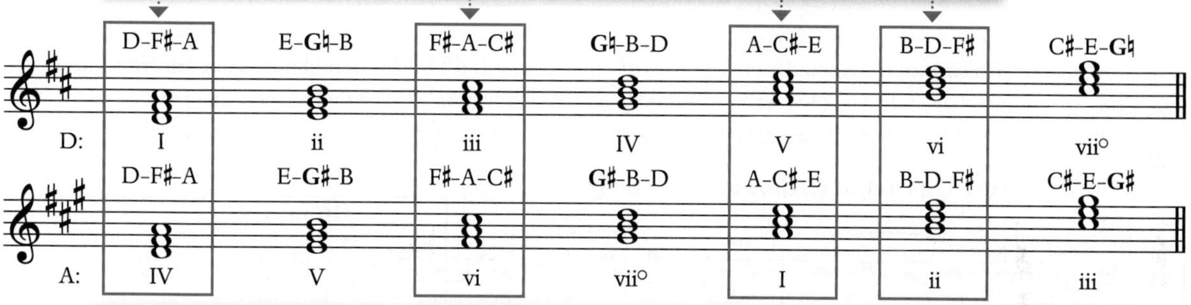

The other harmonies cannot be used as pivot chords: E minor, G major, and C♯ diminished are *not* diatonic chords in the key of A; E major, G♯ diminished, and C♯ minor are *not* diatonic chords in the key of D.

DISTINGUISHING TONICIZATIONS FROM MODULATIONS

As noted above and in Chapter 25, a tonicization occurs when a harmony other than I is briefly treated as a tonic. The appearance of a few chords in a new key in mid-phrase is usually interpreted as a tonicization, rather than a modulation. To be sure, there is no strict dividing line between these two categories, and in some cases a harmonic progression might be characterized either way, as involving a tonicization or a modulation. In general, however, a modulation tends to be a key change that is long and substantial, involves a pivot chord, and—most importantly— is confirmed with a cadence.

27.8 Mozart, "March of the Priests," from *The Magic Flute*

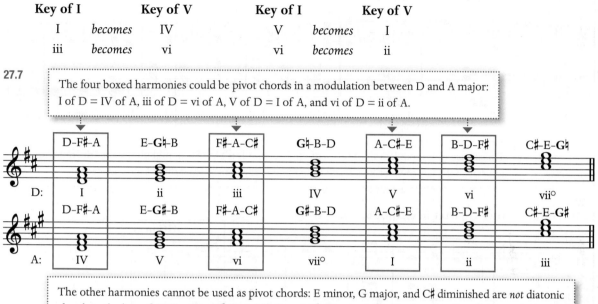

Modulation: The key of C (i.e., the key of V) is introduced with a pivot chord, in mm. 5–8 all the chords and scale degrees function within the key of C, and there is a PAC in C at the end of the phrase.

In contrast, a change of key is regarded as a tonicization if it is brief, not introduced with a pivot chord, and not confirmed with a cadence.

27.9 Mendelssohn, *Kinderstücke* (Children's Pieces), op. 72, no. 6

Tonicization (not modulation): A series of applied chords tonicize C in mid-phrase, but the music does not stay in the key of C for long (note B♭ in the melody in m. 4), and there is no cadence in C.

27.10 Haydn, String Quartet in C, op. 76, no. 3, II

Tonicization (not modulation): Although D (the goal V within the half cadence in the main key) is tonicized at the end of the phrase, there is no pivot chord, nor is there a cadence in D.

HARMONIZING MELODIES

To identify a melody that might be harmonized with a modulation, look for an appearance (or repeated appearance) of an accidental shortly before the end of a phrase, or for a succession of scale degrees that seems more compatible with a progression in a new key.

27.11

***Task*: Harmonize the melody.**

As the leading tone of C major, B normally leads up to C. The downward motion here could be harmonized with a modulation to G, in which the melodic succession B–A is more normal.

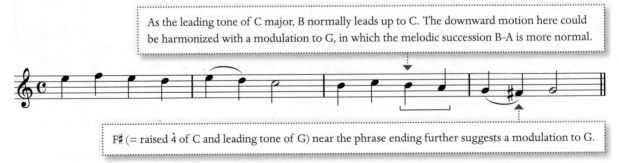

F♯ (= raised $\hat{4}$ of C and leading tone of G) near the phrase ending further suggests a modulation to G.

Possible harmonization:

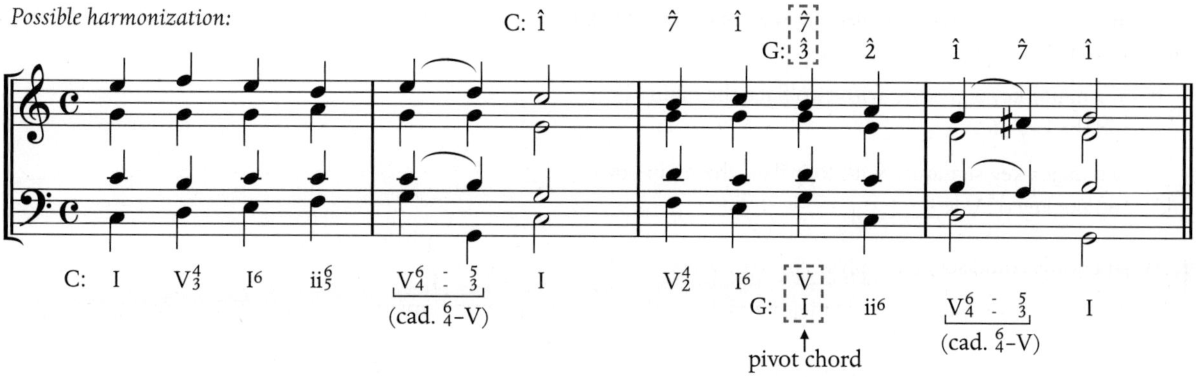

For more on modulating to the dominant key, see A Closer Look.

review and interact

POINTS FOR REVIEW

- **A modulation is a substantial change of key that is confirmed by a cadence.**
- **Modulations are usually signaled by accidentals, rather than by a new key signature.**
- **After a modulation has begun, the harmonies and scale degrees are labeled in the new key.**
- **The key that appears at the start and end of the movement is known as the main key. The keys to which there are modulations are identified by their relationship to the main key.**
- **In a major key piece, the most common modulation is to the dominant key (the key of V).**
- **In modulating between two keys, often the last chord of the first key is the same as the first chord of the new key. This shared chord is known as a pivot chord and must be diatonic to both keys.**
- **Compared to tonicizations, modulations are changes of key that tend to be more substantial, involve a pivot chord, and have a cadence in the new key.**

TEST YOURSELF

1. Name the accidental needed to modulate between the following keys:

Modulate from:	*to:*	*Accidental needed:*	*Modulate from:*	*to:*	*Accidental needed:*
a. G	D		e. D♭	A♭	
b. B♭	F		f. B	F♯	
c. E	B		g. E♭	B♭	
d. A	E				

2. a. In a major key signature with two sharps, the main key is ______ and the key of V is ______.

   b. In a major key signature with two flats, the main key is ______ and the key of V is ______.

   c. In a major key signature with four flats, the main key is ______ and the key of V is ______.

3. What chords could serve as a pivot chord between

   a. B♭ major and F major? b. D major and A major? c. A major and E major?

4. In each of the following three excerpts, what chord functions as the pivot chord? What is the function of that chord in the main key? In the key of V?

a.

b.

c.

Know It? Show It!

Focus by working through the tutorials on:

- Modulation to the dominant key
- Finding pivot chords
- Harmonizing a modulating melody

Learn with inQuizitive.

Apply what you've learned to complete the assignments:

- Determining Possible Pivot Chords
- Realizing Roman Numerals
- Realizing Figured Bass
- Harmonizing Melodies
- Composition
- Analysis

chapter 28

Modulation to Closely Related Keys

Modulations to closely related keys—differing from the main key by no more than one sharp or flat—are common.

CLOSELY RELATED KEYS

Modulations can lead to any key, not just the key of the dominant. The most common modulations are those that lead to closely related keys—that is, keys whose signature differs from that of the main key by no more than one sharp or flat.

28.1

***Task*: Find the closely related keys of C major.**

- Since C major has no sharps or flats, closely related keys include the relative minor, and the major and minor keys that have one sharp or flat:

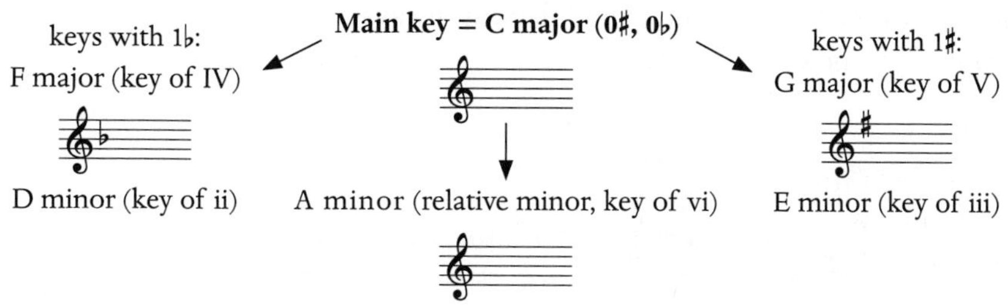

- The closely related keys of C major are A minor, G major, E minor, F major, and D minor.

28.2

***Task*: Find the closely related keys of C minor.**

- Since C minor has three flats, closely related keys include the relative major, and the major and minor keys that have four flats and two flats.

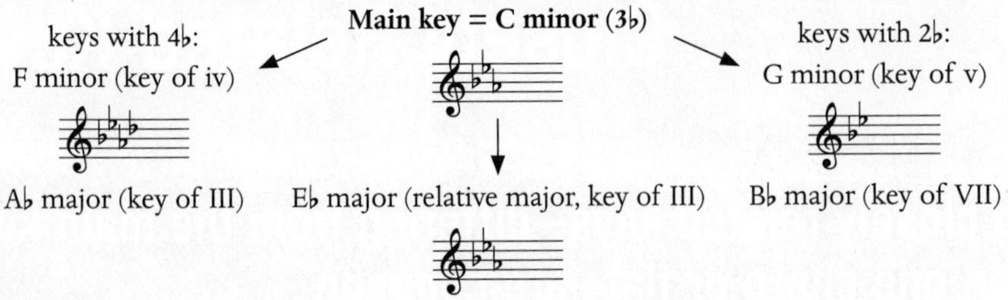

- The closely related keys of C minor are E♭ major, F minor, A♭ major, G minor, and B♭ major.

The tonic chord of each closely related key uses notes—without accidentals—from the scale of the main key.

28.3

The major and minor triads (without accidentals) in a key form the tonic chords of closely related keys.

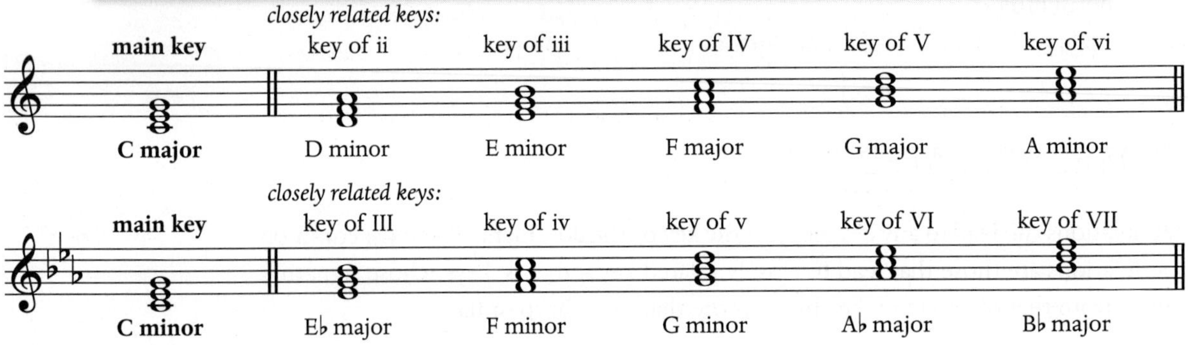

MODULATIONS IN MAJOR-KEY PIECES

After a modulation has begun, scale degrees and harmonies are understood in relation to the new key. A modulation to any key requires a cadence. With the exception of modulation from a minor key to its relative major, modulations always involve accidentals or (much less commonly) a new key signature.

28.4 J. S. Bach, Chorale 148

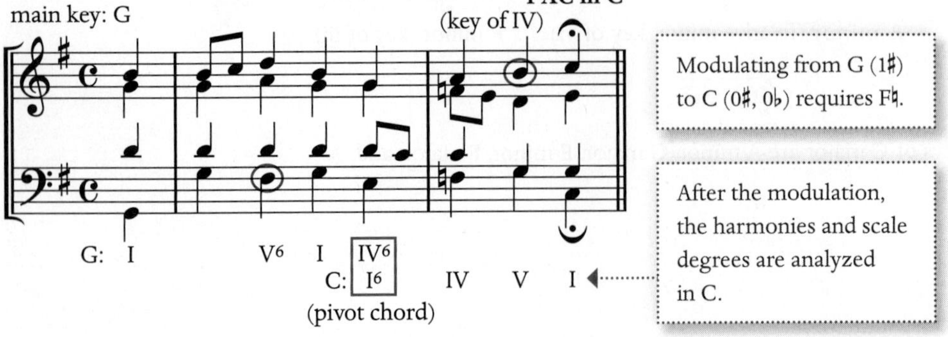

Modulating to the relative minor key requires raising $\hat{7}$ of the new key so that it becomes a leading tone.

28.5 Schubert, *German Dances*, D. 783, no. 13

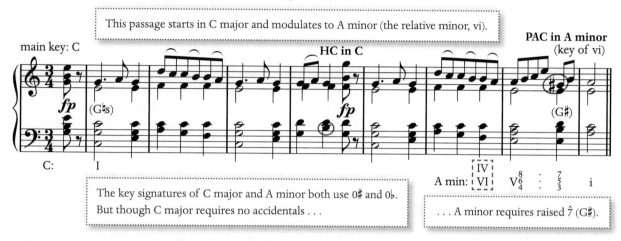

This passage starts in C major and modulates to A minor (the relative minor, vi).

The key signatures of C major and A minor both use 0♯ and 0♭. But though C major requires no accidentals . . .

. . . A minor requires raised $\hat{7}$ (G♯).

Modulation to other minor keys similarly requires a raised $\hat{7}$, in addition to whatever accidentals are needed to reflect the difference in the key signature of the new key.

28.6 Giuliani, *Pièces faciles et agréables* for Flute and Guitar, op. 74, no. 4

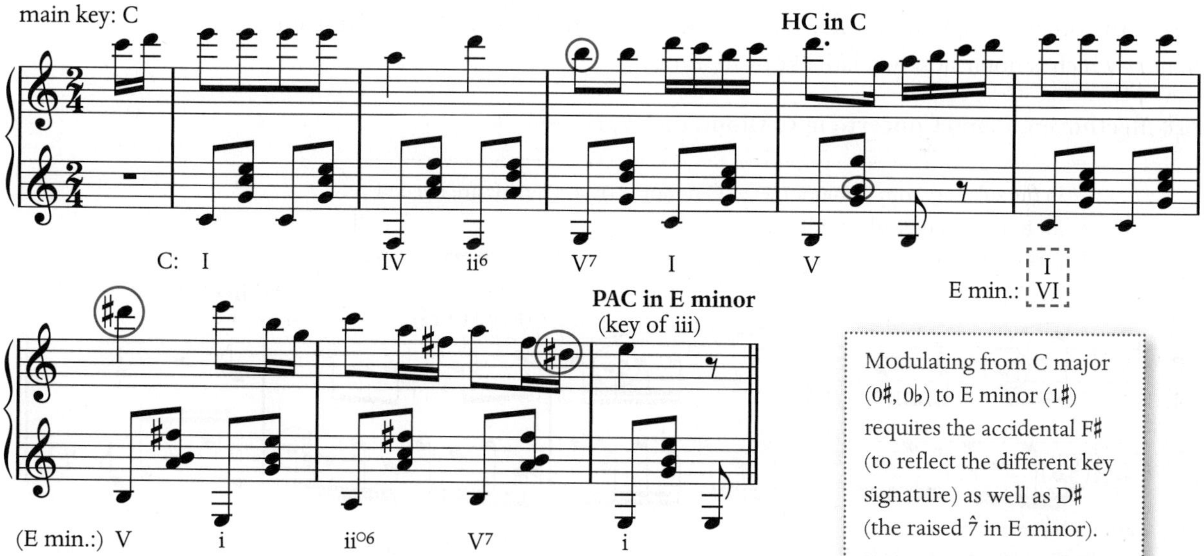

Modulating from C major (0♯, 0♭) to E minor (1♯) requires the accidental F♯ (to reflect the different key signature) as well as D♯ (the raised $\hat{7}$ in E minor).

Simplified harmonic model

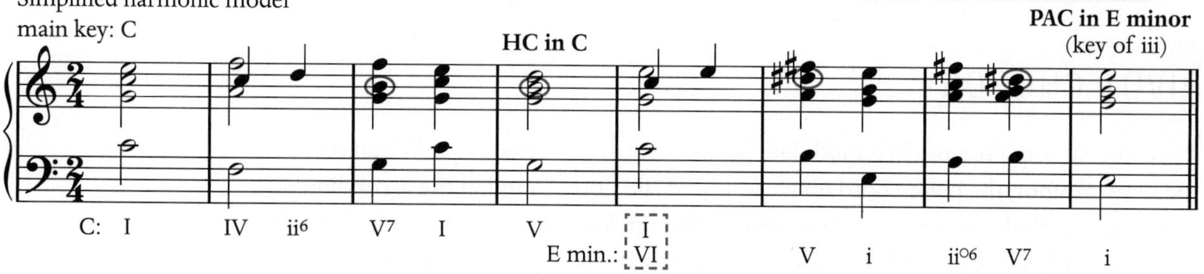

MODULATIONS IN MINOR-KEY PIECES

Within minor-key compositions it is extremely common to modulate to the relative major (III). Although a minor key and its relative major share the same key signature, $\hat{7}$ in minor is almost always raised to form a leading tone. As a result, the prominent and repeated use of $\hat{7}$ that is *not* raised usually indicates a modulation to the relative major, especially if it appears as part of the cadence.

28.7 Purcell, "When monarchs unite," from *Dido and Aeneas*

In the first phrase, $\hat{7}$ is raised to B♮ to form the leading tone in C minor.

The repeated B♭s in the second phrase signal a modulation to E♭.

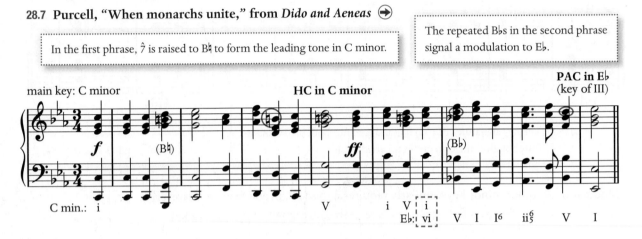

It is also common in minor keys to modulate to the key of the dominant minor, v. (On the other hand, in minor-key pieces modulations to the key of the dominant major—which is not a closely related key—are rare.)

28.8 Beethoven, Piano Concerto in C Minor, op. 37, III

In modulating from C minor (3♭) to G minor (2♭), accidentals are needed for both A♮ and F♯ (the leading tone of G minor).

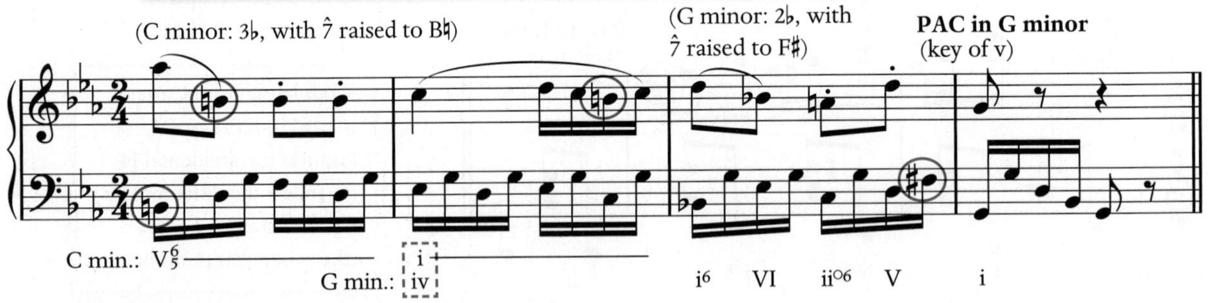

PIVOT CHORDS

Pivot chords are often used to modulate between closely related keys. When one of the keys is minor, the pivot chord may use any of the notes found in the ascending or descending melodic minor scale. Even chords that are less common in simple diatonic passages—such as III, minor v, or subtonic VII—may be used as a pivot chords.

28.9

***Task*: Find the pivot chords that may be used in modulating from G major to A minor.**

- Determine the major, minor, and diminished chords in each key, using the notes in the G major and A melodic minor scales.
- Any chord in the main key that uses the same notes as a chord in the new key can be used as a pivot chord.

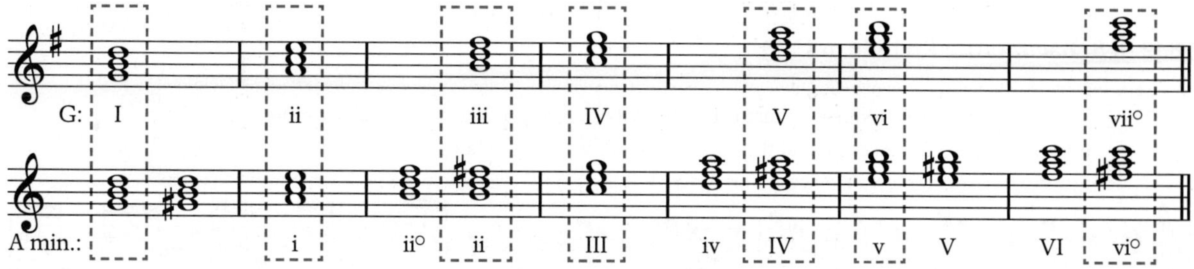

28.10 J. S. Bach, Chorale 249

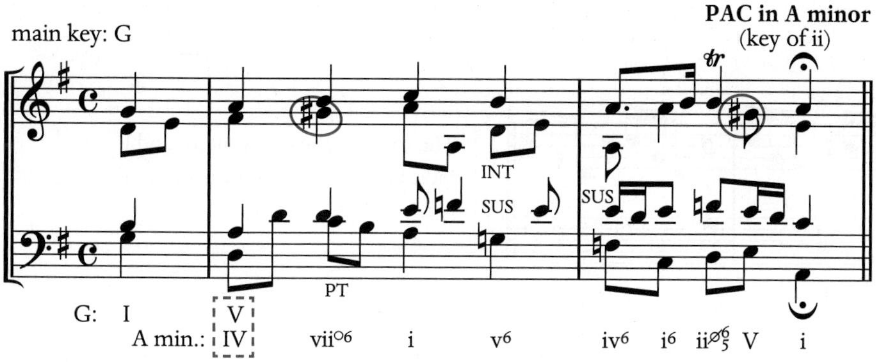

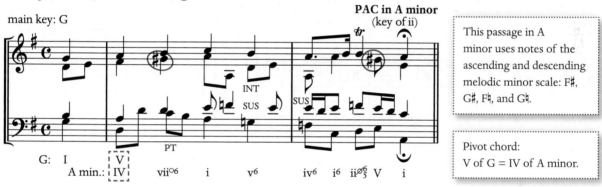

This passage in A minor uses notes of the ascending and descending melodic minor scale: F♯, G♯, F♮, and G♮.

Pivot chord: V of G = IV of A minor.

Pivot chords may be preceded by an applied dominant.

28.11 J. S. Bach, Chorale 88

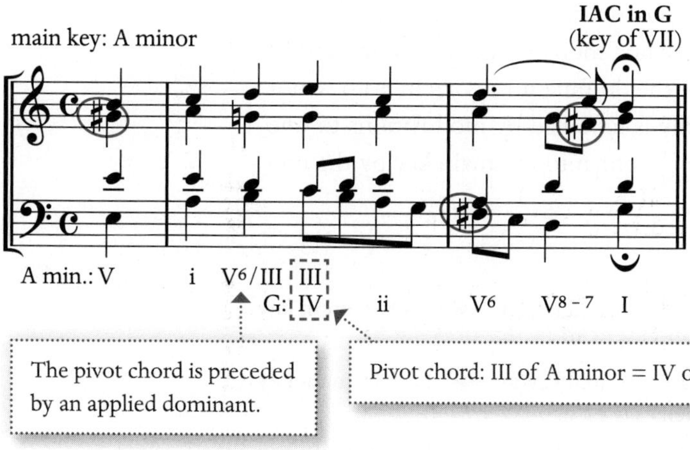

The pivot chord is preceded by an applied dominant.

Pivot chord: III of A minor = IV of G major.

EXTENDED TONICIZATIONS

Some key changes that do not lead to a cadence in the new key—and thus create tonicizations rather than modulations— nonetheless involve *multiple* harmonies that lead toward a goal chord. These may include chords other than applied dominants, including **S**ubdominant harmonies that relate to the goal chord. The chords within these extended tonicizations may be labeled in relation to the tonicized key.

28.12 J. S. Bach, Little Prelude in C

Within this iii-I-vi-IV sequence there are short IV^6_5-V^6_5-I progressions that lead to A minor and F, but there are no cadences in (and thus no modulations to) these keys.

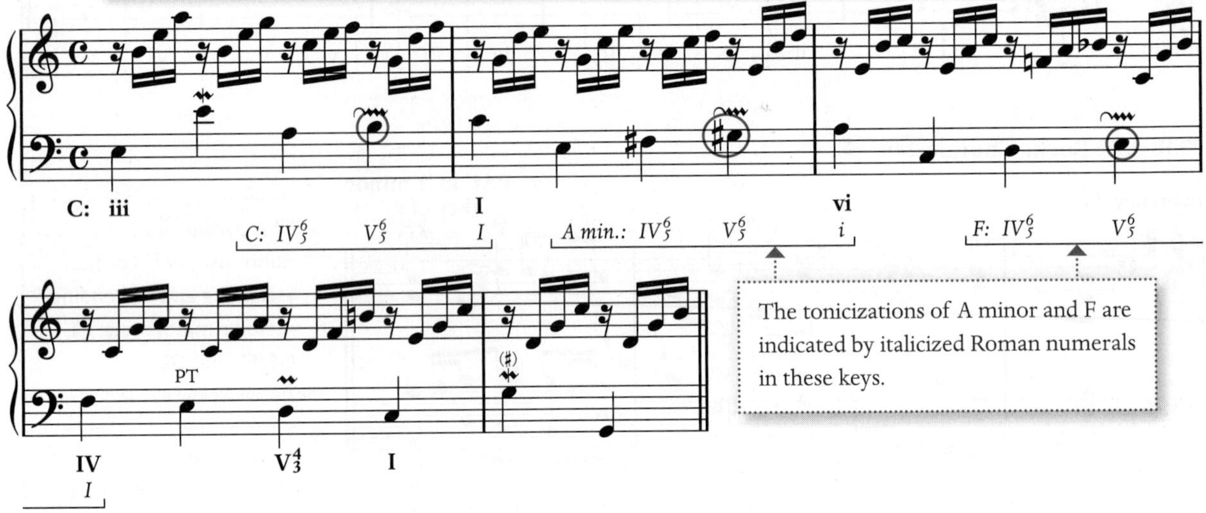

MODULATION SCHEMES

Compositions often modulate to several different keys, frequently following a conventional order. In major-key movements composed before 1800, the first modulation is usually to V. In minor-key movements, the first modulation most often is to III (the relative major), though it can also be to v (the dominant minor). In both major and minor keys, the initial modulation normally is followed by modulations to one or more other closely related keys, and then by a return to the main key by the end of the piece.

28.13 Common modulation schemes

major-key piece: **main key** → V → other closely related key(s) (such as vi or IV) → back to **main key**

minor-key piece: **main key** → III → other closely related key(s) (such as iv or v) → back to **main key**

OR

main key → v → other closely related key(s) (such as III or iv) → back to **main key**

Each key to which there is a modulation is labeled by its relation to the main key. Thus, for instance, in a work in C major a modulation to A minor is labeled as a modulation to the key of vi, even if it is immediately preceded by a modulation to G major.

28.14 J. S. Bach, *Applicatio*

This C-major piece follows a standard modulation scheme: first a modulation to V (G major), then to vi (A minor), and finally back to C.

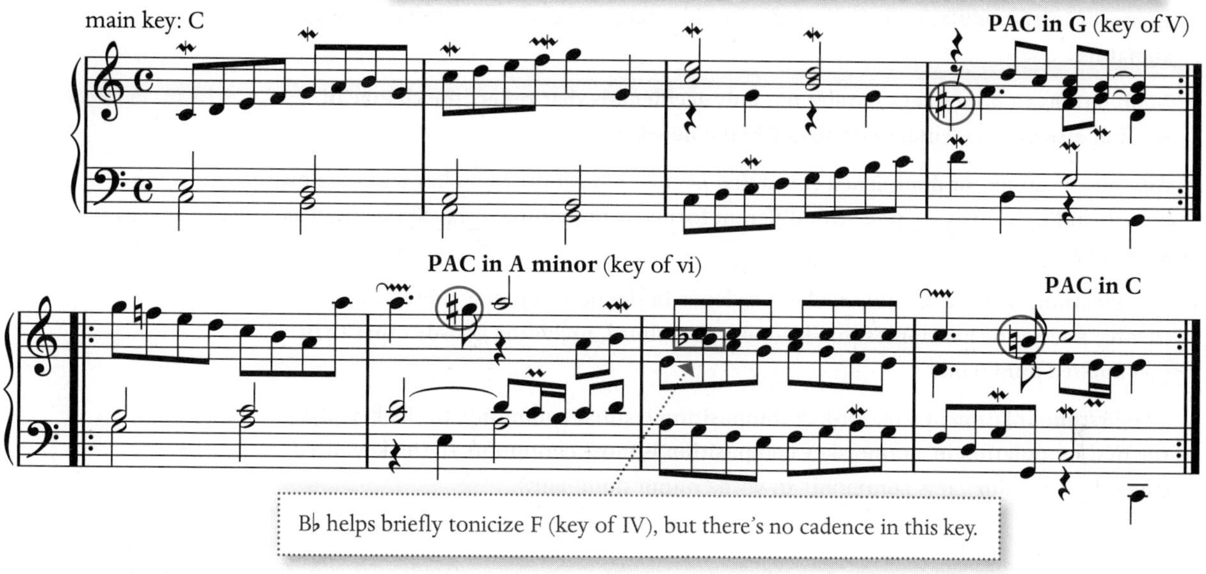

28.15 Handel, Violin Sonata in E, HWV 373, III

This C♯-minor movement follows a standard modulation scheme: first a modulation to III (E major), then to iv (F♯ minor), and finally back to C♯ minor.

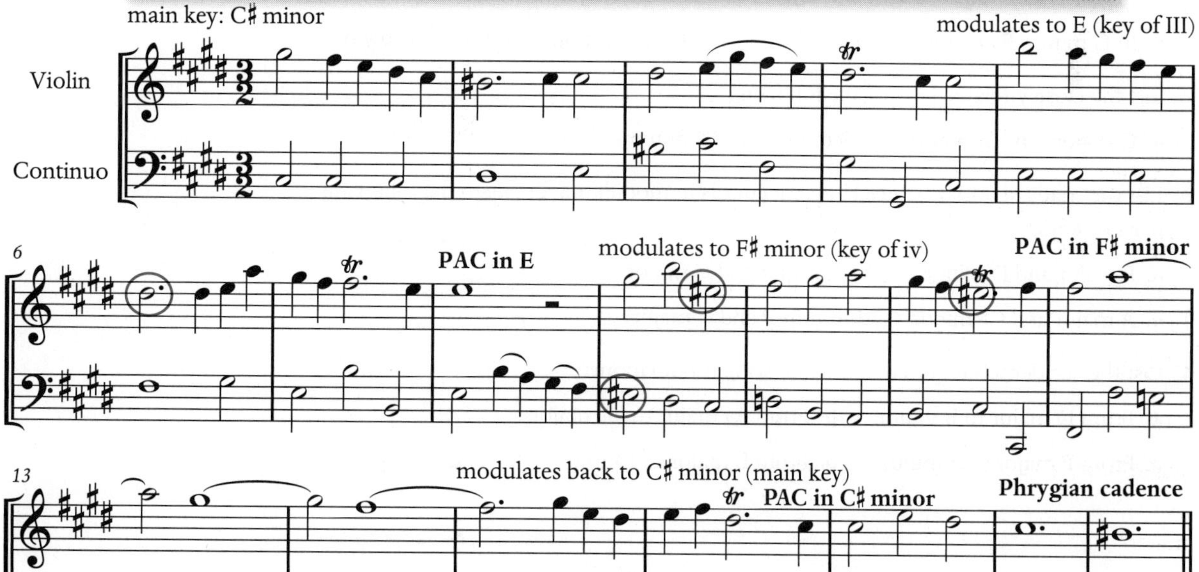

review and interact

POINTS FOR REVIEW

- **It is common to modulate to closely related keys (keys in which the key signature differs from the main key by no more than one sharp or flat).**
- **In most cases, modulation is indicated by accidentals, rather than by a change of key signature.**
- **Modulations to minor keys require not only accidentals that reflect the change of key, but also an accidental that raises $\hat{7}$ in the new key.**
- **Any major, minor, or diminished chord that occurs in both the main key and the new key (including chords created with different forms of the minor scale) can be used as a pivot chord.**
- **Tonicization, which does not involve a cadence in the new key, may nonetheless involve a series of harmonies that lead to a goal chord, including chords other than just applied dominants.**
- **The first modulation in a major-key composition is most commonly to the key of V; the first modulation in a minor-key composition is most commonly to the key of III (the relative major), less commonly to v (the minor dominant).**

TEST YOURSELF

1. In C major, E minor is the key of iii.

   a. In G major, B minor is the key of ____.   b. In A major, D major is the key of ____.

   c. In G minor, E♭ major is the key of ____.   d. In E minor, B minor is the key of ____.

2. List the closely related keys of the following:

   a. G major   b. B♭ major   c. D minor   d. F♯ minor

3. List the triads that may be used as pivot chords in modulating between the following pairs of keys:

   a. F major and D minor   b. G minor and C minor

   c. A major and C♯ minor   d. E minor and C major

4. List the accidentals required in the following modulations:

   a. From D major to B minor.   b. From A♭ major to D♭ major.

   c. From F major to A minor.   d. From E major to F♯ minor.

5. Supply the missing accidentals in the following passages.

a.

b.

c.

Know It? Show It!

Focus by working through the tutorials on:

- Modulation to closely related keys
- Writing a modulating chord progression

Learn with inQuizitive.

Apply what you've learned to complete the assignments:

- Determining Closely Related Keys and Pivot Chords
- Realizing Roman Numerals
- Realizing Figured Bass
- Harmonizing Melodies
- Composition
- Analysis

chapter

29 Modal Mixture

Modal mixture arises when notes, chords, or passages from the parallel minor are used within a major key, or vice versa.

PARALLEL MINOR IN A MAJOR KEY

Modal mixture in a major key results from the appearance of notes, chords, or entire passages drawn from the parallel minor. A shift to the parallel minor can have a powerful expressive effect. It is *not* a modulation, however, because a modulation must involve a change of tonic.

29.1 Schubert, "Thränenregen" (Rain of Tears)

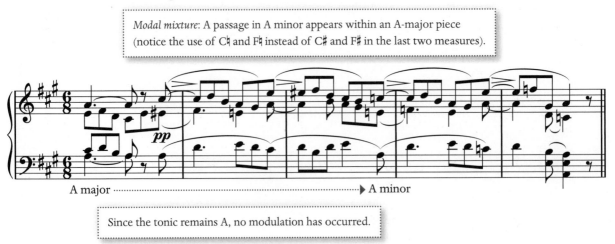

Modal mixture: A passage in A minor appears within an A-major piece (notice the use of C♮ and F♮ instead of C♯ and F♯ in the last two measures).

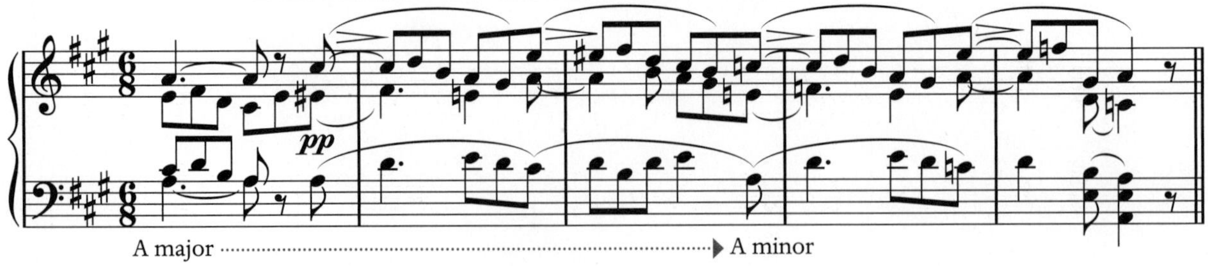

Since the tonic remains A, no modulation has occurred.

BORROWED CHORDS RESULTING FROM MODAL MIXTURE

In a major-key passage, modal mixture may involve only one chord or perhaps just a few harmonies from the parallel minor. In such a case the minor-key harmonies, known as **borrowed chords**, typically use the minor form of either $\hat{3}$ or $\hat{6}$ as one of their chord tones. In each case, the function of the borrowed chord is similar to the diatonic version of the harmony. For instance, within a major key, iv functions like IV, ii$^{\circ 6}$ functions like ii^6, and so on.

29.2

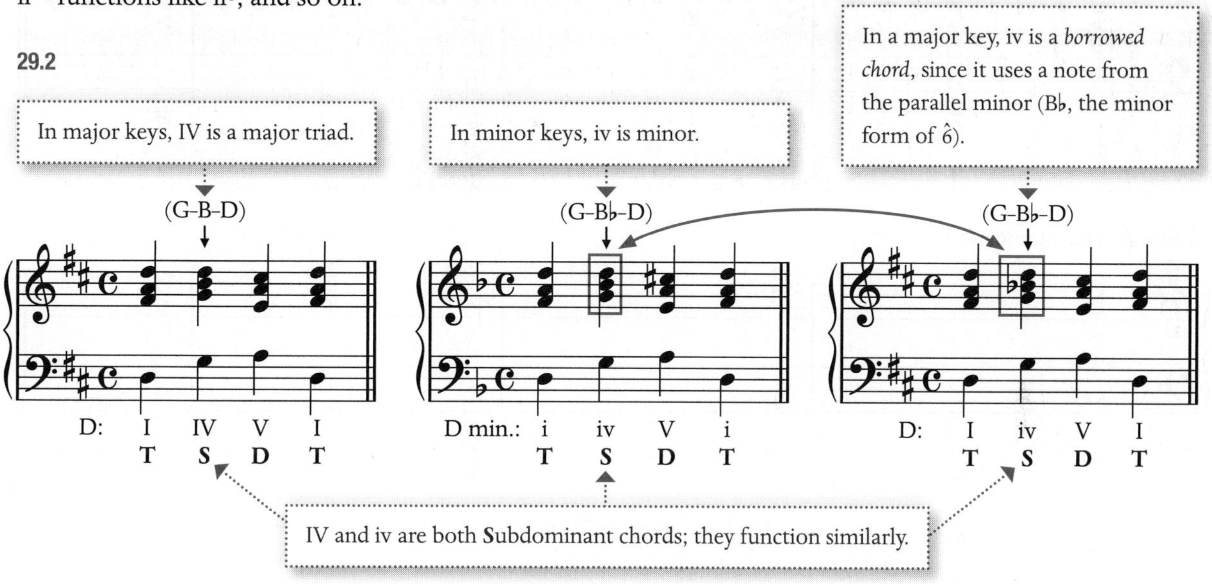

In major keys, IV is a major triad.
In minor keys, iv is minor.
In a major key, iv is a *borrowed chord*, since it uses a note from the parallel minor (B♭, the minor form of 6̂).
(G–B–D)
(G–B♭–D)
(G–B♭–D)
D: I IV V I
T S D T
D min.: i iv V i
T S D T
D: I iv V I
T S D T
IV and iv are both **S**ubdominant chords; they function similarly.

29.3 Dvorak, Waltz, op. 54, no. 4

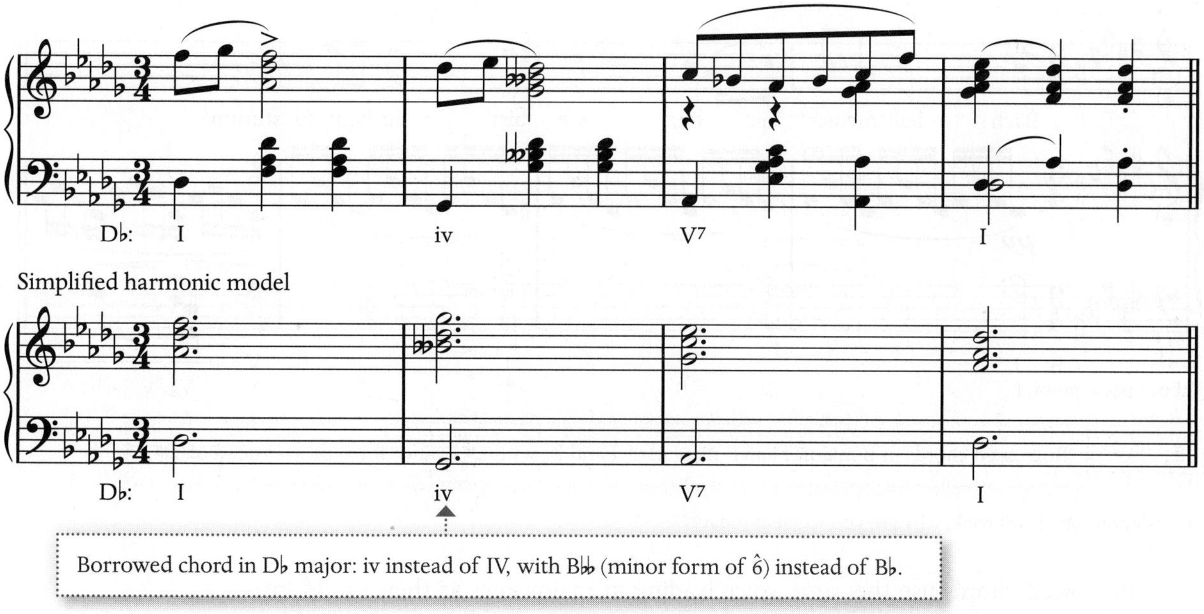

D♭: I iv V7 I
Simplified harmonic model
D♭: I iv V7 I
Borrowed chord in D♭ major: iv instead of IV, with B𝄫 (minor form of 6̂) instead of B♭.

29.4 R. Schumann, "Ich grolle nicht" (I Bear No Grudge)

Simplified harmonic model

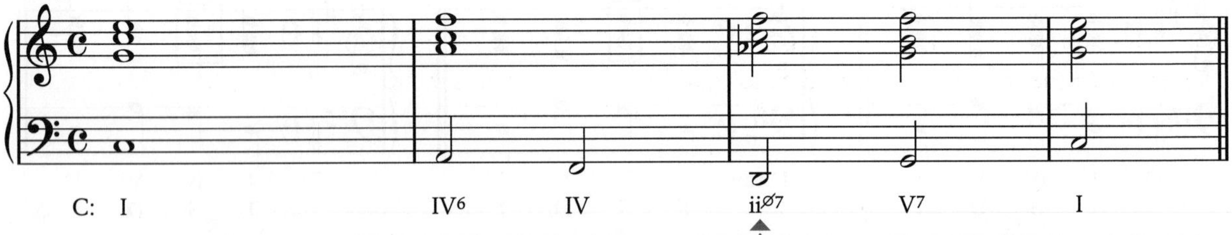

Borrowed chord in C major: iiø7 instead of ii7, with A♭ (minor form of $\hat{6}$) instead of A.

Translation: I bear no grudge, although my heart is breaking.

29.5 Schubert, "Der Neugierige" (The Curious One)

Borrowed chords in B major: i and i6 instead of I and I6, with D♮ (minor form of $\hat{3}$) instead of D♯.

Translation: My dear brook, why are you so silent today?

Borrowed chords use the same voice leading in major keys as they would in their original minor-key context.

29.6

Good Voice-leading from iv is the same in a minor or major key.

Poor Whether in a minor key or in a borrowed chord, the minor form of $\hat{6}$ (B♭) should resolve down to avoid a melodic augmented 2nd.

COMMON BORROWED CHORDS

The most common borrowed chords in major use either the minor form of $\hat{3}$ (such as the i triad), the minor form of $\hat{6}$ (such as iv, ii°6, or iiø7), or both (such as ♭VI—that is, a major triad whose root is the minor form of $\hat{6}$).

29.7

Comparison of diatonic chords and common borrowed chords

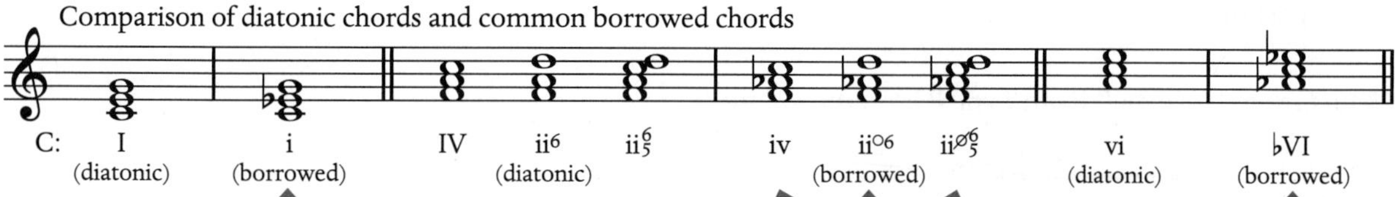

$\hat{3}$ is lowered.

$\hat{6}$ is lowered.

$\hat{3}$ and $\hat{6}$ are lowered (*two* accidentals are needed).

Since $\hat{7}$ is usually raised to form a leading tone in minor keys, borrowed chords that use the subtonic $\hat{7}$ are relatively rare. In the few instances where they do appear, they most often function as passing chords, as parts of sequences, or within lengthy sections in the parallel minor.

29.8

Comparison of diatonic chords and borrowed chords that are relatively uncommon

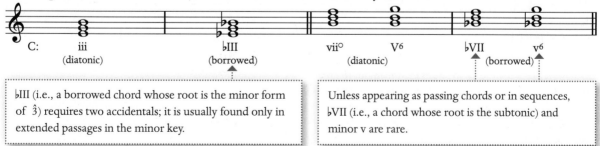

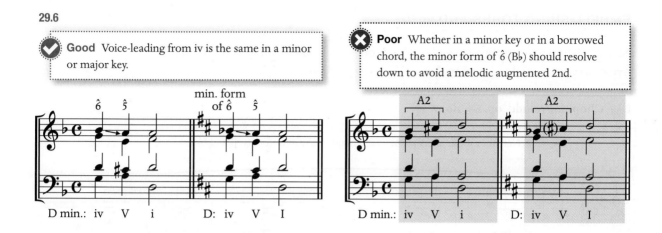

♭III (i.e., a borrowed chord whose root is the minor form of $\hat{3}$) requires two accidentals; it is usually found only in extended passages in the minor key.

Unless appearing as passing chords or in sequences, ♭VII (i.e., a chord whose root is the subtonic) and minor v are rare.

EMBELLISHING TONES AND vii°7

Modal mixture may also involve embellishing tones. For example, the minor form of $\hat{6}$ may serve as a neighbor tone within a major-key passage.

29.9 Chopin, Prelude, op. 28, no. 5

Neighbor tones alternate between major and minor forms (B and B♭) of $\hat{6}$.

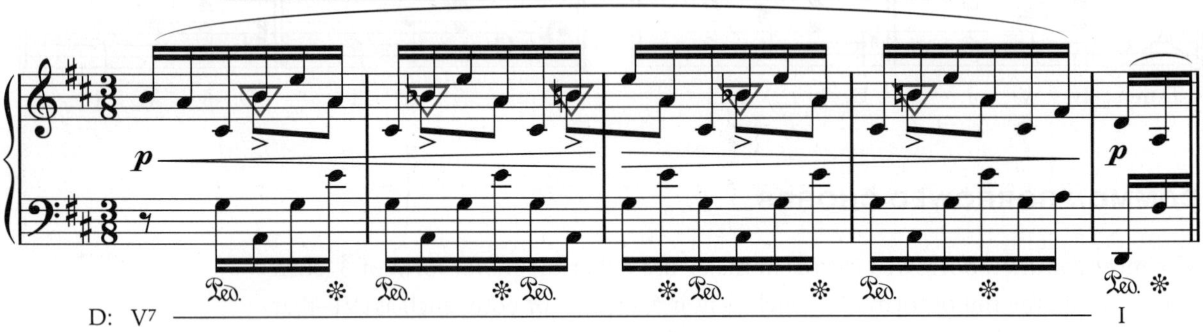

As discussed in Chapter 17, the minor form of $\hat{6}$ may also appear within a major key as part of vii°7.

29.10 Grieg, "Arietta," from *Lyric Pieces*, op. 12, no. 1

Simplified harmonic model

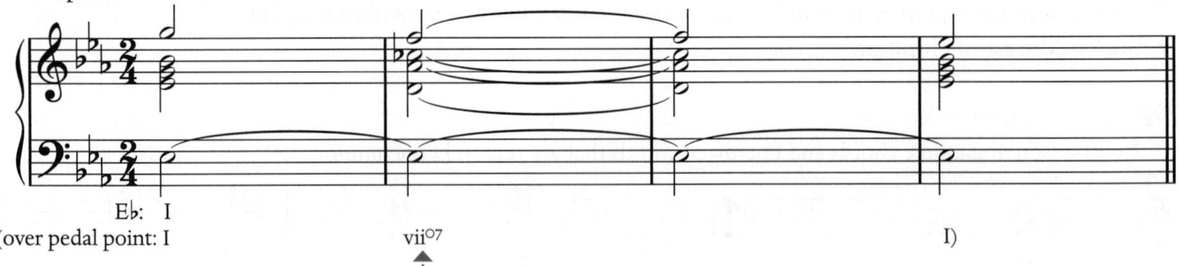

vii°7 uses C♭, the minor form of $\hat{6}$.

PARALLEL MAJOR IN A MINOR KEY

Modal mixture can also occur when a minor-key composition includes a passage in the parallel major.

29.11 Beethoven, "Urians Reise" (Urian's Journey), op. 52, no. 1 ➔

A passage in A major appears in an A-minor piece.

Translation: And so I chose to travel. You have not done badly, so keep on telling your stories, Mister Urian!

Unlike major keys, however, minor keys only rarely use borrowed chords in isolation. After all, $\hat{6}$ and $\hat{7}$ are often raised in minor keys anyway (as in the ascending melodic minor scale), and thus chords that use these raised scale degrees—such as IV or V—are considered to be part of the key rather than borrowed chords.

29.12 J. S. Bach, Chorale 184 ➔

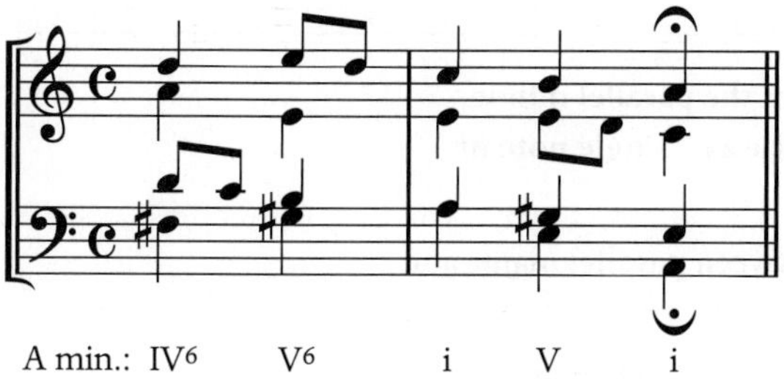

Since $\hat{6}$ and $\hat{7}$ (F♯ and G♯) are part of the ascending melodic minor scale, IV6 and V6 are not borrowed chords.

Likewise, when it appears in the middle of a phrase within a minor-key context, the major form of $\hat{3}$ usually forms part of an applied chord to IV, rather than part of a borrowed chord.

29.13 Jacquet de la Guerre, Suite in D Minor

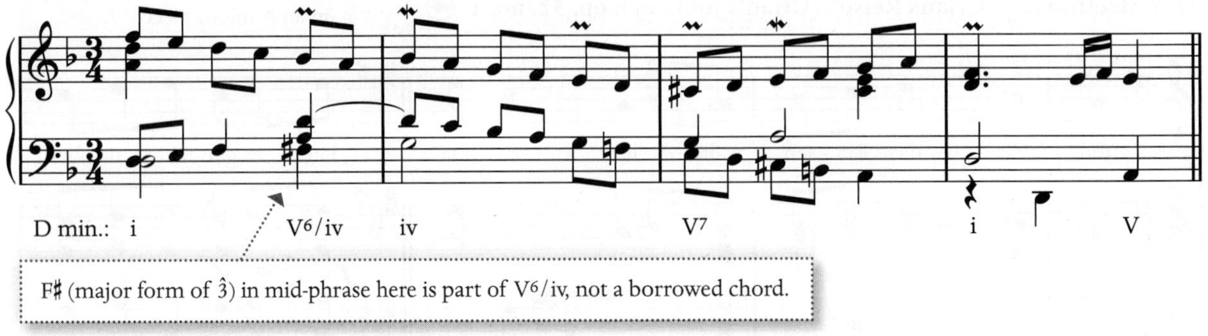
D min.: i
V6/iv
iv
V7
i
V
F♯ (major form of 3̂) in mid-phrase here is part of V6/iv, not a borrowed chord.

The only common instance of a borrowed chord within a minor key arises when the third of a tonic chord is raised at the *end* of a phrase. In this case, the minor form of $\hat{3}$ is replaced by its major form, so that the final tonic chord of the phrase is a major triad rather than a minor one. The raised $\hat{3}$ is known as a **Picardy third**.

29.14 Jacquet de la Guerre, Suite in D Minor

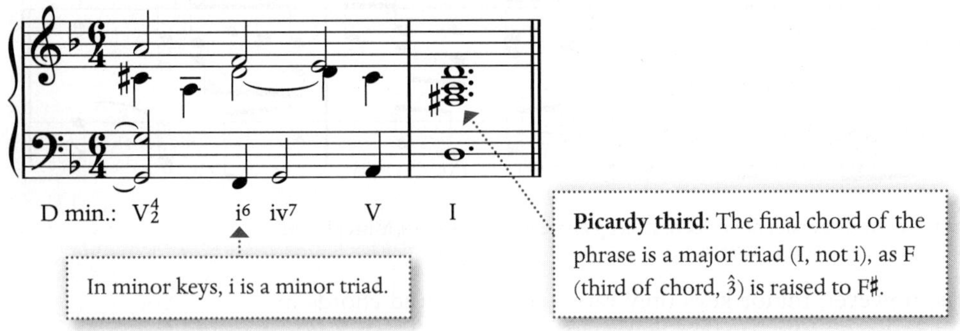
D min.: V4/2
i6
iv7
V
I
In minor keys, i is a minor triad.
Picardy third: The final chord of the phrase is a major triad (I, not i), as F (third of chord, 3̂) is raised to F♯.

review and interact

POINTS FOR REVIEW

- **Modal mixture usually occurs when notes or harmonies from the parallel minor appear within a major key. Modal mixture may involve as little as a single note or chord, or as much as an entire section.**
- **Since modulation involves changing tonic notes, moving between parallel major and minor keys is not considered to be a modulation.**
- **Modal mixture that changes the quality of a single harmony creates a *borrowed chord*. The use of modal mixture in a borrowed chord does not change its harmonic function.**

- **The most common borrowed chords are those that use the minor form of $\hat{3}$, $\hat{6}$, or both within a major key.**
- **Modal mixture may also occur when a section in a major key appears within a minor-key piece.**
- **At the end of a phrase in a minor key, the minor tonic triad may be replaced by a major chord by raising the third of the chord ($\hat{3}$) by a half step. This raised third is known as a *Picardy third*.**

TEST YOURSELF

1. In major keys, which of the following chords involve modal mixture?

   a. iv b. vi c. IV d. ii6 e. ii°6 f. ♭III g. i h. iii

2. What accidentals are missing in the following chords (all of which involve modal mixture)?

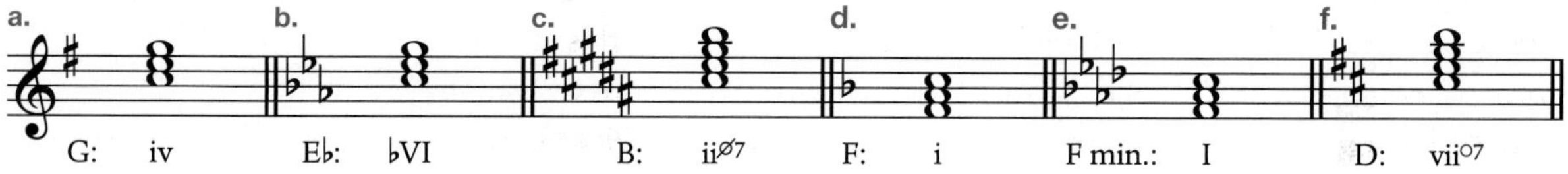

3. Which of the following statements are true?

   a. Modal mixture may arise when there is a move to the parallel minor key within a major-key piece, or vice versa.

   b. There can be a modulation from D major to D minor.

   c. A borrowed chord in a major key always involves using a flat for $\hat{3}$ or $\hat{6}$.

   d. The most common borrowed chords use the minor form of $\hat{3}$, $\hat{6}$, or both within a major-key context.

   e. A Picardy third is found at the end of a phase, rather than in its middle.

Know It? Show It!

Focus by working through the tutorials on:

- Recognizing modal mixture
- Writing a chord progression using mixture

Learn with inQuizitive.

Apply what you've learned to complete the assignments:

- Spelling Borrowed Chords
- Realizing Roman Numerals
- Realizing Figured Bass
- Composition
- Analysis

chapter 30 ♭II6: The Neapolitan Sixth

♭II6 is a first-inversion major triad built on lowered $\hat{2}$; it has a Subdominant function.

BUILDING ♭II6

♭II is a major chord whose root is lowered $\hat{2}$. It usually appears in first inversion, as a **♭II⁶**, also known as a **Neapolitan sixth** (or **N⁶**). ♭II⁶ appears most often in minor keys, in place of a diatonic ii°⁶. The root of ♭II⁶ requires an accidental, which may be either a flat or a natural, depending upon the key signature.

30.1

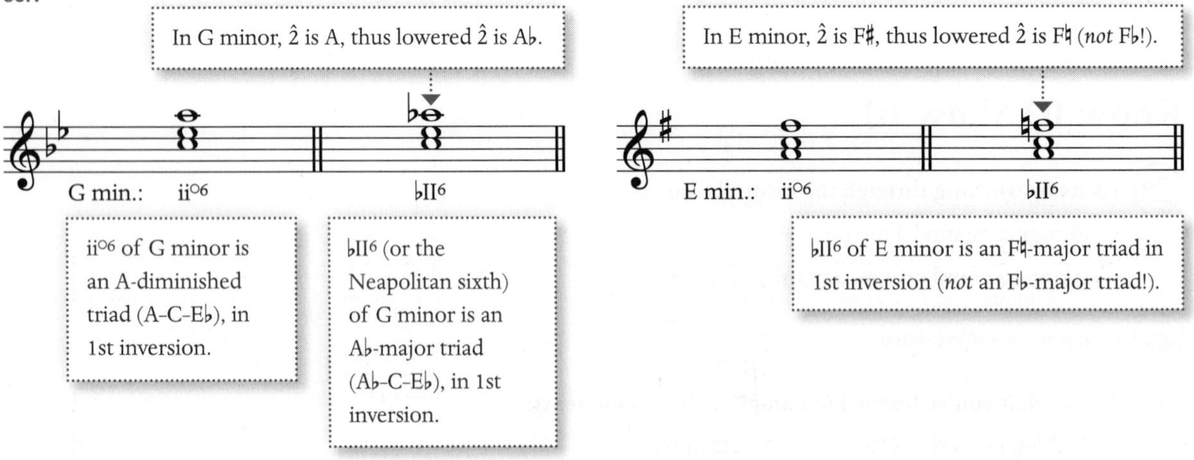

In G minor, $\hat{2}$ is A, thus lowered $\hat{2}$ is A♭.
G min.: ii°6
♭II6
ii°6 of G minor is an A-diminished triad (A–C–E♭), in 1st inversion.
♭II6 (or the Neapolitan sixth) of G minor is an A♭-major triad (A♭–C–E♭), in 1st inversion.
In E minor, $\hat{2}$ is F♯, thus lowered $\hat{2}$ is F♮ (*not* F♭!).
E min.: ii°6
♭II6
♭II6 of E minor is an F♮-major triad in 1st inversion (*not* an F♭-major triad!).

HARMONIC PROGRESSION

Like ii$^{\circ 6}$, ♭II^{6} has a **S**ubdominant function. ♭II^{6} may be preceded by any chord that can go before ii$^{\circ 6}$, such as i, iv, or VI, and it usually leads to a **D**ominant harmony such as V, V^{7}, or their inversions.

30.2 Beethoven, "Sehnsucht" (Longing) ➔

Translation: Only someone who knows longing can understand what I am suffering!

Like ii$^{\circ 6}$, ♭II^{6} can move to V or V^{7}.

30.3 Mozart, Sonata for Violin and Piano in F, K. 377, II ➔

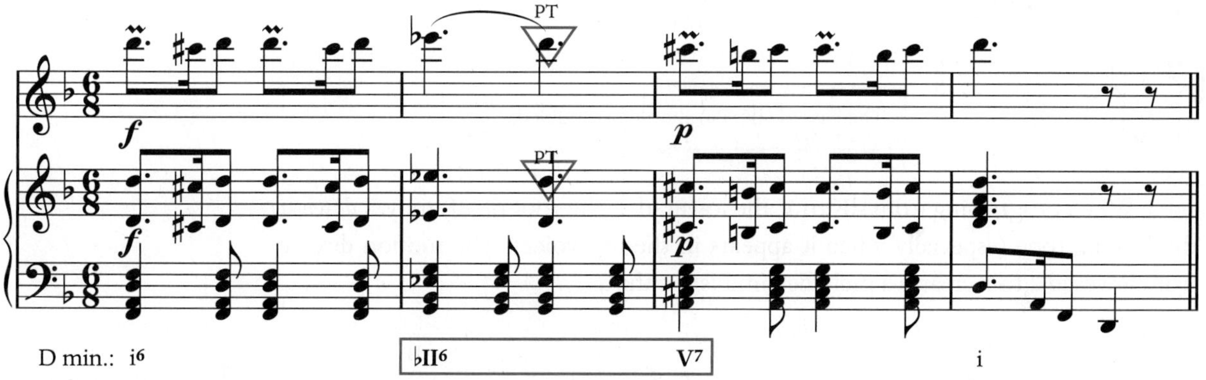

♭II^{6} also may lead to V via a cadential $^{6}_{4}$ or vii$^{\circ 7}$/V.

30.4 Mozart, Sonata for Violin and Piano in E Minor, K. 304, I ➔

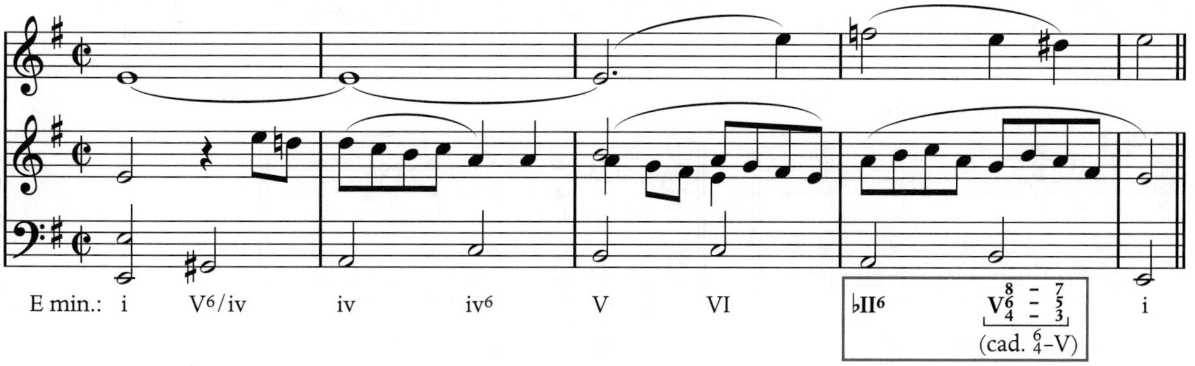

30.5 Handel, *Joseph and His Brethren*, act II ➔

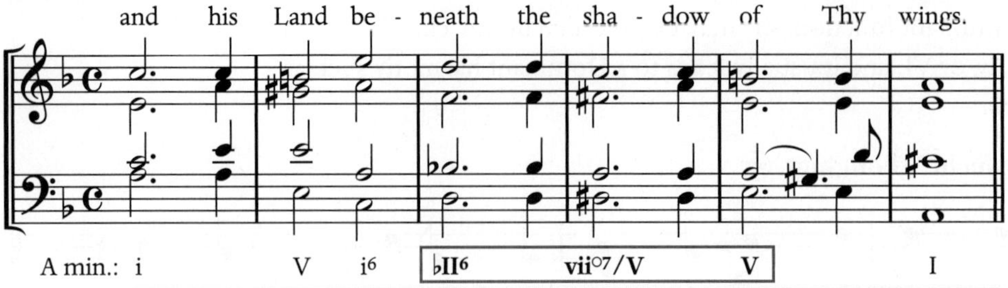

There is a chromatic stepwise ascent in the bass as ♭II6 moves through vii○7/V to V.

VOICE LEADING

♭II6 includes two tendency tones that lead downward: lowered $\hat{2}$ and the minor form of $\hat{6}$. These tones should *not* be doubled. Instead, double the bass of ♭II6 (the third of the chord).

30.6

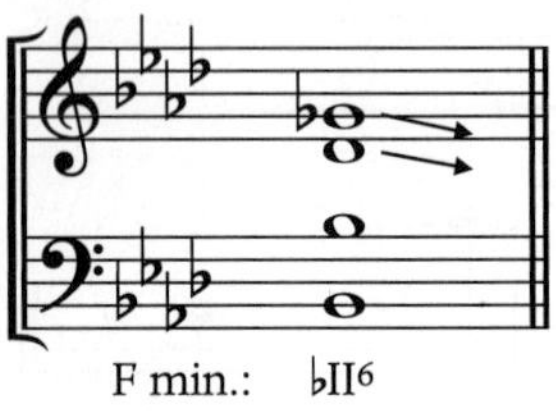

In ♭II6 of F minor, lowered $\hat{2}$ (G♭, the root of the chord) and $\hat{6}$ (D♭, the fifth of the chord) are tendency tones that lead downward and should *not* be doubled.

The bass of ♭II6 (B♭) should be doubled.

When progressing from ♭II6 to V, the lowered $\hat{2}$ (the root of ♭II) moves *down* to the leading tone (especially when it appears in the top voice). The motion directly from lowered $\hat{2}$ to $\hat{7}$ creates a melodic diminished third.

30.7

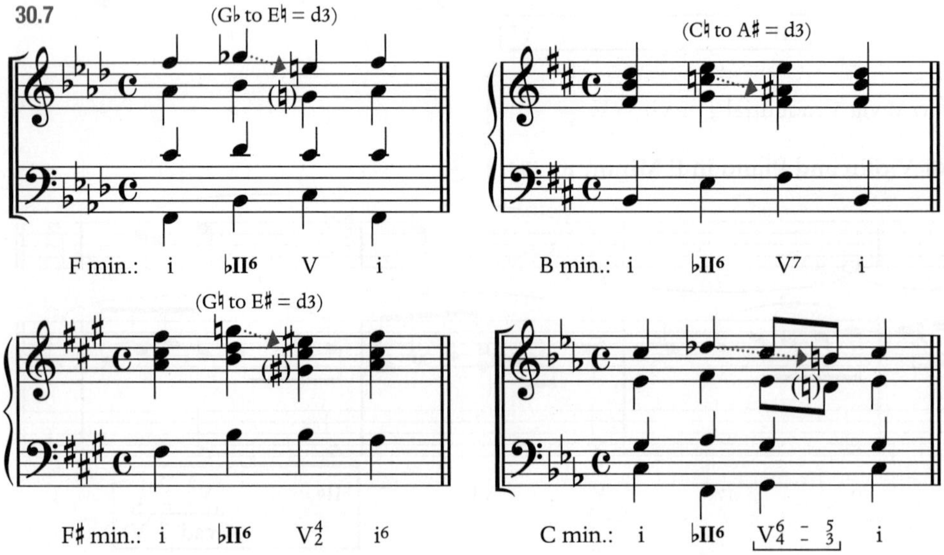

Good Lowered $\hat{2}$ moves down to $\hat{7}$ when ♭II6 moves to a **D**ominant harmony.

Good When ♭II⁶ moves through vii°⁷/V to V, $\hat{6}$ may move to ♯$\hat{6}$.

Poor Lowered $\hat{2}$ should *not* move up to a diatonic $\hat{2}$!

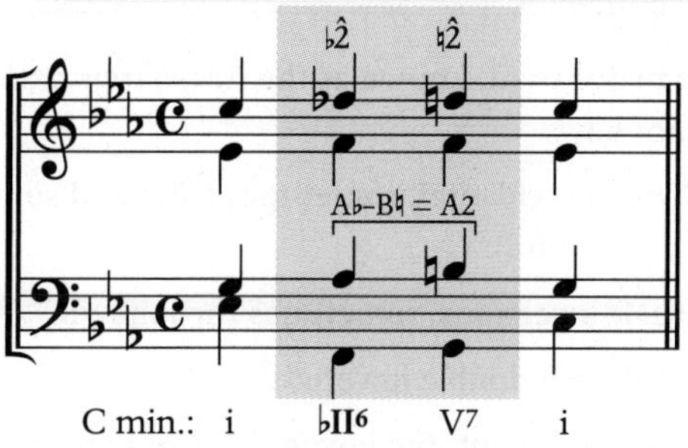

Poor A♭–B♮ creates an augmented 2nd!

30.8 A. Sullivan, "A Many Years Ago," from *H.M.S. Pinafore*

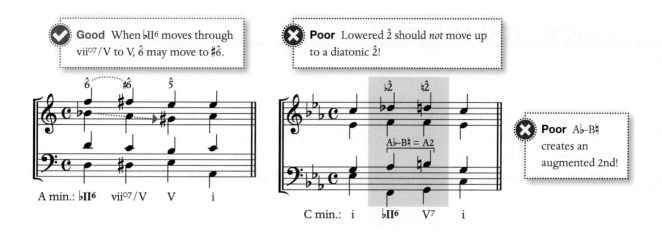

Good Moving from lowered $\hat{2}$ directly to $\hat{7}$ creates a diminished 3rd (F to D♯).

For more on ♭II⁶, see A Closer Look.

review and interact

POINTS FOR REVIEW

- **♭II^6 is a first-inversion major triad, known as the *Neapolitan sixth*. The ♭II^6 almost always appears in minor keys.**
- **The root of ♭II^6 requires an accidental, sometimes a flat and sometimes a natural (depending on the key signature).**
- **♭II^6 leads to V, V^7, or their inversions, sometimes through vii^{o7}/V or a cadential $^6_4$.**
- **Double the bass of ♭II^6; do not double lowered $\hat{2}$ or $\hat{6}$.**
- **When progressing to the dominant, the lowered $\hat{2}$ should move *down*.**

TEST YOURSELF

1. What accidentals need to be added to the following ii^{o6} chords in order to change them into ♭II^6 chords?

a. b. c.

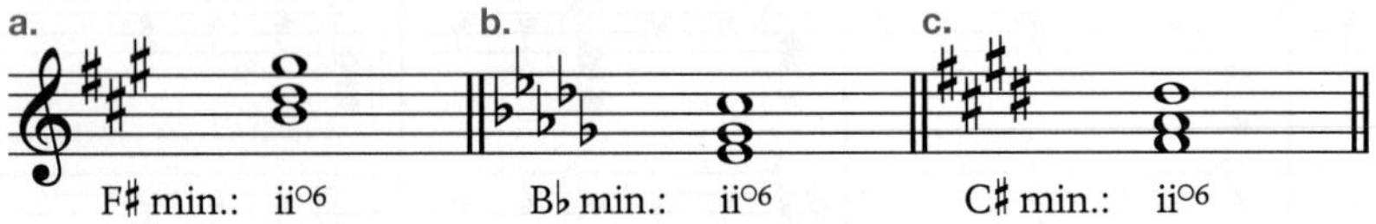

F♯ min.: ii^{o6} B♭ min.: ii^{o6} C♯ min.: ii^{o6}

2. What notes are in the following chords (from the bass up)?

   a. D minor: ii^{o6}: _____, _____, _____ ♭II^6: _____, _____, _____

   b. B minor: ii^{o6}: _____, _____, _____ ♭II^6: _____, _____, _____

   c. F minor: ii^{o6}: _____, _____, _____ ♭II^6: _____, _____, _____

3. Which of the following chords typically might precede ♭II^6?

   a. iv b. V c. vii^{o6} d. i^6 e. VI

4. Fill in the blanks:

   a. ♭II^6 chords usually appear in ________________________ keys.

   b. ♭II^6 is also known as a ________________________.

   c. ♭II^6 is a ________________________ (major, minor, or diminished?) triad.

   d. The root of the ♭II^6 is a tendency tone that leads ________________________.

5. Below is a partly completed harmonization.

   a. Would the best note for the alto voice on beat 2 be E♭, G, or either?

   b. Should the E♭ in the soprano on beat 2 move to an E♮, a C♯, or either?

D min.: i ♭II^6 V

Know It? Show It!

Focus by working through the tutorials on:

- Recognizing ♭II^6: Neapolitan sixth chords
- Writing ♭II^6: (Neapolitan) chords

Learn with inQuizitive.

Apply what you've learned to complete the assignments:

- Spelling ♭II^6 Chords
- Realizing Roman Numerals
- Realizing Figured Bass
- Harmonizing Melodies
- Composition
- Analysis

chapter 31 Augmented Sixth Chords

Augmented sixth chords lead to root-position V and contain tendency tones that are a minor second above and below $\hat{5}$.

FUNCTION AND TENDENCY TONES

Augmented sixth chords are a group of harmonies that share the same tendency tones and the same powerful drive toward V. In eighteenth-century music, augmented sixth chords frequently precede the dominant harmonies of climactic cadences. In later music, augmented sixth chords are used more freely, appearing before a dominant chord at almost any point within a composition.

Unlike most other chords, augmented sixth chords are built not from thirds stacked above a root, but rather by intervals above the *bass*. The bass of an augmented sixth chord is the minor form of $\hat{6}$, a tendency tone that leads *down* to $\hat{5}$. Augmented sixth chords include raised $\hat{4}$, a tendency tone that leads *up* to $\hat{5}$. These two tendency tones—separated by an augmented sixth—resolve to $\hat{5}$ in opposite directions.

31.1

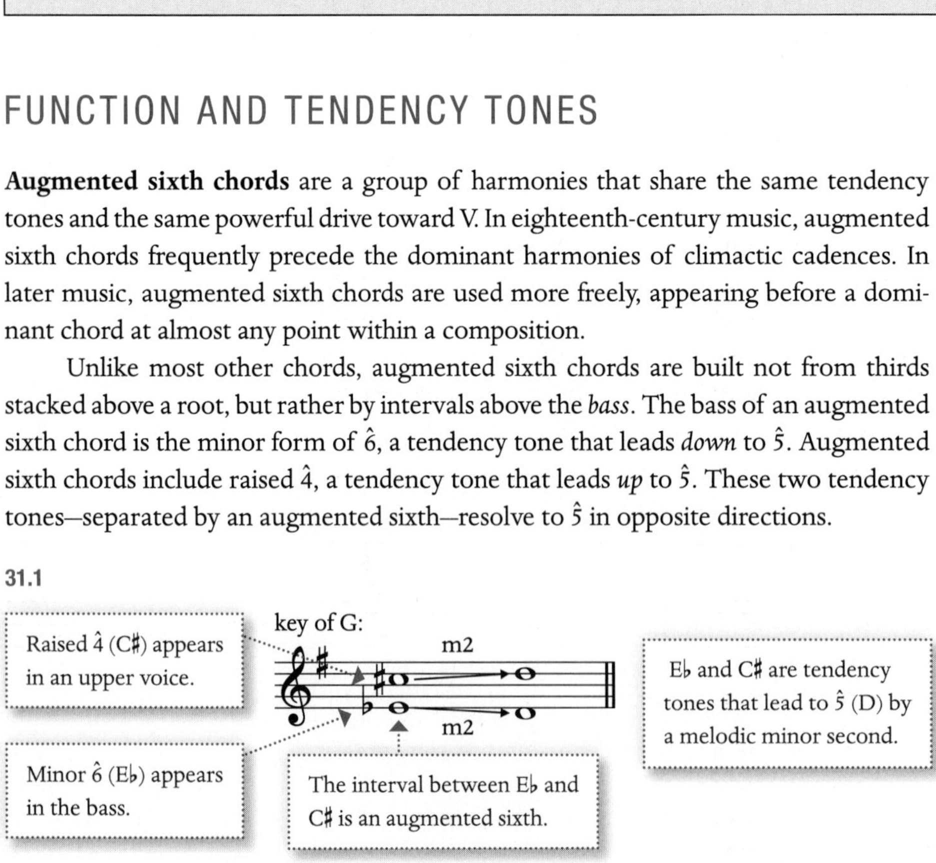

Raised $\hat{4}$ requires an accidental in both major and minor keys. The minor form of $\hat{6}$ requires an accidental in major keys, but not in minor keys. In each case, these tendency tones must be spelled as minor seconds above and below $\hat{5}$—*not* as chromatic semitones.

31.2

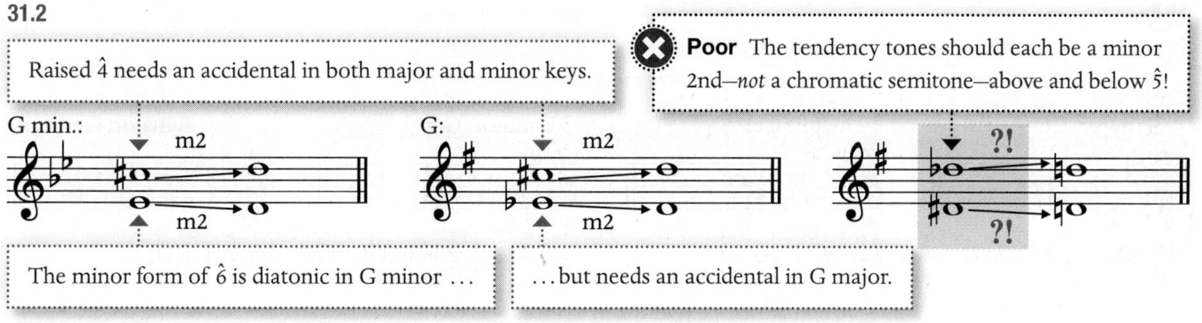

Raised 4̂ needs an accidental in both major and minor keys.
Poor The tendency tones should each be a minor 2nd—not a chromatic semitone—above and below 5̂!
G min.:
m2
m2
G:
m2
m2
?!
?!
The minor form of 6̂ is diatonic in G minor . . .
. . . but needs an accidental in G major.

31.3

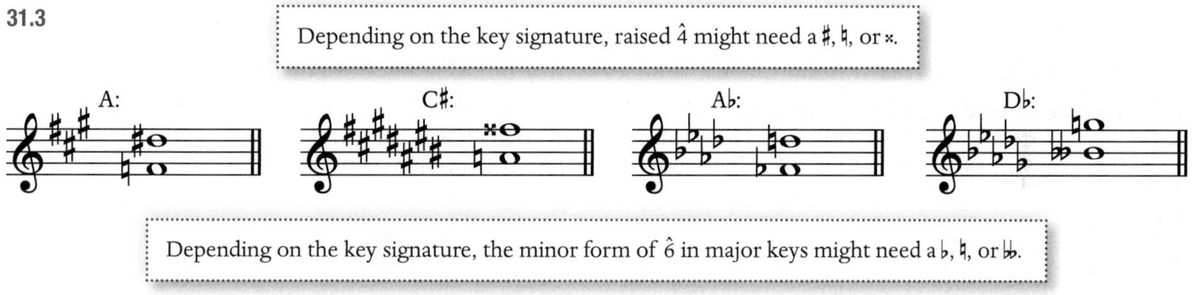

Depending on the key signature, raised 4̂ might need a ♯, ♮, or 𝄪.
A:
C♯:
A♭:
D♭:
Depending on the key signature, the minor form of 6̂ in major keys might need a ♭, ♮, or 𝄫.

TYPES OF AUGMENTED SIXTH CHORDS: ITALIAN, FRENCH, AND GERMAN

The three most common augmented sixth chords are known as the **Italian augmented sixth** (abbreviated as It^{+6}), **French augmented sixth** (Fr^{+6}), and **German augmented sixth** (Ger^{+6}). In addition to raised $\hat{4}$ and minor $\hat{6}$, these chords all include $\hat{1}$. The Italian augmented sixth includes only these three notes; the French augmented sixth also includes $\hat{2}$; and the German augmented sixth includes the minor form of $\hat{3}$.

31.4

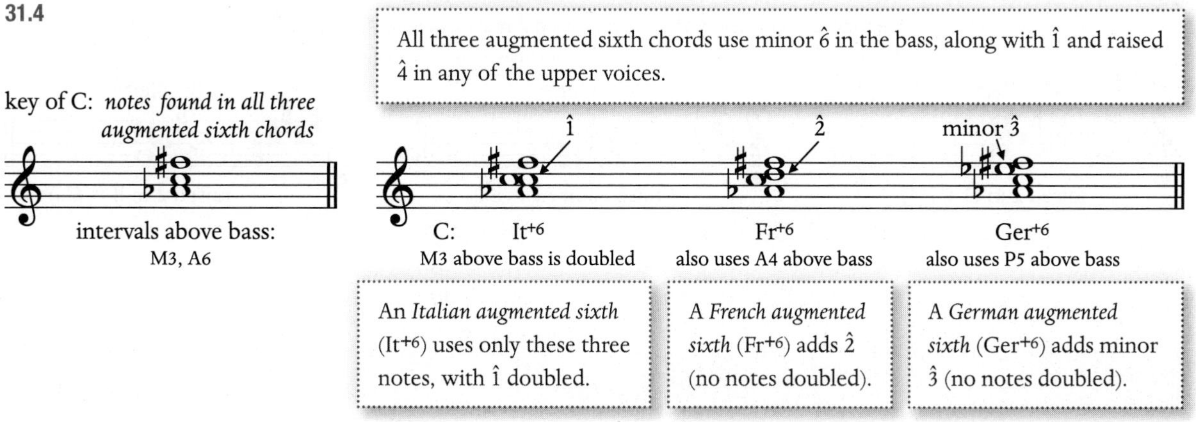

All three augmented sixth chords use minor 6̂ in the bass, along with 1̂ and raised 4̂ in any of the upper voices.
key of C: notes found in all three augmented sixth chords
intervals above bass:
M3, A6
1̂
2̂
minor 3̂
C:
It+6
M3 above bass is doubled
Fr+6
also uses A4 above bass
Ger+6
also uses P5 above bass
An Italian augmented sixth (It+6) uses only these three notes, with 1̂ doubled.
A French augmented sixth (Fr+6) adds 2̂ (no notes doubled).
A German augmented sixth (Ger+6) adds minor 3̂ (no notes doubled).

SPELLING THE GERMAN AUGMENTED SIXTH

The minor $\hat{3}$ in the German augmented sixth is diatonic in minor keys, but requires an accidental in major keys—either a flat or a natural, depending upon the key signature.

31.5

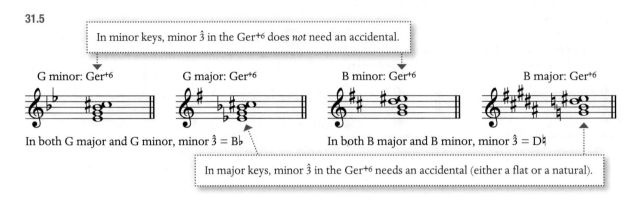

In minor keys, minor $\hat{3}$ in the Ger^{+6} does *not* need an accidental.

G minor: Ger^{+6} G major: Ger^{+6} B minor: Ger^{+6} B major: Ger^{+6}

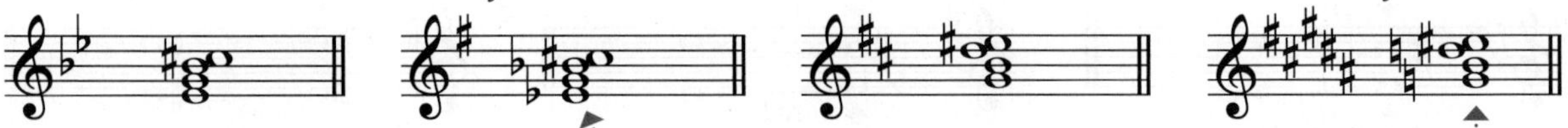

In both G major and G minor, minor $\hat{3}$ = B♭

In both B major and B minor, minor $\hat{3}$ = D♮

In major keys, minor $\hat{3}$ in the Ger^{+6} needs an accidental (either a flat or a natural).

In major keys (but *not* in minor keys), the Ger^{+6} may occasionally be spelled with raised $\hat{2}$ instead of minor $\hat{3}$.

31.6

In major keys, the Ger^{+6} is written with either minor $\hat{3}$ (B♭), a perfect 5th above the bass, or raised $\hat{2}$ (A♯), a *doubly augmented 4th* above the bass.

Poor In minor keys, the Ger^{+6} may *not* be written with raised $\hat{2}$.

G major: Ger^{+6} Ger^{+6}

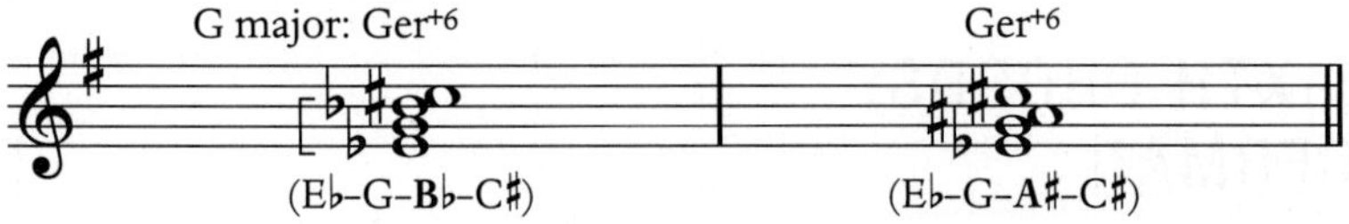

(E♭–G–**B♭**–C♯) (E♭–G–**A♯**–C♯)

(intervals above bass: major third, doubly augmented fourth, augmented sixth)

Raised $\hat{2}$ (A♯) is enharmonic with the minor form of $\hat{3}$ (B♭).

G minor: Ger^{+6} (?!)

In G minor, use B♭ (which is in the key signature), *not* A♯.

31.7

Depending on the key signature, raised $\hat{2}$ may require a ♯, ♮, or 𝄪.

C: Ger^{+6} A♭: Ger^{+6} B: Ger^{+6}

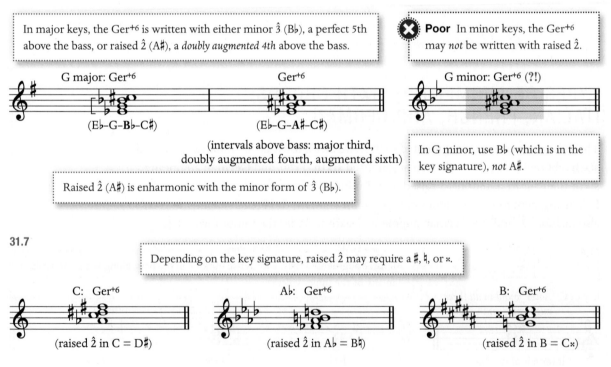

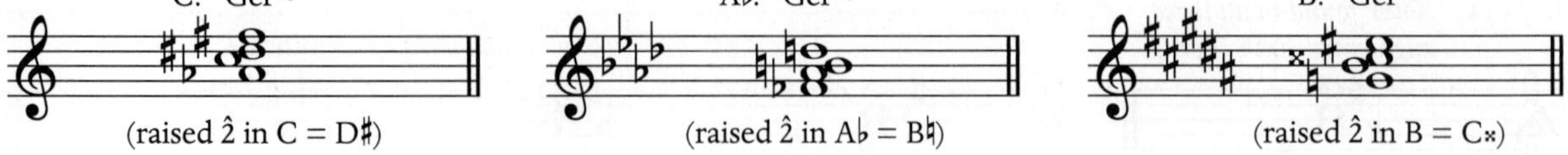

(raised $\hat{2}$ in C = D♯) (raised $\hat{2}$ in A♭ = B♮) (raised $\hat{2}$ in B = C𝄪)

HARMONIC PROGRESSIONS

GERMAN AUGMENTED SIXTH

A German augmented sixth chord most often leads to V through a cadential $^6_4$.

31.8 A Ger+6 normally moves to a cadential $^6_4$–V (i.e., V^{6-5}_{4-3}), with stepwise motion or repeated notes in all voices.

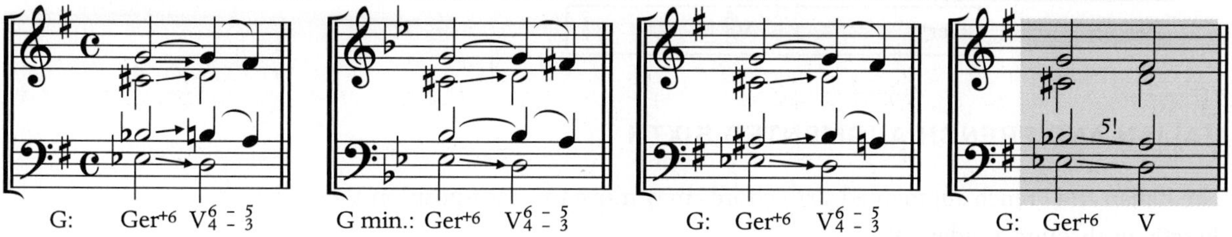

Good Voices move smoothly when Ger+6 goes to a cadential $^6_4$.

Good Good Raised $\hat{2}$ (A♯) moves up to $\hat{3}$ (B).

Poor Moving directly from Ger+6 to V creates parallel 5ths.

31.9 Chopin, Mazurka in A Minor, B. 134

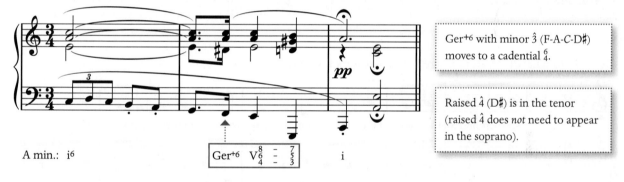

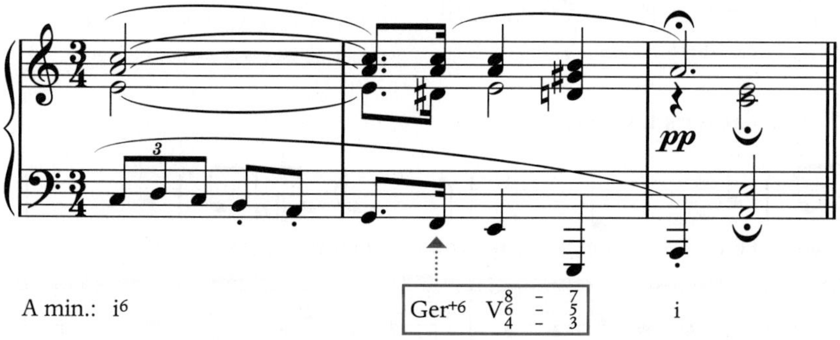

Ger+6 with minor $\hat{3}$ (F-A-C-D♯) moves to a cadential $^6_4$.

Raised $\hat{4}$ (D♯) is in the tenor (raised $\hat{4}$ does *not* need to appear in the soprano).

31.10 Mendelssohn, *Songs without Words*, op. 102, no. 6

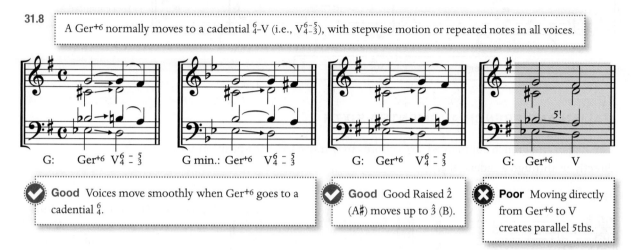

Ger+6 with minor $\hat{3}$ (A♭-C-E♭-F♯) moves to cadential $^6_4$.

31.11 R. Schumann, "Am leuchtenden Sommermorgen" (On a Bright Summer Morning)

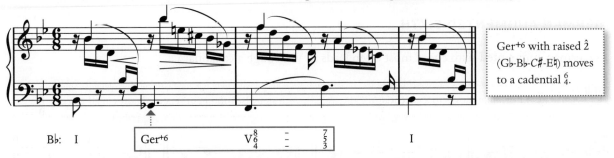

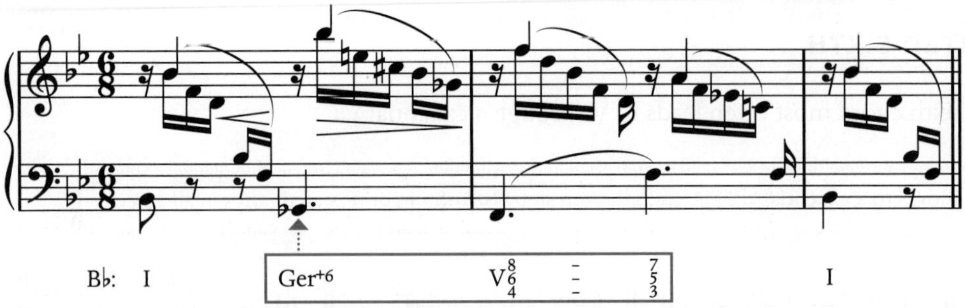

Ger+6 with raised $\hat{2}$ (G♭-B♭-C♯-E♮) moves to a cadential $^6_4$.

ITALIAN AND FRENCH AUGMENTED SIXTH

The Italian and French augmented sixth chords may move to a root-position V either directly or through a cadential $^6_4$.

31.12

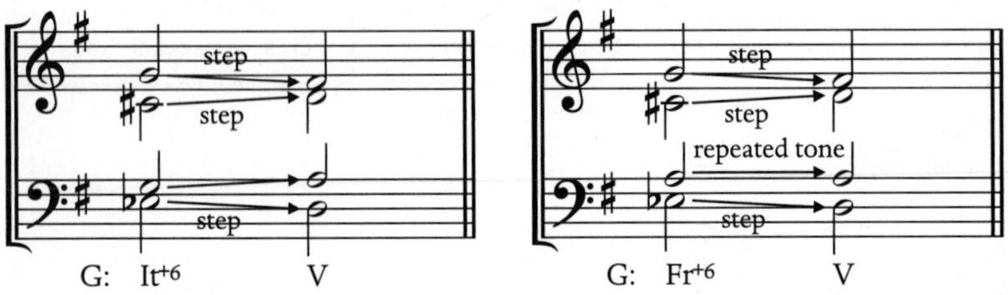

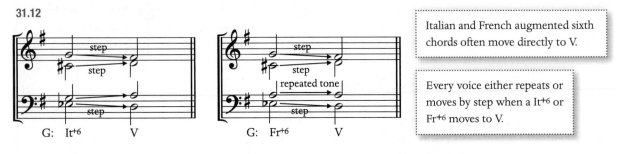

Italian and French augmented sixth chords often move directly to V.

Every voice either repeats or moves by step when a It+6 or Fr+6 moves to V.

31.13 L. Reichardt, "Vaters Klage" (The Father's Lament)

Translation: Three stars shone in the sky, looking sadly down.

31.14 Beethoven, Piano Sonata in C Minor, op. 13 ("Pathétique"), I

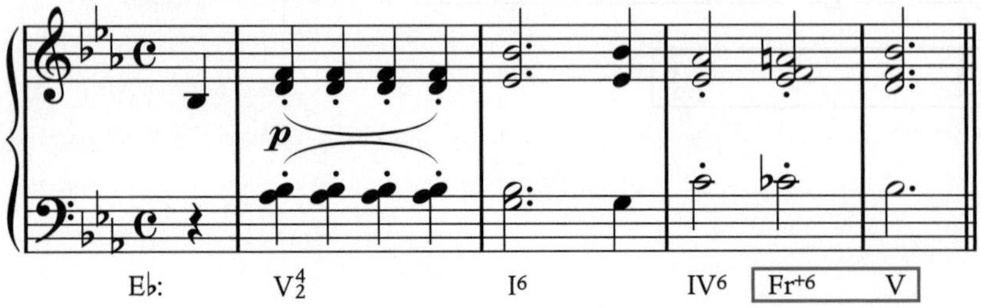

31.15

Italian and French augmented sixth chords can also move through a cadential $^6_4$ to V, with smooth motion in all voices.

31.16 Mozart, Piano Sonata in D, K. 284, III

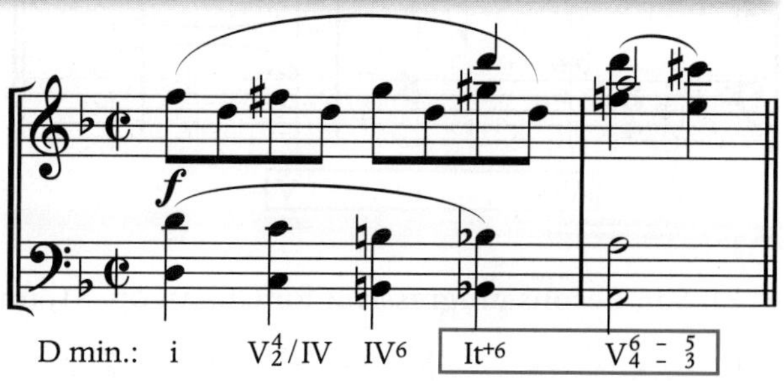

31.17 Beethoven, Piano Sonata in E♭, op. 7, II

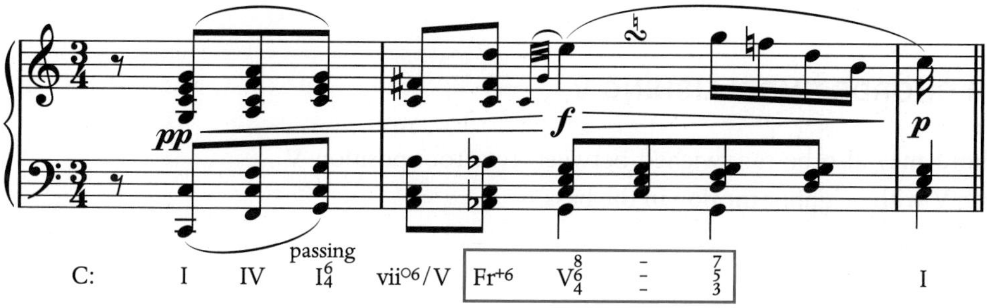

HARMONIES THAT PRECEDE AUGMENTED SIXTH CHORDS

Any harmony that may precede V—such as I, IV6, or vi—may precede an augmented sixth chord.

31.18 Beethoven, Symphony no. 5, I

An augmented sixth chord may be preceded by a tonic chord.

31.19 Schubert, *Moments Musicaux*, op. 94, no. 6

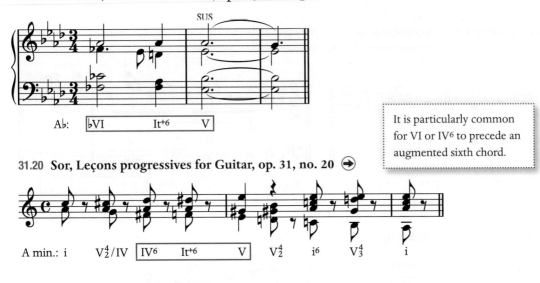

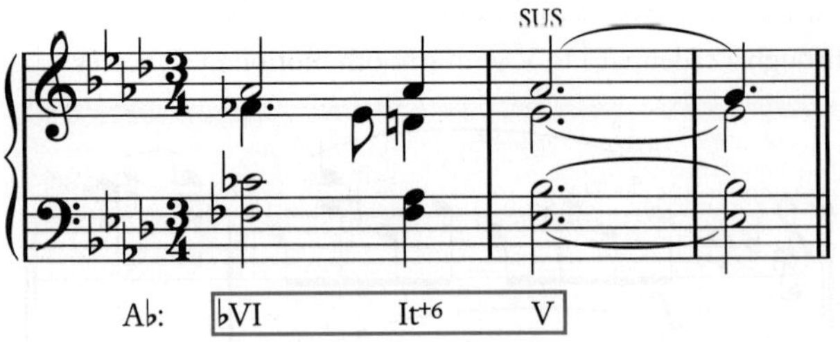

> It is particularly common for VI or IV6 to precede an augmented sixth chord.

31.20 Sor, Leçons progressives for Guitar, op. 31, no. 20

AUGMENTED SIXTH CHORDS EMBELLISHING V

An augmented sixth chord may also be sandwiched between two root-position V chords, so as to embellish V with neighbor motion in the bass.

31.21 Bortniansky, Cherubic Hymn, no. 3

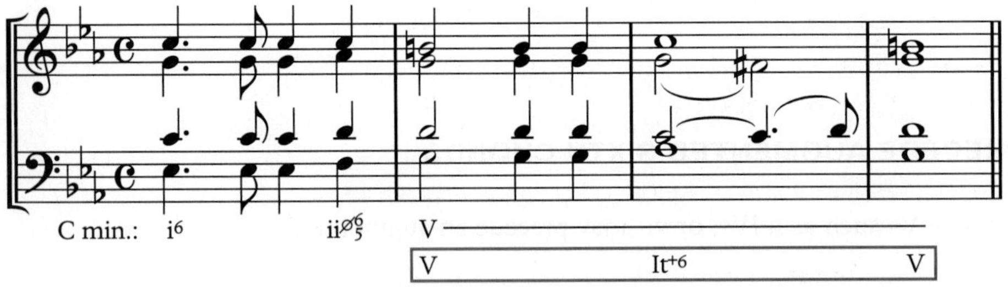

> It+6 embellishes V with a G–A♭–G neighbor motion in the bass.

31.22 Bellini, "Torna, vezzosa Fillide" (Return, charming Phillida)

> Fr+6 embellishes V with E–F–E neighbor motion in the bass.

Translation: Where, Phillida, where?

MOVING BETWEEN AUGMENTED SIXTH CHORDS

Before progressing to V, augmented sixth chords may interchange with one another, as a result of skips or passing motion between chord tones.

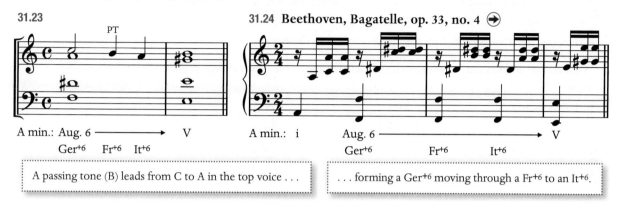

31.23

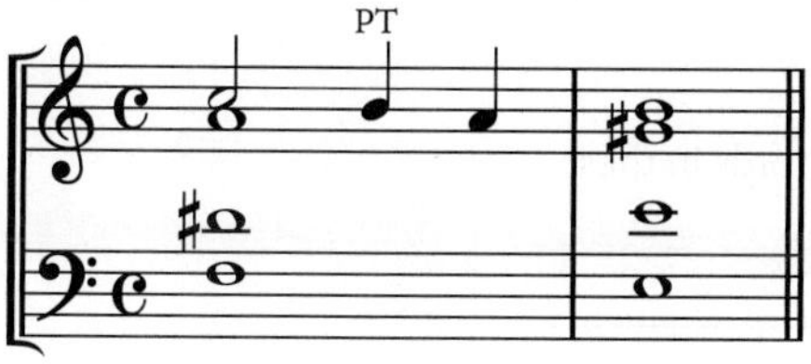

A min.: Aug. 6 ⟶ V

Ger^{+6} Fr^{+6} It^{+6}

A passing tone (B) leads from C to A in the top voice . . .

31.24 Beethoven, Bagatelle, op. 33, no. 4

A min.: i Aug. 6 ⟶ V

Ger^{+6} Fr^{+6} It^{+6}

. . . forming a Ger^{+6} moving through a Fr^{+6} to an It^{+6}.

For more on augmented sixth chords, see A Closer Look.

review and interact

POINTS FOR REVIEW

- **The three main types of augmented sixth chords each include minor $\hat{6}$ in the bass, along with $\hat{1}$ and raised $\hat{4}$ in the upper voices.**
  - An Italian augmented sixth (It^{+6}) uses only these three notes, with $\hat{1}$ doubled.
  - A French augmented sixth (Fr^{+6}) also includes $\hat{2}$, with no notes doubled.
  - A German augmented sixth (Ger^{+6}) also includes minor $\hat{3}$ (or sometimes in major keys raised $\hat{2}$), with no notes doubled.
- **When the augmented sixth chord resolves, its tendency tones—minor $\hat{6}$ and raised $\hat{4}$—resolve to $\hat{5}$ in opposite directions.**
- **A German augmented sixth usually moves through a cadential $^6_4$ to V.**
- **Italian and French augmented sixth chords move either to root-position V or through a cadential $^6_4$ to V.**

Summary of most common types and uses of augmented sixth chords:

key of C: Italian Augmented 6th
♭$\hat{6}$ in bass; $\hat{1}$, ♯$\hat{4}$,
and $\hat{1}$ in other voices

moves to root-position V
(or cad. $^6_4$–V)

French Augmented 6th
♭$\hat{6}$ in bass; $\hat{1}$, ♯$\hat{4}$,
and $\hat{2}$ in other voices

moves to root-position V
(or cad. $^6_4$–V)

German Augmented 6th
♭$\hat{6}$ in bass; $\hat{1}$, ♯$\hat{4}$,
and either ♭$\hat{3}$ **or** ♯$\hat{2}$ in other voices

moves to cadential $^6_4$–V

TEST YOURSELF

1. Name raised $\hat{4}$ and minor $\hat{6}$ in the following keys, and identify which of these notes are not in the key (and thus need accidentals):

   a. F major **b.** F minor **c.** E major **d.** E minor **e.** D♭ major

2. What are the notes in the Italian, French and German augmented sixth chords in these keys?

   a. F major: It+6 = ______________ Fr+6 = ______________ Ger+6 = ______________

   b. F minor: It+6 = ______________ Fr+6 = ______________ Ger+6 = ______________

   c. E major: It+6 = ______________ Fr+6 = ______________ Ger+6 = ______________

   d. E minor: It+6 = ______________ Fr+6 = ______________ Ger+6 = ______________

   e. C♯ minor: It+6 = ______________ Fr+6 = ______________ Ger+6 = ______________

3. Add accidentals to the following harmonies to change them into augmented sixth chords. Identify the augmented sixth chords formed.

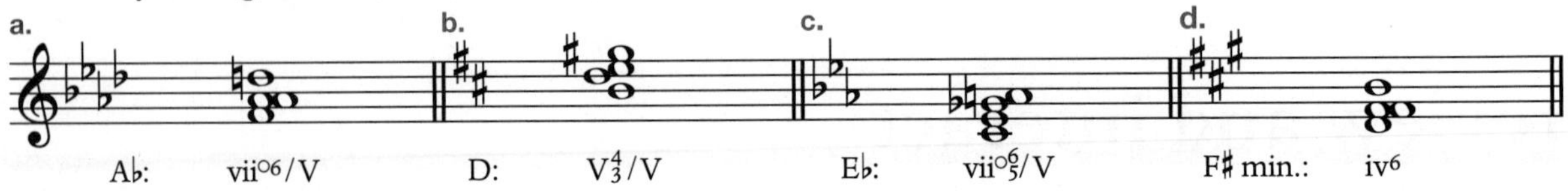

4. The following are augmented sixth chords; label the type of each and identify the keys in which it may appear.

5. In each example below, which of the two augmented sixth chords is incorrect, is notated incorrectly, or uses incorrect doubling? What is the error?

   a. F♯ min.: It+6 **b.** G min.: Ger+6 **c.** F: Fr+6

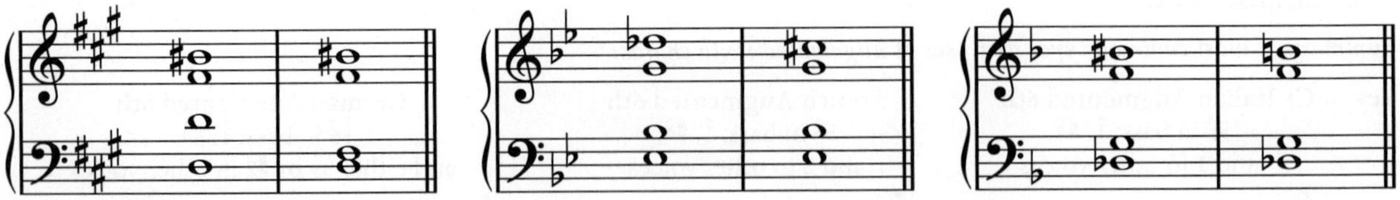

6. In an augmented sixth chord, must minor $\hat{6}$ appear in a particular voice? If so, which voice? Must raised $\hat{4}$ appear in a particular voice? If so, which voice?

Know It? Show It!

Focus by working through the tutorials on:

- Recognizing augmented sixth chords
- Writing Italian augmented sixth (It^{+6}) chords
- Writing French augmented sixth (Fr^{+6}) chords
- Writing German augmented sixth (Ger^{+6}) chords

Learn with inQuizitive.

Apply what you've learned to complete the assignments:

- Spelling Augmented Sixth Chords
- Realizing Roman Numerals
- Realizing Figured Bass
- Harmonizing Melodies
- Analysis

chapter

32 Other Chords: Altered, Common-Tone Chromatic, and Ninth Chords

Chords can be altered with chromatic or added dissonant tones.

- Altered Chords
- Augmented Triads
- ♭II in Root Position and in Major Keys
- Augmented Sixth Chords with Bass Notes Other than $\hat{6}$
- Common-Tone Chromatic Chords
- V^9_7

ALTERED CHORDS

Chromatic alterations that do not lead to a change of key usually involve notes from the parallel major or minor key, creating modal mixture (see Chapter 29). It is also possible, however, for such chromatic alterations to involve notes that are *not* in the parallel key. As with modal mixture, these alterations change the quality of chords but not their function.

32.1

In C major, the A minor triad, vi, is diatonic (it uses no accidentals).

♭VI and iv use modal mixture (A♭ and E♭ are found in the parallel minor of C major).

VI♯ (submediant triad with a raised third) uses C♯, a chromatically altered note *not* found in the parallel key.

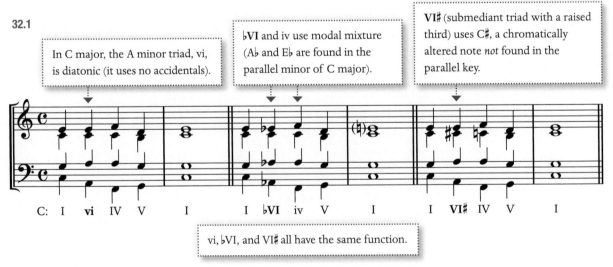

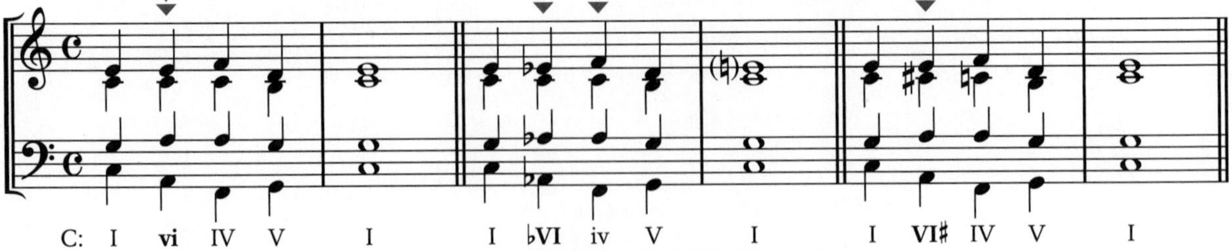

vi, ♭VI, and VI♯ all have the same function.

32.2 R. Schumann, Fantasy in C, op. 17, III ➔

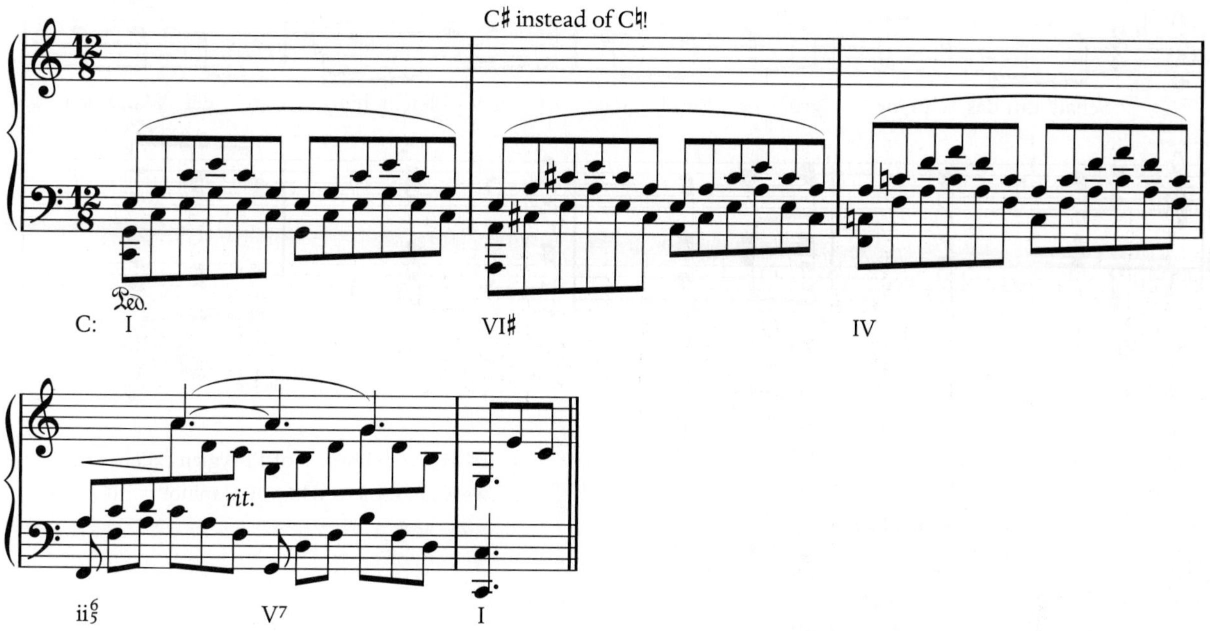

A particularly common chromatically altered chord is **III♯**, a major chord whose root is $\hat{3}$ of a major scale and whose third is raised by a half step with an accidental.

32.3

32.4 Chopin, Polonaise in A♭, op. 53 ➔

Diatonic iii: C-*E♭*-G

III♯: mediant triad with raised third, C-*E♮*-G (*not* C-E♯-G)

32.5 Schubert, "Mit dem grünen Lautenbande" (With the Green Lute-Ribbon)

III♯ as pivot chord: V of Phrygian cadence (iv6–V) in tonicized key of G minor = III♯ of B♭.

Translation: It's too bad that pretty green ribbon is fading there on the wall. I like the color green so much.

AUGMENTED TRIADS

An augmented chord results when an accidental raises the fifth of a major triad (often I, IV, or V) or dominant seventh chord (V^7). The raised fifth of an augmented chord tends to resolve up by step; as a tendency tone, it should not be doubled.

32.6

The raised tone of an augmented chord resolves up by step.

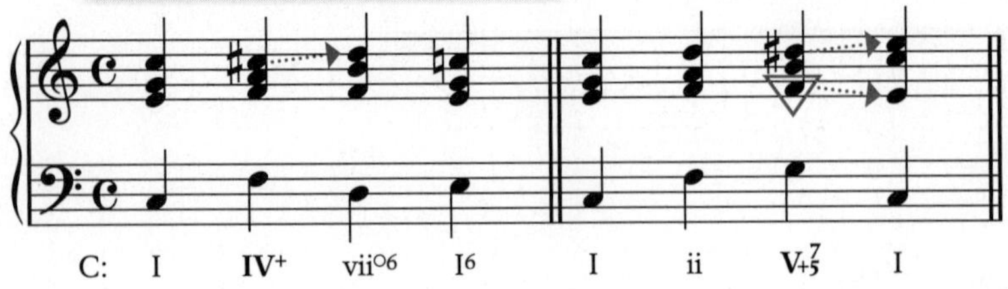

When V^{7+5} (a V^7 chord that includes an augmented triad as a result of its raised fifth) resolves to I, the third of I is doubled (since the fifth of V^7 resolves up and the seventh of V^7 resolves down).

32.7 R. Schumann, "Kleine Studie" (Little Etude)

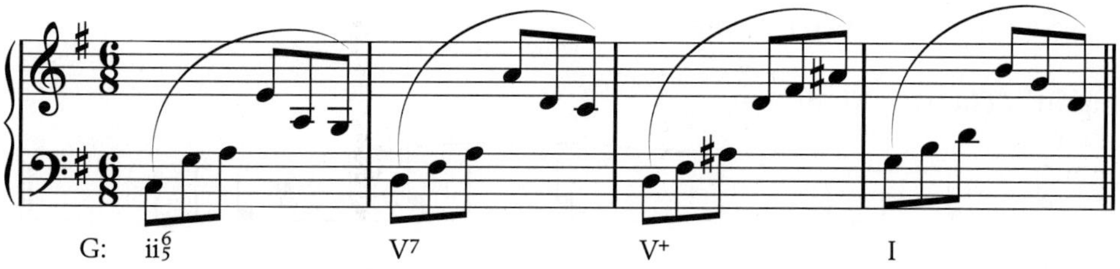

Simplified harmonic model

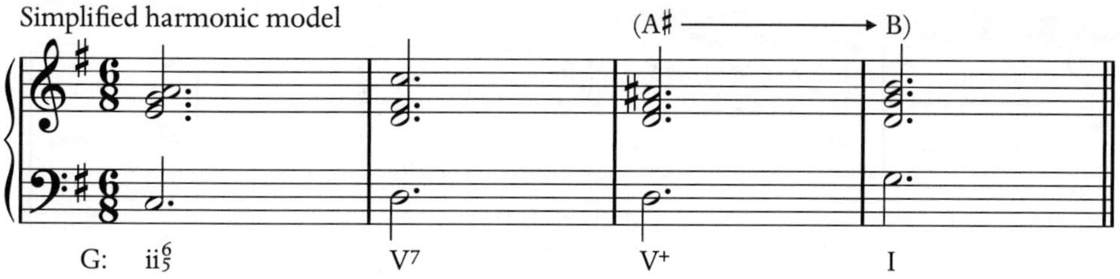

♭II IN ROOT POSITION AND IN MAJOR KEYS

♭II usually appears in first inversion, as a ♭II6 (see Chapter 30). However, it is possible (though far less common) for ♭II to appear in root position. Like ♭II6, ♭II has a **S**ubdominant function.

32.8 Chopin, Prelude in C Minor, op. 28

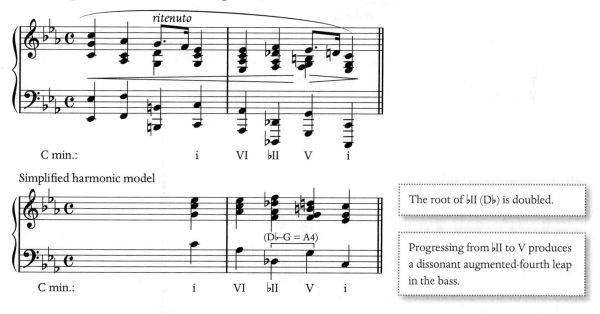

Simplified harmonic model

The root of ♭II (D♭) is doubled.

Progressing from ♭II to V produces a dissonant augmented-fourth leap in the bass.

Although ♭II normally appears in minor keys, it may also appear as a borrowed chord within a major key, where it requires two accidentals.

32.9 Brahms, "Die Mainacht" (The May Night) ➔

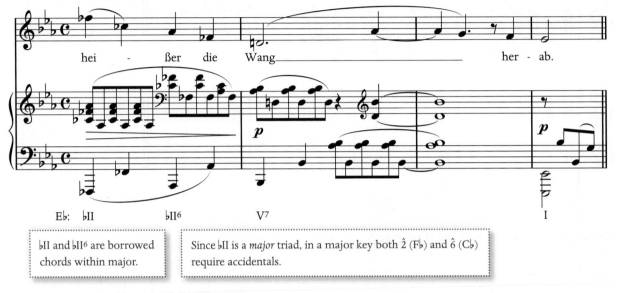

♭II and ♭II6 are borrowed chords within major.

Since ♭II is a *major* triad, in a major key both $\hat{2}$ (F♭) and $\hat{6}$ (C♭) require accidentals.

Translation: [My tears flow] burning down my cheek.

AUGMENTED SIXTH CHORDS WITH BASS NOTES OTHER THAN $\hat{6}$

Although typically the bass of an augmented sixth chord is the minor form of $\hat{6}$ (see Chapter 31), it is also possible for another note to be in the bass. An augmented sixth chord with raised $\hat{4}$ in the bass is sometimes referred to as a **diminished third chord**; otherwise, augmented sixth chords with other notes in the bass do not have standardized labels. No matter what note is in the bass of an augmented sixth chord, minor $\hat{6}$ resolves down and raised $\hat{4}$ resolves up.

32.10

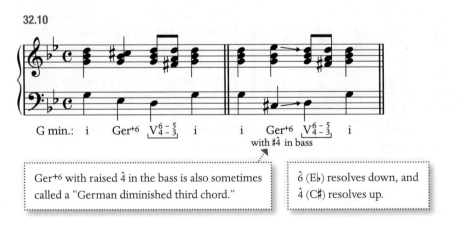

Ger+6 with raised $\hat{4}$ in the bass is also sometimes called a "German diminished third chord."

$\hat{6}$ (E♭) resolves down, and $\hat{4}$ (C♯) resolves up.

32.11 Chopin, Prelude in G Minor, op. 28

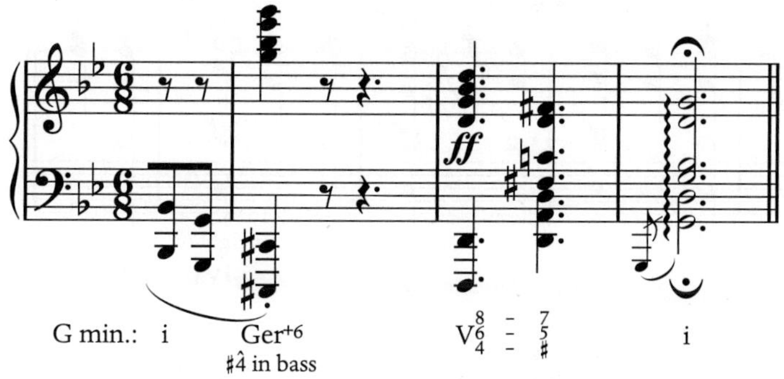

COMMON-TONE CHROMATIC CHORDS

A harmony may be embellished by a chromatic harmony with which it shares a chord tone. The shared tone is usually sustained when the chromatically altered chord resolves to a diatonic harmony, while the other voices are treated as neighbor tones.

32.12 Tchaikovsky, *Souvenir de Hapsal*, op. 2, III

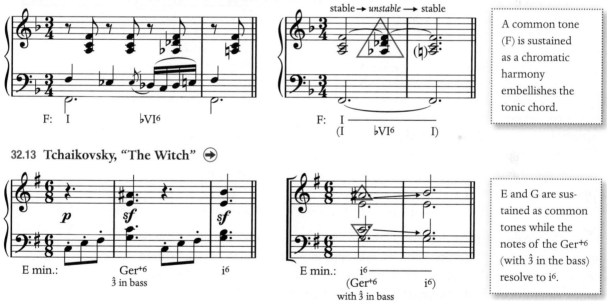

A common tone (F) is sustained as a chromatic harmony embellishes the tonic chord.

32.13 Tchaikovsky, "The Witch"

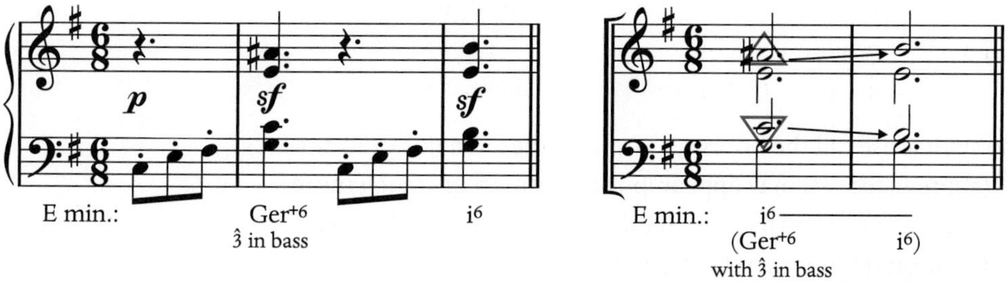

E and G are sustained as common tones while the notes of the Ger+6 (with 3̂ in the bass) resolve to i6.

A particularly common instance of an embellishing common-tone chromatic chord is the **common-tone diminished seventh chord**, which results when the root of a triad is sustained while the third and fifth are decorated by chromatic neighbors. This embellishing sonority is labeled simply as a "common-tone °7" rather than with a Roman numeral.

32.14

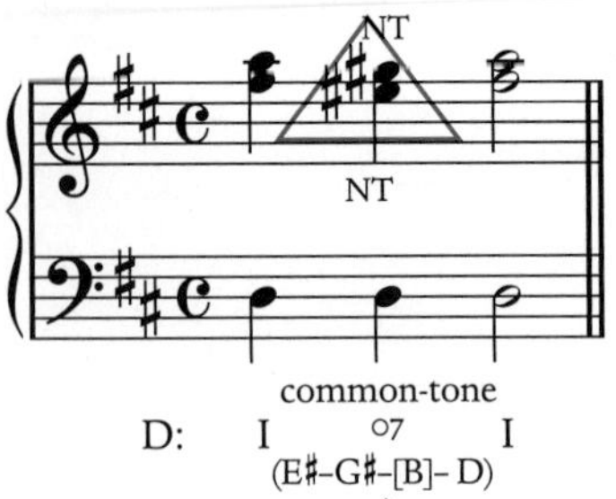

32.15 Haydn, Symphony no. 104, III

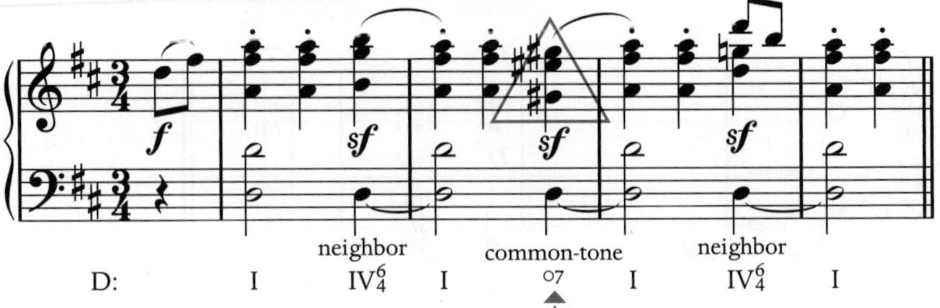

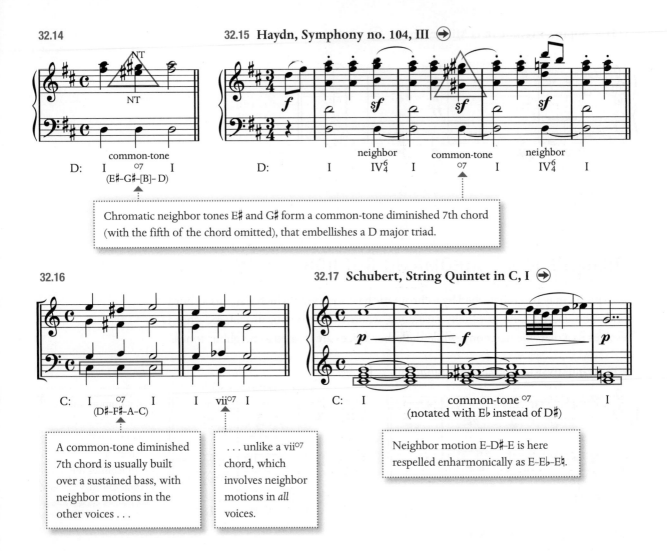

Chromatic neighbor tones E♯ and G♯ form a common-tone diminished 7th chord (with the fifth of the chord omitted), that embellishes a D major triad.

32.16

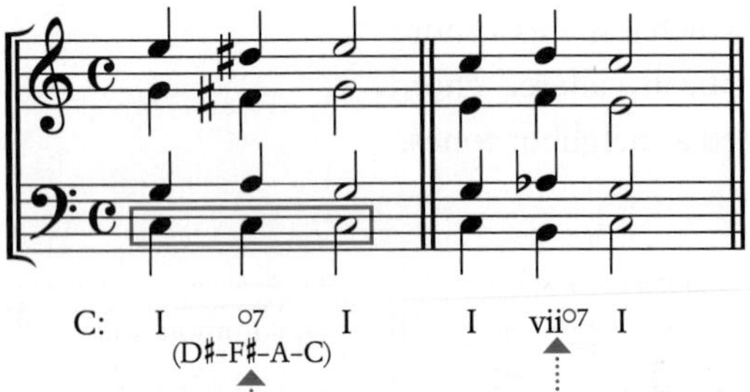

A common-tone diminished 7th chord is usually built over a sustained bass, with neighbor motions in the other voices . . .

. . . unlike a vii°7 chord, which involves neighbor motions in *all* voices.

32.17 Schubert, String Quintet in C, I

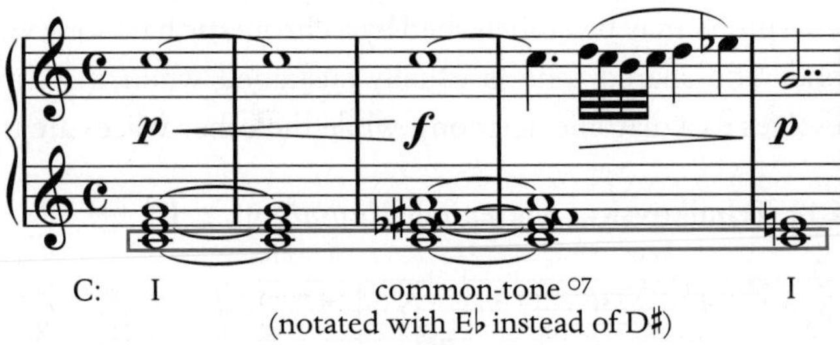

Neighbor motion E–D♯–E is here respelled enharmonically as E–E♭–E♮.

V$^9_7$

V$^9_7$ is a **D**ominant harmony that uses all the notes of V^7 plus either a major or minor ninth above the bass. V$^9_7$ (abbreviated V^9) may appear in root position or (much more rarely) in inversion. The dissonant chordal ninth tends to resolve *down* by step—though in practice this resolution often is merely implied.

32.18

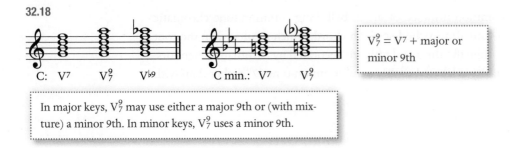

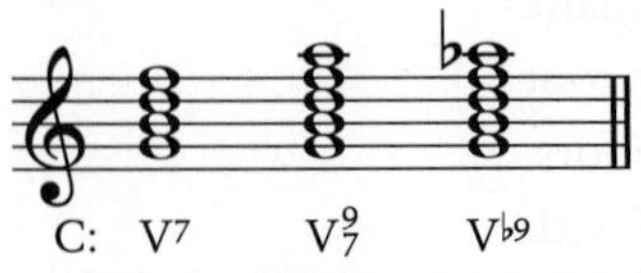

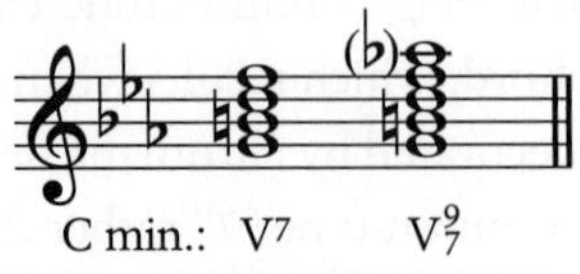

V$^9_7$ = V^7 + major or minor 9th

In major keys, V$^9_7$ may use either a major 9th or (with mixture) a minor 9th. In minor keys, V$^9_7$ uses a minor 9th.

32.19 Schubert, Dances, D. 365, no. 30

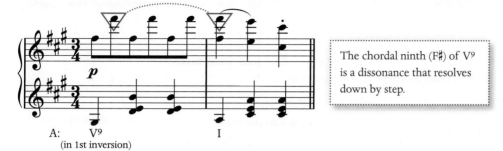

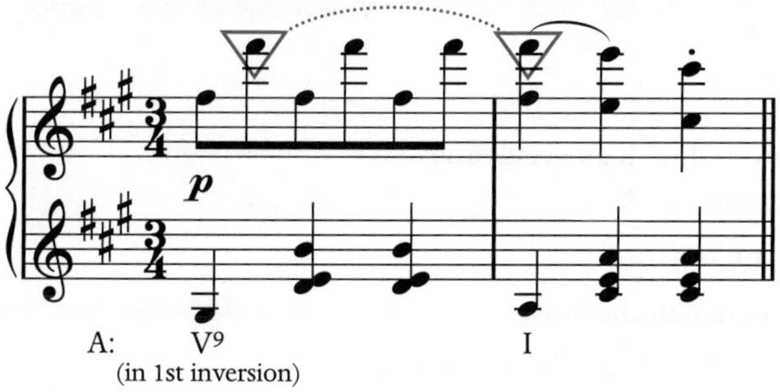

The chordal ninth (F♯) of V9 is a dissonance that resolves down by step.

32.20 Schubert, Dances, D. 365, no. 17

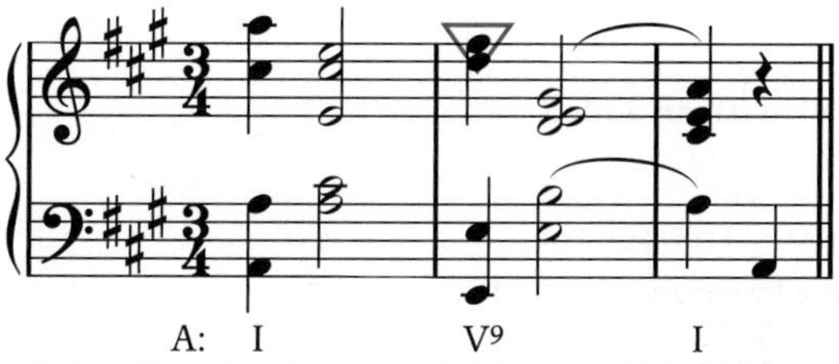

Simplified harmonic model

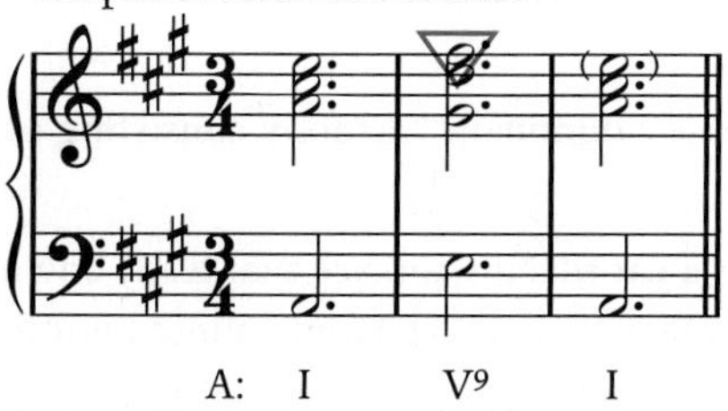

The resolution of the chordal ninth (F♯–E) is implied (although E is in the next chord, it does not appear a step below the F♯).

V^9_7 is most often found in thick textures of more than four voices. Regardless of the number of voices, the chordal ninth should not create a harmonic second or a seventh with the root of chord.

32.21

Poor The root (G) is a seventh above the chordal ninth (A).

Poor The root is a second below the chordal ninth.

Good The chordal ninth is more than an octave above the root.

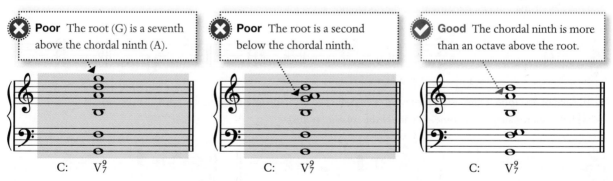

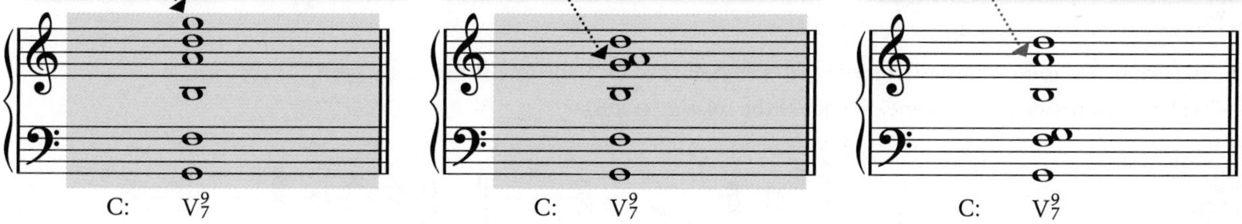

For more about chromatic mediants and submediants, see A Closer Look.

review and interact

POINTS FOR REVIEW

- **The third and fifth of any harmony may be raised or lowered with an accidental, changing the quality of the chord, although not its function.**
- **♭II may appear in root position, in either a major or minor key.**
- **Augmented sixth chords may appear with a note other than $\hat{6}$ in the bass.**
- **A harmony may be decorated by a chromatic chord with which it shares one or more common tones.**
- **A common-tone diminished seventh chord results from a major triad whose third and fifth are decorated by chromatic lower neighbor tones while the root of the chord is sustained.**
- **V^9_7 (abbreviated as V^9) is a dominant harmony consisting of a V^7 with an added ninth.**
- **The ninth of the V^9_7 is a chordal dissonance that leads down by step (though this resolution is often implied); the chordal ninth should not form a harmonic second or seventh with the root.**

TEST YOURSELF

1. What are the notes of the following chords (from the bass up)?

   a. A major: III♯ b. B♭ major: III♯ c. G♭ major: III♯ d. F major: V^+ e. B major: IV^+

   f. G major : ♭II g. E major: ♭II h. D major: Fr^{+6} with raised $\hat{4}$ in bass

   i. B minor: Ger^{+6} with $\hat{1}$ in bass j. E♭ major: V^9

2. For each of the following, name the indicated major key and the chord.

a. b. c. d. e. f.

3. In each of the following, a diatonic chord is embellished by a chromatic harmony with which it shares a common tone. What are the missing notes?

a.

B♭: V ————
(V "♭III⁶" V)

b.

G: I ————
(I common- I)
tone °7

c.

E♭: V ————
(V common- V)
tone °7

4. Which of the following chords is an applied vii°7? Which is a common-tone diminished seventh chord?

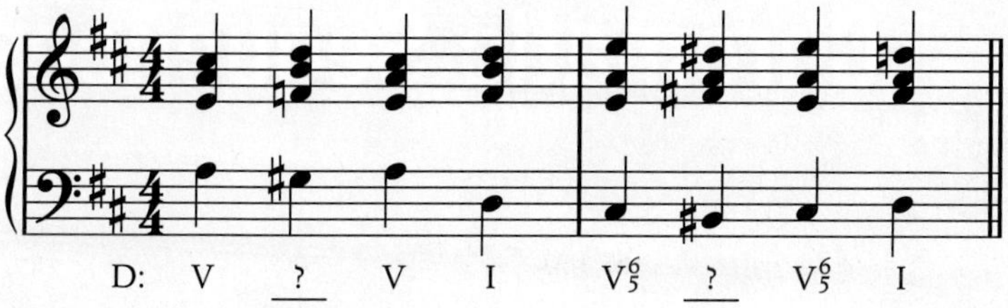

Know It? Show It!

Focus by working through the tutorials on:

- Writing common-tone diminished seventh chords

Learn with inQuizitive.

Apply what you've learned to complete the assignments:

- Spelling Chords
- Realizing Roman Numerals
- Realizing Figured Bass
- Composition
- Analysis

chapter

33 Chromatic Sequences

Chromatic alterations can be used within sequences, sometimes creating a series of applied chords.

CHROMATIC EMBELLISHMENT OF SEQUENCES

Chords within sequences can be chromatically embellished. This changes the qualities of chords within the sequence, but does not disrupt the underlying sequence.

33.1

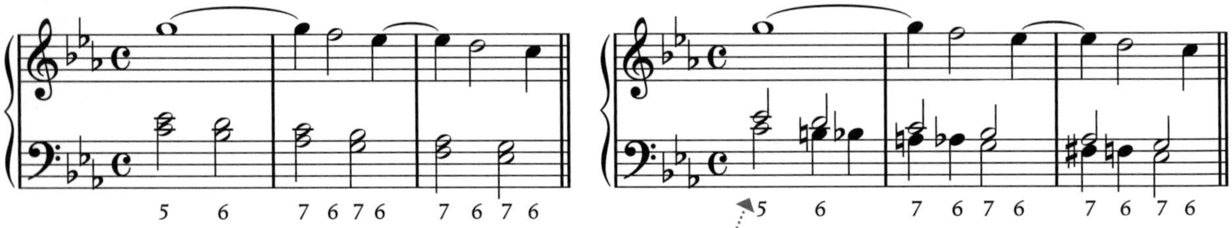

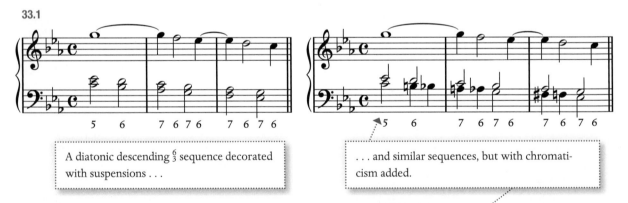

A diatonic descending $^6_3$ sequence decorated with suspensions . . .

. . . and similar sequences, but with chromaticism added.

33.2 Vivaldi, Sonata in C Minor for Violin and Basso Continuo, RV 6, IV

33.3

A diatonic sequence: up 2, down 3 . . .

. . . and the same sequence with chromatic alterations.

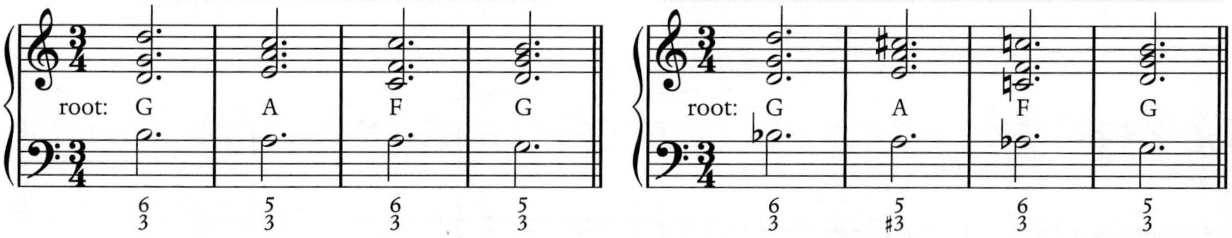

33.4 Schubert, "Morgengruss" (Morning Greetings) ➔

"Up 2, down 3" sequence with chromatic alterations

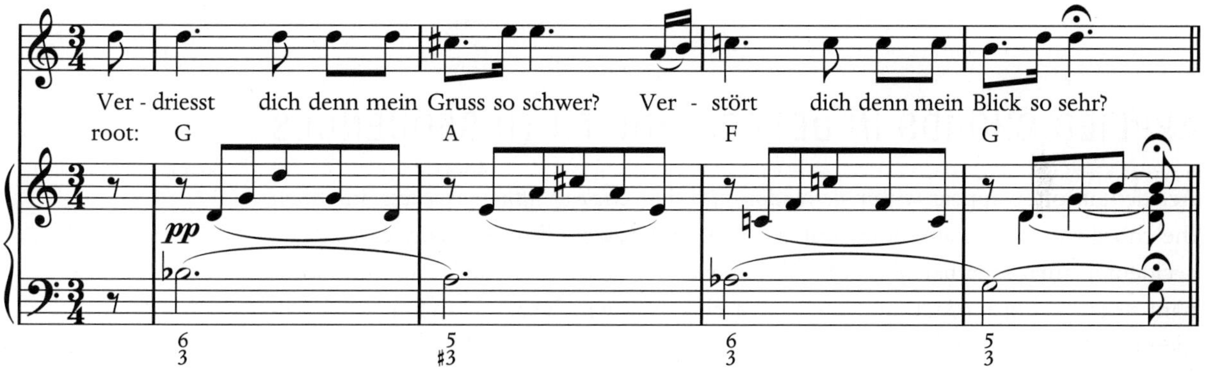

Translation: Do you dislike my greeting so much? Does my gaze disturb you so much?

SEQUENCES AND MODULATION

Adding or subtracting accidentals within a sequence can lead to modulation.

33.5

This diatonic sequence begins and ends in C . . .

. . . while this sequence begins in C and ends in G.

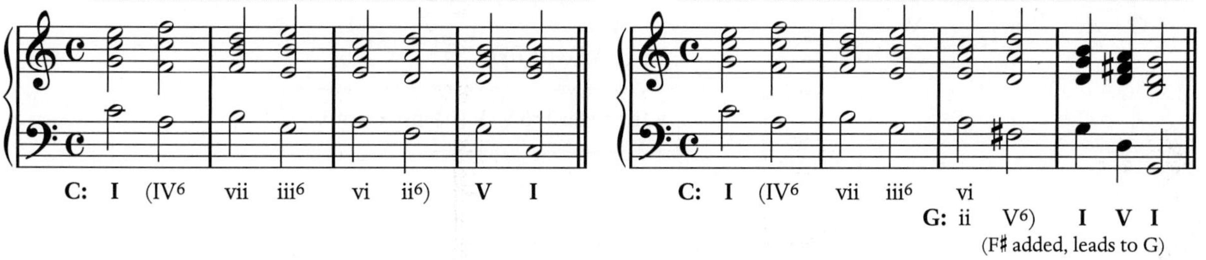

33.6 Handel, Sonata in E for Violin and Basso Continuo, III

This descending fifth sequence (in which every other chord is a seventh chord in first inversion) modulates from F♯ to C♯ minor.

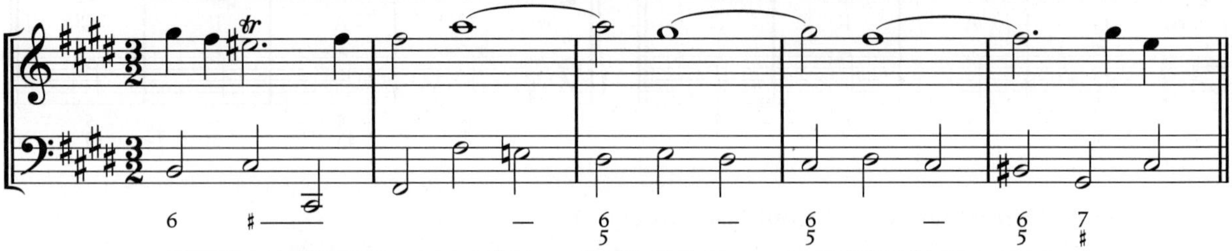

The sequence begins after a cadence in F♯ minor . . .

. . . but it ends in C♯ minor.

APPLIED CHORDS IN DESCENDING FIFTH SEQUENCES

Accidentals often appear within *descending fifth* (i.e., *circle of fifths*) *sequences*, in which the chord roots alternate moving up a fourth and down a fifth. In many cases these accidentals turn each harmony of the sequence into either a major triad or a dominant seventh chord, resulting in a series of chords in which each is an applied dominant to the next.

33.7

A diatonic descending fifth sequence . . .

. . . can be altered to produce a series of major triads that function as applied chords.

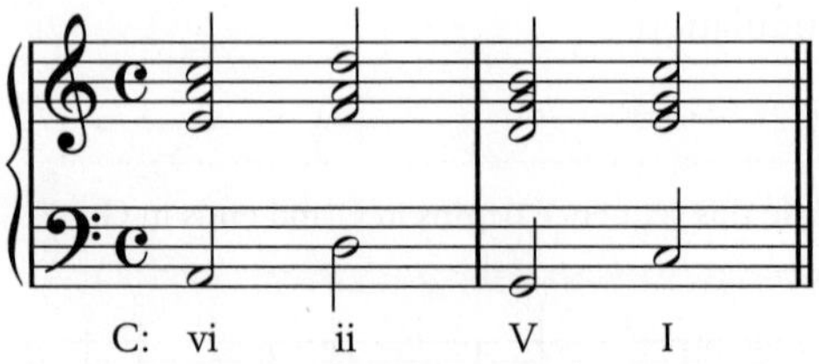

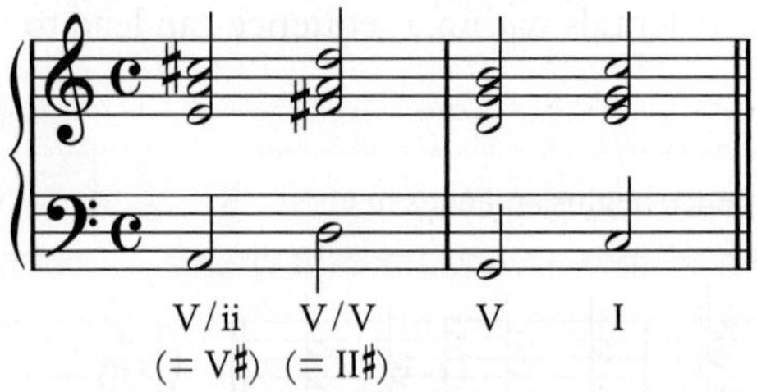

V/ii can lead to V/V (II♯ instead of ii).

33.8

A diatonic descending fifth sequence remains within the key, returning to the starting point on the eighth chord . . .

. . . but chromatically altered notes turn chords within the sequence into applied dominants that can arrive at any key.

In a diatonic descending fifth sequence, one fifth is a diminished fifth (F–B) . . .

. . . but in a chromatic descending fifth sequence, all the fifths are perfect fifths.

A descending fifth sequence can also involve a series of applied dominant seventh chords. If so, the leading tone in each applied dominant does not ascend to the root of the goal chord as expected, but rather slides down by semitone to become the dissonant seventh of the following chord.

33.9

A descending fifth sequence in which every chord is an applied V^{8-7} of the next . . .

. . . and a descending fifth sequence in which every chord is an applied V^7 of the next.

The leading tone in each applied chord resolves up to the root of the goal chord.

The leading tone in each applied chord does *not* resolve up as expected, creating a descending chromatic scale.

33.10 Mozart, String Quartet in D Minor, K. 421, III

Each chord within this descending fifth sequence is an applied dominant seventh of the next chord.

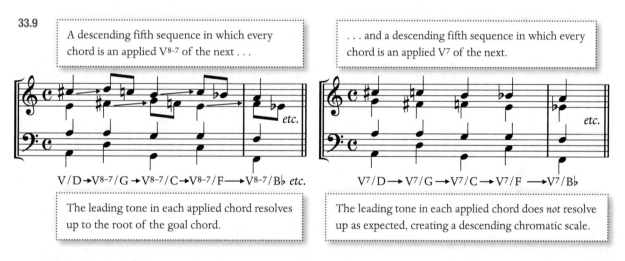

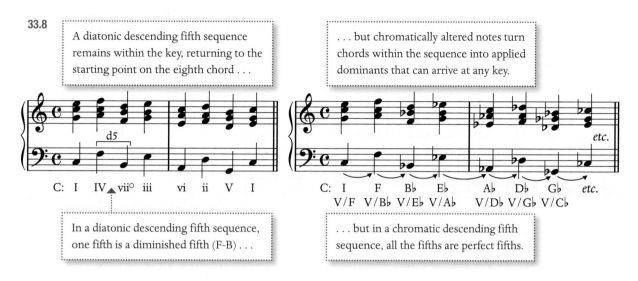

There are also descending fifth sequences in which applied dominant triads alternate with applied dominant sevenths, or in which every chord (or every other chord) is an applied dominant in inversion.

33.11

Chromatic descending 5ths in which every chord is an applied V of the next, using alternating $^6_5$ and $^5_3$ chords . . .

. . . or alternating $^6_5$ and $^4_2$ chords.

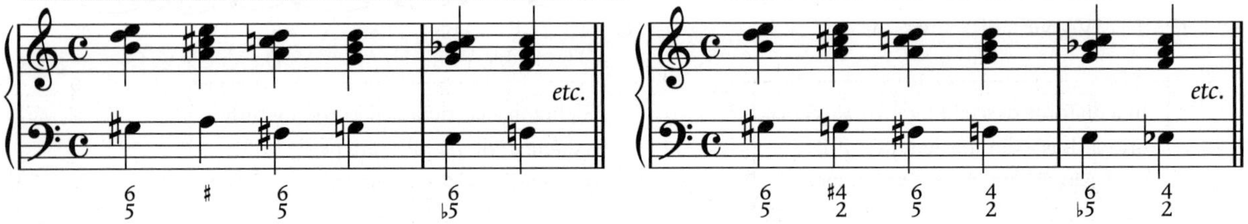

33.12 Chopin, Piano Concerto in F Minor, op. 21, III

A chromatic descending fifth sequence involving applied dominants can modulate through all twelve keys.

Simplified harmonic model (alternating applied V and V7)

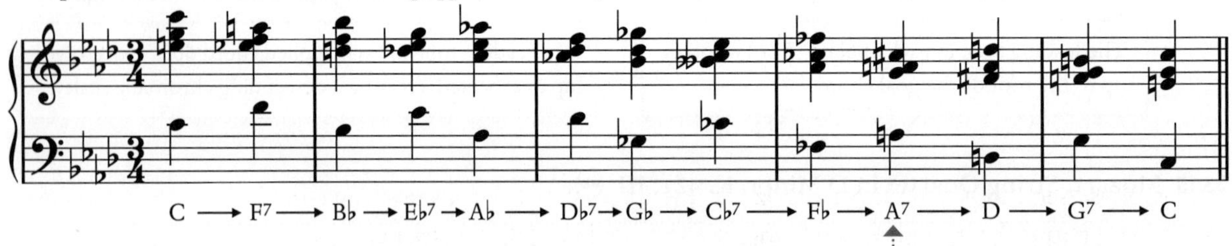

In a complete descending fifth sequence, one chord will need to be enharmonically respelled to return to the beginning point. Here B♭♭ is respelled as A.

APPLIED CHORDS IN OTHER SEQUENCES

Applied chords may appear in any sequence that involves a root motion by ascending fourth (or descending fifth), not just descending fifth sequences. Most notably, applied chords may appear within sequences in which the root moves alternately down a third and up a fourth.

33.13

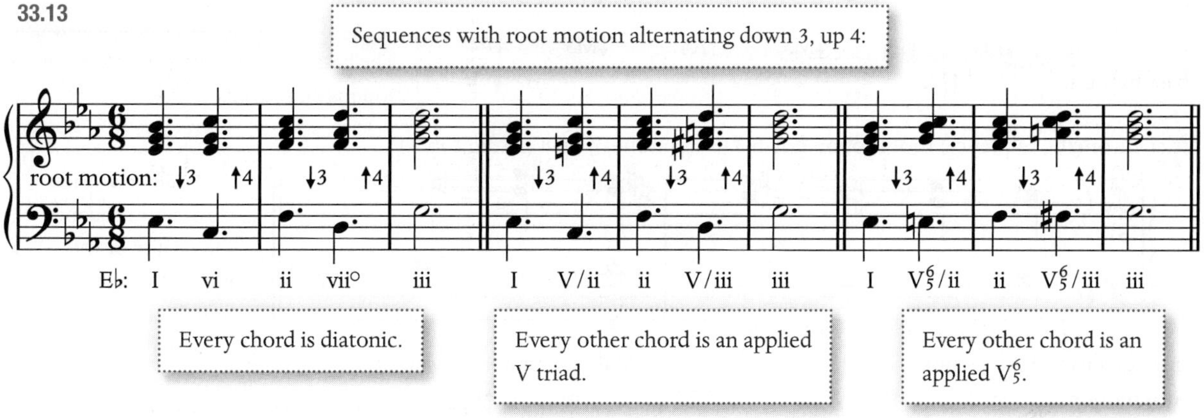

33.14 Beethoven, Piano Sonata in E♭, op. 81a, III

STRICT CHROMATIC SEQUENCES

In a diatonic sequence, the numerical size of the interval of transposition stays the same throughout the sequence, while the quality changes. But in a strict chromatic sequence the interval of transposition always includes the same number of semitones. Strict chromatic sequences became increasingly popular in nineteenth-century music.

33.15

diatonic sequence: root motion down 3, up 4

5 6 5 6 5 6 5

chord quality: Maj. min. min. Maj. dim. Maj. Maj.

root motion: ↓m3 ↑P4 ↓M3 ↑A4 ↓M3 ↑P4

bass motion: ↑M2 ↑M2 ↑m2 ◀

In a diatonic sequence the quality of the intervals in the sequential pattern changes, as does the quality of chords . . .

The bass moves up the scale by major and minor seconds.

strict chromatic sequence: root motion down 3 (3 semitones), up 4 (5 semitones)

5 6 5 6 5 6 5

chord quality: Maj. min. Maj. min. Maj. min. Maj.

root motion: ↓m3 ↑P4 ↓m3 ↑P4 ↓m3 ↑P4

bass motion: ↑2 semitones (= M2) ↑2 semitones ↑2 semitones ◀

. . . while in a strict chromatic sequence the quality of the intervals and chords remain the same throughout.

The bass moves up by major seconds (two semitones).

33.16 Chopin, *Nouvelle Etude*, no. 2 ➔

Each measure is transposed up a semitone, resulting in a strict chromatic sequence.

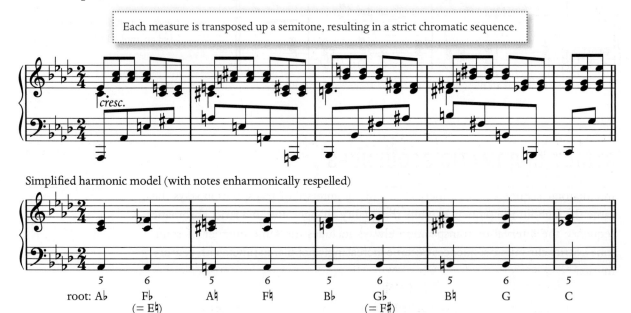

Simplified harmonic model (with notes enharmonically respelled)

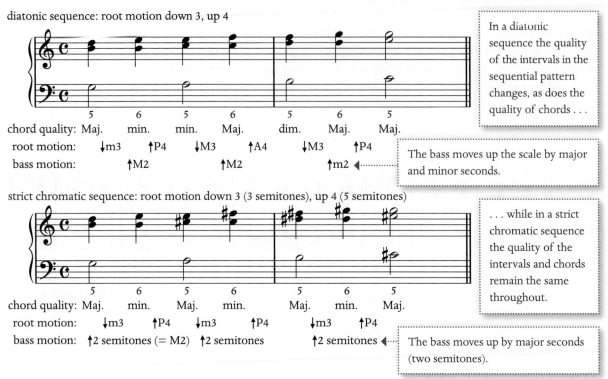

	5	6	5	6	5	6	5	6	5
root:	A♭	F♭ (= E♮)	A♮	F♮	B♭	G♭ (= F♯)	B♮	G	C
chord quality:	Maj.	Aug.	Maj.	Aug.	Maj.	Aug.	Maj.	Aug.	Maj.

Strict chromatic sequences often include enharmonic respelling.

EQUAL DIVISION OF THE OCTAVE

If the sequential pattern is repeated enough times, a strict chromatic sequence returns to its starting harmony. This results in an **equal division of the octave**.

33.17 Bizet, "The Ball," from *Jeux d'enfants* (Children's Games)

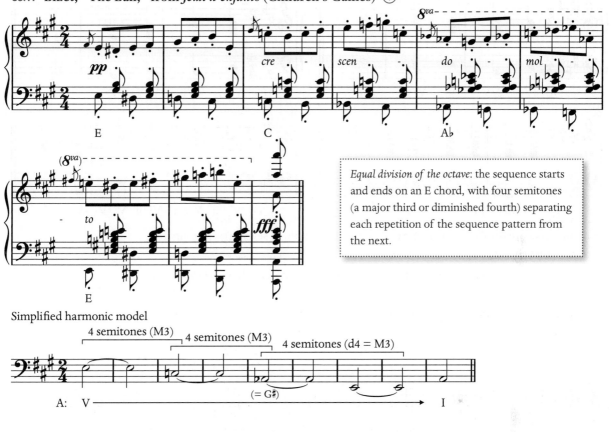

Equal division of the octave: the sequence starts and ends on an E chord, with four semitones (a major third or diminished fourth) separating each repetition of the sequence pattern from the next.

Simplified harmonic model

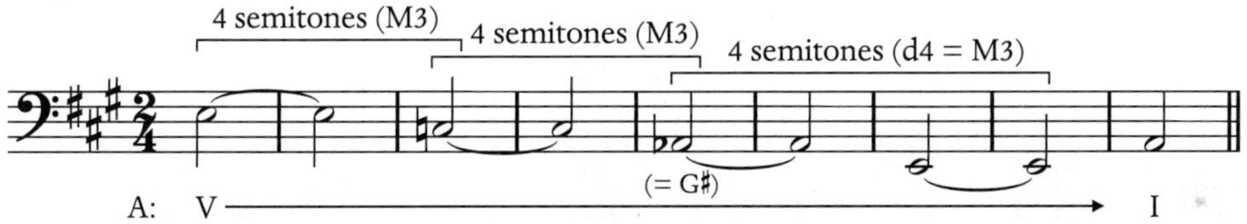

review and interact

POINTS FOR REVIEW

- **Sequences can contain chromatically altered notes.**
- **In descending fifth sequences, altered notes can create a series of applied dominants.**
- **In a descending fifth sequence in which every chord is an applied dominant seventh, the leading tone in each chord slides down by half step to become the seventh of the next chord instead of resolving up by step.**
- **Chromatic alterations can form applied chords in other types of sequences as well.**
- **In strict chromatic sequences each segment of the sequence is transposed by the same number of semitones.**
- **Strict chromatic sequences that return to the first chord of the sequence create an equal division of the octave.**

TEST YOURSELF

1. Add the missing accidentals in the following sequences, and identify each sequence type (descending fifth or "down 3, up 4").

a.

b.

c.

d.

2. In the sequence (d) above, what chord tone (root, third, fifth, or seventh) is missing from every other chord?
3. In a sequence involving a series of applied dominant sevenths, how should each leading tone resolve?
4. In a sequence involving a series of applied dominant sevenths, how should each chordal seventh resolve?

Know It? Show It!

Focus by working through the tutorials on:

- Writing descending fifth sequences using applied chords

Learn with inQuizitive.

Apply what you've learned to complete the assignments:

- Realizing Roman Numerals
- Writing Chromatic Sequences
- Realizing Figured Bass
- Equal Division of the Octave
- Strict Chromatic Sequences
- Analysis

chapter 34

Chromatic Modulation

Modulations between distantly related keys take place through a variety of chromatic techniques.

DISTANTLY RELATED KEYS

Distantly related keys have signatures that differ by more than one accidental. Before the nineteenth century, modulations to distantly related keys occurred primarily in the unstable middle sections of movements, such as the development in sonata form (see Chapter 39). But during the nineteenth century, these modulations became increasingly common. Because distantly related keys usually do not include a pivot chord that is shared by both keys, a variety of chromatic techniques are commonly used for these modulations.

PIVOT CHORDS INVOLVING MIXTURE

A modulation between closely related keys often involves a pivot chord that is diatonic to both keys (see Chapters 27 and 28). In moving between distantly related keys, on the other hand, the pivot chord may be diatonic to only *one* of the keys, functioning within the other key as a chromatic chord derived from modal mixture.

34.1

Modulation between closely related keys: the pivot chord is diatonic to both keys.

Modulation to a distant key: the pivot chord is diatonic in the second key (E♭) but involves modal mixture in the original key (C).

Modulation to a distant key: the pivot chord is diatonic in the original key (C) but involves modal mixture in the second key (E).

34.2 Brahms, Waltz, op. 39, no. 14

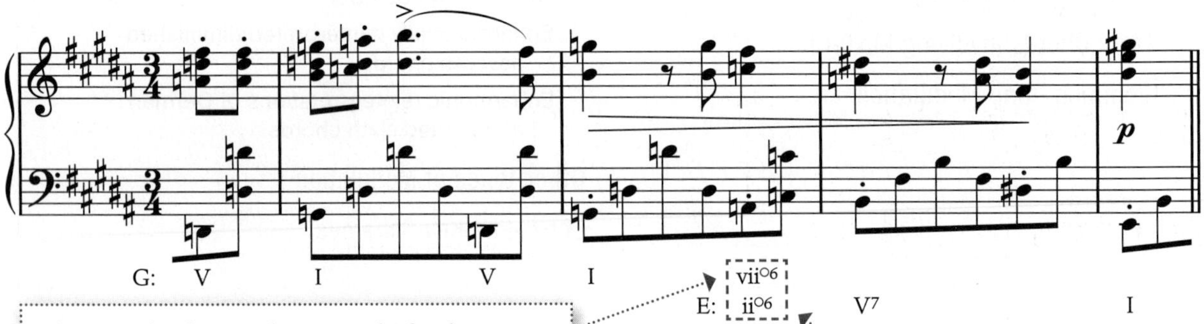

The pivot chord vii°6 is diatonic to the first key (G) . . .

. . . but ii°6 involves modal mixture in the second key (E).

34.3 Schubert, Waltz, D. 365, no. 33

The pivot chord i involves modal mixture in the first key (F) . . .

. . . but vi is diatonic to the second key (A♭).

COMMON-TONE MODULATION

In a **common-tone modulation** the last chord before the modulation shares a tone with the first chord after the modulation, so that just one tone—rather than the entire chord—serves as a pivot. Especially when the shared tone is highlighted in the melody or bass, a common-tone modulation can help ease the transition to a distantly related key, even if there is no pivot chord.

34.4 Bizet, Prelude to *Carmen*

Common-tone modulation from A major to F major: there is no pivot chord leading from one key to the other . . .
pp
A: V
I
F: I
p mais très marqué
. . . but the A in the melody bridges the abrupt connection between these keys.

34.5 Beethoven, String Quartet no. 3, op. 18, no. 3, I

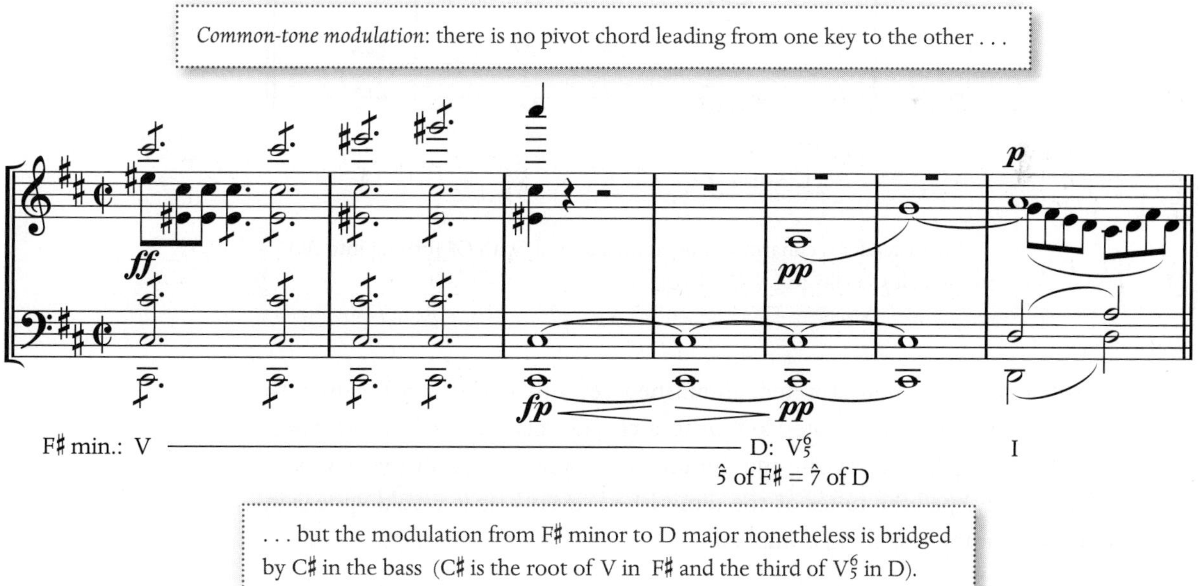
Common-tone modulation: there is no pivot chord leading from one key to the other . . .
ff
pp
p
fp
pp
F♯ min.: V
D: V^6_5
I
$\hat{5}$ of F♯ = $\hat{7}$ of D
. . . but the modulation from F♯ minor to D major nonetheless is bridged by C♯ in the bass (C♯ is the root of V in F♯ and the third of V^6_5 in D).

ENHARMONIC MODULATION

ENHARMONICALLY REINTERPRETED DIMINISHED SEVENTH CHORDS

With the possibility of enharmonic equivalence, any diminished seventh chord might function as vii°7 in four different major keys and their parallel minors.

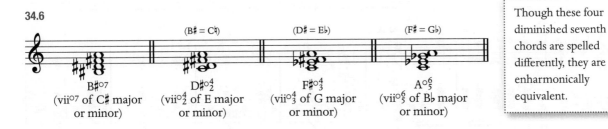

> Though these four diminished seventh chords are spelled differently, they are enharmonically equivalent.

34.6

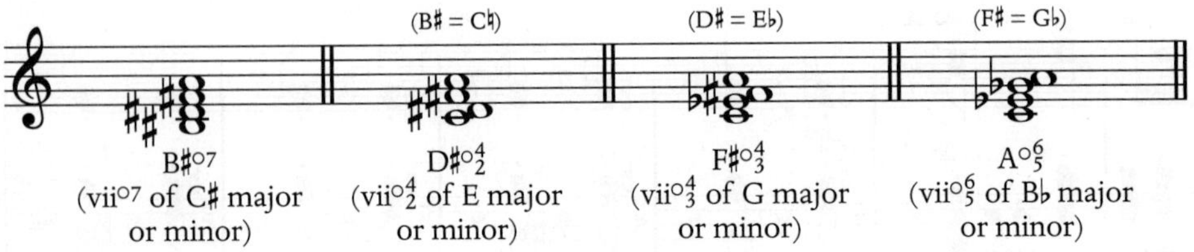
(B♯ = C♮)
(D♯ = E♭)
(F♯ = G♭)
B♯°7
(vii°7 of C♯ major or minor)
D♯°4/2
(vii°4/2 of E major or minor)
F♯°4/3
(vii°4/3 of G major or minor)
A°6/5
(vii°6/5 of B♭ major or minor)

Sometimes an enharmonically reinterpreted diminished seventh chord is used as a pivot chord, so that vii°7 introduced in one key resolves as vii°7 in another key.

34.7

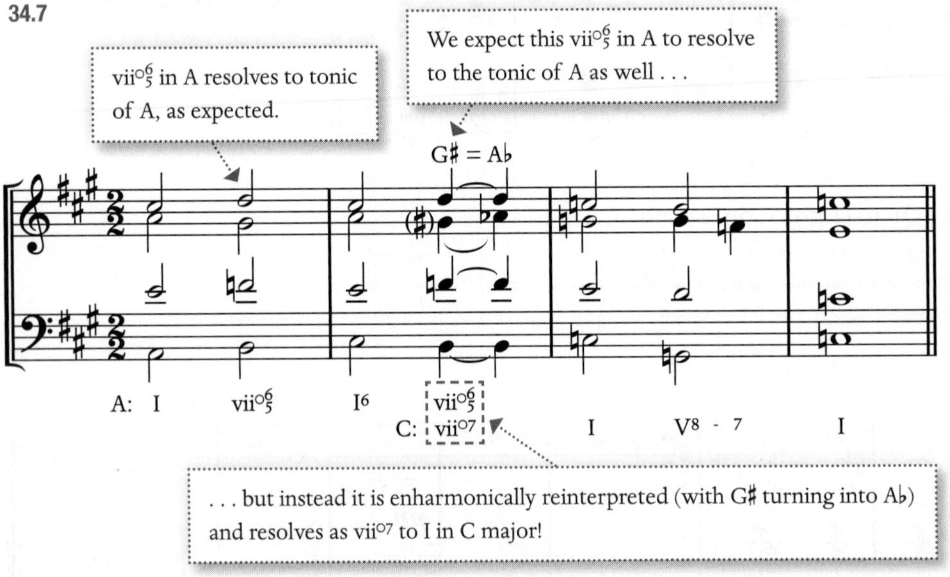
vii°6/5 in A resolves to tonic of A, as expected.
We expect this vii°6/5 in A to resolve to the tonic of A as well . . .
G♯ = A♭
A: I vii°6/5 I6 vii°6/5
C: vii°7 I V8 - 7 I
. . . but instead it is enharmonically reinterpreted (with G♯ turning into A♭) and resolves as vii°7 to I in C major!

An enharmonically reinterpreted diminished seventh chord can be used to modulate either to a distantly related key or to a closely related key. In most cases, composers do not bother to rewrite the diminished seventh chord in the new key. Rather, they simply spell the notes of the diminished seventh as it would appear in the first key, so that the respelling is implied.

34.8 Mozart, Trio for Clarinet, Viola, and Piano, K. 498, I ➔

Simplified harmonic model

We expect vii$^{\circ 4}_{3}$ in C to resolve to i in C, with B♮ ascending to C. . . .

. . . Instead, however, B (functioning as C♭) moves *down* to B♭ so that the preceding diminished seventh chord functions as vii$^{\circ 6}_{5}$ of E♭!

ENHARMONIC REINTERPRETATIONS OF GERMAN AUGMENTED SIXTH CHORDS

German augmented sixth chords may also be enharmonically reinterpreted, since a German augmented sixth is enharmonically equivalent to a dominant seventh chord.

34.9

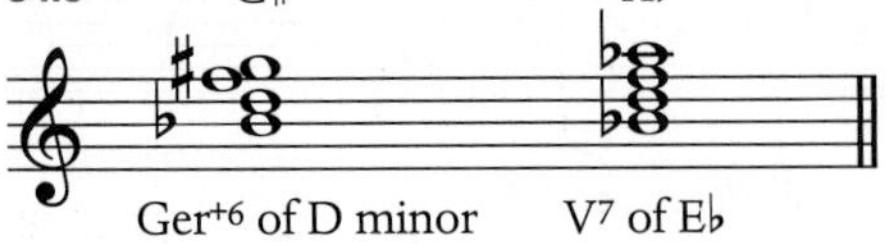

A German augmented sixth and a dominant seventh are enharmonically equivalent.

This enharmonic reinterpretation can lead to a distant modulation, when a harmony introduced as a German augmented sixth resolves as a dominant seventh chord, or vice versa.

34.10

This chord resolves as a Ger+6.

This chord resolves as a dominant seventh.

This chord initially appears as a Ger+6, but then is reinterpreted to resolve as a dominant seventh.

34.11 Haydn, Symphony no. 55, I

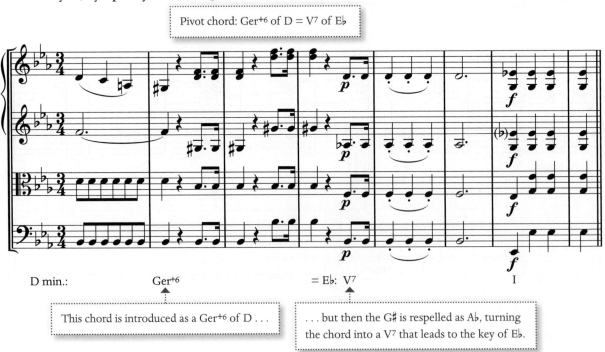

Pivot chord: Ger+6 of D = V7 of E♭

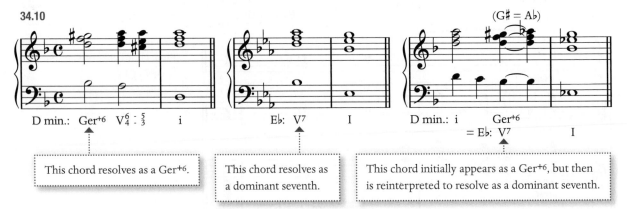

This chord is introduced as a Ger+6 of D . . .

. . . but then the G♯ is respelled as A♭, turning the chord into a V7 that leads to the key of E♭.

34.12 Haydn, Symphony no. 55, I

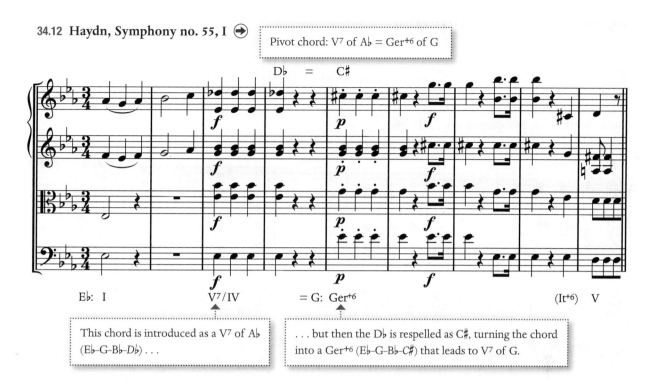

Pivot chord: V7 of A♭ = Ger+6 of G

This chord is introduced as a V7 of A♭ (E♭–G–B♭–*D♭*) . . .

. . . but then the D♭ is respelled as C♯, turning the chord into a Ger+6 (E♭–G–B♭–*C♯*) that leads to V7 of G.

OTHER TYPES OF MODULATION

Not every modulation is approached smoothly. It is certainly possible for a tonal center to shift abruptly, without the use of a pivot chord, enharmonically reinterpreted pivot chord, or common tone. In such cases, the change of key may be partly prepared by chromatically inflected chord tones. Changes of key may also be organized as part of a sequence.

34.13 Dvořák, Symphony no. 8, op. 88, IV

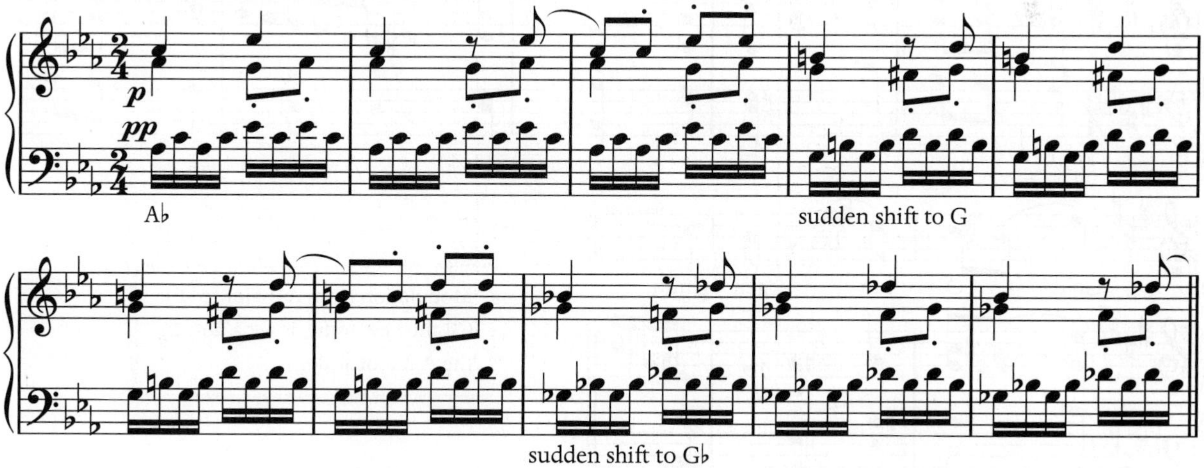

Abrupt changes of key—with no pivot chords or common tones—follow a sequential pattern of descending semitones from A♭ to G to G♭.

CHROMATIC KEY SCHEMES

In music composed after 1800, modulations between distantly related keys became increasingly popular. Modulations involving a chromatic third—such as the modulation in a major-key piece to III♯—are particularly common.

34.14 Beethoven, Symphony no. 7, III ➔

Modulation from F major (1♭) to the key of A major (III♯, 3♯s)

cresc.
sf
sf
f
key of F
→ A

In some more-extreme cases, a modulation may lead to a key whose tonic is not a note in the original key, as in a modulation from I to ♭III or ♭VI.

34.15 Schubert, "Kennst du das Land" (Do You Know the Place) ➔

Kennst du das Land, wo die Ci-tro - nen blühn, im dunk-len Laub die
p
key of A

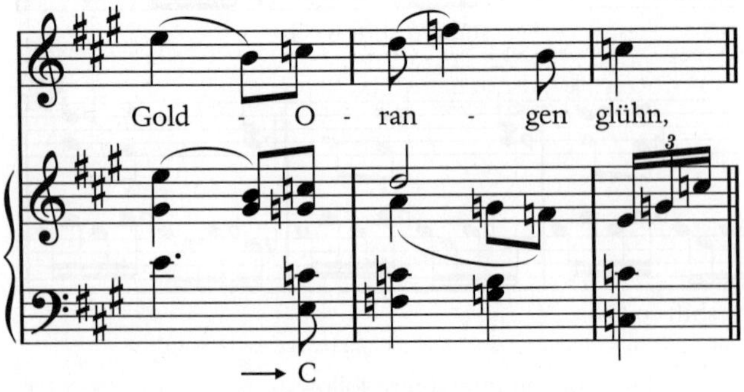
Gold - O - ran - gen glühn,
→ C

Modulation from A major to ♭III. C♮, the new tonic, is *not* a note in the A-major scale.

Translation: Do you know the place where lemon trees grow, where amid dark leaves the gold-colored orange glows . . . ?

Successive modulations or tonicizations by the same interval can lead to a key that is only very distantly related to the original key.

34.16 Schubert, Piano Sonata in D, D. 850, III

Successive tonicizations lead from C (IV of G) up three semitones to E♭, then to G♭, which has no notes in common with the starting key.

If repeated enough times, successive modulations or tonicizations by the same interval can return to the original key. This creates an *equal division of the octave*.

34.17 Chopin, *Nouvelle Etude* no. 2

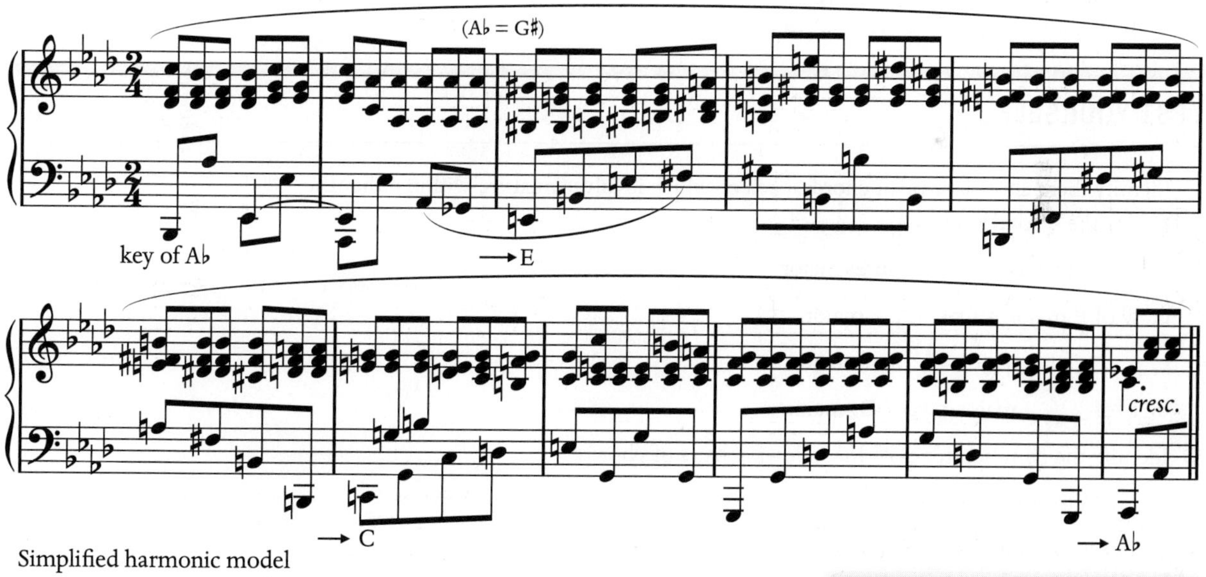

Simplified harmonic model

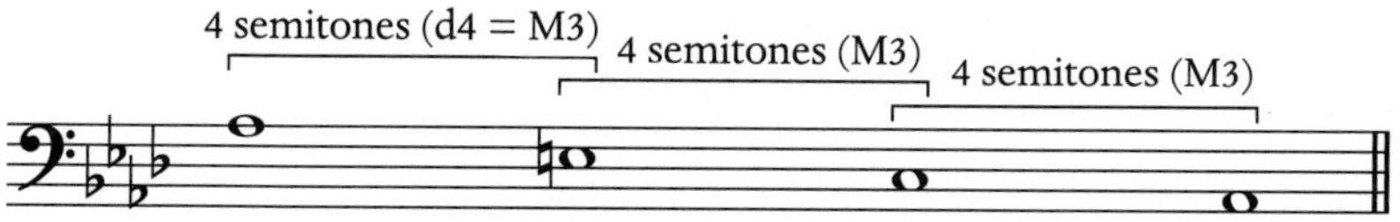

Successive tonicizations, each down by four semitones, lead from A♭, to E, to C, and back to A♭ . . .

. . . creating an equal division of the octave.

review and interact

POINTS FOR REVIEW

- **Distantly related keys are those whose key signatures differ by more than one sharp or flat.**
- **In a modulation between distantly related keys, the pivot chord can involve mixture in either the original key or the new key.**
- **A common-tone modulation involves a shared tone in the chords before and after the modulation.**
- **Each diminished seventh chord is enharmonically equivalent to three other diminished seventh chords and can function as vii$^{\circ 7}$ in four different keys and their parallels. An enharmonically reinterpreted diminished seventh chord can be a pivot chord.**
- **A German augmented sixth chord is enharmonically equivalent to a dominant seventh chord. An enharmonically reinterpreted German augmented sixth chord or enharmonically reinterpreted dominant seventh chord can be a pivot chord.**
- **An abrupt modulation may involve a sudden shift to a key that is not prepared by a pivot chord or common tone.**
- **In music composed after 1800, modulation schemes that involve keys that are distantly related became increasingly common.**
- **Repeated sequential modulation or tonicization by the same interval can lead to a distantly related key or may create an equal division of the octave.**

TEST YOURSELF

1. Identify these chromatic pivot chords, each of which involves mixture within either the first or the second key:

   a. ♭VI of D major = _____ in E♭ major

   b. iv of E major = ii of _____ major.

   c. _____ of C major = V of A♭ major.

   d. iv of _____ major = vi of D♭ major.

2. Identify the common tones of the following pairs of chords.

   a. I of A major and I of F major

   b. I of E major and V^{7} of C major

   c. V of A major and V^{7} of F major

3. vii$^{\circ 7}$ of D is enharmonically equivalent to

   a. vii$^{\circ 6}_{5}$ of _____; b. vii$^{\circ 4}_{3}$ of _____; and c. vii$^{\circ 4}_{2}$ of _____.

4. vii$^{\circ 7}$ of E major is enharmonically equivalent to

   a. vii$^{\circ 6}_{5}$ of _____; b. vii$^{\circ 4}_{3}$ of _____; and c. vii$^{\circ 4}_{2}$ of _____.

5. For each of the following, identify the key of the enharmonically equivalent V^7 or Ger^{+6} chord.

a. Ger^{+6} of E	b. Ger^{+6} of G	c. V^7 of D	d. V^7 of E

= V^7 of ______	= V^7 of ______	= Ger^{+6} of ______	= Ger^{+6} of ______

Know It? Show It!

Focus by working through the tutorials on:

- Enharmonically reinterpreted diminished seventh chords
- Enharmonically reinterpreted German augmented sixth chords

Learn with inQuizitive.

Apply what you've learned to complete the assignments:

- Notating Chromatic Pivot Chords
- Realizing Roman Numerals
- Realizing Figured Bass
- Analysis

part five

Form

chapter

35 Sentences and Other Phrase Types

Many phrases begin with a stable opening followed by increased momentum toward a cadence.

SENTENCES

A phrase is the basic unit of tonal music (see Chapter 6). Phrases conclude with a cadence and do not include a cadence in the middle. Typically, the first half of a phrase begins in a stable fashion, and its second half becomes more active as it leads to a cadence.

One of the most common phrase layouts is a **sentence**. A sentence is typically eight measures, divided into two halves. The opening four measures—the **presentation**—consists of a repeated two-measure melodic segment known as the **basic idea**. The presentation usually embellishes the tonic in a straightforward manner. In the next four measures—the **continuation**—an intensified sense of momentum leads to a cadence. The pace usually quickens in the continuation, often with faster rhythms and more-frequent changes of harmony than in the presentation, and with **fragmentation**, in which a part of the basic idea or a new idea is repeated either exactly or sequentially.

35.1

EIGHT-MEASURE SENTENCE

4 MEASURES		4 MEASURES
presentation (relatively stable)		continuation
2 measures basic idea	**2 measures** repetition (or varied repetition of basic idea	momentum increases, leading to cadence (PAC, IAC, or HC)

35.2 Haydn, Symphony no. 21, III

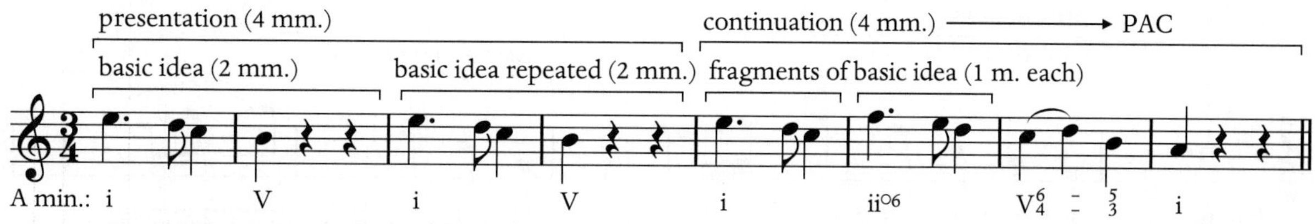

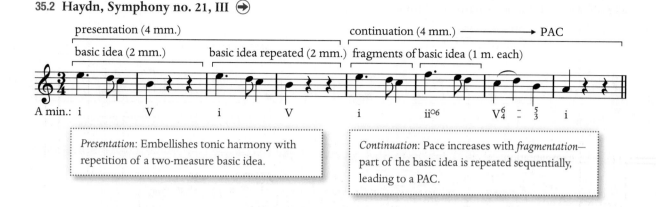

Presentation: Embellishes tonic harmony with repetition of a two-measure basic idea.

Continuation: Pace increases with *fragmentation*—part of the basic idea is repeated sequentially, leading to a PAC.

BASIC IDEA—REPEATED OR VARIED

During the presentation, the basic idea may be repeated exactly, or varied by transposition or elaboration.

35.3 Beethoven, Piano Sonata in A, op. 2, no. 2, III

The basic idea may repeat exactly . . .

35.4 "She'll Be Coming Round the Mountain"

. . . or it may be varied.

A basic idea and its varied repetition can be harmonized differently from one another. For instance, where the varied repetition involves transposition, often the basic idea is harmonized with I and its varied repetition, with V.

35.5 Beethoven, Piano Sonata in F Minor, op. 2, no. 1, I

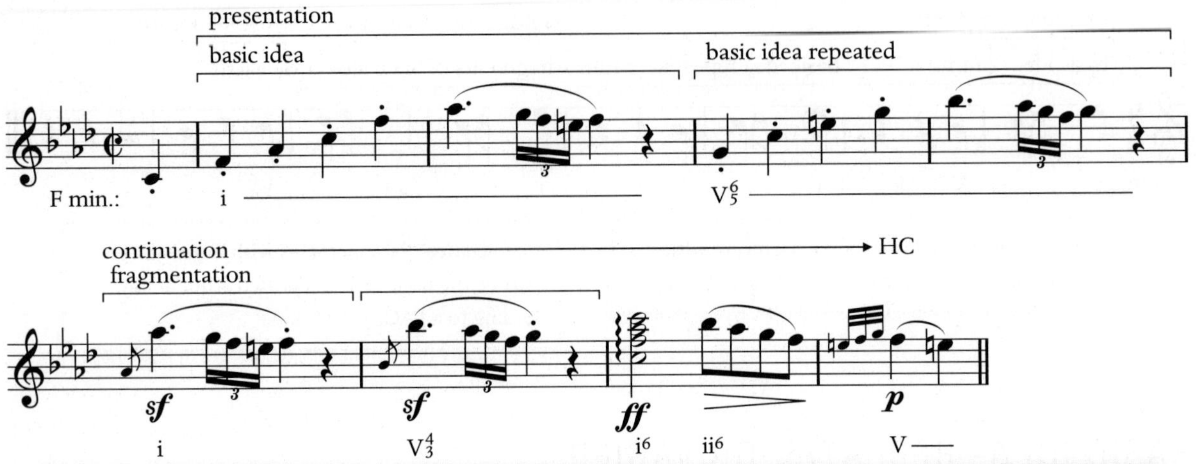

The basic idea is harmonized with Tonic; its varied repetition is a transposition and is harmonized with **D**ominant.

In many other instances, a basic idea harmonized with a I-V progression is answered by a varied repetition harmonized with V-I.

35.6 Mozart, Rondo in D, K. 485

The basic idea is harmonized I-V; its varied repetition is harmonized V-I.

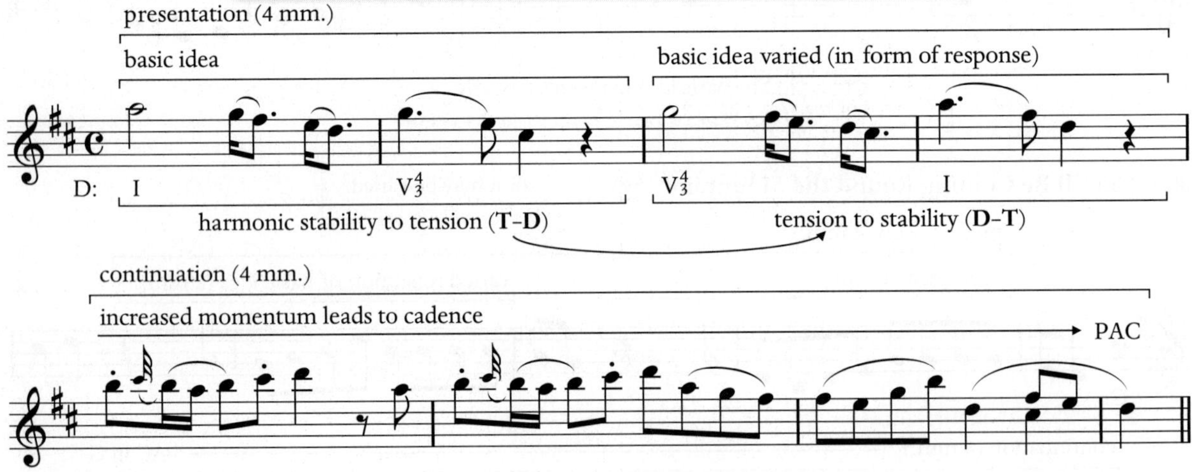

35.7 Mozart, Minuet, K. 1

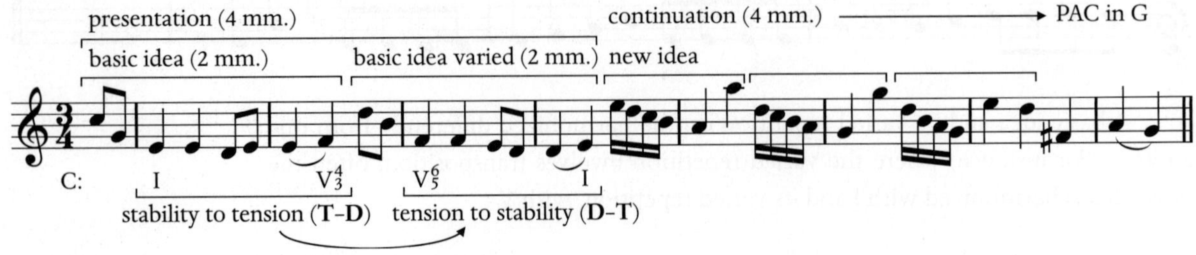

SENTENCE LENGTH

Although most sentences are eight measures long, sentences that are twice as short or long are also possible—provided that the relative proportions of the segments are similar to those of an eight-measure sentence.

35.8 Schubert, "Wasserfluth" (Flood Waters)

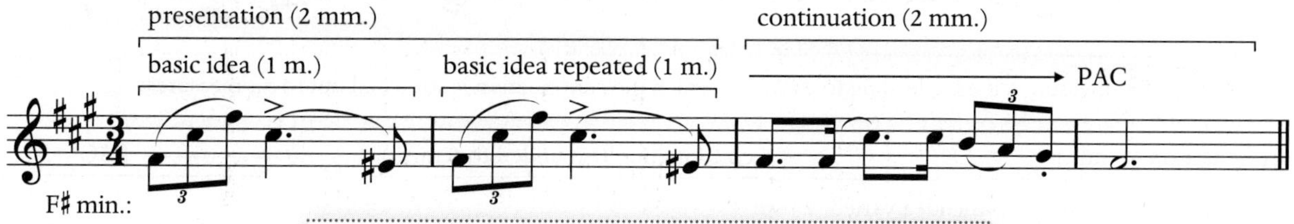

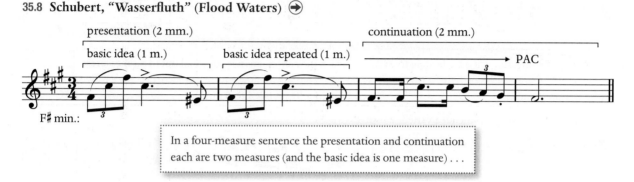

In a four-measure sentence the presentation and continuation each are two measures (and the basic idea is one measure) . . .

35.9 Mozart, Piano Sonata in A Minor, K. 310, III

. . . and in a sixteen-measure sentence the presentation and continuation each are eight measures (and the basic idea is four measures).

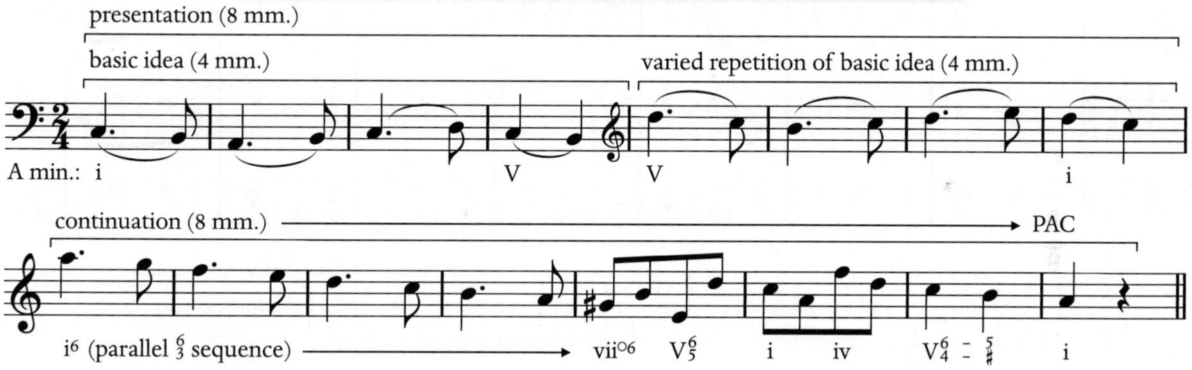

In other situations, the strict proportions of a sentence may be altered by compressing or expanding the segments of the phrase. For instance, a measure or group of measures may be repeated, or a melodic figure inserted in the middle or at the end of a phrase, so that a segment is stretched beyond its normal length.

35.10 Mozart, "Dove sono," from *The Marriage of Figaro*

Eight-measure sentence leading to an HC; the presentation and continuation are four measures each:

Ten-measure sentence leading to a PAC, in which the continuation is stretched out to six measures:

35.11 Beethoven, String Trio in E♭, op. 3, III

Eight-measure sentence:

mm. 1–8

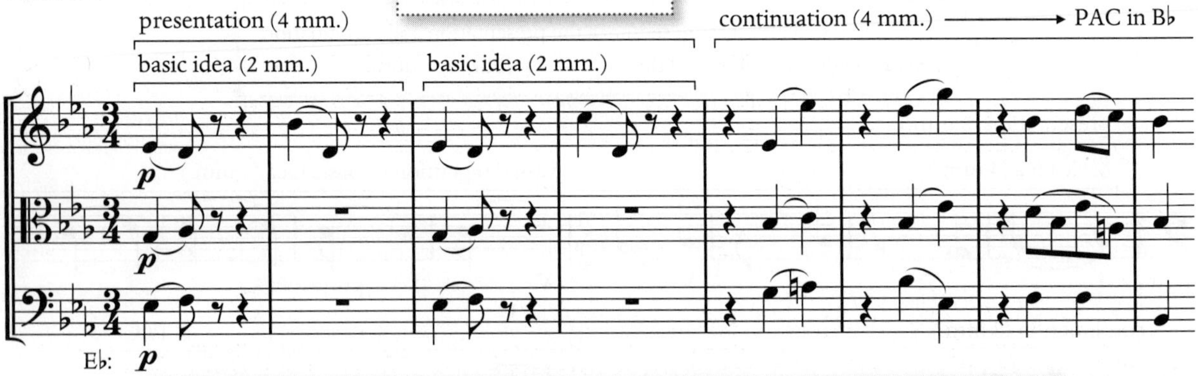

Repetitions expand the sentence to 13 measures when it returns at the end of the movement.

mm. 13–25

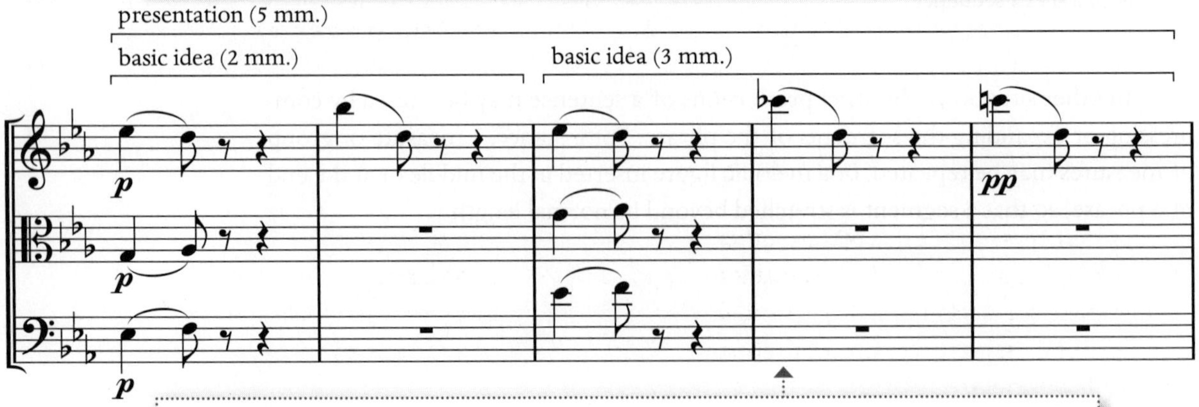

Inserting a varied repetition of part of the basic idea expands the presentation to five measures.

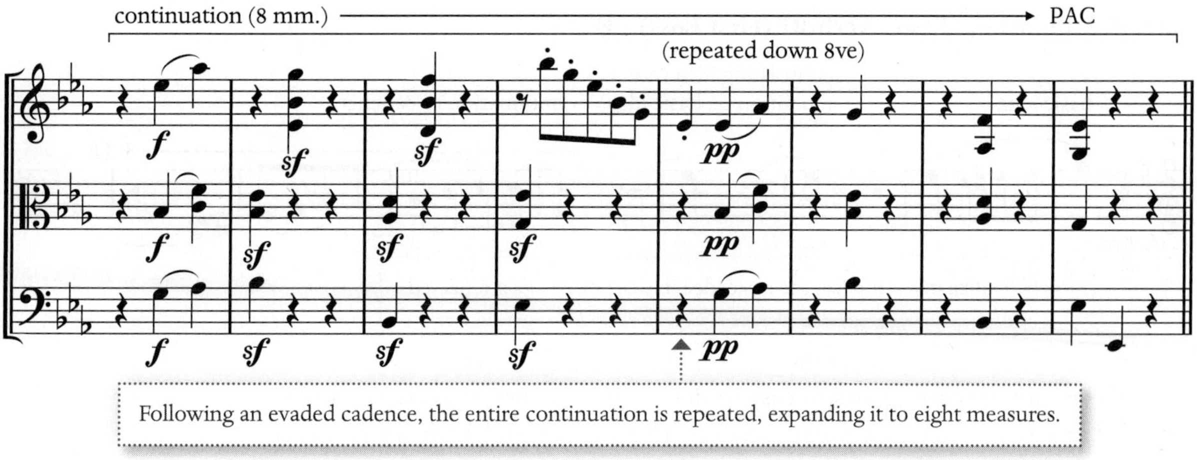

The last measure of a sentence (or any phrase) may also coincide with the first measure of the next phrase, forming a **phrase overlap**.

35.12 Beethoven, Piano Sonata in G, op. 49, no. 2, I

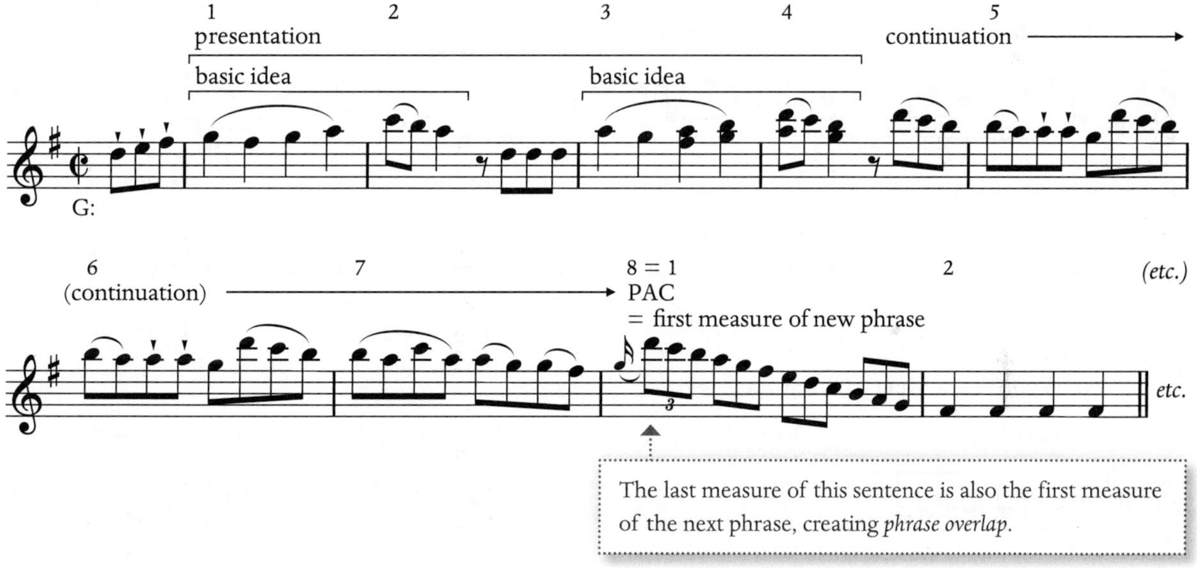

SENTENCE-LIKE PHRASES

In addition to sentences, there are other types of phrase layouts. For instance, a phrase may begin with a basic idea that is followed by a new idea (a **contrasting idea**) rather than by a repetition of the basic idea. A phrase with such a layout is similar to a sentence, since it begins with a relatively stable segment followed by an active passage that leads to a cadence.

35.13 R. Schumann, "Erster Verlust" (First Loss)

Unlike in a sentence, the basic idea in this phrase is *not* repeated.

To be sure, it is not always so easy to determine whether a phrase is properly regarded as a sentence or merely sentence-like. This is especially so when it is unclear whether what follows the basic idea is best understood as a varied repetition or as a contrasting idea, or when the proportions of the phrase seem to radically depart from what is typically found in a sentence.

35.14 Mozart, "Das Veilchen" (The Violet)

Whether this is labeled as a sentence or sentence-like depends on whether mm. 3–4 can be understood as a varied repetition of the basic idea and whether mm. 5–7 can be regarded as a short continuation.

35.15 "We Wish You a Merry Christmas"

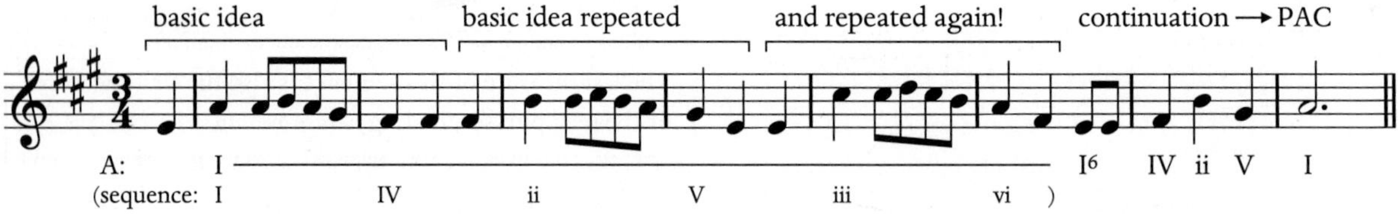

Is this an oddly proportioned sentence, with a six-measure presentation followed by a two-measure continuation? Or is this better understood as a sentence-like phrase?

review and interact

POINTS FOR REVIEW

- **A sentence is a phrase that is usually eight measures long, divided into two halves: the first half (*presentation*) consists of a repeated two-measure segment (*basic idea*); the second half (*continuation*) increases momentum as it leads to a cadence.**
- **In the presentation, the basic idea may be repeated exactly or varied.**
- **Sentences may be longer or shorter than eight measures.**
    - Four- or sixteen-measure sentences maintain the proportions of an eight-measure sentence.
    - Sentences of other lengths may be understood as compressed or expanded.
- **A phrase overlap arises when the last measure of one phrase coincides with the first measure of the next phrase.**
- **In addition to the sentence, other phrase layouts are possible; many of these other layouts resemble sentences, in that they begin stably and increase in momentum leading to a cadence.**

TEST YOURSELF

Determine whether each melody below is a sentence, and explain why.

1.

2.

3.

4.

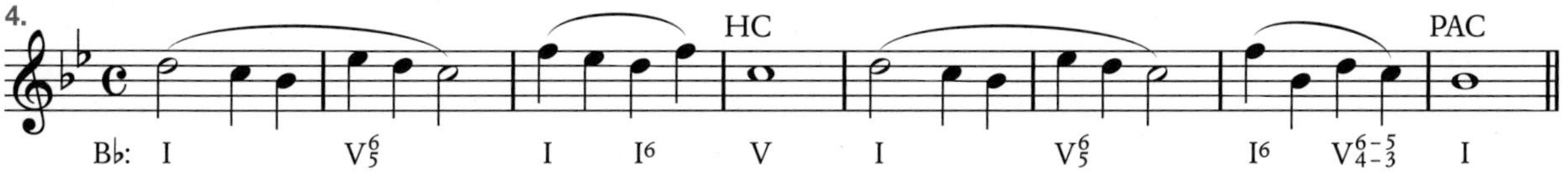

5.

6.

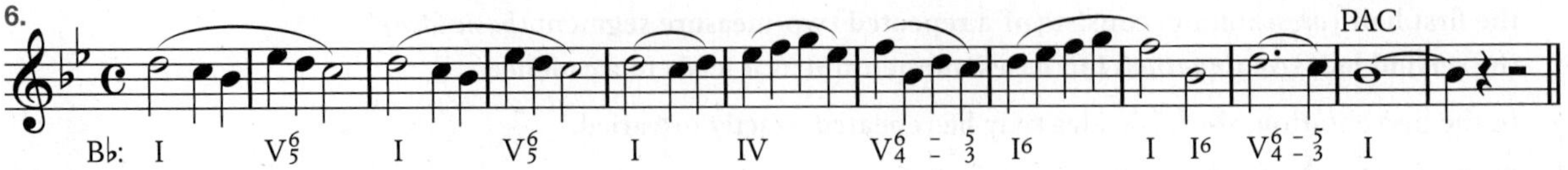

7.

Know It? Show It!

Focus by working through the tutorial on:

- The sentence

Learn with inQuizitive.

Apply what you've learned to complete the assignments:

- Composition
- Analysis

chapter 36

Periods and Other Phrase Pairs

Phrase pairs are classified by the cadences at the end of each phrase and the relationship between the openings of the two phrases.

PERIODS

QUESTION AND RESPONSE

Two successive phrases—each with its own cadence— may combine to form a **phrase pair**. In many phrase pairs, a harmonically unstable cadence at the end of the first phrase (HC or IAC) seems to pose a question that is answered by a harmonically stable cadence at the end of second phrase (PAC). Such a pair of phrases is called a **period**.

36.1 Mozart, Piano Sonata in A, K. 331, I

Period: In this phrase pair, the first phrase ends with an unstable cadence (HC), and the next phrase ends with a stable cadence (PAC).

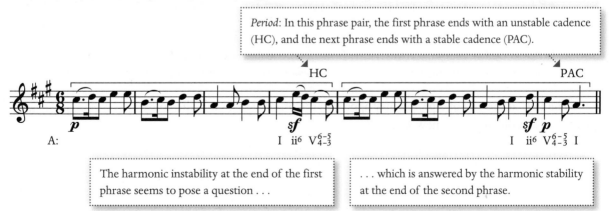

The harmonic instability at the end of the first phrase seems to pose a question . . .

. . . which is answered by the harmonic stability at the end of the second phrase.

The first phrase of a period, which leads to the unstable cadence, is called the **antecedent**. The second phrase, which leads to the stable cadence, is the **consequent**.

36.2 Beethoven, Symphony no. 9, IV

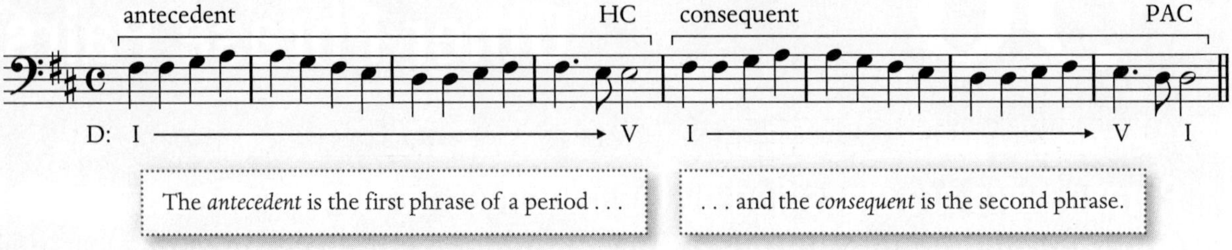
antecedent
HC
consequent
PAC
D: I
V
I
V
I
The *antecedent* is the first phrase of a period . . .
. . . and the *consequent* is the second phrase.

CADENCES WITHIN A PERIOD

Typically, the antecedent of a period ends with a half cadence (HC), and the consequent concludes with a perfect authentic cadence (PAC).

36.3 Foster, "Oh! Susanna"

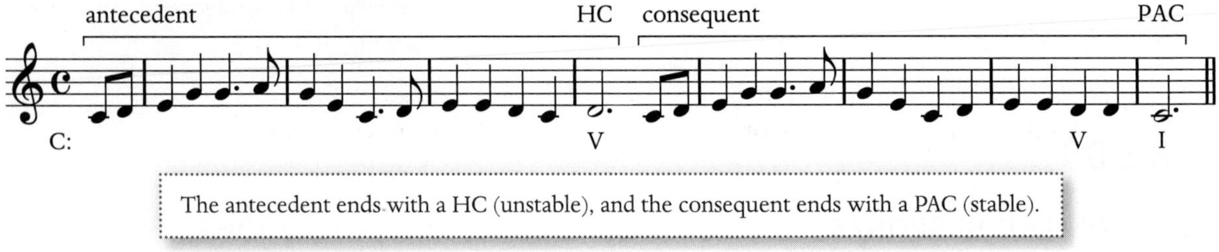
antecedent
HC
consequent
PAC
C:
V
V
I
The antecedent ends with a HC (unstable), and the consequent ends with a PAC (stable).

It is also possible for the antecedent to end with an incomplete authentic cadence (IAC), which is relatively unstable compared to the PAC at the end of the consequent.

36.4 H. Bishop, "Home, Sweet Home"

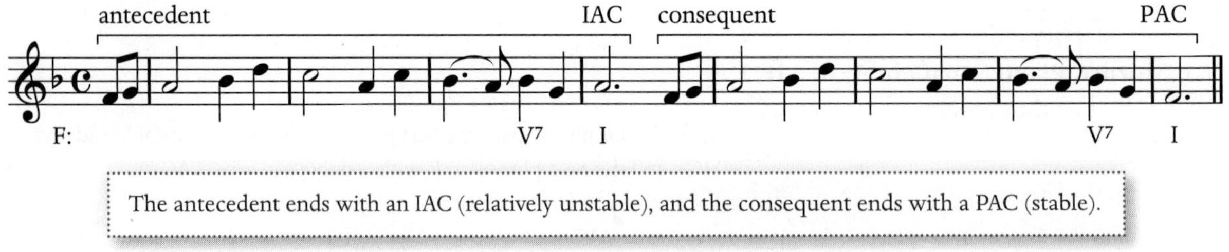
antecedent
IAC
consequent
PAC
F:
V7
I
V7
I
The antecedent ends with an IAC (relatively unstable), and the consequent ends with a PAC (stable).

The PAC at the end of a period may appear in the original key, or (if the consequent phrase modulates) in a new key.

36.5 Tchaikovsky, "The Doll's Funeral" ➔

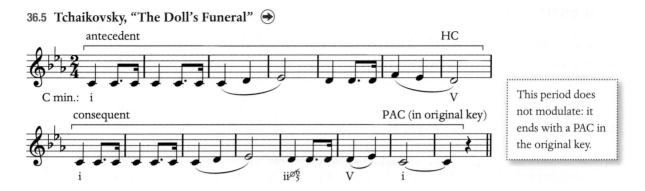

This period does not modulate: it ends with a PAC in the original key.

36.6 Haydn, Symphony no. 104, II ➔

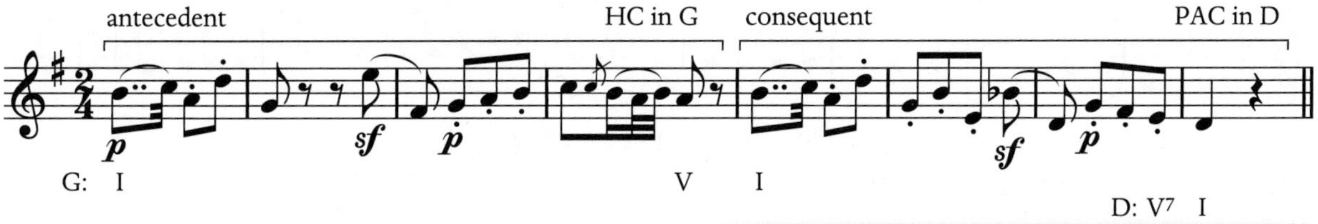

This period modulates, ending with a PAC in V (D).

PARALLEL PERIOD

Periods are classified by how the openings of their two phrases compare with one another. By far the most common type of period is the **parallel period**, in which the two phrases start identically (or nearly identically). All of the periods discussed so far in this chapter are parallel periods.

36.7 "Greensleeves" ➔

Parallel period: Both phrases of the period begin the same way.

36.8 Mozart, Concerto for Horn in E♭, K. 495, III ➔

SEQUENTIAL AND CONTRASTING PERIODS

In a **sequential period**, the melody at the opening of the antecedent returns transposed at the start of the consequent, where it is set with different harmonies. (In contrast, in a parallel period, both the antecedent and consequent begin with the same notes and harmonies.)

36.9 Grieg, "Watchman's Song," *Lyric Pieces*, op. 12 ➔

Sequential period: Although the melodies at the start of both phrases have the same shape and rhythm (as they would in a parallel period), they are on different scale degrees and are harmonized differently from one another.

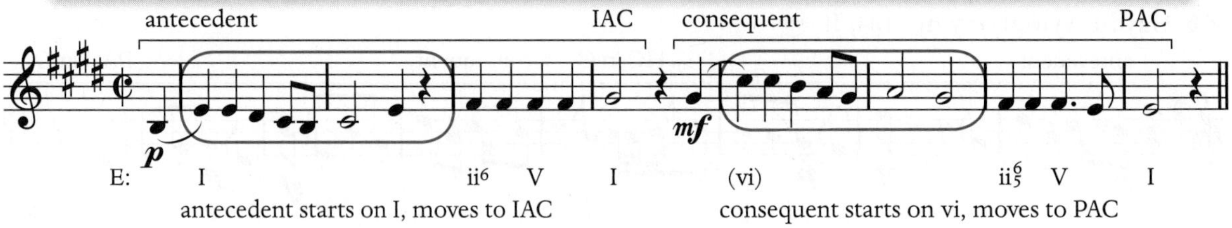

The two phrases of a sequential period often mirror one another harmonically. While the antecedent starts in a harmonically stable manner (on I) and leads to an unstable cadence, the consequent begins unstably (on a chord other than the tonic) and leads to a stable PAC.

36.10 Beethoven, Piano Sonata in A, op. 2, no. 2, III ➔

The antecedent of a sequential period moves from harmonic stability to instability (I to HC) . . .

. . . followed by a consequent that moves from harmonic instability to stability (V to PAC).

In a **contrasting period**, the two phrases begin much differently from one another.

36.11 Haydn, Symphony no. 21 in A, III ➔

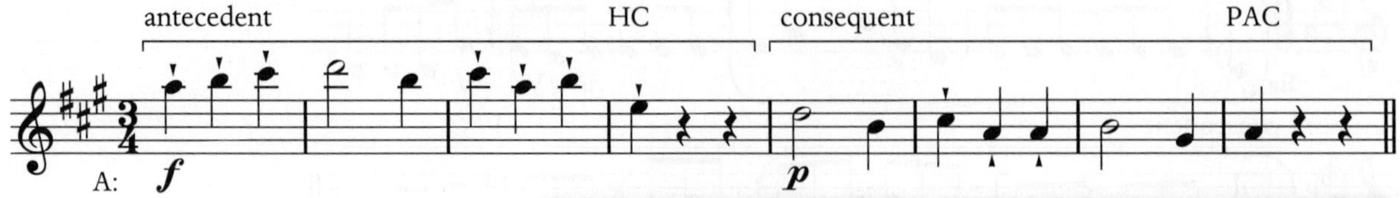

In a *contrasting period* the consequent does *not* begin like the antecedent.

PAIRED PHRASES THAT ARE NOT PERIODS

Because of their cadential layouts, certain phrase pairs do not form periods. This is the case when the first phrase of a pair ends with a PAC, or the second phrase ends with an HC, or both. Such phrase pairs lack the question-answer arrangement of periods.

As with periods, the two phrases within such phrase pairs may begin either similarly or differently.

36.12 R. Schumann, "Soldatenmarsch" (Soldier's March) ➔

Though the two phrases begin similarly, this is *not* a parallel period, since the first phrase ends with a PAC (rather than an HC or IAC).

36.13 Mozart, Minuet, K. 2 ➔

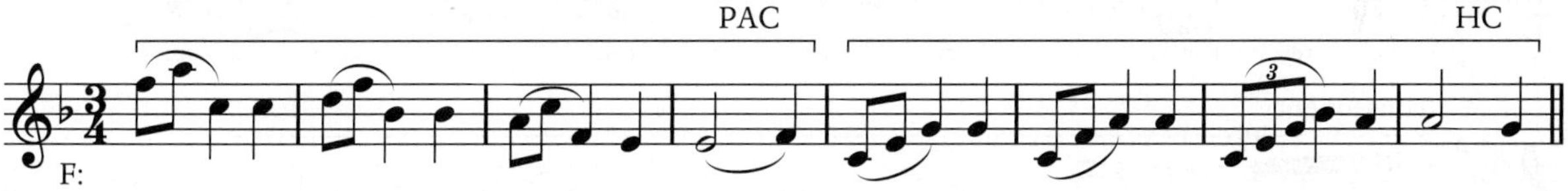

This phrase pair is *not* a period, since the first phrase ends with a PAC (rather than an HC or IAC) and the second phrase with an HC (rather than a PAC).

PHRASES WITHIN PHRASE PAIRS

SENTENCES WITHIN PERIODS AND OTHER PHRASE PAIRS

Within a period (or any phrase pair), each of the two phrases may be a sentence.

36.14 Schubert, Minuet in F Major, D. 41, no. 1 ➔

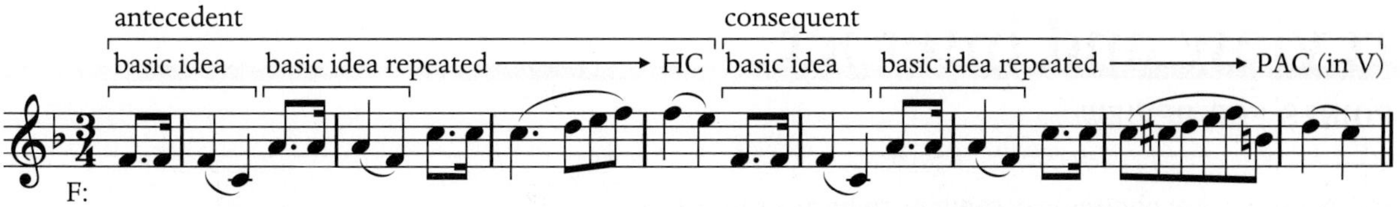

Both the antecedent and consequent of this parallel period are four-measure sentences.

RELATIVE LENGTH OF PHRASES

Typically, the two phrases within a period (or any phrase pair) are the same length as one another, around four or eight measures each. However, it is also possible for one or both of the phrases to be expanded or compressed, in which case one of the phrases (usually the second one) might be longer than the other.

36.15 Mozart, "Là ci darem la mano" (There we will give each other our hands), from *Don Giovanni*

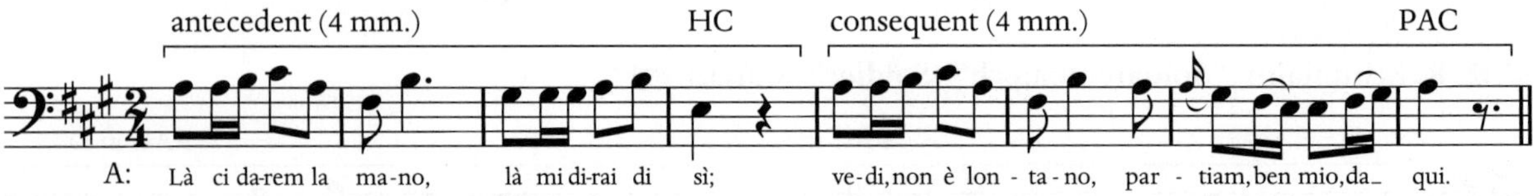

The antecedent and consequent phrases are the same length.

Translation: There we will give each other our hands, there you'll say yes to me; see, it's not far from here, let's go, my dear.

Because of the evaded cadence and subsequent expansion, the consequent is two measures longer than the antecedent.

Translation: I'd like to, and I wouldn't, my heart trembles a little at the thought. True, I could be happy, but he could trick me again!

For more on periods and other phrase pairs, see A Closer Look.

review and interact

POINTS FOR REVIEW

- **Two successive phrases may combine to form a *phrase pair*.**
- **A *period* is a phrase pair in which the first phrase ends with an HC or IAC, and the second phrase ends with a PAC (either in the original key or in a new key).**

- **The first phrase of a period is the *antecedent*, the second phrase the *consequent*.**
  - In a *parallel period*, the antecedent and consequent begin with same notes (or nearly the same notes).
  - In a *sequential period*, the melody at the start of the antecedent is transposed at the start of the consequent, with different harmonies.
  - In a *contrasting period*, the antecedent and consequent begin much differently from each other.
- **Phrase pairs with other cadential layouts—and which thus do not form periods—are also possible.**
- **Each phrase within a period or other phrase pair may be a *sentence*.**

TEST YOURSELF

For each of the following phrase pairs, consider the cadences and identify which are periods and which are not, and why. Which periods are parallel? Sequential? Contrasting? In which is there an expansion?

1.

2.

3.

4.

5.

6.

7.

Know It? Show It!

Focus by working through the tutorial on:

- Periods

Learn with inQuizitive.

Apply what you've learned to complete the assignments:

- Composition
- Analysis

chapter

37 Binary Form

Binary form is a two-part form governed by certain standard tonal and thematic structures.

BINARY FORM

In **binary form** an entire movement is divided into two parts, each of which is usually repeated. Each part of a binary form consists of one or more phrases and ends with a cadence. The first part may end conclusively with an authentic cadence in the main key. Usually, however, it is harmonically open-ended, closing with either a half cadence in the main key or an authentic cadence in another key (most often, the key of V or—in minor-key pieces—the relative major). The second part of a binary form almost always ends with a perfect authentic cadence in the main key.

37.1
BINARY FORM

𝄆 FIRST PART 𝄇	𝄆 SECOND PART 𝄇
Ends with a PAC in the new key, or HC in the main key, or PAC (or IAC) in the main key.	Ends with a PAC in the main key.

BEGINNING EACH PART

The two parts of binary form often begin differently. The first part typically opens in a relatively stable way, embellishing the tonic harmony. The second part, on the other hand, usually begins in an unstable fashion. For instance, the second part might start with a sustained dominant harmony, with a sequence, or with a series of tonicizations, possibly (in longer binary forms) leading to a modulation and cadence in a new key.

37.2 Haydn, String Quartet, op. 33, no. 3, II

The first part begins stably, embellishing the tonic with a simple progression . . .

The end of the first part is harmonically open-ended, with a PAC in V . . .

. . . while the second part begins less stably by sustaining the dominant.

. . . while the second part ends conclusively, with a PAC in I.

37.3 F. Couperin, "Les Brinborions"

The opening of the first part embellishes tonic, while the second part begins with a sequence.

The end of the first part is harmonically open-ended, with an HC in I . . .

. . . while the second part ends conclusively, with a PAC in I.

37.4 Auber, Allegretto

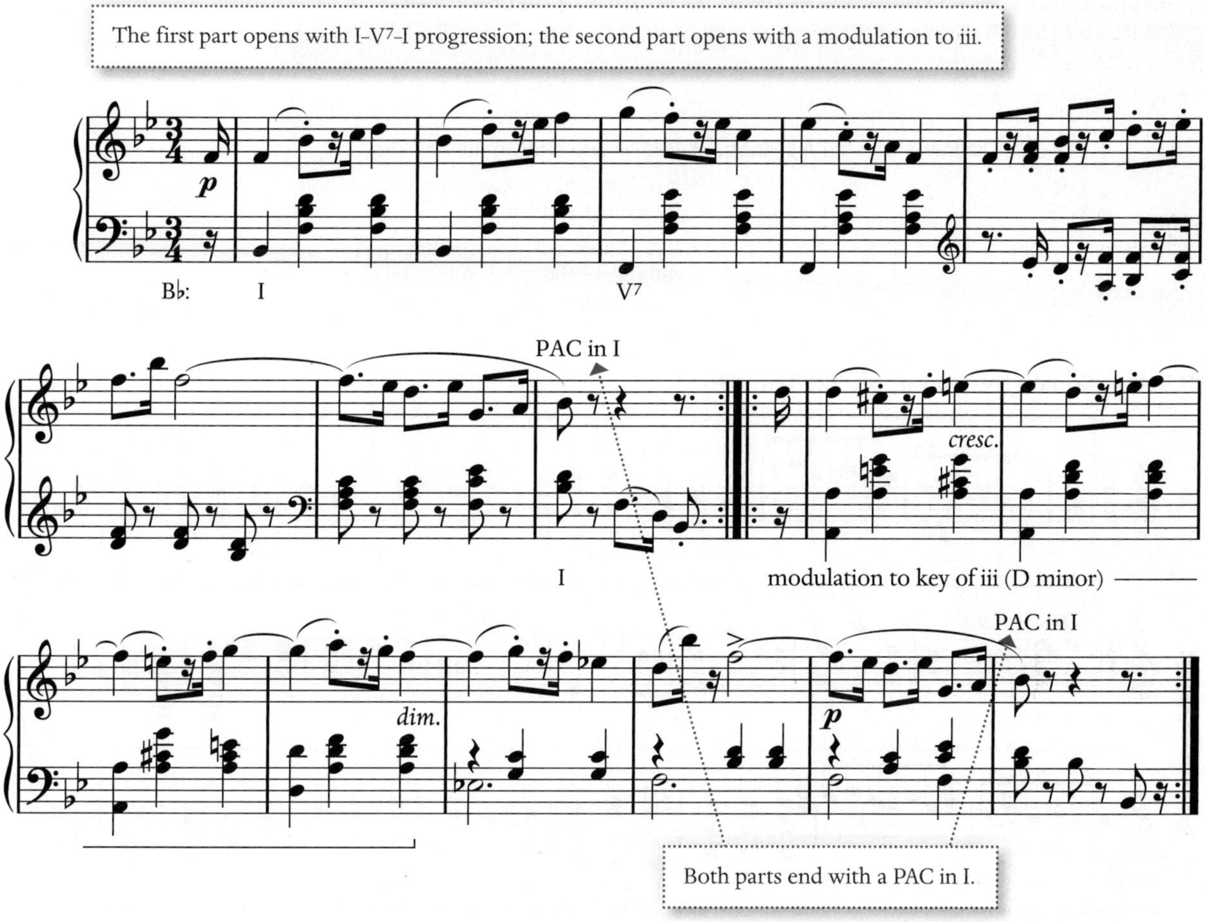

ROUNDED BINARY FORM

Sometimes the opening from the first part of a binary form returns in the original key in the middle of the second part, forming a **rounded binary form**. To be classified as rounded binary, the opening measures from the first part must be repeated either exactly or varied only slightly, so that there is a clear sense of a return. In some cases the entire opening part returns within the second part; at other times only the start of the opening part returns. In every rounded binary, however, the return of the opening must be in the original key.

Letters often are used to designate formal sections; thus rounded binary is labeled **𝄆 A 𝄇 B A 𝄇** or **𝄆 A 𝄇 B A′ 𝄇**. The section designated as **B** contrasts with the opening section, which is labeled as **A**. The repetition of a letter (in this case, **A**) specifies a repetition of that earlier section; a prime mark (′) indicates that the repetition is varied.

37.5

ROUNDED BINARY FORM (OPENING RETURNS IN MIDDLE OF SECOND PART)

FIRST PART	SECOND PART	
𝄆 A 𝄇	𝄆 B	A (or A′) 𝄇
	Contrasts with the **A** section.	• Begins and ends in the main key. • If **A**: The entire **A** section returns exactly (or almost exactly). • If **A′**: Either only the opening of **A** returns, or the entire **A** returns in a much varied form.

37.6 Sor, Sonata for Guitar, op. 22, Trio ➔

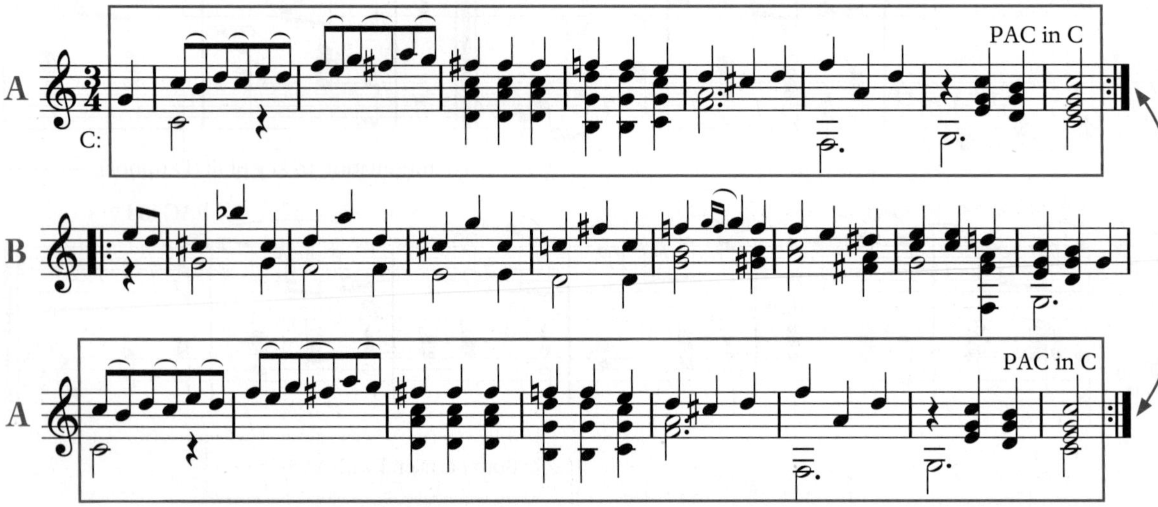

The *entire* first section returns in the tonic key at the end of the second part; this is *rounded binary* (𝄆 **A** 𝄇𝄆 **B A** 𝄇).

37.7 Schubert, Minuet in F ➔

The **A** section is eight measures long and ends in C major; **A′** is shorter (only four measures) and ends in F major . . .

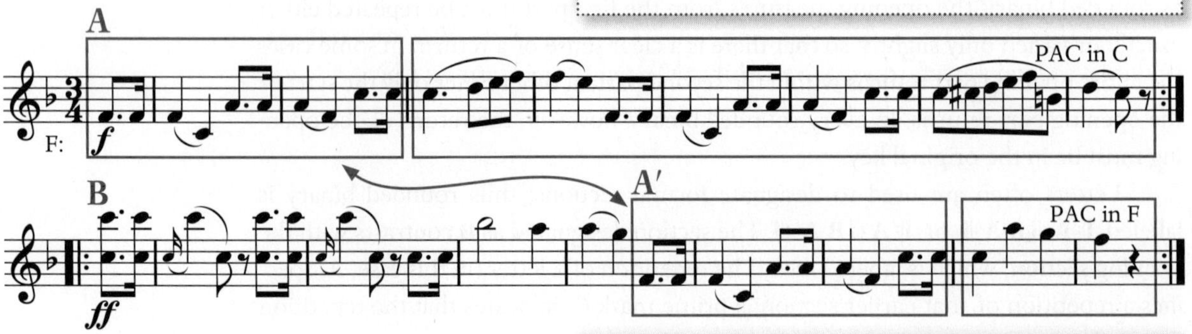

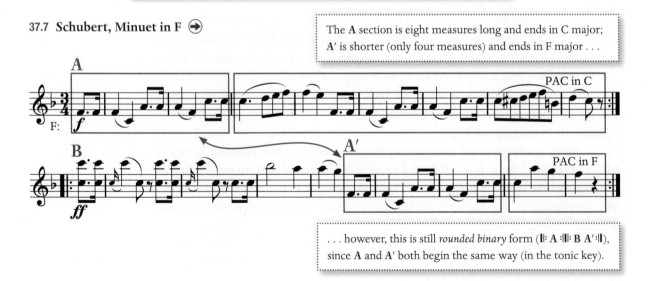

. . . however, this is still *rounded binary* form (𝄆 **A** 𝄇𝄆 **B A′** 𝄇), since **A** and **A′** both begin the same way (in the tonic key).

BALANCED BINARY FORM

In a **balanced binary form**, only the *ending* of the first part (*not* its beginning) returns in the main key at the end of the second part. Almost always, the first part finishes with a segment that leads to a PAC in a new key (such as V or the relative major). This concluding segment then returns transposed to the main key at the end of the second part, where it now leads to a PAC in I.

37.8

BALANCED BINARY FORM (ENDING OF FIRST PART RETURNS AT END OF SECOND PART)

FIRST PART	SECOND PART
𝄆 A 𝄇	𝄆 B 𝄇
First part ends with a PAC in the new key.	The ending segment of the first part returns, transposed to the main key, now leading to a PAC in the main key.

37.9 Mozart, Minuet, K. 1f

The opening of the first part doesn't return in the main key in the second part, so this is not rounded binary form . . .

. . . but the ending of the first part *does* return—now transposed to the main key—to end the second part, thus this is balanced binary form.

SIMPLE BINARY FORM

In many other cases, neither the opening nor the closing of the first part returns within the second part, forming **simple binary form**. Put differently: a binary form that is neither rounded nor balanced is classified as simple binary.

37.10

SIMPLE BINARY FORM (NEITHER ROUNDED NOR BALANCED)

FIRST PART	SECOND PART
𝄆 A 𝄇	𝄆 B 𝄇
	Although the second part is related to the first part, neither the opening nor the ending of the first part returns in the second part.

37.11 Paganini, Caprice no. 24 for Solo Violin

Neither the opening nor the ending of the first part returns in the second part . . .

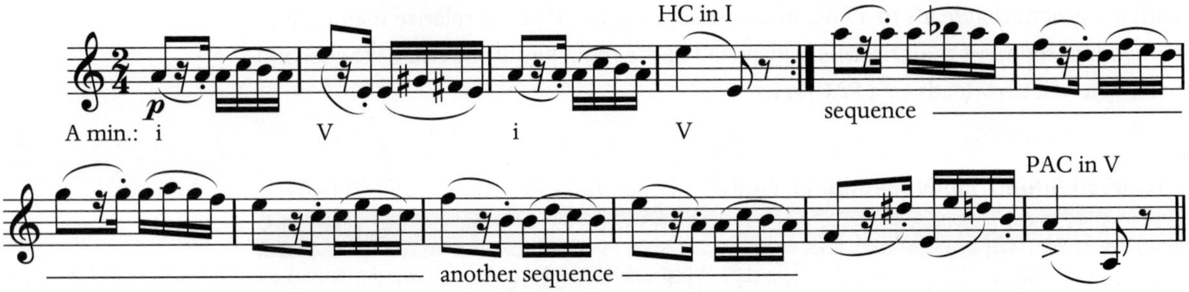

. . . thus, since this is neither rounded nor balanced, it is simple binary form.

RELATIVE LENGTHS OF SECTIONS

In many binary-form pieces, both parts are about the same length.

37.12 Dvořák, Minuet, op. 28, no. 2, III

The two parts of this binary form are each eight measures long.

More often than not, however, the second part of a binary form is considerably longer than the first part, often twice as long or even longer.

37.13 R. Schumann, "Valse Allemande," from *Carnaval*, op. 9

In this binary-form movement, the second part is twice as long as the first.

For more on binary form, see A Closer Look.

review and interact

POINTS FOR REVIEW

- **Binary form is divided into two parts; usually both parts are repeated.**
- **The first part usually ends with an authentic cadence in the tonic key, a half cadence in the tonic key, or a perfect authentic cadence in another key. The second part usually ends with a perfect authentic cadence in the tonic key.**
- **The first part typically begins with an embellishment of the tonic, and the second part typically begins in a relatively unstable harmonic fashion.**
- **In a *rounded binary form*, the opening of the first part returns in the tonic key in the middle of the second part.**
- **In a *balanced binary form*, the ending of the first part returns (transposed to the tonic key) at the end of the second part (but the opening of the first part does not return in the tonic key).**
- **A *simple binary form* is one in which neither the opening nor the ending of the first part returns in the middle of the second part.**
- **The second part of a binary form may be about the same length as the first part, or it may be considerably longer than the first part.**

TEST YOURSELF

1. Are the following statements true or false?
   a. In a rounded binary form, material from the opening measures must return (either exactly or slightly varied) in the tonic key.
   b. In every case, if the last measures of both parts of a binary form are similar, the form will be classified as balanced binary form.
   c. In a simple binary form, the two parts have little in common.
   d. In a binary form usually both parts are repeated.
2. Would you classify each of the following as a rounded, balanced, or simple binary form?

a.

b.

c.

Know It? Show It!

Focus by working through the tutorials on:

- Rounded binary form
- Balanced binary form
- Simple binary form

Learn with inQuizitive.

Apply what you've learned to complete the assignments:

- Composition
- Analysis

chapter

38 Ternary and Rondo Forms

In ternary and rondo forms, a main section recurs one or more times in the tonic key, alternating with one or more contrasting sections.

TERNARY FORM

Ternary form involves three sections in which the first and last sections are similar to one another, with a contrasting section sandwiched in the middle. The resulting form could be described either as **ABA** or **ABA′** (depending on whether the opening section is varied when it returns), with the **B** often taking the form of a departure or digression. A three-part composition in which the main section is not restated at the end (**ABC** format) lacks this sense of departure and return and thus is *not* in ternary form.

KEYS AND CADENCES

In a ternary form, both the **A** and **B** sections usually consist of multiple phrases. The two **A** sections usually begin and end in the tonic key (though the first **A** section may modulate to another key, so that it begins and ends in different keys). Furthermore, both **A** sections typically conclude with a perfect authentic cadence. The **B** section is often either in a different key or in the parallel major or minor. The **B** section usually starts and ends in the same key, and it may conclude with either a perfect authentic cadence or a half cadence. Sometimes a short passage known as a **bridge** leads from the end of the **B** section to the second **A** section.

38.1

TERNARY FORM

A *main section*	**B** *contrasting section*	**A (or A′)** *return of main section*
• Usually multiple phrases. • Starts in the tonic key. • Ends with a PAC, usually in the tonic key.	• Contrasting section. • Often in a new key or in the parallel major or minor key. • Usually starts and ends in the same key. • Ends with a PAC or HC. • A short bridge may lead to the return of **A**.	• Can be varied. • Starts and ends in the tonic key. • Ends with a PAC.

38.2 R. Schumann, "Volksliedchen" (Folk Song)

Ternary form: This opens with a main section (**A**), ending with a PAC in the main (tonic) key (D minor) . . .

. . . followed by a middle section (**B**) in the parallel major (D major) that contrasts with the main section, concluding with a half cadence . . .

. . . and then the main section (in D minor) returns at the end, slightly varied (**A′**).

TERNARY FORM VERSUS ROUNDED BINARY FORM

Although ternary form is similar to rounded binary form, in many cases these two forms can be distinguished from each other. Most notably, the parts of rounded binary form are almost always repeated, and the repeats divide the form into two sections, 𝄆 **A** 𝄇𝄆 **B A** 𝄇. Conversely, whereas there might be repetitions *within* the **A** or **B** section of a ternary form, the **B** and second **A** section are *not* repeated together. Furthermore, the **A** and **B** sections tend to be more self-contained and independent of each other in ternary form than in rounded binary, and more likely to be separated by a strong cadence. Also, the second **A** section is more likely to be the same length as or longer than the first **A** in ternary form than it is in rounded binary form.

38.3

TERNARY VERSUS ROUNDED BINARY FORM

TERNARY FORM	ROUNDED BINARY FORM
ABA or **ABA′**	**‖: A :‖: B A :‖** or **‖: A :‖: B A′ :‖**
• Though there might be repeats *within* **A** or **B**, these sections are *not* repeated together.	• Repeats divide the form into two parts.
• The **A** section and **B** section each typically start and end in the same key, and **A** typically ends with a PAC.	• The first **A** section and the **B** section each often start and end in different keys; the first **A** section may end with a HC.
• The **B** section may end with a PAC.	• The **B** section rarely ends with a PAC.
• Second **A** section is often the same length or even longer than the first **A** section.	• Second **A** section may be the same length or considerably shorter than the first **A**.

COMPOUND TERNARY FORM

In many ternary-form movements, the **A** and **B** sections are themselves in binary or ternary form. This creates what is known as **compound ternary form**. Minuet-and-trio movements are typically in compound ternary form.

38.4 Mozart, Symphony no. 9, K. 73, III

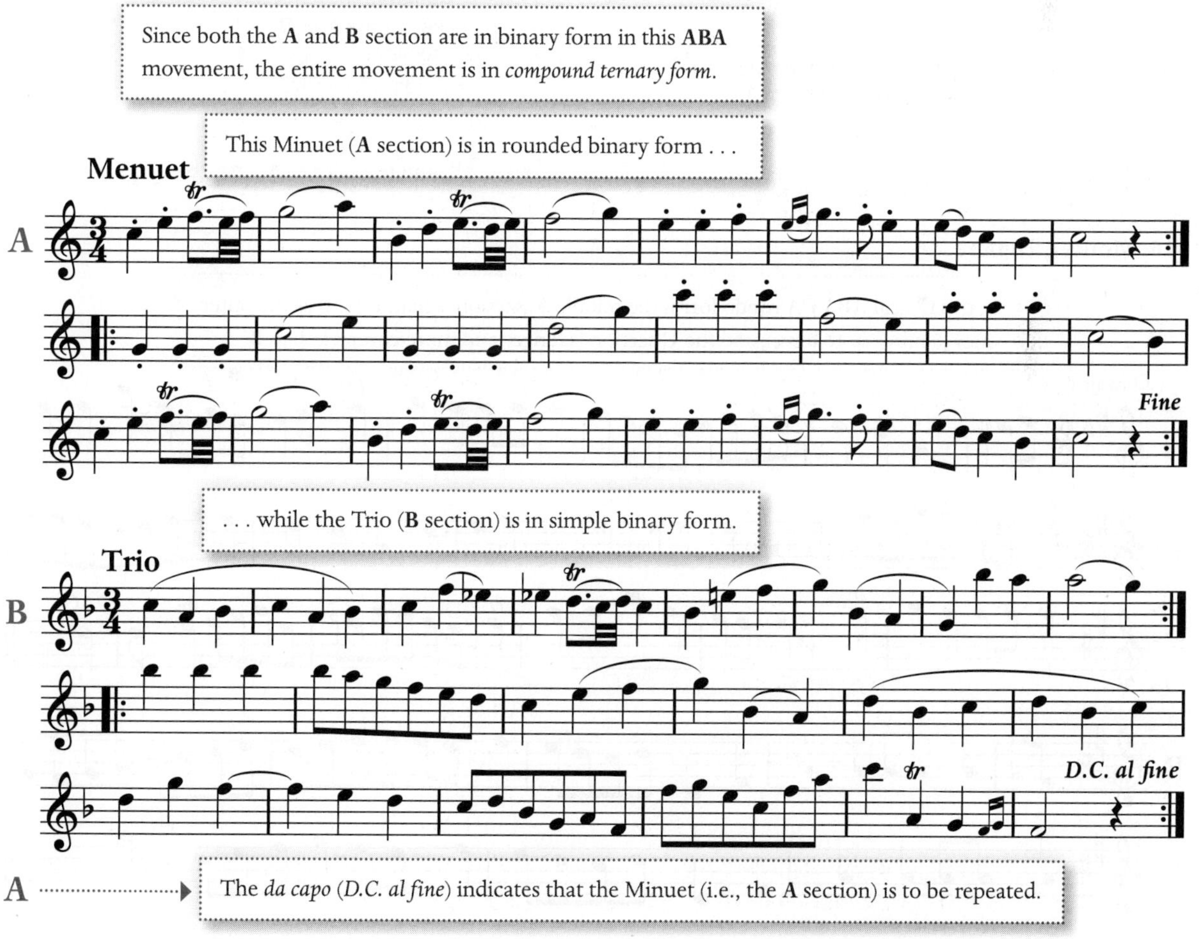
Since both the A and B section are in binary form in this ABA movement, the entire movement is in *compound ternary form*.
This Minuet (A section) is in rounded binary form . . .
Menuet
A
Fine
. . . while the Trio (B section) is in simple binary form.
Trio
B
D.C. al fine
A
The *da capo* (*D.C. al fine*) indicates that the Minuet (i.e., the A section) is to be repeated.

RONDO FORM

In **rondo form**, the initial **A** section returns (either unchanged or slightly varied) two or more times in the tonic key throughout a movement, alternating with two or more contrasting sections. The **A** sections each end with a perfect authentic cadence in the tonic key; the **B** and **C** sections (the contrasting sections) end either with a half cadence in the tonic key, or else with a perfect authentic cadence in a non-tonic key followed by a short bridge that leads back to the tonic key. Usually the **B** section is a bit simpler than the **C** section, which tends to be less stable, longer, and more complex. A common type of rondo form, **ABACA**, is known as a **five-part rondo**.

38.5
FIVE-PART RONDO

A *main section*	**B** *contrasting section*	**A (or A′)** *return of main section*	**C** *another contrasting section*	**A** *main section*
• Starts and ends (with PAC) in the tonic key.	• Relatively simple contrasting section. • May be in a closely related key. • Ends with a PAC or HC. • A short bridge may lead to return of **A**.	• Starts and ends (with PAC) in the tonic key. • May be shorter than first **A**.	• Usually longer and more complex than **B** section. • Usually in a closely related key that is different from the key of the **A** or **B** section. • Ends with a PAC or HC. • A short bridge may lead to return of **A**.	• Starts and ends (with PAC) in the tonic key.

38.6 Mouret, *Fanfare*

In this typical **ABA′CA** rondo form, the middle **A′** section is half as long as the outer ones (8 mm. vs. 16 mm.), and the **C** section is longer and more complex than **B**.

Other types of rondo forms may involve more alternations between the main section in the tonic key and contrasting sections.

38.7

SOME OTHER POSSIBLE SCHEMES FOR MOVEMENTS IN RONDO FORM

ABACAB′A	ABACB′A	ABAB′A	ABACADA . . . (etc.)
Seven-part rondo form: The first **B** section is in a related key (such as V or the relative major) and the second **B** section is in the tonic key. (This is sometimes called *sonata rondo*; see Chapter 39.)	Variant of seven-part rondo.	Variant of five-part rondo.	Sometimes found in French Baroque movements; ends with return of **A** in the tonic key.

For additional forms, see A Closer Look.

review and interact

POINTS FOR REVIEW

- **In ternary form, a contrasting section appears between statements of a main section: ABA (or ABA′).**
- **Both A sections of ternary form usually start and end in the tonic key (though sometimes the first A section modulates to another key). Both conclude with a PAC, and they are often around the same length.**
- **The B section of a ternary form is usually either in a non-tonic key or in the parallel major or minor. It often starts and ends in the same key.**
- **In compound ternary form, the A and B sections are themselves in either binary or ternary form**
- **In rondo form, a main section in the tonic key alternates with two or more contrasting sections; some schemes include ABACA, ABACAB′A, and ABACADA.**

TEST YOURSELF

1. Which of the following are examples of ternary form?
   a. ABA b. ABA′ c. ABC
2. In an **ABA′** ternary form, which of the sections are almost always in the tonic key?
3. In an **ABA′** ternary form, which sections usually end with a PAC?
4. In which key to the **A** sections of a rondo form usually appear: in the tonic key, the dominant key, another key, or in any of these keys?
5. What type of cadence usually appears at the end of the **A** sections of a rondo?
6. In an **ABACA** rondo, which is usually longer: the **B** section, **C** section, or are they usually around the same length?

Know It? Show It!

Focus by working through the tutorials on:
- Ternary form
- Rondo forms

Learn with inQuizitive.

Apply what you've learned to complete the assignments:
- Composition
- Analysis

chapter 39 Sonata Form

Sonata form—consisting of an exposition, a development, and a recapitulation—organizes many instrumental works.

ELEMENTS OF SONATA FORM

Many instrumental works from the second half of the eighteenth century through the nineteenth century (including symphonies, chamber works, and sonatas) are in **sonata form**. Sonata form resembles a large rounded binary form. The opening part, which is usually repeated, consists of the **exposition**. The exposition starts in the tonic key and modulates to a secondary key (a key other than the tonic). The second part of a sonata form movement—which may be repeated as well—consists of two sections, each of which is about as long and substantial as the exposition. The first of these sections is the **development**, which tonicizes various keys before returning to the tonic key. The last section is the **recapitulation**, which starts and ends in the tonic key.

39.1
SONATA FORM

FIRST PART *(usually repeated)*	**SECOND PART** *(often repeated in works composed before 1800)*	
𝄆 **Exposition** 𝄇	𝄆 **Development**	**Recapitulation** 𝄇
(like **A** of rounded binary) begins in the tonic key, ends in a secondary key	(like **B** of rounded binary) tonicizes various keys and ends by returning to the tonic key	(like **A′** of rounded binary, about the same length as **A**)

These three main sections—exposition, development, and recapitulation—themselves are made up of smaller subsections. Although few individual works contain all the characteristic features associated with sonata form, those movements that contain at least most of these features may be regarded as being in sonata form.

EXPOSITION

A sonata form exposition usually consists of two halves. The first half of the exposition starts with a **primary theme** (also known as a *first theme* or *main theme*) that establishes the tonic key. This is followed by a **transition** that leads to a strong half cadence (HC). The second half of the exposition begins and ends in a secondary key. In major-key movements, the secondary key is usually V; in minor-key movements, the secondary key is usually III (the relative major). The opening section of the exposition's second half is the **secondary theme** (also known as the *second theme* or *subordinate theme*). Following a perfect authentic cadence (PAC) at the end of the secondary theme, a **closing section** wraps up the exposition.

39.2

FIRST HALF OF EXPOSITION *Begins in the tonic key; ends with an HC either in the tonic key or a new key*		**SECOND HALF OF EXPOSITION** *Begins and ends in a secondary key*	
primary theme	***transition*** →	***secondary theme***	***closing section***
ends with an HC or a PAC in the tonic key	starts in the tonic key, leads to a big HC	ends with a PAC in a secondary key	wraps up the exposition, ends with a PAC in a secondary key

PRIMARY THEME AND TRANSITION

The primary theme establishes the tonic key with one or more phrases and concludes with either an authentic cadence or a half cadence in this key. The transition that follows starts in the tonic key and leads to a half cadence. In some expositions, the half cadence at the end of the transition is in the tonic key. In most expositions, however (especially in the late eighteenth century and later), the transition modulates to end with a half cadence in the secondary key. The transition typically is more energetic and unstable than the primary theme, involving increased momentum leading to the half cadence at its conclusion.

39.3 Mozart, Piano Sonata no. 5 in G, K. 283, II (mm. 1–8)

primary theme relatively stable, starts and ends in tonic key

First half of exposition:

The *primary theme* (mm. 1–4) establishes the tonic key (C) . . .

transition starts in tonic key; energy builds to lead to HC

. . . the *transition* (mm. 5–8) creates momentum leading to an HC in V, the secondary key (G).

The primary theme and transition may begin similarly, though they always end differently. In many cases, there is a *phrase overlap* between these sections, in which the last chord of the primary theme is also the first chord of the transition. As a result, often there is no sharp break between the end of the primary theme and the start of the transition.

39.4 Mozart, Serenade in G ("Eine kleine Nachtmusik"), K. 525, I (mm. 15–20)

(end of) primary theme **transition**

Phrase overlap: The last chord of the primary theme is also the first chord of the transition.

END OF TRANSITION

The end of the transition is usually strongly demarcated. Typically, the transition ends with a **medial caesura**, a pause or break that marks the end of the exposition's first half and dramatically sets the stage for the secondary theme. The medial caesura may consist of a brief rest in all voices, a sudden thinning of the texture, or some other dramatic change that clearly separates the end of the transition from the start of the ensuing secondary theme.

39.5 Mozart, Serenade in G, K. 525, I (mm. 24–29)

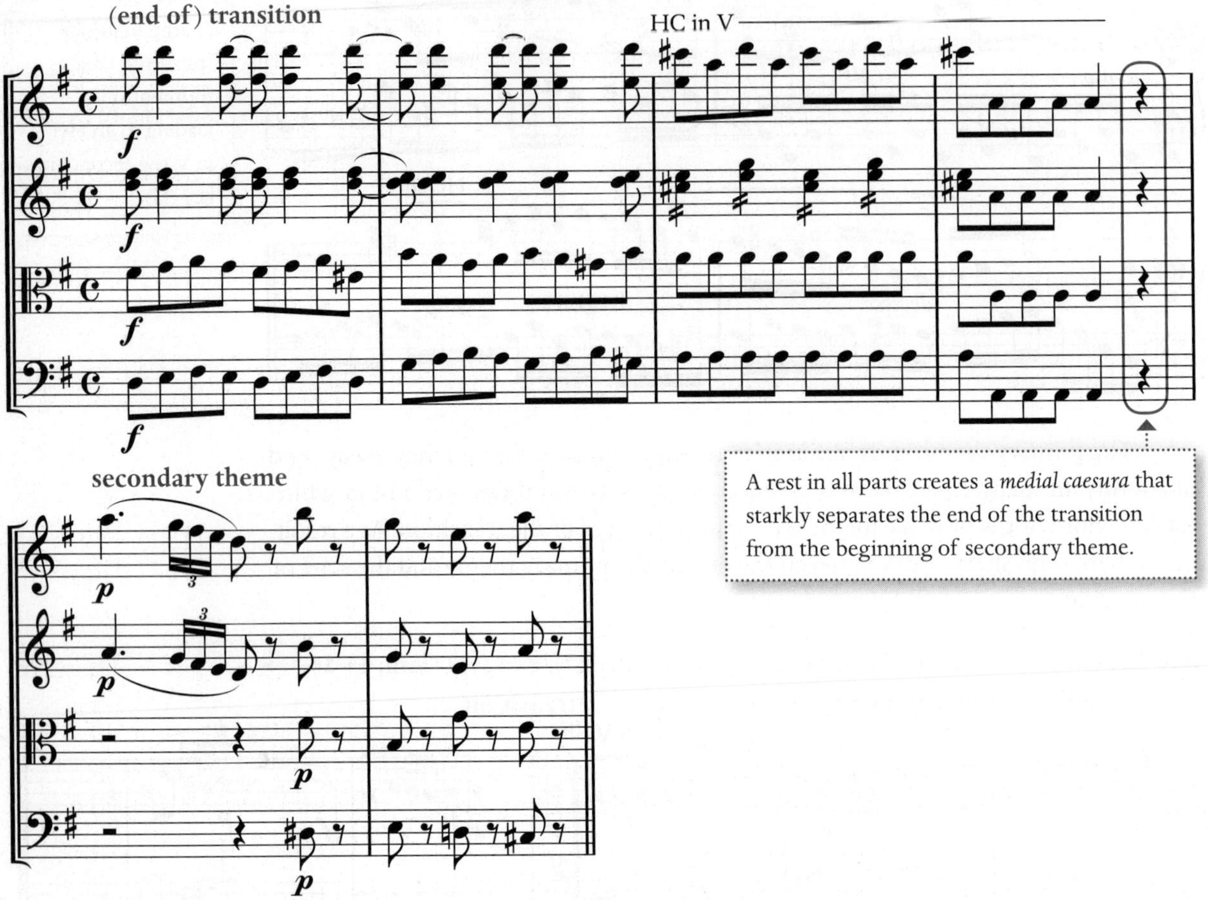

39.6 Beethoven, Piano Sonata in G Minor, op. 49, no. 1, I: Primary Theme and Transition (mm. 1–17)

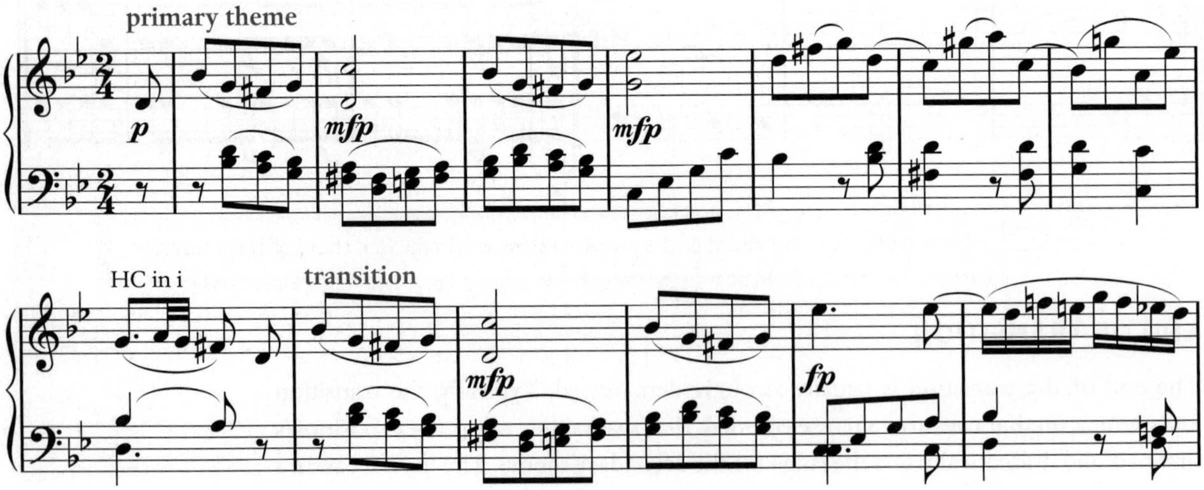

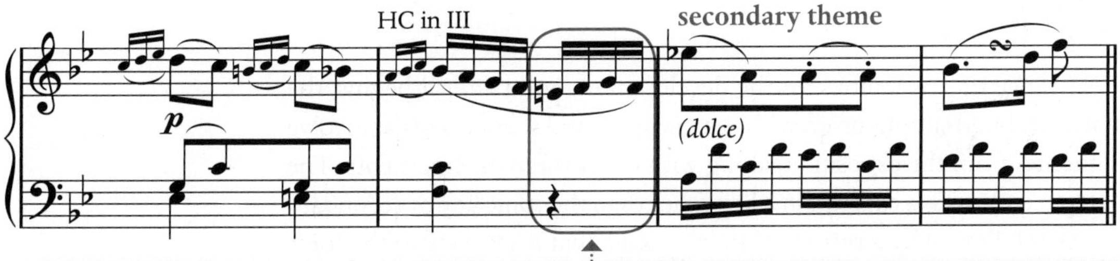
HC in III
secondary theme
p
(dolce)

A sudden rest in the bass creates a medial caesura that separates the end of the transition from the start of the secondary theme.

SECONDARY THEME AND CLOSING SECTION

The secondary theme immediately follows the medial caesura. The secondary theme may present completely new material, or it may be a variant of the primary theme. The secondary theme ends with a perfect authentic cadence in the secondary key. After this cadence, the closing section begins and confirms the conclusion of the exposition with one or more perfect authentic cadences in the secondary key.

39.7 Haydn, Piano Sonata in C, Hob. XVI:10, I: Exposition (mm. 1–21)

This exposition starts in the tonic key and ends with a secondary theme and closing section in V.

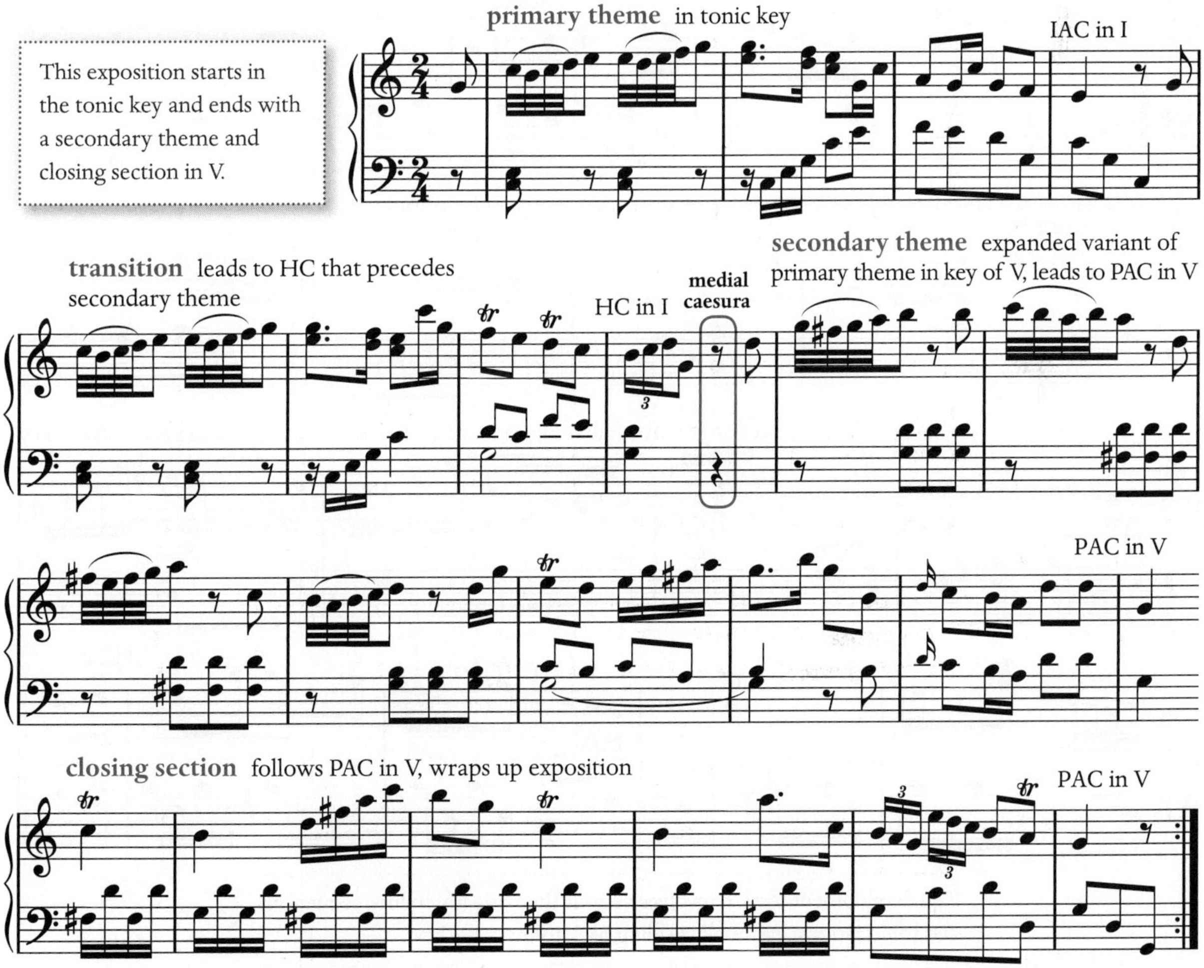
primary theme in tonic key
IAC in I
transition leads to HC that precedes secondary theme
HC in I
medial caesura
secondary theme expanded variant of primary theme in key of V, leads to PAC in V
PAC in V
closing section follows PAC in V, wraps up exposition
PAC in V

DEVELOPMENT

There is a wider range of possibilities for the development. Soon after it begins, the development usually builds momentum with tonicizations and sequences that involve fragments of themes from the exposition, along with other thematic fragments. The development often ends with a cadence in a key other than the tonic key or secondary key. This cadence is followed by a **retransition**, a passage that leads back to the tonic key. Alternately, the development section may end with a dramatic half cadence in the tonic key that prepares for the upcoming recapitulation.

39.8

Development begins stably . . .	. . . it then continues with fragments and variants of themes, using sequences and tonicizations . . .	. . . and ends with either: • PAC in a new key, followed by a retransition leading to the recapitulation, or • a big HC in the tonic key

39.9 Haydn, Piano Sonata in C, Hob. XVI:10, I: Development (mm. 22–38) ➔

development section begins stably, with main theme in key of G (V)
IAC in G
activity increases with sequences, fragments of primary theme, and motion to relative minor
HC in A min.
retransition following cadence in A minor, sequence lead back to tonic key
tr
HC in C
3

The development section involves various thematic fragments, sequences, and tonicizations, eventually leading back to the tonic key.

RECAPITULATION

The recapitulation mostly repeats the music from the exposition, except that the recapitulation both starts *and* ends in the tonic key, with the secondary theme and closing section now transposed to the tonic. The transition is the only section that is usually greatly altered when it reappears in the recapitulation. This is especially so when the transition of the exposition ends with a half cadence in the secondary key: in such a case, the transition must be changed in the recapitulation so as to end with a half cadence in the tonic key.

39.10

FIRST HALF OF RECAPITULATION *Begins and ends in the tonic key*		**SECOND HALF OF RECAPITULATION** *Begins and ends in the tonic key (often a transposition of the second half of the exposition)*	
primary theme	***transition*** →	***secondary theme***	***closing section***
often the same or similar to the primary theme of the exposition	starts and ends in the tonic key; often differs greatly from the transition of the exposition	ends with a PAC in the tonic key	ends with a PAC in the tonic key

39.11 **Haydn, Piano Sonata in C, Hob. XVI:10, I: Recapitulation (mm. 39–59)**

The recapitulation is much like the exposition, except that it begins and ends in the tonic key.

closing section like the closing section of the exposition, but transposed to the tonic key

INTRODUCTION AND CODA

Some sonata form movements open with an **introduction**. The introduction is in a slower tempo than the rest of the movement, and unlike the exposition, it is not repeated. Sonata form movements may also include a **coda**, a concluding section that follows the closing section of the recapitulation. In movements where the development and recapitulation are repeated, the coda is not included within the repeat.

39.12

Introduction	𝄆 Exposition 𝄇	𝄆 Development/Recapitulation 𝄇	Coda
Optional, slower than the rest of the movement, *not* repeated; ends with an HC in the tonic key			Optional, in the tonic key; follows the end of the recapitulation; *not* repeated

SONATA RONDO

The seven-part **ABACABA** rondo is often referred to as a **sonata rondo**. This is especially so if the first **A** and **B** sections are structured like a sonata form exposition, the middle **C** section resembles a sonata form development section, and the following **A** and **B** sections are structured like a recapitulation. Sonata rondos are particularly common in fast final movements of multi-movement works.

39.13

SONATA RONDO

A	B	A′	C	A″	B	A‴
Starts in the tonic key, ends with an HC (like a primary theme + transition)	In a secondary key (like a secondary theme + closing section)	In the tonic key	In a new key, or tonicizes various keys (like a development)	Starts in the tonic key, ends with an HC	In the tonic key (like a secondary theme + closing section)	In the tonic key
Exposition			**Development**	**Recapitulation**		

review and interact

POINTS FOR REVIEW

- Sonata form movements are made up of two large parts: the first part includes just the *exposition* (which is usually repeated); the second part includes the *development* and *recapitulation* (this second part may also be repeated).
- The exposition includes (1) a *primary theme* in the tonic key; (2) a *transition* that ends with an HC in either the tonic key or a new key, followed by a break known as a *medial caesura*; then (3) a *secondary theme* that begins and ends (with a PAC) in the new key, which is usually followed by (4) a *closing section* in the new key.
- The recapitulation revisits the material of the exposition, with the secondary theme and closing section now transposed to the tonic key. In many cases, the material of the transition is significantly revised for the recapitulation so as to end with a half cadence in the tonic key.

EXPOSITION
Starts in the tonic key, ends in a secondary key, usually repeated

1. **Primary theme**: starts and ends in the tonic key; ends with a PAC, IAC, or HC
2. **Transition**: might modulate, ends with an HC in the tonic key or an HC in a secondary key
3. **Secondary theme**: in a secondary key, ends with a PAC
4. **Closing section**: in a secondary key, wraps up the exposition, ends with a PAC

DEVELOPMENT
Tonicizes various keys, ends by returning to the tonic key, sometimes repeated together with the recapitulation

RECAPITULATION
Starts and ends in the tonic key

1. **Primary theme**: like the primary theme of the exposition
2. **Transition**: often a much-revised version of the transition from the exposition, ends with an HC in the tonic key
3. **Secondary theme**: in the tonic key, ends with a PAC
4. **Closing section**: in the tonic key, wraps up the recapitulation, ends with a PAC

- Some sonata form movements also include a slow introduction at the beginning of the movement, and a coda following the recapitulation; neither the introduction nor the coda is repeated.
- A sonata rondo is a seven-part rondo in which the opening sections are structured like a sonata form exposition, the middle section is like a development, and the sections toward the end are structured like a recapitulation.

TEST YOURSELF

1. In what order do the following appear?
   coda, development, exposition, introduction, recapitulation
2. In what key is the primary theme presented in the exposition: the tonic key or the secondary key? In what key does it appear in the recapitulation?
3. In what key does the secondary theme appear in the exposition? In what key does it appear in the recapitulation?
4. In what order do the following appear within both the exposition and recapitulation?
   closing section, primary theme, secondary theme, transition
5. The medial caesura appears at the end of the __________ and precedes the __________.
6. In the exposition, what types of cadence may appear at the end of the closing section, and in what key (tonic or secondary)? At the end of the primary theme? At the end of the secondary theme? At the end of the transition?

Know It? Show It!

Focus by working through the tutorials on:

- Sonata form: Exposition
- Sonata form: Development
- Sonata form: Recapitulation and coda

Learn with inQuizitive.

Apply what you've learned to complete the assignments:

- Composition
- Analysis

Test Yourself Answers

CHAPTER 0. NOTATION OF PITCH AND RHYTHM

1.

F F♯ E B A♭ E B C G♯ C D G C E♭

D♭ D C G F♭ C G G♯ E A♭ B♭ D♯ A C

A♭ A G D C♭ G D D♯ B E♭ F A♯ E G

2.

3.

4.

CHAPTER 1. SCALES

1.

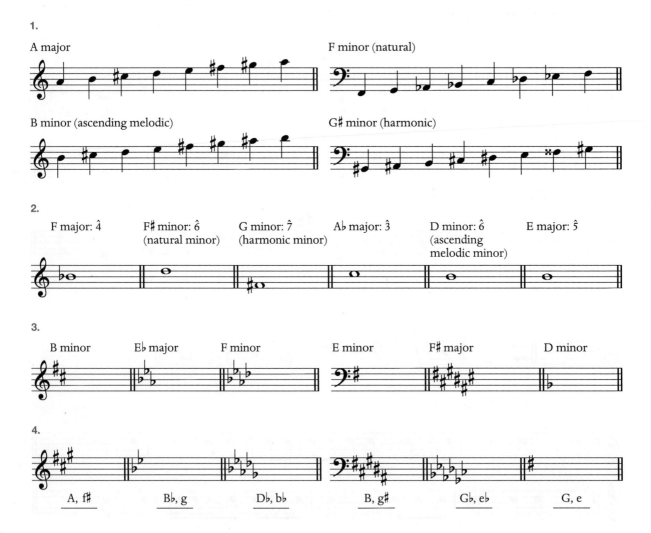

A major | F minor (natural)

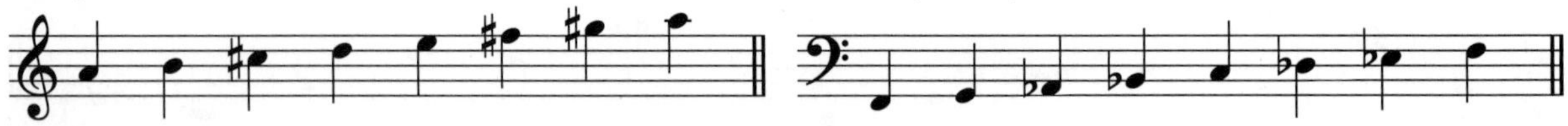

B minor (ascending melodic) | G♯ minor (harmonic)

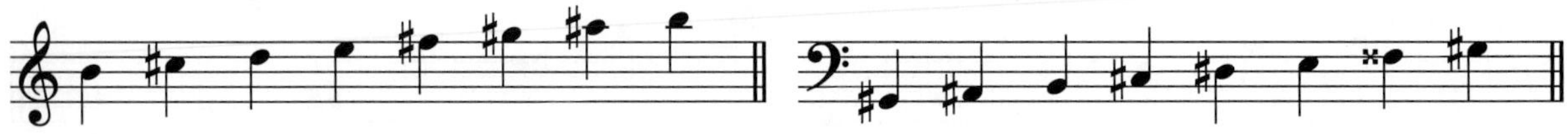

2.

F major: $\hat{4}$ | F♯ minor: $\hat{6}$ (natural minor) | G minor: $\hat{7}$ (harmonic minor) | A♭ major: $\hat{3}$ | D minor: $\hat{6}$ (ascending melodic minor) | E major: $\hat{5}$

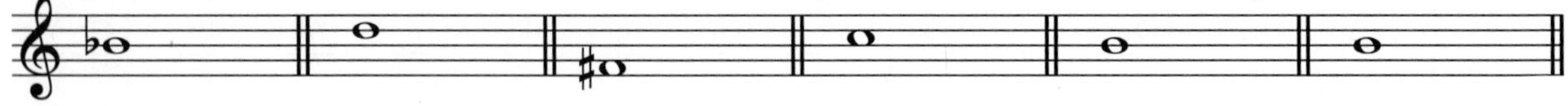

3.

B minor | E♭ major | F minor | E minor | F♯ major | D minor

4.

A, f♯ | B♭, g | D♭, b♭ | B, g♯ | G♭, e♭ | G, e

CHAPTER 2. INTERVALS

1.

2.

3. (**a**) F major: $\hat{2}$–$\hat{6}$: G–D = P5
   (**b**) B♭ major: $\hat{4}$–$\hat{7}$: E♭–A = A4
   (**c**) E major: $\hat{1}$–$\hat{6}$: E–C♯ = M6
   (**d**) D major: $\hat{3}$–$\hat{5}$: F♯–A = m3

4. (**a**) G♯ minor: $\hat{2}$–$\hat{6}$ (natural minor): A♯–E = d5
   (**b**) B♭ minor: $\hat{7}$–$\hat{6}$ (harmonic minor): A–G♭ = d7
   (**c**) D minor: $\hat{1}$–$\hat{5}$: D–A = P5
   (**d**) C♯ minor: $\hat{4}$–$\hat{7}$ (harmonic minor): F♯–B♯ = A4

5. (**a**) C♯–G = D major
   (**b**) D–A♭ = E♭ major
   (**c**) D–G♯ = A major
   (**d**) G–D♭ = A♭ major

6. (**a**) E♭–F♯ = G minor
   (**b**) B♭–C♯ = D minor
   (**c**) A♯–G = B minor
   (**d**) D♯–C = E minor

CHAPTER 3. TRIADS AND SEVENTH CHORDS

1.

2.

Ebm A° Bb+ G#m A

3.

C#ø7 F7 Emaj7 A°7 Gm7

4.

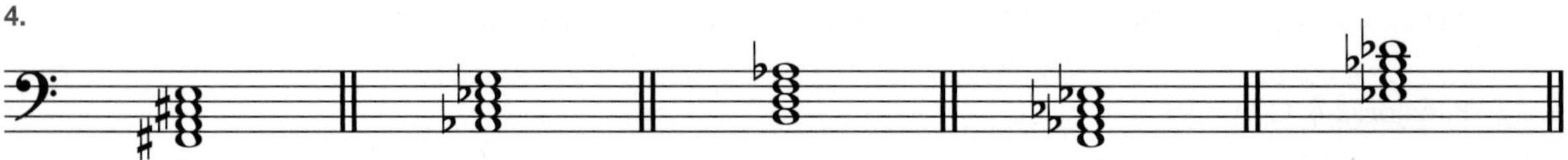

F#m7 Abmaj7 B°7 Fø7 Eb7

5.

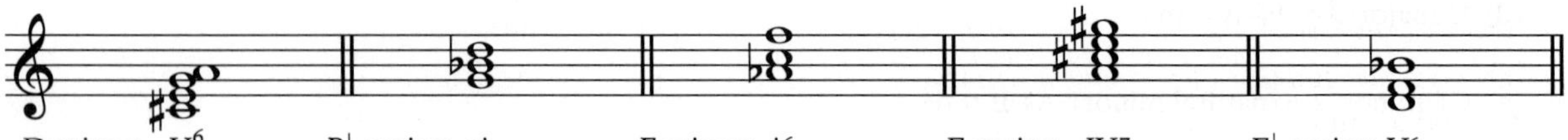

D minor: V^6_5 Bb major: vi F minor: i^6 E major: IV^7 Eb major: V^6

6.

C minor: $ii^{\circ 6}$ D major: V^7 Eb major: IV G minor: V^4_2 A major: I^6

CHAPTER 4. FOUR-PART HARMONY

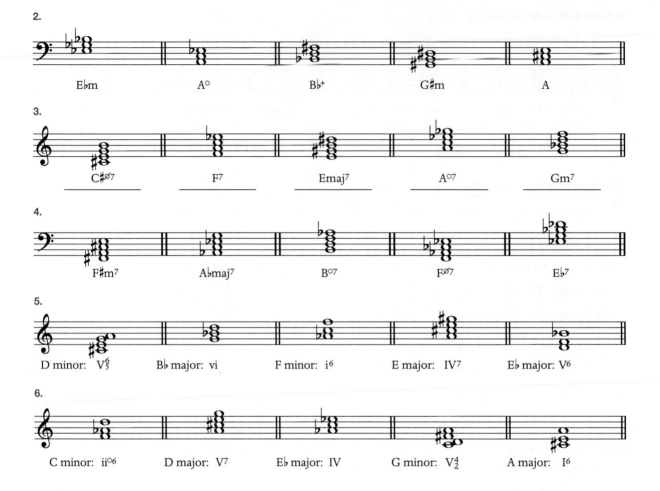

1. (**a**) Soprano. (**b**) Soprano and alto. Tenor and bass may be spaced more than an octave apart. (**c**) Bass: it should always be stemmed downwards in SATB format. (**d**) The root of the chord (Eb) is doubled. (**e**) IV^6_3 or IV^6 (first inversion)
2. (**b**) and (**d**).
3. (**c**). In (**a**) the leading tone should be raised; in (**b**) the third of the chord is omitted.

CHAPTER 5. VOICE LEADING

1. Excerpt (**b**), because the upper voices either repeat their notes, move stepwise, or use the melodic interval of a third. The one big leap of a melodic fourth in the soprano voice—in the beginning of the second measure—is a chord skip, occurring when the chord repeats. The big leaps in the bass voice are also normal. In excerpt (**a**) the upper voices use mostly large melodic leaps; particularly egregious is the leap of a melodic seventh.
2. (**a**) similar; (**b**) contrary; (**c**) stationary; (**d**) parallel; (**e**) oblique.

3. (**a**) and (**c**). In (**b**) the octave and fifth are approached in stationary motion; in (**d**) the octave between the tenor and soprano likewise is approached in stationary motion. In the upper voices of (**e**), the interval of a perfect fifth (F–C in the first chord and C–G in the second) appear between two different pairs of voices.

4. (**a**) F♯ is the leading tone; there is no chordal seventh. The leading tone must resolve up to G because it is in an outer voice (soprano). (**b**) C♯ is the leading tone. Because it is in an inner voice it does not need to resolve up by step. The chordal seventh is the G of the V^7 chord. The final note in the alto should be F♯, since a chordal seventh must resolve down by step.

5. (**b**), (**c**), and (**e**) contain faulty motion to perfect intervals. (**b**) The perfect fifth between soprano and alto on the third beat is arrived at by parallel motion. (**c**) The compound octave between the bass and soprano is arrived at by similar motion between outer voices, with the soprano arriving by leap. (**e**) The octave between alto and tenor is arrived at by similar motion from a dissonant interval (F–G).

   There are no voice-leading errors in (**a**) or (**d**). (**a**) The motion between the soprano and alto on the first two beats involves a perfect fifth (C–G) moving to a diminished fifth (B–F); no perfect interval is approached in parallel motion. The similar approach to the octave in the last two chords is between the bass and alto, not between outer voices. (**d**) Although the compound octave between the bass and soprano involves two outer voices, the soprano moves by step.

CHAPTER 6. HARMONIC PROGRESSION

1. (**a**) Half cadence (HC), ending with V. (**b**) Perfect authentic cadence (PAC), ending V–I with the tonic in the soprano. (**c**) Imperfect authentic cadence (IAC), ending V–I with the soprano voice on $\hat{3}$. (**d**) Perfect authentic cadence (PAC), ending V–I with the soprano voice on the tonic.

2. A normal half cadence ends with a root-position V triad, not an inversion (m. 4). A normal authentic cadence ends with a root-position V (or V^7) to I, not with an inversion of V or V^7 to I (mm. 7–8).

3. (**a**) **T–D–T**. (**b**) **T–D–T** (with the **T**onic and **D**ominant harmonies repeated). (**c**) Neither (faulty **T–D–S–T** progression). (**d**) **T–S–D–T** (the ii^6 is considered a **S**ubdominant harmony).

4. (**a**) Good: **T–S–D–T** pattern, without voice-leading errors. (**b**) Good: **T–D–T** pattern, without voice-leading errors. (**c**) Poor: the final chord is not a root-position I or V; the end of the progression is **D–S**; there are parallel fifths in between the second and third chords. (**d**) Poor: the third note of the melody, B, is $\hat{2}$ and is not in I^6. (**e**) Poor: voice-leading errors (parallel octave between the first two chords, as well as between the last two chords, and a doubled leading tone). (**f**) Good: **T–D–T** pattern, with no voice-leading errors. (**g**) Good: **T–S–D–T** pattern, with no voice-leading errors. (**h**) Poor: contains a **D**ominant that is followed by a **S**ubdominant harmony, and the melody note A is not in IV.

CHAPTER 7. FIGURATION AND EMBELLISHING TONES

1. I–IV–V–I. (The notes of the chords are arpeggiated in the treble clef.)

2. There are five notes in each chord, but only four independent strands of voice leading, since the bottom voice is doubled in parallel octaves throughout.

3. (**a**) approached by step, left by step (**b**) approached by step, left by leap (**c**) approached by leap, left by step (**d**) approached by common tone, left by step (**e**) approached by common tone, left by step (**f**) approached by leap, left by step (**g**) approached by step, left by common tone

4. (**a**) unaccented; PT (**b**) accented; PT (**c**) accented; PT (**d**) accented; SUS (**e**) unaccented; NT (**f**) unaccented; INT (**g**) unaccented; ANT (**h**) accented; RET.

CHAPTER 8. SPECIES COUNTERPOINT

1. First species

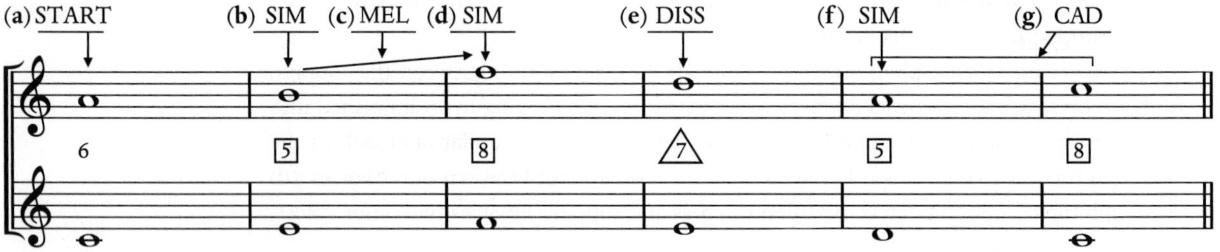

(**a**) START: Must start on $\hat{5}$ or $\hat{8}$.

(**b**) SIM: Similar motion to fifth.

(**c**) MEL: Melody leaps d5.

(**d**) SIM: Similar motion to octave.

(**e**) DISS: Only consonances permitted.

(**f**) SIM: Similar motion to fifth.

(**g**) CAD: Cadence must be sixth to octave.

2. Second species

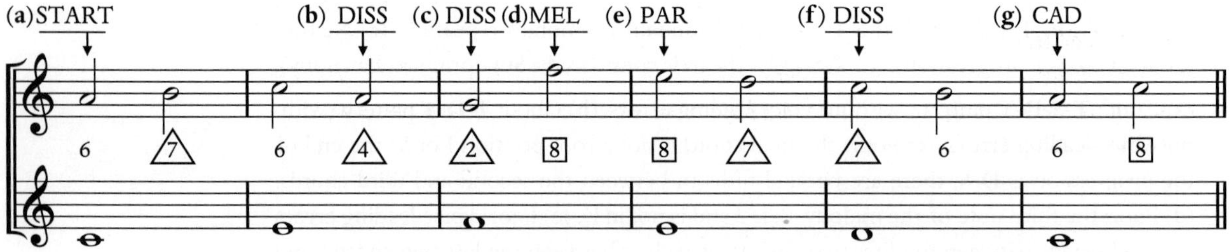

(**a**) START: Must start on $\hat{5}$ or $\hat{8}$.

(**b**) DISS: Must approach dissonance by step.

(**c**) DISS: No dissonance on first beat.

(**d**) MEL: Melody leaps a seventh.

(**e**) PAR: Parallel octaves.

(**f**) DISS: No dissonance on first beat.

(**g**) CAD: Last measure must be a whole note on $\hat{1}$.

3. Fourth species

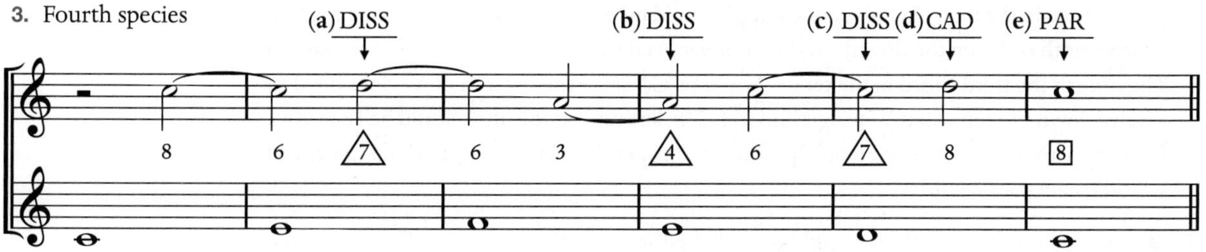

(**a**) DISS: No dissonance on beat 2.

(**b**) DISS: Dissonance must resolve down by step.

(**c**) DISS: Dissonance must resolve down by step.

(**d**) CAD: Penultimate note must be $\hat{7}$.

(**e**) PAR: Parallel octaves.

CHAPTER 9. I AND V

1. (**a**) E♭ major: I = E♭, G, B♭; V = B♭, D, F

   (**b**) E major: I = E, G♯, B; V= B, D♯, F♯

   (**c**) E minor: I = E, G, B; V= B, D♯, F♯

2. The excerpt in (**b**) is better than (**a**), since the melodic intervals of the upper voices are smoother. The excerpt in (**d**) is better than (**c**), since in (**c**) the leading tone (G♯) does not resolve up to the tonic when V progresses to I, even though it is in the soprano. In (**d**), the leading tone is in the alto, and thus does not need to resolve up to the tonic.

3. Tenor: C, C; Alto: A; soprano: F. Keeping the tenor on C provides the smoothest voice leading. The soprano E is the leading tone and must resolve up to the tonic when V progresses to I.

4. (**a**) E♯ (**b**) B♮ (**c**) B♯ (**d**) F𝄪 (**e**) E♮ (**f**) C♯

5. (**a**) $\hat{7}$ of G minor is F, which should be raised by a half step to F♯ in order to form a leading tone. (**b**) The leading tone (which in E major is D♯) should not be doubled. (**c**) There are too many leaps in between the first two chords, which creates faulty parallel octaves and fifths. In (**d**), the leading tone (C♯) should have resolved up to G in the top voice when V goes to I.

CHAPTER 10. THE DOMINANT-SEVENTH CHORD: V^7

1. (**a**) G: D–F♯–A–C (**b**) E: B–D♯–F♯–A (**c**) E♭: B♭–D–F–A♭ (**d**) D♭: A♭–C–E♭–G♭.

2. (**a**) E minor; add D♯ (**b**) F♯ minor; add E♯ (**c**) F minor; add E♮ (**d**) C minor; add B♮ (**e**) B minor; add A♯ (**f**) D♯ minor; add C𝄪

3. (**a**) and (**b**). The last note in the alto could be either E♭ or A♭ (in the latter instance, the fifth of the I chord is omitted, and the root is tripled).

   (**c**) and (**d**). The notes in the alto and tenor in the first chord could either be, respectively, B and G♯, or G♯ and E (in the latter instance, the fifth of V^7 is omitted, and its root is doubled).

(**e**) The note in the tenor in the second chord should be A (since this note is needed for V^7). (The seventh of V^7 on the downbeat does not yet need to resolve, since the V^7 is repeated.) The note in the third chord in the tenor should be G♯, since the seventh of V^7 does need to resolve down by step when V^7 progresses to I. The last note in the alto should be E; using a G♯ in the alto in the last chord would produce improper doubling, and a B in the last chord would create parallel fifths.

4. (**a**), (**b**), and (**c**). Each of these could be labeled either as V–V^7–I or V^{8-7}–I. They also each could be labeled as a V–I in which there is a passing tone in one of the voices.

5. (**a**) G major. The voice leading here is good: the motion of a perfect fifth to a diminished fifth (G–D to F♯–C) is fine. In the last chord, the root of I is tripled and the fifth (D) is omitted; this is also fine.

   (**b**) B♭ major. The voice leading has problems: the chordal seventh in the second chord (E♭) does not resolve down by step; it must do so, even though it is in an inner voice. Also, the third (**d**) is missing from the final I chord. In four-part harmony, you may omit a fifth from a triad, but not a third.

   (**c**) D minor. The voice leading here is good. In the second chord, the root of V^7 is doubled and the fifth (A) is omitted; this is fine.

   (**d**) E♭ major. The voice leading has problems: there are parallel fifths between the bass and alto in the last two chords. Also, the spacing between the alto and tenor in the last chord is more than an octave, which is less than ideal.

6. (**a**) (**i**), (**b**) (**i**), and (**c**) (**ii**) are notated incorrectly. In keyboard style, different rhythms that appear at the same time in the same hand should be stemmed in different directions.

CHAPTER 11. I^6 AND V^6

1. (**a**) Either G, B♭, or D, since any note of I^6 may be doubled. (**b**) Either B or E, since you may double the root or the fifth of V^6. You may not double the third of the chord, G♯, since that is the leading tone. (**c**) Either G or C. You may not double the E, which is the leading tone.

2. Any of these chords may follow I^6.

3. I, I^6, V, or V^7 may follow V^6. I^6 may not follow V^6, however.

4. Of these chords, only I normally follows V^7. It is not common for V^7 to lead directly to a V or V^6 triad or to I^6.

5. (**a**) Bass C should be C♯, since you should raise $\hat{7}$ in a minor key. (**b**) The leading tone (D♯) is doubled in the second chord. (**c**) There are parallel octaves (A to C♯) between the bass and alto beats 2–3: notice that the half note (A) in the alto on beat 1 is sustained through beat 2, thus forming an octave with the bass on this beat. (**d**) V^7–V^6 should be avoided, since it prevents resolution of the chordal seventh (E♭) of V^7. (**e**) V^6 to I^6 should be avoided, since it does not allow the leading (F♯) to resolve up by step in an outer voice.

   In all of these there is an augmented fourth moving to a perfect fourth between a pair of upper voices: an augmented fourth moving to perfect fourth between a pair of upper voices is common when vii^{o6} progresses to I or I^6.

CHAPTER 12. V^6_5 AND V^4_2

1. (**a**) V^6_5. (**b**) It may be followed by I, not by I^6, since then the leading tone in the bass could not resolve up by step. It may be following by either V^7 or V^4_2, not by V or V^6: V^7 in any inversion chord may not lead to a V triad, since then the chordal seventh would not be able to resolve down. (**c**) Any of these chords could precede V^6_5.

2. (**a**) V^4_2. (**b**) V^4_2 must lead directly to i^6 since the prominent chordal seventh in the bass of V $^4_2$ must resolve down by step. (**c**) Any of these chords could precede V^4_2.

3. (**a**) The G in m. 1 could be harmonized with V^6_5, but not V^4_2: V^4_2 of D major uses G in the bass, and thus V^4_2 would double the chordal seventh. The E in m. 2 could be harmonized with either V^6_5 or V^4_2. The C♯ in m. 3 could be harmonized with V^4_2: V^6_5 of D major uses C♯ in the bass, and thus V^6_5 would double the leading tone. (**b**) The E in m. 4 cannot be harmonized with either V^6_5 or V^4_2, since it is part of the cadence: the cadence in this measure should be harmonized V–I or V^7–I. (**c**) A voice exchange could be used in m. 2, with the motion from F♯ to D in the melody set with a motion from D to F♯ in the bass.

4. (**a**) C♯, E, G, A (**b**) F♯, A, C, D (**c**) D♭, E♭, G, B♭ (**d**) B, C♯, E♯, G♯ (**e**) F, G, B♮, D.

CHAPTER 13. V^4_3 AND $vii^{\circ 6}$

1. (**a**) G major: V^4_3 = D, F♯, A, C; bass = A. $vii^{\circ 6}$ = F♯, A, C; bass = A.

   (**b**) B♭ major: V^4_3 = F, A, C, E♭; bass = C. $vii^{\circ 6}$ = A, C, E♭; bass = C.

   (**c**) E major: V^4_3 = B, D♯, F♯, A; bass = F♯. $vii^{\circ 6}$ = D♯, F♯, A; bass = F♯.

   (**d**) E minor: V^4_3 = B, D♯, F♯, A; bass = F♯. $vii^{\circ 6}$ = D♯, F♯, A; bass = F♯ (same as in E major).

2. (**a**) V^6_5 (**b**) V^4_3 (**c**) V^4_2 (**d**) $vii^{\circ 6}$

3. (**a**) fifth (**b**) third (**c**) fifth (**d**) third (**e**) third

4. (**a**) neighbor motion (**b**) passing motion, in parallel motion with bass (**c**) passing motion, in contrary motion with bass (**d**) stationary tone (**e**) passing motion, in contrary motion with bass and with voice exchange between outer voices

5. (**a**) There are no faulty parallel fifths here. The perfect fifth to diminished fifth between the alto and soprano in the first two chords (E♭/B♭–D/A♭) is fine, because it is a diminished fifth, not a perfect fifth, that is approached in parallel motion. The chordal seventh (A♭) properly resolves down by step.

   (**b**) There is a faulty (parallel) approach to the perfect fifth between the alto and soprano in the third chord. The chordal seventh of the V^7 (C) is treated improperly also: it does not resolve down by step.

   (**c**) The diminished fifth to perfect fifth between the alto and soprano in the second and third chords is fine, as is the upward motion of the chordal seventh (E♭), since these are allowed when V^4_3 moves to I^6.

CHAPTER 14. APPROACHING THE DOMINANT: IV, ii^6, AND ii$^6_5$

1. (**a**), (**b**), (**c**), (**f**), (**h**), and (**i**) are correct. (**d**) is poor—V^6 may not progress to ii$^6_5$. (**e**) is poor—V may not progress to ii^6. (**g**) is poor—vii$^{\circ 6}$ is a **Dominant** harmony, and thus may not progress to IV.
2. (**a**) iv, quality = minor (**b**) ii$^{\circ 6}$, quality = diminished (**c**) ii$^{\varnothing 6}_{5}$, quality = half-diminished seventh
3. (**a**) root; $\hat{1}$ (**b**) any note: root, third, or fifth; $\hat{1}$, $\hat{3}$, $\hat{5}$ (**c**) root; $\hat{5}$ (**d**) root or fifth; $\hat{5}$ or $\hat{2}$ (not the third, which is the leading tone) (**e**) root; $\hat{4}$ (**f**) root or third (= bass); $\hat{2}$ or $\hat{4}$
4. (**a**) D; $\hat{1}$ (**b**) A♭; $\hat{4}$ (**c**) B♭; $\hat{1}$ (**d**) D; $\hat{4}$ (**e**) C♯; $\hat{1}$ (**f**) G; $\hat{4}$
5. (**a**) True. (**b**) False: $\hat{4}$ must resolve down by step only if it is a chordal seventh of V^7. (**c**) True. (**d**) True.
6. (**a**) Parallel fifths between bass and alto. (**b**) Chordal seventh within ii$^6_5$ (D) does not resolve down by step. (**c**) Melodic augmented second between A♭ and B♮. (**d**) Parallel octaves between bass and alto. (**e**) $\hat{7}$ is not raised in a minor key.

CHAPTER 15. EMBELLISHING V: CADENTIAL $^6_4$

1. (**a**) B and G (**b**) B♭; G and E♭ (**c**) A; F and D (**d**) B; G and E
2. (**a**) C, F, A (**b**) F♯, B, D♯ (**c**) D, G, B♭ (**d**) E, A, C
3. (**a**) A and C (**b**) E♯ and G♯ (**c**) A (soprano), F♯ (alto), and D (tenor)
4. (**c**) and (**d**). In (**c**), the cadential $^6_4$ follows a **Dominant** harmony (V^6). In (**d**), the cadential $^6_4$ appears on a weaker beat (beat 2) than the notes of the V triad that follow it on beat 3.

CHAPTER 16. LEADING TO THE TONIC: IV

1. All are typical progressions, except for (**d**): I-IV^6-I is uncommon.
2. $\hat{3}$-$\hat{4}$-$\hat{3}$, $\hat{5}$-$\hat{6}$-$\hat{5}$, and $\hat{1}$-$\hat{1}$-$\hat{1}$.
3. All of these could be harmonized with I-IV-I except for (**b**), since the second note, B♭, is not in the IV chord of the key of A♭. Note that though the melodic line of (**c**), $\hat{5}$-$\hat{4}$-$\hat{3}$, is not among the most typical for a I-IV-I progression, it nonetheless would be possible to harmonize this with I-IV-I.
4. (**a**) I-ii^6-V: half cadence. (**b**) iv-V-i: imperfect authentic cadence (it is *imperfect* because the tonic is not in the top voice in the final chord). (**c**) i-iv-i: plagal cadence. (**d**) I^6-V-I: perfect authentic cadence (it is *perfect* because the tonic is in the top voice in the final chord).

CHAPTER 17. THE LEADING-TONE SEVENTH CHORD: vii$^{\circ 7}$ AND vii$^{\varnothing 7}$

1. (**a**) B♭ (**b**) C♯ (**c**) C♮ (**d**) D♯ (**e**) No accidental is needed for a vii$^{\varnothing 7}$ chord in a major key.
2. (**a**) vii$^{\circ 7}$; chordal seventh = F♮; leading tone = G♯

   (**b**) vii$^{\circ 4}_{3}$; chordal seventh = D♭; leading tone = E♮

   (**c**) vii$^{\varnothing 6}_{5}$; chordal seventh = B; leading tone = C♯

(**d**) vii$^{o4}_{2}$; chordal seventh = E♭; leading tone = F♯

(**e**) vii^{ø7}; chordal seventh = C♯; leading tone = D♯

3. (**a**) vii$^{o4}_{3}$; leads to I^{6}. (**b**) vii^{o7}; leads to i (root position). (**c**) vii$^{o6}_{5}$; leads to i^{6} (root-position i would produce faulty parallel fifths with the tenor voice). (**d**) vii$^{o4}_{2}$; leads to V^{7} (because the chordal seventh is in the bass, vii$^{o4}_{2}$ cannot lead to i or i^{6}).

4. (**a**) The next note in the tenor should be B♭, because the chordal seventh of vii^{o7} (C♭) must resolve down by step.

   (**b**) The next note in the tenor should be A, because the leading tone in vii^{ø7} (G♯) should resolve up by step.

   (**c**) The next note in the tenor should be D, even though this would double the third of a root-position I. The E♭ within the vii^{o7} cannot move up to F, since this would cause faulty parallel fifths—that is, a diminished fifth (A-E♭) moving to a perfect fifth (B♭–F).

   (**d**) The next note in the alto should be F, even though this would double the third of a root-position I. The E within the vii^{o7} cannot move down to D, since this would cause faulty parallel fifths—that is, a diminished fifth (E-B♭) moving to a perfect fifth (D-A).

CHAPTER 18. APPROACHING V: IV^{6}, ii, ii^{7}, AND IV^{7}

1. (**a**) I -ii–V–I is good; I–V–ii–I is poor, since V should not progress to ii (**D**ominant moving to **S**ubdominant), and ii should not progress to I.

   (**b**) Although both of these progressions are acceptable, I–IV–ii–V is more standard, since in moving from one **S**ubdominant harmony to another, the bass usually moves down by a third (IV–ii). The I–ii–IV–V progression is less typical, since when moving between ii and IV the bass moves up by third.

   (**c**) Both of these progressions are good.

   (**d**) I–ii–ii^{7}–V–I is good; I–ii^{7}–ii–V–I is poor, since it involves a **S**ubdominant seventh chord that leads to a **S**ubdominant triad.

   (**e**) Both progressions are fine.

   (**f**) Both progressions are fine. Note that a **S**ubdominant seventh chord may move to a V triad, and thus the progression ii^{7}–V (unlike ii^{7}–ii) is fine. Also note that since vii^{o6} is a **D**ominant harmony, the progression ii–vii^{o6} is likewise fine.

2. (**a**) The first progression is good (the doubled G is fine); the second of these progressions is problematic, since the minor form of $\hat{6}$ is doubled and moves up rather than down, giving rise to a faulty melodic augmented second between E♭ and F♯.

   (**b**) The first progression is faulty, since the seventh of the ii^{7} (D) does not resolve down by step. The second progression is good; note that the fifth (E) is omitted from the V^{7} chord—this is fine.

   (**c**) The first progression is good: the seventh of IV^{7} (G) does resolve down by step, although this resolution is momentarily delayed by the cadential $^{6}_{4}$ (which is fine). The second progression is faulty, since the seventh of IV^{7} does not resolve down, but rather moves up to A♭.

3. (**a**) False. It is not good to double the bass of iv^6.The bass of iv^6 is the minor form of $\hat{6}$, which is a tendency tone; doubling it would give rise to voice-leading errors.

   (**b**) True.

   (**c**) False. ii° should not appear in root position.

   (**d**) True.

   (**e**) False.

   (**f**) True.

CHAPTER 19. MULTIPLE FUNCTIONS: VI

1. (**a**) All of these harmonies—even ii^7—may directly follow vi: vi may lead to any **S**ubdominant harmony.

   (**b**) vi often leads to I^6, but it is not common for vi to be followed directly by a root-position I.

   (**c**) vi may occasionally lead to V or V^6 (or even to V^7 or V^6_5); though less common, the vi–V or vi–V^6 progression is not faulty.

2. IV or ii^6 does not normally precede vi: a IV–vi or ii^6–vi progression would involve an unusual motion up by a third in the bass.

3. (**a**) V–vi and (**b**) V^7–vi may form part of a standard deceptive cadence, but the progressions found in (**c**)–(**e**) may not: a deceptive cadence must involve a root-position V (not V in inversion) and a root-position vi (not vi in inversion). The progression I–vi is a good progression, but it does not form a deceptive cadence, which must involve V or V^7 to vi.

4. The progressions found in (**a**), (**b**), (**d**), and (**e**) display good, standard voice leading. Although (**c**) is less typical (since when V moves to vi, normally the third of vi is doubled), this voice leading nonetheless is fine. The progression found in (**f**), on the other hand, does not have good voice leading: the C♯–B♭ in the alto creates a faulty melodic augmented second. The C♯ here should have ascended to D, doubling the third of VI.

CHAPTER 20. EMBELLISHING TONES IN FOUR-PART HARMONY

1. (**a**), (**b**), (**c**) are faulty; (**d**) and (**e**) are fine.

   (**a**) There are parallel octaves between the bass and tenor (the use of a passing tone does not remove these faulty parallels).

   (**b**) The neighbor tone in the alto forms parallel fifths with the bass (D–A, C–G).

   (**c**) The embellishing tones create parallel octaves between the bass and alto (F–E) on the first two beats.

   (**d**) If the chord on the second beat were omitted, there would have been parallel fifths between the tenor and soprano (F–C, G–D). The chord skips on the second beat avert this problem, however.

   (**e**) The passing tones here do not either create or avert faulty parallel octaves or fifths, thus this is fine.

2. (**a**) F, A, D (no note is doubled)

   (**b**) F, G, C (the bass C should be doubled)

(**c**) C, D, F (no note is doubled)

(**d**) D, F, G (no note is doubled; $^{6}_{5}$ is an abbreviated form of $^{6}_{5}_{3}$)

(**e**) D, G, with either D or G doubled (the "2" in the figure indicates that the bass C is dissonant and thus may not be doubled)

3. (**a**) *first beat*: C, D, G; *second beat*: B, D, G

   (**b**) *first beat*: C, D, G; *second beat*: B, D, G (note that this is the same as [**a**])

   (**c**) *first beat*: D, G, A; *second beat*: D, F♯, A

   (**d**) *both beats*: G, C, and either C, E, or G (any note may be doubled; note that this harmony lasts for two beats)

4. *First full measure*: V^{6}_{5} (bass G is a suspension); I (soprano C is a suspension)

   Second full measure: V^{7} (alto G is a suspension); I (soprano and tenor A and C are suspensions, alto F♯ is a retardation)

5. (**a**) The second one is correct. The first one incorrectly uses a third above the bass (A) on the first beat; this note is not indicated in the figures: the third above the bass should not appear until the 4 resolves down to 3.

   (**b**) The second one is correct. The first one incorrectly doubles the bass: when there is a "2" in the figure, you should not double the bass.

   (**c**) The first one is correct. Dashes indicate that the notes in the upper voices should be sustained or repeated; the second one is faulty, since the notes change on the second beat—the "6" does not mean a sixth above C as well.

CHAPTER 21. III AND VII

1. True.
2. False. The leading tone within the iii triad can descend.
3. True.
4. True.
5. False. iii should be rarely—if ever—used within basic melody harmonization exercises, and iii^{6} should never be used in such contexts.
6. False. vii^{o6} is a common chord; you should not use a *root-position* vii^{o} triad in four-part harmony exercises.
7. True—although such a progression is not often found in simple harmonic contexts.

CHAPTER 22. SEQUENCES

1. (**a**) True. (**b**) False. (**c**) True. (**d**) False. (**e**) False. Notice that in each case, the standard rules regarding scale degrees or a chord's position within a key are not relevant within the middle of a sequence. Guidelines regarding faulty parallel intervals and chordal sevenths have nothing to do with scale degrees or a chord's position within a key, and thus these remain relevant in the middle of sequences.

2. From the bass up: (**a**) D, F, A♭, C (descending fifth sequence, in which every chord is a seventh chord). (**b**) F, A♭, C, F ("down 3, up 4" sequence). (**c**) B, D, G (descending parallel $^6_3$ sequence). (**d**) D, A, D, F ("down 4, up 2" sequence). (**e**) F♯, D, A, D (sequence in which the bass descends by step, alternating $^5_3$ and $^6_3$ chords. Although this sequence usually appears in three-voice textures, it may appear in four voices, as is the case here). (**f**) G, A, E♭, C (descending fifth sequence, in which every chord is a seventh chord, alternating $^6_5$ and $^4_2$ chords).

CHAPTER 23. OTHER $^6_4$ CHORDS

1. (**a**) True. (**b**)–(**e**) are all false. Statements (**c**)–(**e**) would be true of a cadential $^6_4$, which has the notes of a tonic chord in second inversion. But I$^6_4$ may also take the form of a passing $^6_4$, a pedal $^6_4$, or a cadential $^6_4$, in which case they would not be true. (**f**) True, in general, but there are exceptional cases in which it is possible to double other notes of I$^6_4$ (unless it is a cadential $^6_4$).
2. (**a**) Passing $^6_4$. (**b**) pedal $^6_4$. (**c**) cadential $^6_4$. (**d**) pedal $^6_4$. This is not a passing $^6_4$, since a passing $^6_4$ must have a passing motion in its bass. (**e**) arpeggiated $^6_4$.

CHAPTER 24. OTHER EMBELLISHING CHORDS

1. m. 1: vi, I^6, V; m. 2: I, ii; m. 3: I^6, ii$^6_5$, V; m. 4: I.
2. ii–I^6 (m. 2, beat 3 to m. 3, beat 1) is an unusual chord succession. The ii is a passing chord, a by-product of a passing tone in the bass (and passing tones in all upper voices).
3. I–V^6–IV^6–V (or V^7).
4. V (or V^7)–vi (or IV^6) –V^6 (or V$^6_5$)–I.
5. V^6 (the third chord) serves as a passing harmony between I and vi. Note the passing motion in the bass (D-C♯-B); note too that V^6 here does not lead to I, as would be more typical. One could properly argue that the IV at the end of the second full measure also serves as a passing chord, within a I^6–IV–V$^{6-5}_{4-3}$ motion. Note that I^6–IV–V$^{6-5}_{4-3}$ is a standard progression, however.

CHAPTER 25. APPLIED DOMINANTS OF V

1. (**a**), (**d**), (**e**), or (**f**). V/V may not be followed by I, IV, ii^6. V/V must be followed by a Dominant harmony (V or V^6; V^7, cadential $^6_4$-V) or by another V/V.
2. (**a**), (**b**), (**c**), (**d**), and (**e**) all are correct. Any chord that may precede V may also precede V/V.
3. (**a**) C♯ (**b**) A♮ (**c**) E♮ (**d**) E♮ and G♮ (**e**) A♯ (**f**) A♯ and C♯. Note that V/V needs two accidentals in minor keys.
4. (**a**) G (**b**) E (**c**) F♯ (**d**) F♯ (**e**) B♭ (**f**) B♭. Note that in each case, the root of V/V is $\hat{2}$ (which is a perfect fifth above $\hat{5}$).
5. (**a**) G, *B♮*, D (**b**) E, *G♯*, B (**c**) F♯, *A♯*, C♯ (**d**) D♯, *F𝄪*, A♯. The italicized tones all require accidentals.

6. (**a**) G, *B♮*, *D♮*, F (**b**) E, *G♯*, *B♮*, D (**c**) F♯, *A♯*, *C♯*, E (**d**) D♯, *F𝄪*, *A♯*, C♯. The italicized notes all require accidentals. Compare with question (5): notice that V^7/V uses the same notes in parallel major and minor keys, but in minor keys V/V requires two accidentals.
7. (**b**), (**c**), and (**d**). The third of V/V (= raised $\hat{4}$) functions like a leading tone in the key of V, and thus when V/V resolves to V (as opposed to moving to another V/V) this note must resolve up if it appears in an outer voice. One exception: if V/V leads to V^7, this note may slide down by chromatic semitone to $\hat{4}$.
8. (**c**) Never: the third of V/V or V^7/V(= raised $\hat{4}$) functions like a leading tone in the key of V, and thus may never be doubled in four-part harmony.

CHAPTER 26. OTHER APPLIED CHORDS

1. (**a**), (**b**), or (**d**): Much as V may be followed by I, I^6, or another V, so V/ii may be followed by ii, ii^6, or another V/ii.
2. (**a**) G♯ (**b**) B♮ (**c**) B♯ (**d**) G♯ and B♮ (**e**) B♮ and A♭ (**f**) F♮
3. (**a**) D♯ (**b**) E♭ (**c**) no accidentals needed (**d**) A♮ (**e**) F♯ and A♮: note that because of the A♭ in the key signature, the A♮ is needed (**f**) no accidentals needed
4. (**a**) C♯ (**b**) A♯ (**c**) G♯ (**d**) D (**e**) D♯ (**f**) B. In each case, the tone that cannot be doubled is the leading tone of the tonicized harmony.
5. (**a**) A; E; E, G♯, B; G♯; G♯

   (**b**) D♭; A♭; A♭, C, E♭, G♭; G♭; C

   (**c**) G♯; D♯; D♯, F𝄪, A♯; F𝄪, A♯; F𝄪

   (**d**) F; C; C, E, G; none; E

CHAPTER 27. MODULATION TO THE DOMINANT KEY

1. (**a**) C♯ (**b**) E♮ (**c**) A♯ (**d**) D♯ (**e**) G♮ (**f**) E♯ (**g**) A♮
2. (**a**) The main key is D; the key of V is A. (**b**) The main key is B♭; the key of V is F. (**c**) The main key is A♭; the key of V is E♭.
3. (**a**) B♭ major; D minor, F major, G minor (**b**) D major; F♯ minor, A major, B minor (**c**) A major; C♯ minor, E major, F♯ minor
4. (**a**) The third chord of m. 1 (B♭ major) is I in B♭ and IV in F.

   (**b**) The fourth chord of m. 1 (E minor) is vi in G and ii in D. You could also read the third chord of m. 1 (G major) as the pivot chord: I in G and IV in D.

   (**c**) The first chord of m. 3 (C♯ minor) is vi in E and ii in B. You also arguably could read the third chord of m. 2 (B major) as the pivot chord: V in E and I in B.

CHAPTER 28. MODULATION TO CLOSELY RELATED KEYS

1. iii; IV; VI; v

2. (**a**) D major, E minor, A minor, B minor, C major

(**b**) C minor, D minor, E♭ major, F major, G minor

(**c**) F major, G minor, B♭ major, A minor, C major

(**d**) A major, B minor, C♯ minor, D major, E major

3. (**a**) F major, G minor, A minor, B♭ major, C major, D minor, E diminished

(**b**) G minor, B♭ major, C minor, E♭ major, F major

(**c**) A major, C♯ minor, E major; F♯ minor

(**d**) E minor, G major, A minor, C major

4. (**a**) A♯; in B minor, the note G♯ might also appear as part of an ascending melodic minor scale. (**b**) G♭. (**c**) B♮ and G♯; in the key of A minor, the note F♯ might also appear as part of an ascending melodic minor scale. (**d**) D♮ and E♯; in the key of F♯ minor, the note D♯ might also appear as part of an ascending melodic minor scale.

5. (**a**) G♮ is missing in m. 2, beat 1; A♯ (needed for a cadence in B minor) is missing in m. 2, beat 2.

(**b**) F♯ (needed within G minor), although used in the first measure, is missing in m. 2, first chord.

(**c**) F𝄪 (needed within G♯ minor) is missing in m. 3, second chord—by which time the key of G♯ minor has returned. The first chord of the second measure does not need an F♯ (since F♯ is in the key signature anyway), but a cautionary accidental here would have been helpful to remind performers that the F𝄪 of the first measure is no longer in force.

CHAPTER 29. MODAL MIXTURE

1. (**a**), (**e**), (**f**), and (**g**) involve mixture; these chords will need an accidental within a major key. The other chords (**b**), (**c**), and (**d**) are diatonic chords within their keys—that is, they do not involve mixture, and do not need an accidental.

2. (**a**) E♭ (**b**) C♭ and G♭ (**c**) G♮ (**d**) A♭ (**e**) A♮ (**f**) B♭

3. (**a**) True. (**b**) False: a move from D major to D minor is not a modulation, since the tonic does not change. (**c**) False: a borrowed chord in a major key down often involves a lowered $\hat{3}$ or $\hat{6}$. However, this chromatic alteration does not always involve the use of a flat: it might also involve the use of a natural or a double flat. (**d**) True. (**e**) True.

CHAPTER 30. ♭II^6: THE NEAPOLITAN SIXTH

1. (**a**) G♮ (**b**) C♭ (**c**) D♮

2. (**a**) ii^{o6} = G, B♭, E; ♭II^6 = G, B♭, E♭

(**b**) ii^{o6} = E, G, C♯; ♭II^6 = E, G, C

(**c**) ii^{o6} = B♭, D♭, G; ♭II^6 = B♭, D♭, G♭

3. (**a**) iv, (**c**) i^6, and (**d**) VI may precede ♭II^6; V and vii^{o6} may not precede ♭II^6, since they function as **D**ominants.

4. (**a**) minor (**b**) Neapolitan sixth (**c**) major (**d**) downward

5. (**a**) The alto should move to G; it is most normal to double the bass (that is, the third of the chord) of the ♭II^6. (**b**) As ♭$\hat{2}$, the E♭ should move down to C♯, not up to E♮.

CHAPTER 31. AUGMENTED SIXTH CHORDS

1. (**a**) and (**b**): ♯$\hat{4}$ = B♮; minor $\hat{6}$ = D♭. Note: these scale degrees are the same in parallel major and minor keys. Note, too, that since both F and F minor have a B♭ in their key signatures, ♯$\hat{4}$ is B♮, *not* B♯.

   (**c**) and (**d**): ♯$\hat{4}$ = A♯; minor $\hat{6}$ = C♮ (*not* C♭).

   (**e**) ♯$\hat{4}$ = G♮; minor $\hat{6}$ = B𝄫 (*not* B♭).

2. (**a**) and (**b**): It^{+6} = D♭, F, B♮; Fr^{+6} = D♭, F, G, B♮; Ger^{+6} = D♭, F, A♭, B♮ (or, in F major only: D♭, F, G♯, B♮). With the exception of the alternate spelling of the Ger^{+6} chord, the augmented sixth chords have the same notes in both F major and F minor.

   (**c**) and (**d**): It^{+6} = C♮, E, A♯; Fr^{+6} = C♮, E, F♯, A♯; Ger^{+6} = C♮, E, G♮, A♯ (or, in E major only: C♮, E, F𝄪, A♯). With the exception of the alternate spelling of the Ger^{+6} chord, the augmented sixth chords have the same notes in both E major and E minor.

   (**e**) It^{+6} = A♮, C♯, F𝄪; Fr^{+6} = A♮, C♯, D♯, F𝄪; Ger^{+6} = A♮, C♯, E, F𝄪.

3. (**a**) Adding F♭ turns this chord into an It^{+6} (**b**) B♭, Fr^{+6} (**c**) C♭, Ger^{+6} (**d**) B♯, It^{+6}

4. (**a**) Key of D major or D minor, It^{+6} (**b**) Key of A major or A minor, Fr^{+6}

   (**c**) Key of G major or G minor, Ger^{+6} (**d**) Key of C major (*not* C minor), Ger^{+6}

   (**e**) Key of E major or E minor, It^{+6}

5. (**a**) The first of the chords has incorrect doubling: in an It^{+6}, you should double the tonic, *not* the bass note (which is a tendency tone).

   (**b**) The first chord is misspelled: an augmented sixth chord requires raised $\hat{4}$—*not* lowered $\hat{5}$—in an upper voice.

   (**c**) The first chord has a wrong note: raised $\hat{4}$ of F is B♮, *not* B♯.

6. In a standard augmented sixth chord, minor $\hat{6}$ must appear in the bass; raised $\hat{4}$ may appear in any upper voice (tenor, alto, or soprano).

CHAPTER 32. OTHER CHORDS: ALTERED, COMMON-TONE CHROMATIC, AND NINTH CHORDS

1. (**a**) C♯, E♯, G♯ (**b**) D, F♯, A (**c**) B♭, D♮, F (**d**) C, E, G♯ (**e**) E, G♯, B♯ (**f**) A♭, C, E♭ (**g**) F♮, A, C♮ (**h**) G♯, B♭, D, E (i) B, D, E♯, G (j) B♭, D, F, A♭, C

2. (**a**) F: ♭II (**b**) E: Ger^{+6} with $\hat{1}$ in the bass (**c**) E♭: V^{+} (**d**) D: III♯ (or V/vi) (**e**) A: IV^{+} (**f**) B♭: V^9

3. (**a**) A♭ and D♭ (**b**) A♯ and C♯ (and optionally also E) (**c**) B♭, C♯, and E♮ (and optionally also G)

4. The first diminished seventh chord is an applied vii^{o7} of V; the second is a common-tone diminished seventh chord that embellishes V. Notice how the root of the V chord (A) is present within the common-tone diminished seventh chord that decorates it.

CHAPTER 33. CHROMATIC SEQUENCES

1. (**a**) m. 1, beat 2: D♯; m. 2, beat 2: E♯; down 3, up 4. (**b**) m. 1, beat 1: F♯; beat 2, B♮; m. 2, beat 2: E♮, descending fifth (with first inversion on alternate chords). (**c**) m. 1, beat 2: G♭s, D♭; m. 2, beat 1: C♭s, G♭; beat 2: C♮; m. 3, beat 1: D♭s; beat 2: D♮; down 3, up 4. (**d**) m. 1, beat 1: E♯; beat 2: E♮, A♯; m. 2, beat 1: D♯ (and courtesy A♮); beat 2: D♮, G♯; (m. 3, beat 1: courtesy G♮); descending fifth (with applied seventh chords).
2. The fifth of every other chord is omitted.
3. The leading tones within the applied dominant sevenths slide down by semitone to the seventh of the following chord instead of resolving up by step.
4. The chordal sevenths must resolve down by step, even within an inner voice and even within a sequence.

CHAPTER 34. CHROMATIC MODULATION

1. (**a**) V (**b**) G (**c**) ♭III (**d**) F
2. (**a**) A (**b**) B (**c**) E
3. (**a**) B (**b**) A♭ (**c**) F
4. (**a**) D♭ or C♯ (**b**) B♭ (**c**) G
5. (**a**) F (V^7 of F = C, E, G, B♭)

   (**b**) A♭ (V^7 of A♭ = E♭, G, B♭, D♭)

   (**c**) C♯ (Ger^{+6} of C♯ = A, C♯, E, F𝄪) or D♭ (Ger+6 of D♭ = B𝄫, D♭, F♭, G♮)

   (**d**) E♭ (Ger^{+6} of E♭ = C♭, E♭, G♭, A♮)

CHAPTER 35. SENTENCES AND OTHER PHRASE TYPES

1. This is a standard sentence, with a presentation in mm. 1–4 (mm. 1–2, basic idea; mm. 3–4, strict repetition) followed by a continuation in mm. 5–8 leading to a cadence.
2. In this standard sentence, the basic idea in mm. 1–2 is repeated in varied form (transposed up a step) in mm. 3–4.
3. This is sentence-like, but *not* a sentence. Although in certain ways similar to a sentence, what is clearly a contrasting idea appears in mm. 3–4; there is no repetition of the basic idea.
4. This is clearly *not* a sentence: a sentence consists of a single phrase, and thus cannot have a cadence in its middle.
5. This standard sentence is four measures long, rather than the more typical eight measures: the presentation is in mm. 1–4 (basic idea in m. 1, varied repetition in m. 2) followed by a continuation leading to a half cadence in mm. 3–4.
6. This standard sentence that is extended to 12 measures as a result of an evaded cadence in m. 8 and rhythmic expansions in the subsequent measures.
7. Whether this is a sentence or merely sentence-like depends on whether mm. 3–4 are understood as a variant of mm. 1–2 (in which case this phrase would be called a sentence) or a contrasting idea (in which case this phrase would be considered sentence-like); one could reasonably argue for either of these interpretations.

CHAPTER 36. PERIODS AND OTHER PHRASE PAIRS

1. Parallel period, with HC in I and PAC in I.
2. Parallel period, with HC in I and PAC in V.
3. Contrasting period, with HC in I and PAC in I; the consequent phrase is motivically new.
4. Parallel period; the first phrase ends with an IAC, which is less stable than the PAC at the end of the following phrase.
5. Parallel period with an expansion; the consequent phrase is extended by two measures.
6. Not a period, since the first phrase ends with a PAC.
7. Sequential period; the consequent phrase starts a step higher.

CHAPTER 37. BINARY FORM

1. (**a**) True.

   (**b**) False: If the opening of the **A** section returns in the tonic key in the middle of the second part, it is classified as rounded binary, even if the endings of the two parts of the same. A binary form is classified as balanced binary only if it cannot be classified as rounded binary.

   (**c**) False: The two parts of a simple binary might share motives and other features, even though there is no large repetition of material from the first part within the second part.

   (**d**) True.

2. (**a**) Balanced binary: The opening measures do not return in the tonic key within the second part, so this is not rounded binary. On the other hand, the last four measures of the first part return—slightly varied and transposed to the tonic key—as the last four measures of the second part; this is typical of balanced binary.

   (**b**) Rounded binary: Although at a different dynamic level (***f*** as opposed to ***mf***), four measures from the end of the second part there is a clear return—in the tonic key—of the first two measures. Note that the last two measures of the second part are a varied repetition of the last two measures of the first part. Even so, this is *not* a balanced binary form, since in balanced binary the opening does not return in the tonic key in the middle of the second part.

   (**c**) Simple binary: Although the two parts share musical materials in common, the opening measures do not return in the tonic key within the second part, and the two parts end differently.

CHAPTER 38. TERNARY AND RONDO FORMS

1. (**a**) **ABA** and (**b**) **ABA′** are examples of ternary form, *not* **ABC**.
2. The **A** and **A′** sections are usually in the tonic key (though it is possible for the first **A** section to end in a different key). The **B** section may also be in the tonic key (or in the parallel key), but often it is not.
3. Both the **A** and **A′** sections usually end with a PAC; the **B** section may end with a PAC (either in the tonic key or in another key), but it may also end with a HC.

4. The **A** sections of a rondo are almost always in the tonic key.
5. The **A** sections of a rondo usually end with a PAC in the tonic key.
6. In an **ABACA** rondo, the **C** section is usually longer than the **B** section.

CHAPTER 39. SONATA FORM

1. Introduction, exposition, development, recapitulation, coda
2. The primary theme appears in the tonic key in both the exposition and recapitulation.
3. The secondary theme appears in the secondary key in the exposition (usually the key of V, or–in minor-key movements–in the relative major), and in the primary key in the recapitulation.
4. Primary theme, transition, secondary theme, closing section
5. The medial caesura appears at the end of the transition and precedes the secondary theme.
6. Closing section of the exposition: PAC in the secondary key; primary theme: PAC, IAC, or HC in the tonic key; secondary theme: PAC in the secondary key; transition: HC in tonic key or HC in primary key.

Glossary

♭II6 First-inversion major triad whose root is lowered $\hat{2}$; functions as a Subdominant and occurs most often in minor keys. Also called *Neapolitan sixth*.

♭III Major triad occurring by modal mixture in a major key, using the minor form of $\hat{3}$ (in the bass) and the minor form of $\hat{7}$.

III♯ Major triad whose root is $\hat{3}$ of a major scale and whose third is raised $\hat{5}$.

♭VI Major triad occurring by modal mixture in a major key, using the minor form of $\hat{6}$ (in the bass) and the minor form of $\hat{3}$.

V of V (V/V) The most common applied dominant, leading to V; may also appear as a seventh chord (as in V^7/V) or in inversion (as in V^6/V).

V^9, V^9_7 Chord that uses the notes of V^7 plus a major or (in a minor key or using modal mixture) a minor ninth above the bass.

VI♯ Major triad whose root is $\hat{6}$ of a major scale and whose third is raised $\hat{1}$.

5-6 sequence Harmonic sequence, most often occurring in a three-voice texture, in which the bass line ascends by step, with each bass note of the sequence supporting a $^5_3$ triad followed by a $^6_3$ triad; a variant of the sequence in which chord roots alternately move down 3, up 4, with every chord in first inversion.

accented Sounding on a relatively strong beat or part of the beat or appearing at the same time (most of) the notes of the chord are sounded.

accidental Any of the signs for sharp, flat, double sharp, or double flat, placed immediately before the notehead on the staff to indicate whether the pitch is to be raised or lowered (generally, for that measure only), or natural, which cancels a sharp or flat.

alto clef C clef 𝄡 indicating that the third line from the bottom of the staff is middle C; used for viola and also called *viola clef.*

anacrusis Note or group of notes forming an incomplete measure and leading to a downbeat; sometimes called a pickup or (if a single beat) an upbeat.

antecedent In a period, the first phrase, which ends with a half cadence or imperfect authentic cadence, requiring an "answer" by the second, *consequent* phrase.

anticipation (ANT) Chord tone that arrives before the beat, as an unaccented non-chord tone, approached by step and left by common tone.

applied dominant Chord that has been chromatically altered to act as V of a note being tonicized. Also called *secondary dominant*.

arpeggiated $^6_4$ Second-inversion triad that results from a chord skip in the bass.

arpeggiation The statement of chord tones in succession instead of together.

ascending fifth sequence Harmonic sequence involving major and minor chords whose roots alternately move up by a fifth and down by a fourth.

ascending melodic minor See *melodic minor scale*.

augmentation dot Dot following a notehead that increases the duration by one half the value of the note.

augmented interval Interval a semitone larger than a perfect or major interval; for example, C–G♯, augmented fifth (A5); B♭–D♯, augmented third (A3).

augmented second (A2) Second that is three semitones in size; characteristic distance between $\hat{6}$ and $\hat{7}$ in a harmonic minor scale.

augmented sixth chord Three- or four-note harmony built on two tendency tones that drive a resolution to V (directly or through cadential $^6_4$); includes the minor form of $\hat{6}$ in the bass (leading down to $\hat{5}$), raised $\hat{4}$ in an upper voice (leading up to $\hat{5}$), plus one or two other notes; see also *Italian augmented sixth*, *French augmented sixth*, and *German augmented sixth*.

augmented triad Triad built of a major third and an augmented fifth.

authentic cadence (AC) Cadence consisting of V or V^7 moving to I; may be perfect (melody ends on $\hat{1}$) or imperfect (melody ends on $\hat{3}$ or $\hat{5}$).

balanced binary form See *binary form*.

barline Vertical line on the staff separating measures.

basic idea See *sentence*.

bass The lowest voice; the bottom note of a chord.

bass clef (F clef) 𝄢 symbol indicating that the fourth line from the bottom of the staff is F below middle C.

beam Horizontal line connecting the stems of two or more notes to indicate durations shorter than a quarter note: a single beam indicates eighth notes, a double beam indicates sixteenth notes, and so forth.

beat Regular pulsation of time at a moderate speed.

binary form Form of a movement or piece divided into two parts, each of which is usually repeated; the first part may be harmonically open-ended (ending with an unstable cadence or a modulation to V or to the relative major), while the second part concludes with an authentic cadence in the main key. In *rounded binary form*, the opening of the first part returns in the middle of the second part, exactly or nearly so and in the main key, creating a sense of return. In *balanced binary form*, the two parts only *conclude* with the same music; generally, the first part ends with a perfect authentic cadence in V or the relative key, and the second part repeats the concluding segment, but transposed to the tonic. Simple binary form does not contain these repetitions.

borrowed chord A chord that uses notes more normally found in the parallel key, such as, in a major key, a chord using the minor form of $\hat{3}$ or $\hat{6}$; a form of modal mixture.

bridge Brief passage (sometimes shorter than a phrase) that follows the cadence at the end of a large section and leads to the beginning of the next section.

C clef 𝄡 symbol indicating the staff line that is middle C; see *alto clef, tenor clef.*

clef Symbol that associates lines and spaces on the staff with specific pitches. See also *treble clef, bass clef, C clef, alto clef, tenor clef.*

cadence Harmonic conclusion of a phrase; cadence types include *authentic, half, Phrygian, plagal,* and *deceptive cadences.*

cadential $^6_4$ Harmony that decorates V with accented embellishing tones, using notes of the tonic chord ($\hat{5}$, $\hat{1}$, and $\hat{3}$), with $\hat{5}$ in the bass.

cantus firmus In species counterpoint, a melody in whole notes.

chord position The arrangement of a chord depending on which note is in the bass.

chord progression *Harmonic progression.*

chord skip Melodic leaps between chord tones while a chord is repeated or sustained.

chord symbol Representation of the root and quality of a chord, as Gm (G-minor triad), E^{o7} (E diminished seventh chord).

chordal dissonance A note of a chord (such as the seventh of a seventh chord) that is dissonant with the root or the bass and thus has a strong tendency to move downward.

chordal seventh The seventh of a seventh chord; in four-part harmony, a tendency tone that should resolve down.

chromatic embellishing tone Embellishing tone that is altered to move by half step.

chromatic passing tone Passing tone that requires an accidental and that leads between two notes that are a major second apart.

chromatic semitone Semitone between two notes with the same letter name, as C–C♯ or B♭–B; unlike a *diatonic semitone,* it cannot occur naturally in a major or minor scale.

circle of fifths Major keys (or minor keys) on each of the twelve chromatic tones, organized in an arrangement a fifth apart, and showing the progression of key signatures; also, the *circle of fifths progression.*

circle of fifths progression See *descending fifth sequence.*

closing section In sonata form, section that usually ends both the exposition and recapitulation, following the perfect authentic cadence that marks the end of the secondary theme.

coda Concluding section of a movement; in sonata form, it follows the recapitulation.

common-tone diminished seventh chord Embellishing chromatic diminished seventh chord resulting from a sustained root and embellishing notes in other voices.

common-tone modulation Modulation between two keys in which one tone shared by two chords is used as a pivot between the keys.

compound interval Interval larger than an octave; identified by the number of steps or by its simple-interval equivalent (e.g., tenth or compound third).

compound meter Meter in which the basic time unit is a dotted-note value; indicated in the upper number of a time signature by 6, 9, or a larger multiple of 3.

compound ternary form Ternary form in which each of the three sections is itself in binary or ternary form (as in a minuet and trio).

consequent In a period, the second phrase, which ends with a perfect authentic cadence and which answers the "question" posed by the first, *antecedent* phrase.

consonant interval Interval that is relatively stable; generally, major or minor third or sixth, perfect unison, octave, fifth, and (in some contexts) fourth.

continuation See *sentence.*

contrary motion Voice leading between two voices in which the voices move in opposite directions.

contrasting idea In a sentence-like phrase, statement of a new idea (usually about two measures long) that follows the *basic idea;* takes the place of the repetition (or varied repetition) that occurs within the presentation of a sentence.

contrasting period Period in which the second (consequent) phrase does not begin like the first (antecedent).

deceptive cadence (DC) Cadence in which V (or V^7) moves to a root-position vi (or VI) instead of the expected I.

descending fifth sequence Common harmonic sequence involving chords whose roots alternately move up by fourth and down by fifth; also called *circle of fifths progression.* In its diatonic version, it can circle through the chords built on all seven scale tones; in its chromatic version, it uses applied dominant chords and can arrive at a distant key.

descending melodic minor See *melodic minor scale.*

development In sonata form, the beginning of the second part, often involving a wide variety of intensifying techniques, including tonicizations, sequences, and fragmentation of themes from the exposition. It may conclude with a cadence in a key other than the main or secondary key, followed by a retransition to the tonic key; or it may prepare the recapitulation with a half cadence in the tonic.

diatonic Staying within the key and using the notes of the scale.

diatonic semitone Semitone between two notes with different names, as C–D♭ or A♯–B; compare *chromatic semitone.*

diminished interval Interval a semitone smaller than a perfect or minor interval; for example, B–F, diminished fifth (d5); B–D♭, diminished third (d3).

diminished third chord "Inversion" of an augmented sixth chord with the raised $\hat{4}$ in the bass, creating a diminished third with the minor form of $\hat{6}$.

diminished seventh chord Seventh chord constructed of a diminished triad and a diminished seventh.

diminished triad Triad built of a minor third and a diminished fifth.

direct fifths *Similar fifths.*

direct octaves *Similar octaves.*

dissonant interval Interval that is relatively unstable; generally, seconds, sevenths, diminished and augmented intervals, and (in some contexts) perfect fourth.

dominant The fifth note in a scale ($\hat{5}$); also, the name of the chord (V) based on that tone, or (as ***Dominant***) any of a group of chords that function as dominants, including vii° and V^7 chords.

dominant key The key in which the dominant chord of a composition's main key is tonic: for example, in a G-major composition, the key of D major.

dominant seventh chord (7) Seventh chord built on the dominant ($\hat{5}$) note of a scale, containing two tendency tones ($\hat{7}$ and the chordal seventh, $\hat{4}$) and functionally leading strongly to the tonic; also, the *chord quality* of a chord constructed of a major triad plus a minor seventh.

double flat 𝄫 Accidental lowering a natural note by a whole step.

double sharp 𝄪 Accidental raising a natural note by a whole step.

doubling In four-part harmony, the appearance of the same chord tone (perhaps separated by one or more octaves) in two voices.

downbeat First beat of a measure.

duple meter Meter with a two-beat grouping (one strong and one weak beat).

eighth note Note written as a solid notehead with a stem and a flag or beam, representing the duration half as long as a quarter note and twice as long as a sixteenth note.

embellishing tone Note that decorates a chord tone and does not belong to the harmony; classified by whether the non-chord tone appears on or off the beat (accented or unaccented) and how it is approached and left.

enharmonic equivalents Notes that have different names ("spellings") but sound the same pitch.

enharmonic intervals Intervals with the same number of semitones but spanning a different number of scale degrees (letter names), as C–D♯ (A2) and C–E♭ (m3).

enharmonic modulation Modulation to a distant key brought about by enharmonically reinterpreting (or respelling) a chord, as when an augmented sixth chord is reinterpreted as a V^7 (or vice versa).

equal division of the octave Repetition of a strict chromatic sequence to return to its starting point, in the process dividing the octave into smaller intervals of the same size, as by three major thirds or four minor thirds.

evaded cadence Technique for extending a phrase by averting a perfect authentic cadence, as when I^6 is substituted for the expected appearance of I.

exposition First part of sonata form. In the exposition the *primary theme* establishes the tonic key; a transition leads to the *secondary theme* in the secondary key and ends with a PAC in this key (usually V or, in minor, III), which is then usually followed by a closing section.

F clef See *bass clef.*

fifth Interval between two tones spanning five scale steps (letter names), as C–G or $\hat{1}$–$\hat{5}$; in a chord, the fifth above the root.

figured bass Keyboard notation in which a bass line is given, with *figures* to indicate upper voices.

figures Arabic numerals, written vertically below bass note, used to indicate chords or intervals above the bass note.

first inversion Chord position in which the third is in the bass; indicated $^6_3$ or ^{6} for a triad, $^6_5$ for a seventh chord.

first theme *Primary theme.*

first-species counterpoint Species counterpoint in which the new melody is written in whole notes against the cantus firmus, using only consonant intervals between the melodies.

five-part rondo form Rondo form in which there are two sections that contrast with the main-key **A** section (**ABACA**).

flag Short line attached to an individual note stem indicating a duration shorter than a quarter note: a single flag indicates an eighth note, a double flag indicates a sixteenth note, and so forth.

flat ♭ Sign (accidental or in the key signature) lowering a natural note by a half step.

four-part harmony Texture of four voices; each chord uses four notes, with mostly the same basic rhythm in all four parts, as in a typical hymn.

fourth Interval between two tones spanning four scale steps (letter names), as C–F or $\hat{1}$–$\hat{4}$.

fourth-species counterpoint Species counterpoint in which the new melody is written in pairs of half notes that are tied across the barline, with dissonances allowed only on the first half of the measure, as suspensions.

fragmentation Technique in which a portion of a previous melodic idea is repeated two or more times, perhaps transposed and presented sequentially.

French augmented sixth (Fr^{+6}) *Augmented sixth chord* that uses the minor form of $\hat{6}$ in the bass and $\hat{1}$, $\hat{2}$, and raised $\hat{4}$ in the upper voices.

fully diminished seventh chord (°7) *Diminished seventh chord.*

function Categories of chords—***Tonic***, ***Dominant***, or ***Subdominant***—that can play a similar role in harmonic progressions.

G clef See *treble clef.*

German augmented sixth (Ger^{+6}) *Augmented sixth chord* that uses the minor form of $\hat{6}$ in the bass, $\hat{1}$, the minor form of $\hat{3}$ (in major keys, sometimes spelled as raised $\hat{2}$), and raised $\hat{4}$ in the upper voices.

grand staff Paired treble and bass clef staves joined by a vertical line and brace.

half cadence (HC) Cadence ending on V.

half note Note written as an open notehead with a stem, representing the duration half as long as a whole note and twice as long as a quarter note.

half step Distance between two adjacent notes on the piano; commonly, the smallest distance between two notes in Western music. There are twelve half steps in an octave.

half-diminished seventh chord (ø7) Seventh chord constructed of a diminished triad and a minor seventh.

harmonic interval Distance (or relationship) between two tones sounding together.

harmonic minor scale Alteration of the minor scale with raised $\hat{7}$ to create a leading tone; there are three half steps, $\hat{2}$–$\hat{3}$, $\hat{5}$–$\hat{6}$, and $\hat{7}$–$\hat{8}$, and an augmented second, $\hat{6}$–$\hat{7}$.

harmonic progression Series of chords that follow each other in a logical manner, with one chord leading to the next.

harmonic sequence See *sequence*.

harmonize Supply bass and harmonies for the notes of a melody.

hidden fifths *Similar fifths*.

hidden octaves *Similar octaves*.

home key *Main key*.

imperfect authentic cadence (IAC) Somewhat unstable cadence, consisting of V or V7 moving to I, ending with $\hat{3}$ or $\hat{5}$ in the melody (soprano voice).

incomplete neighbor tone (INT) *Embellishing tone* that is approached by leap and moves by step to a chord tone, or that is approached by step and left by leap.

interval Distance between two tones, whether sounding together (harmonic interval) or in succession (melodic interval).

interval quality The "flavor" of an interval in terms of number of half steps; in a major key, seconds, thirds, sixths, and sevenths, are major (large) or minor (small); fourths are perfect or augmented (larger), while fifths are perfect or diminished (smaller).

introduction Opening section of a movement; in sonata form, a (usually slow) passage preceding the exposition that is not repeated with the exposition.

inversion (1) For intervals, the interval created when the lower note becomes the upper note (and vice versa); (2) For chords, the arrangement of the chord in which a note other than the root is in the bass.

Italian augmented sixth (It+6) *Augmented sixth chord* built on the minor form of $\hat{6}$ in the bass, with $\hat{1}$ and raised $\hat{4}$ in the upper voices.

key The particular major or minor scale used as the basis of a piece or passage of music.

key of V *Dominant key*.

key signature The sharps or flats needed for a major or minor scale or key, generally indicated immediately after the clef.

keyboard format Notation of four-part harmony in which soprano, alto, and tenor are all written on the treble staff (played by the right hand), the bass on the bass staff (left hand).

lament bass Descending chromatic bass line from $\hat{1}$ to $\hat{5}$, commonly used in minor keys, often to express grief and mourning.

leading tone The seventh note in a major scale ($\hat{7}$), a half step below the tonic, an important tendency tone that often appears as the third of the dominant chord. In minor keys, the leading tone requires an accidental.

ledger line Short horizontal line written above or below the staff to extend the staff for higher or lower notes.

main key The key that begins and ends a movement or piece; also known as home key or tonic key.

main theme *Primary theme*.

major interval The larger natural size of a second, third, sixth, or seventh.

major scale Scale built of whole and half steps, in which the two half steps are $\hat{3}$–$\hat{4}$ and $\hat{7}$–$\hat{8}$.

major seventh chord (M7) Seventh chord constructed of a major triad plus a major seventh.

major triad Triad built of a major third and a perfect fifth above a root.

measure One unit of a meter, consisting of a strong beat (downbeat) followed by weak beats.

medial caesura In sonata form, a pause, break, or other textural demarcation that follows the cadence marking the end of the transition within the exposition or recapitulation and that immediately precedes the secondary theme.

mediant The third note in a scale ($\hat{3}$); also, the name of the chord (III or iii) based on that tone.

melodic interval Distance (or relationship) between two tones sounding in succession.

melodic minor scale Minor scale with raised $\hat{6}$ and $\hat{7}$ (leading tone) in the ascending form, natural $\hat{6}$ and $\hat{7}$ in the descending form.

melodic sequence See *sequence*.

meter Grouping of beats into a regular pattern of strong and weak beats.

middle C The C roughly in the middle of the piano keyboard, notated one ledger line below the treble staff or one ledger line above the bass staff.

minor interval The smaller natural size of a second, third, sixth, or seventh.

minor scale Natural minor scale, with half steps $\hat{2}$-$\hat{3}$ and $\hat{5}$-$\hat{6}$; see also *harmonic minor scale* and *melodic minor scale*.

minor seventh chord (m7) Seventh chord constructed of a minor triad plus a minor seventh.

minor triad Triad built of a minor third and a perfect fifth above a root.

modal mixture The use of elements drawn from the parallel key, recognizably sounding minor in a major key, or sounding major in a minor key.

modulation Change of key that is confirmed by a cadence.

N6 *♭II6*.

natural interval Any interval built on white keys (naturals).

natural minor scale Minor scale with no accidentals, with half steps $\hat{2}$-$\hat{3}$ and $\hat{5}$-$\hat{6}$.

natural seventh chord Any seventh chord built on white keys (naturals).

natural White key of the piano; one of the seven notes A–G, with no sharp or flat; also, the accidental ♮ that cancels a sharp or flat.

natural triad Any triad built on white keys (naturals).

Neapolitan sixth *♭II6*.

neighbor chord Embellishing sonority resulting either from a neighbor tone in the bass (and possibly embellishing tones in other voices) or from neighbor tones in the upper voices above a stationary bass.

neighbor motion See *neighbor tone*.

neighbor tone (NT) Embellishing tone that leaves a chord tone by step and returns to it.

oblique motion Voice leading between two voices in which one voice moves up or down while the other remains on the same pitch.

octave (8va) Interval between two tones spanning eight scale steps and having the same letter name, as C–C or $\hat{1}$–$\hat{8}$.

octave doubling Enrichment of harmonic texture by doubling a voice in parallel octaves.

open-score choral format, open-score format Notation for four-part harmony in which each voice is written on a separate staff, with the tenor part most often written in treble clef but sounding an octave lower.

parallel $^6_3$ chords Harmonic sequence, most often occurring in a three-voice texture, in which a first-inversion chord ($^6_3$) is repeatedly transposed by step.

parallel fifths Fifths approached in parallel motion, permitted in four-part harmony only under extremely special circumstances.

parallel keys The pair of major and minor keys sharing the same tonic.

parallel motion Voice leading between two voices in which the voices move in the same direction and the same distance, so that the intervallic distance between the two voices stays the same.

parallel octaves Octaves approached in parallel motion, forbidden in four-part harmony.

parallel period Period in which the two phrases start identically (or nearly identically).

parallel unisons Unisons approached in parallel motion, forbidden in four-part harmony.

passing $^6_4$ Second-inversion triad whose bass is a passing tone.

passing chord Embellishing sonority resulting from a passing tone in the bass (and possibly embellishing tones in other voices).

passing V^6 Passing chord commonly occurring between I and vi or I and IV^6, as a result of bass stepwise motion.

passing IV^6 Passing chord commonly occurring between V and V^6 (or inversions of V^7), as a result of stepwise bass motion.

passing motion See *passing tone*.

passing tone (PT) Embellishing tone that moves stepwise between two chord tones; may be accented or unaccented.

pedal $^6_4$ $^6_4$ harmony that results when a root-position chord is embellished by motion in the upper voices, with the bass sustaining the root.

pedal point Embellishment of a harmony in which one note (usually the bass) is sustained, while the other voices move, forming different harmonies above or around it; most commonly, a device to embellish a sustained I or V.

perfect authentic cadence (PAC) The most stable cadence, consisting of V or V^7 moving to I, ending with $\hat{1}$ in the melody (soprano voice).

perfect intervals Unisons, octaves, and most fourths and fifths; in any major key, there is one augmented fourth and one diminished fifth; all others are perfect.

period Phrase pair in which a first phrase (antecedent) leads to an unstable cadence, answered by a second phrase (consequent) that concludes with an authentic cadence.

phrase Basic unit of tonal music, often around four or eight measures long, that concludes with a cadence.

phrase overlap Technique of connecting phrases in which the last chord of one phrase also serves as the first chord of the next.

phrase pair The combination of two successive phrases, often about the same length, each with its own cadence.

Phrygian cadence Half cadence that consists of a iv^6–V progression.

Picardy third The use of raised $\hat{3}$ within a minor key to create a major tonic triad at the end of a phrase (especially, at the end of a piece), the most common use of modal mixture in minor.

pitch Specific points on the continuum of audible sound; pitches are measured by the frequency of vibrations.

pivot chord In a modulation, chord that is shared by both keys and is used as a means of transitioning from one key to the next.

plagal cadence IV–I motion occurring at the end of a phrase.

position *Chord position.*

presentation See *sentence.*

primary theme Opening theme of sonata form exposition and recapitulation, establishing the tonic key and ending with a cadence in the tonic key. Also called *first theme* or *main theme.*

quadruple meter Meter with a four-beat grouping (one strong and three weaker beats).

quality See *interval quality; triad quality; seventh quality.*

quarter note Note written as a solid notehead with a stem, and most often used to represent one beat; its duration is half as long as a half note and twice as long as an eighth note.

range Scope of a voice or instrument defined by its lowest and highest notes.

realize To compose a passage based on indicated chords according to Roman numerals or figures.

recapitulation The last section of a piece in sonata form, in which the primary theme and secondary theme are repeated in the main key.

relative keys The pair of major and minor keys sharing a key signature.

rest A duration of silence; notated with signs equivalent to whole note, half note, and so forth.

retardation (RET) Accented embellishing tone that is approached by common tone and resolves up by step; sometime called an "upward resolving suspension."

retransition In sonata form, passage at the end of the development section that leads back to the tonic key of the recapitulation; the retransition usually follows a cadence in a non-tonic key (such as the key of vi) that appears near the end of the development.

Roman numeral Designation of a chord according to the scale degree on which it is built as well as its quality (e.g., ii indicates a minor triad built on $\hat{2}$; ♭III indicates a major triad built on lowered $\hat{3}$).

Romanesca Harmonic sequence in which the chord roots move alternately down a fourth and up a second.

rondo form Multipart form of a movement or piece in which the first section, in the main key, returns after each of two or more contrasting sections, such as **ABACA** or **ABACABA**.

root The pitch on which a triad or other chord is built.

root position The arrangement of a chord in which the root is in the bass; indicated $^5_3$ or no figures for a triad, $^7_{\substack{5\\3}}$ or ^{7} for a seventh chord.

rounded binary form See *binary form.*

SATB (chorale) format Notation of four-part harmony in which soprano and alto are written on the treble staff, tenor and bass on the bass staff.

scale Collection of notes, typically arranged in ascending order, organized with reference to a central pitch (tonic), and used as the basis for a musical composition.

scale degree The step within a scale, indicated as a name or number (e.g., "tonic" or $\hat{1}$).

scale-degree name The name of the step within a scale, as "mediant."

scale-degree number The number of a step within a scale, as $\hat{3}$.

second Interval between two tones spanning two scale steps (letter names), as C-D or $\hat{1}$-$\hat{2}$.

second inversion Chord position in which the fifth is in the bass; indicated $^4_3$ for a seventh chord, $^6_4$ for a triad (and considered dissonant in this form).

second theme *Secondary theme.*

secondary dominant *Applied dominant.*

secondary key In sonata form, the key of the secondary theme in the exposition, most frequently V or the relative major.

secondary theme In sonata form, the theme in the secondary key of the exposition, which ends with a PAC in the secondary key, and which generally is restated in the tonic key when it returns in the recapitulation. Also called *second theme* or *subordinate theme*.

second-species counterpoint Species counterpoint in which the new melody is written in half notes, with dissonances allowed only on the second half of the measure, as passing or neighbor tones.

semitone *Half step.*

sentence Phrase layout typically consisting of eight measures, divided into two halves, *presentation* and *continuation*; the presentation consists of a melodic basic idea (usually about two-measures long) that is repeated, elaborating the tonic. In the continuation, the momentum is intensified in a drive to a cadence, often with *fragmentation* of the basic idea or a new idea.

sequence Harmonic or melodic pattern in which a segment of music is repeated one or more times in succession, transposed in a regular pattern, whether diatonically or (using accidentals) chromatically.

sequential period Period in which the consequent (second phrase) begins with a transposed version of the antecedent (first phrase).

seven-part rondo form Rondo form of the shape **ABACAB′A**, in which the first **B** section is generally in V or the relative major, while the second **B** section is in the main key. Often called sonata rondo when the sections are structured like a sonata form's exposition (**AB**), development (**C**), and recapitulation (**B′A**).

seventh Interval between two tones spanning seven scale steps (letter names), as C-B or $\hat{1}$-$\hat{7}$.

seventh chord Four-note chord constructed of a triad plus a seventh over its root; in figured bass, $^7_{\substack{5\\3}}$, abbreviated to ^{7}.

seventh-chord quality The "flavor" of seventh chord depending on the qualities of the triad and the seventh, as a *minor seventh chord* (minor triad, minor seventh).

sharp (♯) Sign (accidental or in the key signature) raising a natural note by a half step.

similar fifths Fifths approached in similar motion, permitted in four-part harmony with certain restrictions.

similar motion Voice leading between two voices in which the voices move in the same direction but different distances.

similar octaves Octaves approached in similar motion, permitted in four-part harmony with certain restrictions.

simple binary form See *binary form*.

simple interval Interval smaller than an octave.

simple meter Meter in which the basic time unit is not a dotted-note value (compare *compound meter*).

sixteenth note Note written as a solid notehead with a stem and a double flag or beam, representing the duration half as long as an eighth note and twice as long as a thirty-second note.

sixth Interval between two tones spanning six scale steps (letter names), as C-A or $\hat{1}$-$\hat{6}$.

sonata form Extended musical form resembling a large rounded binary form, consisting of two large parts: *exposition*, which modulates to a secondary key (most often V or the relative major), and is usually repeated, and *development* and *recapitulation*, which may also be repeated as one part. There may also be a slow *introduction* at the beginning, and a *coda* at the end.

sonata rondo See *seven-part rondo form*.

spacing Distance between adjacent voices in four-part harmony.

species counterpoint Traditional method for learning voice leading, particularly the treatment of dissonant embellishing tones and perfect consonances, by writing melodies to go with a cantus firmus; the different species are categorized as first through fifth species, depending on the time values in the new melody.

staff Arrangement of five horizontal lines on which pitches are indicated.

stationary motion Voice leading between two voices in which both remain on the same pitch.

step Distance between adjacent scale degrees, either a semitone (half step) or whole tone (whole step).

subdominant The fourth note in a scale ($\hat{4}$); also, the name of the chord (IV or iv) based on that tone, or (as ***Subdominant***) any of a group of chords that function as subdominants, including ii^6, ii$^6_5$, ii^7, and Neapolitan sixth chords.

submediant The sixth note in a scale ($\hat{6}$); also, the name of the chord (VI or vi) based on that tone.

subordinate theme *Secondary theme* of sonata form.

subtonic The seventh note in a scale ($\hat{7}$) as it occurs in natural minor, a whole step below the tonic, or the name of the chord (VII) based on that tone.

subtonic VII Major triad built on the natural minor form of $\hat{7}$; generally occurs as part of a modulation or in a sequence.

supertonic The second note in a scale ($\hat{2}$); also, the name of the chord (ii) based on that tone.

suspension (SUS) Accented embellishing tone that is approached by common tone from a note of the previous chord and resolves down by step.

tendency tone In four-part harmony, a tone with a strong tendency to move stepwise either up or down.

tenor clef C clef (𝄡) indicating that the fourth line from the bottom of the staff is middle C; used for tenor range of cello, trombone, and bassoon.

ternary form Three-part form of a movement or piece (**ABA**) characterized by contrast and return, in which a first section (**A**, generally ending with a perfect authentic cadence in the main key) is followed by a contrasting middle section (**B**, often in or modulating to V or the relative key), with a return of the first section or a variant of it (**A** or **A′**), in the main key. The middle section may end with a bridge that leads back to the main key.

third Interval between two tones spanning three scale steps (letter names), as C-E or $\hat{1}$-$\hat{3}$; in a chord, the third above the root (in a triad, the middle note).

third inversion Position of seventh chord in which the seventh is in the bass, indicated $^4_2$.

tie A curved sign between two noteheads indicating the addition of the time values; can be used to create durations that last across barlines or for which there is no single-note representation.

time signature An indication of notated meter, generally in the form of two stacked numbers indicating the number of beats per measure and the type of note representing one beat.

tonic The central organizing tone in a key, and the first note in a scale ($\hat{1}$).

tonic key *Main key.*

tonicization Momentary change of key, generally indicated by the use of an applied dominant chord but without a cadence to the new key.

transition In sonata form, passage in the exposition that follows the primary theme and precedes the secondary theme; the transition usually concludes with a strong half cadence, either in the tonic or in the secondary key.

transpose To shift a scale, melody, or passage to another note while maintaining its pattern of whole and half steps.

treble clef (G clef) 𝄞 symbol indicating that the second line from the bottom of the staff is G above middle C.

triad Harmonic element consisting of three pitches: a root pitch and a third and fifth above it.

triad quality Quality of a triad: major, minor, augmented, or diminished.

triple meter Meter with a three-beat grouping (one strong and two weak beats).

triplet The division of a note value into three equal parts instead of two: for example, an eighth-note triplet consists of three notes equal in duration to one quarter note.

unaccented Sounding on a relatively weak beat or part of the beat or appearing after (most of) the notes of the chord are sounded.

unison Name of the interval between two notes at the same pitch level, as C-C or $\hat{1}$-$\hat{1}$.

upper voice In four-part harmony, the soprano, alto, or tenor (i.e., not the bass).

viola clef *Alto clef.*

voice In four-part harmony or other part writing, a single melodic part (such as the soprano, alto, tenor, or bass).

voice crossing Harmonic writing in which a voice descends below the next lowest voice, or ascends above the next highest voice.

voice exchange Voice leading in which two chord tones are traded between two voices, as when the bass moves from the root to the third of a chord at the same time that the soprano moves from the third to the root.

voice leading The manner in which one chord, note, or interval moves to the next.

whole note Note written as an open notehead with no stem, representing the duration twice as long as a half note.

whole step, whole tone Distance of two half steps.

Index of Music Examples

Index of Terms and Concepts